SISTER CARRIE

The Pennsylvania Edition

Historical Editors
JOHN C. BERKEY
ALICE M. WINTERS

∞

Textual Editor
JAMES L. W. WEST III

∞

General Editor
NEDA M. WESTLAKE

SISTER CARRIE

THEODORE DREISER

University of Pennsylvania Press

1981

This work was published with the support of the Haney Foundation.

The preparation of this volume was made possible in part by a grant from the Program for Editions of the National Endowment for the Humanities, an independent federal agency.

Library of Congress Cataloging in Publication Data

Dreiser, Theodore, 1871-1945.
  Sister Carrie.

  1. Dreiser, Theodore, 1871-1945. Sister Carrie.
I. Title.
PS3507.R55S5 1981   813'.52   80-50691
ISBN 0-8122-7784-8
ISBN 0-8122-1110-3 (pbk.)

CONTENTS

ILLUSTRATIONS

PREFACE AND
ACKNOWLEDGMENTS

Theodore Dreiser, newspaper reporter and journalist, began his first novel in the early fall of 1899, at the age of twenty-eight. He finished the manuscript in March 1900. In the novel, Dreiser put Carrie Meeber on the afternoon train from Columbia City in Wisconsin to Chicago in August 1889. "She was eighteen years of age, bright, timid and full of the illusions of ignorance and youth." When the story ended, nine years later, Carrie had lost those illusions, and Dreiser had created a novel that would have a publication history and a critical reception as controversial as the career of his heroine.

Dreiser's wife and his friend Arthur Henry cut and revised the manuscript and typescript. The typists and the publisher's house editors made further changes. The *Sister Carrie* that was published in November 1900 was marred by this editorial interference and censorship and has been the basis of American editions and foreign translations until the present. The editors of the Pennsylvania edition of *Sister Carrie*, with recourse to the manuscript and typescript, restore the novel as closely as possible to the author's original version, a more somber and unresolved work of art. The frame of the novel remains; within the picture, like a cleansed portrait, the characters assume the original clarity of the artist's design.

The Pennsylvania edition of *Sister Carrie* has been, from its inception, a collaborative effort. Responsibility for the general editorial strategy employed in this volume is shared equally by the four editors. Historical Editors Berkey and Winters provided the initial impetus for the project; their subsequent responsibilities have included transcription of Dreiser's manuscript, collation of significant forms of the text, explanatory annotation of the novel, and preparation of the maps of Chicago and New York of the era of *Sister Carrie*. Textual Editor West verified the transcription of the manuscript, conceived the editorial principles, emended the copy-text, and compiled the apparatus. West drafted "*Sister Carrie*: Manuscript to Print"; Berkey, Winters, and West collaborated in the expansion, revision, and refinement of the essay. The General Editor has coordinated these efforts and supports the results. Proofreading duties have been assumed by the four editors.

N.M.W.

The editors are grateful, above all, that Theodore Dreiser had the good judgment in 1914, long before his agreement with the University of Pennsylvania, to present the manuscript of *Sister Carrie* to Henry L. Mencken, his friend and mentor; and that Mr. Mencken had the wisdom to place the manuscript for safekeeping in the Manuscripts and Archives Division, the New York Public Library, Astor, Lenox and Tilden Foundations. Paul Rugen, Keeper of Manuscripts, and his staff, and Faye Simkin, Executive Officer, kindly gave us access to the manuscript.

From 1937 until Dreiser's death in 1945, Robert H. Elias had the confidence and encouragement of Dreiser in preparing the pioneer biography. He is the first Dreiser scholar and the editor of the three-volume edition of Dreiser's letters. His work stands as the solid underpinning of this edition. In 1942, influenced by Mr. Elias and E. Sculley Bradley of the English Department of the University of Pennsylvania, Theodore Dreiser assigned the first part of his carefully preserved collection of literary papers to the University. In 1949 Dreiser's second wife, Helen, presented the remaining material then in her possession to the collection. Further manuscripts and correspondence from family and friends have augmented the Dreiser Collection. Without this cooperation, the present volume and any that follow would be impossible. We are especially indebted to Harold J. Dies, the executor of the Dreiser Estate, for his continued interest and good will.

The editors wish to thank Charles W. David, former Director of Libraries, University of Pennsylvania, who enthusiastically sponsored the acquisition of the Dreiser Collection in the 1940s; Richard De Gennaro, Director of Libraries, University of Pennsylvania, for his support and encouragement for the past several years; Joseph Katz, University of South Carolina, for his initial interest in this project and for his helpful suggestions in the formative stage; and William E. Miller, University of Pennsylvania Library, for his assistance in literary identifications.

Historical Editors Berkey and Winters wish to thank Rutgers University Research Council; Gail Casterline, Projects Director, Chicago Historical Society; Gordon Scott, Costume Division, Metropolitan Museum of Art, New York City; Robert Smith, Department of French, Rutgers University, Camden, New Jersey; Thomas Leonard, for his rendering of the Chicago and New York maps; Geraldine Duclow, Theater Department, the Free Library of Philadelphia; Paul Fay, Music Department, Library of Congress; Carl Smith, Department of English, Northwestern Unversity; Edith Mae Smith, Rutgers University, Camden, New Jersey; and Jean Crescensi, Rutgers University Library, Camden, New Jersey.

Textual Editor West wishes to acknowledge with much gratitude the help of the late Ellen Moers and to thank David J. Nordloh, Department of English, Indiana University; Jayne K. Kribbs, Department of English, Temple University; Valarie M. Arms, Department of English, Drexel University; and Arthur D. Casciato, University of Virginia.

SISTER
CARRIE

CHAPTER I.

When Caroline Meeber boarded the afternoon train for Chicago her total outfit consisted of a small trunk, which was checked in the baggage car, a cheap imitation alligator skin satchel holding some minor details of the toilet, a small lunch in a paper box and a yellow leather snap purse, containing her ticket, a scrap of paper with her sister's address in Van Buren Street, and four dollars in money. It was in August, 1889. She was eighteen years of age, bright, timid and full of the illusions of ignorance and youth. Whatever touch of regret at parting characterized her thoughts it was certainly not for advantages now being given up. A gush of tears at her mother's farewell kiss, a touch in the throat when the cars clacked by the flour mill where her father worked by the day, a pathetic sigh as the familiar green environs of the village passed in review, and the threads which bound her so lightly to girlhood and home were irretrievably broken.

To be sure she was not conscious of any of this. Any change, however great, might be remedied. There was always the next station where one might descend and return. There was the great city, bound more closely by these very trains which came up daily. Columbia City was not so very far away, even once she was in Chicago. What pray is a few hours—a hundred miles? She could go back. And then her sister was there. She looked at the little slip bearing the latter's address and wondered. She gazed at the green landscape now passing in swift review until her swifter thoughts replaced its impression with vague conjectures of what Chicago might be. Since infancy her ears had been full of its fame. Once the family had thought of moving there. If she secured good employment they might come now. Anyhow it was vast. There were lights and sounds and a roar of things. People were rich. There were vast depots. This on-rushing train was merely speeding to get there.

When a girl leaves her home at eighteen, she does one of two things. Either she falls into saving hands and becomes better, or she rapidly assumes the cosmopolitan standard of virtue and becomes worse. Of an intermediate balance, under the circumstances, there is no possibility. The city has its cunning wiles no less than the infinitely smaller and more human tempter. There are large forces which allure, with all the soulfulness of expression possible in the most cultured human. The gleam of a thousand lights is often as effective, to all moral intents and purposes, as the persuasive light in a wooing and fascinating eye. Half the undoing of the unsophisticated and natural mind is accomplished by forces wholly superhuman. A blare of sound, a roar of life, a vast array of human hives appeal to the astonished senses in equivocal terms. Without a counselor at hand to whisper cautious interpretations, what falsehoods may not these things breathe into the unguarded ear! Unrecognized for what they are, their beauty, like music, too often relaxes, then weakens, then perverts the simplest human perceptions.

Caroline, or "Sister Carrie" as she had been half affectionately termed by the family, was possessed of a mind rudimentary in its power of observation and analysis. Self-interest with her was high, but not strong. It was nevertheless her guiding characteristic. Warm with the fancies of youth, pretty with the insipid prettiness of the formative period, possessed of a figure which tended toward eventual shapeliness and an eye alight with certain native intelligence, she was a fair example of the middle American class—two generations removed from the emigrant. Books were beyond her interest—knowledge a sealed book. In the intuitive graces she was still crude. She could scarcely toss her head gracefully. Her hands were almost ineffectual for the same reason. The feet, though small, were set flatly. And yet she was interested in her charms, quick to understand the keener pleasures of life, ambitious to gain in material things. A half-equipped little knight she was, venturing to reconnoitre the mysterious city and dreaming wild dreams of some vague, far-off supremacy which should make it prey and subject, the proper penitent, grovelling at a woman's slipper.

"That," said a voice in her ear, "is one of the prettiest little resorts in Wisconsin."

"Is it?" she answered nervously.

The train was just pulling out of Waukesha. For some time she had been conscious of a man behind. She felt him observing her mass of hair. He had been fidgeting, and with natural intuition she felt a certain interest growing in that quarter. Her maidenly reserve and a certain sense of what was conventional under the circumstances called her to forestall and deny this familiarity, but the daring and magnetism of the individual, born of past experiences and triumphs, prevailed. She answered.

He leaned forward to put his elbows upon the back of her seat and proceeded to make himself volubly agreeable.

"Yes, that's a great resort for Chicago people. The hotels are swell. You are not familiar with this part of the country, are you?"

"Oh yes I am," answered Carrie. "That is, I live at Columbia City. I have never been through here though."

"And so this is your first visit to Chicago," he observed.

All the time she was conscious of certain features out of the side of her eye. Flush, colorful cheeks, a light mustache, a gray fedora hat. She now turned and looked upon him in full, the instincts of self-protection and coquetry mingling confusedly in her brain.

"I didn't say that," she said.

"Oh," he answered in a very pleasing way and with an assumed air of mistake. "I thought you did."

Here was a type of the traveling canvasser for a manufacturing house—a class which at that time was first being dubbed by the slang of the day "drummers." He came within the meaning of a still newer term which had sprung into general use among Americans in 1880, and which concisely expressed the thought of one whose dress or manners are such as to impress strongly the fancy, or elicit the admiration, of susceptible young women—a "masher." His clothes were of an impressive character, the suit being cut of a striped and crossed pattern of brown wool, very popular at that time. It was what has since become known as a business suit. The low crotch of the vest revealed a stiff shirt bosom of white and pink stripes, surmounted by a high white collar about which was fastened a tie of distinct pattern. From his coat sleeves protruded a pair of linen cuffs of the same material as the shirt and fastened with large gold-plate buttons set with the common yellow agates known as "cat's-eyes." His fingers bore several rings, one the ever-enduring heavy seal, and from his vest dangled a neat gold watch chain from which was suspended the secret insignia of the Order of

Elks. The whole suit was rather tight-fitting and was finished off with broad-soled tan shoes, highly polished, and the grey felt hat, then denominated "fedora," before mentioned. He was, for the order of intellect represented, attractive; and whatever he had to recommend him, you may be sure was not lost upon Carrie, in this her first glance.

Lest this order of individual should permanently pass, let me put down some of the most striking characteristics of his most successful manner and method. Good clothes of course were the first essential, the things without which he was nothing. A strong physical nature actuated by a keen desire for the feminine was the next. A mind free of any consideration of the problems or forces of the world and actuated not by greed but an insatiable love of variable pleasure—woman—pleasure. His method was always simple. Its principal element was daring, backed of course by an intense desire and admiration for the sex. Let him meet with a young woman twice and upon the third meeting he would walk up and straighten her necktie for her and perhaps address her by her first name. If an attractive woman should deign a glance of interest in passing him upon the street he would run up, seize her by the hand in feigned acquaintanceship and convince her that they had met before, providing of course that his pleasing way interested her in knowing him further. In the great department stores he was at his ease in capturing the attention of some young woman, while waiting for the cash boy to come back with his change. In such cases, by those little wiles common to the type, he would find out the girl's name, her favorite flower, where a note would reach her, and perhaps pursue the delicate task of friendship until it proved unpromising for the one aim in view, when it would be relinquished.

He would do very well with more pretentious women, though the burden of expense was a slight deterrent. Upon entering a parlor car at St. Paul, for instance, he would select a chair next to the most promising bit of femininity and soon inquire if she cared to have the shade lowered. Before the train cleared the yards he would have the porter bring her a footstool. At the next lull in his conversational progress he would find her something to read, and from then on by dint of compliment gently insinuated, personal narrative, exaggeration and service, he would win her tolerance and mayhap regard.

Those who have ever delved into the depths of a woman's conscience must, at some time or other, have come upon that mystery of mysteries—the moral significance, to her, of clothes. A woman should some day write the complete philosophy of that subject. No matter how young she is, it is one of the things she wholly comprehends. There is an indescribably faint line in the matter of man's apparel which somehow divides for her those who are worth glancing at and those who are not. Once an individual has passed this faint line on the way downward he will get no glance from her. There is another line at which the dress of a man will cause her to study her own. This line the individual at her elbow now marked for Carrie. She became conscious of an inequality. Her own plain blue dress with its black cotton tape trimmings realized itself to her imagination as shabby. She felt the worn state of her shoes.

He mistook this thought wave, which caused her to withdraw her glance and turn for relief to the landscape outside, for some little gain his grace had brought him.

"Let's see," he went on. "I know quite a number of people in your town—Morgenroth the clothier and Gibson the dry-goods man."

"Oh, do you," she interrupted, aroused by memories of longings the displays in the latter's establishment had cost her.

At last he had a clue to her interest and followed it up deftly. In a few minutes he had come about into her seat. He talked of sales of clothing, his travels, Chicago and the amusements of that city.

"If you are going there you will enjoy it immensely. Have you relatives?"

"I am going to visit my sister," she explained.

"You want to see Lincoln Park," he said, "and Michigan Avenue. They are putting up great buildings there. It's a second New York, great. So much to see—theatres, crowds, fine houses—oh you'll like that."

There was a little ache in her fancy of all he described. Her insignificance in the presence of so much magnificence faintly affected her. She realized that hers was not to be a round of pleasure, and yet there was something promising in all the material prospect he set forth. There was something satisfactory in the attention of this individual with his good clothes. She could not help smiling as he told her of some popular actress she reminded him of. She was not silly and yet attention of this sort had its weight.

"You will be in Chicago some little time, won't you?" he observed, at one turn of the now easy conversation.

"I don't know," said Carrie vaguely—a flash vision of the possibility of her not securing employment rising in her mind.

"Several weeks anyhow," he said, looking steadily into her eyes.

There was much more passing now than the mere words indicated. He recognized the indescribable thing that made for fascination and beauty in her. She realized that she was of interest to him from the one standpoint which a woman both delights in and fears. Her manner was simple, though, for the very reason that she had not yet learned the many little affectations with which women conceal their true feelings—some things she did appeared bold. A clever companion, had she ever had one, would have warned her never to look a man in the eyes so steadily.

"Why do you ask?" she said.

"Well, I'm going to be there several weeks. I'm going to study stock at our place and get new samples. I might show you 'round."

"I don't know whether you can or not—I mean I don't know whether I can. I shall be living with my sister and—"

"Well, if she minds, we'll fix that." He took out his pencil and a little pocket note book, as if it were all settled. "What is your address there."

She fumbled her purse, which contained the address slip.

He reached down in his hip pocket and took out a fat purse. It was filled with slips of paper, some mileage books, a roll of green-backs and so on. It impressed her deeply. Such a purse had never been carried by any man who had ever been attentive to her before. Indeed a man who traveled, who was brisk and experienced and of the world, had never come within such close range before. The purse, the shiny tan shoes, the smart new suit and the *air* with which he did things built up for her a dim world of fortune around him of which he was the centre. It disposed her pleasantly toward all he might do.

He took out a neat business card on which was engraved "Bartlett, Caryoe and Company," and down in the left-hand corner "Chas. H. Drouet."

"That's me," he said, putting the card in her hand and touching his name. "It's pronounced 'Drew-eh.' Our family was French on my father's side."

She looked at it while he put up his purse. Then he got out a letter from a bunch in his coat pocket.

"This is the house I travel for," he went on, pointing to a picture on it—"corner of State and Lake." There was pride in his voice. He felt that it was something to be connected with such a place, and he made her feel that way.

"What is your address?" he began again, fixing his pencil to write.

She looked at his hand.

"Carrie Meeber," she said slowly, "354 West Van Buren St., care S. C. Hanson."

He wrote it carefully down and got out the purse again. "You'll be at home if I come around Monday night?" he said.

"I think so," she answered.

How true it is that words are but vague shadows of the volumes we mean. Little audible links they are, chaining together great inaudible feelings and purposes. Here were these two, bandying little phrases, drawing purses, looking at cards and both unconscious of how inarticulate all their real feelings were. Neither was wise enough to be sure of the working of the mind of the other. He could not tell how his luring succeeded. She could not realize that she was drifting, until he secured her address. Now she felt that she had yielded something—he, that he had gained a victory. Already they felt that they were somehow associated. Already he took control in directing the conversation. His words were easy. Her manner was relaxed.

They were nearing Chicago. Already the signs were numerous. Trains flashed by them. Across wide stretches of flat open prairie they could see lines of telegraph poles stalking across the fields toward the great city. Away off there were indications of suburban towns, some big smoke stacks towering high in the air. Frequently there were two-story frame houses standing out in the open fields, without fence or trees, outposts of the approaching army of homes.

To the child, the genius with imagination, or the wholly untraveled, the approach to a great city for the first time is a wonderful thing. Particularly if it be evening—that mystic period between the glare and the gloom of the world when life is changing from one sphere or condition to another. Ah, the promise of the night. What does it not hold for the weary. What old illusion of hope is not here forever repeated! Says the soul of the toiler to itself, "I shall soon be free. I shall be in the ways and the hosts of the merry. The streets, the lamp, the lighted chamber set for dining are for me. The theatres, the halls, the parties, the ways of rest and the paths of song—these are mine in the night." Though all humanity be still enclosed in the shops, the thrill runs abroad. It is in the air. The dullest feel something which they may not always express or describe. It is the lifting of the burden of toil.

Sister Carrie gazed out of the window. Her companion, affected by her wonder, so contagious are all things, felt anew some interest in the city and pointed out the marvels. Already vast net-works of tracks—the sign and insignia of Chicago—stretched on either hand. There were thousands of cars and a clangor of engine bells. At the sides of this traffic stream stood dingy houses, smoky mills, tall elevators. Through the interstices, evidences of the stretching city could be seen. Street cars waited at crossings for the train to go by. Gatemen toiled at wooden arms which closed the streets. Bells clanged, the rails clacked, whistles sounded afar off.

"This is North-West Chicago," said Drouet. "This is the Chicago River," and he pointed to a little muddy creek, crowded with the huge, masted wanderers from far-off waters nosing the black, posted banks. With a puff, a clang and a clatter of rails it was gone. "Chicago is getting to be a great town," he went on. "It's a wonder. You'll find lots to see here."

She did not hear this very well. Her heart was troubled by a kind of terror. The fact that she was alone, away from home, rushing into a great sea of life and endeavor, began to tell. She could not help but feel a little choked for breath—a little sick as her heart beat so fast. She half closed her eyes and tried to think it was nothing, that Columbia City was only a little way off.

"Chicago!—Chicago!" called the brakeman, slamming open the door. They were rushing into a more crowded yard, alive with the clatter and clang of life. She began to gather up her poor little grip and closed her hand firmly upon her purse. Drouet arose, kicked his legs to straighten his trousers and seized his clean yellow grip.

"I suppose your people will be here to meet you," he said. "Let me carry your grip."

"Oh no," she said. "I'd rather you wouldn't. I'd rather you wouldn't be with me when I meet my sister."

"All right," he said in all kindness. "I'll be near, though, in case she isn't here, and take you out there safely."

"You're so kind," said Carrie, feeling the goodness of such attention in her strange situation.

"Chicago!" called the brakeman, drawing the word out long. They were under a great shadowy train shed, where lamps were already beginning to shine out, with passenger cars all about and the train moving at a snail's pace. The people in the car were all up and crowding about the door.

"Well, here we are," said Drouet, leading the way to the door. "Goodbye," he said, "till I see you Monday."

"Goodbye," she said, taking his proffered hand.

"Remember I'll be looking till you find your sister."

She smiled into his eyes.

They filed out and he affected to take no notice of her. A lean-faced, rather commonplace woman recognized Carrie on the platform and hurried forward.

"Why Sister Carrie!" she began and there was a perfunctory embrace of welcome.

Carrie realized the change of affectional atmosphere at once. Amid all the maze, uproar and novelty, she felt cold reality taking her by the hand. No world of light and merriment. No round of amusement. Her sister carried with her much of the grimness of shift and toil.

"Why, how are all the folks at home"—she began—"how is Father, and Mother?"

Carrie answered, but was looking away. Down the aisle

toward the gate leading into the waiting room and the street stood Drouet. He was looking back. When he saw that she saw him and was safe with her sister he turned to go, sending back the shadow of a smile. Only Carrie saw it. She felt something lost to her when he moved away. When he disappeared she felt his absence thoroughly. With her sister she was much alone, a lone figure in a tossing, thoughtless sea.

CHAPTER II.

Minnie's "flat," as the one-floor residence apartments were then being called, was in a part of West Van Buren Street which was inhabited by families of laborers and clerks, men who had come and were still coming with the rush of population which was pouring in at the rate of 50,000 a year. It was on the third floor, the front windows looking down into the street where at night the lights of grocery stores were shining and children were playing about. To Carrie the sound of the little bells upon the horse cars as they tinkled in and out of hearing was as pleasing as it was strange and novel. She gazed into the lighted street when Minnie brought her into the front room and wondered at the sounds, the movement, the, to her new ears, audible murmur of the vast city which stretched for miles and miles in every direction.

Mrs. Hanson, after the first greetings were over, gave Carrie the baby and proceeded to get supper. Her husband asked a few questions and then sat down to read the evening paper. He was a silent individual, American-born of a Swede father, and now employed as a cleaner of refrigerator cars at the stock yards. To him the presence or absence of his wife's sister was a matter of indifference. Her personal appearance did not affect him one way or the other. His one observation to the point was concerning the chances of work in Chicago.

"It's a big place," he said. "You can get in somewhere in a few days. Everybody does."

Carrie's coming to live with them would have been prevented by his stolid disapproval if it had not been tacitly understood beforehand that she was to get work and pay her board.

The rent of the flat was only seventeen dollars a month, and with her paying four each week, he figured out that it would not be a bad investment. He was of a clean, saving disposition and had already paid a number of monthly installments upon two lots which were valued at two hundred dollars each, far out on the West Side. His ambition was someday to build a house on them.

In the interval which marked the preparation of the meal, Carrie found time to study the flat. She had some slight gift of observation, and that sixth sense, so rich in every woman, of intuition. She felt the drag of a lean and narrow life. The walls of the rooms were discordantly papered. The floors were covered with matting and the hall laid with a thin rag carpet. One could see that the furniture was of that poor, hurriedly patched-together quality which was then being sold by the installment houses. Too ignorant to understand anything about the theory of harmony, Carrie yet felt the lack of it. Something about the place irritated her, she did not know what. She only knew that these things, to her, were dull and commonplace.

She sat with Minnie in the kitchen, holding the baby until it began to cry. Then she walked and sang to it, until Hanson, disturbed in his reading, came and took it. A pleasant side to his nature came out here. He was patient. One could see that he was very much wrapped up in his offspring.

"Now, now!" he said, walking. "There, there," and there was a certain Swedish accent, noticeable in his voice, which he must have inherited.

"You'll want to see the city first, won't you?" said Minnie, when they were eating. "Well, we'll go out Sunday and see Lincoln Park."

Carrie noticed that Hanson said nothing to this. He seemed to be thinking of something else entirely.

"Well," she said, "I think I'll look around tomorrow. I've got Friday and Saturday and it won't be any trouble. Which way is the business part?"

Minnie began to explain but her husband took this part of the conversation to himself.

"It's that way," he said, pointing east. "That's east." Then he went off into the longest speech he had yet indulged in, concerning the lay of Chicago. "You'd better look in those big manufacturing houses along Franklin Street and just the other side of the river," he concluded. "Lots of girls work there. You could get home easy, too. It isn't very far."

Carrie nodded, and asked her sister about the neighborhood. The latter talked in a subdued tone, telling the little she knew about it, while Hanson concerned himself with the baby. Finally he jumped up and handed the child to his wife.

"I've got to get up early in the morning, so I'll go to bed," and off he went, disappearing into the dark little bedroom off the hall, for the night.

"He works way down at the stockyards," explained Minnie, "and so he's got to get up at half-past five."

"What time do you get up to get breakfast?" asked Carrie.

"At about twenty minutes of five."

Together they finished the labor of the day, Carrie washing the dishes while Minnie undressed the baby and put it to bed. Minnie's manner was one of trained industry and Carrie could see that it was a steady round of toil with her.

One thing which was formulating itself steadily in Carrie's mind was the fact that her relations with Drouet would have to be abandoned. He could not come here. She read from the manner of Hanson, in the subdued air of Minnie and indeed the whole atmosphere of the flat, a settled opposition to anything save a conservative round of toil. If Hanson sat every evening in the front room and read his paper, if he went to bed at nine, and Minnie a little later, what would they expect of her? She saw that she would first need to get work and establish herself on a paying basis before she could think of having company of any sort. Her little flirtation with Drouet seemed now an extraordinary thing.

"No," she said to herself, "he can't come here."

She asked Minnie for ink and paper, which were upon the mantel in the dining room, and when the latter had gone to bed at ten, got out Drouet's card and wrote him.

"I cannot have you call on me here," it ran in part. "You will have to wait until you hear from me again. My sister's place is so small."

She troubled herself over what else to put in the letter. She wanted to make some reference to their relations upon the train but was too timid. She concluded by thanking him for his kindness in a crude way, then puzzled over the formality of signing her name and finally decided upon the severe, winding up with a "Very truly" which she subsequently changed to "Sincerely." She sealed and addressed the letter, and, going in the front room, the alcove of which contained her bed, drew the one small rocking chair up to the open window, and sat looking out upon the night and the streets in silent wonder.

She went over all the ground of the day, listening at the same time to the street cars tinkling by, the occasional voice which rose up in phrase or laughter from out of the street. Finally she wearied herself by her own reflections, began to grow dull in her chair, and feeling the need of sleep, arranged her clothing for the night and went to bed.

When she awoke at eight the next morning, Hanson had gone. Her sister was busy in the dining room, which was also the sitting room, sewing. She worked, after dressing, to arrange a little breakfast for herself and then advised with Minnie as to which way to look. The latter had changed considerably since Carrie had seen her. She was now a thin though rugged woman of twenty-seven, with ideas of life colored by her husband's, and fast hardening into even narrower conceptions of pleasure and duty than had ever been hers in a thoroughly circumscribed youth. She had invited Carrie not because she longed for her presence, but because the latter was dissatisfied at home, and could probably get work and pay her board here. She was pleased to see her in a way, but reflected her husband's point of view in the matter of work. Anything was good enough so long as it paid, say, five dollars a week to begin with. A shop girl was the destiny prefigured for the newcomer. She would get in one of the great shops and do well enough until—well, until something happened. Neither of them knew exactly what. They did not figure on promotion. They did not exactly count on marriage. Things would go on, though, in a dim kind of way until the better thing would eventuate and Carrie would be rewarded for coming and toiling in the city. It was under such auspicious circumstances that she started out this morning to look for work.

Before following her in her round of seeking, let us look at the sphere in which her future was to lie. In 1889 Chicago had the peculiar qualifications of growth which made such adventuresome pilgrimages, even on the part of young girls, plausible.

Its many and growing commercial opportunities gave it widespread fame which made of it a giant magnet, drawing to itself from all quarters the hopeful and the hopeless—those who had their fortunes yet to make and those whose fortunes and affairs had reached a disastrous climax elsewhere. It was a city of over 500,000, with the ambition, the daring, the activity of a metropolis of a million. Its streets and houses were already scattered over an area of seventy-five square miles. Its population was not so much thriving upon established commerce as upon the industries which prepared for the arrival of others. The sound of the hammer engaged upon the erection of new structures was everywhere heard. Great industries were moving in. The huge railroad corporations which had long before recognized the prospects of the place had seized upon vast tracts of land for transfer and shipping purposes. Streetcar lines had been extended far out into the open country in anticipation of rapid growth. The city had laid miles and miles of streets and sewers through regions where perhaps one solitary house stood out alone—a pioneer of the populous ways to be. There were regions, open to the sweeping winds and rain, which were yet lighted throughout the night with long, blinking lines of gas lamps fluttering in the wind. Narrow board walks extended out, passing here a house and there a store at far intervals, eventually ending on the open prairie.

In the central portion was the vast wholesale district and shopping centre to which the uninformed seeker for work usually wended his steps. It was a characteristic of Chicago then, and one not generally shared by other cities, that individual firms of any pretension occupied individual buildings. The presence of ample ground made this possible. It gave an imposing appearance to most of the wholesale houses, whose offices were upon the ground floor and in plain view of the street. The huge plates of window glass, now so common, were then rapidly coming into use, and gave to the ground-floor offices a distinguished and prosperous look. The casual wanderer could see, as he passed, a polished array of office fixtures, much frosted glass, clerks hard at work and gentlemanly business men in "nobby" suits and clean linen lounging about or sitting in groups. Polished brass or nickel signs at the square stone entrances announced the firm and the nature of the business in rather neat and reserved terms. The entire metropolitan centre possessed a high and mighty air calculated to overawe and abash the common applicant, and to make the gulf between poverty and success seem both wide and deep.

Into this important commercial region the timid Carrie now wended her way. She walked east along Van Buren Street through a region of lessening importance until it deteriorated into a mass of shanties and coal yards and finally verged upon the river. She walked bravely forward, led by an honest desire to find employment and delayed at every step by the interest of the unfolding scene, and a sense of helplessness amid so much evidence of power and force which she did not understand. These vast buildings, what were they? These strange energies and huge interests—for what purposes were they there? She could have understood the meaning of a little stone-cutter's yard at Columbia City, whittling little pieces of marble for individual use, but when the yards of some huge stone corporation came into view, filled with spur tracks and flat cars, transpierced by docks from the river and traversed by immense trundling cranes of wood and steel overhead, it lost all significance and applicability to her little world. It was connected with something of which she knew nothing, and was doing things which she could not understand.

It was so with the vast railroad yards, with the crowded array of vessels she saw at the river, and the huge factories which were over the way lining the water's edge. Through the open windows she could see the figures of men and women in working aprons, moving busily about. The great streets were wall-lined mysteries to her. The vast offices, strange mazes which concerned far-off individuals of importance. She could only think of people connected with them as counting money, dressing magnificently and riding in carriages. What they dealt in, how they labored, to what end it all came, she had only the vaguest conception. That it could vitally concern her, other than as regards some little nook in which she might daily labor, never crossed her mind. Each concern in each building must be fabulously rich. Those men in dressy suits such as Drouet wore must be powerful and fashionable—the men the newspapers talked about. It was all wonderful, all vast, all far removed, and she sank in spirits inwardly and fluttered feebly at the heart as she thought of entering any one of these mighty concerns and asking for something to do—something that she could do—anything.

CHAPTER III.

Once across the river and into the wholesale district, she glanced about her for some likely door at which to apply. As she contemplated the wide windows and imposing signs, she became conscious of being gazed upon and understood for what she was—a wage-seeker. She had never done this thing before and lacked courage. To avoid conspicuity and a certain indefinable shame she felt at being caught spying about for some place where she might apply for a position, she quickened her steps and assumed an air of indifference supposedly common to one upon an errand. In this way she passed many manufacturing and wholesale houses without once glancing in. At last, after several blocks of walking, she felt that this would not do, and began to look about again, though without relaxing her pace. A little way on she saw a great door which for some reason attracted her attention. It was ornamented by a small brass sign, and seemed to be the entrance to a vast hive of six or seven floors. "Perhaps," she thought, "they may want some one" and crossed over to enter, screwing up her courage to the sticking point as she went. When she came within a score of feet of the desired goal, she observed a young gentleman in a grey check suit, fumbling his watch-charm and looking out. That he had anything to do with the concern she could not tell, but because he happened to be looking in her direction, her weakening heart misgave her and she hurried by, too overcome with shame to enter in. After several blocks of walking, in which the uproar of the streets and the novelty of the situation had time to wear away the effect of this, her first defeat, she again looked about. Over the way stood a great six-story structure labeled "Storm and King," which she viewed with rising hope. It was a wholesale dry goods concern and employed women. She could see them moving about now and then upon the upper floors. This place she decided to enter, no matter what. She crossed over and walked directly toward the entrance. As she did so two men came out and paused in the door. A telegraph messenger in blue dashed past her and up the few steps which graced the entrance and disappeared. Several pedestrians out of the hurrying throng which filled the sidewalks passed about her as she paused, hesitating. She looked helplessly around and then, seeing herself observed, retreated. It was too difficult a task. She could not go past them.

So severe a defeat told sadly upon her nerves. She could scarcely understand her weakness and yet she could not think of gazing inquiringly about upon the surrounding scene. Her feet carried her mechanically forward, every foot of her progress being a satisfactory portion of a flight which she gladly made. Block after block passed by. Upon street lamps at the various corners she read names such as Madison, Monroe, La Salle, Clark, Dearborn, State; and still she went, her feet beginning to tire upon the broad stone flagging. She was pleased in part that the streets were bright and clean. The morning sun shining down with steadily increasing warmth made the shady side of the streets pleasantly cool. She looked at the blue sky overhead with more realization of its charm than had ever come to her before.

Her cowardice began to trouble her in a way. She turned back along the street she had come, resolving to hunt up Storm and King and enter in. On the way she encountered a great wholesale shoe company, through the broad plate windows of which she saw an enclosed executive department, hidden by frosted glass. Without this enclosure, but just within the street entrance, sat a grey-haired gentleman at a small table, with a large open ledger of some kind before him. She walked by this institution several times hesitating, but finding herself unobserved she eventually gathered sufficient courage to falter past the screen door and stand humbly waiting.

"Well, young lady," observed the old gentleman looking at her somewhat kindly—"what is it you wish?"

"I am, that is, do you—I mean, do you need any help?" she stammered.

"Not just at present," he answered smiling. "Not just at present. Come in sometime next week. Occasionally we need some one."

She received the answer in silence and backed awkwardly out. The pleasant nature of her reception rather astonished her.

She had expected that it would be more difficult, that something cold and harsh would be said—she knew not what. That she had not been put to shame and made to feel her unfortunate position seemed remarkable. She did not realize that it was just this which made her experience easy, but the result was the same. She felt greatly relieved.

Somewhat encouraged, she ventured into another large structure. It was a clothing company, and more people were in evidence—well-dressed men of forty and more, surrounded by brass railings and employed variously.

An office boy approached her.

"Who is it you wish to see?" he asked.

"I want to see the manager," she returned.

He ran away and spoke to one of a group of three men who were conferring together. One broke off and came towards her.

"Well?" he said, coldly. The greeting drove all courage from her at once.

"Do you need any help?" she stammered.

"No," he replied abruptly and turned upon his heel.

She went foolishly out, the office boy deferentially swinging the door for her, and gladly sank into the obscuring crowd. It was a severe set-back to her recently pleased mental state.

Now she walked quite aimlessly for a time, turning here and there, seeing one great company after another but finding no courage to prosecute her single inquiry. High noon came and with it hunger. She hunted out an unassuming restaurant and entered but was disturbed to find that the prices were exorbitant for the size of her purse. A bowl of soup was all that she could feel herself able to afford, and with this quickly eaten she went out again. It restored her strength somewhat and made her moderately bold to pursue the search.

In walking a few blocks to fix upon some probable place she again encountered the firm of Storm and King and this time managed to enter. Some gentlemen were conferring close at hand but took no notice of her. She was left standing, gazing nervously upon the floor, her confusion and mental distress momentarily increasing until at last she was ready to turn and hurry eagerly away. When the limit of her distress had been nearly reached she was beckoned to by a man at one of the many desks within the nearby railing.

"Who is it you wish to see?" he inquired.

"Why any one, if you please," she answered. "I am looking for something to do."

"Oh, you want to see Mr. McManus," he returned. "Sit down!" and he pointed to a chair against the neighboring wall. He went on leisurely writing until after a time a short stout gentleman came in from the street.

"Mr. McManus," called the man at the desk, "this young woman wants to see you."

The short gentleman turned about towards Carrie, and she arose and came forward.

"What can I do for you, Miss," he inquired surveying her curiously.

"I want to know if I can get a position," she inquired.

"As what?" he asked.

"Not as anything in particular," she faltered. "I—"

"Have you ever had any experience in the wholesale dry goods business?" he questioned.

"No sir," she replied.

"Are you a stenographer or typewriter?"

"No sir."

"Well we haven't anything here," he said. "We employ only experienced help."

She began to step backward toward the door, when something about her plaintive face attracted him.

"Have you ever worked at anything before?" he inquired.

"No sir," she said.

"Well now, it's hardly possible that you would get anything to do in a wholesale house of this kind. Have you tried the department stores?"

She acknowledged that she had not.

"Well, if I were you," he said, looking at her rather genially, "I would try the department stores. They often need young women as clerks."

"Thank you," she said, her whole nature relieved by this spark of friendly interest.

"Yes," he said, as she moved toward the door, "you try the department stores," and off he went.

At that time the department store was in its earliest form of successful operation and there were not many. The first three in the United States, established about 1884, were in Chicago. Carrie was familiar with the names of several through the advertisements in the "Daily News," and now proceeded to seek them. The words of Mr. McManus had somehow managed to restore her courage, which had fallen low, and she dared to hope that this new line would offer her something in the way of employment. Some time she spent in wandering up and down thinking to encounter the buildings by chance, so readily is the mind, bent upon prosecuting a hard but needful errand, eased by that self-deception which the semblance of search without the reality gives. At last she inquired of a police officer and was directed to proceed "two blocks up" where she would find The Fair. Following his advice she reached that institution and entered.

The nature of these vast retail combinations, should they ever permanently disappear, will form an interesting chapter in the commercial history of our nation. Such a flowering out of a modest trade principle the world had never witnessed up to that time. They were along the line of the most effective retail organization, with hundreds of stores coordinated into one, and laid out upon the most imposing and economic basis. They were handsome, bustling, successful affairs, with a host of clerks and a swarm of patrons. Carrie passed along the busy aisles, much affected by the remarkable displays of trinkets, dress goods, shoes, stationery, jewelry. Each separate counter was a show place of dazzling interest and attraction. She could not help feeling the claim of each trinket and valuable upon her personally and yet she did not stop. There was nothing there which she could not have used—nothing which she did not long to own. The dainty slippers and stockings, the delicately frilled skirts and petticoats, the laces, ribbons, hair-combs, purses, all touched her with individual desire, and she felt keenly the fact that not any of these things were in the range of her purchase. She was a work-seeker, an outcast without employment, one whom the average employé could tell at a glance was poor and in need of a situation.

It must not be thought that anyone could have mistaken her for a nervous, sensitive, high-strung nature, cast unduly upon a cold, calculating and unpoetic world. Such certainly she was not. But women are peculiarly sensitive to the personal adornment or equipment of their person, even the dullest, and particularly is this true of the young. Your bright-eyed, rosy-cheeked maiden, over whom a poet might well rave for the flowerlike expression of her countenance and the lissome and dainty grace of her body, may reasonably be dead to every evidence of the artistic and poetic in the unrelated evidences of life, and yet not lack in material appreciation. Never, it might be said, does she fail in this. With her the bloom of a rose may pass unappreciated, but the bloom of a fold of silk, never. If nothing in the heavens, or the earth, or the waters, could elicit her fancy or delight her from its spiritual or artistic side, think not that the material would be lost. The glint of a buckle, the hue of a precious stone, the faintest tints of the watered silk, these she would devine and qualify as readily as your poet if not more so. The creak, the rustle, the glow—the least and best of the graven or spun—, these she would perceive and appreciate—if not because of some fashionable or hearsay quality, then on account of their true beauty, their innate fitness in any order of harmony, their place in the magical order and sequence of dress.

Not only did Carrie feel the drag of desire for all of this which was new and pleasing in apparel for women, but she noticed, too, with a touch at the heart, the fine ladies who elbowed and ignored her, brushing past in utter disregard of her presence, themselves eagerly enlisted in the materials which the store contained. Carrie was not familiar with the appearance of her more fortunate sisters of the city. Neither had she before known the nature and appearance of the shop girls, with whom she now compared poorly. They were pretty in the main, some even handsome, with a certain independence and toss of indifference which added, in the case of the more favored, a certain piquancy. Their clothes were neat, in many instances fine, and wherever she encountered the eye of one, it was only to recognize in it a keen analysis of her own position—her individual shortcomings of dress and that shadow of *manner* which she thought must hang about her and make clear to all who and what she was. A flame of envy lighted in her heart. She realized in a dim way how much the city held—wealth, fashion, ease—every adornment for women, and she longed for dress and beauty with a whole and fulsome heart.

On the second floor were the managerial offices, to which

after some inquiry she was now directed. There she found other girls ahead of her, applicants like herself, but with more of that self-satisfied and independent air which experience of the city lends—girls who scrutinized her in a painful manner. After a wait of perhaps three-quarters of an hour she was called in turn.

"Now," said a sharp, quick-mannered Jew who was sitting at a roll-top desk near the window—"have you ever worked in any other store?"

"No sir," said Carrie.

"Oh, you haven't," he said, eyeing her keenly.

"No sir," she replied.

"Well, we prefer young women just now with some experience. I guess we can't use you."

Carrie stood waiting a moment, hardly certain whether the interview had terminated.

"Don't wait!" he exclaimed. "Remember we are very busy here."

Carrie began to move quickly to the door.

"Hold on," he said, calling her back. "Give me your name and address. We want girls occasionally."

When she had gotten safely out again into the street she could scarcely restrain tears. It was not so much the particular rebuff which she had just experienced, but the whole abashing trend of the day. She was tired and rather over-played upon in the nerves. She abandoned the thought of appealing to the other department stores and now wandered on, feeling a certain safety and relief in mingling with the crowd.

In her indifferent wandering she turned into Jackson Street, not far from the river, and was keeping her way along the south side of that imposing thoroughfare, when a piece of wrapping paper written on with marking ink and tacked upon a door attracted her attention. It read "Girls wanted—wrappers and stitchers." She hesitated for the moment, thinking surely to go in, but upon further consideration the added qualifications of "wrappers and stitchers" deterred her. She had no idea of what that meant. Most probably she would need to be experienced in it. She walked on a little way, mentally balancing as to whether or not to apply. Necessity triumphed however and she returned.

The entrance, which opened into a small hall, led to an

elevator shaft, the elevator of which was up. It was a dingy affair, being used both as a freight and passenger entrance, and the woodwork was marked and splintered by the heavy boxes which were tumbled in and out, at intervals. A frowzy-headed German-American, about fourteen years of age, operated the elevator in his shirt sleeves and bare feet. His face was considerably marked with grease and dirt.

When the elevator stopped, the boy leisurely raised a protecting arm of wood and by grace of his superior privilege admitted her.

"Wear do you want to go?" he inquired.

"I want to see the manager," she replied.

"Wot manager?" he returned, surveying her caustically.

"Is there more than one?" she asked. "I thought it was all one firm."

"Naw," said the youth. "Der's six different people. Want to see Speigelheim?"

"I don't know," answered Carrie. She colored a little as she began to feel the necessity of explaining. "I want to see whoever put up that sign."

"Dot's Speigelheim," said the boy. "Fort floor." Therewith he proudly turned to his task of pulling the rope, and the elevator ascended.

The firm of Speigelheim and Co., makers of boys' caps, occupied one floor of fifty feet in width and some eighty feet in depth. It was a place rather dingily lighted, the darkest portions having incandescent lights, filled in part with machines and part with workbenches. At the latter labored quite a company of girls and some men. The former were drabby looking creatures, stained in face with oil and dust, clad in thin shapeless cotton dresses, and shod with more or less worn shoes. Many of them had their sleeves rolled up, revealing bare arms, and in some cases, owing to heat, their dresses were open at the neck. They were a fair type of nearly the lowest order of shop girls,—careless, rather slouchy, and more or less pale from confinement. They were not timid however, were rich in curiosity and strong in daring and slang.

Carrie looked about her, very much disturbed and quite sure that she did not want to work here. Aside from making her uncomfortable by sidelong glances, no one paid her the least attention. She waited until the whole department was aware of her presence. Then some word was sent round and a foreman in an apron and shirt sleeves, the latter rolled up to his shoulders, approached.

"Do you want to see me?" he asked.

"Do you need any help?" said Carrie, already learning directness of address.

"Do you know how to stitch caps?" he returned.

"No sir," she replied.

"Have you ever had any experience at this kind of work?" he inquired.

She owned that she hadn't.

"Well," said the foreman, scratching his ear meditatively, "we do need a stitcher. We like experienced help though. We've hardly got time to break people in." He paused and looked away out of the window. "We might, though, put you at finishing," he concluded reflectively.

"How much do you pay a week?" ventured Carrie, emboldened by a certain softness in the man's manner and his simplicity of address.

"Three and a half," he answered.

"Oh," she was about to exclaim, but checked herself, and allowed her thoughts to die without expression.

"We're not exactly in need of anybody," he went on vaguely, looking her over as one would a package. "You can come Monday morning though," he added, "and I'll put you to work."

"Thank you," said Carrie weakly.

"If you come, bring an apron," he added.

He walked away and left her standing by the elevator, never so much as inquiring her name.

While the appearance of the shop and the announcement of the price paid per week operated very much as a blow to Carrie's fancy, the fact that work of any kind, after so rude a round of experience, was offered her, was gratifying. She could not begin to believe that she would take the place, modest as her aspirations were. She had been used to better than that. Her mere experience and the free out-of-doors life of the country caused her nature to revolt at such confinement. Dirt had never been her share. Her sister's flat was clean. This place was grimy and low; the girls were careless and hardened. They must be bad-minded and -hearted, she imagined. Still a place had been offered her. Surely Chicago was not so bad if she could find one place in one day. She might find another and better later.

Her subsequent experiences were not of a reassuring nature, however. From all the more pleasing or imposing places she was turned away abruptly with the most chilling formality. In others where she applied, only the experienced were required. She met with painful rebuffs, the most trying of which had been in a cloak manufacturing house, where she had gone to the fourth floor to inquire.

"No, no," said the foreman, a rough, heavy-built individual who looked after a miserably lighted work shop, "we don't want anyone. Don't come here."

In another factory she was leered upon by a most sensual-faced individual who endeavored to turn the natural questions of the inquiry into a personal interview, asking all sorts of embarrassing questions and endeavoring to satisfy himself evidently that she was of loose enough morals to suit his purpose. In that case she had been relieved enough to get away and found the busy, indifferent streets to be again a soothing refuge.

With the wane of the afternoon went her hopes, her courage and her strength. She had been astonishingly persistent. So earnest an effort was well deserving of a better reward. On every hand, to her fatigued senses, the great business portion grew larger, harder, more stolid in its indifference. It seemed as if it was all closed to her, that the struggle was too fierce for her to hope to do anything at all. Men and women hurried by in long, shifting lines. She felt the flow of the tide of effort and interest, felt her own helplessness without quite realizing the wisp on the tide that she was. She cast about vainly for some possible place to apply but found no door which she had the courage to enter. It would be the same thing all over. The old humiliation of her pleas rewarded by curt denial. Sick at heart and in body, she turned to the west, the direction of Minnie's flat, which she had now fixed in mind, and began that wearisome, baffled retreat which the seeker for employment at nightfall too often makes. In passing through Fifth Avenue, south towards Van Buren Street, where she intended to take a car, she passed the door of a large wholesale shoe house, through the plate glass window of which she could see a middle-aged gentleman sitting at a small desk. One of those forlorn impulses which often grow out of a fixed sense of defeat, the last sprouting of a baffled and uprooted growth of ideas, seized upon her. She walked deliberately through the door and up to the gentleman who looked at her weary face with partially awakened interest.

"What is it?" he said.

"Can you give me something to do?" asked Carrie.

"Now I really don't know," he said kindly. "What kind of work is it you want—you're not a typewriter, are you?"

"Oh, no," answered Carrie.

"Well, we only employ book keepers and typewriters here. You might go round to the side and inquire upstairs. They did want some help upstairs a few days ago. Ask for Mr. Brown."

She hastened around to the side entrance and was taken up by the elevator to the fourth floor.

"Call Mr. Brown, Willie," said the elevator man to a boy near by.

Willie went off and presently returned with the information that Mr. Brown said she should sit down and that he would be around in a little while.

It was a portion of a stock room which gave no idea of the general character of the floor, and Carrie could form no opinion of the nature of the work.

"So you want something to do," said Mr. Brown, after he inquired concerning the nature of her errand. "Have you ever been employed in a shoe factory before?"

"No sir," said Carrie.

"What is your name?" he inquired, and being informed, "Well, I don't know as I have anything for you. Would you work for four and a half a week?"

Carrie was too worn by defeat not to feel that it was considerable. She had not expected that he would offer her less than six. She acquiesced, however, and he took her name and address.

"Well," he said finally—"you report here at eight o'clock Monday morning. I think I can find something for you to do."

He left her revived by the possibilities, sure that she had found something to do at last. Instantly the blood crept warmly over her body. Her nervous tension relaxed. She walked out into the busy street and discovered a new atmosphere. Behold, the throng was moving with a lightsome step. She noticed that men and women were smiling. Scraps of conversation and notes of laughter floated to her. The air was light. People were already pouring out of the buildings, their labor ended for the day. She noticed that they were pleased, and thoughts of her sister's home, and the meal that would be awaiting her, quickened her steps. She hurried on, tired perhaps, but no longer weary of foot. What would not Minnie say! Ah, long the winter in Chicago—the lights, the crowd, the amusement. This was a great, pleasing metropolis after all. Her new firm was a goodly institution. Its windows were of huge plate glass. She could probably do well there. Thoughts of Drouet returned, of the things he had told her. She now felt that life was better. That it was livelier, sprightlier. She boarded a car in the best of spirits, feeling her blood still flowing pleasantly. She would live in Chicago, her mind kept saying to itself. She would have a better time than she ever had before—she would be happy.

CHAPTER IV.

For the next two days Carrie indulged in the most high-flown speculations. An excellent essay on the art of high living might well be compiled out of the thoughts of those who, like her, are anxiously anticipating the arrival of a small income. In such cases, want runs swiftly before gathering imaginative delights and privileges.

We are all aware that this is not Fancy's novel failing. She has ever borne a full and open purse. Carrie plunged recklessly into privileges and amusements which would have been much more becoming had she been cradled a child of fortune. With ready will and quick mental selection she scattered her meagre four-fifty per week with a swift and graceful hand. It was spent many times over in car fare alone, sight-seeing. Into those vague palaces, of which, to the new arrival, the city is full, and the entrance to which is purchased alone, she now entered. The round of theatres with delightful seats was a simple matter. Her certain income covered it all. Her purse, now unchangingly filled with it, was carried into every avenue and every store. Portions of its fullness were passed over every counter and broken in small change a thousand times, and yet it did not fail. Silks, woolens, lingerie and fine feathers—the necessities and frivolities of fashion as she understood it—all strained its marketing power, but it did not break. Indeed, as she sat in her rocking chair these several evenings before going to bed and looked out upon the pleasantly lighted street, it cleared for its prospective possessor the way to every joy and every bauble which the heart of woman may desire. The lights, the tinkle of car bells, the late murmur of the city, bespoke its power to her. "I will have a fine time," she thought to herself over and over and over.

Her sister Minnie knew nothing of these rather wild cerebrations, though they exhausted the markets of delight. She was too busy scrubbing the kitchen woodwork and calculating the purchasing power of eighty cents for Sunday's dinner. When Carrie had returned home, flushed with her first success and ready, for all her weariness, to discuss the now interesting events which led up to her achievement, the former had merely smiled approvingly and inquired whether she would have to spend any of it for car fare. This consideration had not entered in before, and it did not now for long affect the glow of Carrie's enthusiasm. Disposed as she then was to calculate upon that vague basis which allows the subtraction of one sum from another without any perceptible diminution, she was happy.

When Hanson came home at seven o'clock, he was inclined to be a little crusty,—his usual demeanor before supper. This never showed so much in anything he said, as in a certain solemnity of countenance and the silent manner in which he slopped about. He had a pair of yellow carpet slippers which he enjoyed wearing, and these he would immediately substitute for the solid pair of shoes which he wore. This, and washing his face with the aid of common washing soap, until it glowed a shiny red, constituted his only preparation for his evening meal. He would then get his evening paper and read in silence.

For a young man this was rather a morbid turn of character, and so affected Carrie. Indeed it affected the entire atmosphere of the flat, as such things are inclined to do, and gave to his wife's mind its subdued and tactful turn, anxious to avoid taciturn replies. Under the influence of Carrie's announcement, he brightened up somewhat.

"You didn't lose any time, did you?" he remarked, smiling a little.

"No!" returned Carrie with a touch of pride.

He asked her one or two more questions and then turned to play with the baby, leaving the subject until it was brought up again by Minnie at the table.

Carrie, however, was not to be reduced to the common level of observation which prevailed in the flat.

"It seems to be such a large company," she said, at one place. "Great big plate glass windows and lots of clerks. The man I saw said they hired ever so many people."

"It's not very hard to get work now," put in Hanson, "if you look right."

Minnie, under the warming influence of Carrie's good spirits and her husband's somewhat conversational mood, began to tell Carrie of some of the well-known things to see—things the enjoyment of which cost nothing.

"You'd like to see Michigan Avenue. There are such fine houses. It is such a fine street."

"Where is H. R. Jacob's?" interrupted Carrie, mentioning one of the theatres devoted to melodrama, which went by that name at the time.

"Oh, it's not very far from here," answered Minnie. "It's in Halstead Street, right up here."

"How I'd like to go there. I crossed Halstead today, didn't I?"

At this there was a slight halt in the natural reply. Thoughts are a strangely permeating factor. At her suggestion of going to the theatre, the unspoken shade of disapproval to the doing of those things which involved the expenditure of money—shades of feeling which arose in the mind of Hanson and then in Minnie—slightly affected the atmosphere of the table. Minnie answered "yes," but Carrie could feel that going to the theatre was poorly advocated here. The subject was staved off for a little while until Hanson, through with his meal, took his paper and went into the front room.

When they were alone the two sisters began a somewhat freer conversation, Carrie interrupting it to hum a little, as they worked together at the dishes and putting the things to rights.

"I should like to walk up and see Halstead Street if it isn't too far," said Carrie, after a time. "Why don't we go to the theatre tonight?"

"Oh, I don't think Sven would want to go tonight," returned Minnie. "He has to get up so early."

"He wouldn't mind—he'd enjoy it," said Carrie.

"No, he doesn't go very often," returned Minnie.

"Well I'd like to go," rejoined Carrie. "Let's you and me go."

Minnie pondered awhile, not upon whether she could or would go, for that point was already negatively settled with her, but upon some means of diverting the thoughts of her sister to some other topic.

"We'll go some other time," she said at last, finding no ready means of escape.

Carrie sensed the root of the opposition at once.

"I have some money," she said. "You go with me."

Minnie shook her head.

"He could go along," said Carrie.

"No," returned Minnie softly, rattling the dishes to drown the conversation. "He wouldn't."

It had been several years since Minnie had seen Carrie and in that time the latter's character had developed a few shades. Naturally timid in all things which related to her own advancement, and especially so when without power or resource, her craving for pleasure was so strong that it was the one stay of her nature. She would speak for that when silent on all else.

"Ask him," she pleaded softly.

Minnie was thinking of the resource which Carrie's board would add. It would pay the rent and would make the subject of expenditure a little less difficult to talk about with her husband. But if Carrie was going to think of running around in the beginning, there would be a hitch somewhere. Unless Carrie submitted to a solemn round of industry and saw the need of hard work without longing for play, how was her coming to the city to profit them? These thoughts were not those of a cold, hard nature at all. They were the serious reflections of a mind which invariably adjusted itself without much complaining to such surroundings as its industry could make for it.

At last she yielded enough to ask Hanson. It was a half-hearted procedure without a shade of desire on her part.

"Carrie wants us to go to the theatre," she said, looking in upon her husband. Hanson looked up from his paper and they exchanged a mild look which said as plainly as anything, "This isn't what we expected."

"I don't care to go," he returned. "What does she want to see?"

"H. R. Jacob's," said Minnie.

He looked down at his paper and shook his head negatively.

Carrie, when she saw how they looked upon the proposition, gained a still clearer feeling of their way of life. It weighed on her but took no definite form of opposition.

"I think I'll go down and stand at the foot of the stairs," she said after a time.

Minnie made no objection to this and Carrie put on her hat and went below.

"Where has Carrie gone?" asked Hanson, coming back into the dining room when he heard the door close.

"She said she was going down to the foot of the stairs," answered Minnie. "I guess she just wants to look out awhile."

"She oughtn't to be thinking about spending her money on theatres already, do you think?" he asked.

"She just feels a little curious, I guess," ventured Minnie. "Everything is so new."

"I don't know," said Hanson, and went over to the baby, his forehead slightly wrinkled.

He was thinking of a full career of vanity and wastefulness which a young girl might indulge in and wondering how Carrie could contemplate such a course when she had so little, as yet, to do with.

On Saturday, Carrie went out by herself—first toward the river, which interested her, and then back along Jackson, which was then lined by the pretty houses and fine lawns which subsequently caused it to be made into a boulevard. She was struck with the evidences of wealth, although there was perhaps not a person on the street worth more than a hundred thousand dollars. She was glad to be out of the flat because already she felt that it was a narrow, humdrum place and that interest and joy lay elsewhere. Her thoughts now were of a more liberal character, and she punctuated them with speculations as to the whereabouts of Drouet. She was not sure but that he might call anyhow Monday night, and while she felt a little disturbed at the possibility, there was nevertheless just the shade of a wish that circumstances were such that it might be.

On Monday she arose early and prepared to go to work. She dressed herself in a worn shirtwaist of dotted blue percale, a skirt of light brown serge rather faded, and a small straw hat which she had worn all summer at Columbia City. Her shoes were rather worn at tips and heels, and her necktie was in that crumpled, flattened state which time and much wearing impart. She made a very average-looking shop girl, with the exception of her features. These were slightly more even than is common in women, and gave her a sweet, somewhat reserved air which was pleasing.

It is no easy thing to get up early in the morning when one is used to sleeping until between seven and eight, as Carrie had been at home. She gained some inkling of the character of Hanson's life when, half-asleep, she looked out into the dining room at six o'clock and saw him silently finishing his breakfast. By the time she was dressed he was gone, and she, Minnie and the baby ate together, the latter being just old enough to sit by in a high chair and disturb the dishes with a spoon. Her spirits were greatly subdued now when the fact of entering upon strange and untried duties confronted her. Only the ashes of all her fine fancies were remaining—ashes still concealing, nevertheless, a few red embers of hope. So subdued was she by her weakening nerves that she ate quite in silence, going over imaginary conceptions of the character of the shoe company, the nature of the work, her employer's attitude. She was vaguely feeling that she should come in contact with the great owners, that her work should be where grave, stylishly-dressed men occasionally look on.

"Well, good luck," said Minnie, when she was ready to go. They had agreed it was best to walk, that morning at least, to see if she could do it every day, sixty cents a week for car fare being quite an item under the circumstances.

"I'll tell you how it goes tonight," said Carrie.

Once in the sunlit street, with laborers tramping by in either direction, the horse cars passing, crowded to the rails with the small clerks and floor help in the great wholesale houses, and men and women generally coming out of doors and passing about the neighborhood, Carrie felt slightly reassured. In the sunshine of the morning beneath the wide blue heavens, with a fresh wind astir, what fears, except the most desperate, can find harborage in the human breast? In the night or the gloomy chambers of the day, fears and misgivings wax strong, but out in the sunlight there is for a time cessation even of the terror of death.

Carrie went strongly forward until she crossed the river and turned into Fifth Avenue. The thoroughfare, in this part, was like a walled cañon of brown stone and dark red brick. The big windows of plate glass looked shiny and clean. Trucks were rumbling in increasing numbers; men and women, girls and boys were moving onward in all directions. She met girls her own age who looked at her as if with contempt for her diffidence. She wondered at the magnitude of this life and at the importance of knowing much in order to do anything in it at all. Dread at her own inefficiency crept upon her. She would not know how, she would not be quick enough. Had not all the other places refused her because she did not know something or other? She would be scolded, abused and ignominiously discharged.

It was with but weak knees and a slight catch in her breathing that she came up to the great shoe company at Adams and Fifth Avenue and entered the elevator. When she stepped out on the fourth floor there was no one at hand, only great aisles of boxes piled to the ceiling. She stood, very much frightened, awaiting some one, when a young man with some order slips in his hand got off the elevator.

"Who is it you want?" he asked her.

"Mr. Brown."

"Oh," he said.

Presently Mr. Brown came up. He did not seem to recognize her.

"What is it you want?" he questioned.

Carrie's heart sank.

"You said I should come this morning to see about work—"

"Oh," he interrupted. "Um—yes. What is your name?"

"Carrie Meeber."

"Yes," said he. "You come with me."

He led the way through dark, box-lined aisles which had the smell of new shoes until they came to an iron door which opened into the factory proper. There was a large low-ceiled room with clacking, rattling machines at which men in white shirt sleeves and blue gingham aprons were working. She followed him diffidently through the clattering automatons, keeping her eyes straight before her and flushing slightly. They crossed to a far corner and took an elevator to the sixth floor. Out of the array of machines and benches Mr. Brown signaled a foreman.

"This is the girl," he said, and turning to Carrie, "you go with him." He then returned and Carrie followed her new superior to a little desk in a corner, which he used as a kind of official centre.

"You've never worked at anything like this before, have you?" he questioned rather sternly.

"No sir," she answered.

He seemed rather annoyed at having to bother with such help, but put down her name and then led her across to where a line of girls were sitting on a line of stools in front of a line of clacking machines. On the shoulder of one of the girls who was punching eye holes in one piece of the upper, by the aid of the machine, he put his hand.

"You," he said, "show this girl how to do what you're doing. When you get through, come to me."

The girl so addressed rose promptly and gave Carrie her place.

"It isn't hard to do," she said, bending over. "You just take this so, fasten it with this clamp and start the machine."

She suited action to word, fastened the piece of leather (which was eventually to form the right half of the upper of a man's shoe) by little adjustable clamps, and pushed a small steel rod at the side of the machine. The latter jumped to the task of punching, with sharp, snapping clicks, cutting circular bits of leather out of the side of the upper, leaving the holes which eventually were to hold the laces. After observing a few times, the girl let her work at it alone. Seeing that it was being fairly well done, she went away.

The pieces of leather came from the girl at the machine to her right, and were passed on to the girl at her left. Carrie saw at once that an average speed was necessary or the work would pile up on her and all those below would be delayed. She had no time to look about, and bent anxiously to her task, managing to do fairly well. The girls at her left and right realized her predicament and feelings, and, in a way, tried to aid her as much as they dared by working slower.

At this task she labored incessantly for some time, finding relief from her own nervous fears and imaginings in the humdrum, mechanical movement of the machine. She felt, as the minutes passed, that the room was not very light. It had a thick odor of fresh leather, but that did not worry her. She felt the eyes of the other help upon her and troubled lest she was not working fast enough.

Once when she was fumbling at the little clamp, having made a slight error in setting in the leather, a great hand appeared before her eyes and fastened the clamp for her. It was the foreman. Her heart thumped so that she could scarcely see to go on.

"Start your machine," he said. "Start your machine. Don't keep the line waiting."

This recovered her sufficiently and she went excitedly on, hardly breathing until the shadow moved away from behind her. Then she heaved a great breath.

As the morning wore on the room became hotter. She felt the need of a breath of fresh air and a drink of water but did not venture to stir. The stool she sat on was without a back or footrest and she began to feel uncomfortable. She found after a time that her back was beginning to ache. She twisted and turned from one position to another slightly different, but it did not ease her for long. She was beginning to weary.

"Stand up, why don't you," said the girl at her right, without any form of introduction. "They won't care."

Carrie looked at her gratefully. "I guess I will," she said.

She stood up from her stool and worked that way for awhile, but it was a more difficult position. Her neck and shoulders ached in bending over.

The spirit of the place was one which impressed itself on her in a rough way. She did not venture to look around any, but above the clack of the machines she could hear an occasional remark. She could also note a thing or two out of the side of her eye.

"Did you see Harry last night?" said the girl at her left, addressing her neighbor.

"No."

"You ought to have seen the tie he had on. Gee, but he was a mark."

"S-s-t," said the other girl, bending over her work. The first silenced instantly, assuming a solemn face. The foreman passed slowly along, eyeing each worker distinctly. The moment he was gone, the conversation was resumed again.

"Say," began the girl at her left, "what jeh think he said?"

"I don't know."

"He said he saw us with Eddie Harris at Martin's that night."

"No!" They both giggled.

A youth with tan-colored hair that needed clipping very badly came shuffling along between the machines, bearing a basket of leather findings under his left arm, and pressed against his stomach. When near Carrie he stretched out his right hand and gripped one girl under the arm.

"Aw, let go," she exclaimed angrily—"Duffer."

He only grinned broadly in return.

"Rubber," he called back as she looked after him. There was nothing of the gallant in him.

Carrie got so at last that she could scarcely sit still. Her legs began to tire and she felt as if she would give anything to get up and stretch. Would noon never come? It seemed as if she had worked an entire day already. She was not hungry at all, but weak, and her eyes were tired straining at the one point where the eye-punch came down and clipped the small piece out of the leather. The girl at the right noticed her squirmings and felt sorry for her. She was concentrating herself too thoroughly—what she did really required less mental and physical strain. There was nothing to be done, however. The halves of the uppers came piling steadily down. Her hands began to ache at the wrists and then in the fingers, and toward the last she seemed one mass of dull complaining muscles, fixed in an eternal position and performing a single mechanical movement which became more and more distasteful until at last it was absolutely nauseating. When she was most wondering whether the strain would ever cease, a dull-sounding bell clanged somewhere down an elevator shaft and the end came. In an instant there was a buzz of action and conversation. All the girls instantly left their stools and hurried away into an adjoining room; men passed through, coming from some department which opened on the right. The whirring wheels began to sing in a steadily modifying key until at last they died away in a low buzz. There was an audible stillness in which the common voice sounded strange.

Carrie gladly got up and sought her lunch box. She was stiff, a little dizzy and very thirsty. On the way to the small space portioned off by wood, where all the wraps and lunches were kept, she encountered the foreman, who stared at her hard.

"Well," he said, "did you get along all right?"

"I think so," she replied, very respectfully.

"Um!" he replied, for the want of something better, and walked on.

Under better material conditions this kind of work would not have been so bad, but the new socialism which involves pleasant working conditions for employés had not then taken hold upon manufacturing companies.

The place smelled of the oil of the machines and the new leather—a combination which, added to by the stale odours of the building, was not pleasant even in cold weather. The floor, though regularly swept each evening, presented a littered surface. Not the slightest provision had been made for the comfort of the employés, the idea being that something was gained by giving them as little and making the work as hard and unremunerative as possible. What we know of foot rests, swivel-back chairs, dining rooms for the girls, clean aprons and curling irons supplied free, and a decent cloak room, were unthought of. The wash rooms and lavatories were disagreeable, crude, if not foul places, and the whole atmosphere was one of hard contract.

Carrie looked about her, after she had drunk a tinful of water from a bucket in one corner, for a place to sit and eat. The other girls had ranged themselves about the windows or at the work benches of those of the men who had gone out. She saw no place which did not hold a couple or a group of girls, and being too timid to think of intruding herself and offering friendly overtures, she sought out her machine and, seated upon her stool, opened her lunch on her lap. There she sat, listening to the chatter and comment which went on in different parts of the rooms. It was for the most part silly and graced by the current slang. Several of the men in the room exchanged compliments with the girls at long range.

"Say, Kitty," called one to a girl who was doing a waltz step in a few feet of space near one of the windows—"are you goin' to the ball with me?"

"Look out, Kitty," called another, "you'll jar your back hair."

"Go on, rubber!" was her only comment.

As Carrie listened to this and much more of similar familiar badinage among the men and girls, she instinctively withdrew into herself. She was not used to this type and felt that there was something hard and low about it all. She feared that the young boys about would address such remarks to her—boys who beside Drouet seemed uncouth and ridiculous. She made the average feminine distinction between clothes, putting worth, goodness and distinction in a dress suit, and leaving all the unlovely qualities and those beneath notice in overalls and jumper.

She was glad when the short half-hour was over and the wheels began to whirr again. Though wearied, she would be inconspicuous. This illusion ended when another young man passed along the aisle and poked her indifferently in the ribs with his thumb. She turned about, indignation leaping to her eyes, but he had gone on and only once turned to grin. She found it difficult to conquer an inclination to cry.

The girl next her noticed her state of mind.

"Don't you mind," she said. "He's too fresh."

Carrie said nothing but bent over her work. She felt as though she could hardly endure such a life. Her idea of work had been so entirely different. All during the long afternoon she thought of the city outside with its imposing show, crowds and fine buildings. Columbia City and the better side of her home life came back. By three o'clock she was sure it must be six, and by four it seemed as if they had forgotten to note the hour and were letting all work overtime. The foreman became a true ogre, prowling constantly about, keeping her tied down to her miserable task. What she heard of the conversation about her only made her feel sure that she did not want to make friends with any of these. When six o'clock came she hurried eagerly away, her arms aching and her limbs stiff from sitting in one position.

As she passed out along the hall after getting her hat, a young machine hand, attracted by her looks, made bold to jest with her.

"Say, Maggie," he called, "if you'll wait I'll walk with you."

It was thrown so straight in her direction that she knew who was meant but never turned to look.

In the crowded elevator another dusty, toil-stained youth tried to make an impression on her by leering in her face.

One young man, waiting on the walk outside for the appearance of another, grinned at her as she passed.

"Ain't goin' my way, are you?" he called jocosely.

Carrie turned her face to the west with a subdued heart. As she turned the corner she saw through the great shiny window the small desk at which she had applied. There were the crowds hurrying with the same buzz and energy-yielding enthusiasm. She herself felt a slight relief, but it was only at her escape. She felt ashamed in the face of the better-dressed girls who went by. She felt as though she should be better served, and her heart revolted.

CHAPTER V.

Drouet did not call that evening. That worthy, after receiving the letter, had laid aside all thought of Carrie for the time being and was floating around having what he considered a gay time. On this particular evening he dined at Rector's, a restaurant of some local fame which occupied a basement at Clark and Monroe Streets. Thereafter he visited the resort of Hannah and Hogg's, which was in Adams Street opposite the somewhat imposing Federal Building. There he leaned over the splendid bar which it contained and swallowed a glass of plain whiskey and purchased a couple of cigars, one of which he lighted. This to him represented in part high life—a fair sample of what the whole must be.

Drouet was not a drinker, in the sense that that term is used to express excess. He was not a "monied" man. He only craved the best as his mind conceived it, and such doings seemed to him a part of the best. Rector's, with its polished marble walls and floor, its profusion of lights, its show of china and silverware, and above all its reputation as a resort for actors and professional men, seemed to him the proper place for a successful man to go. He loved fine clothes, good eating, and particularly the company and acquaintanceship of successful men. When dining it was a source of keen satisfaction to him to know that Joseph Jefferson was wont to come to this same place at some time or another, or that Henry E. Dixey, quite a well-known performer of the day, was there only a few tables off. At Rector's he could always obtain this satisfaction, for there, particularly of an evening, one could encounter politicians, brokers, actors, some rich young "rounders" of the town, all eating and drinking amid a buzz of popular, commonplace conversation.

"That's so and so over there," was a common remark of these gentlemen among themselves, particularly among those who had not yet reached, but hoped to do so, the dazzling height which money to dine here, lavishly, represented.

"You don't say so," would be the reply.

"Why yes, didn't you know that? Why he's manager of the Grand Opera House."

When these things would fall upon Drouet's ears, he would straighten himself a little more stiffly and eat with solid comfort. If he had any vanity, this augmented it, and if he had any ambition, this stirred it. He would be able to flash a roll of greenbacks too someday. As it was, he could eat where *they* did.

His preference for Hannah and Hogg's Adams Street place was another yard off the same cloth. This was really a gorgeous saloon from a Chicago standpoint. Like Rector's it also was ornamented with a blaze of incandescent lights held in handsome chandeliers and set in graceful places. The floors were of brightly-colored tiles, the walls a composition of rich, dark-polished wood, which reflected the light, and colored stucco-work, which gave the place a very sumptuous appearance. The long bar was a blaze of lights, polished woodwork, colored and cut glassware and many fancy bottles. It was a truly swell saloon, with rich screens, fancy wines, and a line of bar goods unsurpassed in the country.

At Rector's, Drouet had met Mr. G. W. Hurstwood, manager of the Hannah and Hogg's Adams Street place, the latter having been pointed out as a very successful and well-known man about town. Hurstwood looked the part, for besides being slightly under forty, he had a good stout constitution, an active manner and a solid substantial air, which was composed in part of his fine clothes, his clean linen, his jewels, and, above all, his own sense of his importance. Drouet immediately conceived a notion of him as being someone worth knowing and was glad not only to meet him, but to visit the Adams Street bar thereafter whenever he wanted a drink or a cigar.

Hurstwood was an interesting character after his kind. He was shrewd and clever in many little things and capable of creating a good impression. His position, which was fairly important, was that of manager—a kind of stewardship which was imposing but lacked financial control. He had risen by perseverance and industry, through long years of service, from the position of barkeeper in a commonplace saloon to his present altitude. He had a little office in the place, set off in polished cherry and grillwork, where he kept in a roll-top desk the rather simple accounts of the place—supplies ordered and needed and so on. The chief executive and financial functions devolved upon the owners, Messrs. Hannah and Hogg, and upon a cashier, who looked after the money taken in.

For the most part he lounged about, dressed in excellent, tailored suits of imported goods, several rings upon his fingers, a fine blue diamond in his necktie, a striking vest of some new pattern and a watch chain of solid gold which held a charm of rich design and a watch of the latest make and engraving. He knew by name and could greet personally with a "Well, old fellow," hundreds of actors, merchants, politicians and the general run of successful characters about town, and it was a part of his success to do so. He had a finely graduated scale of informality and friendship, which improved from the "How do you do," addressed to the fifteen-dollar-a-week clerks and office attachés who by long frequenting of the place became aware of his position, to the "Why, old man, how are you," which he addressed to those noted or rich individuals who knew him and were inclined to be friendly. There was a class, however, too rich, too famous, or too successful, with whom he could not attempt any familiarity of address, and with these he was professionally tactful, assuming a grave and dignified attitude, paying them the deference which would win their good feeling without in the least compromising his own bearing and opinions. There were, in the last place, a few good followers, neither rich nor poor, famous nor yet remarkably successful, with whom he was friendly on the score of good fellowship. These were the kind of men whom he would converse with the longest and perhaps the most seriously. He loved to go out and have a good time once in a while,—to go to the races, the theatres, the sporting entertainments at some of the clubs and those more unmentionable resorts of vice—the gilded chambers of shame with which Chicago was then so liberally cursed. He kept a horse and neat trap, had his wife and two children who were well established in a neat house on the North Side, near Lincoln Park, and was altogether a very acceptable individual of our great American upper class—the first grade below the luxuriously rich.

Hurstwood liked Drouet. The latter's genial nature and dressy appearance pleased him. He knew that Drouet was only a traveling salesman, and not one of many years' standing at that, but the firm of Bartlett, Caryoe and Co. was a large and prosperous house, and Drouet stood well. Hurstwood knew Caryoe quite well, having drunk a glass now and then with him, in company with several others, when the conversation was general. Drouet had what was a help in his business, a moderate sense of humor, and could tell a good story when the occasion required. He could talk races with Hurstwood, tell interesting incidents concerning himself and his experiences with women, and report the state of trade in the cities which he visited, and so managed to make himself almost invariably agreeable. To-night he was particularly so, since his report to the company had been favorably commented upon, his new samples had been satisfactorily selected and his trip marked out for the next six weeks.

"Why, hello, Charlie old man," said Hurstwood as Drouet

came in that evening about eight o'clock. "How goes it?" The room was crowded.

Drouet shook hands, beaming good nature, and they strolled toward the bar.

"Oh, all right."

"I haven't seen you in six weeks. When did you get in?"

"Friday," said Drouet. "Had a fine trip."

"Glad of it," said Hurstwood, his black eyes lit with a warmth which half displaced the cold make-believe that usually dwelt in them. "What are you going to take?" he added, as the barkeeper, in snowy jacket and tie, leaned toward them from behind the bar.

"Old Hennessy," said Drouet.

"A little of the same for me," put in Hurstwood.

"How long are you in town this time?" inquired Hurstwood.

"Only until Wednesday. I'm going up to St. Paul."

"George Evans was in here Saturday and said he saw you in Milwaukee last week."

"Yes, I saw George," returned Drouet. "Great old boy, isn't he? We had quite a time there together."

The barkeeper was setting out the glasses and bottle before them, and they now poured out the draught as they talked, Drouet filling his to within a third of full as was considered proper and Hurstwood taking the barest suggestion of whiskey and modifying it with seltzer.

"What's become of Caryoe?" remarked Hurstwood. "I haven't seen him around here in two weeks."

"Laid up, they say," explained Drouet. "Say, he's a gouty old boy!"

"Made a lot of money in his time though, hasn't he?"

"Yes, wads of it," returned Drouet. "He won't live much longer. Barely comes down to the office now."

"Just one boy, hasn't he?" asked Hurstwood.

"Yes, and a swift-pacer," laughed Drouet.

"I guess he can't hurt the business very much though, with the other members all there."

"No, he can't injure that any, I guess."

Hurstwood was standing, his coat open, his thumbs in his pockets, the light on his jewels and rings relieving them with agreeable distinctness. He was the picture of fastidious comfort.

"Hello, George," said a voice, and Hurstwood turned around to put his hand in that of another worthy, resplendent in dress and figure, who had arrived from some other part of the country. They now conversed together in the same pointless phraseology, while Drouet drew out his purse to get a bill. The bartender saw his action however and signaled with his hands.

"It's on the manager," he said, smiling merrily. Hurstwood had them so trained that they knew.

"Let me introduce you to my friend here," Hurstwood said, coming up. He unloaded the newcomer on Drouet, who shook hands and immediately inquired if he would have something. Together they conversed, at first three-handed, with Hurstwood, then alone, while the latter went into his little office to talk with two fat, rosy-cheeked gentlemen who were there waiting to see him. Drouet could see that it was both a genial and interesting meeting for they talked with their heads together, then leaned back and laughed, then talked again and so on, while he exchanged commonplaces.

"What are you doing tonight?" said the newcomer after a time.

"Oh, I think I'll go over to the Grand in a little while," returned Drouet.

"What's there?"

"Hoyt's 'A Hole in the Ground.' "

"Well, if I hadn't seen that several times, I'd join you," he remarked with that spirit of ready companionship which seems to be characteristic of the thoughtless.

Just then a third individual appeared who knew the second and took him away leaving Drouet to gaze, smoke and breathe with smiling satisfaction in the, to him, delightful atmosphere prevailing.

To one not inclined to drink, and gifted with a more serious turn of mind, such a bubbling, chattering, glittering chamber must ever seem an anomaly, a strange commentary on nature and life. Here come the moths in endless procession to bask in the light of the flame. Such conversation as one may hear would not warrant a commendation of the scene upon intellectual grounds. It seems plain that schemers would choose more sequestered quarters to arrange their plans, that politicians would not gather here in company to discuss anything save formalities where the sharp-eared may hear, and it would scarcely be justified on the score of thirst, for the majority of those who frequent these more gorgeous places have no craving for liquor. Nevertheless, the fact that here men gather, here chatter, here love to pass and rub elbows, must be explained upon some grounds. It must be that a strange bundle of passions and vague desires gives rise to such a curious social institution or it would not be.

Drouet, for one, was lured as much by his longing for pleasure as by his desire to shine among his betters. The many friends he met here dropped in because they craved, without perhaps consciously analyzing it, the company, the glow, the atmosphere, which they found. One might take it after all as an augur of the better social order, for the things which they satisfied here, though sensory, were not evil. No evil could come out of the contemplation of an expensively decorated chamber. The worst effect such a thing could have would be perhaps to stir up in the material-minded an ambition to arrange their lives upon a similarly splendid basis. In the last analysis, that would scarcely be called the fault of the decorations, but rather of the innate trend of the mind. That such a scene might stir the less expensively dressed to emulate the more expensively dressed could scarcely be laid at the door of anything save the false ambition of the minds of those so affected. Remove the element so thoroughly and solely complained of, liquor, and there would not be one to gainsay the qualities of beauty and enthusiasm which would remain. The pleased eye with which our modern restaurants of fashion are looked upon is proof positive of this assertion.

Yet here is the fact of the lighted chamber; the dressy, greedy company; the small, self-interested palaver; the disorganized, aimless, wandering mental action which it represents—the love of light and show and finery which, to one outside, under the serene light of the eternal stars, must seem a strange and shiny thing. Under the stars and sweeping night winds, what a lamp-flower it must bloom—a strange, glittering night-flower, odour-yielding, insect-drawing, insect-infested rose of pleasure.

"See that fellow coming in there?" said Hurstwood, returning and glancing at a gentleman just entering, arrayed in a high hat and Prince Albert coat, his fat cheeks puffed and red as with good eating.

"No, where?" said Drouet.

"There," said Hurstwood, indicating the direction by a cast of his eye—"the man with the silk hat."

"Oh, yes," said Drouet, now affecting not to see. "Who is he?"

"That's Jules Wallace, the spiritualist."

Drouet followed him with his eyes, much interested.

"Doesn't look much like a man who sees spirits, does he?" said Drouet.

"Oh, I don't know," returned Hurstwood. "He's got the money, all right," and a little twinkle passed over his eyes.

"I don't go much on those things, do you?" asked Drouet.

"Well, you never can tell," said Hurstwood. "There may be something to it. I wouldn't bother about it myself though. By the way," he added, "are you going anywhere tonight?"

" 'A Hole in the Ground,' " said Drouet, mentioning the popular farce of the time.

"Well, you better be going. It's half after eight already," and he drew out his watch.

The crowd was already thinning out considerably—some bound for the theatres, some to their clubs, and some to that most fascinating of all the pleasures—for the type of man there represented at least—the ladies.

"Yes, I will," said Drouet.

"Come around after the show. I have something I want to show you," said Hurstwood.

"Sure," said Drouet, elated.

"You haven't anything on hand for the night, have you?" added Hurstwood.

"Not a thing!"

"Well, come round then."

"Is she a blonde?" said Drouet, laughing.

"Come around about twelve," said Hurstwood, ignoring the question.

"I struck a little peach coming in on the train Friday," remarked Drouet by way of parting. "By George, that's so. I must go and call on her before I go 'way."

"Oh, never mind her," Hurstwood remarked.

"Say, she was a little dandy, I tell you," went on Drouet confidentially, trying to impress his friend.

"Twelve o'clock," said Hurstwood.

"That's right," said Drouet, going out.

Thus was Carrie's name bandied about in the most frivolous and gay of places, and that also when the little toiler was bemoaning her narrow lot, which was almost inseparable from the early stages of this, her unfolding fate.

CHAPTER VI.

At the flat that evening Carrie felt a new phase of its atmosphere. The fact that it was unchanged, while her feelings were different, increased her knowledge of its character. Minnie, after the good spirits Carrie manifested at the time of securing the place, expected of course a fair report. Hanson supposed that Carrie would be satisfied.

"Well," he said, as he came in from the hall in his working clothes and looked at Carrie through the dining-room door, "how did you make out?"

"Oh," said Carrie, "it's pretty hard. I don't like it."

There was an air about her which showed plainer than any words that she was both weary and disappointed.

"What sort of work is it?" he asked, lingering a moment as he turned upon his heel to go into the bathroom.

"Running a machine," answered Carrie.

It was very evident that it did not concern him much save from the side of the flat's success. He was irritated a shade because it could not have come about in the throw of fortune for Carrie to be pleased.

Minnie worked with less elation than she had just before Carrie arrived. The sizzle of the meat frying did not sound quite so pleasing now that Carrie had reported her discontent. To Carrie the one relief of the whole day would have been a jolly home, a sympathetic reception, a bright supper table, and some one to say, "Oh, well, stand it a little while. You will get something better," but now this was ashes. She began to see that they looked upon her complaint as unwarranted and that she was supposed to work on and say nothing. She knew that she was to pay four dollars for her board and room and now she felt that it would be an exceedingly gloomy round, living with these people. Minnie was no companion for her sister—she was too old. Her thoughts were staid and solemnly adapted to a condition.

Hanson, if he had any pleasant thoughts or happy feelings, concealed them. He seemed to do all his mental operations without the aid of physical expression. He was as still as a deserted chamber. Carrie on the other hand had the blood of youth and some imagination. Her days of love and the mysteries of courtship were still ahead. She could think of things she would like to do, of clothes she would like to wear and of places she would like to visit. These were the things which her mind ran upon, and it was like meeting with opposition at every turn to find no one here to call forth or respond to her feelings.

She had forgotten, in considering and explaining the result of her day, that Drouet might come. Now that she saw how unreceptive these two people were, she hoped he would not. She did not know exactly what she would do or how she would explain Drouet, if he did come, and yet her fear of his arrival after her letter was not great enough to cause her to attempt to clear the way beforehand in case of accident. For want of suitable conversation she thought this over, and after supper changed her clothes. When she was ready she was rather a sweet little being with large eyes and a sad mouth. Her face expressed the mingled expectancy, dissatisfaction and depression she felt, but not as distinctly as would have been the case in more refined mortals. She wandered about after the dishes were put away, talked a little with Minnie and then, struck by a bright idea, decided to go down and stand in the door at the foot of the stairs. There was the way out of the difficulty if Drouet came. She could meet him there. Her face took on the semblance of a look of happiness as she put on her hat to go below.

"Carrie doesn't seem to like her place very well," said Minnie to her husband when the latter came out, paper in hand, to sit in the dining room a few minutes.

"She ought to keep it for a time anyhow," said Hanson. "Has she gone downstairs?"

"Yes," said Minnie.

"I'd tell her to keep it if I were you. She might be here weeks without getting another one."

Minnie said she would and Hanson read his paper awhile.

"If I were you," he said a little later, "I wouldn't let her stand in the door down there. It don't look good."

"I'll tell her," said Minnie.

Meanwhile Carrie was in the door below, looking at the lights in the stores about, the people passing, and the street cars jingling merrily past toward the heart of the city or out toward the suburbs,—directions which to her were interesting mysteries. She enjoyed looking at the boys playing tag about the street, and the young girls who went by in companies laughing and talking. Once in awhile she would see a young girl particularly well-dressed or particularly pretty, or both, which excited her envy and enhanced her longing for nice clothes. Once in awhile a dapper young fellow in his best suit would stride lightly past, bound, she was sure, to call upon some young lady. There were other youths, not so well-dressed, who came in pairs or groups, ogling her, pushing one another and cutting up in such a way as to attract attention. These she gave an assumed look of coldness, or turned her gaze away entirely, which did not, however, seem to faze the young gentlemen in question. They would laugh, whistle, perhaps shout a little and look back still hopeful, but without daring to attempt more intimate overtures—the kind of young men whose faint hearts are concealed behind a show of boisterous enthusiasm. Once in awhile a figure in the distance would look as if it might be that of Drouet and then she would straighten up and become tense in the nerves until, with a nearer approach, her whole flutter and strain would collapse in the face of certain outlines which would prove that the scent was false.

The sprinkling of pedestrians continued for a long time to interest Carrie. She never wearied of wondering where the people in the cars were going or what the enjoyments were which they had. Her imagination trod a very narrow round, always winding up at points which concerned money, looks, clothes or enjoyment. She would have a far-off thought of Columbia City now and then or an irritating rush of feeling concerning her experiences of the present day, but on the whole the little world about her enlisted her whole attention.

The first floor of the building, of which Hanson's flat was

the third, was occupied by a bakery, and to this, while she was standing there, Hanson came down to buy a loaf of bread. She was not aware of his presence until he was quite near her.

"I'm after bread," was all he said as he passed.

The contagion of thought here demonstrated itself. While Hanson really came for bread, the thought dwelt with him that now he would see what Carrie was doing. No sooner did he draw near her with that in his mind than she felt it. Of course she had no understanding of what put it into her head, but nevertheless it aroused in her the first shade of real antipathy to him. She knew now that she did not like him. He was suspicious.

A thought will color a world for us. The flow of Carrie's meditations had been disturbed, and Hanson had not long gone upstairs before she followed. She had realized with the lapse of the quarter hours that Drouet was not coming and somehow she felt a little resentful, a little as if she had been forsaken—was not good enough. She went upstairs, where everything was silent. Minnie was sewing by a lamp at the table. Hanson had already turned in for the night. In her weariness and disappointment Carrie did no more than announce that she was going to bed.

"Yes, you'd better," returned Minnie. "You've got to get up early, you know."

The morning was no better. Hanson was just going out the door as Carrie came out of her room. Minnie tried to talk with her during breakfast but there was not much of interest which they could mutually discuss. As on the previous morning, Carrie walked down town, for she began to realize now that her four-fifty would not even allow her carfare after she paid her board. This seemed a miserable arrangement. But the morning light swept away the first misgivings of the day, as the morning light is ever wont to do.

At the shoe factory she put in a long day, scarcely so wearisome as the preceding, but considerably less novel. The foreman of the room was of Irish extraction—an individual who ruled his mixed brood with frowns, sharp looks and unbending language. Besides him there was a thorough Irishman, who wore exceedingly squeaky shoes, who was over all the floors as head foreman. Carrie made his acquaintance by his own introduction.

"Where did you come from?" he inquired that morning, stopping for the first time beside her machine.

"Mr. Brown hired me," she replied.

"Oh, he did, eh!" And then, "See that you keep things going."

The machine girls impressed her even less favorably. They seemed satisfied with their lot and were in a sense "common." Carrie had more imagination than they. She was not used to slang. Her instinct in the matter of dress was naturally better. She felt bad to have to listen to the girl next to her, who was slangy and rather hardened by experience.

"I'm going to quit this," she heard her remark to her neighbor. "What with the stipend and being up late, it's too much for me health."

They were free with the fellows, young and old, about the place, and exchanged banter in rude phrases which at first shocked her. She saw that she was taken to be of the same sort and addressed accordingly.

"Hello," remarked one of the stout-wristed sole-workers to her at noon. "You're a daisy." He really expected to hear the common "Aw! go chase yourself!" in return and was sufficiently abashed by Carrie's silently moving away to retreat, awkwardly grinning.

That night at the flat she was even more lonely—the dull situation was becoming harder to endure. She could see that the Hansons seldom or never had any company. Standing at the street door looking out, she ventured to walk out a little way. Her easy gait and idle manner attracted the attention of an offensive but common sort. She was slightly taken aback at the overtures of a well-dressed man of thirty who in passing looked at her, reduced his pace, turned back and said:—

"Out for a little stroll, are you, this evening?"

Carrie looked at him in amazement and then summoned sufficient thought to reply, "Why, I don't know you," backing away as she did so.

"Ah, that don't matter," said the other affably.

She bandied no more words with him, but hurried away, reaching her own door quite out of breath. There was something in the man's look which frightened her.

During the remainder of the week it was very much the

same. One or two nights she found herself too tired to walk home and expended carfare. She was not very strong, and sitting all day affected her back. She went to bed one night before Hanson.

Transplantation is not always successful in the matter of flowers or maidens. It requires sometimes a richer soil, a better atmosphere, to continue even a natural growth. It would have been better if her acclimatization had been more gradual—less rigid. She would have done better if she had not secured a position so quickly and had seen more of the city which she constantly troubled to know about.

On the first morning it rained, she found that she had no umbrella. Minnie loaned her one of hers, which was anything but handsome. There was the kind of vanity in Carrie that troubled at this. She went to one of the great department stores and bought herself one, using a dollar and a quarter of her small store to pay for it.

"What did you do that for, Carrie?" asked Minnie when she saw it.

"Oh, I need one," said Carrie.

"You foolish girl," went on Minnie.

Carrie resented this, though she did not reply. She was not going to be a common shop girl, she thought. They need not think it either.

Another thing that was irritating was the stay-at-home-ishness of the Hansons. They would not go anywhere at night, and all day Carrie could not. In the factory she heard the girls talking of many amusements—things which her heart was longing to see. For instance at the noon half-hour, four girls in one of the windows were listening to a story by one of their number of how she had visited the Criterion. There was a farce there called "Eight Bells."

"Oh, it was so funny," exclaimed the relator. "There was one little fat man who was just great. They have a mule which they pull apart and do the strangest things."

Carrie listened to this with ready ears. Why couldn't she go to see that also?

"Gee, I'm so tired," yawned one pretty girl one morning. "I danced till two o'clock last night."

At first Carrie was inclined to look upon these things with misgivings, but in proportion as her own lot impressed her as pointless and difficult, these things took on the hue of withheld delights. She did not crave exactly to dance at the balls of the Plasterers or Woodworkers Unions, but when she heard of outings in the parks and on the lake, visits to the theatres, flirtations with young men and so on, she felt her own life to be exceedingly narrow. She wished she could do something that would give her more money. If she could only get work in The Fair.

On the first Saturday night Carrie paid her board—four dollars—which, Minnie had mentioned in the letter home, she would keep her for. Minnie had a quaver of conscience as she took it, but she did not know how to explain to Hanson if she took less. That worthy gave up just four dollars less toward the household expenses with a smile of satisfaction. He contemplated increasing his building and loan payments. As for Carrie, she studied over the problem of finding clothes and amusement on fifty cents a week with considerable vigor. She brooded over the thing until she was in a state of mental rebellion.

"I'm going up the street for a walk," she said after supper.

"Not alone, are you?" asked Hanson.

"Yes," returned Carrie.

"I wouldn't," said Minnie.

"I want to see something," said Carrie and by the tone she put into the last word they realized for the first time she was not wholly pleased.

"What's the matter with her?" asked Hanson, when she went into the front room to get her hat.

"I don't know," said Minnie.

"Well, she ought to know better than to want to go out alone."

Carrie did not go very far after all. She returned and stood in the door. The next day they went out to Garfield Park, but it did not please her. She did not look well enough. In the shop next day she heard the highly colored reports which girls give of their trivial amusements. They had been happy. On several days it rained and she used up carfare. One night she got thoroughly soaked, going to catch the car at Van Buren Street. All that evening she sat alone in the front room looking out upon the street, where the lights were reflected on the wet pavements, thinking. She had imagination enough to be moody.

On Saturday she paid another four dollars and pocketed her fifty cents in despair. The speaking acquaintanceship which she formed with some of the girls at the shop discovered to her the fact that they had more of their earnings to use for themselves than she did. They had young men of the kind whom she, since her experience with Drouet, felt above, who took them about. She came to thoroughly dislike the light-headed young fellows of the shop. Not one of them had a show of refinement. She saw only their workday side.

There came a day when the first premonitory blast of winter swept over the city. It scudded the fleecy clouds in the heavens, trailed along thin streamers of smoke from the tall stacks, and raced about the streets and corners in sharp and sudden puffs. Carrie now felt the problem of winter clothes. What was she to do? She had no winter jacket, no hat, no shoes. She thought some of asking Minnie to let her keep her money and buy these things. She would need to work a whole month before she would have enough to do anything with. Once she resolved to ask Minnie but every time it came to the point of doing so she lacked courage to bring it up. The increasingly cool mornings constantly reminded her. At last she summoned up the courage.

"I don't know what I'm going to do about clothes," she said one evening when she and Minnie were together. "I need a hat."

Minnie looked serious.

"Why don't you keep a part of your money and buy yourself one?" she suggested, worried over the situation which the withholding of Carrie's money would create.

"I'd like to for a week or so if you don't mind," ventured Carrie.

"Could you pay two dollars?" asked Minnie.

Carrie readily acquiesced, glad to escape the trying situation and liberal now that she saw a way out. She was elated, and began figuring at once. She needed a hat first of all. How Minnie explained to Hanson she never knew. He said nothing at all, but there were thoughts in the air which left disagreeable impressions.

The new arrangement might have worked if sickness had not intervened. It blew up cold after a rain one afternoon, when Carrie was still without a jacket. She came out of the warm shop at six and shivered as the wind struck her. In the morning she was sneezing, and going down town made it worse. That day her bones ached and she felt light-headed. Toward evening she felt very ill and when she reached home was not hungry. Minnie noticed her drooping actions and asked her about herself.

"I don't know," said Carrie. "I feel real bad."

She hung about the stove, suffered a chattering chill and went to bed sick. The next morning she was thoroughly feverish.

Minnie was truly distressed at this but maintained a kindly demeanor. Hanson said perhaps she had better go back home for awhile. When she got up after three days it was taken for granted that her position was lost. The winter was near at hand, she had no clothes and now she was out of work.

"I don't know," said Carrie—"I'll go down Monday and see if I can't get something."

If anything her efforts were more poorly rewarded on this trial than the last. Her clothes were nothing suitable for fall wearing. Her last money she had spent for a hat. For three days she wandered about, utterly dispirited. The attitude of the flat was fast becoming unbearable. She hated to think of going back there each evening. Hanson was so cold. She knew it could not last much longer. Shortly she would have to give up and go back.

On the fourth day she was down town, all day, having borrowed ten cents for lunch from Minnie. She had applied in the cheapest kinds of places, without success. She even answered for a waitress in a small restaurant where she saw a card in the window, but they wanted an experienced girl. She moved through the thick throng of strangers, utterly subdued in spirit. Suddenly a hand pulled her arm and turned her about.

"Well, well," said a voice. In the first glance she beheld Drouet. That worthy was not only rosy-cheeked but radiant. He was the essence of sunshine and good humor.

"Why, how are you, Carrie?" he said. "You're a daisy. Where have you been?"

Carrie smiled under his irresistible flood of geniality.

"I've been out home," she said.

"Well," he said, "I saw you across the street there. I thought it was you. I was just coming out to your place. How are you anyhow?"

"I'm all right," said Carrie, smiling.

Drouet looked her over and saw something different.

"Well," he said, "I want to talk to you. You're not going anywhere in particular, are you?"

"Not just now," said Carrie.

"Let's go up here and have something to eat. George! but I'm glad to see you again."

She felt so relieved in his radiant presence, so much looked after and cared for, that she assented gladly, though with the slightest air of holding back.

"Well," he said as he took her arm—and there was an exuberance of good fellowship in the word which fairly warmed the cockles of her heart.

They went through Monroe Street to the old Windsor dining room, which was then a large, comfortable place, with an excellent cuisine and substantial service. Drouet selected a table close by the window, where the busy rout of the street could be seen. He loved the changing panorama of the street—to see and be seen as he dined.

"Now," he said, getting Carrie and himself comfortably settled, "what will you have?"

Carrie looked over the large bill-of-fare, which the waiter handed her, without really considering it. She was very hungry and the things she saw there awakened her desires, but the high prices held her attention. "Half-broiled spring chicken—$0.75. Sirloin steak with mushrooms—$1.25." She had dimly heard of these things, but it seemed strange to be called to order from the list.

"I'll fix this," exclaimed Drouet. "Sst! Waiter."

That officer of the board, a full-chested, round-faced negro, approached and inclined his ear.

"Sirloin with mushrooms," said Drouet. "Stuffed tomatoes."

"Yassah," assented the negro, nodding his head.

"Hashed brown potatoes."

"Yassah!"

"Asparagus."

"Yassah."

"—And a pot of coffee."

"Um!"—said the colored man.

Drouet turned to Carrie. "I haven't had a thing since break-fast. Just got in from Rock Island. I was going off to dine when I saw you."

Carrie smiled and smiled.

"What have you been doing?" he went on. "Tell me all about yourself. How is your sister?"

"She's well," returned Carrie, answering the last query.

He looked at her hard.

"Say," he said, "you haven't been sick, have you?"

Carrie nodded.

"Well, now that's a blooming shame, isn't it? You don't look very well. I thought you looked a little pale. What have you been doing?"

"Working," said Carrie.

"You don't say so. At what?"

She told him.

"Rhodes, Morgenthau and Scott—why I know that house. Over here on Fifth Avenue, isn't it. They're a close-fisted concern. What made you go there?"

"I couldn't get anything else," said Carrie frankly.

"Well that's an outrage," said Drouet. "You oughtn't to be working for those people. Have the factory right back of the store, don't they?"

"Yes," said Carrie.

"That isn't a good house," said Drouet. "You don't want to work at anything like that anyhow."

He chattered on at a great rate, asking questions, explaining things about himself, telling her what a good restaurant it was and so on, until the waiter returned with an immense tray, bearing the hot, savory dishes which had been ordered. (Drouet fairly shone in the matter of serving.) He appeared to great advantage behind the white napery and silver platters of the table and displaying his arms with a knife and fork. As he cut the meat his rings almost spoke. His new suit creaked as he stretched to reach the plates, break the bread, and pour the coffee. He helped Carrie to a rousing plateful and contributed the warmth of his spirit to her body until she was a new girl. He was a splendid fellow in the true popular understanding of the term and captivated Carrie completely.

That little soldier of fortune took her good turn in an easy way. She felt a little out of place, but the great room soothed her and the view of the well-dressed throng outside seemed a splendid thing. Ah, what was it not to have money. What a thing it was to be able to come in here and dine. Drouet must be fortunate. He rode on trains, dressed in such nice clothes, was so strong and ate in these fine places. He seemed quite a figure of a man and she wondered at his friendship and regard for her.

"So you lost your place because you got sick, eh?" he said— "What are you going to do now?"

"Look around," she said, a thought of the need that hung outside this fine restaurant like a hungry dog at her heels, passing into her eyes.

"Oh, no," said Drouet, "that won't do. How long have you been looking?"

"Four days," she answered.

"Think of that," he said, addressing some problematical individual. "You oughtn't to be doing anything like that. These girls," and he waved an inclusion of all shop and store girls, "don't get anything. Why, you can't live on it, can you?"

He was a brotherly sort of creature in his demeanor. When he had scouted the idea of that kind of toil, he took another tack. Carrie was really very pretty. Even then, in her commonplace garb, her figure was evidently not bad and her eyes were large and gentle. Drouet looked at her and his thoughts reached home. She felt his admiration. It was powerfully backed by his liberality and good humor. She felt that she liked him—that she could continue to like him ever so much. There was something even richer than that running as a hidden strain in her mind.

Every little while her eyes would meet his and by that means the interchanging current of feeling would be fully connected.

"Why don't you stay down town and go to the theatre with me?" he said, hitching his chair closer. The table was not very wide.

"Oh, I can't," she said.

"What are you going to do tonight?"

"Nothing," she answered a little drearily.

"You don't like out there where you are, do you?"

"Oh, I don't know—"

"What are you going to do if you don't get work?"

"Go back home, I guess."

There was the least quaver in her voice as she said this. Somehow the influence he was exerting was powerful. They came to an understanding of each other without words—he of her situation, she of the fact that he realized it.

"No," he said, "you can't make it," genuine sympathy filling his mind for the time. "Let me help you. You take some of my money."

"Oh, no," she said, leaning back.

"What are you going to do?" he said.

She sat meditating, merely shaking her head.

He looked at her quite tenderly for his kind. There were some loose bills in his vest pocket—greenbacks. They were soft and noiseless and he got his fingers about them and crumpled them up in his hand.

"Come on," he said, "I'll see you through all right. Get yourself some clothes."

It was the first reference he had made to that subject, and now she realized how bad off she was. In his crude way he had struck the keynote. Her lips trembled a little.

She had her hand out on the table before her. They were quite alone in their corner and he put his larger, warmer hand over it.

"Aw, come, Carrie," he said, "what can you do alone? Let me help you."

He pressed her hand gently and she tried to withdraw it. At this he held it fast and she no longer protested. Then he slipped the greenbacks he had into her palm, and when she began to protest he whispered:

"I'll loan it to you—that's all right—I'll loan it to you."

He made her take it. She felt bound to him by a strange tie of affection now. They went out and he walked with her far out south toward Polk Street, talking.

"You don't want to live with those people," he said in one

place, abstracted. Carrie heard it but it made only a slight impression.

"Come down and meet me tomorrow," he said, "and we'll go to the matinée. Will you?"

Carrie protested awhile but acquiesced.

"You're not doing anything. Get yourself a nice pair of shoes and a jacket."

She scarcely gave a thought to the complication which would trouble her when he was gone. In his presence she was of his own hopeful, easy-way-out mood.

"Don't you bother about those people out there," he said at parting. "I'll help you."

Carrie left him, feeling as though a great arm had slipped out before her to drive off trouble. The money she had accepted was two soft, green, handsome ten-dollar bills.

CHAPTER VII.

The true meaning of money yet remains to be popularly explained and comprehended. When each individual realizes for himself that this thing primarily stands for and should only be accepted as a moral due—that it should be paid out as honestly stored energy and not as a usurped privilege—many of our social, religious and political troubles will have permanently passed. As for Carrie, her understanding of the moral significance of money was the popular understanding, nothing more. The old definition, "Money: something everybody else has and I must get," would have expressed her understanding of it thoroughly. Some of it she now held in her hand, two soft, green ten-dollar bills, and she felt that she was immensely better off for the having of them. It was something that was a power in itself. One of her order of mind would have been content to be cast away upon a desert island with a bundle of money, and only the long strain of starvation would have taught her that in some cases it could have no value. Even then she would have had no conception of the relative value of the thing; her own thought would undoubtedly have concerned the pity of having so much power and the inability to use it.

The poor girl thrilled as she walked away from Drouet. She felt ashamed in part to have been weak enough to take it, but her need was so dire, she was still glad. Now she would have a nice new jacket. Now she would buy a nice pair of pretty button shoes. She would get stockings, too, and a skirt, and, and— until already, as in the matter of her prospective salary, she had got beyond, in her desires, twice the purchasing power of her bills.

She conceived a true estimate of Drouet. To her and indeed to all the world he was a nice, good-hearted man. There was nothing evil in the fellow. He gave her the money out of a good heart—out of a realization of her want. He would not have given the same amount to a poor young man but we must not forget that a poor young man could not, in the nature of things, have appealed to him like a poor young girl. Femininity affected his feelings. He was the creature of an inborn desire. Yet no beggar could have caught his eye and said, "My God, Mister, I'm starving," but he would have gladly handed out what was considered the proper portion to give beggars and thought no more about it. There would have been no speculation, no philosophizing. He had no mental process in him worthy the dignity of either of those terms. In his good clothes and fine health he was a merry, unthinking moth of the lamp. Deprived of his position and struck by a few of the involved and baffling forces which sometimes play upon man, he would have been as helpless as Carrie—as helpless, as non-understanding, as pitiable, if you will, as she.

Now in regard to his pursuit of women, he meant them no harm, because he did not conceive of the relation which he hoped to hold with them as being harmful. He loved to make advances to women, to have them succumb to his charms, not because he was a cold-blooded, dark, scheming villain, but because his inborn desire urged him to that as a chief delight. He was vain, he was boastful, he was as deluded by fine clothes as any silly-headed girl. A truly deep-dyed villain could have horn-swaggled him as readily as he could have flattered a pretty shop girl. His fine success as a salesman lay in his geniality and the thoroughly reputable standing of his house. He bobbed about among men, a veritable bundle of enthusiasm—no power worthy the name of "intellect," no thoughts worthy the adjective "noble," no feelings long continued in one strain. A Madame

Sappho would have called him a pig; a Shakespeare would have said "my merry child"; old drinking Caryoe thought him a clever, successful business man. In short he was as good as his intellect conceived.

The best proof that there was something open and commendable about the man was the fact that Carrie took the money. No deep, sinister soul with ulterior motives could have given her fifteen cents under the guise of friendship. The unintellectual are not so helpless. Nature has taught the beasts of the field to fly when some unheralded danger threatens. She has put into the small, unwise head of the chipmunk the untutored fear of poisons. "He keepeth His creatures whole" was not written of beasts alone. That is but the religious expression of a material and spiritual truth that has guided the evolution of the race. If not, then what led and schooled the race before it thought logically—before it came into the wisdom to lead itself? Carrie was unwise, and, therefore, like the sheep in its unwisdom, strong in feeling. The instinct of self-protection, strong in all such natures, was roused but feebly if at all by the overtures of Drouet. Evil was not in him. On the contrary there was kindliness, non-understanding, strong physical desire, vainglory, a great admiration for the sex, laughter, even tears, but at these no woman trembles. The moth, the pig, the clown, the butterfly, the actor, the business man and the sensualist mingled in combination. He was an enlivening spectacle of them all.

When Carrie had gone he felicitated himself upon her good opinion of him. Wasn't she pleased, though, poor thing. Pretty too. By George, it was a shame young girls had to be knocked around like that. Cold weather coming on and no clothes. Tough. He would go around to Hannah and Hogg's and get a cigar. He would go over how he persuaded her to take the money and what he would do next. It made him feel light of foot as he thought about it.

Carrie reached home in high good spirits which she could scarcely conceal. The possession of the money involved a number of points which perplexed her seriously. How should she buy any clothes when Minnie knew that she had no money? She had no sooner entered the flat than this point was settled for her. It could not be done. She could think of no way of explaining how she should have come by a new jacket.

"How did you come out?" asked Minnie, referring to the day.

Carrie had none of the small deception which could feel one thing and say something directly opposed. She would prevaricate, but it would be in the line of her feelings at least. So instead of complaining when she felt so good, she said:—

"I have the promise of something."

"Where?"

"At The Boston Store."

"Is it sure promised?" questioned Minnie.

"Well, I'm to find out tomorrow," returned Carrie—disliking to draw out a lie any longer than was necessary.

Minnie felt the atmosphere of good feeling which Carrie brought with her. She felt now was the time to express to Carrie the state of Hanson's feeling about her entire Chicago venture.

"If you shouldn't get it—" she paused—troubled for an easy way.

"If I don't get something pretty soon I think I'll go home."

Minnie saw her chance.

"Sven thinks it might be best, for the winter anyhow."

The situation flashed on Carrie at once. They were unwilling to keep her any longer, out of work. She did not blame Minnie; she did not blame Hanson very much. Now, as she sat there digesting the remark, she was glad she had Drouet's money.

"Yes," she said after a few moments, "I thought of doing that."

She did not explain that the thought, however, had aroused all the antagonism of her nature. Columbia City—what was there for her? She knew its dull little round by heart. Here was the great mysterious city which was still a magnet for her. What she had seen only suggested its possibilities. Now to turn back on it and live the little old life out there—she almost exclaimed against it as she thought.

She had reached home early and went in the front room to think. What could she do? She could not buy new shoes and wear them here. She would need to save part of the twenty to pay her fare home. She did not want to borrow of Minnie for that. And yet how would she explain where she got even that money? If she could only get enough to let her out easy.

She went over the tangle again and again. Here in the morning Drouet would expect to see her in a new jacket, and that couldn't be. Hanson expected her to go home, and she wanted to get away and yet she did not want to go home. In the light of the way they would look on her getting money without work, the taking of it now seemed dreadful. She began to be ashamed. The whole situation depressed her. It was all so clear when she was with Drouet. Now it was all so tangled, so hopeless—much worse than it was before because she had the semblance of aid in her hand which she could not use.

Her spirits sank so that at supper Minnie felt she must have had another hard day. Carrie finally decided that she would give the money back. It was wrong to take it. She would go down in the morning and hunt for work. At noon she would meet Drouet as agreed and tell him. At this decision her heart sank until she was the old Carrie of distress.

Curiously she could not hold the money in hand without feeling some relief. Even after all her depressing conclusions she could sweep away thought about the matter and then the twenty dollars seemed a wonderful and delightful thing. Ah, money, money, money. What a thing it was to have. How plenty of it would clear away all these troubles.

In the morning she got up and started out a little early. Her decision to hunt for work was moderately strong, but the money in her pocket, after all her troubling over it, made the work question seem the least shade less terrible. She walked into the wholesale district, but as the thought of applying came with each passing concern, her heart shrank. What a coward she was, she thought to herself. Yet she had applied so often. It would be the same old story. She walked on and on and finally did go in one place with the old result. She came out feeling that luck was against her. It was no use.

Without much thinking she reached Dearborn Street. Here was the great Fair store, with its multitude of delivery wagons about, its long window display, its crowd of shoppers. It readily changed her thoughts, she who was so weary of them. It was here that she had intended to come and get her new things. Now for relief from distress she thought she would go in and see. She would look at the jackets.

There is nothing in this world more delightful than that middle state in which we mentally balance at times, possessed of the means, lured by desire and yet deterred by conscience or want of decision. When Carrie began wandering around the store amid the fine displays, she was in this mood. Her original experience in this same place had given her a high opinion of its merits. Now she paused at each individual bit of finery, when before she had hurried on. Her woman's heart was warm with desire of them. How would she look in this, how charming that would make her. She came upon the corset counter and paused in rich revery as she noted the dainty concoctions of color and lace there displayed. Ah, if she would only make up her mind she could have one of those now. Where the jewelry was, there also she lingered. She saw the earrings, the bracelets, the pins, the chains. What would she not have given if she could have had them all. She would look fine too, if only she had some of these things.

The jackets were the great attraction—   When she entered the store she already had her heart fixed upon the peculiar little tan jacket, with large mother-of-pearl buttons which were all the rage that fall. Still she delighted to convince herself that there was nothing she would like better. She went about among the glass cases and racks where these things were displayed and satisfied herself that the one she thought of was the proper one. All the time she wavered in mind, now persuading herself that she could buy it right away if she chose, now recalling to herself the actual condition. At last the noon hour was dangerously near and she had done nothing. She must go now and return the money.

Drouet was on the corner when she came up.

"Hello," he said. "Where is the jacket?" And then looking down, "The shoes?"

Carrie had thought to lead up to her decision in some intelligent way, but this swept the whole fore-schemed situation by the board.

"I came to tell you that, that, I can't take the money."

"Oh that's it, is it?" he returned. "Well, you come on with me. Let's go over here to Schlesinger and Mayer's."

Carrie walked with him. Behold, the whole fabric of doubt

and impossibility had slipped from her mind. She could not get at the points that were so serious, the things she was going to make plain to him.

"Have you had dinner yet?—of course you haven't. Let's go in here," and Drouet turned into one of the very nicely furnished restaurants off State Street, in Monroe.

"I mustn't take the money," said Carrie, after they were settled in a cosy corner, and Drouet had ordered. "I can't wear those things out there. They,—they wouldn't know where I got them."

"What do you want to do?" he smiled. "Go without them?"

"I think I'll go home," she said wearily.

"Oh, come," he said, "you've been thinking it over too long. I'll tell you what you do. You say you can't wear them out there. Why don't you rent a furnished room and leave them in that for a week?"

Carrie shook her head. Like all women she was there to object and be convinced. It was up to him to brush the doubts away and clear the path if he could.

"Why are you going home?" he asked.

"Oh, I can't get anything here."

"They won't keep you," he remarked intuitively.

"They can't," said Carrie.

"I'll tell you what you do," he said. "You come with me. I'll take care of you."

Carrie heard this passively. The peculiar state which she was in made it sound like the welcome breath of an open door. Drouet was of her own spirit and was pleasing. He was clean, handsome, well-dressed and sympathetic. His voice was the voice of a friend.

"What can you do back at Columbia City?" he went on, rousing by the words in Carrie's mind a picture of the dull world she had left. "There isn't anything down there. Chicago's the place. You can get a nice room here and some clothes and then you can do something."

Carrie looked out through the window into the busy street. There it was, the admirable great city, so fine when you are not poor. An elegant coach with a prancing pair of bays passed by, carrying in its upholstered depths a young lady.

"What will you have if you go back?" asked Drouet. There

was no subtle undercurrent to the question. He imagined that she would have nothing at all of the things he thought worthwhile.

Carrie sat still, looking out. She was wondering what she could do. They would be expecting her to go home this week.

Drouet turned to the subject of the clothes she was going to buy.

"Why not get yourself a nice little jacket? You've got to have it. I'll loan you the money. You needn't worry about taking it. You can get yourself a nice room by yourself. I won't hurt you."

Carrie saw the drift but could not express her thoughts. She felt more than ever the hopelessness of her case.

"If I could only get something to do," she said.

"Maybe you can," went on Drouet, "if you stay here. You can't if you go 'way. They won't let you stay out there. Now, why not let me get you a nice room? I won't bother you—you needn't be afraid. Then when you get fixed up, maybe you could get something."

He looked at her pretty face and it vivified his mental resources. She was a sweet little mortal to him—there was no doubt of that. She seemed to have some power back of her actions. She was not like the common run of store-girl. She wasn't silly.

In reality Carrie had more imagination than he did, more taste. The thing in her that could sink and sink and make her feel depressed and lonely was a finer mental strain than he possessed. Her poor clothes were neat, and she held her head unconsciously in a dainty way.

"Do you think I could get something?" she asked.

"Sure," he said, reaching over and filling her cup with tea. "I'll help you."

She looked at him and he laughed in a reassuring way.

"Now I'll tell you what we'll do. We'll go over here to Schlesinger and Mayer's and you pick out what you want. Then we'll look around for a room for you. You can leave the things there. Then we'll go to the show tonight."

Carrie shook her head.

"Well, you can go out to the flat, then—that's all right. You don't need to stay in the room. Just take it and leave your things there."

She hung in doubt about this until the dinner was over.

"Let's go over and look at the jackets," he said.

Together they went. In the store they found that shine and rustle of new things which immediately laid hold of Carrie's heart. Under the influence of a good dinner and Drouet's radiating presence, the scheme proposed seemed feasible. She looked about and picked a jacket like the one which she had admired at The Fair. When she got it in her hand, it seemed so much nicer. The saleswoman helped her on with it, and by accident it fitted perfectly. Drouet's face lightened as he saw the improvement. She looked quite smart.

"That's the thing," he said.

Carrie turned before the glass. She could not help feeling pleased as she looked at herself. A warm glow crept into her cheeks.

"That's the thing," said Drouet. "Now pay for it."

"It's nine dollars," said Carrie.

"That's all right—take it," said Drouet.

She reached in her purse and took out one of the bills. The woman asked if she would wear the coat and went off. In a few minutes she was back and the purchase was closed.

From Schlesinger's they went to a shoe store where Carrie was fitted for shoes. Drouet stood by and, when he saw how nice they looked, said, "Wear them." Carrie shook her head, however. She was thinking of returning to the flat. He bought her a purse for one thing and a pair of gloves for another, and let her buy the stockings.

"Tomorrow," he said, "you come down here and buy yourself a skirt."

In all of Carrie's actions there was a touch of misgiving. The deeper she sank into the entanglement, the more she imagined that the thing hung upon the few remaining things she had not done. Since she had not done so and so yet, there was a way out.

Drouet knew a place in Wabash Avenue where there were rooms. He showed Carrie the outside of these and said, "Now, you're my sister." He carried the arrangement off with an easy hand when it came to the selection, looking around, criticizing, opining. "Her trunk will be here in a day or so," he observed to the landlady, who was very pleased.

When they were alone, Drouet did not change in the least. He talked in the same general way as if they were out in the street. Carrie left her things.

"Now," said Drouet, "why don't you move in tonight?"

"Oh, I can't," said Carrie.

"Why not?"

"I don't want to leave them so."

He took that up as they walked along the avenue. It was a warm afternoon. The sun had come out and the wind had died down. As he talked with Carrie he secured an accurate detail of the atmosphere of the flat.

"Come out of it," he said. "They won't care. I'll help you get along."

She listened to this sort of talk until her misgivings vanished. He would show her about a little and then help her get something. For one thing, he half-imagined that he would. He would be out on the road and she would be working.

"Now, I'll tell you what you do," he said. "You go out there and get whatever you want and come away."

She thought a long time about this. Finally she agreed. He would come out as far as Peoria Street and wait for her. She was to meet him at half-past eight. At half-past five she reached home and at six her determination was hardened.

"So you didn't get it," said Minnie, referring to Carrie's story of The Boston Store.

Carrie looked at her out of the corner of her eye. "No," she answered.

"I don't think you'd better try any more this fall," said Minnie. She was feeling that Hanson would want Carrie to go back and she had best urge in that direction at once.

Carrie said nothing.

When Hanson came home, he wore the same inscrutable demeanor. He washed up in silence and went off to read his paper. At dinner Carrie felt a little nervous. The strain of her own plans was considerable, and the feeling that she was not welcome here was strong.

"Didn't find anything, eh?" said Hanson.

Carrie replied negatively.

He turned to his eating again, the thought that it was a burden to have her here dwelling in his mind. She would have to go home, that was all. Once she was away, there would be no more coming back in the spring.

Carrie was afraid of what she was going to do, but she was relieved to know that this condition was ending. They would not care. Hanson particularly would be glad when she went. He would not care what became of her.

After dinner, she went into the bath room where they could not disturb her and wrote a little note.

"Good bye Minnie," it read. "I'm not going home. I'm going to stay in Chicago a little while and look for work. Don't worry. I'll be all right."

In the front room Hanson was reading his paper. As usual she helped Minnie clear away the dishes and straighten up. Then she looked out the front window awhile and wondered at the cars jingling by. When the time drew near, she went back into the dining room.

"I guess I'll stand down at the door a little while," she said. She could scarcely prevent her voice from trembling.

Minnie remembered Hanson's remonstrance.

"Sven doesn't think it looks good to stand down there," she said.

"Doesn't he?" said Carrie. "I won't do it any more after this."

She put on her hat and fidgeted around the table in the little bedroom, wondering where to slip the note. Finally she put it under Minnie's hairbrush.

When she had closed the hall door she paused a moment, and imagined what they would think. Some thought of the queerness of her deed affected her. She went slowly down the stair. Outside, the cars were passing and boys playing. She looked back up the lighted step and then affected to stroll up the street. When she reached the corner she quickened her pace.

As she was hurrying away, Hanson came back to his wife.

"Is Carrie down at the door again?" he asked.

"Yes," said Minnie. "She said she wasn't going to do it any more."

He went over to the baby where it was playing on the floor, and began to poke his finger at it.

Drouet was on the corner waiting in good spirits.

"Hello, Carrie," he said, as a sprightly figure of a girl drew near him. "Got here safe, did you. Well, we'll take a car."

CHAPTER VIII.

Among the forces which sweep and play throughout the universe, untutored man is but a wisp in the wind. Our civilization is still in a middle stage—scarcely beast, in that it is no longer wholly guided by instinct; scarcely human, in that it is not yet wholly guided by reason. On the tiger no responsibility rests. We see him aligned by nature with the forces of life—he is born into their keeping and without thought he is protected. We see man far removed out of the lairs of the jungles, his innate instincts dulled by too near an approach to free will, his free will scarcely sufficiently developed to replace his instincts and afford him perfect guidance. He is becoming too wise to hearken always to instincts and desires; he is still too weak to always prevail against them. As a beast, the forces of life aligned him with them; as a man, he has not yet wholly learned to align himself with the forces. In this intermediate stage he wavers—neither drawn in harmony with nature by his instincts nor yet wisely putting himself into harmony by his own free will. He is even as a wisp in the wind, moved by every breath of passion, acting now by his will and now by his instincts, erring with one only to retrieve by the other, falling by one only to rise by the other—a creature of incalculable variability. We have the consolation of knowing that evolution is ever in action, that the ideal is a light that cannot fail. He will not forever balance thus between good and evil. When this jangle of free will and instinct shall have been adjusted, when perfect understanding has given the former the power to replace the latter entirely, man will no longer vary. The needle of understanding will yet point steadfast and unwavering to the distant pole of truth.

In Carrie, as in how many of our worldlings do they not, instinct and reason, desire and understanding warred for the mastery. In Carrie, as in how many of our worldlings are they not, instinct and desire were yet in part the victors. She followed whither her craving led. She was as yet more drawn than she drew.

When Minnie found the note next morning after a night of mingled wonder and anxiety, which was not exactly touched by yearning sorrow or love, she exclaimed, "Well, what do you think of that?"

"What?" said Hanson.

"Sister Carrie has gone to live somewhere else."

Hanson jumped out of bed with more celerity than he usually displayed and looked at the note. The only indication of his thoughts came in the form of a little clicking sound made by his tongue—the sound some people make when they wish to urge on a horse.

"Where do you suppose she's gone to?" said Minnie, thoroughly aroused.

"I don't know," a touch of cynicism lighting his eye. "Now she has gone and done it."

Minnie moved her head in a puzzled way.

"Oh, oh!" she said. "She doesn't know what she has done."

"Well," said Hanson, after awhile, sticking his hands out before him, "what can you do?"

Minnie's womanly nature was higher than this. She figured the possibilities in such cases.

"Oh," she said at last, "poor Sister Carrie."

At the time of this particular conversation, which occurred at five A.M., that little soldier of fortune was sleeping a rather troubled sleep in her new room, alone.

We are inclined sometimes to wring our hands much more profusely over the situation of another than the mental attitude of that other, towards his own condition, would seem to warrant. People do not grieve so much sometimes over their own state as we imagine. They suffer, but they bear it manfully. They are distressed, but it is about other things as a rule than their actual state at the moment. We see, as we grieve for them, the whole detail of their blighted career, a vast confused imagery of mishaps covering years, much as we read a double decade of tragedy in a ten-hour novel. The victim, meanwhile, for the single day or morrow, is not actually anguished. He meets his unfolding fate by the minute and the hour as it comes.

Carrie's new state was remarkable in that she saw possibilities in it. She was no sensualist, longing to drowse sleepily in the lap of luxury. She turned about, troubled by her daring, glad of her release, wondering whether she would get something to do, wondering what Drouet would do. That worthy had his future fixed for him beyond a peradventure. He could not help what he was going to do. He could not see clearly enough to wish to do differently. He was drawn by his innate desire to act the old pursuing part. He would need to delight himself with Carrie as surely as he would need to eat his heavy breakfast. He might suffer the least rudimentary twinge of conscience in whatever he did, and in just so far he was evil and sinning. But whatever twinges of conscience he might have *would be* rudimentary, you may be sure.

The next day he called upon Carrie and she saw him in her chamber. He was the same jolly enlivening soul.

"Aw," he said, "what you looking so blue about? Come on out to breakfast. You want to get your other clothes today."

Carrie looked at him with the hue of shifting thought in her large eyes.

"I wish I could get something to do," she said.

"You'll get that all right," said Drouet. "What's the use worrying right now? Get yourself fixed up. See the city. I won't hurt you."

"I know you won't," she remarked, half-trustfully.

"Got on the new shoes haven't you? Stick 'em out. George, they look fine! Put on your jacket."

Carrie obeyed.

"Say, that fits like a T, don't it?" he remarked, feeling the set of it at the waist and eyeing it from a few paces with real pleasure. "What you need now is a nice skirt. Let's go out to breakfast."

Carrie put on her hat.

"Where are the gloves?" he inquired.

"Here," she said, taking them out of the bureau drawer.

"Now come on," he said.

Thus the first hour of misgiving was swept away.

It went this way on every occasion. Drouet did not leave her much alone. She had time for some lone wonderings but mostly he filled her hours with sight-seeing. At Carson, Pirie's he bought her a nice skirt and shirtwaist. With his money she purchased the little necessaries of toilet until at last she looked quite another maiden. The mirror convinced her of a few things which she had long believed. She was pretty, yes indeed. How nice her hat set, and weren't her eyes pretty? She caught her little red lip with her teeth and felt her first thrill of power. Drouet was so good.

They went to see "The Mikado" one evening, an opera which was hilariously popular at that time. Before going they made off for the Windsor dining room, which was in Dearborn Street, a considerable distance from Carrie's room. It was blowing up cold, and out of her window, Carrie could see the western sky, still pink with the fading light, but steely blue at the top where it met the darkness. A long, thin cloud of pink hung in mid-air, shaped like some island in a far-off sea. Somehow the swaying of some dead branches of trees across the way brought back the picture she was familiar with, when she looked from their front window in December days at home.

She paused and wrung her little hands.

"What's the matter?" said Drouet.

"Oh, I don't know," she said, her lip trembling.

He sensed something and slipped his arm over her shoulder, patting her arm.

"Come on," he said gently. "You're all right."

She turned to slip on her jacket.

"Better wear that boa about your throat tonight."

They walked north on Wabash to Adams Street and then west. The lights in the stores were already shining out in gushes of golden hue. The arc lights were sputtering overhead, and high up were the lighted windows of the tall office buildings. The chill wind whipped in and out in gusty breaths. Homeward bound, the six o'clock throng bumped and jostled. Light overcoats were turned up about the ears, hats were pulled down. Little shop girls went fluttering by in pairs and fours, chattering, laughing. It was a spectacle of warm-blooded humanity.

Suddenly a pair of eyes met Carrie's in recognition. They were looking out from a group of poorly dressed girls. Their clothes were faded and loose-hanging, their jackets old, their general make-up shabby.

Carrie recognized the glance and the girl. It was one of those who worked at the machines in the shoe-factory. The latter looked, not quite sure, and then turned her head and looked. Carrie felt as if some great tide had rolled between them. The old dress and the old machine came back. She actually started. Drouet never noticed until Carrie bumped into a pedestrian.

"You must be thinking," he said.

They dined and went to the theatre. That spectacle pleased Carrie immensely. The color and grace of it caught her eye. She had vain imaginings about place and power, about far-off lands and magnificent people. When it was over, the clatter of coaches and the throng of fine ladies made her stare.

"Wait a minute," said Drouet, holding her back in the showy foyer, where ladies and gentlemen were moving in a social crush, skirts rustling, lace-covered heads nodding, white teeth showing through parted lips. "Let's see."

"Sixty-seven," the coach-caller was saying, his voice lifted in a sort of euphonious cry. "Sixty-seven."

"Isn't it fine," said Carrie.

"Great," said Drouet. He was as much affected by this show of finery and gaiety as she. He pressed her arm warmly. Once she looked up, her even teeth showing through parted lips, her eyes alight. He felt a keen wave of desire. As they were moving out, he whispered down to her, "You look lovely." They were right where the coach-call was swinging open a coach door and ushering in two ladies.

"You stick to me and we'll have a coach," said Drouet.

Carrie scarcely heard, her head was so full of the swirl of life.

They stopped in at a restaurant for a little after-theatre lunch. Just a shade of a thought of the hour entered Carrie's head, but there was no household law to govern her now. If any habits had ever had time to fix upon her, they would have operated here. Habits are peculiar things. They will drive the really non-religious mind out of bed to say prayers that are only a custom and not a devotion. The victim of habit, when he has neglected the thing which was customary with him to do, feels a little scratching in the brain, a little irritating something which comes of being out of the rut, and imagines it to be the prick of conscience, the still, small voice that is urging him ever to righteousness. If the digression is unusual enough, the drag of habit will be heavy enough and the unreasoning victim will return and perform the perfunctory thing. "Now, bless me," says such a mind, "I have done my duty," when as a matter of fact it has merely done its old unbreakable trick once again.

Carrie had no excellent home principles fixed upon her. If she had, she would have been more consciously distressed. Now the lunch went off with considerable warmth. Under the influence of the varied occurrences, the fine invisible passion which was emanating from Drouet, the food, the still unusual luxury, she relaxed and heard with open ears. She was again the victim of the city's hypnotic influence, the subject of the mesmeric operations of super-intelligible forces. We have heard of the strange power of Niagara, the contemplation of whose rushing flood leads to thoughts of dissolution. We have heard of the influence of the hypnotic ball, a scientific fact. Man is too intimate with the drag of unexplainable, invisible forces to doubt longer that the human mind is colored, moved, swept on by things which neither resound nor speak. The waters of the sea are not the only things which the moon sways. All that the individual imagines in contemplating a dazzling, alluring, or disturbing spectacle is created more by the spectacle than the mind observing it. These strange, insensible inflowings which alternate, reform, dissolve, are, we are beginning to see, foreshadowing the solution of Shakespeare's mystic line, "There are more things in heaven and earth, Horatio, than are dreamt of in your philosophy." We are, after all, more passive than active, more mirrors than engines, and the origin of human action has neither yet been measured nor calculated.

"Well," said Drouet at last, "we had better be going."

They had been dawdling over the dishes and their eyes had frequently met. Carrie could not help but feel the vibration of force which followed, which indeed was his gaze. He had a way of touching her hand in explanation as if to impress a fact upon her. He touched it now as he spoke of going.

They arose and went out into the street. The downtown section was now bare save for a few whistling strollers, a few owl cars, a few open resorts whose windows were still bright. Out Wabash Avenue they strolled, Drouet still pouring forth his volume of small information. He had Carrie's arm in his and held it closely as he explained. Once in awhile, after some witticism, he would look down and his eyes would meet hers. At last they came to the steps, and Carrie stood up on the first one, her head now coming even with his own. He took her hand and held it genially. He looked steadily at her as she glanced about, warmly musing.

At about that hour Minnie was soundly sleeping after a long evening of troubled thought. She had her elbow in an awkward position under her side. The muscles so held irritated a few nerves, and now a vague scene floated in on the drowsy mind. She fancied she and Carrie were somewhere beside an old coal mine. She could see the tall runway and the heap of earth and coal cast out. There was a deep pit which they were looking down into,—they could see the curious wet stones far down where the wall disappeared in vague shadows. An old basket used for descending was hanging there, fastened by a worn rope.

"Let's get in," said Carrie.

"Oh, no!" said Minnie.

"Yes, come on," said Carrie.

She began to pull the basket over, and now in spite of all protest she had swung over and was going down—down.

"Carrie," she called, "Carrie, come back," but Carrie was far down now, and the shadow had swallowed her completely.

She moved her arm.

Now the mystic scenery merged queerly and the place was by waters she had never seen. They were upon some board or ground or something that reached far out, and at the end of this was Carrie. They looked about and now the thing was going down and Minnie heard the low sip of the encroaching water.

"Come on, Carrie," she called, but Carrie was reaching farther out. She seemed to recede and recede and now it was difficult to call to her.

"Carrie," she called, "Carrie," but her own voice was far-away-sounding and the strange waters were blurring everything. She came away suffering as though she had lost something. She was more inexpressibly sad than she had ever been in life.

It was this way through many shifts of the tired brain, those curious phantoms of the spirit slipping in, blurring strange scenes one with the other. The last one made her cry out, for Carrie was slipping away somewhere over a rock, and her fingers had let loose and she had seen her falling.

"Minnie! What's the matter, here, wake up," said Hanson, disturbed and shaking her by the shoulder.

"Wha, what's the matter," said Minnie, drowsily.

"Wake up," he said, "and roll over. You're talking in your sleep."

A week or so later Drouet strolled into Hannah and Hogg's, spruce in dress and manner.

"Hello, Charlie," said Hurstwood, looking out from his office door.

Drouet strolled over and looked in upon the manager at his desk.

"When do you go out on the road again?" he inquired.

"Pretty soon," said Drouet.

"Haven't seen much of you this trip," said Hurstwood.

"Well, I've been busy," said Drouet.

They talked some few minutes on general topics.

"Say," said Drouet, as if struck by a sudden idea, "I want you to come out some evening."

"Out where?" inquired Hurstwood.

"Out to my house, of course," said Drouet, smiling.

Hurstwood looked up, quizzically, the least suggestion of a smile hovering about his lips. He studied the face of Drouet in his wise way and then with the demeanor of a gentleman said, "Certainly, glad to."

"We'll have a nice game of euchre."

"May I bring a nice little bottle of sec?" asked Hurstwood.

"Certainly," said Drouet. "I'll introduce you."

CHAPTER IX.

Hurstwood's residence on the North Side, near Lincoln Park, was a brick building of a very popular type at that time, a three-story affair, with the first floor sunk a very little below the level of the street. It had a large bay window bulging out from the second floor and was graced in front by a small grassy plot twenty-five feet wide and ten feet deep. There was also a small rear yard, walled in by the fences of the neighbors and holding a stable where he kept his horse and trap. The latter faced upon an alley, which paralleled the street, in the rear of the houses.

The ten rooms of the house were occupied by himself, his wife, Julia, and his son and daughter, George Jr. and Jessica. There were besides these a maid servant, represented from time to time by girls of various extraction, for Mrs. Hurstwood was not always easy to please.

"George, I let Mary go yesterday," was not an infrequent salutation at the dinner table.

"All right," was his only reply. He had long since wearied of discussing the rancorous subject.

A lovely home atmosphere is one of the flowers of the world than which there is nothing more tender, nothing more delicate, nothing more calculated to make strong and just the natures cradled and nourished within it. To those who have never experienced the beneficent influence of its delightful seclusion, no words can make clear the power whereby it uplifts. To those who have never found in it the tolerance and love which are chief among its constituents, the song and the literature of the home are dulled. They will not understand wherefore the tear springs glistening to the eyelids at some strange breath in lovely music. The mystic chords which bind and thrill the heart of the nation they will never know.

Hurstwood's residence could scarcely be said to be infused with this home spirit. It lacked that toleration and regard without which the home is nothing. There was fine furniture, arranged as soothingly as the artistic perception of the occupants warranted. There were soft rugs, richly upholstered chairs and divans, a grand piano, a marble carving of some unknown Venus by some unknown artist, and a number of small bronzes gathered up heaven knows where, but generally sold by the large furniture houses along with everything else which goes to make the perfectly appointed house.

In the dining room stood a sideboard laden with glistening decanters and other utilities and ornaments in glass, the arrangement of which could not be questioned. Here was something Hurstwood knew about. He had studied the subject for years in his business. He took no little satisfaction in telling each Mary, shortly after she arrived, something of what the art of the thing required. He was not garrulous by any means. On the contrary, there was a fine reserve in his manner toward the entire domestic economy of his life, which was all that is comprehended by the popular term "gentlemanly." He would not argue, he would not talk freely. In his manner was something of the dogmatist. What he could not correct, he would ignore. There was a tendency in him to walk away from the impossible thing.

There was a time when he had been considerably enamoured of his Jessica, especially when he was younger and more confined in his success. Now, however, in her seventeenth year, Jessica had developed a certain amount of reserve and independence which was not inviting to the richest form of parental devotion. She was still in the high school and had notions of life which were decidedly those of a patrician. She liked nice clothes and urged for them constantly. Thoughts of love and of elegant individual establishments were running in her head. She met girls at the high school whose parents were truly rich and whose fathers had standing locally as partners or owners of solid businesses. These girls gave themselves the airs befitting the thriving domestic establishments from whence they issued. They were the only individuals of the school about whom Jessica concerned herself.

Young Hurstwood Jr. was in his twentieth year and was already connected in a promising capacity with a large real estate firm. He contributed nothing to the domestic expenses of the family but was thought to be saving his money to invest in real estate. He had some ability, considerable vanity and a love of pleasure that had not, as yet, infringed upon his duties, whatever they were. He came in and went out, pursuing his own plans and fancies, addressing a few words to his mother occasionally, relating some little incident to his father, but for the most part confining himself to those generalities with which most conversation concerns itself. He was not laying bare his desires for anyone to see. He did not find anyone in the house who particularly cared to see.

Mrs. Hurstwood was the type of the woman who has ever endeavored to shine and has been more or less chagrined at the evidences of superior capability in this direction elsewhere. Her knowledge of life extended to that little conventional round of society, of which she was not, but longed to be, a member. She was not without realization already that this thing was impossible, so far as she was concerned. For her daughter she hoped better things. Through Jessica she might rise a little. Through George Jr.'s possible success she might draw to herself the privilege of pointing proudly. Even Hurstwood was doing well enough, and she was anxious that his small real-estate adventures should prosper. His property holdings as yet were rather small, but his income was pleasing and his position with Hannah and Hogg was fixed. Both of those gentlemen were on pleasant and rather informal terms with him.

The atmosphere which such personalities would create must be apparent to all. It worked out in a thousand little conversations, all of which were of the same calibre.

"I'm going up to Fox Lake tomorrow," announced George Jr. at the dinner table one Friday evening.

"What's going on up there?" queried Mrs. Hurstwood.

"Eddie Fahrway's got a new steam launch, and he wants me to come up and see how it works."

"How much did it cost him?" asked his mother.

"Oh, over two thousand dollars. He says it's a dandy."

"Old Fahrway must be making money," put in Hurstwood.

"He is, I guess. Jack told me they were shipping Vega-cura to Australia now. Said they sent a whole box to Capetown last week."

"Just think of that," said Mrs. Hurstwood. "And only four years ago they had that basement in Madison Street."

"Jack told me they were going to put up a six-story building next spring in Robey Street."

"Just think of that," said Jessica.

On this particular occasion Hurstwood wished to leave early.

"I guess I'll be going down town," he remarked, rising.

"Are we going to McVicker's Monday?" questioned Julia without rising.

"Yes," he said indifferently.

They went on dining while he went upstairs for his hat and coat. Presently the door clicked.

"I guess he's gone," said Jessica.

The latter's school news was of a particular stripe.

"They're going to give a performance in the lyceum up-stairs," she reported one day, "and I'm going to be in it."

"Are you?" said her mother.

"Yes, and I'll have to have a new dress. Some of the nicest girls in the school are going to be in it. Miss Palmer's going to take the part of Portia."

"Is she?" said Mrs. Hurstwood.

"They've got that Martha Griswold in it again. She thinks she can act."

"Her family doesn't amount to anything, does it?" said Mrs. Hurstwood sympathetically. "They haven't anything, have they?"

"No," returned Jessica, "they're as poor as church mice."

She distinguished very carefully among the young boys of the school, many of whom were attracted by her beauty.

"What do you think," she remarked to her mother, one evening, "that Herbert Crane tried to make friends with me."

"Who is he, my dear?" inquired Mrs. Hurstwood.

"Oh, no one," said Jessica, pursing her pretty lips. "He's just a student there. He hasn't anything."

The other half of this picture came when young Blyford, son of Blyford, the soap manufacturer, walked home with her. Mrs. Hurstwood was on the third floor, sitting in a rocking chair reading, and happened to look out at the time.

"Who was that with you, Jess?" she inquired as Jessica came upstairs.

"It's Mr. Blyford, Mama," she replied.

"Is it?" said Mrs. Hurstwood.

"Yes, and he wants me to stroll over into the park with him," explained Jessica, a little flushed with running up the stairs, and perhaps something else.

"All right, my dear," said Mrs. Hurstwood. "Don't be gone long."

As the two went down the street, she glanced interestedly out the window. It was a most satisfactory spectacle indeed—most satisfactory.

In this atmosphere Hurstwood had moved for a number of years now, not thinking deeply concerning it. His was not the order of nature to trouble for something better, unless the better was immediately and sharply contrasted. As it was he received and gave, irritated sometimes by the little displays of selfish indifference, pleased at others by some show of finery which supposedly made for dignity and social distinction. The life of the resort which he managed was his life. There he spent most of his time. When he went home of an evening, the house looked nice. With rare exceptions the meals were acceptable, being the kind that an ordinary servant can arrange. In fact, he was interested in the talk of his son and daughter, who always looked well. The vanity of Mrs. Hurstwood caused her to keep her person rather showily arrayed, but to Hurstwood this was much better than plainness. There was no love lost between them. There was no great feeling of dissatisfaction. Her opinions on any subjects were not startling. They did not talk enough together to come to the argument of any one point. In the accepted and popular phrase, she had her ideas and he had his. Once in a while he would meet a woman whose youth, sprightliness and humor would make his wife seem rather deficient by contrast, but the temporary dissatisfaction which such an encounter might arouse would be counterbalanced by his social position and a certain matter of policy. He could not complicate his home life, because it might affect his relations with his employers. They wanted no scandals. A man, to hold his position, must have a dignified manner, a clean record, a respectable home anchorage. Therefore he was circumspect in all he did, and whenever he appeared in the public ways of an afternoon on Sunday, it was with his wife and sometimes his children. He would visit the local resorts or those nearby in Wisconsin and spend a few stiff, polished days, strolling about conventional places doing conventional things. He knew the need of it.

When some one of the many middle-class individuals whom he knew, who had money, would get into trouble, he would shake his head. It didn't do to talk about those things. If it came up for discussion among such friends as with him passed for close, he would deprecate the folly of the thing. It was all right to do it—all men do those things—but why wasn't he careful? A man can't be too careful. He lost sympathy for the man that made a mistake and was found out.

On this account he still devoted some time to showing his wife about,—time which would have been wearisome indeed if it had not been for the people he would meet and the little enjoyments which did not depend upon her presence or absence. He watched her with considerable curiosity at times, for she was still attractive in a way, and men looked at her. She was affable, vain, subject to flattery; and this combination, he knew quite well, might produce a tragedy in a woman of her home position. Owing to his order of mind, his confidence in the sex was not great. His wife never possessed the virtues which would win the confidence and admiration of a man of his nature. As long as she loved him vigorously he could see how confidence could be, but when that was no longer the binding chain—well, something might happen.

During the last year or two, the expenses of the family seemed a large thing. Jessica wanted fine clothes, and Mrs. Hurstwood, not to be outshone by her daughter, also frequently enlivened her apparel. Hurstwood had said nothing in the past, but one day he murmured.

"Jess must have a new dress this month," said Mrs. Hurstwood one morning.

Hurstwood was arraying himself in one of his perfection vests before the glass at the time.

"I thought she just bought one," he said.

"That was just something for evening wear," returned his wife complacently.

"It seems to me," returned Hurstwood, "that she's spending a good deal for dresses of late."

"Well, she's going out more," concluded his wife, but the tone of his voice impressed her as containing something she had not heard there before.

He was not a man who traveled much, but when he did he had been accustomed to take her along. Not long after the above conversation, a local alderman's junket had been arranged to visit Philadelphia, a junket that was to last ten days. Hurstwood had been invited by several who were his friends, and he decided to go.

"Nobody knows us down there," said one of these individuals, a gentleman with a face which was a slight improvement over gross ignorance and sensuality. He had on a silk hat of most imposing proportions. "We can have a good time." His left eye moved with just the semblance of a wink. "You want to come along, George," he said concluding.

The next day Hurstwood announced his intention to his wife.

"I'm going away, Julia," he said, "for a few days."

"Where?" she asked looking up.

"To Philadelphia on business."

She looked at him, consciously expecting something else.

"I'll have to leave you behind this time."

"All right," she replied, but he could see that she was thinking that it was a curious thing. Before he went she asked him a few more questions, and that irritated him. He began to feel that she was a disagreeable attachment.

On this trip he enjoyed himself thoroughly, and when it was over he was sorry to get back. He was not willingly a prevaricator and hated thoroughly to make explanations concerning it. The whole incident was glossed over, with general remarks, but Mrs. Hurstwood gave the subject considerable thought. She drove out more, dressed better and attended theatres freely to make up for it.

Such an atmosphere could hardly come under the category of home life. There was not enough spirit in it—not enough soulfulness. It ran along by force of habit, by force of conventional opinion. With the lapse of time it must necessarily become dryer and dryer—must eventually be tinder, easily lighted and destroyed. It was a world apart from Hurstwood's own. It was something he cared very little about. The whole thing might move on in a conventional manner to old age and dissolution. Also, it might not.

CHAPTER X.

In the light of the world's attitude toward woman and her duties, the nature of Carrie's mental state deserves consideration. Actions such as hers are measured by an arbitrary scale. Society possesses a conventional standard whereby it judges all things. All men should be good, all women virtuous. Wherefore, villain, hast thou failed!

For all the liberal analysis of Spencer and our modern naturalistic philosophers we have but an infantile perception of morals. There is more in it than mere conformity to a law of evolution. It is yet deeper than conformity to things of earth alone. It is more involved than we as yet perceive. Answer first why the heart thrills, explain wherefore some plaintive note goes wandering about the world undying, make clear the rose's subtle alchemy, evolving its ruddy lamp in light and rain. In the essence of these facts lie the first principles of morals.

"Oh," thought Drouet, "how delicious is my conquest."

"Ah," thought Carrie, with mournful misgivings, "what is it I have lost?"

Before this world-old proposition we stand, serious, interested, confused; endeavoring to evolve the true theory of morals—the true answer to what is right.

In the view of a certain stratum of society, Carrie was comfortably established—in the eyes of the starveling beaten by every wind and gusty sheet of rain, she was safe in a halcyon harbor. Drouet had taken three rooms furnished, in Ogden Place, facing Union Park, on the West Side. That was a little, green-carpeted breathing spot, than which today there is nothing more beautiful in Chicago. It afforded a vista pleasant to contemplate. The best room looked out upon the lawn of the park, now sear and brown, where a little lake lay sheltered. Across the park were Ashland Boulevard and Warren Avenue, where stood rows of comfortable houses built and occupied by a middle class who were both respectable and moderately well-to-do. Over the bare limbs of the trees, which now swayed in the wintry wind, rose the steeple of the Union Park Congregational Church, and far off the towers of several others. No street cars went by the door, but they were only a block away, at Madison Street, a thoroughfare which was then the most enlivened and prosperous store street of the West Side.

The rooms were comfortably enough furnished. There was a good Brussels carpet on the floor, rich in dull red and lemon shades and representing large jardinières filled with gorgeous impossible flowers. There was a large pier-glass mirror, between the two windows, fitted in when mirrors of that kind were exceedingly popular. A large, soft, green-plush-covered lounge occupied one corner, and several rocking chairs were set carelessly about. Some pictures, several rugs, a few small pieces of bric-a-brac, and the tale of contents is told.

In the bed room, off the front room, was Carrie's trunk, bought by Drouet, and in a wardrobe built into the wall, quite an array of clothing—more than she had ever possessed before and of very becoming designs. There was a third room for possible use as a kitchen, where Drouet had Carrie establish a little portable gas stove for the preparation of small lunches, oysters, Welsh rarebits and the like, of which he was exceedingly fond, and lastly a bath. The whole place was cosy in that it was lighted by gas and heated by furnace registers, possessing also a small grate, set with an asbestos back, a method of cheerful warming which was then first coming into use. By her industry and natural love of order which now developed, the place retained an air pleasing in the extreme.

Here then was Carrie, established in a pleasant fashion, free of certain difficulties which most ominously confronted her, laden with many new ones which were of a mental order, and altogether so turned about in all of her earthly relationships that she might have well been a new and different individual. She looked into her glass and saw a prettier Carrie there than she had seen before; she looked into her mind, a mirror prepared of her own and the world's opinions, and saw a worse. Between these two images she wavered, hesitating which to believe.

"My, but you're a little beauty!" Drouet was wont to exclaim to her.

She would look at him with large, pleased eyes.

"You know it, don't you?" he would continue.

"Oh, I don't know," she would reply, feeling delight in the fact that one should think so, hesitating to believe, though she really did, that she was vain enough to think so much of herself. Thus she wavered.

Her conscience, however, was not a Drouet, interested to praise. There she heard a different voice, with which she argued, pleaded, excused. It was no just and sapient counsellor, in its last analysis. It was only an average little conscience, a thing which represented the world, her past environment, habit, convention, in a confused, reflected way. With it, the voice of the people was truly the voice of God.

"Oh, thou failure," said this voice.

"Why?" she questioned.

"Look at those about," came the whispered answer. "Look

at those who are good. How would they scorn to do what you have done. Look at the good girls, how will they draw away from such as you, when they know you have been weak. You had not tried before you failed."

It was when Carrie was alone looking out across the park that she would be listening to this. It would come infrequently— when something else did not interfere, when the pleasant side was not too apparent, when Drouet was not there. It was somewhat clear in utterance at first, but never wholly convincing. There was always an answer. Always the December days threatened. She was alone; she was desireful; she was fearful of the whistling wind. The voice of want made answer for her.

We do not make sufficient allowance for the natural elements in our philosophy. Our logic is bare of the voice of the wind. How potent is the answer a pang of hunger makes to the cry, "Be good." How subtle is the influence of a dreary atmosphere.

Once the bright days of summer pass by, a city takes on that sombre garb of grey, wrapt in which it goes about its labors during the long winter. Its endless buildings look grey, its sky and its streets assume that sombre hue, the scattered, leafless trees and wind-blown dust and paper but add to the general solemnity of color. There seems to be something in the chill breezes, which scurry through the long narrow thoroughfares, productive of rueful thoughts. Not poets alone, nor artists, nor that superior order of mind which arrogates to itself all refinement, feel this, but dogs and all men. These feel as much as the poet, though they have not the same power of expression. The sparrow upon the wire, the cat in the doorway, the dray horse tugging his weary load, feel the long keen breaths of winter. It strikes to the heart of all life, animate and inanimate. The upsweeping of the dust, the low hanging of the clouds, the smoke of many industries make the late fall and early winter days dull and cheerless. If it were not for the artificial fires of merriment, the rush of profit-seeking trade and pleasure-selling amusements; if the various merchants failed to make the customary displays within and without their establishments; if our streets were not strung with signs of gorgeous hues and thronged with hurrying purchasers, we would quickly discover how firmly the chill hand of winter lays upon the heart;—how dispiriting are the days during which the sun withholds a portion of our allowance of light and warmth. We are more dependent upon these things than is often thought for. We are insects produced by heat and wither and pass without it.

In the drag of such a gray day, the secret voice would reassert itself, feebly and more feebly, as the days passed on.

"Dawdler!" it would exclaim in such language as she would appreciate. "Lingerer in the lap of ease."

"No," she would think. "What else could I do? I was so bad off. Where could I have gone? Not home again—oh, I did not want to go there. I was in danger of being hungry. I had no clothes. Didn't I try?"

"Remember how men look upon what you have done," said the voice.

"I have nice clothes," she would hum to herself in spirit, drowning the urgent voice. "They make me look so nice. I am safe. The world is not so bad now. It is not so dreadful—what have I done?"

The deference of men to one who pays his dues to them confers this belief at times.

"Step into the streets, return to your home, be as you were. Escape!"

"I can't. I can't," was her only reply.

"Out, woman. Into the streets. Preferably be wretched."

"Where may I go?" she would reply. "I am a poor girl. Look how I was treated. What would they think of me, if I came home?"

"Out of it all," the voice would murmur at last, almost indistinct.

"Oh, my nice clothes," the senses were saying. "Oh, the cold streets. Was that the wind whistling I heard? I have a fine cloak. I have gloves. It would be a machine again without these things. Oh, what can I do, what can I do?"

Thus would she sway, thus would all men, similarly equipped, between this truth and that evil—between this right and that wrong. It is all a weighing of advantage. And whoso is it so noble as to ever avoid evil, and who so wise that he moves ever in the direction of truth?

Such mental conflict was not always uppermost. Carrie was not by any means a gloomy soul. More, she had not the mind to get firm hold upon a definite truth. When she could not find her way out of the labyrinth of illogic which thought upon the subject created, she would turn away entirely.

Drouet, all the time, was conducting himself in a model way for one of his sort. He took her about a great deal, spent money upon her to the extent that the state of his finances warranted, and when he traveled took her with him. There were times when she would be alone for two or three days while he made the shorter circuits of his business, but as a rule she saw a great deal of him.

"Say, Carrie," he said one morning shortly after they had so established themselves. "I've invited my friend Hurstwood to come out some day, and spend the evening with us."

"Who is he?" asked Carrie, doubtfully.

"Oh, he's a nice man. He's manager of Hannah and Hogg's."

"What's that?" said Carrie.

"The finest resort in town. It's a way-up swell place."

Carrie puzzled a moment. She was wondering what Drouet had told him, what her attitude would be.

"That's all right," said Drouet, feeling the thought she had. "He doesn't know anything. You're Mrs. Drouet now."

There was something about this which struck Carrie as slightly inconsiderate. She could see that Drouet did not have the keenest sensibilities.

"Why don't we get married?" she inquired, thinking of the voluble promises he had made.

"Well, we will," he said, "just as soon as I get this little deal of mine closed up."

He was referring to some property which he said he had and which required so much attention, adjustment and whatnot, that somehow or other it interfered with his free moral, personal actions.

"Just as soon as I get back from my Denver trip in January, we'll do it."

Carrie accepted this as a basis for hope—it was a sort of salve to her conscience, a pleasant way out. Under the circumstances, things would be righted. Her actions would be justified.

She really was not enamoured of Drouet. A little living with him convinced her of that. She was more clever than he.

In a dim way she was beginning to see where he lacked. If it had not been for this, if she had not been able to measure and judge him in a way, she would have been worse off than she was. She would have adored him. She would have been utterly wretched in her fear of not gaining his affection, of losing his interest, of being swept away and left without an anchorage. As it was, she wavered a little, slightly anxious at first to gain him completely, but later feeling at ease in waiting. She was not exactly sure what she thought of him—what she wanted to do.

When Hurstwood called she met a man who was more clever than Drouet in a hundred ways. Not as insatiably desirous of the feminine, he was yet more successful. He paid that peculiar deference to women which every member of the sex appreciates. He was not overawed, he was not overbold. His great charm was attentiveness. Schooled in winning those birds of fine feather among his own sex, the merchants and professionals who visited his resort, he could use even greater tact when endeavoring to prove agreeable to someone who charmed him. In a pretty woman, of any refinement of feeling whatsoever, he found his greatest incentive. He was mild, placid, assured, giving the impression that he wished to be of service only—to do something which would make the lady more pleased.

Drouet had ability in this line himself when the game was worth the candle, but he was too much the egotist to reach the polish which Hurstwood possessed. He was too buoyant, too full of ruddy life, too assured. He succeeded with many who were not quite schooled in the art of love. He failed dismally where the woman was slightly experienced and possessed innate refinement. In the case of Carrie he found a woman who was all of the latter but none of the former. He was lucky in that opportunity tumbled into his lap, as it were. A few years later with a little more experience, the slightest tide of success, and he had not been able to approach Carrie at all.

Ah, how rapidly women learn. In the main they are Jesuits by instinct. Endow them with beauty, and within the possibilities of their environment they will pick and choose. Show them two men and they will understand which one appreciates women most. Such fine methods of comparison man does not possess. It is an inherited qualification of the sex, developed by ages of necessity.

"You ought to have a piano here, Drouet," said Hurstwood, smiling at Carrie on the evening in question, "so that your wife could play."

Drouet had not thought of that.

"So we ought," he observed readily.

"Oh, I don't play," ventured Carrie.

"It isn't very difficult," returned Hurstwood. "You could do very well in a few weeks."

He was in the best form for entertaining this evening. His clothes were particularly new and rich in appearance. The coat lapels stood out with that medium stiffness which excellent cloth possesses. The vest was of a rich Scotch plaid, set with a double row of round mother-of-pearl buttons. His cravat was a shiny combination of silken threads, not loud, not inconspicuous. What he wore did not strike the eye so forcibly as that which Drouet had on, but Carrie could see the elegance of the material. Hurstwood's shoes were of soft black calf, polished only to a dull shine, while Drouet wore patent leathers, but Carrie could not help feeling that there was a distinction in favor of the soft leather, where all else was so rich. She noticed these things almost unconsciously. They were things which would naturally flow from the situation. She was used to Drouet's appearance.

"Supposing we have a little game of euchre," suggested Hurstwood, after a little round of conversation. He was rather dexterous in avoiding everything that would suggest that he knew anything of Carrie's past. He kept away from personalities altogether and confined himself to those things which did not concern individuals at all. By his manner he put Carrie at her ease, and by his deference and pleasantries he amused her. He pretended to be seriously interested in her replies and kept himself in the background in so far as the making of opportunities for pleasant converse would permit.

"I don't know how to play," said Carrie.

"Charlie, you are neglecting a part of your duty," he observed to Drouet, most affably. "Between us, though," he went on, "we can show you."

By his tact he made Drouet feel that he admired his choice. There was something in his manner that showed that he was pleased to be there. Drouet felt really closer to him than ever before. It gave him more respect for Carrie. Her appearance came into a new light, under Hurstwood's appreciation. The situation livened considerably.

"Now let me see," said Hurstwood, looking over Carrie's shoulder very deferentially. "What have you?" He studied for a moment. "That's rather good," he said. "You're lucky. Now I'll show you how to trounce your husband. You take my advice."

"Here," said Drouet, "if you two are going to scheme together, I won't stand a ghost of a show. Hurstwood's a regular sharp."

"No," said Hurstwood, "it's your wife. She brings me luck. Why shouldn't she win?"

Carrie looked gratefully at Hurstwood and smiled at Drouet. The former took the air of a mere friend. He was simply there to enjoy himself. Anything that Carrie did was pleasing to him, nothing more.

"There," he said, holding back one of his own good cards and giving Carrie a chance to take a trick, "I count that clever playing for a beginner."

The latter laughed gleefully as she saw the hand coming her way. It was as if she were invincible when Hurstwood helped her.

That worthy did not look at her often. When he did, it was with a mild light in his eye. Not a shade there of anything save geniality and kindliness. He took back the shifty, clever gleam and replaced it with one of innocence. Carrie could not guess but that it was pleasure with him in the immediate thing. She felt that he considered she was doing a great deal.

"It's unfair to let such playing go without earning something," he said after a time, slipping his fingers into the little coin pocket of his coat. "Let's play for dimes."

"All right," said Drouet, fishing for bills.

Hurstwood was quicker. His fingers were full of new ten-cent pieces. "Here we are," he said, supplying each one with a little stack.

"Oh, this is gambling," smiled Carrie. "It's bad."

"No," said Drouet, "only fun. If you never play for more than that you will go to heaven."

"Don't you moralize," said Hurstwood to Carrie gently, "until you see what becomes of the money."

Drouet smiled.

"If your husband gets them, he'll tell you how bad it is."

Drouet laughed out loud.

There was such an ingratiating tone about Hurstwood's voice, the insinuation was so perceptible, that even Carrie got the humor of it.

"When do you leave?" said Hurstwood to Drouet.

"On Wednesday," he replied.

"It's rather hard to have your husband running about like that, isn't it?" said Hurstwood, addressing Carrie.

"She's going along with me this time," said Drouet.

"You must both go with me to the theatre before you go."

"Certainly," said Drouet, "eh, Carrie?"

"I'd like it ever so much," she replied.

Hurstwood did his best to see that Carrie won the money. He rejoiced in her success, kept counting her winnings and finally gathered and put them in her extended hands. They spread a little lunch at which he served the wine, and afterwards he used fine tact in going.

"Now," he said, addressing first Carrie and then Drouet with his eyes, "you must be ready at seven-thirty. I'll come and get you." They went with him to the door and there was his cab waiting, its red lamps gleaming cheerfully in the shadow.

"Now," he observed to Drouet, with a tone of good fellowship, "when you leave your wife alone you must let me come out and show her around a little. It will break up her loneliness."

"Sure," said Drouet, quite pleased at the attention shown. By George, Hurstwood was pleased with his Carrie.

"You're so kind," observed Carrie.

"Not at all," he said. "I would want your husband to do as much for me."

He smiled and went lightly away. Carrie was thoroughly impressed. Such grace she had never come in contact with.

As for Drouet, he was equally pleased.

"There's a nice man," he remarked to Carrie as they returned to their cosy chamber. "Good friend of mine, too."

"He seems to be," said Carrie.

CHAPTER XI.

In considering Carrie's mental state, the culmination of reasoning which held her at anchorage in so strange a harbor, we must fail of a just appreciation if we do not give due weight to those subtle influences, not human, which environ and appeal to the young imagination when it drifts. Trite though it may seem, it is well to remember that in life, after all, we are most wholly controlled by desire. The things that appeal to desire are not always visible objects. Let us not confuse this with selfishness. It is more virtuous than that. Desire is the variable wind which blows now zephyrlike, now shrill, filling our sails for some far-off port, flapping them idly upon the high seas in sunny weather, scudding us now here, now there, before its terrific breath, speeding us anon to accomplishment; as often rending our sails and leaving us battered and dismantled, a picturesque wreck in some forgotten harbor. Selfishness is the twin-screw motive power of the human steamer. It drives unchangingly, unpoetically on. Its one danger is that of miscalculation. Personalities such as Carrie's would come under the former category. The art by which her rather confused consciousness of right and duty might be overcome is not easily perceived.

In the progress of all such minds environment is a subtle, persuasive control. It works hand in hand with desire. For instance, by certain conditions which her intellect was scarcely able to control, she was pushed into a situation where for the first time she could see a strikingly different way of living from her own. Fine clothes, rich foods, superior residence, a conspicuously apparent assumption of position in others,—these she saw. She was no more clever in observing this than any shop girl. No matter how dull is the perception in other things, in such matters all women are clear. It is scarcely remarkable also, in view of the struggle for these things which is everywhere apparent, that she should suppose them to be best. If the sight of them aroused a desire in her bosom, is it strange?

It must next be considered that if desire be rife in the mind and no channel of satisfaction is provided; if there be ambition, however weak, and it is not schooled in lovely principle and precept—if no way be shown, be sure it will learn a way of the world. Need it be said that the lesson of the latter is not always uplifting. We know that the common run of mortals *struggle* to be happy. Is not that comment sufficient?

Lastly, let all men remember that in the main, the world's virtue has never been tested. Wherefore was he good—the heavens rained goodness on the soil that nourished him. Where severe tests have been made, there have been some lamentable failures. Too often we move along ignoring the fact of our own advantages in every criticism we make concerning others. We do this because we are ignorant of the subtleties of life. Be sure that the vileness which you attribute to some object is a mirage. It is a sky illumination of your own lack of understanding—the confusion of your own soul.

In the light of these truths, it is well to admit the possibility of persuasion and control other than by men. Did Drouet persuade her entirely? Ah, the magnitude attributed to simple Drouet! The leading strings were with neither of them.

Carrie was an apt student of fortune's ways—of fortune's superficialities. Seeing a thing, she would immediately set to inquiring how she would look properly related to it. Be it known that this is not fine feeling; it is not wisdom. The greatest minds are not so afflicted, and on the contrary the lowest order of mind is not so disturbed. Fine clothes to her were a vast persuasion; they spoke tenderly and Jesuitically for themselves. When she came within earshot of their pleading, desire in her bent a willing ear. Ah, ah! the voices of the so-called inanimate. Who shall yet translate for us the language of the stones.

"My dear," said the lace collar she secured from Pardridge's, "I fit you beautifully; don't give me up."

"Ah, such little feet," said the leather of the soft new shoes, "how effectively I cover them; what a pity they should ever want my aid."

Once these things were in her hand, on her person, she might dream of giving them up; the method by which they came might intrude itself so forcefully that she would ache to be rid of the canker of it, but she would not give them up. "Put on the old clothes—that torn pair of shoes," was called to her by her conscience in vain. She could possibly have conquered the fear of hunger and gone back; the thought of hard work and a narrow round of suffering would, under the last pressure of conscience, have yielded—but spoil her appearance—be old-clothed and poor-appearing—never.

Drouet heightened her opinions on this and allied subjects in such a manner as to weaken her power of resisting their influence. It is so easy to do this when the thing opined is in the line of what we desire. In his hearty way, he insisted upon her good looks. He looked at her admiringly and she took it at its full value. Under the circumstances, she did not need to carry herself as pretty women do. She picked that knowledge up fast enough for herself. Drouet had a habit, characteristic of his kind, of looking after stylishly dressed or pretty women on the street and remarking upon them. He had just enough of the feminine love of dress to be a good judge—not of intellect but of clothes. He saw how they set their little feet, how they carried their chins, with what grace and sinuosity they swayed their bodies. A dainty, self-conscious swaying of the hips by a woman was to him as alluring as the glint of rare wine to a toper. He would turn and follow the disappearing vision with his eyes. He would thrill as a child with the unhindered passion that was in him. He loved the thing that women love in themselves, grace. At this, their own shrine, he knelt with them, an ardent devotee.

"Did you see that woman who went by just now?" he said to Carrie, on the very first day they took a walk together.

It was a very average type of woman they had encountered, young, pretty, very satisfactorily dressed so far as appearances went, though not in style. Drouet had never seen the perfectly groomed ladies of the New York social set, or he would have been conscious of her defects. Carrie had spied her first, though with scarce so single an eye.

"Fine stepper, wasn't she?"

Carrie looked again and observed the grace commended.

"Yes, she is," she returned cheerfully, a little suggestion of possible defect in herself awakening in her mind. If that was so fine she must look at it more closely. Instinctively she felt a desire to imitate it. Surely she could do that too.

When one of her mind sees many things emphasized and

re-emphasized and admired, she gathers the logic of it and applies accordingly. Drouet was not shrewd enough to see that this was not tactful. He could not see that it would be better to make her feel that she was competing with herself, not with others better than herself. He would not have done it with an older, wiser woman; but in Carrie he saw only the novice. Less clever than she, he was naturally unable to comprehend her sensibility. He went on educating and wounding her, a thing rather foolish in one whose admiration for his pupil and victim was apt to grow.

Carrie took the instructions affably. She saw what Drouet liked; in a vague way she saw where he was weak. It lessens a woman's opinion of a man when she learns that his admiration is so pointedly and generously distributed. She sees but one object of supreme compliment in this world and that is herself. If a man is to succeed with many women, he must be all in all to each.

One day he took her driving, as much for his own amusement as her satisfaction. He had a number of things to show her. Principal among these were the fine houses of the millionaires, which were then nearly all on Prairie Avenue. Money to him was a wonderful thing. The application of the term millionaire was as grand as the possession of a title. Like all Americans, he confessed a certain amount of scorn for the latter, but accepted its equivalent, with almost pathetic admiration. He knew where Armour lived and Pullman. The houses of Potter Palmer and Marshall Field he had often seen. Now before them, he gazed with unflagging admiration. To him it was simply wonderful, wonderful.

"Say Carrie," he said, "see that house on ahead there?"

He pointed to a rather awkward brick and stone affair, not at all beautiful in its decorative effect, which was set down in a rather extensive green lawn—a very fair example of the mixed and uncertain architecture characteristic of the city at that time.

Carrie nodded.

"That's Pullman's," he said.

The two gazed at the great sleeping-car magnate's residence with undisguised interest.

"Say, but he's got the money. Twenty million dollars. Think of that!"

In like manner he pointed out many others—bankers, merchants whom he knew of through his business experience.

"Fine, isn't it?" was one of his favorite comments.

Out of one of the imposing gateways of iron, a jingling trap was turning—an elegant pair of bays and a polished and benickeled box surrey. In it were a youth of perhaps twenty-three and a young girl of about Carrie's age. The latter was pretty in a way, the chief impression she made being by grace of a certain hauteur of glance, or better, no glance. She gazed straight before her, pursed up her pretty lips and nodded indifferently to some remark her companion was making.

Drouet was all eyes. There was the woman for him. What a thing to sit up with such a girl as that, behind such a team. Oh, the shine of the polished leather harness—the jingle of the nickeled buckles. He really went with the young lady in fancy, clattering up the broad avenue and holding himself like a millionaire ought to. Carrie felt this, though he said very little. She envied the stiff, dressy slip of a girl. She even saw what was uncomplimentary to Drouet, the distinction of the youth who went along with her. So that was what it was to be rich. A large house with a fine lawn, windows with thick hanging lace curtains, a fine carriage with prancing horses and the ability to turn out of a fine gate behind which a fountain was playing, even in cold weather. Carrie looked and well remembered. She owed her keen impression as much to Drouet's unspoken feelings as to the appearance of the objects themselves. She was being branded like wax by a scene which only made poor clothes, worn shoes, shop application and poverty in general seem more dire, more degraded, more and more impossible. How would she not like to have something like this—what would she not do to avoid the other.

In her own situation there was something even more persuading. It was so much more beautiful than Van Buren Street.

Accidentally, in coming home, Drouet drove through Jackson Street, and before Carrie knew it they were opposite Hanson's flat, a block away. She could see it through some open lots, the front curtains half drawn. Minnie was in the kitchen getting supper.

For a moment Carrie winced perceptibly. It was like a slap in the face.

"Let's not drive down here any further," she said, when they were a block further on.

"All right," he said, turning off. "It isn't as nice as Washington Street. That's the swellest street on the West Side."

In her own apartments Carrie saw things which were lessons in the same school.

In the same house with her lived an official of one of the theatres, Mr. Frank A. Hale, manager of the Standard, and his wife, a pleasing-looking brunette of thirty-five. They were people of a sort very common in America today, who live respectably from hand to mouth. Hale received a salary of forty-five dollars a week. His wife, quite attractive, affected the feeling of youth and objected to that sort of home-life which means the care of a house and the raising of a family. Like Drouet and Carrie, they also occupied three rooms on the floor above.

Not long after Carrie arrived, Mrs. Hale established social relations with her, and together they went about. For a long time this was her only companionship, and the gossip of the manager's wife formed the medium through which she saw the world. Such trivialities, such praises of wealth, such conventional expression of morals as sifted through this passive creature's mind fell upon Carrie and for the while confused her.

On the other hand, her feelings were a corrective influence. The constant drag to something better was not to be denied. By those things which address the heart was she steadily recalled. In the apartments across the hall were a young girl and her mother. They were from Evansville, Indiana, the wife and daughter of a railroad treasurer. The daughter was here to study music, the mother to keep her company.

Carrie did not make their acquaintance, but she saw the daughter coming in and going out. A few times she had seen her at the piano in the parlor, and not infrequently had heard her play. This young woman was particularly dressy for her station, and wore a jeweled ring or two which flashed upon her white fingers as she played.

Now Carrie was affected by music. Her nervous composition responded to certain strains, much as certain strings of a harp vibrate when a corresponding key of a piano is struck. She was not delicately moulded in sentiment, and yet there was enough in her of what is commonly known as feeling to cause her to answer with vague ruminations to certain wistful chords. They awoke longings for those things which she did not have. They caused her to cling closer to things she possessed. One short song the young woman played in a most soulful and tender mood. Carrie heard it through the open door from the parlor below. It was at that hour between afternoon and night when for the idle, the wanderers, things are apt to take on a wistful complexion. The mind wanders forth on far journeys and returns with sheaves of withered and departed joys. Carrie sat at her window looking out. Drouet had been away since ten in the morning. She had amused herself with a walk, a book by Bertha M. Clay, which Drouet had left there, though she did not wholly enjoy the latter, and by changing her dress for the evening. Now she sat looking out across the park, as wistful and depressed as the nature which craves variety and life can be under such circumstances. As she contemplated her new state, the strain from the parlor below stole upward. With it her thoughts became colored and enmeshed. She reverted to the things which were best and saddest within the small limit of her experience. She became for the moment a repentant.

While she was in this mood Drouet came in, bringing an entirely different atmosphere with him. It was dusk and Carrie had neglected to light the lamp. Also the fire in the grate had burned low.

"Where are you, Cad?" he said, using a pet name he had given her.

"Here," she answered.

There was something delicate and lonely in her voice, but he could not hear it. He had not the poetry in him that would seek a woman out under such circumstances and console her for the tragedy of life. Instead, he struck a match and lighted the gas.

"Hello!" he exclaimed, "you've been crying."

Her eyes were still wet with a few vague tears.

"Pshaw," he said, "you don't want to do that."

He took her hand, feeling in his good-natured egotism that it was probably lack of his presence which had made her lonely.

"Come on now," he went on, "it's all right. Let's waltz a little to that music."

He could not have introduced a more incongruous proposition. It made clear to Carrie that he could not sympathize with her. She could not have framed thoughts which would have expressed his defect or made clear the difference between them, but she felt it. It was his first mistake.

What Drouet said about the girl's grace, as she tripped out of an evening accompanied by her mother, caused Carrie to perceive the nature and value of those little modish ways which women adopt when they would presume to be something. She looked in her mirror and pursed up her lips, accompanying it with a little toss of the head as she had seen the railroad treasurer's daughter do. She caught up her skirts with an easy swing, for had not Drouet remarked that in her and several others, and Carrie was naturally imitative. She began to get the hang of those little things which the pretty woman who has vanity invariably adopts. In short, her knowledge of grace doubled, and with it her appearance changed. She became a girl of considerable taste.

Drouet noticed this. He saw the new bow in her hair and the new way of arranging her locks which she affected one morning.

"You look fine that way, Cad," he said.

"Do I?" she replied sweetly. It made her try for other effects that selfsame day.

She used her feet less heavily, a thing that was brought about by her attempting to imitate the treasurer's daughter. How much influence the presence of that young woman in the same house had upon her it would be difficult to say. She saw her in the glamor of a life which was novel to both of them. Chicago was new to this young lady. She was elated over experiences which Evansville did not afford. She moved about, strongly self-conscious of the superior state of her parents which allowed her to come to Chicago and study. Her every action was a testimonial to her pride and self-satisfaction. She played with an air.

Such a personality Carrie could not help but feel. Her chagrin at the coldness and indifference of such natures did not preclude in her the desire to do likewise. If she could only be like that, wouldn't she show such smart creatures!

At night when the tall red-shaded piano lamp stood by the piano, and in its ruddy light the treasurer's daughter played and sang, Carrie saw and felt things which appealed to her imagination. If the melody could, as once it did, arouse thoughts which started the tears, how effectual must have been the impress of the young girl's material state. For Carrie the melody and the light created a halo about nice clothes, showy manners, sparkling rings. It lent an ineffable charm to the world of material display. Accordingly, when Hurstwood called he found a young woman who was much more than the Carrie Drouet had first spoken to. The primary defects of dress and manner had passed. She was pretty, graceful, rich in the timidity born of uncertainty, and with a something childlike in her large eyes which captured the fancy of this starched and conventional poser among men. It was the ancient attraction of the stale to the fresh. If there was a touch of appreciation left in him for the bloom and unsophistication which is the charm of youth, it rekindled now. He looked into her pretty face and felt the subtle waves of young life radiating therefrom. In that large clear eye he could see nothing that his blasé nature could understand as guile. The little vanity, if he could have perceived it there, would have touched him as a pleasant thing.

"I wonder," he said, as he rode away in his cab, "how Drouet came to win her."

He gave the lady credit for feelings superior to Drouet at the first glance.

The cab plopped along between the far receding lines of gas lamps on either hand. He folded his gloved hands and saw only the lighted chamber and Carrie's face. He was pondering over the delight of young beauty.

"I'll have a bouquet for her. Drouet won't mind."

CHAPTER XII.

Drouet was a man whom it was impossible to bind to any one object long. He had but one idol—the perfect woman. He found her enshrined in many a pretty petticoat. On his trade pilgrimages he was like to forget Carrie entirely. She came into his mind when all later divinities were out, or when he was on his way back to Chicago. Then her beauty and the cosy quarters in which she was installed loomed up before him with considerable fascination, and he was delighted to get back. He would enter Carrie's presence with all the spirit of a lover—away from her would forsake her memory with the ease of the unattached masher, which, after all, he was.

With a nature such as Carrie's, which partook somewhat of his own characteristics, there could be no powerful attachment between them. Their very congeniality militated against it, for now that the chief incentive to matrimony had been forced out of its natural achievement and result, by conditions over which Carrie had little control, she viewed her companion in a modified light. He was good, he was genial, he was agreeable, but he was not the man either to win or retain her affection. She felt, though she could not frame them in any connected and logical form of thought, the points wherein he failed as a man.

Drouet on the contrary went merrily forward, pursuing the routine of his satisfactory employment and brooding not at all upon his companion's situation. He stinted himself nothing in the way of flirtation and observation of the other sex. His friends called him out to this or that sortie upon the susceptibilities of the fair sex in various cities and he seldom failed to respond. There was no compunction in the matter—there was no detailed thought upon the subject. Women were made for men—and there was an end to it. The glance of a coquetish eye was sufficient reason for any deviltry. He had no other conception of its meaning.

Hurstwood, however, was a man who was less light-minded and consequently more subtle. He saw a trifle more clearly the necessities of our social organization, but he was more unscrupulous in the matter of sinning against it. He did not, as a matter of fact, conduct himself so loosely as Drouet, but it was entirely owing to a respect for his situation. In the actual matter of a decision and a consummation, he was worse than Drouet. He more deliberately set aside the canons of right as he understood them.

Hurstwood was attracted by Carrie. He never for a moment concealed the fact from himself. He troubled himself not at all about Drouet's priority or individuality. He was merely floating those gossamer threads of thought, which like the spider's, he hoped would lay hold somewhere. He did not know, he could not guess, what the result would be.

A few days later, Drouet in his peregrinations encountered one of his well-dressed lady acquaintances in Chicago on his return from a short trip to Omaha. He had intended to hurry out to Ogden Place and surprise Carrie, but now he fell into an interesting conversation and soon modified his original intention.

"Let's us go to dinner," he said, little recking any chance meeting which might trouble his way.

"Certainly," said his companion.

They visited one of the better restaurants for a social chat. It was five in the afternoon when they met; it was seven-thirty before the last bone was picked.

Drouet was just finishing a little incident he was relating and his face was expanding into a smile when Hurstwood's eye caught his own. The latter had come in with several friends and, seeing Drouet and some woman not Carrie, drew his own conclusion.

"Ah, the rascal," he thought; and then with a touch of righteous sympathy, "that's pretty hard on the little girl."

Drouet jumped from one easy thought to another as he caught Hurstwood's eye. He felt but very little misgiving until he saw that Hurstwood was cautiously pretending not to see the little situation. Then some of the latter's impression forced itself upon him. He thought of Carrie and their last meeting.

By George, he would have to explain this to Hurstwood. Such a chance half-hour with an old friend must not have anything more attached to it than it really warranted.

For the first time he was troubled. Here was a moral complication of which he could not possibly get the ends. Hurstwood would laugh at him for being a fickle boy. He would laugh with Hurstwood. Carrie would never hear, his present companion at table would never know, and yet he could not help feeling that he was getting the worst of it—there was some faint stigma attached and he was not guilty. He broke up the dinner by becoming dull, and saw his companion on her car. Then he went home.

"He hasn't talked to me about any of these later flames," thought Hurstwood to himself. "He thinks I think he cares for the girl out there."

"He ought not to think I'm knocking around, since I have just introduced him out there," thought Drouet.

"I saw you," Hurstwood said genially, the next time Drouet drifted into his polished resort, from which he could not stay away. He raised his forefinger indicatively, as parents do to children.

"An old acquaintance of mine that I ran into just as I was coming up from the station," explained Drouet. "She used to be quite a beauty."

"Still attracts a little, eh!" returned the other, affecting to jest.

"Oh, no," said Drouet, "just couldn't escape her this time."

"How long are you here?" asked Hurstwood.

"Only a few days."

"You must bring the girl down and take dinner with me," he said. "I'm afraid you keep her cooped up out there. I'll get a box for Joe Jefferson."

"Not me," answered the drummer. "Sure I'll come."

This pleased Hurstwood immensely. He gave Drouet no credit for any feeling towards Carrie whatever. He envied him, and now as he looked at the well-dressed, jolly salesman whom he so much liked, the cold gleam of the rival glowed in his eye. He began to size up Drouet from the standpoints of wit and fascination. He began to look to see where he was weak. There was no disputing that whatever he might think of him as a good fellow, he felt a certain amount of contempt for him as a lover. He could hoodwink him all right. Why, if he would just let Carrie see one such little incident as that of Thursday, it would settle the matter. He ran on in thought, almost exulting the while he laughed and chatted, and Drouet felt nothing. He had no power of analyzing the glance and the atmosphere of a man like Hurstwood. He stood and smiled and accepted the invitation, while his friend examined him with the eye of a hawk.

The object of this peculiarly involved comedy was not thinking of either. She was busy adjusting her thoughts and feelings to newer conditions and was not in danger of suffering disturbing pangs from either quarter.

That evening Drouet found her dressing herself before the glass.

"Cad," said he, catching her, "I believe you're getting vain."

"Nothing of the kind," she retorted, smiling.

"Well, you are mighty pretty," he went on, slipping his arm around her. "Put on that navy blue dress of yours, and I'll take you to the show."

"Oh, I've promised Mrs. Hale to go with her to The Exposition tonight," she returned apologetically.

"You did, eh," he said, studying the situation abstractly. "I wouldn't care to go to that myself."

"Well, I don't know," answered Carrie, puzzling but not offering to break her promise in his favor.

Just then a knock came at their door and the maid-servant handed a letter in.

"He says there's an answer expected," she explained.

"It's from Hurstwood," said Drouet, noting the superscription as he tore it open.

"You two are to come down and see Joe Jefferson with me tonight," it ran in part. "It's my turn as we agreed the other day. All other bets are off."

"Well, what do we say to this?" asked Drouet innocently, while Carrie's mind bubbled with favorable replies.

"You had better decide, Charlie," she said reservedly.

"I guess we had better go, if you can break that engagement upstairs," said Drouet.

"Oh, I can," returned Carrie, without thinking.

Drouet selected writing paper, while Carrie moved to change her dress. She hardly explained to herself why this latest invitation appealed to her most.

"Shall I wear my hair as I did yesterday?" she asked as she came out with several articles of apparel pending.

"Um huh," he returned pleasantly.

She was relieved to see that he felt nothing. She did not credit her willingness to go to any fascination Hurstwood held for her. It seemed that the combination of Hurstwood, Drouet and herself was more agreeable than anything else which had been suggested. She arrayed herself most carefully and they started off, extending excuses upstairs.

"I say," said Hurstwood as they came up the theatre lobby, "we are exceedingly charming this evening."

Carrie fluttered under his approving glance.

"Now then," he said, leading the way up the foyer into the theatre.

If ever there was dressiness it was here. It was the personification of the old term "spick and span."

"Did you ever see Jefferson?" he questioned as he leaned toward Carrie in the box.

"I never did," she returned.

"He's delightful, delightful," he went on, giving the commonplace rendition of approval which such men know. He sent Drouet after a program and then discoursed to Carrie concerning Jefferson as he had heard of him. The former was pleased beyond expression and was really hypnotized by the environment, the trappings of the box, the elegance of her companion. Several times their eyes accidentally met and then there poured into hers such a flood of feeling as she had never before experienced. She could not for the moment explain it, for in the next glance or the next move of the hand there was seeming indifference mingled only with the kindliest attention.

Drouet shared in the conversation but he was almost dull in comparison. Hurstwood entertained them both and now it was driven into Carrie's mind that here was the superior man. She instinctively felt that he was stronger and higher and yet withal so simple. By the end of the third act she was sure that Drouet was only a kindly soul but otherwise defective. He sank every moment in her estimation by the strong comparison.

"I have had such a nice time," said Carrie when it was all over and they were coming out.

"Yes, indeed," added Drouet, who was not in the least aware that a battle had been fought and his defences weakened. He was like the Emperor of China who sat glorying in himself, unaware that his fairest provinces were being wrested from him.

"Well, you have saved me a dreary evening," returned Hurstwood. "Goodnight."

He took Carrie's little hand and some feelable current swept from one to the other.

"I'm so tired," said Carrie, leaning back in the car when Drouet began to talk.

"Well, you rest a little while I smoke," he said, rising, and then he foolishly went to the forward platform of the car and left the game as it stood.

CHAPTER XIII.

If there was one quality which might be predicated more than another of Hurstwood at this time it was circumspectness, which the state of his home life and the tenure of his position depended upon. While there was in him no feeling of affection which could bind him to his wife and children, there was, as has been pointed out, a certain vanity in the good showing which his home life made. He was respected. His family was on speaking terms with his immediate neighbors, several of whom had considerable money. When he rode down town in the cars of a morning, he had the satisfaction of brushing elbows with numerous plethoric-pursed merchants and of answering solicitations concerning his wife and children which were made in that perfunctory manner common to Americans of the money-making variety. These things seemed to give him standing and as such they were worth while.

At the same time, there were moral guy ropes of a more subtle character. His wife was of a cold, self-satisfied disposition which he did not quite comprehend. For a truth he had never really understood the woman. Passion and self-advantage were mixed attributes of the courtship which had terminated in their marriage. When the former had been satisfied, they drifted along together bound by those mutual interests which married people feel. There was no reason for dissatisfaction since they had enough to live on and were saving money. Both saw something ahead and their relations were for many years cordial if not enthusiastic.

In these latter days, however, the dispositions and habits of each had intensified owing to the fact that they were very much separated during the hours of the day and evening. Mrs. Hurstwood centered more and more of her interest in her children, particularly her daughter. Hurstwood depended more and more upon the artificial gaiety of the resort over which he presided for his individual amusement. The children were not sufficiently refined in feeling or interesting in motive to draw the twain together. This common object—the success of the children—how many homes have owed their stability to it.

Mrs. Hurstwood was not aware of any of her husband's moral defections, though she might readily have suspicioned his tendencies, which she well understood. She was a woman upon whose action, under provocation, you could never count. Hurstwood, for one, had not the slightest idea of what she would do under certain circumstances. He had never seen her thoroughly aroused. In fact she was not a woman who would fly into a passion. She had too little faith in mankind not to know that they were erring. She was too calculating to jeopardize any advantage she might gain in the way of information by fruitless clamor. Her wrath would never wreak itself in one fell blow. She would wait and brood, studying the details and adding to them until her power might be commensurate with her desire for revenge. At the same time she would not delay to inflict any injury big or little which would wound the object of her revenge and still leave him uncertain as to the source of the evil. She was a cold, self-centered woman with many a thought of her own which never found expression, not even so much as in the glint of an eye.

Hurstwood felt some of this in her nature though he did not actually perceive it. He dwelt with her in peace and some satisfaction. He did not fear her in the least—there was no cause for it. She still took a faint pride in him, which was augmented by her desire to have her social integrity maintained. She was secretly somewhat pleased by the fact that much of her husband's property was in her name, a precaution which Hurstwood had taken when his home interests were somewhat more alluring than at present. His wife had not the slightest reason to feel that anything would ever go amiss with their household, and yet the shadows which run before gave her a thought of the good of it now and then. She was in a position to become refractory with considerable advantage, and Hurstwood conducted himself circumspectly because he felt that he could not be sure of anything once she became dissatisfied.

It so happened that on the night when Hurstwood, Carrie and Drouet were in the box at McVicker's, George Jr. was in the sixth row of the parquet with the daughter of H. B. Carmichael, the third partner of a wholesale drygoods house of that city. Hurstwood did not see his son, for he sat, as was his wont, as far back as possible, leaving himself just partially visible when he bent forward to those within the first six rows in question. It was his wont to sit this way in every theatre—to make his personality as inconspicuous as possible, where it would be no advantage to him to have it otherwise.

He never moved but what, if there was any danger of his conduct being misconstrued or ill-reported, he looked carefully about him and counted the cost of every inch of conspicuity. He moved in ways mysterious, saw to it that he was not seen, except by those whose sight was welcome.

On this occasion his son saw him and the next morning at breakfast said:—

"I saw you, Governor, last night."

"Were you at McVicker's?" said Hurstwood with the best grace in the world.

"Yes," said young George.

"Who with?"

"Miss Carmichael."

Mrs. Hurstwood directed an inquiring glance at her husband, but could not judge from his appearance whether it was any more than a casual look into the theatre which was referred to.

"How was the play?" she inquired.

"Very good," returned Hurstwood, "only it's the same old thing, 'Rip Van Winkle.' "

"Who did you go with?" queried his wife, with assumed indifference.

"Charlie Drouet and his wife. They are friends of Hogg's visiting here."

Owing to the peculiar nature of his position, such a disclosure as this would ordinarily have created no difficulty. His wife took it for granted that his situation called for certain social movements in which she might not be included. Beside this, there had been a growth of indifference on the part of his family as to what disposition he made of his days and nights, so long as his managerial duties demanded the extended hours they did. But of late he had pleaded office duty on several occasions when his wife had asked for his company to an evening's entertainment. He had done so in regard to the very evening in question only the morning before.

"George," his wife had asked, "will you be busy this evening?"

"Yes," he said. "I've got some bills to make out tonight."

"I thought you were going to be busy," she now remarked very carefully.

"So I was!" he exclaimed. "I couldn't help the interruption, but I made up for it afterward by working until two."

This settled the discussion for the time being, but there was a residue of opinion which was not satisfactory. There was no time at which the claims of his wife could have been more unsatisfactorily pushed. For years he had been steadily modifying his matrimonial devotion, and found her company dull. Now that a new light shone upon the horizon, this older luminary paled in the west. He was satisfied to turn his face away entirely, and any call to look back was irksome.

She, on the contrary, was not at all inclined to accept anything less than a complete fulfillment of the letter of their relationship though the spirit might be wanting.

"We are coming down town this afternoon," she remarked a few days later. "I want you to come over to Kinsley's and meet Mr. Phillips and his wife. They're stopping at the Tremont and we're going to show them around a little."

After the occurrence of Wednesday he could not refuse, though the Phillips were about as uninteresting as vanity and ignorance could make them. He agreed, but it was with short grace. He was angry when he left the house.

"I'll put a stop to this," he thought. "I'm not going to be bothered fooling around with visitors when I have work to do."

Not long after this, Mrs. Hurstwood came with a similar proposition, only it was to a matinée this time.

"My dear," he returned, "I haven't time. I'm too busy."

"You find time to go with other people though," she replied with considerable irritation.

"Nothing of the kind," he answered. "I can't avoid business relations and that's all there is to it."

"Well, never mind!" she exclaimed, her lips tightening, and the feeling of mutual antagonism was thereafter "on."

On the other hand, his interest in Drouet's little shop girl increased in an almost evenly balanced proportion. That young lady, under the stress of her situation and the tutelage of her new friend, changed effectively. She had the aptitude of the struggler who seeks emancipation. The glow of a more showy life was not lost upon her. She did not grow in knowledge so much as she awakened in the matter of desire. Mrs. Hale's extended harangues upon the subjects of wealth and position taught her to distinguish between degrees of wealth.

Mrs. Hale loved to drive of an afternoon in the sun when it was fine and to satisfy her soul with a sight of those mansions and lawns which she could not afford. On the North Side had been erected a number of elegant mansions along what is now known as the North Shore Drive. The present lake wall of stone and granitoid was not then in place, but the road had been well laid out, the intermediate spaces of lawn were lovely to look upon and the houses were thoroughly new and imposing. When the winter season had passed and the first fine days of the early spring appeared, Mrs. Hale secured a buggy for an afternoon and invited Carrie. They rode first through Lincoln Park and on far out toward Evanston, turning back at four and arriving at the north end of the Shore Drive at about five o'clock. At that time of year the days were still comparatively short and the shadows of the evening were beginning to settle down upon the great city. Lamps were beginning to burn with that mellow radiance which seems almost watery and translucent to the eye. There was a softness in the air which speaks with an infinite delicacy of feeling to the flesh as well as to the soul. Carrie felt that it was a lovely day. She was ripened by it in spirit for many suggestions. As they drove along the smooth pavement, an occasional carriage passed. She saw one stop and the footman dismount, opening the door for a gentleman who seemed to be leisurely returning from some afternoon pleasure. Across the broad lawns, now first freshening into green, she saw lamps faintly glowing upon rich interiors. Now it was but a chair, now a table, now an ornate corner which met her eye, but it appealed to her as almost nothing else could. Such childish fancies as she had had of fairy palaces and kingly quarters now came back. She imagined that across these richly carved entranceways where the globed and crystalled lamps shone upon paneled doors, set with stained and designed panes of glass, was neither care nor unsatisfied desire. She was perfectly certain that here was happiness. If she could but stroll up yon broad walk, cross that rich entranceway, which to her was of the beauty of a jewel, and sweep in grace and luxury to possession and command—oh! how quickly would sadness flee; how, of an instant, would the heartaches end. She gazed and gazed, wondering, delighting, longing, and all the while the siren voice of the unrestful was whispering in her ear.

"If we could have such a home as that," said Mrs. Hale sadly, "how delightful it would be."

"And yet they do say," said Carrie, "that no one is ever happy."

She had heard so much of the canting philosophy of the grapeless fox.

"I notice," said Mrs. Hale, "that they all try mighty hard, though, to take their misery in a mansion."

When she came to her own rooms Carrie saw their comparative insignificance. She was not so dull but that she could perceive that they were but three small rooms in a moderately well-furnished boarding house. She was not contrasting it now with what she had had, but what she had so recently seen. The glow of the palatial doors was still in her eye, the roll of cushioned carriages still in her ears. What, after all, was Drouet. What was she. At her window she thought it over, rocking to and fro and gazing out across the lamplit park toward the lamplit houses on Warren Avenue and Ashland Boulevard. She was too wrought up to care to go down to eat, too pensive to do aught but rock and sing. Some old tunes crept to her lips and as she sang them her heart sank. She longed and longed and longed. It was now for the old cottage room in Columbia City, now the mansion up on the Shore Drive, now the fine dress of some lady, now the elegance of some scene. She was sad beyond measure and yet uncertain, wishing and fancying. Finally it seemed as if all her state was one of loneliness and forsakenness and she could scarce refrain from trembling at the lip. She hummed and hummed as the moments went by, sitting in the shadow by the window, and was therein as happy, though she could not perceive it, as ever she would be.

While Carrie was still in this frame of mind, the house

servant brought up the intelligence that Mr. Hurstwood was in the parlor asking to see Mr. and Mrs. Drouet.

"I guess he doesn't know that Charlie is out of town," thought Carrie.

She had seen comparatively little of the manager during the winter but had been kept constantly in mind of him by one thing and another—principally by the strong impression he made. She was quite disturbed for the moment as to her appearance but soon satisfied herself by the aid of the mirror and went below.

Hurstwood was in his best form as usual. He hadn't heard that Drouet was out of town. He was but slightly affected by the intelligence and devoted himself to the more general topics which would interest Carrie. It was surprising—the ease with which he conducted a conversation. He was like every man who has had the advantage of practice, and knows he is sympathized with. He knew that Carrie listened to him pleasurably, and without the least effort he fell into a train of observation which absorbed her fancy. He drew up his chair and modulated his voice to such a degree that what he said seemed wholly confidential. He confined himself almost exclusively to his observation of men and pleasures. He had been here and there, he had seen so and so. Somehow he made Carrie wish to see similar things, and all the while kept her aware of himself. She could not shut out the consciousness of his individuality and presence for a moment. He would raise his eyes slowly in smiling emphasis of something, and she was fixed by their magnetism. He would draw out with the easiest grace her approval. Once he touched her hand for emphasis and she only smiled. He seemed to radiate an atmosphere which suffused her being. He was never dull for a minute and seemed to make her clever. At least she brightened under his influence until all her best side was exhibited. She felt that she was cleverer with him than with others. At least he seemed to find so much in her to applaud. There was not the slightest touch of patronage. Drouet was full of it.

There had been something so personal, so subtle in each meeting between them, both when Drouet was present and when he was absent, that Carrie could not speak of it without feeling a sense of difficulty. She was no talker. She could never arrange her thoughts in fluent order. It was always a matter of feeling with her, strong and deep. Each time there had been no sentence of importance which she could relate, and as for the glances and sensations—what woman would reveal them. Such things had never been between her and Drouet. As a matter of fact they could never be. She had been dominated by distress and the enthusiastic forces of relief, which Drouet represented at an opportune moment, when she yielded to him. Now she was persuaded by secret current feelings which Drouet had never understood. Hurstwood's glance was as effective as the spoken words of a lover and more. They called for no immediate decision and could not be answered.

People in general attach too much importance to words. They are under the illusion that talking effects great results. As a matter of fact, words are as a rule the shallowest portion of all the argument. They but dimly represent the great surging feelings and desires which lie behind. When the distraction of the tongue is removed, the heart listens.

In this conversation she heard instead the voices of the things which he represented. How suave was the counsel of his appearance. How feelingly did his superior state speak for itself. The growing desire he felt for her lay upon her spirit as a gentle hand. She did not need to tremble at it, because it was invisible—she did not need to worry over what people would say—what she herself would say, because it had no tangibility. She was being pleaded with, persuaded, led into denying old rights and assuming new ones, and yet there were no words to prove it. Such conversation as was indulged in held the same relationship to the actual mental enactments of the twain, that the low music of the orchestra does to the dramatic incident which it is used to color.

Let me not be quarreled with for predicating these psychologic truths of these two individuals. The great forces of nature must not be arrogated by the intellectual alone. Refinement is nothing more than the perception and understanding of these things, and whoso understands and feels that these things are true is refined. But the forces themselves may be perceived by the wise, working in the commonest moulds. The forces which regulate the pig are subtle, strange and wonderful, and require refinement of thought in the observer to understand.

The forces which regulate two individuals of the character of Carrie and Hurstwood are as strange and as subtle as described. We have been writing our novels and our philosophies without sufficiently emphasizing them—we have been neglecting to set forth what all men must know and feel about these things before a true and natural life may be led. We must understand that not we, but the things of which we are the evidence, are the realities. That it is not true of beauty alone that

> ". . . it speaketh through the landscape
> And it speaketh through the sky."

but that

> "All its realms are earth and heaven
> Good and evil, thou and I."

"Have you ever seen the houses along the lake shore on the North Side?" asked Hurstwood.

"Why, I was just over there this afternoon—Mrs. Hale and I. Aren't they beautiful?"

"They're very fine," he answered.

"Oh, me," said Carrie pensively, "I wish I could live in such a place."

"You're not happy," said Hurstwood, slowly, after a slight pause. He had raised his eyes solemnly and was looking into her own. He assumed that he had struck a deep chord. Now was a slight chance to say a word in his own behalf. He leaned over quietly and continued his steady gaze. He felt the critical character of the period. She endeavored to stir but it was useless. The whole strength of the man's nature was working. He had good cause to urge him on. He looked and looked and the longer the situation lasted the more difficult it became. The little shop girl was getting into deep water. She was letting her few supports float away from her.

"Oh," she said at last, "you mustn't look at me like that."

"I can't help it," he answered.

She relaxed a little and let the situation endure, giving him strength.

"You are not satisfied with life, are you?"

"No," she answered weakly.

He saw he was the master of the situation—he felt it. He reached over and touched her hand.

"You mustn't," she exclaimed, jumping up.

"I didn't intend to," he answered easily.

She did not run away, as she might have. She did not terminate the interview, but he drifted off into a pleasant field of thought with the readiest grace. Not long after, he rose to go and she felt that he was in power.

"You mustn't feel bad," he said kindly. "Things straighten out in the course of time."

She made no answer because she could think of nothing to say.

"We are good friends, aren't we," he said, extending his hand.

"Yes," she answered.

"Not a word then until I see you again."

He retained a hold on her hand.

"I can't promise," she said doubtfully.

"You must be more generous than that," he said in such a simple way that she was touched.

"Let's not talk about it any more," she returned.

"All right," he said, brightening.

He went down the steps and into his cab. Carrie closed the door and ascended to her room. She undid her broad lace collar before the mirror and unfastened a pretty alligator belt which she had recently bought.

"I'm getting terrible," she said, honestly affected by a feeling of trouble and shame—"I don't seem to do anything right."

She unloosed her hair after a time and it was good to look upon. Her mind was going over the events of the evening.

"I don't know," she murmured at last, "what I can do."

"Well," said Hurstwood as he rode away, "she likes me all right, that I know."

The aroused manager whistled merrily for a good four miles to his office, an old melody that he had not recalled for fifteen years—if a day.

CHAPTER XIV.

It was not quite two days after the subtle scene between Carrie and Hurstwood in the Ogden Place parlor before that worthy again put in his appearance. He had been thinking almost uninterruptedly of her during the meantime. Her leniency had in a way enflamed his regard. He felt that he must succeed with her, and that speedily.

The reason for this experienced individual's interest, not to say fascination, was deeper than mere desire. It was a flowering out of feelings which had been wintering in dry and almost barren soil for many years. It is probable that Carrie represented a better order of woman than had ever attracted him before. He had had no love affair since that which culminated in his marriage, and since then, time and the world had taught him how raw and erroneous was his original judgment. Whenever he thought of it he told himself that if he had it to do over again he would never marry such a woman. At the same time his experiences with women in general had lessened his respect for the sex. He maintained a cynical attitude which was well-grounded on numerous experiences. Such women as he had known were of nearly one type, selfish, ignorant, flashy. The wives of his friends were not inspiring to look upon. His own wife had developed a cold, commonplace nature which to him was anything but pleasing to contemplate. What he knew of that underworld where grovel the beast-men of society—and he knew a great deal—had hardened his nature. He looked upon most women with suspicion—a single eye to the utility of beauty and dress. He followed them with a keen, suggestive glance. At the same time he was not so dull but that a good woman commanded his respect. Personally he did not attempt to analyze the marvel of a saintly woman. He would take off his hat, and would silence the light-tongued and the vicious in her presence—much as the Irish keeper of a Bowery Hell will humble himself before a Sister of Mercy, and pay toll to charity with a willing and reverent hand—but he would not think much upon the question of why he did so.

A man in his situation, who comes, after a long round of worthless or hardening experiences, upon a young, unsophisticated, innocent soul, is apt either to hold aloof out of a sense of his own remoteness, or to draw near and become fascinated and elated by his discovery. It is only by a roundabout process that such men ever do draw near a girl of the kind described. They have no method, no understanding of how to ingratiate themselves in youthful favor, save when they find virtue in the toils. If, unfortunately, the fly has got caught in the net, the spider can come forth and talk business upon its own terms. So when maidenhood has wandered into the moil of the city, when it is brought within the circle of the rounder and the roué, even though it be at the outermost rim, they can come forth and use their alluring arts.

"Ah," exclaims such a mind, "here is innocence within my reach. I can now go forth and try my luck."

Forthwith it adventures, with what result we may guess, where innocence has neither wisdom nor counsel at its call.

It must be readily seen that by a roundabout process, Carrie had been brought within Hurstwood's reach. He went forth at Drouet's invitation to meet a new baggage of fine clothes and pretty features. He entered expecting to indulge an evening of lightsome frolic and then lose track of the newcomer forever. Instead he found a woman whose youth and beauty attracted him. In the mild light of Carrie's eye was nothing of the calculation of the mistress. In the diffident manner was nothing of the art of the courtezan. He saw at once that a mistake had been made—that some difficult conditions had pushed this troubled creature into his presence, and his interest was enlisted. Here sympathy sprang to the rescue, but it was not unmixed with selfishness. He wanted to win Carrie because he thought her fate mingled with his was better than if it was united with Drouet's. He envied the drummer his conquest as he had never envied any man in all the course of his experience.

Carrie was certainly better than this man, as she was superior, mentally, to Drouet. She came fresh from the air of the village, the light of the country still in her eye. Here was neither guile nor rapacity. There were slight inherited traits of both in her, but they were rudimentary. She was too full of wonder and desire to be greedy. She still looked about her upon the great maze of the city without understanding. Hurstwood felt the bloom and the youth. He picked her as he would the fresh fruit of a tree. Ah, how different she was from his wife—how far removed from the flashy creatures, fashioned in the same mold, who were experienced in the ways of the city. He drew near to this young lady as a thirsty traveler draws nigh to a fountain. He felt as fresh in her presence as one who is taken out of the flash of summer to the first cool breath of spring.

Carrie, left alone since the scene in question and having no one to counsel with, had at first wandered from one strange mental conclusion to another until at last, tired out, she gave it up. She owed something to Drouet, she thought. It did not seem more than yesterday that he had aided her when she was worried and distressed. She had the kindliest feelings for him in every way. She gave him credit for his good looks, his generous feelings, and even, in fact, failed to recollect his egotism, when he was absent; but she could not feel any binding influence keeping her for him as against all others. In fact such a thought had never had any grounding, even in Drouet's desires.

The truth is that this goodly drummer carried the doom of all enduring relationships, with the female sex at least, in his own lightsome manner and unstable fancy. No woman could long observe him and not feel that he was one with whom it was "out of sight, out of mind." He could not for a moment be pulled down from the light upper world in which he existed to the vale of serious feeling. He went merrily on, assured that he was alluring all, that affection followed tenderly in his wake, that things would endure unchangingly for his pleasure. When he missed some old face, or found some door finally shut to him, it did not grieve him deeply. The man had no such depth of feeling as ached when old delights take flight. He was too young yet, too successful. He was one who would remain thus young in spirit until he was dead.

Carrie was about as closely bound to Drouet as such a nature as his could bind anyone. She did not know his habits well enough to form any opinion on that score. Nothing he had done since their first meeting had as yet irritated her. If there was anything she might have regarded as defective in him, it was owing to what he had not done—what he did not have it in him to do.

As for Hurstwood, he was alive with thoughts and feelings concerning Carrie. He had no definite plans regarding her, but he was determined to make her confess an affection for him. He thought he saw in her drooping eye, her unstable glance, her wavering manner, the symptoms of a budding passion. He wanted to stand near her and make her lay her hand in his—he wanted to find out what her next step would be—what the next sign of feeling for him would be. Such anxiety and enthusiasm had not affected him for years. He was a youth again in feeling—a cavalier in action.

In his position, opportunity for taking his evenings out was excellent. He was a most faithful worker in general and a man who commanded the confidence of his employers, in so far as the distribution of his time was concerned. He could take such hours off as he chose, for it was well known that he fulfilled his managerial duties successfully, whatever time he might take. His grace, tact, ornate appearance gave the place an air which was most essential, while at the same time his long experience made him a most excellent judge of its stock necessities. Bartenders and assistants might come and go, singly or in groups, but so long as he was present, the host of old-time customers would barely notice the change. He gave the place the air which they were used to. Consequently he arranged his hours very much to suit himself—taking now an afternoon, now an evening off, but invariably returning between eleven and twelve to witness the last hour or two of the day's business and look after the closing details, which were a part of his duties.

"You see that things are safe and all the employees are out when you go home, George," Hogg had once remarked to him, and he never once, in all the period of his long service, neglected to do this. Neither of the owners had for years been in the resort after five in the afternoon, and yet their manager as faithfully fulfilled this request as if they had been there regularly to observe.

On this Friday afternoon, scarcely two days after his previous visit, he made up his mind that he would go out and talk with Carrie. He could not stay away longer. He had tried to work at his desk all morning but with little result. He had shaken hands with several old friends, had joined in one or two conversational circles which had been formed, and otherwise fulfilled the routine functions of the place, but his thoughts were not upon what he was doing. All the while he fancied what a delightful feeling he would have if he could again sit in Carrie's presence. At last he made up his mind that he would go, and after that he kept his eye on the clock which moved for him unmercifully slowly.

At 12:30 he went for lunch but his appetite was poor, and by 1:15 he was back, nervous to make up his mind as to the moment he would start. At a quarter of two he took down his light grey overcoat and dark derby hat.

"Evans," he said, addressing the head barkeeper, "if anyone calls I will be back between four and five."

He hurried to Madison Street and boarded a horse car, which carried him to Ogden Place in half an hour.

Carrie had thought some of going for a walk and had put on a light grey woolen dress, the jacket of which was set with a double row of large grey buttons. She had gotten out her hat and gloves, which were before her upon the chiffonier, and was fastening a white lace tie about her throat when the housemaid brought up the information that Mr. Hurstwood wished to see her.

She started slightly at the announcement but told the girl to say that she would come down in a moment, and proceeded to hasten her dressing.

Carrie could not have told herself at this moment whether she was glad or sorry that the impressive manager was awaiting her presence. She was slightly flurried and tingling in the cheeks, but it was more nervousness than either fear or favor. She did not try to conjecture what the drift of the conversation would be. She only felt that she must be careful, and that Hurstwood had an indefinable fascination for her. Then she gave her tie its last touch with her fingers, and went below.

The deep-feeling manager was himself a little strained in the nerves by the thorough consciousness of his mission. He felt that he must make a strong play on this occasion, but now that the hour was come, and he heard Carrie's feet upon the stair, his nerve failed him. He sank a little in determination for he was not so sure after all of what her opinion might be.

When she entered the room, however, her appearance gave him courage. She looked simple and charming enough to strengthen the daring of any lover. Her apparent nervousness dispelled his own.

"How are you?" he said easily. "I could not resist the temptation to come out this afternoon, it was so pleasant."

"Yes," said Carrie, halting before him, "I was just preparing to go for a walk myself."

"Oh, were you?" he said. "Supposing then you get your hat and we both go."

"Very well," she answered, and turning, left the room.

In this slight meeting she was reassured concerning Hurstwood's interest for her. There was no doubt now but that she was attracted to him. His grace and good looks kept his person from being conspicuous. It took away her sensibility concerning his body, and left her affected only by his thoughts. These were exceedingly alluring and magnetic.

"Well," he said, "I'm glad I got here when I did or I'd have missed you."

"Yes," she answered, "I was just going."

They crossed the park and went west along Washington Street, which was then good to look upon with its broad macadamized road and large frame houses set back from the sidewalks. It was a street where many of the more prosperous residents of the West Side lived, and Hurstwood could not help feeling nervous over the publicity of it. He was known to a great many merchants on all sides of the city, and although he consoled himself with the thought that at this time of the day most merchants would be in their offices, and with the additional thought that in most cases he was not known to their wives and children, still he could not help wishing that his presence was not so conspicuous. They had gone but a few blocks when a livery stable sign in one of the side streets solved the difficulty for him.

"Supposing we drive instead of walk," he said.

"I shouldn't mind," said Carrie.

"You have never seen the new boulevard about the city, have you?" he asked.

"No," she answered.

"Well, we'll look at that," he went on, very much pleased with the idea.

The boulevard in question was at that time little more than a country road. The part he intended showing her was much farther out on this same West Side, where there was scarcely a house. It connected Douglas Park with Washington, or South Park, and was nothing more than a neatly *made* road, running due south for some five miles over an open grassy prairie, and then due east, over the same kind of prairie for the same distance. There was not a house to be encountered anywhere along the larger part of the route, and any conversation would be pleasantly free of interruption.

At the stable he picked a gentle horse and neat buggy and together they soon traveled out of range of either public observation or hearing.

"Can you drive?" he said after a time.

"I never tried," said Carrie.

He put the reins in her hand and folded his arms.

"You see, there's nothing to it much," he said smilingly.

"Not when you have a gentle horse," said Carrie.

"You could handle a horse as well as any one after a little practice," he added encouragingly.

He had been looking for some time for a break in the conversation when he could give it a serious turn. Once or twice he had held his peace, hoping that in silence her thoughts would take the color of his own, but she had lightly continued the subject. Presently, however, his silence controlled the situation. The drift of his thoughts began to tell. He gazed fixedly at nothing in particular, as if he were thinking of something which concerned her not at all. His thoughts, however, spoke for themselves. She was very much aware that a climax was pending.

"Do you know," he said, "I have spent the happiest evenings in years since I have known you." The situation had become almost tense.

"Have you?" she said with assumed airiness, but still excited by the conviction which the tone of his voice carried.

"I was going to tell you the other evening," he added, "but somehow the opportunity slipped away."

Carrie was listening without reply. She could think of nothing worth while to say. Despite all the ideas concerning right which had troubled her vaguely since she had last seen him, she was now influenced again strongly in his favor.

"I came out here today," he went on solemnly, "to tell you just how I feel—to see if you wouldn't listen to me."

Hurstwood was something of a romanticist after his kind.

He was capable of strong feelings—often poetic ones, and under a stress of desire, such as the present, he waxed eloquent. That is, his feelings and his voice were colored with that seeming repression and pathos which is the essence of eloquence.

"You know," he said, putting his hand on her arm, and keeping a strained silence while he formulated words, "that I love you."

Carrie did not stir at the words. She was bound up completely in the man's atmosphere. He would have churchlike silence in order to express his feelings, and she kept it. She did not move her eyes from the flat, open scene before her. Hurstwood waited for a few moments and then repeated the words.

"You must not say that," she said weakly.

The words were not convincing at all. They were the result of a feeble thought that something ought to be said. He paid no attention to them whatever.

"Carrie," he said, using her first name with sympathetic familiarity, "I want you to love me. You don't know how much I need someone to waste a little affection on me. I am practically alone. There is nothing in my life that is pleasant or delightful. It's all work and worry with people who are nothing to me."

As he said this Hurstwood really imagined that his state was pitiful. He had the ability to get off at a distance and view himself objectively—of seeing what he wanted to see in the things which made up his existence. Now, as he spoke, his voice trembled with that peculiar vibration which is the result of tensity. It went ringing home to his companion's heart.

"Why, I should think," she said, turning upon him large eyes which were full of sympathy and feeling, "that you would be very happy. You know so much of the world."

"That is it," he said, his voice dropping to a soft minor— "I know so much of the world."

It was an important thing to her to hear one so well-positioned and powerful speaking in this manner. She could not help feeling the strangeness of her situation. How was this that in so little a while, the narrow life of the country had fallen from her as a garment and the city, with all its mystery, taken its place. Here was its greatest mystery, the man of money and affairs, sitting beside her—appealing to her. Behold, he had ease and comfort, his strength was great, his position high, his garments rich, and yet he was appealing to her. It affected her much as the magnificence of God affects the mind of the Christian when he reads of His wondrous state and finds at the end an appeal to him to come and make it perfect. She could think no thought which would be just and right. She troubled herself no more upon the matter. She only basked in the warmth of his feeling, which was as a grateful blaze to one who is cold. Hurstwood glowed with his own intensity, and the heat of his passion was already melting the wax of his companion's scruples.

"You think," he said, "I am happy, that I ought not to complain. If you were to meet all day with people who care absolutely nothing about you—if you went day after day to a place where there was nothing but show and indifference, if there was not one person in all those you knew whom you could appeal to for sympathy or talk to with pleasure—perhaps you would be unhappy too."

He was striking a chord now which found sympathetic response in her own situation. She knew what it was to meet with people who were indifferent, to walk alone amid so many who cared absolutely nothing about you. Had not she? Was not she at this very moment quite alone? Who was there among all whom she knew to whom she could appeal for sympathy? Not one. She was left to herself to brood and wonder.

"I could be content," went on Hurstwood, "if I had you to love me. If I had you to go to, you for a companion. As it is I simply move about from place to place without any satisfaction. Time hangs heavily on my hands. Before you came I did nothing but idle and drift into anything that offered. Since you came— well, I've had you to think about."

The old illusion that here was someone who needed her aid began to grow in Carrie's mind. She truly pitied this sad, lonely figure. To think that all his fine state should be so barren for want of her; that he needed to make such an appeal when she herself was lonely and without anchor. Surely this was too bad.

"I am not very bad," he said apologetically, as if he owed it to her to explain on this score. "You think probably that I roam around and get into all sorts of evil. I have been rather reckless, but I could easily come out of that. I need you to draw me back if my life ever amounts to anything."

Carrie looked at him with the tenderness which virtue ever feels in its hope of reclaiming vice. How could such a man need reclaiming? His errors, what were they that she could correct? Small they must be where all was so fine. At worst they were gilded affairs, and ah, with what leniency are gilded errors ever viewed.

He put himself in such a lonely light that she was deeply moved.

"Is it that way," she mused.

He slipped his arm about her waist and she could not find the heart to draw away. With his free hand he seized upon her fingers. A breath of soft spring wind went bounding over the road, rolling some brown twigs of the previous autumn before it. The horse paced leisurely on, unguided.

"Tell me," he said softly, "that you love me."

Her eyes fell consciously.

"Own to it, dear," he said feelingly—"you do, don't you?"

She made no answer but he felt his victory.

"Tell me," he said richly, drawing her so close that their lips were near together. He pressed her hand warmly and then released it to touch her cheek.

"You do," he said, pressing his lips to her own.

For answer her lips replied.

"Now," he said joyously, his fine eyes ablaze, "you're my own girl, aren't you."

By way of further conclusion her head lay softly upon his shoulder.

CHAPTER XV.

When Carrie was set down at her rooms that evening she was in a fine glow physically and mentally. She was deeply rejoicing in her affection for Hurstwood and his love, and looked forward with fine fancy to their next meeting which was scheduled for Sunday night. They had agreed, without any feeling of enforced secrecy, that she should come down town to meet him, though, after all, the need of it was the cause.

Mrs. Hale, from her upper window, saw her come in.

"Um!" she thought to herself, "she goes riding with another man when her husband is out of the city. He had better keep an eye on her."

The truth is that Mrs. Hale was not the only one who had a thought on this score. The housemaid who had welcomed Hurstwood had her own opinion also. She had no particular regard for Carrie, whom she took to be cold and disagreeable. At the same time, she had a fancy for the merry, easy-mannered Drouet, who threw her a pleasant remark now and then and in other ways extended her the evidence of that regard which he had for all members of the sex. Hurstwood, on the contrary, was more reserved and critical in his manner. He did not appeal to this bodiced functionary in the same pleasant way. Consequently, after he had called a few times, the housemaid had little which was pleasing to think of him. She wondered that he came so frequently, that Mrs. Drouet should go out with him this afternoon when Mr. Drouet was absent. She gave vent to her opinions in the kitchen where the cook was. As a result, a train of gossip was set going which moved about the house in that secret manner common to gossip. In a short time there were more than two people who had their opinions, not to say all.

Carrie was in a mental state which was exceedingly satisfactory to herself. Now that she had yielded sufficiently to Hurstwood to confess her affection, she no longer troubled about her attitude toward him. Temporarily she gave little thought to Drouet, thinking only of the dignity and grace of her lover and of his consuming affection for her. On the first evening she did little but go over the details of the afternoon, always winding up at that delicious climax when she had confessed, by action, her too full sympathy for his lonely state. It was the first time her sympathies had ever been thoroughly aroused, and they threw a new light on her character. She had some power of initiative, latent before, which now began to exert itself. She looked more practically upon her state and began to see glimmerings of a way out. Hurstwood seemed a drag in the direction of honor. Her feelings were exceedingly creditable in that they constructed out of these recent developments something which augered freedom from dishonor. She had no idea of what Hurstwood's next word would be. She only took his affection to be a fine thing and appended better, more generous results accordingly.

That worthy, on the contrary, had formulated no plan of action, though he listened, almost unreservedly, to his desires. He was in fine feather now that his suit had prospered so well. There was no question but that Carrie's fascination for him was genuine. He felt deeply attached to her and only awaited their next meeting to prosper his relationship. He was lured exceedingly by the joy he felt in her presence. The thought of her affectionate glance was sufficient to send pleasing thrills throughout his body. He awaited his next opportunity to see her with impatience. In short, for the time being he walked in a lighter atmosphere and saw all things through a more rosy medium. It might have been said of him, under these circumstances, that he was truly in love.

What his intentions were we may readily guess from our knowledge of men. Many individuals are so constituted that their only thought is to obtain pleasure and shun responsibility. They would like, butterfly-like, to wing forever in a summer garden, flitting from flower to flower, and sipping honey for their sole delight. They have no feeling that any result which might flow from their action should concern them. They have no conception of the necessity of a well-organized society wherein all shall accept a certain quota of responsibility and all realize a reasonable amount of happiness. They think only of themselves because they have not yet been taught to think of society. For them pain and necessity are the great taskmasters. Laws are but the fences which circumscribe the sphere of their operations. When, after error, pain falls as a lash, they do not comprehend that their suffering is due to misbehavior. Many such an individual is so lashed by necessity and law that he falls fainting to the ground, dies hungry in the gutter or rotting in the jail and it never once flashes across his mind that he has been lashed only in so far as he has persisted in attempting to trespass the boundaries which necessity sets. A prisoner of fate, held enchained for his own delight, he does not know that the walls are tall, that the sentinels of life are forever pacing, musket in hand. He cannot perceive that all joy is within and not without. He must be for scaling the bounds of society, for overpowering the sentinel. When we hear the cries of the individual strung up by the thumbs, when we hear the ominous shot which marks the end of another victim who has thought to break loose, we may be sure that in another instance life has been misunderstood—we may be sure that society has been struggled against until death alone would stop the individual from contention and evil.

As yet Hurstwood had only a thought of pleasure without responsibility. He did not feel that he was doing anything which could introduce a complication into his life. His position was secure; his home life, if not satisfactory, was at least undisturbed; his personal liberty rather untrammeled. Carrie's love represented only so much added pleasure. He would enjoy this new gift over and above his ordinary allowance of pleasure. He would be happy with her and his own affairs would go on as they had—undisturbed.

On Sunday evening Carrie dined with him at a place he had selected in East Adams Street, and thereafter they took a cab to what was then a pleasant evening resort out on Cottage Grove Avenue near 39th Street. In the process of his declarations, he soon realized that Carrie took his love upon a higher basis than he had anticipated. She kept him at a distance in a rather earnest way and submitted only to those tender tokens of affection which better become the inexperienced lover. Hurstwood saw that she was not to be possessed for the asking and deferred pressing his suit too warmly. He made love to her in a form which was more youthful than seductive. She was made to feel that all favors were for her giving. At the same time his interest was heightened. Now that the game was only to be won by artifice, it seemed much more entrancing. Her beauty was heightened for him by her aloofness—her desire to entangle herself no further—to leave things stand as they were. Since he had feigned to believe in her married state, he found that he had to carry out the part. His triumph, he saw, was still a little distance hence. How far he could not possibly guess.

It was only ten o'clock by the timepiece at one end of the hall where they were listening to the concert when Carrie said:—

"We must be going."

"Why it's only ten," returned Hurstwood.

"I know, but it will be after eleven when we get to Ogden Place. I can't stay out late."

"Do they keep early hours over there?"

"Oh yes," she said. "I must get in by eleven if possible."

Hurstwood reluctantly yielded to her opinion, though he was too tactful to show it. They were nearing Ogden Place in the cab when he asked:—

"When will I see you again?"

"I don't know," she answered, wondering herself.

"Why not come down to The Fair," he suggested, "next Tuesday."

She shook her head.

"Not so soon," she answered.

"I'll tell you what I'll do," he added. "I'll write you care of this West Side post office. Could you call there Tuesday?"

Carrie assented.

The cab stopped one door out of the way, according to his call.

"Goodnight," he whispered.

Unfortunately for the smooth progression of this affair, Drouet returned. Hurstwood was sitting in his imposing little office the next afternoon when he saw Drouet enter.

"Why hello, Charlie!" he called affably. "Back again, eh!"

"Yes," smiled Drouet, approaching and looking in the door. Hurstwood arose.

"Well," he said, looking the drummer over, "rosy as ever."

They began talking of people they knew and things that had happened.

"Been home yet?" finally asked Hurstwood.

"No. I am going, though," said Drouet.

"I remembered the little girl out there," said Hurstwood, "and called once. Thought you wouldn't want her left quite alone."

"Right you are," agreed Drouet. "How was she?"

"Very well," said Hurstwood. "Rather anxious about you, though. You'd better go out now and cheer her up."

"I will," said Drouet, smilingly.

"Like to have you both come down and go to the show with me Wednesday—" concluded Hurstwood at parting.

"Thanks, old man," said his friend. "I'll see what the girl says and let you know."

They separated in the most cordial manner.

"There's a nice fellow," Drouet thought to himself as he turned the corner toward Madison.

"Drouet's a good fellow," Hurstwood thought to himself as he went back into his office, "but he's no man for Carrie."

The thought of the latter turned his mind into a most pleasing vein, and he wondered how he would get ahead of the drummer.

When Drouet entered Carrie's presence he caught her in his arms as usual but she responded to his kiss with a tremor of opposition.

"Well," he said, "I had a great trip."

"Did you?" she responded. "How did you come out with that La Crosse man you were telling me about?"

"Oh, fine. Sold him a complete line. There was another fellow there representing Burnstein—a regular hook-nosed sheeny, but he wasn't in it. I made him look like nothing at all."

As he undid his collar and unfastened his studs preparatory to washing his face and changing his clothes, he dilated upon his trip. Carrie could not help listening with amusement to his animated descriptions.

"I tell you," he said, "I surprised the people at the office. I've sold more goods this last quarter than any man of our house on the road. I sold three thousand dollars' worth in La Crosse."

He plunged his face in a basin of water and puffed and blew as he rubbed his neck and ears with his hands, the while Carrie gazed upon him with mingled thoughts of recollection and present judgement. He was still wiping his face when he continued.

"I'm going to strike 'em for a raise in June. They can afford to pay it, as much business as I turn in. I'll get it too, don't you forget."

"I hope you do," said Carrie.

"And then if that little real estate deal I've got on goes through, we'll get married," he said with a great show of earnestness, the while he took his place before the mirror and began brushing his hair.

He dragged in the reference to the fictitious real estate deal as a sop to Carrie's matrimonial desires. He wanted her to feel contented with her state, the while he winged his merry, thoughtless round.

"I don't believe you ever intend to marry me, Charlie," Carrie said ruefully. The recent protestations of Hurstwood had given her courage to say this.

"Oh, yes I do—course I do—what puts that in your head."

He had stopped his trifling before the mirror now and crossed over to her. For the first time Carrie felt as if she must move away from him.

"But you've been saying that so long," she said, looking with her pretty face upturned into his.

"Well, and I mean it too, but it takes money to live as I want to. Now when I get this increase I can come pretty near fixing things all right and I'll do it. Now don't you worry, girlie."

He patted her reassuringly upon the shoulder, but Carrie felt how really futile were her hopes. She could clearly see that this easy-going soul intended no move in her behalf. He was simply letting things drift because he preferred the free round of his present state to any legal trammelings. In contrast, Hurstwood loomed up beside him quite strong and sincere. There was more to him, she felt, in every way. He had no easy manner of putting her off. He sympathized with her and showed her what her true value was. He needed her, while Drouet did not care.

"Oh, no," she said half-remorsefully, her tone reflecting some of her own success and more of her helplessness—"you never will."

"Well, you wait a little while and see," he concluded—"I'll marry you all right."

Carrie looked at him and felt justified. She was looking for something which would salve her conscience and here it was— a light, airy disregard of her claims upon his justice. He had faithfully promised to marry her and this was the way he fulfilled his promise.

"Say," he said, after he had, as he thought, pleasantly disposed of the marriage question, "I saw Hurstwood today and he wants us to go to the theatre with him."

Carrie started at the name, but recovered quickly enough to avoid notice.

"When?" she asked, with assumed indifference.

"Wednesday. We'll go, won't we?"

"If you think so," she answered, her manner being so enforcedly reserved as to almost excite suspicion. Drouet noticed something, but he thought it was due to her feelings concerning their talk about marriage.

"He called once," he said.

"Yes," said Carrie, "he was out here Sunday evening."

"Was he?" said Drouet. "I thought from what he said that he had called a week or so ago."

"So he did," answered Carrie, who was wholly unaware of what conversation her lovers might have held. She was all at sea mentally and fearful of some entanglement which might ensue from what she would answer.

"Oh, then he called twice," said Drouet, the first shade of misunderstanding showing in his face.

"Yes," said Carrie innocently, feeling now that Hurstwood must have mentioned but one call.

Drouet imagined that he must have misunderstood his friend. He did not attach particular importance to the information after all.

"What did he have to say?" he queried with slightly increased curiosity.

"He said he came because he thought I might be lonely. You hadn't been in there so long he wondered what had become of you."

"George is a fine fellow," said Drouet, rather gratified by his conception of the manager's interest. "Come on and we'll go out to dinner."

When Hurstwood saw that Drouet was back he wrote at once to Carrie, saying in part:

"I told him I called on you, dearest, when he was away. I did not say how often but he probably thought once. Let me know of anything you may have said. Answer by special messenger when you get this. And, darling, I must see you. Let me know if you can't meet me at Jackson and Throop Streets Wednesday afternoon at two o'clock. I want to speak with you before we meet at the theatre."

Carrie received this Tuesday morning when she called at the West Side branch of the post office and answered at once.

"I said you called twice," she wrote. "He didn't seem to mind. I will try and be at Throop Street if nothing interferes. I seem to be getting very bad. It's wrong to act as I do, I know."

Hurstwood, when he met her as agreed, reassured her on this score.

"You mustn't worry, sweetheart," he said. "Just as soon as he goes on the road again we will arrange something. We'll fix it so that you won't have to deceive any one."

Carrie imagined that he would marry her shortly, though he had not directly said so, and her spirits rose. She proposed to make the best of the situation until Drouet left again. Her heart was wholly with her handsome manager who seemed so sincere, so considerate, so much more tactful than the drummer.

When a young girl finds herself in such a tangled and anomalous position, she either develops commensurate resources of tact and daring or she fails utterly. In the case of Carrie, the sight of wealth and the merry life of the city had awakened in her a desire to reach something higher and to live better. The vacillation and indifference of Drouet made it perfectly plain to her that the door of escape was closed in that quarter. The dress and manner of Hurstwood deluded her as to the height and luxury of his position. She imagined that his attraction to her could only mean that entrance for her in a higher world which she craved. So now when he promised a plan of some sort, her mind rested itself.

"Don't show any more interest in me than you ever have," Hurstwood counseled concerning the evening at the theatre.

"You mustn't look at me steadily then," she answered, mindful of the power of his eyes.

"I won't," he said, squeezing her hand at parting and giving the glance she had just cautioned against.

"There," she said playfully, pointing a finger at him.

"The show hasn't begun yet," he returned.

He watched her walk from him with a tender solicitation. Such youth and prettiness reacted upon him far more subtly than wine.

At the theatre, things passed as they had—in Hurstwood's favor. If he had been pleasing to Carrie before, how much more so was he now. His grace was more permeating because it found a readier medium. Carrie watched his every movement with pleasure. She almost forgot poor Drouet, who babbled on as if he were the host. Hurstwood was too clever to give the slightest indication of a change. He paid, if anything, more attention to his old friend than usual, and yet in no way held him up to that subtle ridicule which a lover in favor may so secretly practice before the mistress of his heart. If anything, he felt the injustice of the game as it stood and was not cheap enough to add to it the slightest mental taunt.

Only the play produced an ironical situation, and this was due to Drouet alone.

The scene was one in "The Covenant," in which the wife listened to the seductive voice of a lover, in the absence of her husband.

"Served him right," said Drouet, afterward, even in view of her keen expiation of her error. "I haven't any pity for a man who would be such a chump as that."

"Well, you never can tell," returned Hurstwood gently. "He probably thought he was right."

"Well, a man ought to be more attentive than that to his wife if he wants to keep her."

They had come out of the lobby and made their way through the showy crush about the entrance way.

"Say, mister," said a voice at Hurstwood's side—"would you mind giving me the price of a bed?"

Hurstwood was interestedly remarking to Carrie.

"Honest to God, mister, I'm without a place to sleep."

The plea was that of a gaunt-faced man of about twenty-eight, who looked the picture of privation and wretchedness. Drouet was the first to see. He handed over a dime with an upwelling feeling of pity in his heart. Hurstwood scarcely noticed the incident. Carrie quickly forgot.

"Well sir," concluded Hurstwood, just before leaving them, "there isn't anything better than a good play, is there?"

"I like a comedy best," said Drouet.

CHAPTER XVI.

The complete ignoring by Hurstwood of his own home came with the growth of his affection for Carrie. His actions, in all that related to his family, were of the most perfunctory kind. He sat at breakfast mornings with his wife and children, absorbed in his own fancies, which reached far without the realm of their interests. He read his paper, which was heightened in interest by the shallowness of the themes discussed by his son and daughter. Between himself and his wife ran a river of indifference.

Oh, the drag of the culmination of the wearisome. How it delays,—sapping the heart until it is dry. In this state he had lived since long ago when first it was enlivened by the spirit of affection; in this he had lingered long after it had become the dusty shell of departed beauty. Now he had become indifferent. To some things he had shut his ears, to others closed his eyes. The rest he shed as garments when crossing the threshold. Life was keen again when he was outside.

Now that Carrie had come, he was in a fair way to be blissful again. There was delight in going down town of an evening. When he walked forth in the short days, the street lamps had a merry twinkle. He began to experience the almost forgotten feeling which hastens the lover's feet. When he looked at his fine clothes he saw them with her eyes—and her eyes were young.

When in the flush of such feelings he heard his wife's voice, when the insistent demands of matrimony recalled him from dreams to a stale practice, how it grated. He then knew that this was a chain which bound his feet.

"George," said Mrs. Hurstwood in that tone of voice which had long since come to be associated in his mind with demands, "we want you to get us a season ticket to the races."

"Do you want to go to all of them?" he said with a rising inflection.

"Yes," she answered.

The races in question were soon to open at Washington Park, on the South Side, and were considered quite society affairs among those who did not affect religious rectitude and conservatism. Mrs. Hurstwood had never asked for a whole season ticket before, but this year certain considerations decided her to get a box. For one thing, one of her neighbors, a certain Mr. and Mrs. Ramsey, who were possessors of money made out of the coal business, had done so. In the next place, her favorite physician, Dr. Beale, a gentleman inclined to horses and betting, had talked with her slightly concerning his intention to enter a two-year-old in the Derby. In the third place, she wished to exhibit Jessica, who was rapidly gaining in maturity and beauty, and whom she hoped to marry to a man of means. Her own desire to be about in such things and parade among her acquaintances and the common throng was as much an incentive as anything.

Hurstwood thought over the proposition a few moments without answering. They were in the sitting room on the second floor, waiting for supper to be called. It was the evening of his engagement with Carrie and Drouet to see "The Covenant," which had brought him home to make some alterations in his dress.

"You're sure separate tickets wouldn't do as well?" he asked, hesitating to say anything more rugged.

"No," she replied impatiently.

"Well," he said, taking offence at her manner, "you needn't get mad about it. I'm just asking you."

"I'm not mad," she snapped. "I'm merely asking for a season ticket."

"And I'm telling you," he returned, fixing a clear, steady eye on her, "that it's no easy thing to get. I'm not sure whether the manager will give it to me."

He had been thinking all the time of his pull with the racetrack magnates.

"We can buy it then!" she exclaimed sharply.

"You talk easy," he said. "A season family ticket costs one hundred and fifty dollars."

"I'll not argue with you," she replied with determination. "I want the ticket and that's all there is to it."

She had risen and now walked angrily out of the room.

"Well, you get it then," he said grimly, though in a modified tone of voice.

As usual, the table was one short that evening.

The next morning he had cooled down considerably, and later the ticket was duly secured, though it did not heal matters. He had long been giving a thought now and then to the growing expenditures of his wife, and now that Carrie had usurped his affection he looked upon these things with even greater feeling. His wife made no better showing in his presence because of them.

She paid for parties for Jessica, carriages for Jessica, dresses for Jessica and the like until the latter began to loom up in Hurstwood's mind as a pampered and petted creature who was receiving an unjust allowance of the perquisites of fortune. He thought he did not mind giving his children a fair share of all that he earned, but he did not like to be forced to provide against his will. More, he missed that filial affection in his children which he had never inspired. Jessica was so self-contented that she scarcely missed her father. Whenever she came into his presence she was usually primped up to go somewhere. He was too shrewd an observer not to notice the vanity which possessed her soul. He forgot his own failing in this respect, and now attributed his daughter's to the influence of her mother.

"Did you know, Mother," said Jessica another day, "the Spencers are getting ready to go away."

"No. Where, I wonder?"

"Europe," said Jessica. "I met Georgine yesterday and she told me. She just put on more airs about it."

"Did she say when?"

"Monday, I think. They'll get a notice in the papers again—they always do."

"Never mind," said Mrs. Hurstwood consolingly—"we'll go one of these days."

Hurstwood moved his eyes over the paper slowly but said nothing.

" 'We sail for Liverpool from New York!' " Jessica exclaimed, mocking her acquaintance. " 'Expect to spend most of the "summah" in France'—vain thing. As if it was anything to go to Europe."

"It must be if you envy her so much," put in Hurstwood.

It grated upon him to see the feeling his daughter displayed.

"Don't worry over them, my dear," said Mrs. Hurstwood.

"Did George get off?" asked Jessica of her mother another day, thus revealing something that Hurstwood had heard nothing about.

"Where has he gone?" he asked, looking up. He had never before been kept in ignorance concerning departures.

"He was going to Wheaton," said Jessica, not noticing the slight put upon her father.

"What's out there?" he asked, secretly irritated and chagrined to think that he should be made to pump for information in this manner.

"A tennis match," said Jessica.

"He didn't say anything to me," Hurstwood concluded, finding it difficult to refrain from a bitter tone.

"I guess he must have forgot," explained his wife blandly.

In the past he had always commanded a certain amount of respect, which was a compound of appreciation and awe. The familiarity which in part still existed between himself and his daughter he had courted. As it was, it did not go beyond the light assumption of words. The *tone* was always modest. Whatever had been, however, had lacked affection, and now he saw that he was losing track of their doings. His knowledge was no longer intimate. He saw them at table and sometimes he did not.

He heard of their doings occasionally; more often he did not. Some days he found that he was all at sea as to what they were talking about—things they had arranged to do, or that they had done in his absence. More affecting was the feeling that there were little things going on which he no longer heard of. Jessica was beginning to feel that her affairs were her own. George Jr. flourished about as if he were a man entirely and must needs have private matters. All this Hurstwood could see and it left a trace of feeling, for he was used to being considered—in his official position at least, and felt that his importance should not begin to wane here. To darken it all he saw the same indifference and independence growing in his wife, while he looked on and paid the bills.

Out of the house, however, his mind was engrossed with other subjects and he did not give it much thought. In the matter of the quarrel recorded, his feelings were almost entirely put in order by his pleasant evening with Carrie. He consoled himself with the thought that after all he was not without affection. Things might go as they would at his house, but he had Carrie outside of it. With his mind's eye he looked into her comfortable room in Ogden Place, where he had spent several such delightful evenings, and thought how charming it would be when Drouet was disposed of entirely and she was waiting evenings in cozy little quarters for him. That no cause would come up whereby Drouet would be led to inform Carrie concerning his married state, he felt hopeful. Things were going so smoothly that he believed it would not change. Shortly now he would persuade Carrie and all would be satisfactory.

The day after their theatre visit he began writing her regularly—a letter every morning, and begging her to do as much for him. These he addressed care of the West Side post office where Carrie called for them. He was not literary by any means, but experience of the world and his growing affection gave him somewhat of a style. This he exercised at his office desk with perfect deliberation. He purchased a box of delicately colored and scented writing paper in monogram, which he kept locked in one of the drawers. His friends now wondered at the cleric and very official-looking nature of his position. The five bartenders viewed with respect the duties which could call a man to so much desk work and penmanship.

Hurstwood surprised himself with his fluency. By the natural law which governs all effort, what he wrote reacted upon him. He began to feel those subtleties which he could find words to express. With every expression came increased conception. Those inmost breathings which thus found words took hold upon him. He thought Carrie worthy of all the affection he could thus express.

An essay might be written to illuminate this one point in a passion which is neither young nor idyllic. The man of the world of experience, who considers many points of his affection, who imagines he has all the ends of his passion, who can lead, master and destroy, is still drawn and controlled by these very thoughts. He is the moth who knows all about his own feelings, all about the attraction of the flame, but who cannot bring himself to even wish to keep away. So much for the human conception of the natural forces which work in them.

Carrie was indeed worth loving if ever youth and grace are to command that token of acknowledgment from life, in their bloom. Experience had not yet taken away that freshness of the spirit which is the charm of the body. Her soft eyes contained in their liquid lustre no suggestion of the knowledge of disappointment. She had been troubled in a way by doubt and longing, but these had made no deeper impression than could be traced in a certain open wistfulness of glance and speech. The mouth had the expression at times, in talking and in repose, of one who might be upon the verge of tears. It was not that grief was thus ever-present. The pronunciation of certain syllables gave to her lips this peculiarity—a formation as suggestive and moving as pathos itself.

More, there was nothing bold in her manner. Life had not taught her domination—the superciliousness of grace which is the lordly power of some women. Her longing for consideration was not sufficiently powerful to move her to demand it. Even now she lacked self-assurance, but there was that in what she had already experienced which left her a little less than timid. She wanted pleasure, she wanted position, and yet she was confused as to what these things might be. Every hour the kaleidoscope of human affairs threw a new lustre upon something, and therewith it became for her the desired—the all. Another shift of the box and lo, some other had become the beautiful, the perfect.

On her spiritual side also, she was rich in feeling, as such a nature well might be. Sorrow in her was aroused by many a spectacle—an uncritical upwelling of grief for the weak and the helpless. She was constantly pained by the sight of the white-faced, ragged men who slopped desperately by her in a sort of wretched mental stupor. The poorly clad girls who went blowing by her window evenings—coming from some of the shops of the West Side, she pitied from the depths of her heart. She would stand and bite her lips as they passed, shaking her little head and wondering. They had so little, she thought. It was so sad to be ragged and poor. The hang of faded clothes pained her eyes.

"And they have to work so hard!" was her only comment.

On the street sometimes she would see men working—Irishmen with picks, coal heavers with great loads to shovel, Americans busy about some work which was a mere matter of strength—and they touched her fancy. Toil, now that she was free of it, seemed even a more desolate thing than when she was of it. She saw it through a mist of fancy—a pale, sombre half-light which was the essence of poetic feeling. Her old father, in his flour-dusted miller's suit, sometimes returned to her in memory—revived by a face in a window. A shoemaker pegging at his last, a blastman seen through a narrow window in some basement where iron was being melted, a bench worker seen high aloft in some window, his coat off, his sleeves rolled up—

these took her back in fancy to the details of the mill. She felt, though she seldom expressed them, sad thoughts upon this score. Her sympathies were ever with that underworld of toil from which she had so recently sprung and which she best understood.

Though Hurstwood did not know it, he was dealing with one whose feelings were as tender and as delicate as this. He did not know, but it was this in her, after all, which attracted him. He never attempted to analyze the nature of his affection. It was sufficient that there was tenderness in her eye, weakness in her manner, good nature and hope in her thoughts. He drew near this lily which had sucked its waxen beauty and perfume from below a depth of waters which he had never penetrated, and out of ooze and mold which he could not understand. He drew near because it was waxen and fresh. It lightened his feelings for him. It made the morning worth while.

In a material way she was considerably improved. Her awkwardness had all but passed, leaving if anything a quaint residue which was as pleasing as perfect grace. Her little shoes now fitted her smartly and had high heels. She had learned much about laces and those little neckpieces which add so much to a woman's appearance. Her form had filled out until it was admirably plump and well-rounded. With Drouet's experience and opinion for a guide she had learned to select colors and shades which had value in relation to her complexion. Her dresses draped her becomingly, for she wore excellent corsets and laced herself with care. Her hair had grown out even more luxuriantly than before, and she knew considerable concerning dressing it. She had always been of cleanly instincts and now that opportunity afforded, she kept her body sweet. Her teeth were white, her nails rosy, her hair always done up clear of her forehead. She had some color in her cheeks, a large soft eye, a plump, dainty chin and a round, full neck. Altogether, and at all times, she was pleasing to look upon.

Hurstwood wrote her one morning asking her to meet him in Jefferson Park, Monroe Street. He did not consider it policy to call any more, even when Drouet was at home.

The next afternoon he was in the pretty little park by one— had found a rustic bench beneath the green leaves of a lilac bush which bordered one of the paths. It was at that season of the year when the fullness of spring had not yet worn quite away. At a little pond nearby, some cleanly dressed children were sailing white, canvassed boats. In the shade of a green pagoda, a be-buttoned officer of the law was resting, his arms folded, his club at rest in his belt. An old gardener was upon the lawn with a pair of pruning shears looking after some bushes. High overhead was the clear blue sky of the new summer, and in the thickness of the shiny green leaves of the trees hopped and twittered the busy sparrows.

Hurstwood had come out of his own home that morning feeling much of the same old annoyance. At his store he had idled, there being no need to write. He had come away to this place with the lightness of heart which characterizes those who put weariness behind. Now in the shade of this cool, green bush he looked about him with the fancy of the lover. He heard the carts go lumbering by upon the neighboring streets, but they were far off and only buzzed upon his ear. The hum of the surrounding city was faint; the clang of an occasional bell was as music. He looked and dreamed a new dream of pleasure which concerned his present fixed conditions not at all. He got back in fancy to the old Hurstwood who was neither married nor fixed in a solid position for life. He remembered the lightsome spirit in which he once looked after the girls—how he had danced, escorted them home, hung over their gates. He almost wished he was back there again—here in this pleasant scene he felt as if he were wholly free.

At two Carrie came tripping along the walk toward him, rosy and clean. She had just recently donned a sailor hat for the season with a band of pretty white-dotted blue silk. Her skirt was of a rich blue material and her shirt waist matched it with a thin stripe of blue upon a snow white ground, stripes that were as fine as hairs. On her feet were yellow shoes and in her hands her gloves.

Hurstwood looked up at her with delight.

"You came, dearest," he said eagerly, standing to meet her and taking her hand.

"Of course," she said smiling. "Did you think I wouldn't?"

"I didn't know," he replied, so wrapped up in her charms that words meant little.

"Have you been waiting long?" she inquired.

"Not very."

"I thought I never would get away," she went on.

"Did you have much trouble?" he put in, thinking that Drouet was probably there and she had to make excuses. She understood in the question the thought that prompted it.

"Oh, Drouet," she said. "He went down at ten o'clock this morning. Said he wouldn't be home till five."

Hurstwood smiled the smile of satisfaction.

"Sit down a minute and cool off." He looked at her forehead which was moist from her brisk walk. Then he took out one of his own soft, scented silk handkerchiefs and touched her face here and there.

"Now," he said affectionately, "you're all right."

They indulged for a little while in that play of subtle feelings for which conversation is but a fence—those feelings, the spoken words of which very often make love scenes sound ridiculous. They were happy in being near one another—in looking into each other's eyes. Finally, when the long flush of delight had subsided slightly, he said:—

"When is Charlie going away again?"

"I don't know," she answered. "He says he has some things to do for the house here now."

Hurstwood grew serious and he lapsed into quiet thought. He looked up after a time to say:—

"Why wouldn't you come away and leave him."

He turned his eyes to the boys with the boats, as if the question were of little importance.

"Where would we go?" she asked in much the same manner, rolling her gloves and looking into a neighboring tree.

"Where do you want to go?" he inquired.

There was something in the tone in which he said this which made her feel as if she must record her feelings against any local habitation.

"We can't stay in Chicago," she replied.

He had not thought this was in her mind, that any removal would be suggested.

"Why not?" he asked softly.

"Oh, because," she said, "I wouldn't want to."

He listened to this with but dull perception of what it meant. It had no serious ring to it. The question was not up for immediate decision.

"I would have to give up my position," he said.

The tone he used made it seem as if the matter deserved only slight consideration. Carrie thought a little, the while enjoying the pretty scene.

"I wouldn't like to live in Chicago and him here," she said, thinking of Drouet.

"It's a big town, dearest," Hurstwood answered. "It would be as good as moving to another part of the country to move to the South Side."

He had fixed upon that region as an objective point.

"Anyhow," said Carrie, "I shouldn't want to get married as long as he is here. I wouldn't want to run away."

The getting married suggestion struck Hurstwood forcibly. He saw clearly that this was her idea—he felt that it was not to be gotten over easily. Bigamy lightened the horizon of his shadowy thoughts for a moment. He wondered for the life of him how it would all come out. He could not see that he was making any progress save in her regard. When he looked at her now he thought her beautiful. What a thing it was to have her love him, even if it be entangling. She increased in value in his eyes because of her objection. She was something to struggle for, and that was everything. How different from the women who yielded willingly. He swept the thought of them from his mind.

"And you don't know when he'll go away?" asked Hurstwood quaintly.

She shook her head.

He sighed.

"You're a determined little miss, aren't you?" he said after a few moments, looking up into her eyes.

She felt a wave of feeling sweep over her at this. It was pride at what seemed his admiration—affection for the man who could feel thus concerning her.

"No," she said coyly, "but what can I do?"

Again he folded his hands and looked away over the lawn into the street.

"I wish," he said pathetically, "you would come to me. I don't like to be away from you this way. What good is there in waiting? You're not any happier are you?"

"Happier!" she exclaimed softly. "You know better than that."

"Here we are then," he went on in the same tone, "wasting

our days. If you are not happy, what do you think I am? I sit and write to you the biggest part of the time. I'll tell you what, Carrie!" he exclaimed, throwing sudden force of expression into his voice and fixing her with his eyes—"I can't live without you and that's all there is to it. Now," he concluded, showing the palm of one of his white hands in a sort of at-an-end helpless expression—"what shall I do?"

This shifting of the burden to her appealed to Carrie. The semblance of the load, without the weight, touched the woman's heart.

"Can't you wait a little while yet?" she said tenderly. "I'll try and find out when he is going."

"What good will it do?" he asked, holding the same strain of feeling.

"Well, perhaps we can arrange to go somewhere."

She really did not see anything clearer than before, but she was getting into that frame of mind, where, out of sympathy, a woman yields.

Hurstwood did not understand. He was wondering how she was to be persuaded—what appeal would move her to forsake Drouet. He began to wonder how far her affection for him would carry her. He was thinking of some question which would make her tell.

Finally he hit upon one of those problematical propositions which often disguise our own desires, while leading us to an understanding of the difficulties which others make for us, and so discover for us a way. It had not the slightest connection with anything intended on his part and was spoken at random before he had given it a moment's serious thought.

"Say," he said, looking into Carrie's face and assuming a serious look which he did not feel, "supposing I were to come to you next week, or this week for that matter—tonight say, and tell you I had to go away—that I couldn't stay another minute and wasn't coming back any more, would you come along with me?"

His sweetheart viewed him with the most affectionate glance, affecting to think, though her answer had been ready before the words were out of his mouth.

"Yes," she said.

"You wouldn't stop to argue or arrange?"

"Not if you couldn't wait."

He smiled when he saw that she took him seriously, and he thought what a chance it would afford for a possible junket of a week or two. He had a notion to tell her that he was joking and so brush away her sweet seriousness, but the effect of it was too delightful. He let it stand.

"Supposing we didn't have time to get married here," he added, an afterthought striking him.

"If we got married as soon as we got to the other end of the journey it would be all right."

"I meant that," he said.

"Yes."

The morning seemed peculiarly bright to him now. He wondered whatever could have put such a thought into his head. Impossible as it was, he could not help smiling at its cleverness. It showed how she loved him. There was no doubt in his mind now, and he would find a way to win her.

"Well," he said jokingly, "I'll come and get you one of these evenings," and then he laughed.

"I wouldn't live with you, though, if you didn't marry me," Carrie added reflectively.

"I don't want you to," he said tenderly, taking her hand.

She was extremely happy now that she understood. She loved him the more for thinking that he would rescue her so. As for him, the marriage clause did not dwell in his mind. He was thinking that with such affection there could be no bar to his eventual happiness.

"Let's stroll about," he said gaily, rising and surveying all the lovely park.

"All right," said Carrie.

They passed the young Irishman, who looked after them with envious eyes.

" 'Tis a foine couple," he observed to himself. "They must be rich."

CHAPTER XVII.

In the course of his present stay in Chicago, Drouet paid some slight attention to the secret order to which he belonged, attending one of the monthly meetings which occurred at this time and otherwise interesting himself in the doings of his local branch for the nonce. This interest was the result of a conversation he had overheard in Minneapolis, in which the value of lodge standing and the great influence of secret insignia, when representing a high degree of fellowship, was set forth.

"I tell you," he remembered the speaker as saying quite confidentially to his friend, "it's a great thing. Look at Hazenstab. He isn't so deuced clever. Of course he's got a good house behind him, but that won't do alone. I tell you it's his degree. He's a way-up Mason and that goes a long way. He's got a secret sign that stands for something."

Drouet resolved then and there that he would take more interest in lodge matters. So when he got back to Chicago he repaired to his local lodge headquarters.

"I say, Drouet," said Mr. Harry Quincel, an individual who was very prominent in this local branch of the Elks, "you're the man that can help us out."

It was after the business meeting, and things were now going socially with a hum. Drouet was bobbing around, chatting and joking with a score of individuals whom he knew.

"What are you up to?" he inquired genially, turning a smiling face upon his secret brother.

"We're trying to get up some theatricals for two weeks from today, and we want to know if you don't know some young lady who could take a part—it's an easy one."

"Sure," said Drouet, "what is it?" He did not trouble to remember that he scarcely knew anyone whom he could appeal to on this score. His innate good nature, however, dictated a favorable reply.

"Well now, I'll tell you what we are trying to do," went on Mr. Quincel. "We are trying to get a new set of furniture for the lodge. There isn't enough money in the treasury at the present time, and we thought we would raise it by a little entertainment."

"Sure," interrupted Drouet, "that's a good idea."

"Several of the boys around here have got talent. There's Harry Burbeck—he does a fine black-face turn. Mac Lewis is all right at heavy dramatics. Did you ever hear him recite 'Over the Hills'?"

"Never did."

"Well I tell you he does it fine."

"And you want me to get you some woman to take a part?" questioned Drouet, anxious to terminate the subject and get on to something else. "What you going to play?"

" 'Under the Gaslight,' " said Mr. Quincel, mentioning Augustin Daly's famous production, which had worn from a great public success down to an amateur theatrical favorite, with many of the troublesome accessories cut out and the dramatis personae reduced to the smallest possible number.

Drouet had seen this play at some time or other in his past.

"That's it," he said. "That's a fine play. It will go all right. You ought to make a lot of money out of that."

"We think we'll do very well," Mr. Quincel replied. "Don't you forget now," he concluded, Drouet showing signs of restlessness. "Some young woman to take the part of Pearl."

"Sure. I'll tend to it."

He moved away, forgetting almost all about it the moment Mr. Quincel had ceased talking. He had not even thought to ask the time or place. It was more important with Mr. Quincel, however, and before Drouet got out of the door for the night, Mr. Quincel had button-holed him.

"I forgot to tell you," he said, "that it's going to be held in Avery Hall in West Madison Street on the sixteenth. Don't forget now, will you?"

"Not me."

"Some woman with experience if you can," called the interested director as Drouet went down the steps.

"That's right, Harry. I'll tend to it," and forth he went as conscience-free of any duty in the matter as if the conversation had never occurred.

The energetic director was more thorough and conscientious in these matters than is usually the case. He was just large enough mentally to rejoice in the small honors of a secret lodge and to take great pride in fulfilling any such arduous commission as the present. He was not one to make a request and then sit down and worry because of its possible non-fulfillment. With him it was merely the initiative of a series of notices, requests, urgent calls, and so forth, which usually followed in quick succession until some definite information had arrived concerning the proper fulfillment of the detail in question. He was the true functionary for such an undertaking as the present, for he not only gained the promise of assistance from all and every influential quarter, but saw that he secured their value by going and attending to these things himself.

"Quincel is a clever fellow," was the common remark after the successful conclusion of some such entertainment. "He manages to get so much work out of other people."

Drouet was reminded of his promises a day or two later by the receipt of a letter announcing that the first rehearsal was set for the following Friday evening and urging him to kindly forward the young lady's address at once in order that the part might be delivered to her.

"Now who the deuce do I know?" asked the drummer reflectively, scratching his rosy ear. "I don't know anyone that knows anything about amateur theatricals."

He went over in memory the names of a number of women he knew and finally picked on one, largely because of the convenient location of her house on the West Side, and promised himself that as he came out that evening he would "drop in" and see her. When, however, he started west on the car, he had forgotten and was only reminded of his delinquency by an item in the "Evening News," a small three-line affair under the head of "Secret Society Notes" which stated that the Custer Lodge of the Order of Elks would give a theatrical performance in Avery Hall on Friday the sixteenth, when "Under the Gaslight" would be produced.

"George!" exclaimed Drouet, "I forgot that."

"What?" inquired Carrie.

They were at their little table in the room which might have been used for a kitchen, where Carrie occasionally served a meal. Tonight the fancy had caught her, and the little table was spread with a pleasing repast.

"Why, my lodge entertainment. They're going to give a play and they wanted me to get them some young lady to take a part."

"What is it they're going to play?"

" 'Under the Gaslight.' "

"When?"

"On the sixteenth."

"Well, why don't you?" asked Carrie.

"I don't know anyone," he replied.

Suddenly he looked up.

"Say," he said, "how would you like to take the part?"

"Me?" said Carrie. "I can't act."

"How do you know?" questioned Drouet, reflectively.

"Because," answered Carrie, "I never did."

Nevertheless she was pleased to think he would ask. Her eyes brightened, for if there was anything that enlisted her sympathies, it was the art of the stage.

True to his nature Drouet clung to this idea as an easy way out.

"That's nothing. You can act all you have to down there."

"No, I can't," said Carrie weakly, very much drawn toward the proposition and yet fearful.

"Yes you can. Now why don't you do it? They need someone, and it will be lots of fun for you."

"Oh, no it won't," said Carrie seriously.

"You'd like that. I know you would. I've seen you dancing around here and giving imitations, and that's why I asked you. You're clever enough all right."

"No, I'm not," said Carrie shyly.

"Now I'll tell you what you do. You go down and see about it. It'll be fun for you. The rest of the company isn't going to be any good. They haven't any experience. What do they know about theatricals?"

He frowned as he thought of their ignorance.

"Hand me the coffee," he added.

"I don't believe I could act, Charlie," Carrie went on pettishly. "You don't think I could, do you?"

"Sure. Out o' sight. I bet you make a hit. Now you want to go, I know you do. I knew it when I came home. That's why I asked you."

"What is the play, did you say?"

" 'Under the Gaslight.' "

"What part would they want me to take?"

"Oh, one of the heroines—I don't know."

"What sort of a play is it?"

"Well," said Drouet, whose memory for such things was not the best, "it's about a girl who gets kidnapped by a couple of crooks—a man and a woman that live in the slums. She had some money or something and they wanted to get it. I don't know now how it did go exactly."

"Don't you know what part I would have to take?"

"No I don't, to tell the truth." He thought a moment. "Yes, I do, too. Pearl, that's the thing—you're to be Pearl."

"And you can't remember what the part is like?"

"To save me, Cad, I can't," he answered. "I ought to, too; I've seen the play enough. There's a girl in it that was stolen when she was an infant, or picked off the street, or something, and she's the one that's hounded by the two old criminals I was telling you about." He stopped with a mouthful of pie poised before his face on a fork. "She comes very near getting drowned—no, that's not it. I'll tell you what I'll do," he concluded hopelessly. "I'll get you the book. I can't remember now for the life of me."

"Well, I don't know," said Carrie when he had concluded, her interest and desire to shine dramatically struggling with her timidity for the mastery. "I might go if you thought I'd do all right."

"Of course you'll do," said Drouet, who in his efforts to enthuse Carrie had interested himself. "Do you think I'd come home here and urge you to do something that I didn't think you would make a success of? You can act all right. It'll be good for you."

"When must I go?" said Carrie, reflectively.

"The first rehearsal is Friday night. I'll get the part for you tonight."

"All right," said Carrie resignedly, "I'll do it, but if I make a failure now it's your fault."

"You won't fail," assured Drouet. "Just act as you do around here. Be natural. You're all right. I've often thought you'd make a corking good actress."

"Did you, really?" asked Carrie.

"That's right," said the drummer.

He little knew as he went out of the door that night what a secret flame he had kindled in the bosom of the little girl he left behind. Carrie was possessed of that sympathetic, impressionable nature, which, even in its most developed form, has been the glory of the drama. She was created with that passivity of soul which is always the mirror of the active world. She possessed an innate taste for imitation and no small ability. Even without practise, she could sometimes restore dramatic situations she had witnessed by recreating, before her mirror, the expressions of the various faces taking part in the scene. She loved to modulate her voice after the conventional manner of the distressed heroine, and repeat such pathetic fragments as appealed most to her sympathies. Of late, seeing the airy grace of the ingénue in several well-constructed plays, she had been moved to secretly imitate it, and many were the little movements and expressions of the body which she indulged in from time to time in the privacy of her chamber. On several occasions when Drouet had caught her admiring herself, as he imagined, in the mirror, she was doing nothing more than recalling some little grace of the mouth or the eyes which she had witnessed in another. Under his airy accusation she mistook this for vanity and accepted the blame with a faint sense of error, though as a matter of fact it was nothing more than the first subtle outcroppings of an artistic nature, endeavoring to recreate the perfect likeness of some phase of beauty which appealed to her. In such feeble tendencies, be it known, such outworking of desire to reproduce life, lies the basis of all dramatic art.

Now when Carrie heard Drouet's laudatory opinion of her dramatic ability, her body tingled with satisfaction. Like the flame which welds the loosened particles into a solid mass, his words united those floating wisps of feeling which she had felt, but never believed, concerning her possible ability, and made them into a gaudy shred of hope. Like all human beings she had a touch of vanity. She felt that she could do things if she only had a chance. How often had she looked at the well-dressed actresses on the stage and wondered how she would look, how delightful she would feel, if only she were in their places. The glamour, the tense situations, the fine clothes, the applause—

these had lured her until she felt that she, too, could act—that she, too, could compel acknowledgment of power. Now she was told that she really could—that little things she had done about the house had made even him feel her power. It was a delightful sensation, while it lasted.

Dramatic art is most peculiar in this respect, that it inspires thoughts of emulation in the most hopeless of its observers and arouses a feeling of equal ability. This is due no doubt to the fact that it is at once the most natural as well as the most understandable of the graces. It presents that which its observers daily live and feel. It scarcely occurs to the inexperienced on-looker that it must be difficult to be natural—to do as we see each and all others doing about us. They see, mirrored upon the stage, scenes which they would like to witness, situations in which they would rejoice to be placed, passions which they would be happy to feel. The simulation of merriment and grief, laughter and tears, affection and hate are so real, that the art of the thing itself is lost. The observer sees what, with the flight of years, will be presented to him outside—everyday human nature and events, heightened and crowded together for his temporary delectation. These things, while they attract, de-ceive. They allure the languorously inclined, the luxuriants of all classes, promising ease and that shift and play of feeling which is the hope of all.

Carrie could scarcely be numbered among the latter. Rather, she would have been classed among the elect of the field by reason of her sensitive, receptive nature, her barometric feelings and almost hopeless lack of logic. Her impressionable feelings were the actor's own—her lack of initiative and decision were also characteristic of the tribe. In short, she could feel without reasoning therefrom, and this has ever been the true state of the thespians, since dramatic representation began.

When Drouet was gone, she sat down in her rocking chair by the window to think about it. As usual, imagination exag-gerated the possibilities for her. It was as if he had put fifty cents in her hand and she had exercised the thoughts of a thousand dollars. She saw herself in a score of pathetic situations in which she exercised a tremulous voice and suffering manner. Her mind delighted itself with scenes of luxury and refinement, situations in which she was the cynosure of all eyes, the arbiter of all fates. As she rocked to and fro, she felt the tensity of woe in abandonment, the magnificence of wrath after deception, the languor of sorrow after defeat. Thoughts of the young lady she had seen walking with Scanlan came back. Thoughts of all the charming women she had seen in plays—every fancy, every illusion which she had concerning the stage, now came back, as a returning tide after the ebb. She built up feelings and a determination which the occasion did not warrant.

The part which Drouet brought her was not *Pearl,* but *Laura.* He had dropped in at the lodge when he went down town and swashed around with a great *air,* as Quincel met him.

"Where is that young lady you were going to get for us?" asked the latter.

"I've got her," said Drouet.

"Have you?" said Quincel, rather surprised by his promptness. "That's good. What's her address?" and he pulled his note book, in order to be able to send her her part.

"You want to send her her part?" asked the drummer.

"Yes."

"Well, I'll take it. I'm going right by her house in the morning."

Both drummer and manager were confronted by a little situation. The latter cleared up his at once.

"I told you," he said, "that your lady friend would take the part of Pearl. When I said that, I thought the woman Harrison was going to bring would take the part of Laura, but she is sure now that she could not do it right. So I gave her Pearl's part. Do you suppose your friend could do Laura?"

"Well, I don't know," returned the drummer, who was not in the least troubled about the matter. "I guess so. I'll take it and let her see it. Then if she can't do it, she can come down and see you."

"That's the way," said Quincel—"only we haven't any time to waste."

"I know it," returned Drouet.

"What did you say her address was—we only want it in case we have any information to send her."

"29 Ogden Place."

"And her name?"

"Carrie Madenda," said the drummer, firing at random. The lodge members knew him to be single.

"That sounds like somebody that can act, doesn't it?" said Quincel.

"Yes, it does."

He took home the part to Carrie and handed it to her with the air of one who does a favor.

"There you are, Cad."

"This is it, is it?" said Carrie, turning the pages.

"He says that's the best part. Do you think you can do it?"

"I don't know until I look it over. You know I'm afraid, now that I've said I would."

"Ah, go on. What have you got to be afraid of? It's a cheap company. The rest of them aren't as good as you are."

"Well, I'll see," said Carrie, pleased to have the part, for all her misgivings.

He sidled around dressing and fidgeting before he arranged to make his next remark.

"They were getting ready to print the programs," he said, "and I gave them the name of Carrie Madenda—was that all right?"

"Yes, I guess so," said his companion, looking up at him. She was thinking it was slightly strange.

"If you didn't make a hit, you know—" he went on.

"Oh, yes," she answered, rather pleased now with his caution. It was clever for Drouet.

"I didn't want to introduce you as my wife because you'd feel worse then if you didn't 'go.' They all know me so well. But you'll 'go' all right. Anyhow, you'll probably never meet any of them again."

"Oh, I don't care," said Carrie desperately. She was determined now to have a try at the fascinating game.

Drouet breathed a sigh of relief. He had been afraid that he was about to precipitate another conversation upon the marriage question.

The part of *Laura*, as Carrie found out when she began to examine it, was one of suffering and tears. As delineated by Mr. Daly, it was true to the most sacred traditions of melodrama as he found it when he began his career. The sorrowful demeanor, the tremolo music, the long, explanatory, cumulative addresses, all were there.

"Poor fellow," read Carrie, consulting the text and drawing her voice out pathetically. "Martin, be sure and give him a glass of wine before he goes."

She was surprised at the briefness of the entire part, not knowing that she must be on the stage while others were talking, and not only be there, but also keep herself in harmony with the dramatic movement of the scenes.

She read further.

"Ha! Ha! from some goose who has made one call too many today. Read it, Ray—" (*Offering letter*).

Carrie struck an attitude after the lines in which Ray refused to read it and gave it back to Pearl, who handed it to Laura. What she emphasized with some force and feeling ran as follows:—

Laura. (*Looks at it a moment, when the whole expression of face changes. Then reads slowly and deliberately.* RAY *down* R. C. *with* PEARL.) "*I respectfully beg you to grant me the favor of an interview to-night. I have waited until your company retired. I am waiting across the street, now.*"

She skipped the part which said:—

Pearl. (*Runs to window.*) *A tall man in black is just walking away.—*

—and went on with her own:—

" '*If you will have the door opened as soon as you get this, I will step over; if you don't, I will ring; under all circumstances I will get in. There is no need to sign my name; you will remember me as the strange man whom you once saw talking with your mother in the parlor, and who frightened you so much.*' What can be the meaning of this?—Pearl—no—"

Carrie caught the force of this rather fully. She read the thing with remarkable expression for a novice.

"I think I can do that," she said.

For the benefit of those who are not familiar with "Under the Gaslight," it must be related here that Laura is the adopted daughter of the rich, fashionable Courtland family of New York. She had been picked up off the streets by Mrs. Courtland, whom she tried to rob, when only six years old. She has been cared for until nineteen years old, and now the villain appears—the man who knows that she was a waif and a pickpocket. He arrives just when fashionable Mr. Ray Trafford is about to marry her. His object is deviltry and cash. The letter just read was from him, announcing his mysterious arrival upon a blissful scene. Of course, when young Trafford finds this out, he hesitates. Society would not brook a marriage with so low a creature. He writes a letter to Laura, mentioning this discovery and breaking off the engagement. Affection modifies his decision and he decides to go on as before, but fails to destroy this letter. This neglect forms the basis for the second scene of Act I in which Laura's part is exceedingly brief but strong. She comes in at the last moment.

Trafford has come into the ball room where she is expected and has accidentally dropped the note. A society leader has found it, read and published the information there and then.

"What can it mean?" questions one of her hearers.

"It means," says this character, "that the rumors of ten years ago are proven. It was then suspected that the girl whom Mrs. Courtland brought every year from some unnamed place in the country, and introduced to everybody as her niece, was an imposter, which that foolish woman, in a freak of generosity, was thrusting upon society. The rumors died out for want of proof—and before Laura's beauty and dignity—but now they are confirmed. She is some beggar's child."

"What do you think we ought to do?" asks one.

"Tell it—tell it everywhere, of course. The best blood of New York is insulted by the girl's presence."

Upon this company, when they are ready to spurn her, Laura is supposed to walk in. Her own lover now hesitates to receive her. Her cousin is equally shy. She stands quiet—alone before the scornful, departing throng.

As the lines have it:—

(Music low as LAURA enters, continues while all except PEARL [her cousin] and RAY pass out, eyeing her superciliously.)

"Ray, Ray, why do you not come to her?" cries Pearl.

"Are you not coming with us?" says Mrs. Van Dam, the woman who has read the note to him.

"Let us go home," says Pearl to Laura.

"No; stay with him," cries the heroine, pointing to Ray, who has held off. "He shall not suffer the disgrace long!"

She is about to faint as he runs toward her, but she waves him proudly away.

"It is Heaven's blow!" are her closing words, upon which the curtain descends.

This part affected Carrie deeply. It reminded her somehow of her own state. She caught the infection of sorrow, sympathized with it wholly and consequently mastered it easily. Her lines were very few indeed, but as in all such cases, everything depended upon the expression.

When Drouet came that night she was very much satisfied with her day's study.

"Well, how goes it, Caddie?" he said.

"All right," she laughed. "I think I've got it memorized nearly."

"That's good," he said. "Let's hear some of it."

"Oh, I don't know whether I can get up and say it off here," she said bashfully.

"Well, I don't know why you shouldn't. It'll be easier here than it will there."

"I don't know about that," she answered.

Eventually, she took off the ball room episode with considerable feeling, forgetting as she got deeper in the scene all about Drouet, and letting herself rise to a fine state of feeling.

"Good," said Drouet, "fine, out o' sight. You're all right, Caddie. I tell you."

He was really moved by her excellent representation and the general appearance of the pathetic little figure as it swayed and finally fainted to the floor. He had bounded up to catch her and now held her laughing in his arms.

"Ain't you afraid you'll hurt yourself?" he asked.

"Not a bit."

"Well, you're a wonder. Say, I never knew you could do anything like that."

"I never did either," said Carrie, merrily, her face flushed with delight.

"Well you can bet that you're all right," said Drouet. "You can take my word for that. You won't fail."

CHAPTER XVIII.

The, to Carrie, very important theatrical performance was to be "pulled off on schedule time" at the Avery under conditions which were to make it more noteworthy than was at first anticipated. The little dramatic student had written to Hurstwood the very morning her part was brought her that she was going to take part in a play.

"I really am," she wrote, feeling that he might take it as a jest. "I've got my part now, honest truly."

Hurstwood smiled in an indulgent way as he read this.

"I wonder what it is going to be. I must see that."

He answered at once, making a pleasant reference to her ability. "I haven't the slightest doubt you will make a success. You must come to the park tomorrow morning and tell me all about it."

Carrie gladly complied and revealed all the details of the undertaking as she understood it.

"Well," he said, "that's fine. I'm glad to hear it. Of course you will do well. You're so clever."

He had truly never seen so much spirit in the girl before. Her tendency to discover a touch of sadness had for the nonce disappeared. As she spoke, her eyes were bright, her cheeks red. She radiated much of the pleasure which her undertaking gave her. For all her misgivings, and they were as plentiful as the moments of the day, she was still happy. She could not repress her delight in doing this little thing which to an ordinary observer had no importance at all.

Hurstwood was charmed by the development of the fact that the girl had capabilities. There is nothing so inspiring in life as the sight of a legitimate ambition, no matter how incipient. It gives color, force and beauty to the possessor.

Carrie was now lightened by a touch of this divine afflatus. She drew to herself commendations from her two admirers which she had not earned. Their affection for her naturally heightened their perception of what she was trying to do and their approval of what she did. Her inexperience conserved her own exuberant fancy which ran riot with every straw of opportunity, making of it a golden divining rod, whereby the treasure of life was to be discovered.

"Let's see," said Hurstwood. "I ought to know some of the boys in the Custer Lodge. I'm an Elk myself."

"Oh, you mustn't let him know I told you."

"That's so," said the manager.

"I'd like for you to be there, if you want to come, but I don't see how you can unless he asks you."

"I'll be there," said Hurstwood affectionately. "I can fix it so he won't know you told me.   You leave it to me."

This interest of the manager was a large thing in itself for the performance, for his standing among the Elks was something worth talking about. Already he was thinking of a box with some friends, and flowers for Carrie. He would make it a dress-suit affair and give the little girl a chance.

Within a day or two Drouet dropped into the Adams Street resort, and he was at once spied by Hurstwood. It was at five in the afternoon and the place was crowded with merchants, actors, managers, politicians—a goodly company of rotund, rosy figures, silk-hatted, starchy-bosomed, be-ringed and be-scarf-pinned to the queen's taste. John L. Sullivan, the pugilist, was at one end of the glittering bar, surrounded by a company of loudly dressed sports who were holding a most animated conversation. Drouet came across the floor with a festive stride, a new pair of tan shoes squeaking audibly his progress.

"Well sir," said Hurstwood, "I was wondering what had come of you. I thought you had gone out of town again."

Drouet laughed.

"If you don't report more regularly we'll have to cut you off the list."

"Couldn't help it," said the drummer. "I've been busy."

They strolled over toward the bar amid the noisy, shifting company of notables. The dressy manager was shaken by the hand three times in as many minutes.

"I hear your lodge is going to give a performance," observed Hurstwood in the most off-hand manner.

"Yes, who told you?"

"No one," said Hurstwood. "They just sent me a couple of tickets which I can have for two dollars. Is it going to be any good?"

"I don't know," replied the drummer. "They've been trying to get me to get them some woman to take a part."

"I wasn't intending to go," said the manager easily. "I'll subscribe of course. How are things over there?"

"All right. They're going to fit things up out of the proceeds."

"Well," said the manager, "I hope they make a success of it—have another."

He did not intend to say any more. Now, if he should appear on the scene with a few friends, he could say that he had been urged to come along. Drouet had a desire to wipe out the possibility of confusion.

"I think the girl is going to take a part in it," he said abruptly, after thinking it over.

"You don't say so. How did that happen?"

"Well, they were short and wanted me to find them someone. I told Carrie and she seems to want to try."

"Good for her," said the manager. "It'll be a real nice affair. Do her good, too.—Has she ever had any experience?"

"Not a bit."

"Oh, well, it isn't anything very serious."

"She's clever though," said Drouet, casting off any imputation against Carrie's ability. "She picks up her part quick."

"You don't say so," said the manager.

"Yes sir, she surprised me the other night—by George if she didn't."

"We must give her a nice little send-off," said the manager. "I'll look after the flowers."

Drouet smiled at his good nature.

"After the show you must come with me and we'll have a little lunch—"

"I think she'll do all right," said Drouet.

"I want to see her. She's got to do all right. We'll make her," and the manager gave one of his quick, steely half-smiles, which was a compound of good nature and shrewdness.

Carrie meanwhile attended the first rehearsal. At this performance Mr. Quincel presided, aided by Mr. Millice, a young man who had some qualifications of past experience which were not exactly understood by anyone. He was so experienced and so business-like, however, that he came very near being rude—failing to remember, as he did, that the individuals he was trying to instruct were volunteer players and not salaried underlings.

"Now Miss Madenda," he said, addressing Carrie, who stood in one part uncertain as to what move to make—"you don't want to stand like that. Put expression in your face. Remember you are troubled over the intrusion of the stranger. Walk so—" and he struck out across the Avery stage in a most drooping manner.

Carrie did not exactly fancy the suggestion, but the novelty of the situation, the presence of strangers, all more or less nervous, and the desire to do anything rather than make a failure made her timid. She walked in imitation of her mentor, as requested, inwardly feeling that there was something strangely lacking.

"Now Mrs. Morgan," said the director to one young married woman who was to take the part of Pearl. "You sit here. Now Mr. Bamberger—you stand here, so. Now, what is it you say?"

"Explain," said Mr. Bamberger, feebly. He had the part of Ray, Laura's lover, the society individual who was to waver in his thoughts of marrying her, upon finding that she was a waif and a nobody by birth.

"How is that—what does your text say?"

"Explain," repeated Mr. Bamberger, looking intently at his part.

"Yes, but it also says," the director remarked, "that you are to look shocked. Now say it again and see if you can't look shocked."

"Explain!" demanded Mr. Bamberger vigorously.

"No, no, that won't do. Say it this way—*Explain!*"

"Explain!" said Mr. Bamberger, giving a modified imitation.

"That's better, now go on."

"One night," resumed Mrs. Morgan, whose lines came next, "Father and Mother were going to the Opera. When they were crossing Broadway, the usual crowd of children accosted them for alms—"

"Hold on," said the director, rushing forward, his arm extended. "Put more feeling into what you are saying."

Mrs. Morgan looked at him as if she feared a personal assault. Her eye lightened with resentment.

"Remember, Mrs. Morgan," he added, ignoring the gleam, but modifying his manner, "that you're detailing a pathetic story. You are now supposed to be telling something that is a grief to you. It requires feeling, repression, thus: 'the usual crowd of children accosted them for alms.' "

"All right," said Mrs. Morgan.

"Now go on."

"As mother felt in her pocket for some change, her fingers touched a cold and trembling hand which had clutched her purse."

"Very good," interrupted the director, nodding his head significantly.

"A pickpocket! Well," exclaimed Mr. Bamberger, speaking the lines that here fell to him.

"No, no, Mr. Bamberger," said the director, approaching, "not that way. 'A pickpocket,—Well'—so. That's the idea."

"Don't you think," said Carrie weakly, noticing that it had not been proven yet whether the members of the company knew their lines, let alone the details of expression, and feeling that it would be better if the company could go through once and gain the assurance of knowledge on this score, "that it would be better if we just went through our lines once to see if we know them? We might pick up some points."

"A very good idea, Miss Madenda," said Mr. Quincel, who sat at the side of the stage, looking serenely on and volunteering opinions which the director did not heed.

"All right," said the latter, somewhat abashed. "It might be well to do it." Then brightening with a show of authority, "Supposing we run right through, putting in as much expression as we can."

"Good," said Mr. Quincel.

"This hand," resumed Mrs. Morgan, glancing up at Mr. Bamberger and down at her book, as the lines proceeded, "my mother grasped in her own, and so tightly that a small, feeble voice uttered an exclamation of pain. Mother looked down, and there beside her was a little ragged girl."

"Very good," observed the director, now hopelessly idle.

"The thief!" exclaimed Mr. Bamberger.

"Louder," put in the director, finding it almost impossible to keep his hands off.

"The thief!" roared poor Bamberger.

"Yes, but a thief hardly six years old, with a face like an angel's. 'Stop!' said my mother. 'What are you doing?' 'Trying to steal,' said the child. 'Don't you know that it's wicked to do so?' asked my father. 'No,' said the girl, 'but it's dreadful to be hungry.' 'Who told you to steal?' asked my mother. 'She—there!' said the child, pointing to a squalid woman in a doorway opposite, who fled suddenly down the street. 'That is Old Judas,' said the girl."

Mrs. Morgan read this rather flatly and the director was in despair. He fidgeted around and then went over to Mr. Quincel.

"What do you think of them?" he asked.

"Oh, I guess we'll be able to whip them into shape," said the latter, with an air of strength under difficulties.

"I don't know," said the director. "That fellow Bamberger strikes me as being a pretty poor shift for a lover."

"He's all we've got," said Quincel, rolling up his eyes. "Harrison went back on me at the last minute. Who else can we get?"

"I don't know," said the director. "I'm afraid he'll never pick up."

At this moment Bamberger was exclaiming, "Pearl, you are joking with me."

"Look at that now," said the director, whispering behind his hand. "My Lord! what can you do with a man who drawls out a sentence like that."

"Do the best you can," said Quincel consolingly.

The rendition ran on in this wise until it came to where Carrie, as Laura, supposedly comes into the room to explain to Ray, who, after hearing Pearl's statement about her birth, had written the letter repudiating her, which, however, he did not deliver. Bamberger was just concluding the words of Ray: "I must go before she returns. Her step—too late!" and was cramming the letter in his pocket when she began sweetly with:

"Ray."

"Miss—Miss Courtland," Bamberger faltered weakly.

Carrie looked at him a moment and forgot all about the company present. She began to feel the part and summoned an indifferent smile to her lips, turning as the lines directed and going to a window, as if he were not present. She did it with a grace which was fascinating to look upon.

"Who is that woman?" asked the director, watching Carrie in her little scene with Bamberger.

"Miss Madenda," said Quincel.

"I know her name," said the director, "but what does she do?"

"I don't know," said Quincel. "She's a friend of one of our members."

"Well she's got more gumption than anyone I've seen here so far—seems to take an interest in what she's doing."

"Pretty, too, isn't she?" said Quincel.

The director strolled away without answering.

In the second scene where she was supposed to face the company in the ball-room, she did even better, winning the smile of the director, who volunteered, because of her fascination for him, to come over and speak with her.

"Were you ever on the stage?" he asked insinuatingly.

"No," said Carrie.

"You do so well I thought you might have had some experience."

Carrie only smiled consciously.

He walked away to listen to Bamberger, who was feebly spouting some ardent lines.

Mrs. Morgan saw the drift of things and gleamed at Carrie with envious and snapping black eyes.

"She's some cheap professional," she gave herself the satisfaction of thinking, and scorned and hated her accordingly.

The rehearsal ended for one day and Carrie went home feeling that she had acquitted herself satisfactorily. The words of the director were ringing in her ears, and she longed for an opportunity to tell Hurstwood. She wanted him to know just how well she was doing. Drouet, too, was an object for her confidences. She could hardly wait until he should ask her, and yet she did not have the vanity to bring it up.

The drummer, however, had another line of thought tonight and her little experience did not appeal to him as important. He let the conversation drop, save for what she chose to recite without solicitation, and Carrie was not good at that. He took it for granted that she was doing very well, and he was relieved of further worry. Consequently he threw Carrie into repression which was irritating. She felt his indifference keenly and longed to see Hurstwood. It was as if that worthy were now the only friend she had on earth. The next morning Drouet was interested again, but the damage had been done.

She got a pretty letter from the manager saying that by the time she got it he would be waiting for her in the park. When she came, he shone upon her as the morning sun.

"Well, my dear," he asked, "how did you come out?"

"Well enough," she said, still somewhat reduced after Drouet.

"No, tell me now just how you did. Was it pleasant?"

Carrie related the incidents of the rehearsal, warming up as she proceeded.

"Well, that's delightful," said Hurstwood. "I'm so glad. I must get over there to see you—when is the next rehearsal?"

"Tuesday," said Carrie, "but they don't allow visitors."

"I imagine I could get in," said Hurstwood significantly.

She was completely restored and delighted by his consideration, but she made him promise not to come around.

"Now you must do your best to please me," he said encouragingly. "Just remember that I want you to succeed. We will make the performance worth while. You do that now."

"I'll try," said Carrie, brimming with affection and enthusiasm.

"That's the girl," said Hurstwood fondly. "Now remember," shaking an affectionate finger at her, "your best."

"I will," she answered, looking back.

The whole earth was brimming sunshine that morning. She tripped along, the clear sky pouring liquid blue into her soul. Oh blessed are the children of endeavor in this—that they try and are hopeful. And blessed also are they who knowing, smile and approve.

CHAPTER XIX.

A very Hall was a three-story red brick building containing stores and a lobby upon the ground floor and a few offices upstairs, the larger portion being devoted to disuse, for it was not very popular any more as a theatre. It had originally been built as part of a larger summer garden, when the ground upon which it was located was not more than a mile from the city limits. The city had grown so rapidly and extended its borders so far that the summer garden idea had been abandoned and the surrounding ground parceled out into one-story store buildings which were largely vacant. The hall itself, like much other Chicago property, was not in demand. It was rented occasionally, at a very nominal rate, for lectures, entertainments and theatricals and was really very well adapted for the purpose. The original decorations of white, blue and gold, the conventional daubery of every one-horse paper hanging company, were still pleasing to look upon, and the scenic properties of the small stage were not so aged as to be disagreeable. They were freely patched and repaired in many places, but after all they were infinitely better than most of the performances which they were compelled to help out.

By the evening of the sixteenth the subtle hand of Hurstwood had made itself apparent in more than one little matter which related to the improvement of the occasion. He had given the word among his friends, and they were many and influential, that here was something which they ought to attend, and as a consequence the sale of tickets by Mr. Quincel, acting for the lodge, had been large. Small four-line notes had appeared in all of the daily newspapers from time to time, mentioning the fact that the Elks were preparing a very interesting performance, or that arrangements were now almost completed and the performance promised to be a success in every way. These he had arranged for by the aid of one of his newspaper friends on the "Times,"—Mr. Harry McGarren, the managing editor.

"Say, Harry," Hurstwood said to him one evening as the latter stood at the bar drinking before wending his belated way homeward, "you can help the boys out, I guess."

"What is it?" said McGarren, pleased to be consulted by the opulent manager.

"The Custer Lodge is getting up a little entertainment for their own good, and they'd like a little newspaper notice. You know what I mean—a squib or two saying that it's going to take place."

"Certainly," said McGarren. "I can fix that for you, George."

"They're all good people," suggested the manager, indicating thereby that merchants and well-positioned individuals belonged. "They're not looking for any taffy you know—just a clean little announcement."

"The paper would probably notice it anyhow," said McGarren, happy to be of service—"Elks, you know, but I'll tend to it for you."

"Thanks, old man," said Hurstwood, and therewith was an end of that.

Faithful to his word, McGarren posted the papers, and a number of little squibs in the club and secret order notes was the consequence.

If any one doubts the efficacy of such things, he should attempt to engineer a small affair of this sort, depending upon the good nature rather than the need or desire of some class or sect, and he will discover how dismal is progress without publicity. He will also discover that individuals love more to bask in the sunshine of popularity than they do to improve in some obscure intellectual shade. Merit is no object, conspicuity all.

No one realized this better than Hurstwood. At the same time he kept himself wholly in the background. The members of Custer Lodge could scarcely understand why their little affair was taking so well. Mr. Harry Quincel was looked upon as quite a star for this sort of work. His friends were calling for tickets, and quite a number of members from other lodges. If he could have seen Hurstwood quietly using a word now and then with those who were his friends he would have seen a light.

"What have you got on, Mark, for the sixteenth?" he asked of a fellow Elk who drifted into the forum of trade over which he so graciously presided.

"Nothing. What's up?" replied that worthy.

"I want you to come out and see a little performance at Avery Hall that night. Bring your wife."

"Certainly," said Mark. "What is it—full dress?"

"That's it."

"Where do I get the tickets?"

"Custer Lodge, I guess."

The mere fact that Hurstwood should ask that he should come out was sufficient indication to the newcomer that there was something more back of the request than the mere performance. It was nothing to him, though, one way or another. The performance would probably be passable, he would meet with a number of well-known friends, and the aim, whatever it was, would be satisfied. What was an evening or ten dollars?

"I saw something about that in the 'Times' the other morning," said another Elk whom Hurstwood addressed. "What is it?"

"Just a little theatrical performance. It may not amount to much, but it's got to go."

"All right, I'll be there—full dress, did you say?"

By the time the sixteenth had arrived Hurstwood's friends had rallied like Romans to a senator's call. He was a man of few words but he had considerable influence, owing to his long standing with the Elks, who were rather influential locally, and to his stable and showy position. He was of a social disposition and distributed pleasures with a liberal hand when the turn fell to him. Among many men of his own kind—prosperous, dressy, convivial—he, to use a bit of picturesque slang, pulled a great stroke. On occasions of this sort he was in his element, and the very fact that he was tipping it off as worthy of attention was sufficient to make it an Elk night among his many acquaintances. A well-dressed, good-natured, flatteringly inclined audience was assured from the moment he thought of assisting Carrie.

That little student had mastered her part to her own satisfaction, much as she trembled for her fate when she should once face the gathered throng, behind the glare of the footlights. She tried to console herself with the thought that a score of other persons, men and women, were equally tremulous concerning the outcome of their efforts, but she could not disassociate the general danger from her own individual liability. She feared that she would forget her lines, that she might be unable to muster the feeling which now she felt concerning her own movements in the play. At times she wished that she had never gone in on the affair; at others she trembled lest she should be paralyzed with fear and stand white and gasping, not knowing what to say and spoiling the entire performance.

She communicated some of her fears to Drouet but he only made light of them:—

"Nonsense," he said. "You'll do nothing of the kind. Why the audience won't amount to anything. They're not there to hiss you down. Besides, look at the other people. They're just as much frightened as you are."

"I know it," said Carrie, "but I feel as if my heart would come right up in my throat and choke me if I should forget a word."

"But you won't," he explained. "Don't bother about the audience—don't think that they are there. Just go on about your part as if there wasn't another soul around. You'll come out all right—see if you don't."

"Oh, I don't know," said Carrie. "I'm so nervous."

She brooded over her lines the livelong day on Friday—reporting first for a final rehearsal and later studying alone in her room.

"Oh, dear! dear!" she said, "I just know I won't succeed."

At the rehearsal Hurstwod put in an appearance. He could not resist the temptation. Fortunately Drouet was not there.

"Well," he said, "I thought I had better run out and see how you felt."

"Oh, I don't know," said Carrie. "I'm rather shaky."

"Well, don't you be now," he said cordially. "It isn't worth it. These people will be indulgent with you. Besides it will be nothing if you do miss some of your lines. Just drive on—you'll come out all right."

"I do hope so," said Carrie.

"You will that—now be easy."

In the matter of the company, Mr. Bamberger had disappeared. That hopeless example had fallen under the lance of the director's criticism. Mrs. Morgan was still present, but envious and determined, if for nothing more than spite, to do as well as Carrie at least. A loafing professional had been called in to assume the role of Ray, and while he was a poor stick after his kind, he was not troubled by any of those qualms which attack the spirit of those who have never faced an audience. He swashed about, cautioned though he was to maintain silence concerning his past theatrical relationships, in such a self-confident manner, that he was like to convince everyone of his identity by mere matter of circumstantial evidence.

"It is so easy," he said to Mrs. Morgan, in the usual affected stage voice. "An audience would be the last thing to trouble me. It's the spirit of the part, you know, that is difficult."

Carrie disliked his appearance, but she was too much the actress not to swallow his qualities with complaisance, seeing that she must suffer his fictitious love for the evening.

At six she was ready to go. Theatrical paraphernalia had been provided over and above her care. From lack of dressing-room space, there being only twelve cubby holes set aside for dressing purposes, she was assigned with Mrs. Hoagland, a widow of thirty, who was scheduled to take the part of Mrs. Van Dam, one of the voices of society. Carrie had practised make-up in the morning, had rehearsed and arranged her material for the evening by one o'clock, and had gone home to have a final look at her part, waiting the evening to come.

On this occasion the lodge sent a carriage. Drouet rode with her as far as the door and then went about the neighboring stores looking for some good cigars. The little actress marched nervously into her dressing room and began that painfully anticipated matter of make-up which was to transform her, a simple maiden, to Laura, the Belle of Society.

The life of the world behind the curtain is a fascinating thing to every outsider with theatrical leanings, as we well know. It would require the pen of a Hawthorne and the spirit of the "Twice-Told Tales" to do justice to that mingled atmosphere of life and mummery which pervades the chambers of the children of the stage. The flare of the gas jets, the open trunks suggestive of travel and display, the scattered contents of the make-up box—rouge, pearl-powder, whiting, burnt cork, India ink, pencils for the eyelids, wigs for the head, scissors, looking glasses, drapery—in short all the nameless paraphernalia of disguise have a remarkable atmosphere of their own. They breathe of the other half of life in which we have no part, of doors that are closed, and mysteries which may never be revealed. Through these we may be admitted—through these get a glimpse of the joys and sorrows which we may never be permitted to feel on our own behalf.

Carrie had not known this atmosphere before, but now it made a deep impression upon her. Since her arrival in the city, many things had influenced her but always in a far-removed manner. This new atmosphere was more friendly. It was wholly unlike the great, brilliant mansions which waved her coldly away, permitting her only awe and distant wonder. This took her by the hand kindly, as one who says, "My dear, come in." It opened for her as if for its own. She had wondered at the greatness of the names upon the billboards, the marvel of the long notices in the papers, the beauty of the dresses upon the stage—the atmosphere of carriages, flowers, refinement. Here was no illusion. Here was an open door to all of that. She had come upon it as one who stumbles upon a secret passage, and, behold, she was in the chamber of diamonds and delight.

As she dressed with a flutter in her little stage room, hearing the voices outside, seeing Mr. Quincel hurrying here and there, noting Mrs. Morgan and Mrs. Hoagland at their nervous work of preparation, seeing all the twenty members of the cast moving about and worrying over what the result would be, she could not help thinking what a delight this would be if it would endure, how perfect a state, if she could only do well now, and then sometime get a place as a real actress. The thought had taken a mighty hold on her. It hummed in her ears as the melody of an old song. Ah! ah! to be rid of idleness and the drag of loneliness—to be doing and rising—to be admired, petted, raised to a state where all was applause, elegance, assumption of dignity. Her head swam as she thought of it—her little lines assumed great importance in the world. If she could only represent them as she should.

Outside in the little lobby, another scene was being enacted. The dwellers in the flats across the way were interested in seeing the little theatre lighted up. It being a warm night, a number of children were playing about the street. Storekeepers stood out in front of their brightly lighted shops and enjoyed the pleasant progress of the night. Street cars went jingling by in great number, for this, of all the streets on the West Side, was the most important. By seven the ushers and functionaries, together with the participants in the production, had all arrived.

By seven-thirty the members of Custer Lodge and their friends began to put in an appearance.

Without the interest of Hurstwood, the little hall would have probably been comfortably filled, for the members of the lodge were moderately interested in its welfare. Hurstwood's word, however, had gone the rounds. It was to be a full-dress affair. The four boxes had been taken. Dr. Norman McNeill Hale and his wife were to occupy one. This was quite a card, for Dr. Hale was well and favorably known. G. R. Walker, dry goods merchant and possessor of at least two hundred thousand dollars, had taken another, a well-known coal merchant had been induced to take the third and Hurstwood and his friends the fourth. Among the latter was Drouet. The people who were now pouring in here were not celebrities, nor even local notabilities in a general sense. They were the lights of a certain circle—the circle of small fortunes and secret order distinctions. These gentlemen Elks knew the standing of one another. They had regard for the ability which could amass a small fortune, own a nice home, keep a barouche or carriage perhaps, wear fine clothes and maintain a good mercantile position. Anyone who did this and belonged to their lodge was quite a figure. Naturally, Hurstwood, who was a little above the order of mind which accepts this standard as perfect, who had shrewdness and much assumption of dignity, who held an imposing and authoritative position and commanded friendship by intuitive tact in handling people, was quite a figure among these. He was more generally known than most others in the same circle, and was looked upon as someone whose reserve covered a mine of influence and solid financial prosperity.

Tonight he was in his element. He came with several gentleman friends directly from Rector's in a carriage. In the lobby he met Drouet, who was just returning from a trip for more cigars. All five now joined in an animated conversation concerning the company present, and the general drift of lodge affairs.

"Who's here?" said Hurstwood, passing into the theatre proper, where the lights were turned up and a goodly company of gentleman Elks were laughing and talking in the open space back of the seats.

"Why, how do you do, Mr. Hurstwood?" came from the first individual recognized.

"Glad to see you," said the latter, grasping his hand lightly.

"Looks like quite an affair, doesn't it?"

"Yes, indeed," said the manager.

"Custer seems to have the backing of its members," observed the friend.

"So it should," said the knowing manager—"I'm glad to see it."

"Well, George," said another rotund citizen, whose avoirdupois made necessary an almost alarming display of starched shirt bosom, "how goes it with you?"

"Excellent," said the manager.

"What brings you over here—you're not a member of Custer."

"Good nature," returned the manager. "Like to see the boys, you know."

"Wife here?"

"She couldn't come tonight. She's not well."

"Sorry to hear it—nothing serious, I hope."

"No, just feeling a little unwell."

"I remember Mrs. Hurstwood when she was traveling once with you over to St. Joe—" and here the newcomer launched off in a trivial recollection which was terminated by the arrival of more friends.

"Why George—how are you?" said another genial West Side politician and lodge member. "My, but I'm glad to see you again—how are things anyhow?"

"Very well—I see you got that nomination for alderman."

"Yes, we whipped them out over there without much trouble."

"What do you suppose Hennessy will do now?"

"Oh, he'll go back to his brick business. He has a brick yard you know."

"I didn't know that," said the manager. "Felt pretty sore, I suppose, over his defeat."

"Perhaps," said the other, winking shrewdly.

Some of the more favored of his friends whom he had invited began to roll up in carriages now. They came shuffling in with a great show of finery and much evident feeling of content and importance.

"Here we are," said Hurstwood, turning to one from a group he was talking with.

"That's right," returned the newcomer, a gentleman of about forty-five.

"And say," he whispered jovially, pulling Hurstwood over by the shoulder so that he might whisper in his ear—"if this isn't a good show I'll punch your head."

"You ought to pay for seeing your old friends. Bother the show."

To another who inquired, "Is it something really good?" the manager replied, "I don't know, I don't suppose so." Then lifting his hand graciously, "For the lodge."

"Lot of boys out, eh?"

"Yes, look up Shanahan. He was just asking for you a moment ago."

It was thus that the little theatre resounded to a babble of successful voices, the creak of fine clothes, the commonplace of good nature, and all largely because of this man's bidding. Look at him any time within the half hour before the curtain was up;—he was a member of an eminent group—a rounded company of five or more, whose stout figures, large white bosoms and shining pins bespoke the character of their success. The gentlemen who brought their wives called him out to shake hands. Seats clicked; ushers bowed while he looked blandly on. He was evidently a light among them, reflecting in his personality the ambitions of those who greeted him. He was acknowledged, fawned upon, in a way lionized. Through it all one could see the standing of the man. It was greatness in a way, small as it was.

CHAPTER XX.

At last the curtain was ready to go up. All the details of the make-up had been completed and the company settled down as the leader of the small hired orchestra tapped significantly upon his music rack with his baton and began the soft curtain-raising strain. Hurstwood ceased talking and went with Drouet and his friend Sagar Morrison around to the box.

"Now we'll see how the little girl does," he said to Drouet, in a tone which no one else could hear.

On the stage, six of the characters had already appeared in the opening parlor scene. Drouet and Hurstwood saw at a glance that Carrie was not among them and went on talking in a whisper. Mrs. Morgan, Mrs. Hoagland and the actor who had taken Bamberger's part were representing the principal roles in this scene. The professional, whose name was Patton, had little to recommend him outside of his assurance, but this at the present moment was most palpably needed. Mrs. Morgan, as Pearl, was stiff with fright. Mrs. Hoagland was husky in the throat. The whole company was so weak-kneed that the lines were merely spoken and nothing more. It took all the hope and uncritical good nature of the audience to keep from manifesting pity by that unrest which is the agony of failure.

Hurstwood was perfectly indifferent. He took it for granted that it would be worthless. All he cared for was to have it endurable enough to allow for pretensions and congratulations afterward.

After the first rush of fright, however, the players got over the danger of collapse. They rambled weakly forward, losing nearly all the expression which was intended and making the thing dull in the extreme, when Carrie came in.

One glance at her and both Hurstwood and Drouet saw plainly that she also was weak-kneed. She came faintly across the stage, saying:—

"And you, Sir, we have been looking for you since eight o'clock," but with so little color and in such a feeble voice that it was positively painful.

"She's frightened," whispered Drouet to Hurstwood.

The manager made no answer.

She had a line presently which was supposed to be funny:—

"Well, that's as much as to say I'm a sort of Life Pill."

It came out so flat, however, that it was a deathly thing. Drouet fidgeted. Hurstwood moved his toe the least bit.

There was another place in which Laura was to rise and, with a sense of impending disaster, say sadly:—

"I wish you hadn't said that, Pearl. You know the old proverb: 'Call a maid by a married name.' "

The lack of feeling in the thing was ridiculous. Carrie did not get it at all. She seemed to be talking in her sleep. It looked as if she were certain to be a wretched failure. She was more hopeless than Mrs. Morgan, who had recovered somewhat and was now saying her lines clearly at least. Drouet looked away from the stage at the people. The latter held out silently, hoping for a general change, of course. Hurstwood fixed his eye on Carrie as if to hypnotize her into doing better. He was pouring determination of his own in her direction. He felt sorry for her.

In a few more minutes it fell to her to read the letter sent in by the strange villain. The audience had been slightly diverted by a conversation between the professional actor and a character called Snorkey, impersonated by a short little American who really developed some humor as a half-crazed one-armed soldier, turned messenger for a living. He bawled his lines out with such defiance, that, while they really did not partake of the humor intended, they were funny. Now he was off, however, and it was back to pathos, with Carrie as the chief figure. She did not recover. She wandered through the whole scene between herself and the intruding villain, straining the patience of the audience and finally exiting, much to their relief.

"She's too nervous," said Drouet, feeling in the mildness of the remark that he was lying for once.

"Better go back and say a word to her."

Drouet was glad to do anything for relief. He fairly hustled around to the side entrance and was let in by the friendly door keeper. Carrie was standing in the wings, weakly waiting her next cue, all the snap and nerve gone out of her.

"Say, Cad," he said, looking at her, "you mustn't be nervous. Wake up. Those guys out there don't amount to anything. What are you afraid of?"

"I don't know," said Carrie. "I just don't seem to be able to do it."

She was grateful for the drummer's presence, though. She had found the company so nervous that her own strength had gone.

"Come on," said Drouet. "Brace up. What are you afraid of? Go on out there now and do the trick. What do you care?"

Carrie revived a little under the drummer's electrical nervous condition.

"Did I do so very bad?"

"Not a bit. All you need is a little more ginger. Do it as you showed me. Get that toss of your head you had the other night."

Carrie remembered her triumph in the room. She tried to think she could do it.

"What's next?" he said, looking at her part which she had been studying.

"Why, the scene between Ray and me, when I refuse him."

"Well now you do that lively," said the drummer. "Put in the snap, that's the thing. Act as if you didn't care."

"Your turn next, Miss Madenda," said the prompter.

"Oh, dear," said Carrie.

"Well you're a chump for being afraid," said Drouet. "Come on now, brace up. I'll watch you from right here."

"Will you?" said Carrie.

"Yes. Now go on. Don't be afraid."

The prompter signaled her.

She started out, weak as ever, but suddenly her nerve partially returned. She thought of Drouet looking.

"Ray," she said gently, using a tone of voice much more calm than when she had last appeared. It was the scene which had pleased the director at the rehearsal.

"She's easier," thought Hurstwood to himself.

She did not do the part as she had at rehearsal, but she was better. The audience was at least not irritated. The improvement of the work of the entire company took away direct observation of her. They were making very fair progress, and now it looked as if the play would be passable, in the less trying parts at least.

Carrie came off warm and nervous.

"Well," she said, looking at him, "was it any better?"

"Well, I should say so. That's the way. Put life into it. You did that about a thousand per cent better than you did the other scene. Now go on and fire up. You can do it. Knock 'em."

"Was it really better?"

"Better, I should say so. What comes next?"

"That ballroom scene."

"Well you can do that all right," he said.

"I don't know," answered Carrie.

"Why woman!" he exclaimed. "You did it for me. Now you go out there and do it. It'll be fun for you. Just do as you did in the room. If you'll reel it off that way I'll bet you make a hit. Now what'll you bet? You do it."

The drummer usually allowed his ardent good nature to get the best of his speech. He really did think that Carrie had acted this particular scene very well, and he wanted her to repeat it in public. His enthusiasm was due to the mere spirit of the occasion.

When the time came he buoyed Carrie up most effectually. He began to make her feel as if she really had done very well. The old melancholy of desire began to come back as he talked at her, and by the time the situation rolled 'round she was running high in feeling.

"I think I can do this."

"Sure you can. Now you go ahead and see."

On the stage Mrs. Van Dam was making her proud insinuations against Laura.

Carrie listened and caught the infection of something—she did not know what. Her nostrils sniffed thinly.

"It means," the professional actor began, speaking as Ray, "that society is a terrible avenger of insult. Have you ever heard of the Siberian wolves? When one of the pack falls through weakness, the others devour him. It is not an elegant comparison—but there is something wolfish in society. Laura has mocked it with a pretence, and society, which is made up of pretences, will bitterly resent the mockery."

At the sound of her stage name, Carrie started. She began to feel the bitterness of the situation. The feelings of the outcast descended upon her. She hung at the wing's edge, rapt in her own mounting thoughts. She hardly heard anything more, save her own rumbling blood.

"Come girls!" said Mrs. Van Dam, solemnly. "Let us look after our things. They are no longer safe when such an accomplished thief enters."

"Cue," said the prompter, close to her side, but she did not hear. Already she was moving forward with a steady grace, born of inspiration. She dawned upon the audience, handsome and proud, shifting with the necessity of the situation to a cold, white, helpless object as the social pack moved away from her scornfully.

Hurstwood blinked his eyes and caught the infection. The radiating waves of feeling and sincerity were already breaking against the farthest walls of the chamber. The magic of passion, which will yet dissolve the world, was here at work.

There was a drawing, too, of attention, a riveting of feelings, heretofore wandering.

"Ray, Ray! why do you not come to her?" was the cry of Pearl.

"Are you not coming with us, Trafford?"

Every eye was fixed on Carrie, still, proud and scornful. They moved as she moved. Their eyes were with her eyes.

Mrs. Morgan, as Pearl, approached her.

"Let us go home," she said.

"No," answered Carrie, her voice assuming for the first time a penetrating quality which it had never known. "Stay with *him.*"

She pointed an almost accusing hand toward her lover. Then with a pathos which struck home because of its utter simplicity, "He shall not suffer long."

Hurstwood realized that he was seeing something extraordinarily good. It was heightened for him by the applause of the audience as the curtain descended and the fact that it was Carrie. He thought now that she was beautiful. She had done something which was above his sphere. He felt a keen delight in realizing that she was his.

"Fine," he said, and then, seized by a sudden impulse, jumped up and went about to the stage door.

When he came in upon Carrie she was still with Drouet. His feelings for her were most exuberant. He was almost swept away by the strength and feeling she exhibited. His desire was to pour forth his praise with the unbounded feelings of a lover, but here was Drouet, whose feelings of affection were also rapidly reviving. The latter was more fascinated, if anything, than Hurstwood. At the least, in the nature of things, his feelings took a more ruddy form.

"Well, well," said Drouet, "you did out of sight. That was simply great. I knew you could do it. Oh but you're a little daisy."

Carrie's eyes flamed with the light of achievement. She was warm and pulsating. Her lips were aglow, her cheeks rosy.

"Did I do all right?"

"Did you? Well I guess, didn't you hear the applause?"

There was some faint sound of clapping yet.

"I thought I got it something like—I felt it."

Just then Hurstwood came in. Instinctively he felt the change in Drouet. He saw that the drummer was near to Carrie, and jealousy leaped alight in his bosom. In a flash of thought he reproached himself for having sent him back. Also, he hated him as an intruder. He could scarcely pull himself down to the level where he would have to congratulate Carrie as a friend. Nevertheless the man mastered himself, and it was a triumph. He almost jerked the old subtle light to his eyes.

"I thought," he said, looking at Carrie, "that I would come around and tell you how well you did, Mrs. Drouet. It was delightful."

Carrie took the cue and replied:—

"Oh, thank you."

"I was just telling her," put in Drouet, now delighted with his possession, "that I thought she did fine."

"Indeed you did," said Hurstwood, turning upon Carrie eyes in which she read more than the words.

Carrie laughed luxuriantly.

"If you do as well in the rest of the play, you will make us all think you're a born actress."

Carrie smiled again. She felt the acuteness of Hurstwood's position and wished deeply that she could be alone with him, but she did not understand the change in Drouet. Hurstwood found that he could not talk, repressed as he was, and grudging Drouet every moment of his presence. He bowed himself out with the elegance of a Faust. Drouet did not come along. Outside, Hurstwood set his teeth with envy.

"Damn it," he said, " is he always going to be in the way?" He was moody when he got back to the box and could not talk for thinking of his wretched situation.

As the curtain for the next act arose, Drouet came back.

He was very much enlivened in temper and inclined to whisper, but Hurstwood pretended interest. He fixed his eyes on the stage, although Carrie was not there, a short bit of melodramatic comedy preceding her entrance. He did not see what was going on, however. He was thinking his own thoughts, and they were wretched.

The progress of the play did not improve matters for him. Carrie, from now on, was easily the centre of interest. The audience, which had been inclined to feel that nothing could be good, after the first gloomy impression, now went to the other extreme and saw power where it was not. The general feeling reacted on Carrie. She presented her part with some felicity, though nothing like the intensity which had aroused the feeling at the end of the long first act. Her part was one of distress, being hidden away, as she was supposed to be, in a miserable quarter in New York, to avoid old acquaintances and at the same time being hunted by her terrible old criminal step-mother—Judas, who wished to kidnap her and hold her for ransom.

Both Hurstwood and Drouet viewed her pretty figure with rising feelings. The fact that such ability should reveal itself in her—that they should see it set forth under such effective circumstance—framed almost in massy gold and shone upon by the appropriate lights of sentiment and personality, heightened her charm for them. She was more than the old Carrie to Drouet. He longed to be at home with her until he could tell her. He awaited impatiently the end when they should go home alone. Hurstwood, on the contrary, saw in the strength of her new attractiveness his miserable predicament. He could have cursed the man beside him. By the Lord, he could not even applaud feelingly as he would. For once, he must simulate when it left a taste in his mouth.

In the second act Carrie had two good situations—one with her lover, Ray, who came to win her back—one with her supposed mother, Judas, who, with her criminal pal, forced her to come along against her will. In the third act she was tried in a police court for disobedience to her fake father, forced into a carriage, and finally rescued, by some water rats and her lover, when being brought down to the river at the dead of night. In the fourth act, she was seen under the old circumstances, among friends, but still hounded by designing villains and still refusing to take back her lover, who wished to restore himself in her regard. A most difficult situation was presented her in her attempts to leave home, in order that she might no longer be a temptation to her old lover, who had since become engaged,— nor to her friends, anxious to protect her against further designs.

It was in this act that Carrie's fascination for her lovers assumed its most effective character. Drouet had been so satisfied with the performance that he went around at the end of the second and third acts to compliment her, although in the latter act her part had been insignificant and almost wholly passive. He was not quite recovered from the warmth of his original awakening and saw all that she did in a rosy light.

Hurstwood, meanwhile, found that he must talk with his many friends, who made it impossible for him to maintain his grey shade of feelings between the acts. He pulled himself together and fairly maintained his standard of good fellowship, though his thoughts and desires were with the girl behind the scenes.

Drouet came out after his short visit at the end of the third act.

"She's in good spirits," he said pleasantly.

"That's good," said Hurstwood.

The fourth act, on which the curtain now rose, was supposed to take place at "Long Branch"—on the ground floor of the elegant summer home of the Courtlands. Quite an effect had been secured by using tall, open windows in the back, extending from floor to ceiling, and by installing a piece of canvas painted blue, and slightly sprinkled with silver dust, in the far recess of the stage, to represent the sea. A balcony or promenade was also outside, making a summery prospect, not wholly devoid of realism.

The audience viewed the unfolding story with considerable interest, for the entire company had improved in feeling and were doing work which at least did not obscure the natural attractions of the good old melodrama. Mrs. Morgan, as Pearl, had caught some of the feeling of the light-minded coquette— not difficult, since she looked the part. Mr. Patton, as Ray Trafford, once and still Laura's lover, but now engaged to Pearl, was passable. Mrs. Hoagland, as Mrs. Van Dam, had grown easy in her manner owing to the praise of Carrie, who had assured her repeatedly in the dressing room that she was doing excellently. The applause and good nature of the audience, which, in its surprise at finding itself not tortured, went to the extreme of hilarious commendation, reacted upon the mediocre talent and produced ease and consequent better results.

Hurstwood listened to the progress of the act, wondering when Carrie would come on. He could not tell when she would appear, and like Drouet he was now interested to get the connection in order to judge of her work in the matter. He had not long to wait, for after a little scene in which Pearl showed that she really did not care much for Ray, that she was merry and soulless, and much interested in a certain nobleman who was infatuated with her, Carrie entered. The author had used the artifice of sending all the merry company for a drive, and now Carrie came in alone. It was the first time that Hurstwood had had a chance to see her facing the audience quite alone, for nowhere else had she been without a foil of some sort. He suddenly felt as she entered that her old strength—the power that had grasped him at the end of the first act, had come back. She seemed to be gaining feeling, now that the play was drawing to a close and the opportunity for great action was passing.

"Poor Pearl," she said, speaking with natural pathos. "It is a sad thing to want for happiness, but is is a terrible thing to see another groping about blindly for it when it is almost within the grasp."

She was gazing now sadly out upon the open sea, her arm resting listlessly upon the polished door post.

Hurstwood began to feel a deep sympathy for her and for himself. He could almost feel that she was talking to him. He was, by a combination of feelings and entanglements, almost deluded by that quality of voice and manner, which, like a pathetic strain of music, seems ever a personal and intimate thing. Pathos has this quality—that it seems ever addressed to one alone.

"And yet she can be very happy with him," went on the little actress. "Her sunny temper, and her joyous face, will brighten any home."

She turned slowly toward the audience without seeing. There was so much simplicity in her movements that she seemed

SISTER CARRIE · 189

wholly alone. Then she found a seat by a table and turned over some books, devoting a thought to them.

"With no longings for what I may not have," she breathed in conclusion—and it was almost a sigh, "my existence hidden from all, save two in the wide world, and making my joy out of the joy of that innocent child who will soon be his wife."

Hurstwood was sorry when a character known as Peach-blossom interrupted her. He stirred irritably, for he wished her to go on. He was charmed by the pale face, made so by a touch of blue under the eyes, the lissome figure, draped in pearl gray, with a coiled string of imitation pearls at the throat. Carrie had the air of one who was weary and in need of protection, and under the fascinating make-believe of the moment, he rose in feeling until he was ready, in spirit, to go to her and ease her of her misery by adding to his own delight.

This character of little Peachblossom was interesting enough in the run of the melodrama, being an urchin whom Laura had cared for and who had consequently followed her about, revealing the secrets of the plotters against her, and doing other impossible but plot-aiding things usually attributed to street urchins in melodramas. But Hurstwood did not fancy the interruption and only followed Carrie, whose part was much less pathetic here. When it was over he pricked his ears for a keener note in the play.

Carrie was alone again and was saying with animation:—

"I must return to the city, no matter what dangers may lurk there. I must go—secretly if I can—openly if I must—"

—when there was a sound of horse's hoofs outside and then Ray's voice saying:—

"No, I shall not ride again. Put him up."

He entered and then began a scene which had as much to do with the creation of the tragedy of affection in Hurstwood as anything in his peculiar and involved career. For Carrie had resolved to make something of this scene, and now that the cue had come, it began to take a feeling hold upon her. Both Hurst-wood and Drouet noted the rising sentiment as she proceeded.

"I thought you had gone with Pearl," she said to her lover.

"I did go part of the way, but I left the party a mile down the road."

"You and Pearl had no disagreement?"

"No—yes; that is, we always have. Our social barometers always stand at 'cloudy' and 'overcast.' "

"And whose fault is that?" she said easily.

"Not mine," he answered pettishly. "I know I do all I can—I say all I can—but she—"

This was rather awkwardly put by Patton, but Carrie redeemed it with a grace which was inspiring.

"But she is to be your wife," she said, fixing her whole attention upon the stilted actor and softening the quality of her voice until it was again low and musical. "Ray—my friend—courtship is the text from which the whole solemn sermon of married life takes its theme. Do not let yours be discontented and unhappy."

She put her two little hands together and pressed them appealingly.

Hurstwood gazed with slightly parted lips. Drouet was fidgeting with satisfaction.

"To be my wife; yes," went on the actor in a manner which was weak by comparison but which could not now spoil the tender atmosphere which Carrie had created and maintained. She did not seem to feel that he was wretched. She would have done nearly as well with a block of wood. The accessories she needed were within her own imagination. The acting of others could not affect them.

"And you repent already?" she said slowly.

"I lost you," he said, seizing her little hand, "and I was at the mercy of any flirt that chose to give me an inviting look. It was your fault—you know it was! Why did you leave me?"

Carrie turned slowly away and seemed to be mastering some impulse in silence. Then she turned back.

"Ray," she said, "the greatest happiness I have ever felt has been the thought that all your affections were forever bestowed upon a virtuous lady, your equal in family, fortune and accomplishments. What a revelation do you make to me now! What is it makes you continually war with your happiness?"

The last question was asked so simply that it came to the audience and the lover as a personal thing.

At last it came to the part where the lover exclaimed, "Be to me as you used to be!"

Carrie answered with affecting sweetness, "I cannot be that

to you; but I can speak as the spirit of the Laura who is dead to you forever."

"Be it as you will," said Patton.

Hurstwood leaned forward. The whole audience was now affected by the grace of her demeanor. It looked like another repetition of the climax of the first act—so moving was the feeling about.

"Let the woman you look upon be wise or vain," said Carrie, her eyes bent sadly upon the lover, who had sunk into a seat, "beautiful or homely, rich or poor, she has but one thing she can really give or refuse—her heart."

Drouet felt a scratch in his throat.

"Her beauty, her wit, her accomplishments, she may sell to you—but her love is the treasure without money and without price."

The manager suffered this as a personal appeal. It came to him as if they were alone, and he could hardly restrain the tears for sorrow over the hopeless, pathetic and yet dainty and appealing woman whom he loved. Drouet also was beside himself. He was resolving that he would be to Carrie what he had never been before. He would marry her, by George. She was worth it.

"She only asks in return," said Carrie, scarcely hearing the small, scheduled reply of her lover, and putting herself even more in harmony with the plaintive melody now issuing from the orchestra, "that when you look upon her, your eyes shall speak a mute devotion; that when you address her, your voice shall be gentle, loving and kind. That you shall not despise her because she cannot understand, all at once, your vigorous thoughts and ambitious designs; for when misfortune and evil have defeated your greatest purposes—her love remains to console you. You look to the trees," she continued, while Hurstwood restrained his feelings only by the grimmest repression, "for strength and grandeur—do not despise the flowers because their fragrance is all they have to give. Remember," she concluded tenderly, "love is all a woman has to give," and she laid a strange sweet accent on the *all*, "but it is the only earthly thing which God permits us to carry beyond the grave."

The two men were in a most harrowed state of affection. They scarcely heard the few remaining words with which the scene concluded. They only saw their idol, moving about with

appealing grace, continuing a power which to them was a revelation.

Hurstwood resolved a thousand things—Drouet as well.
They joined equally in the burst of applause which called Carrie
out. Drouet pounded his hands until they ached. Then he
jumped up again and started out. As he went, Carrie came out,
and seeing an immense basket of flowers being hurried down the
aisle toward her, she waited. They were Hurstwood's. She
looked toward the manager's box for a moment, caught his eye
and smiled. He could have leaped out of the box to enfold her.
He forgot the need of circumspectness which his married state
enforced. He almost forgot that he had with him in the box
those who knew him. By the Lord, he would have that lovely
girl if it took his all. He would act at once. This should be the
end of Drouet and don't you forget it. He would not wait another
day. The drummer should not have her.

He was so excited that he could not stay in the box. He
went into the lobby and then into the street thinking. Drouet
did not return. In a few minutes, the last act was over and he
was crazy to have Carrie alone. He cursed the luck that could
keep him smiling, bowing, shamming, when he wanted to tell
her that he loved her, when he wanted to whisper to her alone.
He groaned as he saw that his hopes were futile. He must even
take her to dinner, shamming. He finally went about and asked
how she was getting along. The actors were all dressing, talking,
hurrying about. Drouet was palavering with the looseness of
excitement and passion. The manager mastered himself only by
a superhuman effort. He could have groaned aloud.

"We are going to supper, of course," he said with a voice
that was a mockery of his heart.

"Oh yes," said Carrie, smiling.

The little actress was in fine feather. She was realizing now
what it was to be petted. For once she was the admired, the
sought-for. The independence of success now made its first faint
showing. With the tables turned, she was looking down, rather
than up, to her lover. She did not fully realize that this was so,
but there was something in condescension coming from her
which was infinitely sweet. When she was ready, they climbed
into the waiting coach and drove down town. Once only did
she find an opportunity to express her feeling and that was when

the manager preceded Drouet in the coach and sat beside her. Before Drouet was fully in she had squeezed Hurstwood's hand in a gentle, impulsive manner. The manager was beside himself with affection. He could have sold his soul to be with her alone.

"Ah," he thought, "the agony of it."

Drouet hung on, thinking he was all in all. The dinner was spoiled by his enthusiasm. Hurstwood went home feeling as if he should die if he did not find affectionate relief. He whispered "tomorrow" passionately to Carrie and she understood. He walked away from the drummer and his prize, at parting feeling as if he could slay him and not regret. Carrie also felt the misery of it.

"Goodnight," he said, simulating a grace he could not feel, and longing towards Carrie.

"Goodnight," said the little actress tenderly.

"The fool," he said, now hating Drouet. "The idiot. I'll do him yet. And that quick. We'll see tomorrow."

"Well, if you aren't a wonder," Drouet was saying complacently, squeezing Carrie's arm. "You're the dandiest little girl on earth."

CHAPTER XXI.

Passion in a man of Hurstwood's nature takes a vigorous form. It is no musing, dreaming thing. There is none of the tendency to sing outside of my lady's window—to languish and repine in the face of difficulties. In the night he was long getting to sleep because of too much thinking, and in the morning he was early awake, seizing with alacrity upon the same dear subject and pursuing it with vigor. He was out of sorts physically as well as disordered mentally, for did he not delight in a new way in his Carrie, and was not Drouet in the way? Never was man more harassed by the thoughts of his love being held by the elated, flush-mannered drummer. He would have given anything, it seemed to him, to have the complication ended—to have Carrie acquiesce to an arrangement which would dispose of Drouet effectually and forever.

What to do. He dressed thinking. He moved about in the same chamber with his wife, unmindful of her presence.

At breakfast he found himself without an appetite. The meat to which he helped himself remained on his plate un-touched. His coffee grew cold, while he scanned the paper in-differently. Here and there he read a little thing but remembered nothing. He was in a mood which might well have been called conflicting.

It was a time when the affairs of his own home concerned him very little, and that little disagreeably. Jessica had not yet come down. His wife sat at one end of the table, revolving thoughts of her own in silence. A new servant had been recently installed and had forgot the napkins. On this account the silence was irritably broken by a reproof.

"I've told you about this before, Maggie," said Mrs. Hurst-wood. "I'm not going to tell you again."

Hurstwood took a glance at his wife. She was frowning. Just now her manner irritated him excessively. Her next remark was addressed to him.

"Have you made up your mind, George, when you will take your vacation?"

It was customary for them to discuss the regular summer outing at this season of the year.

"Not yet," he said. "I'm very busy just now."

"Well, you'll want to make up your mind pretty soon, won't you, if we're going?" she returned.

"I guess we have a few days yet," he said.

"Hmf," she returned. "Don't wait until the season's over."

She stirred in aggravation as she said this.

"There you go again," he observed. "One would think I never did anything, the way you begin."

"Well, I want to know about it," she reiterated.

"You've got a few days yet," he insisted. "You'll not want to start before the races are over."

He was irritated to think that this should come up when he wished to have his thoughts for other purposes.

"Well, we may. Jessica doesn't want to stay until the end of the races."

"What did you want with a season ticket then?"

"Uh!" she said, using the sound as an exclamation of disgust—"I'll not argue with you," and therewith arose to leave
the table.

"Say," he said rising, putting a note of determination in
his voice which caused her to delay her departure—"what's the
matter with you of late? Can't I talk with you any more?"

"Certainly, you can *talk* with me," she replied, laying emphasis on the word.

"Well you wouldn't think so by the way you act. Now you
want to know when I'll be ready—not for a month yet. Maybe
not then."

"We'll go without you!"

"You will, eh?" he sneered.

"Yes, we will."

He was astonished at the woman's determination but it
only irritated him the more.

"Well, we'll see about that. It seems to me you're trying to
run things with a pretty high hand of late. You talk as though
you settled my affairs for me. Well, you don't. You don't regulate
anything that's connected with me. If you want to go, go, but
you won't hurry me any by such talk as that."

He was thoroughly aroused now. His dark eyes snapped,
and he crunched his paper as he laid it down. Mrs. Hurstwood
said nothing more. He was just finishing when she turned on
her heel and went out into the hall and upstairs. He paused for
a moment as if hesitating—then sat down and drank a little
coffee and thereafter arose and went for his hat and gloves, upon
the main floor.

His wife had really not anticipated a row of this character.
She had come down to the breakfast table feeling a little out of
sorts with herself and revolving a scheme which she had in her
mind. Jessica had called her attention to the fact that the races
were not what they were supposed to be. The social opportunities were not what they had thought they would be this year.
The beautiful girl found going every day a dull thing. There was
an earlier exodus this year, of people who were anybody, to the
watering places and Europe. In her own circle of acquaintances
several young men in whom she was interested had gone to
Waukesha. She began to feel that she would like to go too, and

her mother agreed with her. Why shouldn't they. The fact of having secured a season ticket was nothing.

"Do you know," said Jessica one afternoon, when they were preparing to drive out to the track, "the Lamberts are already up there? They went Tuesday."

She was referring to Waukesha.

"Is that so? I thought they weren't going for some time yet."

"So did I," returned the daughter, "but they've gone. So have the Fahrways. I wish we could go."

"We can, if we want to," returned her mother.

"Oh, I wish you would arrange it, Mamma!" cried the radiant girl. "It would be so much nicer. These old races are not a bit interesting."

Accordingly Mrs. Hurstwood decided to broach the subject. She was thinking this over when she came down to the table, but for some reason the atmosphere was wrong. She was not sure after it was all over just how the trouble had begun. She was determined now, however, that her husband was a brute and that under no circumstances would she let this go by unsettled. She would have more ladylike treatment or she would know why.

For his part, the manager was loaded with the care of this new argument until he reached his office and started from there to meet Carrie. Then the other complication of love, desire and opposition possessed him. His thoughts fled on before him upon eagle's wings. He could hardly wait until he should meet Carrie face to face. What was the night after all without her—what the day? She must and should be his.

For her part, Carrie had experienced a world of fancy and feeling since she had left him the night before. She had listened to Drouet's enthusiastic maunderings, with much regard for that part which concerned herself, with very little for that which affected his own gain. She did not love him. She kept him at such lengths as she could, because her thoughts were with her own triumph. She felt Hurstwood's passion as a delightful background to her own achievement, and she wondered what he would have to say. She was sorry for him, too, with that peculiar sorrow which finds something complimentary to itself in the misery of another. She was now experiencing the first shades of feeling of that subtle change which removes one out of the ranks of the suppliants into the lines of the dispensers of charity. She was, all in all, exceedingly happy.

On the morrow, however, there was nothing in the papers concerning the event, and in view of the flow of common, everyday things about, it now lost a shade of the glow of the previous evening. Drouet himself was not talking so much *of* as *for* her. He felt instinctively that for some reason or other, he needed reconstruction in her regard.

"I think," he said, as he spruced around their chambers the next morning, preparatory to going down town, "that I'll straighten out that little deal of mine this month and then we'll get married. I was talking with Mosher about that yesterday."

"No you won't," said Carrie, who was coming to feel a certain faint power to jest with the drummer.

"Yes I will!" he exclaimed more feelingly than usual, adding with the tone of one who pleads, "Don't you believe what I've told you?"

Carrie laughed a little.

"Of course I do," she answered.

Drouet's assurance now misgave him. Shallow as was his mental observation, there was that in the things which had happened which made his little power of analysis useless. Carrie was still with him, but not helpless and pleading. There was a lilt in her voice which was new. She did not study him with eyes expressive of dependence. The drummer was feeling the shadow of something which was coming. It colored his feelings and made him develop those little attentions and say those little words which were mere forefendations against danger. He moved about unenlightened but still alive to something, and drawn by a desire which was now entirely revived.

"Say," he said in one place, as he was studying the effect of a new puff tie before the mirror, "how did you do that?"

"What?" asked Carrie.

"That scene in the ball room—how'd you work it up—I mean. You looked as if you really were miserable."

"Oh! I don't know," answered Carrie.

The question let in a flood of light on the matter of superiority. She began to see the things which he did not understand. He was fixing his place in her estimation.

"You don't imagine the thing is so, do you?" he went on.

"No-o," said Carrie, "I don't exactly imagine it. I just feel how it ought to be."

He looked at her curiously for a moment and then added— "Well, you did it as though you felt it."

Shortly afterward he departed, and Carrie prepared for her meeting with Hurstwood. She hurried at her toilet, which was soon made, and hastened down the stairs. At the corner she passed Drouet but they did not see each other.

The drummer had forgotten some bills which he wished to turn in to his house. He hastened up the stairs and burst into the room but found only the chambermaid who was cleaning up.

"Hello!" he exclaimed, half to himself. "Has Carrie gone?"

"Your wife? Yes, she went out just a few minutes ago."

"That's strange," thought Drouet. "She didn't say a word to me. I wonder where she went."

He hastened about rummaging in his valise for what he wanted and finally pocketing it. Then he turned his attention to his fair neighbor who was good-looking and kindly disposed towards him.

"What are you up to?" he said smiling.

"Just cleaning," she replied, stopping and winding a dusting towel about her hand.

"Tired of it?"

"Not so very."

"Let me show you something," he said affably, coming over and taking out of his pocket a little lithographed card which had been issued by a wholesale tobacco company. On this was printed a picture of a pretty girl holding a striped parasol, the colors of which could be changed by means of a revolving disk in the back which showed red, yellow, green and blue through little interstices made in the ground occupied by the umbrella top.

"Isn't that clever," he said, handing it to her and showing her how it worked. "You never saw anything like that before."

"Isn't it nice," she answered.

"You can have it if you want it," he remarked.

He was forever laying hold of just such little things and using them in this way.

"That's a pretty ring you have," he said, touching a commonplace setting which adorned the hand which was holding the card he had given her.

"Do you think so?"

"That's right," he answered, making use of a pretence at examination to secure her finger. "That's fine."

The ice being then broken, he launched into further observation, pretending to forget that her fingers were still retained by his. She soon withdrew them, however, and retreated a few feet to rest against the window sill.

"I didn't see you for a long time," she said coquetishly, repulsing one of his exuberant approaches—"You must have been away."

"I was," said Drouet.

"Do you travel far?"

"Pretty far—yes."

"Do you like it?"

"Oh, not very well. You get tired of it after awhile."

"I wish I could travel," said the girl, gazing idly out of the window.

"What has become of your friend Mr. Hurstwood?" she suddenly asked, bethinking herself of the manager, who from her own observation seemed to contain promising material.

"He's here in town. What makes you ask about him?"

"Oh, nothing, only he hasn't been here since you got back."

"How did you come to know him?"

"Didn't I take up his name a dozen times in the last month?"

"Get out," said the drummer lightly. "He hasn't called more than half-a-dozen times since we've been here."

"He hasn't, eh?" said the girl smiling. "That's all you know about it."

Drouet took on a slightly more serious tone. He was uncertain as to whether she was joking or not.

"Tease!" he said. "What makes you smile that way?"

"Oh, nothing."

"Have you seen him recently?"

"Not since you came back," she laughed.

"Before?"

"Certainly."

"How often?"

"Why, nearly every day."

She was a mischievous newsmonger and was keenly wondering what the effect of her words would be.

"Who did he come to see?" asked the drummer, incredulously.

"Mrs. Drouet."

He looked rather foolish at this answer, and then attempted to correct himself so as not to appear a dupe.

"Well," he said, "what of it?"

"Nothing," replied the girl, her head cocked coquetishly on one side.

"He's an old friend," he went on, getting deeper into the mire.

He would have gone on further with his little flirtation but the taste for it was temporarily removed. He was quite relieved when the girl's name was called from below.

"I've got to go," she said, moving away from him airily.

"I'll see you later," he said, with a pretence of disturbance at being interrupted.

When she was gone he gave freer play to his feelings. His face, never easily controlled by him, expressed all the perplexity and disturbance which he felt. Could it be that Carrie had received so many visits and yet said nothing about them? Was Hurstwood lying? What did the chambermaid mean by it, anyway? He had thought there was something odd about Carrie's manner at the time. Why did she look so disturbed when he had asked her how many times Hurstwood had called? By George! he remembered now. There was something strange about the whole thing.

He sat down in a rocking chair to think the better, drawing up one leg on his knee and frowning mightily. His mind ran on at a great rate.

And yet Carrie hadn't acted out of the ordinary. It couldn't be, b' George, that she was deceiving him. She hadn't acted that way. Why even last night she had been as friendly towards him as could be, and Hurstwood too. Look how they acted. He could hardly believe they would try to deceive him.

His thoughts burst into words.

"She did act sort of funny at times. Here she has dressed and gone out this morning and never said a word."

He scratched his head and prepared to go down town. He was still frowning. As he came into the hall he encountered the girl, who was now looking after another chamber. She had on a white dusting cap beneath which her chubby face shone good-naturedly. Drouet almost forgot his worry in the fact that she was smiling on him. He put his hand familiarly on her shoulder as if only to greet her in passing.

"Got over being mad?" she said, still mischievously inclined.

"I'm not mad," he answered.

"I thought you were," she said, smiling.

"Quit your fooling about that," he said in an off-hand way. "Were you serious?"

"Certainly," she answered. Then with an air of one who did not intentionally mean to create trouble, "He came lots of times. I thought you knew."

The game of deception was up with Drouet. He did not try to simulate indifference further.

"Did he spend the evening here?" he asked.

"Sometimes. Sometimes they went out."

"In the evening?"

"Yes. You mustn't look so mad though."

"I'm not," he said. "Did anyone else see him?"

"Of course," said the girl, as if, after all, it were nothing in particular.

"How long was this ago?"

"Just before you came back."

The drummer pinched his lip nervously.

"Don't say anything, will you?" he asked, giving the girl's arm a gentle squeeze.

"Certainly not," she returned. "I wouldn't worry over it."

"All right," he said, passing on, seriously brooding for

once, and yet not wholly unconscious of the fact that he was making a most excellent impression upon the chambermaid.

"I'll see her about that," he said to himself passionately, feeling that he had been unduly wronged. "I'll find out, b' George, whether she'll act that way or not."

CHAPTER XXII.

To understand the power of Hurstwood's affection one must understand the man of the world. He was no longer young. He was no longer youthful in spirit, but he carried in his memory some old fancies which were of the day of his love time. His observation was keen, his affections lively. His love of the light of youth intense.

In Carrie he saw the embodiment of old experiences and old dreams. There was in her fresh cheeks something of the old garden of spring. He had loved—yes, long ago, and once in awhile there came a sense of the round moon that hung in a serene heaven of a May night, of odours that were sweet because wafted to nostrils young and sensitive, of rare feelings which came because love had loosened his mind and strengthened the springs of perception. In short he had been in love, and what feelings of that old time came back, cut as a knife and stung as a whip, for he feared—and oh, how keenly the man of exuberant passions ever fears—that the like might never come again.

And now, lo, it was come. In a fading, an almost desolate garden here, was sprung up a new flower. Eyes of soft radiance. Form of graceful, attractive lines, cheeks soft and colorful, hair that was pleasant to look upon—a lightsome step, a youthful fancy, a radiant fire of feeling as he had so recently seen. Here was something which was new, something which took him back.

When Carrie came he had been waiting many minutes. His blood was warm. His nerves wrought up. He was anxious to see the woman who had stirred him so profoundly the night before.

"Here you are," he said, repressedly, feeling a spring in his limbs and an elation which was tragic in itself.

"Yes," said Carrie.

They walked on as if bound for some objective point, while Hurstwood drank in the radiance of her presence. The rustle of her pretty skirt was like music to him.

"Are you satisfied?" he asked, thinking of how well she did the night before.

"Are you?"

He tightened his fingers as he saw the smile she gave him.

"You did splendidly," he answered, "fine."

Carrie laughed ecstatically.

"That was one of the best things I've seen in a long time," he added.

He was dwelling on her attractiveness as he had felt it the evening before and mingling it with the feeling her presence inspired now.

"I'm glad you liked it," she said affectedly.

"I did," he said, "I did."

Carrie was dwelling in the atmosphere which this man created for her. Already she was enlivened and suffused with a glow. His intense affection for her acted like wine. She felt his drawing toward her in every sound of his voice. There was more in the little looks and breathings than a volume could explain.

"Those were such nice flowers you sent me," she said, after a moment or two. "They were beautiful."

"Glad you liked them," he answered simply.

He was thinking all the time that the subject of his desire was being delayed. He was anxious to turn the talk to his own feelings. All was ripe for it. His Carrie was beside him. He wanted to plunge in and expostulate with her, and yet he found himself fishing for words and feeling for a way.

"You got home all right," he said gloomily of a sudden, his tone modifying itself to one of self-commiseration.

"Yes," said Carrie easily.

He looked at her steadily for a moment, slowing his pace and fixing her with his eye.

She felt the flood of feeling.

"How about me?" he asked.

This confused Carrie considerably, for she realized the flood gates were open. She didn't know exactly how *to* answer.

"I don't know," she answered.

He took his lower lip between his teeth for a moment and then let it go. He stopped by the walk side and kicked the grass with his toe. He searched her face with a tender, appealing glance.

"Don't you think you ought to?" he asked.

Carrie hesitated for want of understanding. She was realizing a difficult situation, without perceiving a way to modify it. She was between the falling back and the dragging forward of two things—she knew not what.

"Why don't you?" he asked after a time.

"Why don't I what?"

"Why don't you know?"

"Oh, I didn't know," she said helplessly.

He looked at her pretty face and new feeling came to him. It was a strong, deep wave such as rises and falls in the frame of every lover. He realized what a delight she would be to him, how she would console him for all the distresses and wearinesses of a complex home situation—how his life would be brightened if she were his own. Yet, he found also, as what lover has not, that he could not talk. There was no simple or involved way of making clear this intensity which he felt. He tightened his fibres as he sought what he thought he needed—expression.

"Won't you come away from him?" he said intensely, bearing down upon his left foot and looking aimlessly away.

"I don't know," returned Carrie, still illogically drifting and finding nothing to catch at.

As a matter of fact, she was in a most hopeless quandary. Here was a man whom she thoroughly liked, who exercised an influence over her sufficient almost to delude her into the belief that she was possessed of a lively passion for him. She was still the victim of his keen eyes, his suave manners, his fine clothes. She looked and saw before her a man who was most gracious and sympathetic, who leaned toward her with a feeling which it was a delight to observe. She could not resist the glow of his temperament, the light of his eye. She could hardly keep from feeling what he felt.

And yet she was not without thoughts which were disturbing. What did he know? What had Drouet told him? Was she a wife in his eyes, or what? Would he marry her? Even while he talked and she softened and her eyes were lighted with a tender glow, she was asking herself had Drouet told him they were not married. She was not at all sure whether he had or not. There was never anything at all convincing about what Drouet said.

And yet she was not grieved at Hurstwood's love. No strain of bitterness was in it, for her, whatever he knew. He was evidently sincere. His passion was real and warm. There was power in what he said. What would she do? She went on thinking this, answering vaguely, languishing affectionately, and altogether drifting illogically, until she was on a borderless sea of speculation.

"Why don't you come away," he said tenderly. "I will arrange for you whatever—"

"Oh don't," said Carrie.

"Don't what?" he asked. "What do you mean?"

There was a look of confusion and pain in her face. She was wondering why that miserable thought must be brought in. She was struck, as by a blade, with the miserable provision which was outside the pale of marriage.

He himself realized that it was a wretched thing to have dragged in. He wanted to weigh the effects of it, and yet he could not see. He went beating on, flushed by her presence, clearly awakened, intensely enlisted in his plan.

"Won't you come?" he said, beginning over and with a more reverent feeling. "You know I can't do without you—you know it—it can't go on this way—can it?"

"I know," said Carrie.

"I wouldn't ask if I—I wouldn't argue with you if I could help it. Look at me, Carrie. Put yourself in my place. You don't want to stay away from me do you?"

She shook her head, as if in deep thought.

"Then why not settle the whole thing, once and for all?"

"I don't know," said Carrie.

"Don't know! Ah, Carrie, what makes you say that? Don't torment me. Be serious."

"I am," said Carrie, softly.

"You can't be, dearest, and say that. Not when you know how I love you. Look at last night."

anner, as he said this, was the most quiet imaginable.
nd body retained utter composure. Only his eyes
d they flashed a subtle, dissolving fire. In them the
ensity of the man's nature was distilling itself.

ie made no answer.

ow can you act this way, dearest?" he inquired after a
You love me, don't you?"

He turned on her such a storm of soul feeling that she was
overwhelmed. For the moment all doubts were cleared away.

"Yes," she answered frankly and tenderly.

"Well then, you'll come, won't you?"

"I don't know whether I can or not," she answered, troubled by the old thought and her present situation. She was not
one to whom change was agreeable. She had not the shifting
and daring of an adventuress. She was too uncertain of herself,
too much afraid of the world. This man, while she liked him,
possessed qualities which awed her. She felt safer with the easy
Drouet, to whom she was used. She had got the hang of that
simple-souled individual's personality. She saw shades of its
weakness wherever she was strong. Moreover, she was fixed in
a comfortable apartment, where she could at least house herself
and speculate. How would it be somewhere else? She seemed
called upon to loosen her moorings, uncertain and unsatisfying
as they were, and drift somewhere else. She was being called to
come and could scarcely make answer.

"Last night," he said, "I was thinking—"

Then he stopped. His eyes were bent upon the ground.
The intensity of his affection touched her deeply.

"What?" she said softly, seeing that he did not continue.
In her voice was all the persuasion of one who denies with words
but makes evident by action what she feels.

"Nothing," he answered.

"Oh yes there was. What were you going to say?"

He went strolling on, desire for expression growing.

"What?" she said, tenderly.

"You," he said at last with repressed vehemence—"You—
I was thinking that I must have you. Don't you see where I
stand—how much I want you—"

The situation had been brought back to where it was before,

SISTER CARRIE · 207

only they were more warmly inclined to one another. Carrie was finding it more and more difficult to see him longing thus without offering the consolation which he so much desired. Her own quandary became less and less important. Her doubts were dissolving in the fire of his affection.

"Can't you wait awhile," she said, "until—"

Then she paused.

He also waited, hearing her every word with delight.

"What?" he said at last, finding that she could not go on.

"Until I see what I can do."

"What do you want to see about?" he asked eagerly.

"Oh—I don't know."

"There you go again," he said mournfully. "You don't want to see about anything."

"Yes I do," she answered.

"Well now, what?"

In the face of this direct question she could not make clear to herself what. She began to feel that she was, after all, merely playing at excuse and delay. The great fact which loomed up in the background, the huge solid reality he was asking her to abandon for the problematical, began to lose importance. She could not formulate the consideration she owed it. It had only the value of a gloomy certainty from which she might move away.

"What?" he repeated.

"You don't know how hard it is to decide right off," she said weakly. "I don't know just what to do. I'd like to think it over."

"You won't come, then," he said sadly.

"Oh yes I will," she answered with a sudden burst of feeling.

"When?"

"Well, pretty soon."

He was very close to her now, straining at her with all of his reserve affection and feeling. He took her hand tightly in his own.

"Tomorrow?" he asked.

"Oh no."

"You could if you wanted to."

"I couldn't get ready."

"Saturday?"

She looked intently into the future, her pretty lips slightly parted, her even teeth showing.

"Why not Saturday?" he asked, breathing a world of feeling into his tones.

"Can't you wait any longer?" she asked, a wave of feeling animating her body and coloring her cheeks. She was making manifest that affection ruled.

"No, no," he said, "I want you today."

She hesitated while he pressed his suit without word or action. His great desire was fighting for him without aid of word or deed.

"I might come then," she said slowly.

"Will you?" he said, bounding with joy. "Oh, that's great. Now you're my own Carrie," and he squeezed her hand passionately.

Almost instantly the reaction came. She had gone too far. Somehow she had bound herself to something. The problem of her marriage affected her. She troubled again to secure her rights as a good woman.

"When will we be married?" she asked diffidently, forgetting in her difficult situation that she had hoped he took her to be Drouet's wife.

The manager started, hit as he was by a problem which was more difficult than hers. He gave no sign of the thoughts that flashed like messages to his mind.

"Any time you say," he said with ease, refusing to discolor his present delight with this miserable problem.

"Saturday?" asked Carrie.

He nodded his head.

"Well, if you will marry me then," she said, "I'll go."

The manager looked at his lovely prize, so beautiful, so winsome, so difficult to be won, and resolved strange resolutions. His passion had gotten to that stage now where it was no longer colored with reason. He did not trouble over little barriers of this sort in the face of so much loveliness. He would accept the situation with all its difficulties—he would not try to answer the objections which cold truth thrust upon him. He would promise anything, everything, and trust to fortune to disentangle him.

He would make a try for Paradise, whatever might be the result. He would be happy, by the Lord, if it cost all honesty of statement, all abandonment of truth.

Carrie looked at him tenderly. She could have laid her head upon his shoulder, so delightful did he seem.

"Well," she said, "I'll try and get ready then."

Hurstwood looked into her pretty face, crossed with little shadows of wonder and misgiving, and thought he had never seen anything more lovely.

"I'll see you again tomorrow," he said joyously, "and we'll talk over the plans."

He walked on with her, elated beyond words, so delightful had been the result. He impressed a long story of joy and affection upon her, though there was but here and there a word. After a half-hour he began to realize that the meeting must come to an end, so exacting is the world.

"Tomorrow," he said at parting, a gayety of manner adding wonderfully to his brave demeanor.

"Yes," said Carrie, tripping elatedly away.

There had been so much enthusiasm engendered that she was believing herself deeply in love. She sighed as she thought of her handsome adorer. Yes, she would get ready by Saturday. She would go and they would be happy.

CHAPTER XXIII.

The misfortune of the Hurstwood household was due to the fact that jealousy, having been born of love, did not perish with it. Mrs. Hurstwood retained this in such form that subsequent influences could transform it into hate. Hurstwood was still worthy in a physical sense of the affection his wife had once bestowed upon him, but in a social sense he fell short. With his regard died his power to be attentive to her, and this, to a woman, is much greater than outright crime toward another. Our self-love dictates our appreciation of the good or evil in another. In Mrs. Hurstwood it discolored the very hue of her husband's indifferent nature. She saw design in deeds and phrases which sprung only from a faded appreciation of her presence.

As a consequence she was resentful and suspicious. The jealousy that prompted her to observe every falling away from the little amenities of the married relation, on his part, served to give her notice of the airy grace with which he still took the world. She could see from the scrupulous care which he exercised in the matter of his personal appearance that his interest in life had abated not a jot. No one could spruce about and exhibit so much interest in everything which pertained to himself without awakening a feeling in the close observer that the world still contained many a prize worth struggling for. Indeed no one who had as much to enlist his sympathies, as did Hurstwood at present, could possibly conceal the feelings he felt, providing the observer was sensitive to atmospheres. Every motion, every glance, had something in it of the pleasure he felt in Carrie, of the zest this new pursuit of pleasure lent to his days. He was too much the lover and consequently too sensitive of his graces and Chesterfieldian arts not to make some sign in his own home. Such oil could not forever be unmixed in such water and not be observed—or at least felt. He brought a world of thought and color into the house which did not belong there, and, as a consequence, it attracted observation, if not detection. Mrs. Hurstwood felt something, she knew not what, sniffing change as animals do danger, afar off.

This feeling was strengthened by actions of a direct and more potent nature on the part of Hurstwood. We have seen with what irritation he shirked those little duties which no longer contained any amusement or satisfaction for him, and open snarls with which, more recently, he resented her irritating goads. These little rows were really precipitated by an atmosphere which was surcharged with dissension. That it should shower with a sky so full of blackening thunder-clouds would scarcely be thought worthy of comment. Thus, after leaving the breakfast table this morning, raging inwardly at his blank declaration of indifference to her plans, Mrs. Hurstwood encountered Jessica in her dressing room, very leisurely arranging her hair. Hurstwood had already left the house.

"I wish you wouldn't be so late coming down to breakfast,"

she said, addressing Jessica, while making for her crochet basket. "Now here the things are quite cold and you haven't eaten."

Her natural composure was sadly ruffled, and Jessica was doomed to feel the fag end of the storm.

"I'm not hungry," she answered.

"Then why don't you say so and let the girl put away the things—instead of keeping her waiting all morning."

"She doesn't mind," answered Jessica coolly.

"Well I do, if she doesn't," returned her mother, "and anyhow I don't like you to talk that way to me. You're too young to put on such an air with your mother."

"Oh, Mamma, don't row," answered Jessica. "What's the matter this morning, anyway?"

"Nothing's the matter and I'm not rowing. You mustn't think because I indulge you in some things that you can keep everybody waiting. I won't have it."

"I'm not keeping anybody waiting," returned Jessica sharply, stirred out of a cynical indifference to a sharp defence. "I said I wasn't hungry. I don't want any breakfast."

"Mind how you address me, missy. I'll not have it. Hear me now, I'll not have it."

Jessica heard this last while walking out of the room, with a toss of her head and a flick of her pretty skirts, indicative of the independence and indifference she felt. She did not propose to be quarreled with.

Such little arguments were all too frequent, the result of the growth of natures which were largely independent and selfish. George Jr. manifested even greater touchiness and exaggeration in the matter of his individual rights and attempted to make all feel that he was a man with a man's privileges—an assumption which of all things is most groundless and pointless in the youth of nineteen.

Hurstwood was a man of authority and some fine feeling, and it irritated him excessively to find himself surrounded more and more by a world upon which he had no hold and of which he had a lessening understanding. He could not brook this air of secretiveness and planning without his interest. He could not help noting that things were going on very effectually without him. This was a grievous thing, in as much as it was his desire to retain all the prestige he had ever held, while at the same time devoting himself to other and more agreeable affairs. In short, he wished to eat his cake and have it too.

Now when little things, such as the proposed earlier start to Waukesha, came up, they made clear to him his position. He was being made to follow—was not leading. When, in addition, a sharp temper was manifested, and to the process of shouldering him out of his authority was added a rousing intellectual kick such as a sneer or a cynical laugh, he was unable to keep his temper. He flew into hardly repressed passion and wished himself clear of the whole household. It seemed a most irritating drag upon all his desires and opportunities.

For all this he still retained the semblance of leadership and control, even though his wife was straining to revolt. Her display of temper and open assertion of opposition were based upon nothing more than the feeling that she could do it. She had no special evidence wherewith to justify herself—the knowledge of something which would give her both authority and excuse. The latter was all that was lacking, however, to give a solid foundation to what in a way seemed groundless discontent. The clear proof of one overt deed was the cold breath needed to convert the lowering clouds of suspicion into a rain of wrath.

An inkling of untoward deeds on the part of Hurstwood had come sometime before the occasion of the last quarrel in the shape of a social encounter. Dr. Beale, the handsome resident physician of the neighborhood, had met Mrs. Hurstwood at her own doorstep two days after Hurstwood and Carrie had taken the drive west on Washington Street which resulted in their acknowledging a mutual attachment. Dr. Beale, coming east on the same drive, had recognized Hurstwood, but not before he was quite past him. He was not so sure of Carrie—did not know whether it was Hurstwood's wife or daughter.

"You don't speak to your friends when you meet them out driving, do you?" he said jocosely to Mrs. Hurstwood.

"If I see them I do. Where was I?"

"On Washington Street," he answered, expecting her eye to light with immediate remembrance.

She shook her head.

"Yes, out near Hayne Avenue. You were with your husband."

"I guess you're mistaken," she answered. Then remembering her husband's part in the affair, she immediately fell prey to a host of young suspicions, of which, however, she gave no sign.

"I know I saw your husband," he went on. "I wasn't so sure about you. Perhaps it was your daughter."

"Perhaps it was," said Mrs. Hurstwood, knowing full well that such was not the case, as Jessica had been her companion for weeks. She had recovered herself sufficiently to wish to know more of the details.

"Was it the afternoon?" she asked artfully, assuming an air of acquaintanceship with the matter.

"Yes, about two or three."

"It must have been Jessica," said Mrs. Hurstwood, not wishing to seem to attach any importance to the incident.

The physician had a thought or two of his own, but dismissed the matter as worthy of no further discussion, on his part at least.

Mrs. Hurstwood gave this bit of information considerable thought during the next few hours and even days. She took it for granted that the doctor had really seen her husband and that he had been riding, most likely with some other woman, after announcing himself as *busy* to her. As a consequence she recalled with rising feeling how often he had refused to go places with her, to share in little visits or, indeed, take part in any of the social amenities which furnished the diversion of her existence. He had been seen at the theatre with people whom he called Hogg's friends; now he was seen driving, and most likely would have an excuse for that. Perhaps there were others she did not hear of, or why should he be so busy, so indifferent of late? In the last six weeks he had become strangely irritable—strangely satisfied to pick up and go out, whether things were right or wrong in the house—why?

She recalled, with more subtle emotions, that he did not look at her now with any of the old light of satisfaction or approval in his eye. Evidently, along with other things, he was taking her to be getting old and uninteresting. He saw her wrinkles perhaps. She was fading while he was still preening himself in his elegance and youth. He was still an interested factor in the merry makings of the world while she— but she did not pursue the thought. She only found the whole situation bitter and hated him for it thoroughly.

Nothing came of this incident at the time, for the truth is, it did not seem conclusive enough to warrant any discussion. Only the atmosphere of distrust and ill-feeling was strengthened, precipitating, every now and then, little sprinklings of irritable conversation, enlivened by flashes of wrath. The matter of the Waukesha outing was merely a continuation of other things of the same nature.

The day after Carrie's appearance on the Avery stage, Mrs. Hurstwood visited the races with Jessica and a youth of her acquaintance, Mr. Bart Taylor, the son of the owner of a local house-furnishings establishment. They had driven out early, and as it chanced, encountered several friends of Hurstwood, all Elks, and two of whom had attended the performance the evening before. A thousand chances the subject of the performance had never been brought up, had Jessica not been so engaged by the attentions of her young companion who usurped as much time as possible. This left Mrs. Hurstwood in the mood to extend the perfunctory greetings of some who knew her into short conversations, and the short conversations of friends into long ones. It was from one who meant but to greet her perfunctorily that the interesting intelligence came.

"I see," said this individual, who wore sporting clothes of the most attractive pattern, and had a field glass strung over his shoulder, "that you did not get over to our little entertainment last evening."

"No?" said Mrs. Hurstwood inquiringly, and wondering why he should be using the tone he did in noting the fact that she had not been to something she did not know anything about. It was on her lips to say, "What was it?" when he added, "I saw your husband."

Her wonder was at once replaced by the more subtle quality of suspicion.

"Yes," she said cautiously. "Was it pleasant—he did not tell me much about it."

"Very—really one of the best private theatricals I ever attended. There was one actress who surprised us all."

"Indeed," said Mrs. Hurstwood.

"It's too bad you couldn't have been there, really. I was sorry to hear you weren't feeling well."

Feeling well. Mrs. Hurstwood could have echoed the words

after him open-mouthed. As it was, she extricated herself from her mingled impulse to deny and question and said, almost raspingly:

"Yes, it is too bad."

"Looks like there will be quite a crowd here today, doesn't it?" the aquaintance observed, drifting off upon another topic.

The manager's wife would have questioned further but she saw no opportunity. She was for the moment wholly at sea, anxious to think for herself and wondering what new deception was this which would cause him to give out that she was ill when she was not. Another case of her company not wanted and excuses being made. She resolved to find out more.

"Were you at the performance last evening?" she asked of the next of Hurstwood's friends who greeted her, as she sat in her box.

"Yes. You didn't get around?"

"No," she answered. "I was not feeling very well."

"So your husband told me," he answered. "Well, it was really very enjoyable. Turned out much better than I expected."

"Were there many there?"

"The house was full. It was quite an Elk night. I saw quite a number of your friends—Mrs. Harrison, Mrs. Barnes, Mrs. Collins."

"Quite a social gathering."

"Indeed it was. My wife enjoyed it very much."

Mrs. Hurstwood bit her lip.

"So," she thought, "that's the way he does. Tells my friends I am sick and cannot come."

She wondered what could induce him to go alone. There was something back of this. She rummaged her brain for a reason.

By evening when Hurstwood reached home she had brooded herself into a state of sullen desire for explanation and revenge. She wanted to know what this peculiar action of his imported. She was certain there was more behind it all than what she had heard, and evil curiosity mingled well with distrust and the remnants of her wrath of the morning. She, impending disaster itself, walked about with gathered shadow at the eyes and the rudimentary muscles of savagery fixing the hard lines of her mouth.

On the other hand, as we may well believe, the manager came home in the sunniest mood. His conversation and agreement with Carrie had raised his spirits until he was in the frame of mind of one who sings joyously. He was proud of himself, proud of his success, proud of Carrie. He could have been genial to all the world, and he bore no grudge against his wife. He meant to be pleasant, to forget her presence, to live in the atmosphere of youth and pleasure which had been restored to him. His entrance had something of that feeling about it, but it did not last long.

If we think of the approach of a thunderstorm we shall get a very good impression of the Hurstwood household at this stage of the game—the thunderstorm that rolls up at even on a warm, halcyon summer's day. At such times, though the atmosphere be heavily charged with electricity and the air ominously still, there is nothing disagreeable about it. It does not come like the sinking, enveloping fog of the sea to lower both the temperature and the spirits. Rather, its approach enlivens the nervous system, makes wires of the muscles and plays upon the whole body such a symphony of activity as to stir the blood and create pleasurable feeling. Even after it has broken, when in the midst of the clatter and crash, the flare of flame, the long peals of thunder, the puffs of wind and capfuls of rain, one stands bewildered but not wretched. Even then it does not depress the spirits, like the long dreary drizzle of foul weather, but sets us jumping and wondering, keenly awakened to sound and murmur, but lively and enspirited as one should be who is involved in tumult and disorder.

So here, when he entered, the house to his mind had a most pleasing and comfortable appearance. In the hall he found an evening paper, laid there by the maid and forgotten by Mrs. Hurstwood. In the dining room was the table, clean-laid with linen and napery and shiny with glasses and pink-flowered china. Through an open door he saw into the kitchen where the fire was crackling in the stove and the evening meal already well under way. Out in the small back yard was George Jr., frolicking with a young dog he recently purchased, and in the parlor Jessica playing at the piano, the sounds of a merry waltz filling every nook and corner of the comfortable house. Everyone, like himself, seemed to have regained his good spirits, to be in sympathy with youth and beauty, to be inclined to joy and merrymaking. He felt as if he could say a good word to all around himself, and took a most genial glance at the spread table and polished sideboard before going upstairs to read his paper in the comfortable arm chair of the sitting-room which looked through the open windows into the street. When he entered there, however, he found his wife, brushing her hair and musing to herself the while.

He came lightly in, thinking to smooth over any feeling that might still exist by a kindly word and a ready promise, but Mrs. Hurstwood said nothing. He seated himself in the large chair, stirred lightly in making himself comfortable, opened his paper and began to read. In a few moments he was smiling merrily over a very comical account of a baseball game which had taken place between the Chicago and Detroit teams.

The while he was doing this, Mrs. Hurstwood was observing him casually through the medium of the mirror which was before her. She noticed his pleasant and contented manner, his airy grace and smiling humor, and it merely aggravated her the more. She wondered how he could think to carry himself so in her presence after the cynicism, indifference and neglect he had heretofore manifested and would continue to manifest so long as she should endure it. She thought how she should like to tell him—what stress and emphasis she would lend her assertions, how she should drive over this whole affair until satisfaction should be rendered her. Indeed, the shining sword of her wrath was but weakly suspended by a thread of thought.

In the meanwhile Hurstwood encountered a humorous item concerning a stranger who had arrived in the city and become entangled with a bunko-steerer. It amused him immensely and at last he stirred and chuckled to himself. He wished that he might enlist his wife's attention and read it to her.

"Ha, ha," he exclaimed softly, as if to himself, "that's funny."

Mrs. Hurstwood kept on arranging her hair, not so much as deigning a glance.

He stirred again and went on to another subject. At last he felt as if his good humor must find some outlet. Julia was probably still out of humor over that affair of this morning, but that could easily be straightened. As a matter of fact she was in the wrong, but he didn't care. She could go to Waukesha, right away if she wanted to. The sooner the better. He would tell her that as soon as he got a chance, and the whole thing would blow over.

"Did you notice," he said at last, breaking forth concerning another item which he had found, "that they have entered suit to compel the Illinois Central to get off the lake front, Julia?" he asked.

She could scarcely force herself to answer, but managed to say "no" sharply.

Hurstwood pricked up his ears. There was a note in her voice which vibrated keenly.

"It would be a good thing if they did," he went on, half to himself, half to her, though he felt that something was amiss in that quarter. He withdrew his attention to his paper very circumspectly, listening mentally for the little sounds which should show him what was on foot.

As a matter of fact, no man as clever as Hurstwood—as keenly observant and sensitive to atmospheres of many sorts, particularly upon his own plane of thought, would have made the mistake which he did in regard to his wife, wrought up as she was, had he not been occupied mentally with a very different train of thought. Had not the influence of Carrie's regard for him, the elation which her promise aroused in him, lasted over, he would not have seen the house in so pleasant a mood. It was not extraordinarily bright and merry this evening. He was merely very much mistaken and would have been much more fitted to cope with it had he come home in his normal state.

After he had studied his paper a few moments longer, he felt that he ought to modify matters in some way or other. Evidently his wife was not going to patch up peace at a word. So he said:—

"Where did George get the dog he has there in the yard?"

"I don't know," she snapped.

He put his paper down on his knees and gazed idly out the window. He did not propose to lose his temper, but merely to be persistent and agreeable and by a few questions bring around a mild understanding of some sort.

"Why do you feel so bad about that affair of this morning?" he said at last. "We needn't quarrel about that. You know you can go to Waukesha if you want to."

"So you can stay here and trifle around with someone else?" she exclaimed, turning to him a determined countenance upon which was drawn a sharp and wrathful sneer.

He stopped as if slapped in the face. In an instant his persuasive, conciliatory manner fled. He was on the defensive at a wink and puzzled for a word to reply.

"What do you mean?" he said at last, straightening himself and gazing at the cold, determined figure before him, who paid no attention, but went on arranging herself before the mirror.

"You know what I mean," she said finally, as if there were a world of information which she held in reserve—which she did not need to tell.

"Well, I don't," he said stubbornly, yet nervous and on the *qui vive* for what should come next. The finality of the woman's manner took away his feeling of superiority in battle.

She made no answer.

"Humph!" he murmured, with a movement of his head to one side. It was the weakest thing he had ever done. It was totally unassured.

Mrs. Hurstwood noticed the lack of color in it. She turned upon him animal-like, able to strike an effectual second blow.

"I want the Waukesha money tomorrow morning," she said.

He looked at her in amazement. Never before had he seen such cold, steely determination in her eye—such a cruel look of indifference. She seemed a thorough master of her mood—thoroughly confident and determined to wrest all control from him. He felt that all his resources could not defend him. He must attack.

"What do you mean?" he said, jumping up. "*You* want! I'd like to know what's got into you tonight."

"Nothing *got* into me," she said, flaming. "I want that money. You can do your swaggering afterwards."

"Swaggering, eh! What! You'll get nothing from me. What do you mean by your insinuations anyhow?"

"Where were you last night," she answered. The words were hot as they came. "Who were you driving with on Washington Street? Who were you with at the theatre when George saw you? Do you think I'm a fool to be duped by you? Do you think I'll sit at home here and take your 'too busy's' and 'can't come's' while you parade around and make out that I'm unable to come? I want you to know that lordly airs have come to an end so far as I am concerned. You can't dictate to me nor my children. I'm through with you entirely."

"It's a lie," he said, driven to a corner and knowing no other excuse.

"Lie, eh," she said fiercely but with returning reserve. "You may call it a lie if you want to, but I know."

"It's a lie, I tell you," he said in a low sharp voice. "You've been searching around for some cheap accusation for months and now you think you have it. You think you'll spring something and get the upper hand. Well I tell you, by God, you can't. As long as I'm in this house I'm master of it and you nor any one else will dictate to me—do you hear?"

He crept towards her with a light in his eye that was ominous. Something in the woman's cool, cynical, upperhandish manner, as if she were already master, caused him to feel for the moment as if he could strangle her.

She gazed at him—a pythoness in humor.

"I'm not dictating to you," she returned. "I'm telling you what I want."

The answer was so cool, so rich in bravado, that somehow it took the wind out of his sails. He could not attack her; he could not ask her for proofs. Somehow he felt evidence, law, the remembrance of all his property which she held in her name, to be shining in her glance. He was like a vessel, powerful and dangerous, but rolling and floundering without sail.

"And I'm telling you," he said in the end, slightly recovering himself, "what you'll not get."

"We'll see about it," she said. "I'll find out what my rights are. Perhaps you'll talk to a lawyer if you won't to me."

It was a magnificent play and had its effect. Hurstwood fell back beaten. He knew now that he had more than mere bluff to contend with. He felt that he was face to face with a dull proposition. What to say he hardly knew. All the merriment had gone out of the day. He was disturbed, wretched, resentful. What should he do?

"Do as you damn please," he said at last. "I'll have nothing more to do with you," and out he strode.

CHAPTER XXIV.

When Carrie reached her own room she had already fallen a prey to those doubts and misgivings which are ever the result of a lack of decision. She could not persuade herself as to the advisability of her promise, or that now, having given her word, she ought to keep it. She went over the whole ground in Hurstwood's absence, and discovered little objections which had not occurred to her in the warmth of the manager's argument. She saw where she had put herself in a peculiar light—namely, that of agreeing to marry, when she was already supposedly married and without giving time for divorce. She remembered a few things Drouet had done, and now that it came to walking away from him without a word, she felt as if she were doing wrong. More, she was comfortably situated, and to one who is more or less afraid of the world, this is an urgent matter and one which puts up strange, uncanny arguments. "You do not know what will come. There are miserable things outside. People go a-begging. Women are wretched. You never can tell what will happen. Remember the time you were hungry. Stick to what you have."

Curiously, for all her leaning towards Hurstwood, he had not taken a firm hold on her understanding. She was listening, smiling, approving, and yet not finally agreeing. This was due to a lack of power on Hurstwood's part, a lack of that majesty of passion that sweeps the mind from its seat, fuses and melts all arguments and theories into a tangled mass and destroys, for the time being, the reasoning power. This majesty of passion is possessed by nearly every man once in his life, but it is usually an attribute of youth and conduces to the first successful mating.

Hurstwood, being an older man, could scarcely be said to retain the fire of youth, though he did possess a passion warm and unreasoning. It was strong enough to induce the leaning toward him, which, on Carrie's part, we have seen. She might have been said to be imagining herself in love when she was not. Women frequently do this. It flows from the fact that in each exists a bias toward affection, a craving for the pleasure of being loved. The longing to be shielded, bettered, sympathized with, is one of the attributes of the sex. This, coupled with sentiment and a natural tendency to emotion, often makes refusing difficult. It persuades them that they are in love. The more so is this true since we know that the passions are the only advocates which invariably persuade.

Like all women Carrie hearkened tenderly to those things which wished her joy. She was most readily inflamed with the feelings of another, for her nature was tender and sympathetic. Thus Hurstwood, himself powerfully imbued with his affection for her, was able in the flower of his fancy, and while she was with him, to make her feel that she was really in love. Away from him she was not so certain. This unfortunate predicament was the cause of her present distress.

Once at home she changed her clothes and straightened the rooms for herself. In the matter of the arrangement of the furniture, she never took the housemaid's opinion. That young lady invariably put one of the rocking chairs in the corner, and Carrie as regularly moved it out. Today she hardly noticed that it was in the wrong place, so absorbed was she in her own thoughts. Still she kept working about until Drouet put in an appearance at five o'clock. The drummer was flushed and excited, and full of great resolve to know all about her relations with Hurstwood. He had taken several drinks and was warm for his purpose. Nevertheless, after going over the subject in his mind the live-long day, he was rather weary of it and wished it over with. He did not foresee serious consequences of any sort, and yet he rather hesitated to begin. Carrie was sitting by the window when he came in, rocking and looking out.

"Well," she said innocently, weary of her own mental discussion and wondering at his haste and ill-concealed excitement, "what makes you hurry so?"

Drouet hesitated, now that he was in her presence, uncertain as to what course to pursue. He was no diplomat. He could neither read nor see.

"When did you get home?" he asked foolishly.

"Oh, an hour or so ago: what makes you ask that?"

"You weren't here," he said, "when I came back this morning, and I thought you had gone out."

"So I did," said Carrie simply. "I went for a walk."

Drouet looked at her wonderingly. For all his lack of dignity in such matters, he did not know how to begin. He stared at her in the most flagrant manner until at last she asked:—

"What makes you stare at me so,—what's the matter?"

"Nothing," he answered. "I was just thinking."

"Just thinking what?" she returned smilingly, puzzled by his attitude.

"Oh, nothing—nothing much."

"Well then, what makes you look so?"

Drouet was standing by the dresser, gazing at her in a comic manner. He had laid off his hat and gloves and was now fidgeting with the little table pieces which were nearest him. He hesitated to believe that the pretty woman before him was involved in anything so unsatisfactory to himself. He was very much inclined to feel that it was all right after all. Yet the knowledge imparted to him by the chambermaid was rankling in his mind. He wanted to plunge in with a straight remark of some sort, but he knew not what.

"Where did you go this morning?" he finally asked, weakly.

"Why, I went for a walk," said Carrie.

"Sure you did?" he asked.

"Yes, what makes you ask?"

She was beginning to see by now that something which she had not anticipated was the matter. He knew something.

Instantly she drew herself into a more reserved position. Her cheeks blanched slightly.

"I thought maybe you didn't," he said, beating about the bush in the most useless manner.

Carrie gazed at him and as she did so her ebbing courage halted. She saw that he himself was hesitating and with a woman's intuition realized that there was no occasion for great alarm.

"What makes you talk like that?" she asked, wrinkling her pretty forehead. "You act so funny tonight."

"I feel funny," he answered.

They looked at one another for a moment and then Drouet plunged desperately into his subject.

"What's this about you and Hurstwood?" he asked.

"Me and Hurstwood, what do you mean?"

"Didn't he come here a dozen times while I was away?"

"A dozen times," repeated Carrie guiltily. "No, but what do you mean?"

"Somebody said that you went out riding with him and that he came here every night."

"No such thing," answered Carrie—"It isn't true—who told you that?"

She was flushing scarlet to the roots of her hair, but Drouet did not catch the full hue of her face owing to the modified light of the room. He was regaining much confidence as Carrie defended herself with denials.

"Well, someone," he said. "You're sure you didn't?"

"Certainly," said Carrie. "You know how often he came."

Drouet paused for a moment and thought.

"I know what you told me," he said finally.

He fumbled his watch charm while Carrie looked at him confusedly.

"Well, I know that I didn't tell you any such thing as that," said Carrie, recovering herself.

"If I were you," went on Drouet, ignoring her last remark, "I wouldn't have anything to do with him. He's a married man, you know."

"Who—who is?" said Carrie, stumbling at the word.

"Why, Hurstwood," said Drouet, noting the effect and feeling that he was delivering a telling blow.

"Hurstwood!" exclaimed Carrie, rising. Her face had changed several shades since this announcement was made. She looked within and without herself in a half-dazed way.

"Who told you this?" she asked, forgetting that her interest was out of order and exceedingly incriminating.

"Why, I know it. I've always known it," said Drouet.

Carrie was feeling about for a right thought. She was making a most miserable showing and yet feelings were generating within her which were anything but crumbling cowardice.

"I thought I told you," he added.

"No you didn't," she contradicted, suddenly recovering her voice. "You didn't do anything of the kind."

Drouet listened to her in astonishment. This was something new.

"I thought I did," he said.

Carrie looked around her, very solemnly, and then went over to the window.

"You oughtn't to have had anything to do with him," said Drouet in an injured tone, "after all I've done for you."

"You," said Carrie—"you—what have *you* done for me?"

Her little brain had been surging with contradictory feelings—shame at exposure, shame at Hurstwood's perfidy, anger at Drouet's deception—the mockery he had made of her. Now one clear idea came into her head. He was at fault. There was no doubt about it. Why did he bring Hurstwood out—Hurstwood, a married man, and never say a word to her. Never mind now about Hurstwood's perfidy—why had he done this? Why hadn't he warned her? There he stood now, guilty of this miserable breach of confidence and talking about what he had done for her.

"Well I like that!" exclaimed Drouet, little realizing the fire his remark had generated—"I think I've done a good deal."

"You have, eh?" she answered. "You've lied to me—that's what you've done. You've brought your old friends out here under false pretences. You've made me out to be—oh," and with this her voice broke and she pressed her two little hands together tragically.

"I don't see what that's got to do with it," said the drummer quaintly.

"No," she answered, recovering herself and shutting her little teeth. "No, of course you don't see. There isn't anything you see. You couldn't have told me in the first place, could you? You had to make me out wrong until it was too late. Now you come sneaking around with your information and your talk about what you've done."

Drouet had never suspected this side of Carrie's nature. She was alive with feeling, her eyes snapping, her lips quivering, her whole body sensible of the injury she felt and partaking of her wrath.

"Who's sneaking?" he asked, mildly conscious of error on his part but certain that he was wronged.

"You are," stamped Carrie. "You're a big conceited braggart, that's what you are. If you had any sense of manhood you wouldn't have thought of doing any such thing."

The drummer stared.

"I'm not conceited," he said. "What do you mean by going with other men anyway?"

"Other men!" exclaimed Carrie. "Other men—you know better than that. I did go with Mr. Hurstwood, but whose fault was it? Didn't you bring him here? You told him yourself that he should come out here and take me out. Now after it's all over you come and tell me that I oughtn't to go with him and that he's a married man."

She paused at the sound of the last two words and wrung her hands. The knowledge of Hurstwood's perfidy wounded her like a knife.

"Oh," she sobbed, repressing herself wonderfully and keeping her eyes dry. "Oh, oh!"

"Well, I didn't think you'd be running around with him when I was away," insisted Drouet.

"Didn't think!" said Carrie, now angered to the core by the man's peculiar attitude. "Of course not. You thought only of what would be to your satisfaction. You thought you'd make a toy of me. Well, I'll show you that you won't. I'll have nothing more to do with you at all. You can take your old things and keep them," and unfastening a little pin which he had given her from her throat, she flung it vigorously upon the floor and began to move about as if to gather the things which belonged to her.

By this Drouet was not only irritated but fascinated the more. He looked at her in amazement and finally said:—

"I don't see where your wrath comes in. I've got the right of this thing. You oughtn't to have done anything that wasn't right after all I did for you."

"What have you done for me?" asked Carrie, blazing, her head thrown back and her lips parted.

"I think I've done a good deal," said the drummer looking around. "I've given you all the clothes you wanted, haven't I?

I've taken you everywhere you wanted to go. You've had as much as I've had and more too."

Carrie was not ungrateful, whatever else might be said of her. In so far as her mind could construe, she acknowledged benefits received. She hardly knew how to answer this, and yet her wrath was not placated. She felt that the drummer had injured her irreparably.

"Did I ask you to?" she returned.

"Well, I did it," said Drouet, "and you took it."

"You talk as though I had persuaded you," answered Carrie. "You stand there and throw up what you've done. I don't want your old things. I'll not have them. You take them tonight and do what you please with them. I'll not stay here another minute."

"That's nice!" he answered, becoming angered now at the sense of his own approaching loss. "Use everything and abuse me and then walk off. That's just like a woman. I take you when you haven't got anything, and then when someone else comes along, why, I'm no good. I always thought it would come out that way."

He felt really very sad as he thought of his treatment and looked as if he saw no way of obtaining justice.

"It's not so," said Carrie, "and I'm not going with anybody else. You've been as miserable and inconsiderate as you can be. I hate you, I tell you, and I wouldn't live with you another minute. You're a big, insulting," here she hesitated and used no word at all—"or you wouldn't talk that way."

She had secured her hat and jacket and slipped the latter on over her little evening dress. Some wisps of wavy hair had loosened from the bands at the side of her head, and were straggling over her hot, red cheeks. She was angry, mortified, grief-stricken. Her large eyes were full of the anguish of tears, but her lids were not yet wet. She was distracted and uncertain, deciding and doing things without aim or conclusion, and she had not the slightest conception of how the whole difficulty would end.

"Well that's a fine finish," said Drouet. "Pack up and pull out, eh! You take the cake. I bet you were knocking around with Hurstwood or you wouldn't act like that. I don't want the old rooms. You needn't pull out for me. You can have 'em for all I care, but, b'George! you haven't done me right."

"I'll not live with you," said Carrie. "I don't want to live with you. You've done nothing but brag around ever since you've been here."

"Aw, I haven't anything of the kind," he answered.

Carrie walked over to the door.

"Where're you going?" he said, stepping over and heading her off.

"Let me out," she said.

"Where are you going?" he repeated.

He was, above all, sympathetic, and the sight of Carrie wandering out, he knew not where, affected him, despite his grievance.

Carrie merely pulled at the door.

The strain of the situation was too much for her, however. She made one more vain effort and then burst into tears.

"Now be reasonable, Cad," said Drouet gently. "What do you want to rush out for this way? You haven't any place to go. Why not stay here now and be quiet. I'll not bother you. I don't want to stay here any longer."

Carrie had gone sobbing from the door to the window. She was so overcome that she could not speak.

"Be reasonable now," he said. "I don't want to hold you. You can go if you want to, but why don't you think it over. Lord knows, I don't want to stop you."

He received no answer. Carrie was quieting, however, under the influence of his plea.

"You stay here now and I'll go," he added at last.

Carrie listened to this with mingled feelings. Her mind was shaken loose from the little mooring of logic that it had. She was stirred by this thought, angered by that—her own injustice, Hurstwood's, Drouet's, their respective qualities of kindness and favor, the threat of the world outside in which she had failed once before, the impossibility of this state inside, where the chambers were no longer justly hers—the effect of the argument upon her nerves, all combined to make her a mass of jangling fibres—an anchorless, storm-beaten little craft which could do absolutely nothing but drift.

"Say," said Drouet, coming over to her after a few moments, with a new idea, and putting his hand upon her.

"Don't," said Carrie, drawing away, but not removing her handkerchief from her eyes.

"Never mind about this quarrel now. Let it go. You stay here until the month's out anyhow, and then you can tell better what you want to do. Eh?"

Carrie made no answer.

"You better do that," he said. "There's no use your packing up now. You can't go anywhere."

Still he got nothing for his words.

"If you'll do that we'll call it off for the present, and I'll get out."

Carrie lowered her handkerchief slightly and looked out of the window.

"Will you do that?" he asked.

Still no answer.

"Will you?" he repeated.

She only looked vaguely into the street.

"Aw! come on," he said, "tell me. Will you?"

"I don't know," said Carrie softly, forced to answer.

"Promise me you'll do that," he said, "and we'll quit talking about it. It'll be the best thing for you."

Carrie heard him but she could not bring herself to answer reasonably. She felt that the man was gentle and that his interest in her had not abated, and it made her suffer a pang of regret. She was in a most hopeless plight.

As for Drouet, his attitude had been that of the jealous lover. Now his feelings were a mixture of anger at deception, sorrow at losing Carrie, misery at being defeated. He wanted his rights in some way or other, and yet his rights included the retaining of Carrie, the making her feel her error.

"Will you?" he urged.

"Well, I'll see," said Carrie.

This left the matter as open as before, but it was something. It looked as if the quarrel would blow over, if they could only get some way of talking to one another. Carrie was ashamed and Drouet aggrieved. He pretended to take up the task of packing some things in a valise.

Now as Carrie watched him, out of the corner of her eye, certain sound thoughts came into her head. He had erred—true, but what had she done? He was kindly and good-natured, for all his egotism. Throughout this argument he had said nothing very harsh. On the other hand there was Hurstwood—a greater deceiver than he. He had pretended all this affection, all this passion, and he was lying to her all the while. Oh, the perfidy of men! And she had loved him. There could be nothing more in that quarter. She would see Hurstwood no more. She would write him and let him know what she thought. Thereupon, what would she do? Here were these rooms. Here was Drouet, pleading for her to remain. Evidently things could go on here, somewhat as before, if all were arranged. It would be better than the street without a place to lay her head.

All this she thought of as Drouet rummaged the drawers for collars, and labored long and painstakingly at finding a shirt stud. He was in no hurry to rush this matter. He felt an attraction by Carrie which would not down. He could not think that the thing would end by his walking out of the room. There must be some way round, some way to make her own up that he was right and she was wrong—to patch up a peace and shut out Hurstwood forever. Mercy, how he turned at the man's shameless duplicity.

"Do you think," he said, after a few moments' silence, "that you'll try and get on the stage?"

He was wondering what she was intending.

"I don't know what I'll do yet," said Carrie.

"If you do, maybe I can help you—I've got a lot of friends in that line."

She made no answer to this.

"Don't go and try to knock around now without money. Let me help you," he said. "It's no easy thing to go on your own hook here."

Carrie only rocked back and forth in her chair.

"I don't want you to go up against a hard game that way."

He bestirred himself about some other details and Carrie rocked on.

"Why don't you tell me all about this thing," he said, after a time, "and let's call it off. You don't really care for Hurstwood, do you?"

"What do you want to start on that for again?" said Carrie. "You were to blame."

"No, I wasn't," he answered.

"Yes, you were too," said Carrie. "You shouldn't have ever told me such a story as that."

"But you didn't have much to do with him, did you?" went on Drouet, anxious for his own peace of mind to get some direct denial from her.

"I won't talk about it," said Carrie, pained at the quizzical turn the peace arrangement had taken.

"What's the use of acting like that now, Cad?" insisted the drummer, stopping in his work and putting up a hand expressively. "You might let me know where I stand at least."

"I won't," said Carrie, feeling no refuge but in anger. "Whatever has happened is your own fault."

"Then you do care for him," said Drouet, stopping completely and experiencing a rush of feeling.

"Oh, stop," said Carrie.

"Well I'll not be made a fool of!" exclaimed Drouet. "You may trifle around with him if you want to, but you can't lead me. You can tell me or not just as you want to, but I won't fool any longer."

He shoved the last few remaining things he had laid out into his valise and snapped it with a vengeance. Then he grabbed his coat, which he had laid off to work, picked up his gloves and started out.

"You can go to the deuce as far as I am concerned," he said as he reached the door—"I'm no sucker." And with that he opened it with a jerk and closed it equally vigorously.

Carrie listened at her window view, more astonished than anything else at this sudden rise of passion in the drummer. She could hardly believe her senses, so good-natured and tractable had he invariably been. It was not for her to see the wellspring of human passion. A real flame of love is a subtle thing. It burns as a will-o'-the-wisp, dancing onward to fairy lands of delight. It roars as a furnace. Too often jealousy is the quality upon which it feeds.

CHAPTER XXV.

That night Hurstwood remained downtown entirely, going to the Palmer House for a bed after his work was through. He was in a fevered state of mind, owing to the blight his wife's action threatened to cast upon his entire fortune. While he was not sure how much significance might be attached to the threat she had made, he was sure that her attitude, if long continued, would cause him no end of trouble. She was determined and had worsted him in a very important contest. How would it be from now on? He walked the floor of his little office and later that of his room, putting one thing and another together, but to no avail. He could not see how things were to be adjusted now.

Mrs. Hurstwood, on the contrary, had decided that her advantage should not be lessened by inaction. Now that she had practically cowed him, she would follow up her work with de-mands, the acknowledgement of which would make her word *law* in the future. He would have to pay her the money which she would now regularly demand, or she would make trouble for him. It did not matter what he did. She really did not care whether he came home any more or not. The household would move along much more pleasantly without him, and she could do as she wished without consulting anyone. Now she proposed to consult a lawyer and hire a detective. She would find out at once just what advantages she could gain.

Hurstwood walked the floor, mentally arranging the chief points of his situation. "She has that property in her name," he kept saying to himself. "What a fool trick that was. Curse it! What a fool move that was."

He also thought of his managerial position. "If she raises a row now, I'll lose this thing. They won't have me around if my name gets in the papers. My friends, too!" He bit his lip as he thought of the talk any action on her part would create. How would the papers talk about it? Every man he knew would be wondering. He would have to explain and deny and make a general mark of himself. Then Hogg would come and confer with him and there would be the devil to pay.

Many little wrinkles gathered between his eyes as he con-templated this, and his brow moistened. He saw no solution of anything—not a loop-hole left.

Through all this, thoughts of Carrie flashed upon him, and the approaching affair of Saturday. Tangled as all his matters were, he did not worry over that. It was the one pleasing thing in this whole rout of trouble. He could arrange that satisfacto-rily, for Carrie would be glad to wait, if necessary. He would see how things turned out tomorrow and then he would talk to her. They were going to meet as usual. He saw only her pretty face and neat figure, and wondered why life was not arranged so that such joy as he found with her could be steadily maintained. How much more pleasant it would be. Then he would take up his wife's threat again, and the wrinkles and moisture would return.

In the morning he came over from the hotel and opened his mail, but there was nothing in it outside the ordinary run. For some reason he felt as if something might come that way, and was relieved when all the envelopes had been scanned and nothing suspicious noticed. He began to feel the appetite that had been wanting before he had reached the office, and decided, before going out to the park to meet Carrie, to drop in at the Grand Pacific and have a pot of coffee and some rolls. While the danger had not lessened, it had not as yet materialized, and with him, no news was good news. If he could only get plenty of time to think, perhaps something would turn up. Surely, surely, this thing would not drift along to catastrophe and he not find a way out.

His spirits fell, however, when upon reaching the park, he waited and waited and Carrie did not come. He held his favorite post for an hour or more, then arose and began to walk about restlessly. Could something have happened out there to keep her away? Could she have been reached by his wife—surely not. So little did he consider Drouet, that it never once occurred to him to worry about his finding out. He fumbled at his watch charm as he ruminated and then decided that it was nothing. She had not been able to get away this morning. That was why no letter notifying him had come. He would get one yet today. It would probably be on his desk when he got back. He would look for it at once.

Such thoughts were only momentarily reassuring, however. He was subject, at other moments, to the most painful misgivings. The humiliating altercation with his wife returned with galling distinctness. He could see again the superior gleam in her eye. He could see her saying, "Perhaps you'll talk to a lawyer if you won't to me." Oh, the cold demon. To think that he should have married a woman like that. He shook his head as he contemplated her.

After a time, he gave up waiting and drearily headed for the Madison car. To add to his distress, the bright blue sky became overcast, with little fleecy clouds which shut out the sun. The wind veered to the east, and by the time he reached his office it was threatening to drizzle all afternoon.

He went in and examined his letters, but there was nothing from Carrie. Fortunately, there was nothing from his wife either. He thanked his stars that he did not have to confront that proposition just now when he needed to think so much. He walked the floor again, pretending to be in an ordinary mood, but secretly troubled beyond the expression of words.

At one-thirty he went to Rector's for lunch, and when he returned, a messenger was waiting for him. He looked at the little chap with a feeling of doubt.

"I'm to bring an answer," said the boy.

Hurstwood recognized the paper and writing of his wife. He tore it open and read without a show of feeling. It began in the most formal manner and was sharply and coldly worded throughout.

"I want you to send the money I asked for at once. I need it to carry out my plans. You can stay away if you want to. It doesn't matter in the least. But I must have some money. So don't delay, but send it by the boy."

When he had finished it, he stood holding it in his hands. The audacity of the thing took his breath. It roused his ire also—the deepest element of revolt in him. His first impulse was to write but four words in reply—"Go to the devil!"—but he compromised by telling the boy that there would be no reply. Then he sat down in his chair and gazed without seeing, contemplating the result of his work. What would she do after that? The confounded bitch! Was she going to try to bull-doze him into submission? He would go up there and have it out with her, that's what he would do. She was carrying things with too high a hand. No, by God, he wouldn't be ordered like that. She could do what she damn pleased. He would let her take care of herself. She could wait now until he got good and ready. These were his first thoughts.

Later, however, his old discretion asserted itself. Something had to be done. A climax was near, and she would not sit idle. He knew her well enough to know that when she had decided upon a plan, she would follow it up. Possibly matters would go into a lawyer's hands at once.

"Damn her," he said softly, with his teeth firmly set. "Damn her. I'll make it hot for her if she causes me trouble. I'll make her change her tone if I've got to wring her neck."

He arose from his chair and went and looked out into the street. The long drizzle had begun. Pedestrians had turned up collars and trousers at the bottom. Hands were hidden in the pockets of the umbrella-less—umbrellas were up. The street looked like a sea of round, black-cloth roofs, twisting, bobbing, moving. Trucks and vans were rattling in a noisy line, and everywhere men were shielding themselves as best they could. He scarcely noticed the picture. He was forever confronting his wife, demanding of her to change her attitude toward him before he worked her bodily harm.

At four o'clock another note came which simply said that if the money were not forthcoming that evening, the matter would be laid before Hannah and Hogg on the morrow, and other steps would be taken to get it.

Hurstwood was almost made to exclaim out loud by the insistency of this thing. Yes, he would send her the money. He'd take it to her—he would go up there and have a talk with her and that at once.

He put on his hat and looked around for his umbrella. By the Lord, he would have some arrangement of this thing.

He called a cab and was driven through the dreary rain to the North Side. On the way his temper cooled as he thought of the details of the case. What did she know? What had she done? Maybe she'd got hold of Carrie, who knows—or—or Drouet. Perhaps she really had evidence and was prepared to drop him, as a man does another from secret ambush. She was shrewd. Why should she taunt him this way unless she had good grounds?

He began to wish that he had compromised in some way or other—that he had sent the money. Perhaps he could do it up here. He would go in and see anyhow. He would have no row.

By the time he reached his own street he was keenly alive to the difficulties of his situation and wished over and over that some solution would offer itself—that he could see his way out. He alighted and went up the steps to the front door, but it was with a nervous palpitation of the heart. He pulled out his key and tried to insert it, but another key was on the inside. He shook at the knob, but the door was locked. Then he rang the bell. No answer. He rang again—this time harder. Still no answer. He jangled it fiercely several times in succession, but without avail. Then he went below.

There was a door which opened under the steps into the kitchen, protected, however, by an iron grating which was intended as a safeguard against burglars. When he reached there he noticed that it also was bolted and that the kitchen windows were down. What could it mean? He rang the bell and then waited. Finally seeing that no one was coming, he turned and went back to his cab.

"I guess they've gone out," he said apologetically to the cabby, who was hiding his red face in a loose tarpaulin rain coat.

"I saw a young girl up in that winder," returned the cabby.

Hurstwood looked but there was no face there now. He climbed moodily into the cab, relieved and distressed.

So this was the game was it. Shut him out and make him pay. Well, by the Lord, that did beat all.

CHAPTER XXVI.

When Hurstwood got back to his office again, he was in a greater quandary than ever. What to do, was with him the all-important question. He was shut out from his home, his wife would not see him, and yet he must send her money or there would be trouble at the office in the morning. He took her to be as good as her word. If she said she would lay the matter before Hannah and Hogg, she would do it, and there would be another and a worse situation by far.

He studied and studied the thing over and went without his supper. He was worried, angered, impatient. He was like a fly in a web, wearying itself by beating its wings. He could think of nothing to do save send her the money she asked for and acknowledge himself beaten. Even after he had done that, he was not through. She had the reins in her hands and could drive him. She would give him no peace but would demand more and more. He would be skulking around like a criminal, evading her presence and complying with her demands. Lord, Lord, he thought, what had he got into? How could things have taken such a violent turn and so quickly? He could hardly realize how it had all come about. It seemed a monstrous, unnatural, un-warranted condition, which had suddenly descended upon him without his let or hindrance.

Meanwhile he gave a thought now and then to Carrie. What could be the trouble in that quarter? No letter had come, no word of any kind, and yet here it was late in the evening and she had agreed to meet him that morning. Tomorrow they were to have met and gone off—where,— He saw that in the excitement of recent events he had not formulated a plan upon that score. He was desperately in love and would have taken great chances to win her under ordinary circumstances, but now—now what? Supposing she had found out something? Supposing she, too, wrote him and told him that she knew all. That she would have nothing more to do with him. It would be like things, as they were going now, for this to happen. And meanwhile he had not sent the money.

He strolled up and down the polished floor of the resort, his hands in his pockets, his brow wrinkled, his mouth set. He was getting some vague comfort out of a good cigar, but it was no panacea for the ill which affected him. Every once in a while he would clinch his fingers and tap his foot—signs of the stirring mental process he was undergoing. His whole nature was vig-orously and powerfully shaken up, and he was finding what limits the mind has to endurance. He drank more brandy and soda than he had any evening in months. He was altogether a fine example of great mental perturbation.

For all his study, nothing came of the evening except this— he sent the money. It was with great opposition, after two or three hours of the most urgent mental affirmation and denial, that at last he got out an envelope, placed in it the requested amount and slowly sealed it up. He did it with many mental reservations. He would just put it in the envelope and think it over. Perhaps he would not send it after all. Perhaps he would just hold it in that shape a little while and then put it back in his pocket. She would never know. She couldn't see him doing it.

At last he got it well-sealed and then, tipped back in his chair and smoking, decided that he had better do it. It would save a row in the morning and give him time for some other ideas. Surely something would come up. He would find out what she was going to do. Maybe she didn't have so much information. He thought and thought and finally called Harry, the boy of all work around the place.

"You take this to this address," he said, handing him the envelope, "and give it to Mrs. Hurstwood."

"Yes, sir," said the boy.

"If she isn't there, bring it back."

"Yes, sir."

"You've seen my wife?" he asked as a precautionary measure, as the boy turned to go.

"Oh, yes sir. I know her."

"All right now. Hurry right back."

"Any answer?"

"I guess not."

The boy hastened away and the manager fell to his musings. Now he had done it. There was no use speculating over that. He was beaten for tonight and he might just as well make the best of it. But oh, the wretchedness of being forced this way. He could see her meeting the boy at the door and smiling sardonically. She would take the envelope and know that she had triumphed. Lord, Lord, but this was tough business. If he only had that letter back. So help him, he wouldn't send it. He breathed heavily and wiped the moisture from his face. It was something awful.

For relief he arose and joined, in conversation, a few friends who were drinking. He tried to get the interest of things about him, but it was not to be. All the time a thought or two would run out to his home and see the scenes being therein enacted. All the time he was wondering what she would say when the boy handed her the envelope.

In about an hour and three-quarters, the boy returned. He had evidently delivered the package, for as he came up, he made no sign of taking anything out of his jacket.

"Well?" said Hurstwood.

"I gave it to her."

"My wife?"

"Yes, sir."

"Any answer?"

"She said it was 'high time.' "

Hurstwood bit his lip fiercely.

There was more to be done upon that score. He went on brooding over his situation until midnight, when he repaired again to the Palmer House. He wondered what the morning would bring forth and slept anything but soundly upon it.

Next day he went again to the office and opened his mail, suspicious and hopeful of its contents. No word from Carrie. Nothing from his wife, which was pleasant.

The fact that he had sent the money, and that she had received it, eventually worked to the ease of his mind, for as the fact that he had backed down and sent the money receded, his chagrin at it grew less and his hope of peace more. He fancied, as he sat at his desk, that nothing would be done for a week or two. Meanwhile he should have time to think.

This process of *thinking* began by a reversion to Carrie and the arrangement by which he was to get her away from Drouet. How about that now? His pain at her failure to meet or write him rapidly increased as he devoted himself to this subject. He decided to write her care of the West Side post office and ask for an explanation, as well as to have her meet him. The thought that this letter would probably not reach her until Monday chafed him exceedingly. He must get some speedier method—but how?

He thought upon it for a half-hour, not contemplating a messenger or a call direct to the house, owing to the exposure of it; but finding that time was slipping away to no purpose, he wrote the letter and then began to think again.

The valuelessness of speculation in the face of certain patent facts is often one of the humorous phases of life. It has the quality of futility which is a fine ingredient of humor. The cleverest mind sits down before certain obvious conditions much as the philosopher takes his stand before the Sphinx and proceeds to reason concerning them. The uselessness of it all is sometimes comic, sometimes pathetic. The situation is seldom altered thereby. Man frequently imagines, when a change for the better takes place, that his reasoning has done it. As a matter of fact, all such complications are largely modified by the inherent qualities of the things themselves. They change, and by exposing new phases give the watchful a chance. The strain of thinking has done little except keep the interested one in touch.

This is a good exposition of Hurstwood's predicament. Shrewd as he was, he could do nothing. He well knew where Carrie was, but in the face of her silence and the possibility of a complication unfavorable to him out there, he could not venture to call. For the same reason he did not think it politic to call. Thus he brooded, hand to brow as it were, thinking to alter matters, but without avail. The hours slipped by and with them the possibility of the union he had contemplated. He had thought to be joyously aiding Carrie by now, about the task of joining her interests to his, and here was the afternoon and nothing done. Three o'clock came, four, five, six and no letter. The helpless manager paced the floor and grimly endured the gloom of defeat. He saw a busy Saturday ushered out, the Sabbath in, and nothing done. All day, the bar being closed, he brooded alone, shut out from home, from the excitement of his resort, from Carrie, and without the ability to alter his condition one iota. It was the worst Sunday he had spent in his life.

In Monday's second mail he encountered a very legal-looking letter which held his interest for some time. It had the imprint of the law offices of McGreggor, James and Hay, and with a very formal "Dear Sir" and "We beg to state," went on to inform him briefly that they had been retained by Mrs. Julia Hurstwood to adjust certain matters which related to her sustenance and property rights, and would he kindly call and see them about the matter at once?

He read it through carefully several times and then merely shook his head. It seemed as if his family troubles were just beginning.

"Well!" he said after a time, quite audibly, "I don't know."

Then he folded it up and put it in his pocket.

To add to his misery there was no word from Carrie. He was quite certain now that she knew he was married and was angered at his perfidy. His loss seemed all the more bitter now that he needed her most. He thought he would go out and burst in upon her if she did not send him word of some sort soon. He was really affected most miserably of all by this desertion. He had loved her earnestly enough, but now that the possibility of losing her stared him in the face, she seemed much more attractive. He really pined for a word, and looked out upon her with his mind's eye in the most wistful manner. He did not propose to lose her, whatever she might think. Come what might, he would adjust this matter, and soon. He would go to her and tell her all his family complication. He would explain to her just where he stood and how much he needed her. Surely she couldn't go back on him now. It wasn't possible. He would plead until her anger would melt—until she would forgive him.

Suddenly he thought—"Supposing she isn't out there—suppose she has gone."

He was forced to take his feet. It was too much to think and sit still.

Nevertheless his rousing availed him nothing. On Tuesday it was the same way. He did manage to bring himself into the mood to go out to Carrie's, but when he got in Ogden Place, he thought he saw a man watching him and went away. He did not go within a block of the house.

One of the galling incidents of this visit was that he came back on the Randolph Street car, and without noticing, arrived almost opposite the building of the concern with which his son was connected. This sent a pang through his heart when he noticed it. There was the place. He had called on his boy there several times. Now the lad had not sent him a word. His absence did not seem to be noticed by either of his children. Well, well—fortune plays a man queer tricks. He got back to his office and joined in a conversation with friends. It was as if idle chatter deadened the sense of misery.

That night he dined at Rector's and returned at once to his office. In the bustle and show of the latter was his only relief. He troubled over many little details and talked perfunctorily to everybody. He stayed at his desk long after all others had gone and only quitted his desk when the night watchman, on his round, pulled at the front door to see if it was safely locked.

On Wednesday he received another polite note from McGreggor, James and Hay. It read—

Dear Sir:—

We beg to inform you that we are instructed to wait until tomorrow (Thursday) at one o'clock, before filing suit against you, on behalf of Mrs. Julia Hurstwood, for divorce and alimony. If we do not hear from you before that time we shall consider that you do not wish to compromise the matter in any way, and act accordingly.

Very Truly Yours, Etc.

"Compromise!" exclaimed Hurstwood bitterly. "Compromise!"

Again he shook his head.

So here it was, spread out clear before him, and now he knew what to expect. If he didn't go and see them, they would sue him promptly. If he did, he would be offered terms that would make his blood boil. He folded the letter and put it with the other one. Then he put on his hat and went for a turn about the block.

The trouble with his present situation was that there were too many ends to consider. Whichever way he might move, he would not gain anything. It was all so sudden that he had not yet recovered from the dazing effect of it—from a curious desire he had to study it out. This last was due to a more or less speculative turn of mind. He had never been given to instantaneous decisions.

With the last proposition to contemplate he hastened not a little. He could not bring himself to go to this firm's office. He could not agree to talk with them about this matter which seemed such a personal thing. He had a crude feeling about something turning up—the hope of it—certain as he was that it would not. He even thought of his wife's compromising the thing after a talk with him, and then he remembered his visit in the rain. His whole, strong, passionate nature rebelled at being forced, and he was too much the lover of power to play the part of the suppliant.

"I ought to go over there," he brought himself once to admit, and later, "I ought to get a lawyer."

"What good would that do?" said another voice in his mind. "They'll sue tomorrow, lawyer or no lawyer, if you don't see them. What are you going to do about that?"

"I don't know what I'm going to do," he admitted to himself secretly, and then started to consider other parts of the situation, which would, by a circuitous method, lead around to the same conclusion not ten minutes later.

CHAPTER XXVII.

Carrie, left alone by Drouet, listened to his retreating steps, scarcely realizing what had happened. She knew that he had stormed out. It was some moments before she questioned whether he would return—not now exactly, but ever. She looked around her upon the rooms, out of which the evening light was dying, and wondered why she did not feel quite the same towards them. She went over to the dresser and struck a match, lighting the gas. Then she went back to her rocker to think.

It was some time before she could collect her thoughts, but when she did, this truth began to take on importance. She was quite alone. Suppose Drouet did not come back. Suppose she should never hear anything more of him. This fine arrangement of chambers would not last long. She would have to quit them.

To her credit be it said she never once counted on Hurstwood. She could only approach that subject with a pang of sorrow and regret. For a truth, she was rather shocked and frightened by this evidence of human depravity. He would have tricked her without turning an eyelash. She would have been led into a newer and worse situation. And yet she could not keep out the pictures of his looks and manners. Only this one deed seemed strange and miserable. It contrasted sharply with all she felt and knew concerning the man.

But she was alone. That was the greater thought just at the present moment. How about that? Would she go out to work again? Would she begin to look around in the business district? The stage—oh, yes. Drouet had spoken about that. Was there any hope for her there? She moved to and fro, in deep and varied thoughts, while the minutes slipped away and night fell completely. She had had nothing to eat and yet there she sat, thinking it over.

About that time she remembered that she was hungry, and went to the little cupboard in the rear room, where were the remains of one of their breakfasts. She looked at these things with certain misgivings. The contemplation of food had more significance than usual.

While she was eating, she began to wonder how much money she had. It struck her as exceedingly important, and without ado she went to look for her purse. It was on the dresser, and in it were seven dollars in bills and some change. She quailed as she thought of the insignificance of the amount and rejoiced when the thought struck her that the rent was paid until the end of the month. She began also to think what she would have done if she had gone out into the street when she first started. By the side of that situation, as she looked at it now, the present seemed agreeable. She had a little time at least, and then perhaps everything would come out all right after all.

Drouet had gone, but what of it? He did not seem seriously angry. He only acted as if he was huffy. He would come back— of course he would. There was his cane in the corner. Here also was one of his collars. He had left his light overcoat in the wardrobe. She looked about and tried to assure herself with the sight of a dozen such details, but alas, the secondary thought arrived. Supposing he did come back. Then what?

Here was another proposition, nearly if not quite as disturbing. She would have to talk with and explain to him. He would want her to admit that he was right. The details of the whole liaison would come out in such a manner that it would be impossible for her to live with him, even if he would. She could not think of facing his knowledge of her guilt. Anyhow, she did not care for him. Her quarrel proved that. He had acted ungenerously towards her in the matter of Hurstwood—egotistically in others. It would be impossible to know this and go on simulating friendship. She saw that if he came back, she could not think of staying there—and then what? The world of struggle was only a few days removed, come what may. That she felt. She did not yet understand what mortals may forego in order to dwell together. The lion and lamb would be joyous bed fellows compared to some.

After she had assured herself as to her resources, she went

back to her food, but not to eat. It had lost its value in the interim, and she put away the pieces and closed the door. Then she went back to her chair.

Drouet had rushed out under the impetus of the feeling that he was being made a fool of. He took his grip, and rode straight for the Palmer House. B'George, he would not be treated this way, if he never saw her again. He had been good to her. He had done everything he could think of and yet she wasn't satisfied. She had to go knocking around with other people.

He brooded, head down, all the way to State and Madison and registered his name with little thought of what he was doing —"Charles Drouet, City."

"Just for tonight, Mr. Drouet?" asked the night clerk.

"No, I'll keep it a day or two," said the drummer.

He went upstairs and deposited his grip. Then he washed his face and hands and went out to dine. He was in the lowest sort of spirits and wished repeatedly that things were different.

"To think of that damned Hurstwood," he thought, and sometimes said to himself. "After all the time I've known him."

For that evening he walked the lobby of the Palmer House and cudgeled his brains with the evidence before him. What rotten treatment. Oh, Lord, to think a woman should do a man like that. And Carrie too—little Carrie. He would have never thought anything like that of her.

At last he went upstairs to get some bills, and, bringing them down into the comfortable writing room, tried to work, but it was no use. He couldn't do it. The more he tried the more his thoughts wandered to his hard luck, and at last he gave it up in despair.

"It's no use," he said. "I can't do it."

He finally went around to one of the theatres but came away disgusted. It wasn't funny. Then he tried to read and, finding that useless, went to bed,—only to dream of being fired from his position and injured in every possible way, for the rest of the night.

On the morrow he was in no better mood. He went about his duties for the day, which concerned the city trade of the house which he represented, but found no cessation of feeling concerning what he considered Carrie's perfidy. He tried to make himself believe that he was breaking away from her—that he could be strong and punish her by leaving her forever. He tried to quell his longing to be with her by recounting the chief points in this trick she had played him, but alas, it was a sorry fight. He was ever remembering that he had certain things to get out there—his extra linen, his light overcoat, his shoes. He would go and tend to that. Also, he recalled that Carrie had no money. What would she do now? If he didn't act at once, perhaps she would be hard up. Perhaps—ah, agonizing thought—she would go to Hurstwood. Maybe she had gone already. It was this thought which caused him the most suffering of all. It was a galling thing—whether he cared for her or not, that the wrong done him should be augmented in this manner—that Hurstwood should triumph. B'George, it was an outrage—a shame.

This mood lasted him for a goodly period, but it was assuming a more and more modified form all the time. He could not get a line on what he would consider the proper thing to do. To go out to Carrie was one thing, to stay away another, to head off Hurstwood was a third. He let hour after hour slip by, hoping that Carrie would write him or call—she knew his business address—and make some statement. Ah, if she had only called—what a reconciliation there would have been. He came to the office several evenings, his feet hastening that he might see. Invariably he felt gloomy as he realized that the solution of the problem still rested upon him. No letter, no acknowledgement of error, no pleading for forgiveness. His nights at the Palmer House were dreary indeed.

At the same time Carrie was in a very similar state. She did not know what to do. On Friday she remembered her appointment with Hurstwood but was too angry and distressed to think of keeping it. Nevertheless, the passing of the hour when she should by all right of promise have been in his company served to keep the calamity which had befallen her exceedingly fresh and clear in her mind. She thought of it a dozen times, but she thought also of her state and of what would happen if she were again thus rudely thrown upon her own resources. In her nervousness and stress of mind she felt it necessary to act, and consequently she put on a brown street dress and at eleven o'clock started to visit the business portion once again.

The rain, which threatened at twelve and began at one,

served equally as well to cause her to retrace her steps and remain within doors as it did to reduce Hurstwood's spirits and give him a wretched day.

The morrow was Saturday, a half-holiday in many business quarters, and besides, it was a balmy, radiant day, with the trees and grass shining exceedingly green after the rain of the night before. The sparrows were twittering merrily in joyous chorus. Carrie was in no mood to rise early, after the long freedom she had enjoyed from workseeking. She could not help feeling, as she looked out across the lovely park, that life was a joyous thing for those who did not need to worry, and she wished over and over that something might interfere now to preserve for her the comfortable state which she had occupied. She did not want Drouet or his money, when she thought of it, nor anything more to do with Hurstwood, but only the content and ease of mind she had experienced—for after all she had been happy—happier at least than she was now when confronted by the necessity of making her way alone. She looked out of the window and grieved that this lovely day would be fraught with worry for her. She would have to go forth in the sunshine and seek for a livelihood. She would have to walk the hard streets in a vain attempt to rescue herself from a position which was fraught with all the miseries the flesh is heir to. She could not keep from referring to her few remaining dollars and the fact that she was utterly alone.

When she arrived in the business part it was quite eleven o'clock and the business had little longer to run. She did not realize this at first, being affected by some of the old distress, which was a result of her earlier adventure into this strenuous and exacting quarter. She wandered about, assuring herself that she was making up her mind to look for something and at the same time feeling that perhaps it was not necessary to be in such haste about it. The thing was difficult to encounter, and she had a few days. Also she was not sure that she was really face to face again with the bitter problem of self-sustenance. Anyhow there was one change for the better. She knew that she had improved in appearance. Her manner had vastly changed. Her clothes were becoming, and men—well-dressed men—some of the kind who before had gazed at her indifferently from behind their polished railings and imposing office partitions, now glanced into her face with a soft light in their eyes. In a way she felt the power and satisfaction of the thing, but it did not wholly reassure her. She looked for nothing save what might come legitimately and without the appearance of special favor. She wanted something, but no man should buy her by false protestations or favor. She proposed to earn her living honestly.

She walked about quite a little, realizing that something must be done, but more and more succumbing to the excuse which her timidity made, that today was not the day to try. Little cards placed in doorways indicated that business was soon to be called off until Monday at least.

"This store closes at one on Saturdays" was a pleasing and satisfactory legend to see upon doors at which she felt she ought to enter and inquire for work. It gave her an excuse, and, after encountering quite a number of them and noting that the clocks registered twelve-fifteen, she decided that it would be no use to seek further today, so she got on a car and went to Lincoln Park. There was always something to see there—the flowers, the animals, the lake, and she flattered herself that on Monday she would be up betimes and searching. Besides, many things might happen between now and Monday.

Sunday passed with equal doubts, worries, assurances and heaven knows what vagaries of mind and spirit. Every half-hour in the day the thought would come to her most sharply, like the tail of a swishing whip, that she could not stop to think—that action—immediate action—was imperative. At other times she would look about her, and assure herself that things were not so bad—that certainly she would come out safe and sound. At such times she would think of Drouet's advice about going on the stage and would see some chance for herself in that quarter. She decided to take up that opportunity on the morrow and search until she found something.

Accordingly she arose early Monday morning and dressed herself in a way which she thought would make a good impression. She did not know just how such applications were made, but she took it to be a matter which related more directly to the theatre buildings. All you had to do was to inquire of some one about the theatre for the manager and ask for a position. If there was anything you might get it—or at least he could tell you how.

She had had no experience with this class of individuals whatsoever and did not know the salacity and humor of the theatrical tribe. She only knew of the position which Mr. Hale occupied, but of all things she did not wish to encounter that personage, on account of her intimacy with his wife. Besides, she had no liking for the man, who was a stout, over-experienced, fakish sort of an individual, who had one type of woman in mind when the name of woman was mentioned, and who was forever on the *qui vive* for some little encounter with the fair sex which might work to his advantage. She therefore gave the Standard a wide berth, even in thought.

There was, however, at this time, one theatre, the Chicago Opera House, which was considerably in the public eye; and its manager, David A. Henderson, had a fair local reputation. Carrie had seen one or two elaborate performances there and had heard of several others. She knew nothing of Henderson nor of the methods of applying, but she instinctively felt that this would be a likely place and accordingly strolled about in that neighborhood. She came bravely enough to the showy entrance-way, with the polished and be-gilded lobby, set with framed pictures out of the current attraction, leading up to the quiet box office, but she could get no further. Mr. Francis Wilson was holding forth that week and the air of distinction and prosperity overawed her. She could not imagine that there would be any-thing in such a lofty sphere for her. She almost trembled at the audacity which might have carried her on to a terrible rebuff. She could find heart only to look at the pictures, which were showy, and then walk out. It seemed to her as if she had made a splendid escape and that it would be foolhardy to think of applying in that quarter again.

This little experience settled her hunting for one day. She looked around elsewhere, but it was from the outside. She got the location of several playhouses fixed in her mind, notably the Grand Opera House and McVicker's, both of which were leading in attractions, and then came away. Her spirits were materially reduced, owing to the newly restored sense of the magnitude of the great interests and the insignificance of her claims upon society, such as she understood them to be.

That night she was visited by Mrs. Hale, whose chatter

and protracted stay made it impossible to dwell upon her predicament or the fortune of the day. Before retiring, however, she sat down to think and gave herself up to the most gloomy forebodings. Drouet had not put in an appearance. She had had no word from any quarter. She had spent a dollar of her precious sum in procuring food and paying car fare. It was evident that that would not endure long. Besides she had discovered no resource.

In this situation her thoughts went out to her sister in Van Buren Street, whom she had not seen since the night of her flight, and to her home at Columbia City which seemed now a part of a something that could not be again. She looked for no refuge in that direction. Nothing but sorrow was brought her by thoughts of Hurstwood, which would return. That he could have chosen to dupe her in so ready a manner seemed a cruel thing.

Tuesday came and with it appropriate indecision and speculation. She was in no mood, after her failure of the day before, to hasten forth upon her work-seeking errand, and yet she rebuked herself for what she considered her weakness the day before. Accordingly she started out to revisit the Chicago Opera House, but possessed scarcely enough courage to approach.

She did manage to inquire at the box office, however.

"Manager of the company or the house?" asked the smartly dressed individual who took care of the tickets. He was favorably impressed by Carrie's looks.

"I don't know," said Carrie, taken back by the question.

"You couldn't see the manager of the house today anyhow," volunteered the young man. "He's out of town."

He noted her puzzled look and then added—"What is it you wish to see about?"

"I want to see about getting a position," she answered.

"You'd better see the manager of the company," he returned, "but he isn't here now."

"When will he be in?" asked Carrie, somewhat relieved by this information.

"Well, you might find him in between eleven and twelve. He's here after two o'clock."

Carrie thanked him and walked briskly out while the young

man gazed after her through one of the side windows of his gilded coop.

"Good-looking," he said to himself and proceeded to visions of condescensions on her part which were exceedingly flattering to himself.

Once outside Carrie decided that there was nothing for it but to stroll about and wait, but upon reflecting that nothing was assured in this quarter and that she ought to make sure of something, she applied at one of the other theatres—the Grand Opera House. Here one of Charles Frohman's comedy companies was playing an engagement. This time Carrie asked to see the manager of the company, reasoning that he would be most likely to engage assistants for his own play. She little knew the trivial authority of this individual, or that had there been a vacancy, an actor would have been sent on from New York to fill it.

"His office is upstairs," said the individual who had charge of the box office.

In the manager's office were several individuals, two lounging near a window, another talking to an individual sitting at a roll-top desk—the manager. Carrie glanced nervously about and began to fear that she should have to make her appeal before the assembled company, two of whom, the occupants of the window, were already observing her carefully.

"I can't do it," the manager was saying—"it's a rule of Mr. Frohman's never to allow visitors back of the stage—no—no."

Carrie timidly waited, standing. There were chairs but no one motioned her to be seated. The individual to whom the manager had been talking went away quite crestfallen. That luminary gazed earnestly at some papers before him, as if they were of the greatest concern.

"Did you see that in the 'Herald' this morning about Nat Goodwin, Harris?"

"No," said one of the individuals so addressed, "what was it?"

"Made quite a curtain address at Hooley's last night. Better look it up."

Harris reached over to a table and began to look for the "Herald."

"What is it?" asked the manager of Carrie, apparently noticing her for the first time. He thought he was going to be held up for free tickets.

Carrie summoned up all her courage, which was little at best. She realized that she was a novice and felt as if a rebuff were certain. Of this she was so sure that she only wished now to make out as if she had called for advice.

"Can you tell me how to go about getting on the stage?"

It was the best way after all to have gone about the matter. She was interesting, at least, to the occupant of the chair from a physical point of view, and the simplicity of her request and manner took his fancy. He smiled, as did the other individuals in the room, who, however, made some slight effort to conceal their humor.

"I don't know," he answered, looking her brazenly over. "Have you ever had any experience upon the stage?"

"A little," answered Carrie. "I have taken part in a number of amateur performances."

She thought she had to make some sort of showing in order to retain his interest.

"Never studied for the stage?" he said, putting on an air, intended as much to impress his friends with his discretion as Carrie.

"No sir."

"Well, I don't know," he answered, tipping lazily back in his chair while she stood before him. "What makes you want to get on the stage?"

She felt abashed at the man's daring but could only smile in answer to his engaging smirk, and say:

"I need to make a living."

"Oh," he answered, rather taken by her trim appearance and feeling as if he might scrape up an acquaintance with her. "That's a good reason, isn't it. Well, Chicago is not a good place for what you want to do. You ought to be in New York. There's more chance there. You could hardly expect to get started out here."

Carrie smiled genially, grateful that he should condescend to advise her even so much. He noticed the smile and put a slightly different construction on it. He thought he saw an easy chance for a little flirtation.

"Sit down," he said, pulling a chair forward from the side

of his desk and dropping his voice so that the two men in the room should not hear. Those two gave each other the suggestion of a wink.

"Well, I'll be going, Barney," said one, breaking away and so addressing the manager. "See you this afternoon."

"All right," said the manager.

The remaining individual took up a paper as if to read.

"Did you have any idea what sort of part you would like to get?" asked the manager softly.

"Oh no," said Carrie. "I would take anything to begin with."

"I see," he said. "Do you live here in the city?"

"Yes, sir," answered Carrie, not wishing to communicate facts on that score.

The manager smiled most blandly.

"Have you ever tried to get in as a chorus girl?" he asked, assuming a more confidential air.

Carrie began to feel that there was something exuberant and unnatural in his manner.

"No," she said.

"That's the way most girls begin," he went on, "who go on the stage. It's a good way to get experience."

He was turning on her a glance of the companionable and persuasive manner.

"I didn't know that," said Carrie.

"It's a difficult thing," he went on, "but there's always a chance, you know." Then as if he suddenly remembered, he pulled out his watch and consulted it. "I've an appointment at two," he said, "and I've got to go to lunch now. Would you care to come and dine with me? We can talk it over there."

"Oh no," said Carrie, the whole motive of the man flashing on her at once. "I have an engagement myself."

"That's too bad," he said, realizing that he had been a little beforehand in his offer and that Carrie was about to go away. "Come in later—I may know of something."

"Thank you," she answered with some trepidation, and went out.

"She was good-looking, wasn't she?" said the manager's companion, who had not caught all the details of the little game.

"Yes, in a way," said the other, sore to think the game had been lost. "She'd never make an actress though. Just another pair of tights, that's all."

CHAPTER XXVIII.

This little experience nearly destroyed her ambition to call upon the manager of Mr. Wilson's company at the Chicago Opera House, but she decided to do so after a time. That individual was of a more sedate turn of mind. He said at once that there was no opening of any sort, and seemed to consider that her search was foolish.

"Chicago is no place to get a start," he said. "You ought to be in New York."

Still she persisted and went to McVicker's where she could not find anyone. "The Old Homestead" was running there, but the individual to whom she was referred was not to be found.

These little expeditions took up her time until quite four o'clock when she was weary enough to go home. She felt as if she ought to continue and inquire elsewhere, but the results so far were too dispiriting. She took the car and arrived at Ogden Place in three-quarters of an hour, but decided to ride on to the West Side branch of the post office, where she was accustomed to receive Hurstwood's letters. There was one there now, written Saturday, which she tore open and read with mingled feelings. There was so much warmth in it and such tense complaint at her having failed to meet him and her subsequent silence, that she rather pitied the man. That he loved her was evident enough. That he had wished and dared to do so, married as he was, was the evil. She felt as if the thing deserved an answer and consequently decided that she would write and let him know that she knew of his married state and was justly incensed at his deceptions. She would tell him that it was all over between them.

At her room, the wording of this missive occupied her for some time, for she fell to the task at once. It was most difficult.

"You do not need to have me explain why I did not meet you," she wrote in part. "How could you deceive me so? You cannot expect me to have anything more to do with you. I wouldn't under any circumstances.

"Oh, how could you act so," she added in a burst of feeling. "You have caused me more misery than you can think. I hope you will get over your infatuation for me. We must not meet anymore. Goodbye."

She signed the letter "Carrie."

She took the letter the next morning and at the corner dropped it reluctantly into the letter box, still uncertain as to whether she should do so or not. Then she took the car and went down town.

This was the dull season with the department stores, but she was listened to with more consideration than was usually accorded to young women applicants, owing to her neat and attractive appearance. She was asked the same old questions with which she was already familiar.

"What can you do?" "Have you ever worked in a retail store before?" "Are you experienced?"

In her desperation Carrie decided not to jeopardize her chances by admitting inexperience, so she boldly declared that she was experienced.

"Where have you worked before?" asked the man in The Boston Store.

"At The Fair," she answered.

"Were you discharged?" he inquired.

"No," she answered. "I quit because I thought I was to move away from Chicago."

"Um!" he replied. "Well, there isn't anything open just now. This is the dull season, you know. You might give us your name and address."

He looked at her pretty face and figure and then added, "We would like to have you a little later on, but we're full up now."

At The Fair, Sea and Co., Siegel, Cooper and Co., and Schlesinger and Mayer's, it was much the same. It was the dull season, she might come in a little later, possibly they would like to have her.

There was one thing which was an improvement over her original experience in these places—she was treated with more consideration. It was plain that comely features and good looks went for something with these people. At one store the man was most kindly in his attentions, asked her to have a chair, carefully took her address and said there might be something next week—he would try and remember her. He smiled at her in a most covert manner as she went out, and Carrie knew well enough why he did it. She was resolved, however, that such as he should get no consideration from her, but was grieved to think that her necessary bread might be bought by such favor.

In all the smaller stores her treatment accorded with the age, the dinner or the mood of the proprietor. She entered several millinery stores, where only experienced help was required by the women proprietors. She tried the fur houses, but they were doing nothing at all. One or two music stores caught her eye and into these she ventured, but here only male help was employed. At last she entered a picture-framing establishment—the "Great American Art Company" as the window indicated—and was directed to the manager's office in the rear. This was one of those fake crayon-portrait companies which were then doing a flourishing business by a system of solicitation and trickery which was later exposed and stopped by the police. It was a method of forgery and blackmail, the victims agreeing to pay a very reasonable sum for the crayon portrait, but learning afterward that the frame was not included and also that they had ordered and agreed to pay for that separately. The individual who managed this was a young man of about twenty-six years of age, keen, calculating, and unprincipled as any youth of his age could be. He had an eye to cheapness and service in most of his employés, but he was nevertheless anxious to get near him some girl of good looks and weak principles on whom he might practice his art of seduction.

When Carrie walked in upon him, he surveyed her closely with a lightening eye as he asked her what she wanted.

There was something in his manner which was extremely disagreeable to Carrie. He was not by any means handsome and there was the imprint of all his innermost thoughts upon his features. Something oily and crooked characterized his manner, the smirk of his mouth and the way in which he rubbed his hands.

"What can I do for you?" he asked.

"I am looking for a position," said Carrie.

"Ever work at anything like this before?" he asked, noting her large eyes and her colorful cheeks.

"No," she replied.

"But you have had some business experience," he went on graciously, as if to help her.

"Very little," said Carrie.

"Can you keep books?"

Carrie's color rose as she acknowledged that she could not.

"Do you live on the South Side?"

"No—on the West Side," she returned.

"With your parents?"

She answered "No" before she thought, wondering at the youth's oily and ingratiating air. Then she added, "With my sister."

"Ah," he said, "just so." There was much of the lordly egotist about his manner.

"Well, I hire some girls as you see," he observed, "but most of them do clerical work. How much would you expect a week?"

Carrie hesitated a moment and then said, "Whatever you would think reasonable."

"Well," he went on, "most of these girls work for four and five dollars a week. It isn't very hard work. I do pay a little more sometimes," he added, "but this is our dull season just now."

He was looking at Carrie with a very soft air, to see if he could not detect some sign of compliance which would further his desires.

"Would you work for five?" he went on, rocking back and forth in his spring chair, and with the air of one who had known her for some time.

"Yes," said Carrie.

"I might," he said, studying his shoes and then her face, "make room for you. As I say, I'm not in any special need of help, but I might give *you* a place."

He put the suggestion of an accent on the word, and then smiled what he intended to be sweetly. Carrie noticed the inflection and began to realize his intentions. Nevertheless she answered simply enough, "I should like a place very much."

"Supposing," he said, "you give me your address. I will see what I can do."

He wrote down her address and then said, "I live out your

way—on Washington Boulevard. If I find I can make a place for you, I may drop in to tell you."

"Thank you very much," said Carrie, while thinking directly the opposite. She understood the whole trend of the man's mind, for he was at little pains to conceal it. He ogled her most salaciously and rose with an affectation of politeness to show her out. In short, he tacitly conveyed to her one of the most brazen propositions imaginable—seeking to buy her services and favor for five dollars per week.

She was relieved to get out of that, for the man was repulsive to her. She could not help thinking of his lips, which were of a bluish hue, nor of the queer eyes that were slightly tainted with yellow. She knew that if she took that place it would be to put herself in the way of disagreeable familiarity and solicitation, and she hesitated to think that anything could bring her to it. Still the day had gone by and five dollars was five dollars. Insignificant as the sum seemed compared with what had been her allowance and state of living, she thought in her fear that it might be necessary to take it. She had not had the refusal of it so far, but it was a proposition which worried her as much as the want of it had before.

Another thing that galled her was the thought that even if she did get a place, when her remaining money was gone she would be in a difficult position. She could not live until the end of the first week without a dollar. Then she thought of her trinkets and the pawn-shop, and her mind was relieved. She could help herself out on that score. This thought gave her a little relief, and she went home feeling as if she had still a few days' lease of life.

When she arrived, she discovered that some one had been there—evidently Drouet. His umbrella was gone—likewise his light overcoat. She thought she missed other things but could not be sure. Everything had not been taken.

So, his going was crystallizing into a staying. What was she to do now? Evidently she would be facing the world in the same old way within a day or two. Her clothes would get poor. She would have to work hard. She would be forced to take the miserable five dollars a week offered this afternoon and under such intolerable circumstances. She almost thanked her stars that such an offer, wretched as it was, had been made. She put her two hands together in her customary expressive way and pressed her fingers. Large tears gathered in her eyes and broke hot across her cheeks. She was alone, very much alone.

Drouet really had called, but it was with a very different mind from that which Carrie imagined. He expected to find her, to justify his return by claiming that he came to get the remaining portion of his wardrobe, and before he got away again to patch up a peace.

Accordingly, when he arrived he was disappointed to find Carrie out. He trifled about, hoping that she was somewhere in the neighborhood and would soon return. He constantly listened, expecting to hear her foot on the stair. When he did so, it was his intention to make believe that he had just come in and was disturbed at being caught. Then he would explain his need of his clothes and find out how things stood.

Wait as he did, however, Carrie did not come. From puttering around among the drawers, in momentary expectation of her arrival, he changed to looking out the window and from that to resting himself in the rocking chair. Still no Carrie. He began to grow restless and lit a cigar. After that he walked the floor. Then he looked out the window and saw clouds gathering. He remembered an appointment at three. He began to think that it would be useless to wait and got hold of his umbrella and light coat, intending to take these things anyway. It would scare her, he hoped. Tomorrow he would come back for the others. He would find out how things stood.

As he started to go, he felt truly sorry that he had missed her. There was a little picture of her on the wall, showing her arrayed in the little jacket he had first bought her—her face a little more wistful than he had seen it lately. He was really touched by it and looked into the eyes of it with rather rare feeling for him.

"You didn't do me right, Cad," he said, as if he were addressing her in the flesh.

Then he went to the door, took a good look around and went out.

CHAPTER XXIX.

It was when he returned from his disturbed stroll about the streets, after receiving the decisive note from McGreggor, James and Hay, that Hurstwood found the letter Carrie had written him that morning. He thrilled intensely as he noted the handwriting and rapidly tore it open.

"There," he thought. "She loves me or she would not have written me at all."

He was slightly depressed at the tenor of the note for the first few minutes, but soon recovered. "She wouldn't write at all if she didn't care for me."

This was his one resource against the vague depression which held him. He could extract little from the wording of the letter, but the spirit he thought he knew.

There was really something exceedingly human if not pathetic in his being thus relieved by a clearly worded reproof. He, who had for so long remained satisfied with himself, now looked outside of himself for comfort—and to such a source. The mystic chords of affection!—how they bind us all.

He had not read it through for the first time before he had decided to get some way of seeing Carrie. He would write her or watch for her, or call. She should not remain away from him long. Oh no, that should not be. She would not want to if he could only talk with her.

He went over this ground with such rapidity of thought that color came to his cheeks. For the moment he forgot the letter from McGreggor, James and Hay. Ah, if he could only have Carrie, perhaps he could get out of the whole entanglement—perhaps it would not matter. He wouldn't care what his wife did with herself if only he might not lose here. He stood up and walked about, dreaming his delightful dream of a life continued with this lovely possessor of his heart. It seemed it would not really matter what became of his present difficulties if only he could have her. Ah, ah! if only he could have her.

It was not long, however, before the old worry was back for consideration, and with it, what weariness! He thought of the morrow and the suit. He had done nothing and here was the afternoon slipping away. It was now a quarter of four. At five the attorneys would have gone home. He still had the morrow until noon. Even as he thought, the last fifteen minutes passed away and it was five. Then he abandoned the thought of seeing them any more that day and turned to Carrie.

It is a singular thing to note that his thoughts were all the more ardent, for the temporary lapse of the other problem. He was so weary of that, so disgusted with trying to reach a solution. Here had Carrie written him, and now he had some hope. Supposing she did know—what of it? Didn't she love him? Was he not content to give up all? He forgot to credit his home complications with a considerable share in the matter of making it easy for him to give them up, but he was too wrought-up for that. He could only think of Carrie and the fact that he would probably be forced to find refuge in her company entirely. If his home were to be broken up this way, to whom else would he turn? They could now lead a lovely, quiet life together.

As he made this matter clear to himself, he hastened in thought to Carrie. He saw himself finding her surprised, affecting to be astonished, withdrawing fearfully from him, but secretly leaning toward him. Yes, that would be the way—she would secretly lean toward him—he knew. She could do nothing else when he loved her so. Then he would listen to all her charges humbly and say nothing. She could pour out upon him all her accusations until she were satiated, and he would not interrupt. Only when all had been listened to would he begin, and then—Oh, he would tell her the whole misery of his situation. She should realize how hopeless it was for him to help loving her. It was Drouet's fault. He did not want to go out there. He had every thought of never going again. But once he had seen her, how could he resist? Was he to blame? Oh, surely not, when she was so winning. He had tried—but there. His own self-justification failed him at this point. He would wait until he saw her. She should be made to understand.

It is to be observed that the man did not justify himself to himself. He was not troubling about that. His whole thought was the possibility of persuading Carrie. Nothing was wrong in that. He loved her dearly. Their mutual happiness depended upon it. Would that Drouet were only away.

While he was thinking thus elatedly he remembered that he wanted some clean linen in the morning. He had promised to bring some with him back to the hotel that night. All his other clothes were up at the house, and he had not made up his mind what to do on that account. He decided to go out and purchase some at once, not knowing where he would wind up tonight. He was thinking of Carrie and would probably visit her. Surely he could get some way of seeing her, he thought.

He purchased the linen together with a half-dozen ties and went to the Palmer House. As he entered he thought he saw Drouet ascending the stairs with a key. Surely not Drouet. The first thought that flashed into his mind, after the impossibility of it, was that he might be there with Carrie. Perhaps they had changed their abode temporarily. He went straight up to the desk and looked over the register. No name familiar to him had been written in it that day. He turned to the one before. Still none. "Is Mr. Drouet stopping here?" he asked of the clerk.

"I think he is," said the latter, consulting his private registry list—"yes."

"Is that so!" exclaimed Hurstwood, otherwise concealing his astonishment.

"Alone?" he added.

"Yes," said the clerk.

Hurstwood turned away and set his eyes so as best to express and conceal his feelings.

"How's that?" he thought. "They've had a row."

He hastened to his room, with rising spirits, and changed his linen. As he did so, he made up his mind that if Carrie was alone or if she had gone to another place, it behooved him to find out. He decided to call at once.

"I know what I'll do," he thought. "I'll go to the door and ask if Mr. Drouet is at home. That will bring out whether he is there or not and where Carrie is."

He was almost moved to some muscular display as he thought of it. He decided to go immediately after supper.

On coming down from his room at six, he looked carefully about to see if Drouet were present and then went out to lunch. He could scarcely eat, however—he was so anxious to be about his errand. Before starting, he thought it well to discover where Drouet would be, and returned to his hotel.

"Has Mr. Drouet gone out?" he asked of the clerk.

"No," answered the latter, "he's in his room. Do you wish to send up a card?"

"No, I'll call around later," answered Hurstwood and strolled out.

He took a Madison car and went direct to Ogden Place, this time walking boldly up to the door. The chambermaid answered his knock.

"Is Mr. Drouet in?" said Hurstwood blandly.

"He is out of the city," said the girl, who had heard Carrie tell this to Mrs. Hale.

"Is Mrs. Drouet in?"

"No, she has gone to the theatre."

"Is that so?" said Hurstwood, considerably taken back. Then, as if burdened with something important, "You don't know to which theatre?"

The girl really had no idea where she had gone, but not liking Hurstwood and wishing to cause him trouble, answered, "Yes, Hooley's."

"Thank you," returned the manager, and tipping his hat slightly he went away.

Carrie was not at Hooley's, but she had gone out with Mrs. Hale to the Columbia where one of William Gillette's earliest comedies was running.

"I'll look in there," thought the manager as he wended his steps toward the car, considerably disappointed by his errand; but as a matter of fact he did not. Before he had reached the central portion of the city, he had thought the whole matter over again and decided it would be useless. As much as he longed to see Carrie, he knew she would be with some one, and did not wish to intrude with his plea there. A little later he might do so—in the morning. Only in the morning he had the lawyer question before him.

This little pilgrimage threw quite a wet blanket upon his rising spirits. He was soon down again to his old worry and reached the resort anxious to find relief. Quite a company of gentlemen were making the place lively with their conversation. A group of Cook County politicians were conferring about a round, cherry-wood table in the rear portion of the room. Several young merrymakers were chattering at the bar before making a belated visit to the theatre. A shabby-genteel individual with a red nose and an old high hat was sipping a quiet glass of ale alone at one end of the bar. Hurstwood nodded to the politicians and went into his office.

About ten o'clock a friend of his, Mr. Frank L. Taintor, a local sporter and racing man, dropped in and, seeing Hurstwood alone in his office, came to the door.

"Hello, George!" he exclaimed.

"How are you, Frank," said Hurstwood, somewhat relieved by the sight of him. "Sit down," and he motioned him one of the chairs in the little room.

"What's the matter, George?" asked Taintor. "You look a little glum. Haven't lost at the track, have you?"

"I'm not feeling very well tonight—I had a slight cold the other day."

"Take whiskey, George," said Taintor. "You ought to know that."

Hurstwood smiled.

They went off into a short talk on racing and wound up by stepping out toward the bar together. While they were still conferring there, several other of Hurstwood's friends entered, and not long after eleven, the theatres being out, some actors began to drop in—among them several notabilities. There were Scanlan, Denman Thompson of the "Old Homestead" company, and Frank Bush, then first coming into note on the variety stage as an impersonator.

"Hello, George," observed the latter to Hurstwood.

It was the first time he had met the manager on this trip. Hurstwood greeted him most cordially. He had not yet become acquainted with Thompson, whom he knew by reputation. Scanlan he knew but slightly. It so happened that Mark Kennedy, a well known rounder of the city, also dropped in. He was one who by his wealth and moderate taste had come into personal relationship with a great many celebrities who visited the city. The three actors he knew.

"Let me introduce you to Mr. Thompson," he said to Hurstwood, after he had rounded up the three notabilities and the manager. Then began one of those pointless social conversations so common in American resorts where the would-be gilded attempt to rub off gilt, from those who have it in abundance. If Hurstwood had one leaning, it was toward notabilities. He considered that, if anywhere, he belonged among them. He was too proud to toady, too keen not to strictly observe the plane he occupied, when there were those present who did not appreciate him, but in situations like the present—where he could shine as a gentleman and be received without equivocation as a friend and equal among men of known ability, he was most delighted. It was on such occasions, if ever, that he would "take something." When the social flavor was strong enough, he would even unbend to the extent of drinking glass for glass with his associates, punctiliously observing his turn to pay as if he were an outsider like the others. If ever he approached intoxication, or rather that ruddy warmth and comfortableness which precedes the more sloven state, it was when individuals such as these were gathered about him—when he was one of a circle of chatting celebrities. Tonight, disturbed as was his state, he was rather relieved to find company, and now that notabilities were gathered, he laid aside his troubles for the nonce, and joined in right heartily.

It was not long before the imbibing began to tell. Stories began to crop up—those ever-enduring droll stories which form the major portion of the conversation among American men under such circumstances.

"Did you ever hear the story of," and "That reminds me," were the most repeated phrases. Scanlan led all with his humor. Hurstwood was not to be outdone. He was no humorist, but he heard constantly a great many stories and had a good memory for them as well as fair discrimination in the matter of selection. So he told story for story as the turn came.

The result was that twelve o'clock came, the hour for closing, and with it the company took leave. Hurstwood shook hands with them most cordially. He was in a very roseate state, physically. He had arrived at that state where his mind, being clear, was nevertheless warm in its fancies. He felt as if his troubles were not very serious. Going into his office he began to turn over certain accounts, awaiting the departure of the bartenders and the cashier, who soon left.

It was the manager's duty as well as his custom, after all were gone, to see that everything was safely closed up for the night. As a rule, no money except the cash taken in after banking hours was kept about the place; and that was locked in the safe by the cashier, who with the owners was joint keeper of the secret combination; but nevertheless, Hurstwood nightly took the precaution to try the cash drawers and the safe in order to see that they were tightly closed. Then he would lock his own little office and set the proper light burning near the safe, after which he would take his departure.

Never in his experience had he found anything out of order, but tonight, after shutting down his desk, he came out and tried the safe. His way was to give a sharp pull. This time the door responded. He was slightly surprised at that and, looking in, found the money cases, as left for the day, apparently unprotected. His first thought was of course to inspect the drawers and shut the door.

"I'll speak to Mayhew about this, tomorrow," he thought.

The latter had certainly imagined upon going out a half-hour before that he had turned the knob on the door so as to spring the lock. He had never failed to do so before. But tonight Mayhew had had other thoughts. He had been revolving the problem of a business of his own.

"I'll look in here," thought the manager, pulling out one of the money drawers. He did not know why he wished to look in there. It was quite a superfluous action, which another time might not have happened at all.

As he did so a layer of bills, in parcels of a thousand, such as banks issue, caught his eye. He could not tell how much they represented but paused to view them. Then he pulled out the second of the cash drawers. In that were the receipts of the day.

"I didn't know Hannah or Hogg ever left any money this way," his mind said to itself. "They must have forgotten it."

He looked at the other drawer again and paused again.

"Count them," said a voice in his ear.

He put his hand into the first of the boxes and lifted the stack, letting the separate parcels fall. They were bills of fifty and one hundred dollars, done in packages of a thousand. He thought he counted ten such.

"Why don't I shut the safe?" his mind said to itself, lingering. "What makes me pause here?"

For answer there came the strangest words, "Did you ever have ten thousand dollars in ready money?"

Lo, the manager remembered that he had never had so much. All his property had been slowly accumulated, and now his wife owned that. He was worth more than forty thousand all told—and she would get that.

He puzzled as he thought of these things—then pushed in the drawers and closed the door, pausing with his hand upon the knob which might so easily lock it all beyond his temptation. Still he paused. Finally he went to the windows and pulled down the curtain. Then he tried the door, which he had previously locked. What was this thing making him suspicious? Why did he wish to move about so quietly? He came back to the end of the counter as if to rest his arm and think. Then he went and unlocked his little office door and turned on the light. He also opened his desk, sitting down before it, only to think strange thoughts.

"The safe is open," said a voice. "There is just the least little crack in it. The lock has not been sprung."

The manager floundered among a jumble of thoughts. Now all the entanglement of the day came back. Also the thought that here was a solution. That money would do it. If he had that and Carrie. He rose up and stood stock still, looking at his shoes.

"What about it?" his mind asked, and for answer he put his hand slowly up and scratched his ear.

The manager was no fool, to be led blindly away by such an errant proposition as this, but his situation was peculiar. Wine was in his veins. It had crept up into his head and given him a warm view of the situation. It also colored the possibilities of ten thousand for him. He could see great opportunities with that. He could get Carrie—oh, yes he could. He could get rid of his wife. That letter, too, was waiting discussion tomorrow morning. He would not need to answer that. He went back to the safe and put his hand on the knob. Then he pulled the door open and took the drawer, with the money, quite out.

With it once out and before him it seemed a foolish thing to think about leaving it. Certainly it would. Why he could live quietly with Carrie for years.

Lord! what was that. For the first time he was tense, as if a stern hand had been laid upon his shoulder. He looked fearfully around. Not a soul was present. Not a sound. Some one was shuffling by on the side walk. He took the box and the money and put it back in the safe. Then he partly closed the door again.

To those who have never wavered in conscience, the predicament of the individual whose mind is less strongly constituted, and who trembles in the balance between duty and desire, is one which is scarcely appreciable, unless graphically portrayed. Those who have never heard that solemn voice of the ghostly clock of the mind which ticks with awful distinctness "thou shalt," "thou shalt not," "thou shalt," "thou shalt not," are in no position to judge. Not alone in sensitive, highly organized natures is such a mental conflict possible. The dullest specimen of humanity, when drawn by desire toward evil, is recalled by a sense of right, which is proportionate in power and strength to his evil tendency. We must remember that it may not be a knowledge of right, for no knowledge of right is predicated of the animal's instinctive recoil at evil. Men are still led by instincts before they are regulated by knowledge. It is instinct which recalls the criminal—it is instinct, (where highly organized reasoning is absent), which gives the criminal his feeling of danger, his fear of wrong.

At every first adventure, then, into some untried evil, the mind wavers. The clock of thought ticks out its wish and its denial. To those who have never experienced such a mental dilemma, the following will appeal on the simple ground of revelation.

When Hurstwood put the money back, his nature again resumed its ease and daring. No one had observed him. He was quite alone. No one could tell what he wished to do. He could work this thing out for himself.

The imbibation of the evening had not yet worn off. Moist as was his brow, tremble as did his hand once after the nameless fright, he was still flushed with the fumes of liquor. He scarcely noticed that the time was passing. He went over his situation once again, always his eye seeing the money in a lump, always his mind seeing what it would do. He strolled into his little room, then to the door, then to the safe again. He put his hand on the knob and opened it. There was the money. Surely no harm could come from looking at the money.

He took out the drawer again and lifted the bills—they were so smooth, so compact, so portable. How little they made after all. He decided he would take them. Yes, he would, he would put them in his pocket. Then he looked at that and saw they would not go there. His hand satchel! To be sure, his hand satchel. They would go in that—all of it would. No one would think anything of it either. He went into the little office and took it from the shelf in the corner. He remembered, as he did so, the little junket he had made the last time he used it. Now he set it upon his desk and went out toward the safe. For some reason he did not want to fill it out in the big room.

First he brought the bills and then the loose receipts of the day. He would take it all. He put the empty drawers back and pushed the iron door almost to—then he stood beside it meditating.

The wavering of a mind under such circumstances is an almost inexplicable thing and yet it is absolutely true. Hurstwood could not bring himself to act definitely. He wanted to think about it—to ponder it over, to decide whether it were best. He was drawn by such a keen desire for Carrie, driven by such a state of turmoil in his own affairs, that he thought constantly that it would be best, and yet he wavered. He did not know what evil might result from it to him—how soon he might come to grief. The true ethics of the situation never once occurred to him. It is most certain that they never would have, under any circumstances.

After he had all the money in the hand bag, a revulsion of feeling seized him. He would not do it—no. Think of what a scandal it would make. The police, they would be after him. He would have to fly, and where? Oh, the terror of being a fugitive from justice. He took out the two boxes and put all the money back. In his excitement he forgot what he was doing and put the sums in the wrong boxes. Then he pushed the door to, but in doing so he thought he remembered doing it wrong and opened the door again. There were the two boxes mixed.

He took them out and straightened the matter, but now the terror had gone. Why be afraid? Could he not get away? What would be the use of remaining? He would never get such a chance again. He emptied the good money into the satchel. There was something fascinating about the soft green stack—the loose silver and gold. He felt sure now that he could not leave that. No, no. He would do it. He would lock the safe before he had time to change his mind.

He went over and restored the empty boxes. Then he pushed the door to for somewhere near the sixth time. He wavered, thinking, putting his hand to his brow.

While the money was in his hand, the lock clicked. It had sprung. Did he do it? He grabbed at the knob and pulled vigorously. It had closed. Heavens! he was in for it now, sure enough.

The moment he realized that the safe was locked for a surety, the sweat burst out upon his brow and he trembled. He looked about him and decided instantly. There was no delaying now.

"Supposing I do lay it on the top," he said, "and go away. They'll know who took it. I'm the last to close up. Besides, other things will happen."

At once he became the man of action.

"I must get out of this," he thought.

He hurried into his little room, took down his light coat and hat, locked his desk and grabbed the satchel. Then he turned out all but the one light and opened the door. He tried to put on his old assured air, but it was almost gone. He was repenting rapidly.

"By the Lord," he said, "I wish I hadn't done that. By the Lord, that was a mistake."

He walked steadily down the street, greeting a night watchman, whom he knew, who was trying the doors. He must get out of the city and that quickly.

"I wonder how the trains run," he thought.

Instantly he pulled out his watch and looked. It was nearly half past one.

At the first drug store he stopped, seeing a long-distance telephone booth inside. It was a famous drug store and contained one of the first private telephone booths ever erected.

"I want to use your phone a minute," he said to the night clerk.

The latter nodded.

"Give me 1643," he called to Central, after looking up the Michigan Central Depot number. Soon he got the ticket agent.

"How do the trains leave here for Detroit?" he asked.

The man explained the hours.

"No more tonight?"

"Nothing with a sleeper. Yes, there is too," he added. "There's a mail train out of here at three o'clock."

"All right," said Hurstwood. "What time does that get to Detroit?"

He was thinking, if he could only get there and cross the river, into Canada, he could take his time about getting to Montreal. He was relieved to learn that it would reach there by noon.

"Mayhew won't open the safe till nine," he thought. "They can't get on my track before noon."

Then he thought of Carrie. With what speed must he get her, if he got her at all. She would have to come along. He jumped into the nearest cab standing by.

"To Ogden Place," he said sharply. "I'll give you a dollar more, if you make good time."

The cabby beat his horse into a sort of imitation gallop, which was fairly fast however. On the way, Hurstwood thought out what to do. Reaching the number he hurried up the steps and did not spare the bell in waking the servant.

"Is Mrs. Drouet in?" he asked.

"Yes," said the astonished girl.

"Tell her to dress and come to the door at once. Her husband is in the hospital injured, and wants to see her."

The servant girl hurried upstairs, convinced by the man's strained and emphatic manner.

"What?" said Carrie, lighting the gas and searching for her clothes.

"Mr. Drouet is hurt and in the hospital. He wants to see you. The cab's down stairs."

Carrie dressed very rapidly and soon appeared below, forgetting everything save the necessaries.

"Drouet is hurt," said Hurstwood, quickly. "He wants to see you. Come quickly."

Carrie was so bewildered that she swallowed the whole story.

"Get in," said Hurstwood, helping her and jumping after.

The cabby began to turn the horse around.

"Michigan Central Depot," he said, standing up and speaking so low that Carrie could not hear. "As fast as you can go."

CHAPTER XXX.

The cab had not traveled a short block before Carrie, settling herself and thoroughly waking in the night atmosphere, asked, "What's the matter with him? Is he hurt badly?"

The fact that Drouet was ill and in a hospital displaced the feeling of estrangement which had been growing, and aroused her sympathies. She was anxious to know.

"It isn't anything very serious," Hurstwood said solemnly. He was very much disturbed over his own situation and, now that he had Carrie with him, only wanted to get safely out of the reach of the law. Therefore he was in no mood for anything save such words as would further his plans distinctly.

Carrie did not forget that there was something to be settled between her and Hurstwood, but it did not seem very important. The one thing was to finish this strange midnight pilgrimage.

"Where is he?"

"Way out on the South Side," said Hurstwood. "We'll have to take the train. It's the quickest way."

Carrie said nothing and the horse gamboled on. The weirdness of the city by night held her attention. She looked at the long receding rows of lamps and studied the dark, silent houses with a feeling of awe. It seemed very good to be in a cab with a man for a companion.

"How did he hurt himself?" she asked—meaning what was the nature of his injuries. Hurstwood understood. He hated to lie any more than necessary, and yet he wanted no protests until he was out of danger.

"I don't know exactly," he said. "They just called me up and asked me to go and get you and bring you out. They said there wasn't any need for alarm, but that I shouldn't fail to bring you."

The man's serious manner convinced Carrie and she became silent, wondering.

Hurstwood examined his watch and urged the man to

hurry. For one in so delicate a position he was exceedingly cool. He could only think of how needful it was to make the train and get quietly away. Carrie seemed quite tractable and he congratulated himself.

In due time they reached the depot and after helping Carrie out he handed the man a five-dollar bill and hurried in.

"You wait here," he said to Carrie, when they reached the waiting room, "while I get the tickets."

"Have I much time to catch that train for Detroit?" he asked of the agent.

"Four minutes," said the latter.

He paid for two tickets as circumspectly as possible.

"Is it far?" said Carrie, as he hurried back.

"Not very," he said. "We must get right in."

He pushed her before at the gate, stood between her and the ticket man while the latter punched their tickets, so that she could not see, and then hurried after.

There was a long line of express and passenger cars and one or two common day-coaches. As the train had only recently been remade, and few passengers were expected, there were only one or two brakemen waiting. They entered the rear day-coach and sat down. Almost immediately "All aboard" resounded faintly from the outside and the train started.

Carrie began to think it was a little bit curious—this going to a depot, but said nothing. The whole incident was so out of the natural that she did not attach too much weight to anything she imagined.

"How have you been?" asked Hurstwood gently, for he now breathed slightly easier.

"Very well," said Carrie, who was so disturbed that she could not bring a proper attitude to bear in the matter. She was still nervous to reach Drouet and see what could be the matter. Hurstwood contemplated her and felt this. He was not disturbed that it should be so. He did not trouble because she was moved sympathetically in the matter. It was one of the qualities in her which pleased him exceedingly. He was only thinking how he should explain. Even this was not the most serious thing in his mind, however. His own deed and present flight were the great shadows which weighed upon him.

"What a fool I was to do that," he said over and over. "By the Lord, what a mistake!"

In his sober senses he could scarcely realize that the thing had been done. He could not begin to feel that he was a fugitive from justice. He had often read of such things and had thought they must be terrible, but now that the thing was upon him he only sat and looked into the past. The future was a thing which concerned the Canadian line. He wanted to reach that. As for the rest, he surveyed his actions for the evening and counted them parts of a great mistake.

"Still," he said, "what could I have done?"

Then he would decide to make the best of it, and would begin to do so: by starting the whole inquiry over again. It was a fruitless, harassing round and left him in a queer mood to deal with the proposition he had in the presence of Carrie.

The train clacked through the yards along the lake front and ran rather slowly to 24th Street. Brakes and signals were visible without. The engine gave short calls with its whistle, and frequently the bell rang. Several brakemen came through, bearing lanterns. They were locking the vestibules and putting the cars in order for a long run.

Presently it began to gain speed and Carrie saw the silent streets flashing by in rapid succession. The engine also began its whistle calls of four parts, with which it signaled danger to important crossings.

"Is it very far?" asked Carrie.

"Not so very," said Hurstwood. He could hardly repress a smile at her simplicity. He wanted to explain and conciliate her, but he wanted to be well out of Chicago.

In the lapse of another half-hour, it became apparent to Carrie that it was quite a run to wherever he was taking her anyhow.

"Is it in Chicago?" she asked nervously. They were now far beyond the city limits and the train was scudding across the Indiana line at a great rate.

"No," he said, "not where we are going."

There was something in the way he said this which aroused her in an instant.

Her pretty brow began to contract.

"We are going to see Charlie, aren't we?" she asked.

He felt that the time was up. An explanation might as well come now as later. Therefore he shook his head in the most gentle negative.

"What," said Carrie. She was nonplussed at the possibility of the errand being different from what she had thought.

He only looked at her in the most kindly and mollifying way.

"Well, where are you taking me, then?" she asked, her voice showing the quality of fright.

"I'll tell you, Carrie, if you'll be quiet. I want you to come along with me to another city."

"Oh," said Carrie, her voice rising into a weak cry. "Let me off. I don't want to go with you."

She was quite appalled at the man's audacity. This was something which had never for a moment entered her head. Her one thought now was to get off and away. If only the flying train could be stopped, the terrible trick would be amended.

She arose and tried to push out into the aisle—anywhere. She knew she had to do something. Hurstwood laid a gentle hand on her.

"Sit still, Carrie," he said. "Sit still. It won't do you any good to get up here. Listen to me and I'll tell you what I'll do. Wait a moment."

She was pushing at his knees, but he only pulled her back. No one saw this little altercation, for very few persons were in the car, and they were attempting to doze.

"I won't," said Carrie, who was nevertheless complying against her will. "Let me go," she said. "How dare you," and large tears began to gather in her eyes.

Hurstwood was now fully aroused to the immediate situation, and let go his thinking upon his own situation. He must do something with this girl or she would cause him trouble. He tried the art of persuasion, with all his powers aroused.

"Look here now, Carrie," he said. "You mustn't act this way. I didn't mean to hurt your feelings. I don't want to do anything to make you feel bad."

"Oh," sobbed Carrie. "Oh, oh-ou-o."

"There, there," he said, "you mustn't cry. Won't you listen to me? Listen to me a minute and I'll tell you why I came to do this thing. I couldn't help it. I assure you I couldn't. Won't you listen?"

Her sobs disturbed him so that he was quite sure she did not hear a word he said.

"Won't you listen?" he asked.

"No, I won't," said Carrie flashing up. "I want you to let me out of this or I'll tell the conductor. I won't go with you. It's a shame," and again sobs of fright cut off her desire for expression.

Hurstwood listened with some astonishment. He felt that she had just cause for feeling as she did and yet he wished deeply that he could straighten this thing out quickly. Shortly the conductor would come through for the tickets. He wanted no noise, no trouble of any kind. Lord, if he could only make her quiet.

"You couldn't get out until the train stops again," said Hurstwood. "It won't be very long until we reach another station. You can get out there if you want to. I won't stop you. All I want you to do is to listen a moment. You'll let me tell you, won't you?"

Carrie seemed not to listen. She only turned her head toward the window, where outside all was black. The train was speeding with steady grace across the fields and through patches of wood. The long whistle came with sad, musical effect as the lonely woodland crossings were approached.

Now the conductor entered the car and took up the one or two fares that had been added at Chicago. He approached Hurstwood, who handed out the tickets. Poised as she was to act, Carrie made no move. She did not look about. She was in such a state that she did not know what to do.

When the conductor had gone again Hurstwood felt relieved.

"You're angry at me because I deceived you," said Hurstwood. "I didn't mean to, Carrie. As I live I didn't. I couldn't help it. I couldn't stay away from you after the first time I saw you."

He was ignoring the last deception as something that might go by the board. He wanted to convince her that his wife could no longer be a factor in their relationship. The money he had stolen he tried to shut out of his mind.

"Don't talk to me," said Carrie. "I hate you. I want you to go away from me. I am going to get out at the very next station."

She was in a tremble of excitement and opposition as she spoke.

"All right," he said, "but you'll hear me out, won't you?

After all you have said about loving me, you might hear me. I don't want to do you any harm. I'll give you the money to go back with when you go. I merely want to tell you, Carrie. You can't stop me from loving you, whatever you may think."

He looked at her tenderly but received no reply.

"You think I deceived you badly, but I haven't. I didn't do it willingly. I'm done with my wife. She hasn't any claims on me. I'll never see her any more. That's why I'm here tonight. That's why I came and got you."

"You said Charlie was hurt," said Carrie savagely. "You lied to me. You've been lying all the time and now you want to force me to run away with you."

She was so excited that she got up and tried to get by him again. He let her and she took another seat. Then he followed.

"Don't run away from me, Carrie," he said gently. "Let me explain. If you will only hear me out, you will see where I stand. I tell you my wife is nothing to me. She hasn't been anything for years or I wouldn't have ever come near you. I'm going to get a divorce just as soon as I can. I'll never see her again. I'm done with all that. You're the only person I want. If I can have you, I won't ever think of another woman again."

Carrie heard all this in a very ruffled state. It sounded sincere enough, however, despite all he had done. There was a tenseness in Hurstwood's voice and manner which could not but have some effect. He actually felt deeply what he was saying and wished sincerely that he could overcome Carrie's distress and make her love him as before. Still, she did not want anything to do with him. He was married, he had deceived her once, and now again most cruelly, and she thought him terrible. Still, there is something in such daring and power which is fascinating to a woman, especially if she can be made to feel that it is all prompted by a love of her.

The progress of the train was having a great deal to do with the solution of this difficult situation. The speeding wheels and disappearing country put Chicago farther and farther behind. Carrie could feel that she was being borne a long distance off— that the engine was making an almost stopless run to some distant city. She felt at times as if she could cry out and make such a row that someone would come to her aid; at other times it seemed an almost useless thing—so far was she from any aid, no matter what she did. All the while Hurstwood was endeavoring to formulate his plea in such a way that it would strike home and bring her into sympathy with him.

"You see," he said, "I couldn't help it. You wouldn't have anything more to do with me—you said you wouldn't. I couldn't accept that, Carrie. I knew you loved me once and I just couldn't give you up. It was no use trying. I got where I couldn't live without you. I didn't want to deceive you, I won't any more. I was simply put where I didn't know what else to do."

Carrie deigned no suggestion of hearing this.

"When I saw you wouldn't come unless I could marry you, I decided to put everything else behind me and get you to come away with me. I'm going off now to another city. I want to go to Montreal for awhile and then anywhere you say, if you will come. I'll do anything you want to. We'll go and live in New York, if you say."

"I'll not have anything to do with you," said Carrie. "I want to get off this train. Where are we going?"

"To Detroit," said Hurstwood.

"Oh!" said Carrie, in a real burst of anguish. So distant and definite a point seemed to increase the difficulty.

"You'll never want for anything if you'll only let me take care of you, Carrie. I'll give you a good home. You don't need to decide right away. You can come along with me and when you get ready, we'll get married. I'll not trouble you, I promise you that. You can be to yourself all you want to, only I want to have you near where I can see you, at least."

Still Carrie made no answer.

"Won't you come along with me?" he said, as if there was great danger that she would not. "You won't need to do anything but travel with me. I'll not trouble you in any way. You can see Montreal and New York, and then if you don't want to stay you can go back. It will be better than trying to go back tonight."

The first gleam of fairness shone in this proposition for Carrie. It seemed a plausible thing to do, much as she feared his opposition if she tried to carry it out. Montreal and New York. Even now she was speeding toward those strange lands and could see them if she liked. She thought, but made no sign.

Hurstwood thought he saw a shade of compliance in this. He redoubled his ardor.

"Think," he said, "what I'm giving up. I can't go back to Chicago any more. I've got to stay away and live alone now, if you don't come with me. You won't go back on me entirely will you, Carrie?"

"I don't want you to talk to me," she answered forcibly.

Hurstwood kept silence for awhile.

"Won't you even go as far as Montreal?" he asked.

They were nearing Michigan City, the first station where the engine stopped for coal and water. The engine whistled the long announcement of its coming, the sound fleeing like a piteous wail through the night.

"Won't you?" he said softly. "I don't think I can go without you."

Carrie felt the train to be slowing down. It was the moment to act if she was to act at all. She stirred uneasily.

"Don't think of going, Carrie," he said. "If you ever cared for me at all, come along and let's start right. I'll do whatever you say. I'll marry you or I'll let you come back. Give yourself time to think it over. I wouldn't have wanted you to come if I hadn't loved you. I tell you, Carrie, before God, I can't live without you, I won't."

There was a tensity and fierceness in the man's plea which appealed deeply to Carrie's sympathies. It was a dissolving fire which was actuating him now. He was loving her too intensely to think of giving her up in this, his hour of distress. He clutched her hand nervously and pressed it with all the force of an appeal.

The train was now all but stopped. It was running by some cars on a side track. Everything outside was dark and dreary. A few sprinkles on the window began to indicate that it was raining. Carrie hung in a quandary, balancing between decision and helplessness. Now the train stopped, and she was listening to his plea. The engine backed a few feet, and all was still.

"Think how I love you, Carrie," said the ex-manager. "Think how miserable you'll make me if you go."

Still she wavered, totally unable to make a move. Minute after minute slipped by and still she hesitated, he pleading. At last the opportunity was drawing to a close. She had admitted the possibility of getting off at another station.

"Will you let me come back if I want to?" she asked, as if

she now had the upper hand, and her companion were utterly subdued.

"Of course," he answered, "you know I will."

The engine bell clanged clearly and the wheels began to grate with a slow, onward movement.

"You'll come," he said, "won't you?" as she still wavered. He realized the softened manner. "Oh, you can have anything you want," he went on. "I'll show you how good I can be."

Carrie only listened as one who has granted a temporary amnesty. She began to feel as if the matter were in her hands entirely.

The train was again in rapid motion. Hurstwood changed the subject.

"Aren't you very tired?" he said.

"No," she answered.

"Won't you let me get you a berth in the sleeper?"

She shook her head, though for all her distress and his trickery, she was beginning to notice what she had always admired, his thoughtfulness.

"Oh, yes," he said, "you will feel so much better."

She shook her head.

"Let me fix my coat for you anyway," and he arose and arranged his light coat in a comfortable position to receive her head.

"There," he said tenderly, "now see if you can't rest a little." He could have kissed her for her compliance. He took his seat beside her and thought a moment.

"I believe we're in for a heavy rain," he said.

"So it looks," said Carrie, whose nerves were slightly quieting under the sound of the rain drops, driven by a gusty wind, as the train swept on frantically through the shadow to a newer world.

CHAPTER XXXI.

During the onward flight of the train Carrie brooded over her situation, which was by no means pleasing. She tried to aid herself by means of ideas, of which she was not short. Indeed, it was to a surplus of them which might be attributed her hesitation and doubt. The discovery that Drouet was not ill modified her sympathy in that direction as much as it irritated her with regard to Hurstwood's. She had readily forgiven or put out of consciousness the feeling she had against Drouet when she heard he was ill. Now that she realized that he was not injured in any way she recalled that he had never returned— that he had cast her off, as it were, to shift and struggle alone. This was not complimentary to the drummer. Only that very afternoon had she wrung her hands in misery as she realized that he had been there and removed his few belongings.

Also she remembered, lying disconsolately back against the car seat and listening to the swift, clicking sound of the rails, that she had had no resource for the morrow, save the position in the art portrait office at five dollars a week; that if she returned, she had no one to whom she might repair. Drouet had cast her off. Hurstwood was not there. She had no friends and no acquaintances. It would be a hopeless situation in which she might suffer and come to—she knew not what. All this affected her deeply, for she was a sensitive soul and grieved over many things. The fact that she was in a train and being hurried away, perforce, to other situations and other scenes was the one contrast to all the Chicago misery, and that in itself was no relief. She knew that even here she was being unjustly dealt with and made baggage of. It was a shame and a disgrace, and yet what could she do? Not infrequently after such meditations, tears came into her eyes and she wept silently. It was all wrong with her, no matter what she tried to do.

Hurstwood, this first trouble apparently over, went back to his own situation. He could not sleep. The little grip containing the stolen money he kept beside him, slightly concealed behind his coat. He was very much worried lest something should happen. What telegrams might come? How soon in the early morning might they search the train? Then as to his wife and his children. He hated the former thoroughly for the trouble she had caused him, but he felt sorry for Jessica. Tomorrow the papers would be full of his theft—the afternoon papers. He could hear the news boys crying about in the down town streets. He could see Hannah's frown and Hogg's wrath. The bartenders, what amazement would be theirs. He saw the swell resort as it would be when the discovery of the defalcation was made. How the cashier would stare; how he would report to the owners; how to the police. Then his wife would be notified. What a blow to her social ambitions. He bit his lip as he thought of all the mess he had created—the wrath, the anger, the distress. Yet here he was safe out of it all, but going he knew not where, afraid of the money he had with him, afraid of the future, and his Carrie unwilling to accompany him. What would she think when she learned that he was a safe-robber, when she learned that she had been compelled to run away in the dead of night with a man who was fleeing from justice. He would try to keep the papers from her. She should not know of it, if it were possible.

Ah, his fine position, his elegant office; how had he cut himself off from that. Tomorrow his friends would come—Marvin, Phillips, Anderson, the whole fine, well-dressed, well-situated throng which he knew. What would they think, how would they look, what would they say? Oh, the fineness of the thing from which he had cut himself—the friends, the standing. Yes, the wrath of his wife—her lawyers' letter—he knew all about that, but what was it after all? Certainly no excuse for such a crazy, idiotic, horrible thing like this he had fallen into. He could have gotten out all right. He could have acceded to his wife's demands; he could have given in and straightened it out with her. Why had he not done so—oh, why had he not done so? What would he do now, far off in Canada without anyone he knew. He could not meet his old friends; he could not use his own name. He would have to drop that and adopt some other. He would have to explain to Carrie. Oh, what a mixup. How had he jumped from the frying pan into the fire. The ills he had borne: how much easier it would have been to have borne them than to fly thus to these he knew not of. He could not understand how he had come to do it. He must have been mad, drunk and demoniac. He could not explain it upon any grounds whatever.

This train of thought was a burden to carry. It rocked his brain and dampened his brow. It made his head ache and caused him to be nervous and fearful. He was in a subdued mood and yet staringly clear. He could not sleep, could not feel good enough to stay awake. In short he was wretched and waited with dogged patience until he could get into Canada. Maybe, over there, he would feel better.

The minutes passed and with them came fitful, nervous dozing to both. Carrie imagined all sorts of things and so did he. They were brought to by the early light of the morning, which now glimmered in the east. The rain had ceased. On either hand, wet green fields and lovely woodland prospects were scudding by. Carrie was too troubled and weary to appreciate such things, much as they usually appealed to her. Hurstwood had no taste for such things at all. It was Canada for him or nothing.

By half-past five he was sitting up again, bright and clear in the head. So was Carrie. She was no less distressed and not inclined to consider him as present. He, however, found his one consolation in looking at her. She was so pretty in her distress. He would have given a great deal to have restored her to confidence and affection.

"Let's have a cup of coffee," he said, "and lunch. You'll feel better."

"If you want to," she replied.

He called the porter, who brought a table board, and ordered the coffee. Carrie scarcely ate anything, but drank the coffee. It made her stronger for the time being.

Hurstwood's vitality was very much restored by what he ate. The approaching sunlight encouraged him. He proposed at once to say more concerning his action of the night and win Carrie over to his side. His love for her was no trivial thing and he longed to feel that she, at least, would be with him in this dim future of which he could foretell nothing. Accordingly he addressed her with even greater tenderness.

"Don't you think you can ever forgive me, Carrie?" he said, "for deceiving you this way?"

"No," she answered, without looking at him, "I can't."

"Even if I make every amend in my power?"

She did not answer.

"Can't you see," he said, ignoring her silence, "that I wouldn't have done as I did if I didn't love you. I wouldn't want you with me if I didn't care for you."

He stopped, but she only looked out upon the moving panorama of rural life.

"If you will only believe in me again," he went on, "I'll lead a life that you can be proud of. I'll go into business of some kind," he said, "and we'll live in a nice home."

Carrie thought of this but did not wish to do so. Hurstwood waited a few moments, studying the profile of her face, which was turned away.

"Don't you care for me at all?" he asked.

She was comparing this picture of the future with that which lay behind. Here was offered her a chance for a decent life in another city. She would be away from all past associations, she would be in a new world. Hurstwood was not an evil individual. As yet he had worked her no harm. He had deceived her, but he was not attempting to brutally force her to do something which she seriously objected to. So far he had given her liberty to act for herself. He had promised to let her return, to give her money to do so if she wished. Also he wished to do the only thing possible, get a divorce and marry her. It was a pleasing thing to see him so attentive, so anxious. He was offering everything except her absence from him, and that was because he loved her too much to let her go away. More, he opened a kindly door out of many troubles, and that was something. She could not well forget that she had nowhere else to go.

"Won't you stay with me?" he went on, "if I do everything I can to make things right again? You certainly can't hate me after all I have done."

She felt that he was not looking at her and took a secret glance. He was sitting head down, staring at his shoes. He was the same handsome Hurstwood she had so long admired, only now apparently sorrowful. His clothes were as neat as ever, his whole appearance as perfect as clothes could make it. Carrie wanted to make some answer, but could not bring herself to do so. She turned her head away.

"Look at me, Carrie," he said gently, turning toward her. "You don't really hate me do you?"

Carrie took a shy glance at him, but looked quickly down.

"No," she said, "I don't hate you."

"Well, don't you think you can forgive me, and we'll start all over again?"

She shook her head unwillingly.

"Why not?" he asked.

"You know why," she answered.

He dropped again into his old attitude. Minutes rolled away before he spoke, for he realized that she would soon make up if he would plead enough.

"Can't you forget that and let me start all over again?"

She did not answer.

"Can't you?" he said.

She still looked away.

"Please look at me, Carrie," he said. "I mean to do everything that's right. Won't you try and forgive me?"

She almost smiled to herself mentally as she heard this. It was a pleasing thing.

"I'll think about it," she said coolly.

He looked at her most merrily and said, "Will you come to Montreal?"

She paused awhile and then nodded her head.

"Oh," he said nervously, "I knew you would. You wouldn't turn me down altogether." He pressed her hand which was near him, but she drew it away.

"Won't you tell me that you care for me the least little bit?" he said.

"No, I won't," she said sharply, but there was something else in the voice besides wrath.

"Let's go back in the sleeper," he said, "where it's more comfortable. Will you?"

"If you want to," she answered.

He went off to hunt up the Pullman conductor and purchase day seats.

"Come on," he said, "I've arranged all right."

He gathered up his overcoat and the small satchel full of money.

"Mighty little baggage, isn't it?" he said playfully.

Carrie only smiled.

"This hasty traveling makes one forget lots of things, don't it?" he added.

Carrie could scarcely resist his humor. She was beginning to see things with his eyes.

"Now then," he said, when they were seated in the new

section, "I wonder when they put on the dining car. We get to Detroit by noon."

Carrie looked about her on the luxurious furnishings. It was the second time she had ever been in a Pullman car in her life.

"Do we change cars there?" she asked.

"Yes, we go over to Walkerville, I think," he said, knowing full well that it was Canada he wished to reach without waiting for any train unless one left at once.

The fact that he had, in a measure, mollified Carrie, was a source of satisfaction to Hurstwood, but it furnished only the most temporary relief. Now that her opposition was out of the way, he had all of his time to devote to the consideration of his own error, which he did. He wished he could see something in the future which lay before him. Already he was wondering what sort of a position he could get. Ten thousand dollars was nothing. Besides, he was beginning to feel that he had no right to it, that he could never use it.

His condition was bitter in the extreme, for he did not want the miserable sum he had stolen. He did not want to be a thief. That sum, or any other, could never compensate for the state which he had thus foolishly doffed. It could not give him back his host of friends, his name, his house and family, nor Carrie as he had meant to have her. He was shut out from Chicago, from his easy comfortable state. He had robbed himself of his dignity, his merry meetings, his pleasant evenings. And for what? The more he thought of it, the more unbearable it became. He began to think that he would try to restore himself to his own state. He would return the miserable thievings of the night and explain. Perhaps Hogg would understand. Perhaps they would forgive him and let him come back.

Wild as this imagining was, it seemed plausible enough in the face of the wilder actualities in which he had figured. It could not be worse than this future which lay before him—dark, friendless, exiled. He had no profession. Managing was nothing which could be had for the asking. He would have to explain his experience, and how could he do that without telling what he had done? The money he had taken he did not want to use. He ought to send it back. Then he remembered how ridiculous it would have seemed the day before if anyone had told him that today he would be worrying about money. The horrible truth that he, anyone, everyone could be where they needed money and could not get it flashed upon him with a sickening panoramic effect. He felt that his position was most difficult. He would have to look about at once and get started. Ah, and how. And oh, worst of all, it would need to be done in a strange city and among strange people. He would not have his friends. Nostalgy began to affect his vitals. That dread yearning for the fixed, the stable, the accustomed, which seizes those who reflect an atmosphere in their blood, began to make its way in him. He longed for Chicago, for his old ways and pleasant places. He wanted to go back and remain there, let the cost be what it would.

These were his feelings, among others. In one place he looked out of the window and saw a great sign on some long factory or other which read "George B. Murdoch." He looked at it casually and saw little points in the scene which struck him agreeably. "George B. Murdoch," done in large white letters, stayed before his eye. Why wouldn't that be a good name for him to use. George B. Murdoch. No, George H. Murdoch, or just George Murdoch. He thought about this quite some time and half-felt that that would be the name he would use. It struck him as being much the sort of name he would like to have.

By noon the train rolled into Detroit and he began to feel exceedingly nervous. The police must be on his track by now. They had probably notified all the police of the big cities, and detectives would be watching for him. He remembered instances in which defaulters had been captured. Consequently, he breathed heavily and paled somewhat. His hands felt as if they must have something to do. He simulated interest in several scenes without, which he did not feel. He repeatedly beat his foot upon the floor.

Carrie noticed his agitation, but said nothing. She had no idea what it meant or that it was important.

He wondered now why he had not asked whether this train went on through to Montreal or some Canadian point. Perhaps he could have saved time. He jumped up and sought out the conductor.

"Does any part of this train go to Montreal?" he asked.

"Yes, the next sleeper back does."

He would have asked more but it did not seem wise, so he decided to inquire at the depot.

The train rolled into the yards, clanging and puffing.

"I think we had better go right on through to Montreal," he said to Carrie. "I'll see what the connections are when we get off."

He was exceedingly nervous but did his best to put on a calm exterior. Carrie only looked at him with large, troubled eyes. She was drifting mentally, unable to say to herself what to do.

The train stopped and Hurstwood led the way out. He looked warily around him, pretending to look after Carrie. Seeing nothing that indicated studied observation, he made his way to the ticket office.

"The next train for Montreal leaves when?" he asked.

"In twenty minutes," said the man.

He bought two tickets and Pullman berths. Then he hastened back to Carrie.

"We go right out again," he said, scarcely noticing that Carrie looked tired and weary.

"I wish I was out of this all," she exclaimed gloomily.

"You'll feel better when we reach Montreal," he said.

"I haven't an earthly thing with me," said Carrie, "not even a handkerchief."

"You can buy all you want as soon as you get there, dearest," he explained. "You can call in a dressmaker."

Carrie said nothing and Hurstwood breathed easy. He saw no detectives anywhere.

Now the crier called the train ready and they got on. Hurstwood breathed a sigh of relief as it started. There was a short run to the river and then they were ferried over. They had barely pulled the train off the ferry boat when he settled back with a sigh.

"It won't be so very long now," he said, remembering her in his relief. "We get in the first thing in the morning."

Carrie scarcely deigned to reply.

"I'll see if they haven't got on a dining car," he added. "I'm hungry."

CHAPTER XXXII.

To the untraveled, territory other than their own familiar heath is invariably fascinating. Next to love it is the one thing which solaces and delights. It is a boon to the weary and distressed, the one thing, which, because of its boundless pro-digality of fact and incident, causes the mind to forget. Not even wounded love can long wander to and fro amid new scenes without in a measure forgetting its wound. The things to see are too important to be neglected, and mind, which is a mere re-flection of sensory impressions, succumbs to this flood of objects. It is so busy storing new ideas that there is scarcely any time for old ones. Thus lovers are forgotten, sorrows laid aside, death hidden from view. There is a world of accumulated feeling back of the trite dramatic expression—"I am going away." To the untraveled, that is the only equivalent for love lost—the one partial compensation, the thing which, if it cannot restore, can make us forget. Let us not forget therefore that Carrie, the untraveled, was traveling.

As she looked out upon the flying scenery, she almost forgot that she had been tricked into this long journey against her will, and that she was without the necessary apparel for traveling. She quite forgot Hurstwood's presence at times, and looked away to lonely farm houses and cosy cottages in villages with won-dering eyes. It was an interesting world to Carrie. Her life had just begun. She did not feel herself defeated at all. Neither was she blasted in hope. The great city held something, she knew not what. Possibly she would come out of bondage into free-dom—who knows? Perhaps she would be happy. These were thoughts, which in the thinking raised her above the level of the erring. She was saved in that she was hopeful.

Hurstwood conversed some with her after leaving Detroit, but as the day waned, both grew weary and slept. By eight-thirty the porter began to let down the berths, and by nine many were retired. Hurstwood was the first to suggest that she retire early. After she had gone he went forward to smoke a cigar but found no comfort. Before long he sought his berth, and so the night was passed.

The following morning the train pulled safely into Montreal and they stepped down, Hurstwood glad to be out of danger, Carrie wondering at the novel atmosphere of the northern city. Long before, Hurstwood had been here, and now he remembered the name of the hotel at which he had stopped. As they came out of the main entrance of the depot, he heard it called anew by a busman.

"We'll go right up and get rooms," he said to Carrie, moving with her toward the welcoming busman.

Carrie acquiesced and he helped her in. The bus drove through streets radically different from those of Chicago to the large hotel, which they entered by the ladies' way.

"Sit down a moment," said Hurstwood as they reached the little waiting room. "I'll go and see about the room."

Carrie, however, preferred to walk about and look at the few pictures on the walls.

At the clerk's office Hurstwood swung the register about while the clerk came forward. He was thinking what name he would put down. With the latter before him, he found no time for hesitation. The name he had seen out of the car window came swiftly back. It was pleasing enough. With an easy hand he wrote "G. W. Murdoch and wife." It was the largest concession he felt like making to necessity. His initials he could not spare.

"Anything on the second floor with a bath?" he asked.

The clerk studied his list.

"Yes, number eleven."

"Let me see it," he said.

A boy was called and he went to look. For a wonder it was eminently satisfactory, being decorated in dark green, with furniture to match, and having three outside windows. He kept the key and went down for Carrie.

"I think I've got a suitable room for you," he said quietly.

Carrie also liked it. She was soothed by the simple, decorative treatment of the place. She felt at once that he had secured her a lovely chamber.

"You have a bath there," said he. "Now you can clean up when you get ready."

Carrie went over and looked out the window, while Hurstwood looked at himself in the glass. He felt dusty and unclean. He had no trunk, no change of linen, not even a hair brush.

"I'll ring for soap and towels," he said, "and send you up a hair brush. Then you bathe and get ready for breakfast. I'll go for a shave and come back and get you, and then we'll go out and look for some clothes for you."

He smiled goodnaturedly as he said this.

"All right," said Carrie.

She sat down in one of the rocking chairs, while Hurstwood waited for the boy, who soon knocked.

"Soap, towels and a pitcher of ice water."

"Yes, sir."

"I'll go now," he said to Carrie, coming towards her and holding out his hands, but she did not move to take them.

"You're not mad at me, are you?" he asked softly.

"Oh, no," she answered, rather indifferently.

"Don't you care for me at all?"

She made no answer but looked steadily toward the window.

"Don't you think you could love me a little?" he pleaded, taking one of her hands, which she endeavored to draw away. "You once said you did."

"What made you deceive me so?" asked Carrie.

"I couldn't help it," he said. "I wanted you too much."

"You didn't have any right to want me," she answered, striking cleanly home.

"Oh, well, Carrie," he answered, "here I am. It's too late now. Won't you try and care for me a little?"

He looked rather worsted in thought as he stood before her.

She shook her head negatively.

"Let me start all over again. Be my wife from today on."

Carrie rose up as if to step away, he holding her hand. Now he slipped his arm about her and she struggled, but in vain. He held her quite close. Instantly there flowed up in his body the all-compelling desire. His affection took an ardent form.

"Let me go," said Carrie, who was folded close to him.

"Won't you love me?" he said. "Won't you be mine from now on?"

Carrie had never been ill-disposed toward him. Only a moment before she had been listening with some complacency, remembering her old affection for him. He was so handsome, so daring.

Now, however, this feeling had changed to one of oppo-sition, which rose futilely. It mastered her for a moment, and then, held close as she was, began to wane. Something else in her spoke. This man to whose bosom she was being pressed was strong, he was passionate, he loved her and she was alone. If she did not turn to him—accept of his love, where else might she go? Also the physical claims its own. Her resistance half-dissolved in the flood of his strong feeling.

"Won't you love me a little?" he asked. "I'll start over. Won't you own that you love me?"

Carrie was relaxing her struggle. She found him lifting her head and looking into her eyes. What magnetism there was, she could never know. His many sins, however, were for the mo-ment all forgotten.

He pressed her closer and kissed her, and she felt that further opposition was useless.

"Will you marry me?" she asked, forgetting *how*.

"This very day," he said with all delight.

Now the hall boy pounded on the door, and he released his hold upon her regretfully.

"You get ready now, will you?" he said. "At once."

"Yes," she answered.

"I'll be back in three-quarters of an hour."

Carrie, flushed and excited, moved away, as he admitted the boy.

Below stairs he halted in the lobby to look for a barber-shop. For the moment he was in fine feather. His recent victory over Carrie seemed to atone for much he had endured during the last few days. Life seemed worth fighting for. The eastward flight from all things customary and attached seemed as if it might have happiness waiting at the end of it. The storm showed a rainbow, at the end of which might be a pot of gold.

He was about to cross to a little red and white striped bar which was fastened up beside a door, when a voice greeted him familiarly. Instantly his heart sank.

"Why hello, George, old man," said the voice. "What are you doing down here?"

Hurstwood was already confronted and recognized his friend Kenny, the stock broker.

"Just tending to a little private matter," he answered, his

mind working like the keyboard of a telephone station. This man evidently did not know—he had not read the papers.

"Well, it seems strange to see you way up here," said Mr. Kenny genially. "Stopping here?"

"Yes," said Hurstwood uneasily, thinking of his handwriting on the register.

"Going to be in town long?"

"No, only a day or so."

"Is that so. Had your breakfast?"

"Yes," said Hurstwood, lying blandly. "I'm just going for a shave."

"Won't come have a drink?"

"Not until afterwards," said the ex-manager. "I'll see you later. Are you stopping here?"

"Yes," said Mr. Kenny, and then turning the word again added, "How are things out in Chicago?"

"About the same as usual," said Hurstwood, smiling genially.

"Wife with you?"

"No."

"Well, I must see more of you today. I'm just going in here for breakfast. Come in when you're through."

"I will," said Hurstwood, moving away. The whole conversation was a trial to him. It seemed to add complications with every word. This man called up a thousand memories. He represented everything he had left. Chicago, his wife, the elegant resort—all these were in his greeting and inquiries. And here he was in this same hotel, expecting to confer with him, unquestionably waiting to have a good time with him. All at once the Chicago papers would arrive. The local papers would have accounts in them this very day. He forgot his triumph with Carrie in the possibility of soon being known for what he was, in this man's eyes, a safe-breaker. He could have groaned as he went into the barber-shop. He decided to escape this friend and stay with Carrie—to seek a more secluded hotel.

Accordingly, when he came out, he was glad to see the lobby clear, and hastened toward the stairs. He would get Carrie and go out by the ladies' entrance. They would have breakfast in some more inconspicuous place.

Across the lobby, however, another individual was surveying him. He was of a commonplace Irish type, small of stature, cheaply dressed and with a head that seemed a smaller edition of some huge ward politician's. This individual had been evidently talking with the clerk, but now he surveyed the ex-manager keenly.

Hurstwood felt the long-range examination and recognized the type. Instinctively he felt that the man was a detective, that he was being watched. He hurried across, pretending not to notice, but in his mind were a world of thoughts. What would happen now? What could these people do? He began to trouble concerning the extradition laws. He did not understand them absolutely. Perhaps he could be arrested. Oh, if Carrie should find out. Montreal was too warm for him. He began to long to be out of it.

Carrie had bathed and was waiting when he arrived. She looked refreshed—more delightful than ever, but reserved. Since he had gone she had resumed somewhat of her cold attitude toward him. Love was not blazing in her heart. He felt it and his troubles seemed increased. He could not take her in his arms; he did not even try. Something about her forbade it. In part his opinion was the result of his own experiences and reflections below stairs.

"You're ready, are you?" he said kindly.

"Yes," she answered.

"We'll go out for breakfast. This place down here don't appeal to me very much."

"All right," said Carrie.

They went out and turned into the main street, but at the corner the commonplace Irish individual was standing, eyeing him. Hurstwood could scarcely refrain from showing that he knew of this chap's presence. The insolence in the fellow's eye was galling. Still they passed, and he explained to Carrie concerning the city. Another restaurant was not long in showing itself, and here they entered.

"What a queer town this is," said Carrie, who marveled at it solely because it was not like Chicago.

"It isn't as lively as Chicago," said Hurstwood. "Don't you like it?"

"No," said Carrie, whose feelings were already localized in the great western city.

"Well, it isn't as interesting," said Hurstwood.

"What's here?" asked Carrie, wondering at his choosing to visit this town.

"Nothing much," returned Hurstwood. "It's quite a resort. There's some pretty scenery about here."

Carrie listened but with a feeling of unrest. This city did not appeal to her. There was much about her situation which destroyed the possibility of appreciation.

"We won't stay here long," said Hurstwood, who was now really glad to note her dissatisfaction. "You pick out your clothes as soon as breakfast is over and we'll run down to New York soon. You'll like that. It's a lot more like a city than any place outside Chicago."

He was really planning to slip out and away. He would see what these detectives would do—what move his employers at Chicago would make—then he would slip away—down to New York where it was easy to hide. He knew enough about that city to know that its mysteries, and possibilities of mystification, were infinite.

The more he thought, however, the more wretched his situation became. He saw that getting here did not exactly clear up the ground. The firm would probably employ detectives to watch him—Pinkerton men or agents of Mooney and Boland. They might arrest him the moment he tried to leave Canada. So he might be compelled to remain here months, and in what a state! His heart revolted at it. Nothing in Montreal appealed to him. It was comparatively small—comparatively provincial. Worst of all it was not Chicago—and now that he was threatened with long separation from that place and his daily duties and greetings, the misery of it became great. He began to feel the first faint touches of nostalgy—as old and experienced as he was.

After breakfast he went with Carrie to several large dry-goods stores and waited while she ordered a number of things. Young as she was, Carrie had already a fund of experience to draw upon. Thrown thus upon her own responsibility in the matter of selecting clothing, she arose and met the occasion with admirable determination. Her selection was altogether good, because while following her feelings, she had not forgotten the advice of Mrs. Hale. She selected with fair rapidity and finally came away.

"Got all you want?" asked Hurstwood.

"All I need just now," answered Carrie.

At the hotel Hurstwood was anxious and yet fearful to see the morning papers. He wanted to know how far the news of his criminal deed had spread. So he told Carrie he would be up in a few moments, and went to secure and scan the dailies. No familiar or suspicious faces were about, and yet he did not like reading in the lobby, so he sought the main parlor on the floor above and, seated by a window there, looked them over. Very little was given to his crime, but it was there, several "sticks" in all, among all the riff-raff of telegraphed murders, accidents, marriages and other news items from out the length and breadth of the land. He wished deeply, as he read, that all his eyes followed were not true. He wished half-sadly that he could undo it. Every moment of his time in this far-off abode of safety but added to his feeling that he had made a great mistake. There could have been an easier way out, if he had only known.

He left the papers before going to the room, thinking thus to keep them out of the hands of Carrie.

"Well, how are you feeling?" he asked of her. She was engaged in looking out of the window.

"Oh, all right," she answered.

He came over and was about to begin a conversation with her when a knock came at their door.

"Maybe it's one of my parcels," said Carrie.

Hurstwood opened the door, outside of which stood the individual whom he so thoroughly suspected.

"You're Mr. Hurstwood, are you?" said the latter with a volume of affected shrewdness and assurance.

"Yes," said Hurstwood calmly. He knew the type so thoroughly that some of his old familiar indifference to it returned. Such men as these were of the lowest stratum welcomed at the resort. He stepped out and closed the door.

"Well, you know what I am here for, don't you?" said the man confidentially.

"I can guess," said Hurstwood softly.

"Well, do you intend to try and keep the money?"

"That's my affair," said Hurstwood grimly.

"You can't do it, you know," said the detective, eyeing him coolly.

"Look here, my man," said Hurstwood authoritatively. "You don't understand anything about this case, and I can't explain to you. Whatever I intend to do I'll do without advice from the outside. You'll have to excuse me."

"Well, now there's no use of your talking that way," said the man, "when you're in the hands of the police. We can make a lot of trouble for you, if we want to. You're not registered right in this house, you haven't got your wife with you and the newspapers don't know you're here yet. You might as well be reasonable."

"What do you want to know?" asked Hurstwood.

"Whether you're going to send back that money or not."

Hurstwood paused and studied the floor.

"There's no use explaining to you about this," he said at last. "There's no use of your asking me. I'm no fool, you know. I know just what you can do and what you can't. You can create a lot of trouble if you want to—I know that all right, but it won't help you to get the money. Now, I've made up my mind what to do—I've already written Hannah and Hogg, so there's nothing I can say. You wait until you hear more from them."

All the time he had been talking, he had been moving away from the door, down the corridor, out of the hearing of Carrie. They were now near the end where the corridor opened into the large general parlor.

"You won't give it up?" said the man.

The words irritated Hurstwood greatly. Hot blood poured into his brain. Many thoughts formulated themselves. He was no thief. He didn't want the money. If he could only explain to Hannah and Hogg, maybe it would be all right again.

"See here," he said, "there's no use my talking about this at all. I respect your power all right, but I'll have to deal with the people who know."

"Well, you can't get out of Canada with it," said the man.

"I don't want to get out," said Hurstwood. "When I get ready, perhaps there'll be nothing to stop me for."

He turned back and the detective watched him closely. It seemed an intolerable thing. Still he went on and into the room.

"Who was it?" asked Carrie.

"A friend of mine from Chicago."

The whole of this conversation was such a shock, that

coming as it did after all the other worry of the past week, it sufficed to induce a deep gloom and moral revulsion in Hurst-wood. What hurt him worst was the fact that he was being pursued as a thief. He began to see the nature of that social injustice which sees but one side, often but a single point in a long, cumulative tragedy. All the newspapers noted but one thing, his taking the money. How and wherefore were but indifferently dealt with. All the complications which led up to it were unknown. He was accused without being understood.

What began to take clearest form in his mind was the fact that he did not want to keep the money. It was a wretched piece of business, the taking of it, and he did not care to keep it. Besides, if he retained it, he sold for a paltry sum all his connections with the past—his rights, privileges and desires. If he kept it, he bought nothing but suffering and the necessity to sneak about in by-ways and secret places. He would be watched; some day he would be caught. Canada would be his only refuge and it was cold, different, un-American. Already he missed the clang and clatter of Chicago life. The absence of the show and shine of the resort was telling deeply upon his spirits.

Sitting in his room with Carrie the same day, he decided to send the money back. He would write Hannah and Hogg, explain all and then send it by express. Maybe they would forgive him. Perhaps they would invite him back. He would make good the false statement he had made about writing them. Then he would leave this peculiar town.

"I think I'll write a few letters," he said to Carrie, after ringing for a boy.

She acquiesced and picked up a book.

For an hour he brooded over this particular missive, trying to formulate a plausible statement of the tangle. He wanted to tell them about his wife but couldn't. He finally narrowed it down to an assertion that he was light-headed from entertaining friends, had found the safe open and having gone so far as to take the money out, had accidentally closed it. This act he regretted ever so much. He was sorry he had put them to so much trouble. He would undo what he could by sending the money back—the major portion of it. The remainder he would pay up as soon as he could. Was there any possibility of his being restored?—this he only hinted at.

The troubled state of the man's mind may be judged by the very construction of this letter. For the nonce he forgot what a painful thing it would be to resume his old place, even if it were given him. He forgot that he had severed himself from the past as by a sword, and that if he did manage to in some way reunite himself with it, the jagged line of separation and reunion would always show. He was always forgetting something—his wife, Carrie, his need of money, his present situation or something, and so did not reason clearly. Nevertheless he sent the letter, waiting a reply before sending the money.

Meanwhile, he accepted his present situation with Carrie, getting what joy out of it he could, which was great when the past did not interfere. Carrie's purchases, which included among other things a trunk, duly arrived and were arranged. By three o'clock she had managed to array herself somewhat differently and much more becomingly. In her new raiment she felt better and more hopeful, as what woman would not? Hurstwood drew near, in a wooing spirit, and longed for a complete matrimonial union with her. He very gradually restored her good feeling for him by the most assiduous attention.

One thing that worked for the obvious result of this flight was the glory of the day. Out came the sun by noon, for it had been raining here, and poured a golden flood through their open windows. Sparrows were twittering. There was laughter and song in the air. Hurstwood could not keep his eyes from Carrie. She seemed the one ray of sunshine in all his trouble. Oh, if she would only love him wholly—only throw her arms around him in the blissful spirit in which he had seen her in the little park in Chicago, how happy he would be. It would repay him; it would show him that he had not lost all. He would not care.

"Carrie," he said, getting up once and coming over to her, "are you going to stay with me from now on?"

She looked at him quizzically, but melted with sympathy as the value of the look upon his face forced itself upon her. It was love now, keen and strong, love enhanced by difficulty and worry. She could not help smiling.

He dropped down on one knee beside her chair. The beauty of the day was enhancing the feeling of both.

"Let me be everything to you from now on," he said. "Don't make me worry any more. I'll be true to you. We'll go to New York and get a nice flat. I'll go into business again and we'll be happy. Won't you be mine?"

Carrie listened quite solemnly. There was no great passion in her, but the drift of things and this man's proximity created a semblance of affection. She felt rather sorry for him, a sorrow born of what had only recently been a great admiration. True love she had never felt for him. She would have known as much if she could have analyzed her feelings, but this thing which she now felt, aroused by his great feeling, broke down the barriers between them.

"You'll stay with me, won't you?" he asked.

"Yes," she said, nodding her head.

He gathered her to himself, imprinting kisses upon her lips and cheeks.

"You must marry me, though," she said.

"I'll get a license today," he said.

"How?" she asked.

"Under a new name," he answered. "I'll take a new name and live a new life. From now on I'm Murdoch."

"Oh, don't take that name," said Carrie.

"Why not?" he said.

"I don't like it."

"Well, what shall I take?" he asked.

"Oh, anything, only don't take that."

He thought awhile, still keeping his arms about her, and then said, "How would Wheeler do?"

"That's all right," said Carrie.

"Well then, Wheeler," he said. "I'll get the license the first thing in the morning."

The next day they were married by a Baptist minister, the first divine they found convenient. Hurstwood showed Carrie the city, pending the arrival of Hannah and Hogg's answer. He had good occasion to know that he was watched, for the form of the detective turned up at odd moments to convince him. Personally he became exceedingly weary of the Canadian city because it was slow and because he was idle. He constantly remembered that if he sent the money back, he would have little enough to live on. Altogether he had fled with eleven thousand and some forty-five dollars, ten thousand of which was the special sum left unguarded in the safe, and eight hundred the busy change of the day. The other two hundred and forty-five was his own. Of this he already spent over a hundred and twenty-five.

He decided that unless he should go back to Chicago, (and in his saner moments he had little hopes of that), he would only return nine thousand five hundred dollars, keeping thirteen hundred of the stolen money as a loan, until such time as he could repay it. He did not want to do this and yet he did not want to leave himself stranded. He hoped to go into the saloon business in New York—to buy into some resort and build it up as he had the Chicago house. He would again be a manager, have a nice little home and Carrie. So each day that passed, eating up the sum which he proposed to reserve to himself, troubled him.

At last the Chicago firm answered. It was Mr. Hogg's dictation. He was astonished that Hurstwood had done this, very sorry that it had come about as it had. If the money were returned they would not trouble to prosecute him, as they really bore him no ill will. As for his returning or their restoring him to his former position, they had not quite decided what the effect of it would be. They would think it over and correspond with him later. Possibly, after a little time, and so on.

The sum and substance of it was that there was no hope, and they wanted the money with the least trouble possible. Hurstwood read his doom. He decided to pay the agent whom they said they would send—some representative of a banking firm with whom they dealt here, and go on to New York. He telegraphed his acquiescence, explained to the representative who called at the hotel the same day, took a certificate of payment and told Carrie to pack her trunk. He was slightly depressed over this newest move at the time he began to make it, but eventually restored himself. He feared that even yet he might be seized and taken back, so he tried to conceal his movements, but it was scarcely possible. He ordered Carrie's trunk sent to the depot, where he had it sent by express to New York. No one seemed to be observing him, but he left at night. He was greatly agitated lest at the first station across the border, or at the depot in New York, there should be waiting for him an officer of the law.

Carrie, ignorant of his theft and his fears, enjoyed the entry into the latter city in the morning. The round green hills sentineling the broad, expansive bosom of the Hudson held her attention by their beauty as the train followed the line of the stream. She had heard of the Hudson, the Harlem River, the great city of New York, and now she looked out, filling her mind with the wonder of it. She thought of what a thing it was to travel, to ride in such fine cars and see new scenes. She began to pride herself on her experience, in this particular at least. It was a thing people liked to do and she had done it—was doing it.

As the train turned east at Spuyten Duyvil and followed the east bank of the Harlem River, Hurstwood nervously called her attention to the fact that they were on the edge of the city. After her experience with Chicago she expected long lines of cars—a great highway of tracks—and noted the difference. The sight of a few boats in the Harlem and more in the East River tickled her young heart. It was the first sign of the great sea. Next came a plain street with five-story brick flats, and then the train plunged into the tunnel.

"Grand Central Station," called the trainman as, after a few minutes of darkness and smoke, daylight reappeared.

Hurstwood arose and gathered up his small grip. He was screwed up to the highest tension. With Carrie he waited at the door and then dismounted. No one approached him, but he glanced furtively to and fro as he made for the street entrance. So excited was he that he forgot all about Carrie, who fell behind, wondering at his self-absorption. As he passed through the depot proper, the strain reached its climax and began to wane. All at once he was on the side-walk and none but cabmen hailed him. He heaved a great breath and turned, remembering Carrie.

"I thought you were going to run off and leave me," she said.

"I was trying to remember which car takes us to the Gilsey," he answered.

Carrie hardly heard him, so interested was she in the busy scene.

"How large is New York?" she asked.

"Oh, a million or more," said Hurstwood.

He looked around and hailed a cab, but he did so in a changed way.

For the first time in years the thought that he must count these little expenses flashed through his mind. It was a disagreeable thing.

He decided he would lose no time living in hotels but would rent a flat. Accordingly, he told Carrie and she agreed.

"We'll look today, if you want to," she said.

Suddenly he thought of his experience in Montreal. At the Gilsey he would be certain to meet Chicagoans whom he knew. He stood up and spoke to the driver.

"Take me to the Continental," he said, knowing it to be less frequented by those whom he knew. Then he sat down.

"Where is the residence part?" asked Carrie, who did not take the tall five-story walls on either hand to be the abode of families.

"Everywhere," said Hurstwood, who knew the city fairly well. "There are no lawns in New York. All these are houses."

"Well, then I don't like it," said Carrie, who was coming to have a few opinions of her own.

CHAPTER XXXIII.

The social atmosphere of the city at that time has interest in that, if rightly understood, it at once fixes the station of any given individual. Already the great money kings had arrived—Vanderbilt, Gould, Russell Sage, and with them an imposing company of millionaires, whose residences were in Fifth Avenue and whose offices were in or near Wall Street. Theatrical genius was represented by Augustin Daly, the Frohmans and Lester Walker. Literature and art had its kings in the persons of Howells, Z. G. A. Ward, John LaFarge. Such figures as Edison, Dana, Conklin, John Kelly ruled in their respective spheres. Tammany Hall was an all-controlling power. The gaudy pleasures of the surging metropolis were taxed then, as they are today, to make that organization rich and strong.

Whatever a man like Hurstwood could be in Chicago, it

is very evident that he would be but an inconspicuous drop in an ocean like New York. In Chicago, whose population still ranged about 500,000, the Armours, Pullmans, Palmers, Fields had not yet arrived, as it were. Millionaires were not numerous. The rich had not become so conspicuously rich as to drown all moderate incomes in obscurity. The attention of the inhabitants was not so distracted by local celebrities in the dramatic, artistic, social and religious fields as to shut the well-positioned man from view. In Chicago the two roads to distinction were politics and trade. In New York the roads were any one of a half-hundred and each had been diligently pursued by hundreds, so that celebrities were numerous. The sea was already full of whales. A common fish must needs disappear wholly from view, remain unseen. In other words, Hurstwood was nothing.

There is a more subtle result of such a situation as this, which, though not always taken into account, produces the tragedies of the world. The great create an atmosphere which reacts badly upon the small. This atmosphere is easily and quickly felt. Walk among the magnificent residences, the splendid equipages, the gilded shops, restaurants, resorts of all kinds. Scent the flowers, the silks, the wines; drink of the laughter springing from the soul of luxurious content, of the glances which gleam like light from defiant spears; feel the quality of smiles which cut like glistening swords and of strides born of place and power, and you shall know of what is the atmosphere of the high and mighty. Little need to argue that of such is not the kingdom of greatness, but so long as the world is attracted by this and the human heart views this as the one desirable value which it must attain, as long, to that heart, will this remain the realm of greatness. So long, also, will the atmosphere of this realm work its desperate results in the soul of man. It is like a chemical reagent. One day of it, like one drop of the other, will so affect and discolor the views, the aims, the desires of the mind, that it will thereafter remain forever dyed. A day of it to the untried mind is like opium to the untried body. A craving is set up which, if gratified, shall eternally result in dreams and death. Aye, dreams unfilled—gnawing, luring, idle phantoms which beckon and lead, beckon and lead, until death and dissolution dissolve their power and restore us blind to nature's heart.

A man of Hurstwood's age and temperament is not subject to the illusions and burning desires of youth, but neither has he the strength of hope which gushes as a fountain in the heart of youth. Such an atmosphere could not incite in him the cravings of a boy of eighteen, but in so far as they were excited, the lack of hope made them proportionately bitter. He could not fail to notice the signs of affluence and luxury on every hand. He had been to New York before and knew the resources of its folly. In fact it was an awesome place to him for here gathered all that he most respected on this earth—wealth, place and fame. The majority of the celebrities with whom he had tipped glasses in his day as manager of Hannah and Hogg's hailed from this self-centered and populous spot. The most inviting stories of pleasure and luxury had been told of places and individuals here. He knew it to be true that unconsciously he was brushing elbows with fortunes the livelong day; that a hundred or five hundred thousand gave no one the privilege of living more than comfortably in so wealthy a place. Fashion and pomp required more ample sums, so that the poor man was nowhere. All this he realized, now quite sharply, as he faced the city, cut off from his friends, despoiled of his modest fortune and even his name, and forced to begin the battle for place and comfort all over again. He was not old, but he was not so dull but that he could feel he soon would be. Of a sudden, then, this show of fine clothes, place and power took on peculiar significance. It was emphasized by contrast with his own distressing state.

And it was distressing. He soon found that freedom from fear of arrest was not the sine qua non of his existence. That danger dissolved, the next necessity became the grievous thing. The paltry sum of thirteen hundred and some odd dollars, set against the need of rent, clothing, food and pleasure for years to come, was a spectacle little calculated to induce peace of mind in one who had been accustomed to spend five times that sum in the course of a year. He thought upon the subject rather actively the first few days he was in New York and decided that he must act quickly. As a consequence he consulted the business opportunities advertised in the morning papers and began investigations on his own account.

That was not before he had become settled, however. Carrie and he went looking for a flat, as arranged, and found one in 78th Street, near Amsterdam Avenue. It was a five-story building, and their flat was on the third floor. Owing to the fact that the street was not yet built solidly up, it was possible to see east to the green tops of the trees in Central Park and west to the broad waters of the Hudson, a glimpse of which was to be had out of the west windows. For the privilege of six rooms and a bath, running in a straight line, they were compelled to pay thirty-five dollars a month—an average and yet exorbitant rent for a home at the time. Carrie noticed the difference between the size of the rooms here and in Chicago and mentioned it.

"You'll not find anything better, dear," said Hurstwood, "unless you go into one of the old-fashioned houses, and then you won't have any of these conveniences."

Carrie picked the new abode because of its newness and bright woodwork. It was one of the very new ones supplied with steam-heat, which was a great advantage. The stationary range, bath with hot and cold water, dumb-waiter, speaking tubes and call bell for the janitor pleased her very much. She had enough of the instincts of a housewife to take great satisfaction in these things.

"Suppose we take it," suggested Hurstwood, who liked the location.

"All right," answered Carrie. "It will be real nice, won't it?"

Hurstwood made an arrangement with one of the installment houses, whereby they furnished the flat complete and accepted fifty dollars down and ten dollars a month. He then had a little plate bearing the name "G. W. Wheeler" made, which he placed on his letter box in the hall. It sounded exceedingly odd to Carrie to be called "Mrs. Wheeler" by the janitor, but in time she became used to it, and looked upon the name as her own.

These home details settled, Hurstwood visited some of the advertised opportunities to purchase an interest in some flourishing downtown bar. After the palatial resort in Adams Street, he could not stomach the commonplace saloons which he found advertised. He lost a number of days looking up these and finding them disagreeable. He did, however, gain considerable knowledge by talking, for he discovered the influence of Tammany Hall and the value of standing in with the police. The most profitable and flourishing places he found to be those which conducted anything but a legitimate business such as that controlled by Hannah and Hogg. Elegant back rooms and private drinking booths on the second floor were usually adjuncts of very profitable places. He saw, by portly keepers whose shirt fronts shone with large diamonds and whose clothes were properly cut, that the liquor business, here as elsewhere, yielded the same golden profit.

At last he found an individual who had a resort in Warren Street which seemed an excellent venture. It was fairly well-appearing and susceptible of improvement. The owner claimed the business to be excellent, and it certainly looked so.

"We deal with a very good class of people," he told Hurstwood, "merchants, salesmen and professionals. It's a well-dressed class. No bums. We don't allow 'em in the place."

Hurstwood listened to the cash-register ring and watched the trade for a while.

"It's profitable enough for two is it?" he asked.

"You can see for yourself, if you're any judge of the liquor trade," said the owner. "This is only one of two places I have. The other is down in Nassau Street. I can't tend to them both alone. If I had some one who knew the business thoroughly, I wouldn't mind sharing with him in this one and letting him manage it."

"I've had experience enough," said Hurstwood blandly, but he felt a little diffident about referring to Hannah and Hogg.

"Well, you can suit yourself, Mr. Wheeler," said the proprietor.

He only offered a third-interest in the stock, fixtures and good will, and this in return for a thousand dollars and managerial ability on the part of the one who should come in. There was no property involved, because the owner of the saloon merely rented from an estate.

The offer was genuine enough, but it was a question with Hurstwood of whether a third-interest in that locality would be made to yield one hundred and fifty dollars a month, which he figured that he must have in order to meet the ordinary family expenses and be comfortable. It was not the time, however, (after many failures to find what he wanted) to hesitate. It looked as though a third would pay a hundred a month now. By judicious management and improvement, it might be made to pay more. Accordingly he agreed to enter into partnership and made over his thousand dollars, preparing to enter the next day.

His first inclination was to be elated, and he confided to Carrie that he thought he had made an excellent arrangement. Time, however, introduced food for reflection. He found his partner to be a very disagreeable individual, who was not infrequently the worse for liquor, which made him surly. This was the last thing which Hurstwood was used to in business. Besides, the business varied. It was nothing like the class of patronage which he had enjoyed in Chicago. Moreover, he found that it would take a long time to make friends. These people hurried in and out, without seeking the pleasures of friendship. It was no gathering or lounging place. Whole days and weeks passed without one such hearty greeting as he had been wont to enjoy every day in Chicago.

For another thing Hurstwood missed the celebrities—those well-dressed, elite individuals who lend grace to the average bars and bring news from far off and exclusive circles. He did not see one such in a month. Of an evening when still at his post, he would occasionally read in the evening papers incidents concerning celebrities whom he knew—whom he had drunk a glass with many times. They would visit a bar like Hannah and Hogg's in Chicago, or the Hoffman House uptown, but he knew he would never see them down here. It was too much out of the way. The patronage was good enough, but the class he was used to roamed in different fields. Such interesting company would never come here.

Again, the business did not pay as well as he had thought. It increased a little but he found he would have to watch his household expenses, which was humiliating. He would have to put Carrie on an allowance or caution her against extravagance, should it develop. He did not know what she would think or do about that. Still, he could see that the time was coming when he would have to do it.

In the very beginning it was a delight to go home late at night, as he did, and find Carrie. He managed to run up and take dinner with her between six and seven, and to remain at home until nine o'clock in the morning, but the novelty of this waned after a time, and he began to feel the drag of his duties.

In the next place, he began to long for the society of male company such as he had enjoyed. New York was rather strange to him, on the whole, and he longed to join in its merry whirl. The "Morning World," which he read, was full enough of accounts of various gaieties and amusements, which put an edge on his craving for the pleasures which the city might contain.

The first month had scarcely passed before Carrie said in a very natural way, "I think I'll go down town this week and buy me a dress."

"What kind?" said Hurstwood.

"Oh, something for street wear."

"All right," said Hurstwood smiling, although he noted mentally that it would be more agreeable to his finances if she didn't. Nothing was said about it the next day, but the following morning he asked, "Have you done anything about your dress?"

"Not yet," said Carrie.

He paused a few moments as if in thought and then said:—

"Would you mind putting it off a few days?"

"No," replied Carrie, who did not catch the drift of his remarks. She had never thought of him in connection with money troubles before. "Why?"

"Well I'll tell you," said Hurstwood. "This investment of mine is taking a lot of money just now. I expect to get it all back shortly, but just at present I am running close."

"Oh," answered Carrie, "why certainly, dear. Why didn't you tell me before?"

"It wasn't necessary," said Hurstwood.

For all her ready acquiescence there was something about the way Hurstwood spoke of his investment which reminded Carrie of Drouet and his little deal, which he was always about to put through. It was only the thought of a second, but it was a beginning. It was something new in her thinking of Hurstwood.

Other things followed from time to time, little things of the same sort, which in their cumulative effect were eventually equal to a full revelation. Carrie was not dull by any means. Hurstwood was not remarkably keen. Anyhow, two persons cannot long dwell together without coming to an understanding of one another. The mental difficulties of an individual reveal themselves whether he voluntarily confesses them or not. Trouble gets in the air and contributes gloom, which speaks for itself. The color of a glance, the shade of a word, a chance remark— all tell, unite and resuggest one another until at last the story is out. This was the way with Hurstwood. He dressed as nicely as usual but they were the same clothes which he had in Canada. Carrie noticed that he did not install a large wardrobe, though his own was anything but large. She noticed also that he did not suggest many amusements, said nothing about the food, seemed concerned about his business. This was not the easy Hurstwood of Chicago—not the liberal, opulent Hurstwood she had known. The change was too obvious to escape detection.

In time she began to feel that a change had come about, and also that she was not in his confidence. He was evidently secretive and kept his own counsel. She found herself asking him questions about little things. This is a disagreeable state to a woman. Great love makes it seem reasonable—sometimes plausible, but never satisfactory. When great love is not, a more definite and less satisfactory conclusion is reached.

As for Hurstwood, he was making a great fight against the difficulties of a changed condition. He was too shrewd not to realize the tremendous mistake he had made, and appreciate that he had done well in getting where he was, and yet he could not help contrasting his present state with his former—hour after hour and day after day. It became a natural method of mentation with him—to think of doing a thing now, and then quickly remembering how he did it formerly. He tried to think that the new state would not endure, that he would get something better, but it was hard. Most difficult of all was the curbing of his desire to spend. Every time it became necessary he felt that he was making a most paltry showing. For instance he one day saw new fall patterns for suits displayed in a Broadway tailor's window. For the first time in years he felt an inclination to halt and examine them on the outside without going in—without putting himself in a position where he would have to buy. It was a miserable way to be compelled to think and it hurt him exceedingly. He could have cursed his luck openly—did, in fact, mentally.

Besides, he had the disagreeable fear of meeting old-time friends, ever since one such encounter which he made shortly after his arrival in the city. It was in Broadway that he saw a man approaching him whom he knew. There was no time for simulating non-recognition—the exchange of glances had been too sharp, the knowledge of each other too apparent. So the friend, a buyer for one of the Chicago wholesale houses, felt, perforce, the necessity of stopping.

"How are you?" he said, extending his hand with an evident mixture of feelings and a lack of plausible interest.

"Very well," said Hurstwood, equally embarrassed. "How is it with you?"

"All right. I'm down here doing a little buying. Are you located here now?"

"Yes," said Hurstwood, "I have a place down in Warren Street."

"Is that so?" said the friend. "Glad to hear it. I'll come down and see you."

"Do," said Hurstwood.

"So long," said the other, smiling affably and going on.

It was a most trying affair. Not a word about Chicago, not a suggestion of the robbery, and yet the whole thing avoided with so much difficulty that it was worse than talked about. "He never even asked for my number," thought Hurstwood. "He wouldn't think of coming." He wiped his forehead, which had grown damp, and hoped sincerely he would meet no one else. All those people would act alike—all who had once chatted and made merry with him as this individual had. He hoped he would meet no more of them.

These things told upon his good nature, such as it was. His one hope was that things would change for the better in a money way. He had Carrie. His furniture was being paid off. He was maintaining his position. As for Carrie, the amusements he could give her would have to do for the present. He could probably keep up his pretensions sufficiently long without exposure to make good, and then all would be well. He failed, therein, to take account of the frailties of human nature—the difficulties of matrimonial life. Carrie was young. With him and with her, varying mental states were common. At any moment the extremes of feeling might be anti-polarized at the dinner table. This often happens in the best regulated families. Little things brought out on such occasions need great love to obliterate them afterward. Where that is not, both parties count two and two and make a problem after awhile. Between Hurstwood and Carrie, as we have shown, was no mutual great love. It was not even reasonable appreciation. Hence the incidents which follow.

CHAPTER XXXIV.

The effect of the city and his own situation on Hurstwood was paralleled in the case of Carrie, who accepted the things which fortune provided with the most genial good nature. New York, despite her first expression of disapproval, soon interested her exceedingly. Its clear atmosphere, more populous thoroughfares and peculiar indifference struck her forcibly. She had never seen such a little flat as hers and yet it soon enlisted her affection. The new furniture made an excellent showing; the side board, which Hurstwood himself arranged, gleamed brightly. The furniture for each room was appropriate and in the so-called parlor, or front room, was installed a piano, because Carrie said she would like to learn to play. There was a maid or servant, also, hired by the week, who helped do the cooking and did nearly all of the cleaning under Carrie's supervision.

The latter developed rapidly in household tactics and information. As suggested before, she was instinctively clean and the personality of her new home appealed to her. For the first time in her life she felt settled and somewhat justified in the eyes of society, as she conceived of it. Her thoughts were merry and innocent enough. For a long while she concerned herself over the arrangement of New York flats and marveled at ten families living in one building and all remaining strange and indifferent to one another. Also she marveled at the whistles of the hundreds of vessels in the harbor—the long, low cries of the Sound steamers and ferry boats when fog was on. The mere fact that these things spoke from the sea made them wonderful. She looked much at what she could see of the Hudson from her west windows and of the great city building up rapidly on either hand. It was much to ponder over, and would have sufficed to entertain her for a year without becoming stale.

For another thing, Hurstwood was exceedingly interesting

in his affection for her. Troubled as he was, he never exposed his difficulties to her. He carried himself with the same self-important air, took his new state with easy familiarity and rejoiced in Carrie's household proclivities and successes. Each evening he arrived promptly to dinner and found the little dining room a most inviting spectacle. In a way, the smallness of the room added to its luxury. It looked full and replete. The white-covered table was arranged with pretty dishes and lighted with a four-armed candelabra, each light of which was topped with a red shade. Between Carrie and the girl, the steaks and chops came out all right, and canned goods did the rest for a while. Carrie studied up on the art of making biscuit and soon reached the stage where she could show a plate of light, palatable morsels for her labor.

This evening scene and Carrie's personal appearance went far to atone to Hurstwood for the miserable predicament he had gotten himself into. His first opinion was that such a lovely little flat and agreeable little wife would atone for any scurvy flings of fortune. Once in the circle of its influence, he forgot his old situation and habits and would assure himself that he was better off for being out of it all. Even when the time approached in which, by the natural wear and tear of things, expenditures suggested themselves which he could not readily make, he felt that if he could retain Carrie everything would be well.

In this manner the second, third and fourth months passed. Winter came and with it a feeling that indoors was best, so that the attending of theatres was not much talked of. Hurstwood made great efforts to meet all expenditures without a show of feeling one way or the other. He pretended that he was reinvesting his money in strengthening the business for greater ends in the future. He contented himself with a very moderate allowance of personal apparel and rarely suggested anything for Carrie. Thus the first winter passed.

In the second year of their married life the business which Hurstwood managed did increase somewhat. He got out of it regularly the one hundred and fifty dollars per month which he had anticipated. Unfortunately, by this time Carrie had reached certain conclusions, and he had scraped up a few acquaintances. The process by which Carrie had come to see that he was no longer well-to-do was simple enough. His stay-at-homishness, curbed tendencies to dress well, or, rather, over-dress, and his avoidance of all money questions, sufficed in the course of a year to open her eyes.

Curiously, being of passive and receptive rather than active and aggressive nature, Carrie accepted the change. Her state seemed satisfactory enough. Once in awhile they would go to a theatre together, occasionally in season to the beaches and different points about the city, but they picked up no acquaintances. Hurstwood naturally abandoned his show of fine manners with her and modified his attitude to one of easy familiarity. There were no misunderstandings, no apparent differences of opinion. In fact, without money or visiting friends, he led a life which could neither arouse jealousy nor comment. Carrie rather sympathized with his efforts and thought nothing upon her lack of entertainment such as she had enjoyed in Chicago. New York, as a corporate entity, and her flat temporarily seemed sufficient.

However, as Hurstwood's business increased, he, as stated, began to pick up acquaintances. Also, he began to allow himself more for clothes. He convinced himself that his home-life was very precious to him, but also allowed that he could occasionally stay away from dinner. The first time he did this he sent a message saying that he would be detained. Carrie ate alone and wished that it might not happen again. The second time, also, he sent word, but at the last moment. The third time he forgot entirely and explained afterwards. These events were months apart, each.

"Where were you, George?" asked Carrie, after the first absence.

"Tied up at the office," he said genially. "There were some accounts I had to straighten."

"I'm sorry you couldn't get home," she said kindly. "I was fixing to have such a nice dinner."

The second time he gave a similar excuse, but the third time, the feeling about it in Carrie's mind was a little bit out of the ordinary.

"I couldn't get home," he said, when he came in later in the evening. "I was so busy."

"Couldn't you have sent me word?" asked Carrie.

"I meant to," he said, "but you know I forgot it until it was too late to do any good."

"And I had such a good dinner," said Carrie.

Now, it so happened, that from his observations of Carrie he began to imagine that she was of the thoroughly domestic type of mind. He really thought, after a year, that her chief expression in life was finding its natural channel in household duties. Notwithstanding the fact that he had observed her acting in Chicago, and that during the past year he had only seen her, limited in her relations to her flat and him, by conditions which he made, and that she had not gained any friends or associates, he drew this peculiar conclusion. With it came a feeling of satisfaction in having a wife who could thus be content, and this satisfaction worked its natural result. That is, since he imagined he saw her satisfied, he felt called upon to give only that which contributed to such satisfaction. He supplied the furniture, the decorations, the food and the necessary clothing. Thoughts of entertaining her, leading her out into the shine and show of life, grew less and less. He felt attracted to that outer world but did not think she would care to go along. Once he went to the theatre alone. Another time he joined a couple of his new friends at an evening of poker. He began to look again into the eyes of women and to take cognizance of the pleasures of the tenderloin. Since his money-feathers were beginning to grow again, he felt like sprucing about. All this, however, in a much less imposing way than had been his wont in Chicago. He avoided the gay places where he would be apt to meet those who had known him.

Now, Carrie began to feel this in various sensory ways. She was not the kind to be seriously disturbed by his actions. Not loving him greatly, she could not be jealous in a disturbing way. In fact she was not jealous at all. Hurstwood was pleased with her placid manner, when he should have duly considered it. When he did not come home, it did not seem anything like a terrible thing to her. She gave him credit for having the usual allurements of men—people to talk to, places to stop at, friends to consult with. She was perfectly willing that he should enjoy himself in his way, but she did not care to be neglected herself. As pointed out, she did not feel that thus far she had been neglected. Her state seemed fairly reasonable. All she did observe was that Hurstwood was somewhat different.

When, however, after a year, the novelty of her surroundings wore off and the flat had become a very pleasant but no longer remarkable thing; after the city as a geographic and corporate entity had ceased to allure her and she began to wonder concerning its details; after she had noticed Hurstwood's changed state and had assured herself that he was doing the very best under given conditions, then came the slight change in his money affairs, and the operation of the opinion which he had formed concerning her house-wifely instincts.

"Dearest," he said on a number of occasions now, "I don't think I'll be up to dinner this evening," or, "Dearest, I shall be working late tonight."

"All right," said Carrie very pleasantly, taking the excuse as natural and turning to her novel for resource against ennui. Heretofore he had taken her much about the city, but now she noticed that she occasionally asked him. Often she thought that it was because they had seen most all of the general details and he was weary of them or averse to walking. At any rate, she asked him. This thing went on until at last, in addition, she began to see that she was getting along with only such clothes as she seemed really to need. She went out so little that what she had lasted her a long while and Hurstwood, schooled in saving by his year of adversity, said nothing. Still he forgot the lessons of adversity when it came to himself, and by contrast with his new blossoming, she began to see that she was, comparatively, rather poorly dressed. This was the proper lever to move her mind. It awoke her to keener observations and consequent decisions.

Sometime in the second year of their residence in 78th Street, the flat across the hall from Carrie became vacant and into it moved a very handsome young woman and her husband, both of whom Carrie afterwards became acquainted with. This was brought about solely by the arrangement of the flats, which were united in one place, as it were, by the dumb-waiter. This useful elevator, by which fuel, groceries and the like were sent up from the basement, and garbage, waste and the like sent down, was used by both residents of one floor—that is, a small door opened into it from each flat.

It so happened both Carrie and the newcomer took milk and cream in the morning, as well as the "Morning World" and "Sunday Herald." Both, or their servants, at least, had the habit

of sending down the waste ashes and paper by the same convenience, after they took off the cream. If both servants or both
housewives answered the whistle of the janitor at the same time,
and came to get their papers, the result was that when they
opened their little dumb-waiter doors, they would stand face to
face in their respective flats. One morning Carrie's servant, having gone home the night before, did not put in an appearance,
and she herself answered the janitor's whistle notifying her that
her paper was waiting to be taken off. When she arrived there,
the newcomer, a handsome brunette of perhaps twenty-three
years of age, was also removing her paper. She was in a night-
gown and dressing robe, with her hair very much tousled, but
she looked so pretty and good-natured that Carrie instantly conceived a liking for her. The newcomer did no more than smile
shame-facedly, but it was sufficient. Carrie felt that she would
like to know her, and a similar feeling stirred in the mind of
the other, who admired Carrie's innocent face.

"That's a real pretty woman who has moved in next door,"
said Carrie to Hurstwood at the breakfast table.

"Has someone moved in there?" said the manager.

"Yes," said Carrie.

"Where did you see her?"

"Through the dumb-waiter this morning. She looked real
sweet."

"Who are they?" asked Hurstwood.

"I don't know," said Carrie. "The name on the bell is
Vance. Some one over there plays beautifully. I guess it must
be her."

"I've never heard her," said Hurstwood.

"She doesn't seem to play when you're here," said Carrie.

"Well, you never can tell what sort of people you're living
next to in this town, can you?" said Hurstwood, expressing the
customary New York opinion about neighbors.

"Just think," said Carrie, "I have been in this house with
nine other families for over a year and I don't know a soul.
These people have been here over a month and I haven't seen
any one before this morning."

"It's just as well," said Hurstwood. "You never know who
you're going to get in with. Some of these people are pretty bad
company."

"I expect so," said Carrie agreeably.

The conversation turned to other things and Carrie thought no more upon the subject, until a day or two later, when going out to market, she encountered Mrs. Vance coming in. The latter recognized her and nodded, for which Carrie returned a smile. This settled the probability of acquaintanceship. If there had been no faint recognition on this occasion, there would have been no future association.

Carrie saw no more of Mrs. Vance for several weeks but she heard her play through the thin walls which divided the front rooms of the flats and was pleased by the merry selection of pieces and the brilliance of their rendition. She could play only moderately herself, and such variety as Mrs. Vance exercised, bordered, for Carrie, upon the verge of great art. Everything she had seen and heard thus far,—the merest scraps and shadows—indicated that these people were in a measure refined and in comfortable circumstances. So Carrie was ready for any extension of the friendship which might follow.

One day Carrie's bell rang and the servant, who was in the kitchen, pressed the button which caused the front door of the general entrance on the ground floor to be electrically unlatched. When Carrie waited at her own door on the third floor, to see who it might be coming up to call on her, Mrs. Vance appeared.

"I hope you'll excuse me," she said. "I went out a while ago and forgot my outside key. So I thought I'd ring your bell."

This was a common trick of other residents of the building who, whenever they had forgotten their outside keys, and no one was at home in their own flats to spring the lower door for them, would press some one else's button. They did not apologize for it, however.

"Certainly," said Carrie. "I'm glad you did. I do the same thing sometimes."

"Isn't it just delightful weather?" said Mrs. Vance, pausing for a moment.

"Perfectly beautiful," said Carrie. "I've been thinking of going for a walk myself."

"I often wonder what you do with yourself," said Mrs. Vance, "when you're alone. I've noticed that your husband leaves rather early in the morning. I know that time hangs heavy on my hands."

"I don't do much of anything," said Carrie, "outside of

taking care of my flat. I shouldn't think you would be lonely, when you can play so well."

"I get tired of that," said Mrs. Vance. "But you play, don't you?"

"A very little," said Carrie.

"I thought I heard you. A piano isn't company all of the time, though."

"No," said Carrie, rather solemnly.

"I should be very glad if you would run in and see me," said Mrs. Vance. "I do so much want a neighbor. New York is such a queer place."

"Thank you," said Carrie, "I should be delighted. You must come over and see me."

Thus after a few more preliminaries, this visiting acquaintanceship was well launched, and in the young Mrs. Vance, Carrie found an agreeable companion.

This woman was the typical New Yorker in many things, some of which were dressiness, jollity, love of metropolitan life, crowds, theatres and gentleman companions. She was primarily an importation from Ohio, the daughter of a doctor in one of the southern counties. At seventeen she made a runaway match with a young student of one of the schools there and went to Cleveland, Ohio, but that had turned out badly. Toward the conclusion of her illusions concerning her first love, she had met the present keeper of her heart and honor, Mr. William B. Vance, the secretary of a large tobacco company whose general office was in New York. This individual had brought her out of Cleveland some three years before, and they had been living in New York ever since, having changed their location to suit the desires of the wife, who had never as yet been exactly located to her taste. Mrs. Vance, seeing Hurstwood in his recently rehabilitated condition, as he departed for his store in the morning, and noting Carrie's innocent look through the dumbwaiter, had conceived favorably of both of them. Also, the more she saw of Carrie, the better she liked her.

On several occasions Carrie visited her and was visited. Both flats were good to look upon, though that of the Vances tended somewhat more to the luxurious.

"I want you to come over this evening and meet my husband," said Mrs. Vance, not long after their intimacy began. "He wants to meet you. You play cards, don't you?"

"A little," said Carrie.

"Well, we'll have a game of cards. If your husband comes home, bring him over."

"He's not coming to dinner tonight," said Carrie.

"Well, when he does come we'll call him in."

Carrie acquiesced and that evening met the portly Vance, an individual a few years younger than Hurstwood who owed his seemingly comfortable matrimonial state much more to his money than to his good looks. He thought well of Carrie upon the first glance and laid himself out to be genial, teaching her a new game of cards and talking to her about New York and its pleasures. Mrs. Vance played some upon the piano and at last Hurstwood came.

"I'm very glad to meet you," he said to Mrs. Vance when Carrie introduced him, showing much of the old grace which had captivated Carrie.

"Did you think your wife had run away?" said Mr. Vance, extending his hand upon introduction.

"I didn't know but what she might have found a better husband," said Hurstwood.

He now turned his attention to Mrs. Vance, and in a flash Carrie saw again what she had for some time subconsciously missed in Hurstwood, the adroitness and flattery of which he was capable. She also saw that she was not well-dressed—not nearly as well-dressed as Mrs. Vance. These were not vague ideas any longer. Her situation was cleared up for her. She felt that her life was becoming stale, and therein she felt cause for gloom. The old helpful, urging melancholy was restored. The desirous Carrie was whispered to concerning her possibilities.

The party broke up not long after Hurstwood arrived, and back in their own flat Carrie found that her husband approved of his neighbors.

"She's quite a nice little woman," he said of Mrs. Vance.

"I think she's awfully clever," said Carrie, with an undertone of feeling.

"She is," said Hurstwood. "She's very attractive."

There were no immediate results to this awakening, for Carrie had little power of initiative, but nevertheless she seemed ever capable of getting herself into the tide of change where she would be easily borne along. Hurstwood noticed nothing. He had been unconscious of the marked contrasts which Carrie had observed. He did not even detect the shade of melancholy which settled in her eyes. Worst of all she now began to feel the loneliness of the flat, and seek the company of Mrs. Vance, who liked her exceedingly.

"Let's go to the matinée this afternoon," said Mrs. Vance, who had stepped across into Carrie's flat one morning, still arrayed in a soft pink dressing gown, which she had donned upon arising. Hurstwood and Vance had gone their separate ways nearly an hour before.

"All right," said Carrie, noticing the air of the petted and well-groomed woman in Mrs. Vance's general appearance. She looked as though she was dearly loved and her every wish gratified. "What shall we see?"

"Oh, I do want to see Nat Goodwin," said Mrs. Vance. "I do think he is the jolliest actor. The papers say this is such a good play."

"What time will we have to start?" asked Carrie.

"Let's go at one and walk down Broadway from 34th," said Mrs. Vance. "It's such an interesting walk. He's at the Madison Square."

"I'll be glad to go," said Carrie. "How much will we have to pay for seats?"

"Not more than a dollar," said Mrs. Vance.

The latter soon departed and at one o'clock reappeared, stunningly arrayed in a dark blue walking dress, with a nobby hat to match. Carrie had gotten herself up charmingly enough but this woman pained her by contrast. She seemed to have so many dainty little things which Carrie had not. There were trinkets of gold, an elegant green leather purse, set with her initials, a fancy handkerchief exceedingly rich in design, and the like. Carrie felt that she needed more and better clothes to compare with this woman, and that anyone looking at the two would pick Mrs. Vance for her raiment alone. It was a trying though rather unjust thought, for Carrie had now developed an equally pleasing figure, and had grown in comeliness until she was a thoroughly attractive type of her color of beauty. There was some difference in the clothing of the two, both of quality and age, but this difference was not especially noticeable. It served, however, to augment Carrie's dissatisfaction with her state.

The walk down Broadway, then as now, was one of the remarkable features of the city. There foregathered, before the matinée and afterwards, not only all the pretty women who love a showy parade, but the men who love to gaze upon and admire them. It was a very imposing procession of pretty faces and fine clothes. Women appeared in their very best hats, shoes and gloves, and walked arm in arm on their way to the fine shops or theatres strung along from 14th to 34th. Equally the men paraded with the very latest they could afford. A tailor might have secured hints on suit measurements, a shoemaker on proper lasts and colors, a hatter on hats. It was literally true that if a lover of fine clothes secured a new suit, it was sure to have its first airing on Broadway. So true and well understood was this fact, that several years later a popular song detailing this and other facts concerning the afternoon parade on matinée days and entitled "What Right Has He On Broadway?" was published and had quite a vogue about the music halls of the city.

In all her stay in the city, Carrie had never heard of this showy parade, had never even been on Broadway when it was taking place. On the other hand, it was a familiar thing to Mrs. Vance, who not only knew of it as an entity, but had often been in it, going purposely to see and be seen, to create a stir with her beauty and dispel any tendency to fall short in dressiness by contrasting herself with the beauty and fashion of the town.

Carrie stepped along easily enough after they got out of the car at 34th Street, but soon fixed her eyes upon the lovely company which swarmed by and with her as they proceeded. She noticed of a sudden that Mrs. Vance's manner had rather stiffened under the gaze of handsome men and elegantly dressed ladies, whose glances were not modified by any rules of propriety. To stare seemed the proper and natural thing. Carrie found herself stared at and ogled. Men in flawless top coats, high hats and silver-headed walking sticks elbowed near and looked too often into conscious eyes. Ladies rustled by in dresses of stiff cloth, shedding affected smiles and perfume. Carrie noticed among them the sprinkling of goodness and the heavy percentage of vice. The rouged and powdered cheek and lips, the scented hair, the large, misty and languorous eye were common enough. With a start she awoke to find that she was in fashion's throng, on parade in a showplace—and such a showplace. Jewelers' windows gleamed along the path with remarkable frequency. Florist shops, furriers, haberdashers, confectioners, all followed in rapid procession. The street was full of coaches. Pompous doormen, in immense coats with shiny brass belts and buttons, waited in front of expensive salesrooms. Coachmen in tan boots, white tights and blue jackets waited obsequiously for the mistresses of carriages, who were shopping inside. The whole street bore the flavor of riches and show and Carrie felt that she was not of it. She could not, for the life of her, assume the attitude and smartness of Mrs. Vance, who in her beauty was all assurance. She could only imagine that it must be evident to many that she was the less handsomely dressed of the two. It cut her to the quick, and she resolved that she would not come here again until she looked better. At the same time she longed to feel the delight of parading here as an equal. Ah, then she would be happy.

CHAPTER XXXV.

Such feelings as were generated in Carrie by this walk put her in an exceedingly receptive mood for the pathos which followed in the play. The actor whom they had gone to see had achieved his popularity by presenting a mellow type of comedy in which sufficient sorrow was introduced to lend contrast and relief to humor. For Carrie, as we well know, the stage had great attraction. She had never forgotten her one histrionic achievement in Chicago. It dwelt in her mind and occupied her consciousness during many long afternoons in which her rocking chair and her latest novel contributed the only pleasures of her state. Never could she witness a play without having her own ability vividly brought to consciousness. Some scenes made her long to be a part of them—to give expression to the feelings which she, in the place of the character represented, would feel. Almost invariably she would carry the vivid imaginations away with her and brood over them the next day alone. She lived as much in these imaginary things as in the realities which made up her daily life.

It was not often that she came to the play stirred to her heart's core by actualities. Today a low song of longing had been set singing in her heart by the finery, the merriment, the beauty she had seen. Oh, these women who had passed her by hundreds and hundreds strong, who were they? Whence came the rich, elegant dresses, the astonishingly colored buttons, the knick-knacks of silver and gold? Where were these lovely creatures housed? Amid what elegancies of carved furniture, decorated walls, elaborate tapestries, did they move? Where were their rich apartments, loaded with all that money could provide? In what stables champed these sleek nervous horses and rested the gorgeous carriages? Where lounged the richly groomed footmen? Oh, the mansions, the lights, the perfume, the loaded boudoirs and tables. New York must be filled with such bowers or the beautiful, insolent, supercilious creatures could not be. Some hot-houses held them. It ached her to know that she was not of them—that alas, she had dreamed a dream and it had not come true. She wondered at her own solitude these two years past—her indifference to the fact that she had never achieved what she had expected.

The play was one of those drawing-room concoctions in which charmingly overdressed ladies and gentlemen suffer the pangs of love and jealousy amid gilded surroundings. Such bon mots are ever enticing to those who have all their days longed for such material surroundings and have never had them grati-fied. They have the charm of showing suffering under ideal con-ditions. Who would not grieve upon a gilded chair? Who would not suffer amid perfumed tapestries, cushioned furniture and liv-eried servants? Grief under such circumstances becomes an en-ticing thing. Carrie longed to be of it. She wanted to take her sufferings, whatever they were, in such a world, or failing that, at least to simulate them under such charming conditions upon the stage. So affected was her mind by what she had seen that the play now seemed an extraordinarily beautiful thing. She was soon lost in the world it represented and wished that she might never return. Between the acts she studied the galaxy of matinée attendants in front rows and boxes, and conceived a new idea of the possibilities of New York. She was sure she had not seen it at all—that the city was one whirl of pleasure and delight.

Going out, the same Broadway taught her a sharper lesson.

The scene she had witnessed coming down was now augmented and at its height. Such a crush of finery and folly she had never seen. It clinched her convictions concerning her state. She had not lived, could not lay claim to having lived, until something of this had come into her own life. Women were spending money like water. She could see that in every elegant shop she passed. Flowers, candy, jewelery seemed the principal things in which the elegant dames were interested. And she,—she had scarcely enough pin money to indulge in such outings as this a few times a month.

That night the pretty little flat seemed a commonplace thing. It was not what the rest of the world was enjoying. She saw the servant working at dinner with an indifferent eye. In her mind were running scenes of the play. Particularly she remembered one beautiful actress—the sweetheart who had been wooed and won. The grace of this woman had won Carrie's heart. Her dresses had been all that art could suggest, her sufferings had been so real. The anguish which she had portrayed Carrie could feel. It was done as she was sure she could do it. There were spots in which she could even do better. Hence she repeated the lines to herself. Oh, if she could only have such a part, how broad would be her life. She too could act appealingly.

When Hurstwood came, Carrie was moody. She was sitting, rocking and thinking and did not care to have her enticing imaginations broken in on. So she said little or nothing.

"What's the matter, Carrie?" said Hurstwood after a time, noticing her quiet, almost moody state.

"Nothing," said Carrie. "I don't feel very well tonight."

"Not sick are you?" he asked, approaching very close.

"Oh, no," she said, almost pettishly. "I just don't feel very good."

"That's too bad," he said, stepping away and adjusting his vest, after his slight bending over. "I was thinking we might go to the show tonight."

"I don't want to go," said Carrie, annoyed that her fine visions should all have thus been broken into and driven out of her mind. "I've been to the matinée this afternoon."

"Oh, you have?" said Hurstwood. "What was it?"

" 'A Gold Mine.' "

"How was it?"

"Pretty good," said Carrie.

"And you don't want to go again tonight?"

"I don't think I do," she said.

Nevertheless, wakened out of her melancholia and called to the dinner table, she changed her mind. A little food in the stomach does wonders. She went again, and in so doing, temporarily recovered equanimity. The great awakening blow had, however, been delivered. As often she might be recovered from these discontented thoughts now, they would occur again. Time and repetition—ah, the wonder of it. The dripping water and the solid stone—how utterly it yields at last.

Not long after this matinée experience, perhaps a month, Mrs. Vance invited Carrie to an evening at the theatre with them. She heard Carrie say that Hurstwood was not coming home to dinner.

"Why don't you come with us? Don't get dinner for yourself. We're going down to Sherry's for dinner and then over to Wallack's. Come along with us."

"I think I will," answered Carrie.

She prepared that afternoon at three o'clock for the departure at half-past five for the noted dining room, which was crowding Delmonico's for position in the favor of society. In this dressing, Carrie showed the influence of her association with the dashing Mrs. Vance. She had constantly had her attention called by the latter to novelties in everything which pertains to a woman's apparel.

"Are you going to get such and such a hat?" or, "Have you seen the new gloves with the oval pearl buttons?" were but sample phrases out of a large selection.

"The next time you get a pair of shoes, dearie," said Mrs. Vance, "get button, with thick soles, and patent leather tips. They're all the rage this fall."

"I will," said Carrie.

"Oh, dear, have you seen the new shirtwaists at Altman's? They have some of the loveliest patterns. I saw one there that I know would look stunning on you. I said so when I saw it."

Carrie listened to these things with considerable interest, for they were suggested with more of friendliness than is usually common between pretty women. Mrs. Vance liked Carrie's stable good nature so well that she really took pleasure in tipping her off to the latest things.

"Why don't you get yourself one of those nice serge skirts they're selling at Stewart's?" she said one day. "They're the circular style and they're going to be worn from now on. A dark blue one would look so nice on you."

Carrie listened with eager ears. These things never came up between her and Hurstwood. Nevertheless she began to suggest one thing and another, which Hurstwood agreed to without any expression of opinion. He noticed the new tendency on Carrie's part, and finally, hearing much of Mrs. Vance and her delightful ways, suspected from whence the change came. He was not at all inclined so soon to offer the slightest objection, but he felt that Carrie's wants were expanding. This did not appeal to him exactly, but he cared for her in his own way, and so the thing stood. Still there was something in the details of the transactions which caused Carrie to feel that her requests were not a delight to him. He did not enthuse over her purchases. This led her to believe that neglect was creeping in, and so another small wedge was entered.

Nevertheless, one of the results of Mrs. Vance's suggestions was the fact that on this occasion Carrie was dressed somewhat to her own satisfaction. She had on her best, but there was comfort in the thought that if she must confine herself to a *best*, it was meet and fitting. She looked the well-groomed woman of twenty-one, and Mrs. Vance praised her, which brought color to her plump cheeks and a noticeable brightness into her large eyes. It was threatening to rain and Vance, at his wife's request, had called a coach.

"Your husband isn't coming?" suggested Vance as he met Carrie in his little parlor.

"No, he said he wouldn't be home for dinner."

"Better leave a little note for him, telling him where we are. He might turn up."

"I will," said Carrie, who had not thought of it before.

"Tell him we'll be at Sherry's, Fifth Avenue and 28th Street, until eight o'clock. He knows, though, I guess."

Carrie crossed the hall with rustling skirts, and scrawled the note, gloves on. When she returned, a newcomer was in the Vance flat.

"Mrs. Wheeler, let me introduce Mr. Ames, a cousin of mine," said Mrs. Vance. "He's going along with us, ain't you, Bob?"

"I'm very glad to meet you," said Ames, bowing politely to Carrie.

The latter caught in a glance the dimensions of a very stalwart figure. She also noticed that he was smooth-shaven, good-looking and young, but nothing more.

"Mr. Ames is just down in New York for a few days," said Vance, putting in, "and we're trying to show him around a little."

"Oh, are you?" said Carrie, taking another glance at the newcomer.

"Yes, I am just on here from Indianapolis for a week or so," said young Ames, dropping to the edge of a chair to wait, while Mrs. Vance completed the last touches of her toilet.

"I guess you find New York quite a thing to see, don't you?" said Carrie, venturing something to avoid a possible deadly silence.

"It is rather large to get around in a week," answered Ames, pleasantly.

He was an exceedingly genial soul, this young man, and wholly free of affectation. It seemed to Carrie he was as yet only overcoming the last traces of the bashfulness of youth. He did not seem apt at conversation, but he had the merit of being well-dressed and wholly courageous. Carrie felt as if it were not going to be hard to talk to him.

"Well, I guess we're ready now. The coach is outside."

"Come on, people," said Mrs. Vance, coming in smiling. "Bob, you'll have to look after Mrs. Wheeler."

"I'll try to," said Bob, smiling and edging closer to Carrie. "You won't need much watching, will you?" he volunteered in a sort of ingratiating and help-me-out kind of way.

"Not very, I hope," said Carrie.

They descended the stairs, Mrs. Vance offering suggestions, and climbed into the open coach.

"All right," said Vance, slamming the coach door, and the conveyance rolled away.

"What is it we're going to see?" asked Mr. Ames.

"Florence," said Vance, "in 'Judge Dockitt.' "

"Oh, he's so good," said Mrs. Vance. "He's just the funniest man."

"I notice the papers praise it," said Ames.

"I haven't any doubt," put in Vance, "but we'll all enjoy it very much."

Ames had taken a seat beside Carrie, and accordingly he felt it his bounden duty to pay her some attention. He was interested to find her so young a wife, and so pretty, though it was only a respectful interest. There was nothing of the dashing ladies' man about him. He had respect for the married state and thought only of some pretty marriageable girls in Indianapolis.

"Are you a born New Yorker?" asked Ames of Carrie.

"Oh, no, I've only been here two years."

"Oh, well, you've had time to see a great deal of it, anyhow."

"I don't seem to have," answered Carrie. "It's about as strange to me as when I first came here."

"You're not from the West, are you?"

"Yes, I'm from Wisconsin," she answered.

"Well, it does seem as if most people in this town haven't been here so very long. I hear of lots of Indiana people in my line who are here."

"What is your line?" asked Carrie.

"I'm connected with an electrical company," said the youth.

Carrie followed up this desultory conversation, with occasional interruptions from the Vances. Several times the conversation became general and partially humorous, and in that manner Sherry's was reached.

Carrie had noticed the appearance of gayety and pleasure-seeking in the streets which they were following. Coaches were numerous, pedestrians many, and in 59th Street the street cars were crowded. At 59th Street and Fifth Avenue, a blaze of lights from several new hotels which bordered the Plaza Square gave a suggestion of sumptuous hotel life. Fifth Avenue, the home of the wealthy, was noticeably toned with carriages and gentlemen in evening dress. At Sherry's an imposing doorman opened the coach door and helped them out. Young Ames held Carrie's elbow as he helped her up the steps. They stepped into a lobby

already swarming with patrons, and then after divesting themselves of their wraps, went into a sumptuous dining room.

In all Carrie's experience she had never seen anything like
this. In the whole time she had been in New York, Hurstwood's
modified state had not permitted his bringing her to such a
place. There was an almost indescribable atmosphere about it
which convinced the newcomer that this was the proper thing.
Here was the place where the matter of expense limited the
patrons to the monied or pleasure-loving class. Carrie had read
of it often in the "Morning World" and "Evening World." She
had seen notices of dances, parties, balls, suppers at Sherry's.
The Misses So-and-So would give a party on Wednesday evening
at Sherry's. Young Mr. So-and-So would entertain a party of
friends at a private lunch on the sixteenth, at Sherry's. The
common run of conventional, perfunctory notices of the doings
of society, which she could scarcely refrain from scanning each
day, had given her a distinct idea of the gorgeousness and luxury
of this wonderful temple of gastronomy. Now, at last, she was
really in it. She had come up the imposing steps guarded by the
large and portly doorman. She had seen the lobby, guarded also
by another large and portly gentleman, and waited upon by
uniformed youths who took care of canes, overcoats and the
like. Here was the splendid dining chamber, all decorated and
aglow, where the wealthy ate. Ah, how fortunate was Mrs.
Vance; young, beautiful and well-off—at least sufficiently so to
come here in a coach and bring her. What a wonderful thing
it was to be rich.

Vance led the way through lanes of shining tables at which
were seated parties of two, three, four, five and six. The air of
assurance and dignity about it all was exceedingly noticeable to
the novitiate. Incandescent lights, the reflection of their glow
in polished glasses, and the shine of gilt upon the walls combined
into one tone of light which it required minutes of complacent
observation to separate and take particular note of. The white
shirt fronts of the gentlemen, the bright costumes of the ladies,
diamonds, jewels, fine feathers, all were exceedingly noticeable.

Carrie walked with an air equal to that of Mrs. Vance and
accepted the seat which the head waiter provided for her. She
was keenly aware of all the little things that were done—the

little genuflections and attentions in the waiters and head waiter which Americans pay for. The air with which the latter pulled out each chair and the wave of the hand with which he motioned her to be seated were worth several dollars in themselves.

Once seated, there began that exhibition of showy, wasteful and unwholesome gastronomy as practised by wealthy Americans which is the wonder and astonishment of true culture and dignity the world over. The large bill-o'-fare held an array of dishes sufficient to feed an army, sidelined with prices which made reasonable expenditure a ridiculous impossibility. An order of soup at fifty cents or a dollar, with a dozen kinds to choose from. Oysters in forty styles and at sixty cents the half-dozen. Entrées, fish and meats at prices which would house one overnight in an average hotel. A dollar fifty and two dollars seemed to be the most common figures upon this most tastefully printed bill-o'-fare.

Carrie noticed this and in scanning it, the price of spring chicken carried her back to that other bill-o'-fare and far different occasion when, for the first time, she sat with Drouet in a good restaurant in Chicago. It was only momentary—a sad note as out of an old song, and then it was gone. But in that flash was seen the other Carrie, poor, hungry, drifting at her wits' ends, and all Chicago a cold and closed world, which she only wandered away from because she could not find work.

On the walls were designs in color, square spots of robin's-egg blue, set in ornate frames of gilt, whose corners were elaborate mouldings of fruits and flowers, with fat, naked cupids hovering in angelic comfort. On the ceilings were colored traceries with more gilt, leading to a centre where spread a broad circle of light—incandescent globes mingled with glittering prisms and stucco tendrils of gilt. The floor was of a reddish hue, waxed and polished, and in every direction were mirrors—tall, brilliant, bevel-edged mirrors, reflecting and re-reflecting forms, faces and candelabra a score and a hundred times.

The tables were not so remarkable in themselves, and yet the imprint of "Sherry" upon the napery, the name of "Tiffany" upon the silverware, the name of "Haviland" upon the china, and over all the glow of the small red-shaded candelabra, and the reflected tints of the walls on garments and faces, made them seem remarkable. Each waiter added an air of exclusiveness and elegance by the manner in which he bowed, scraped, touched and trifled with things. The exclusively personal attention which he devoted to each one, standing half-bent, ear to one side, elbows akimbo, saying "soup—green turtle, yes—One portion, yes. Oysters—certainly—half-dozen—yes. Asparagus! Olives—yes."

It would be the same with each one, only Vance essayed to order for all, inviting counsel and suggestions. Carrie studied the company with open eyes. So this was high-life in New York. It was so that the rich spent their days and evenings. Her poor little mind could not rise above applying each scene to all society. Every fine lady must be in the crowd on Broadway in the afternoon, in the theatre at the matinée, in the coaches and dining halls at night. It must be glow and shine everywhere, with coaches waiting, and footmen attendant, and she was out of it all. In two long years she had never even been in such a place as this.

Vance was in his element here, as Hurstwood would have been in former days. He ordered freely of soup, oysters, roast meats and side dishes, and had several bottles of wine brought, which were set down beside the table in a wicker basket.

Young Ames volunteered the information that they knew he did not drink.

"I don't care for wine either," said Carrie.

"You poor things," said Mrs. Vance. "You don't know what you're missing. You ought to drink a little, anyhow."

"No," said Carrie, "I don't believe I will."

Ames was looking away rather abstractedly at the crowd and showed an interesting profile to Carrie. His forehead was high, his nose rather large and strong, the chin moderately pleasing. He had a good, wide, well-shaped mouth, and his dark brown hair was slightly long and parted on one side. He seemed to have the least touch of boyishness to Carrie, and yet he was a man full grown.

"Do you know," he said turning back to Carrie, after his reflection, "I sometimes think it's a shame for people to spend so much money this way."

Carrie looked at him a moment, with the faintest touch of surprise at his seriousness. He seemed to be thinking about something which she had never pondered over.

"Do you?" she answered interestedly.

"Yes," he said, "they pay so much more than these things are worth. They put on so much show."

"I don't know why people shouldn't spend when they have it," said Mrs. Vance.

"It doesn't do any harm," said Vance who was still studying the bill-o'-fare, though he had ordered.

Ames was looking away again and Carrie was again looking at his forehead. To her he seemed to be thinking about strange things. Also, as he studied the crowd, his eye was mild.

"Look at the woman's dress over there," he said again, turning to Carrie and nodding in a direction.

"Where?" said Carrie, following his eyes.

"Over there in the corner—way over—do you see that brooch?"

"Isn't it large," said Carrie.

"One of the largest clusters of jewels I have ever seen," said Ames.

"It is, isn't it," said Carrie. She felt as if she would like to be agreeable to this young man and also there came with it, or perhaps preceded it, the slightest shade of a feeling that he was better educated than she was—that his mind was better. He seemed to look it, and the saving grace in Carrie was that she could understand that people could be wiser. She had seen a number of people in her life who reminded her of what she had vaguely come to think of as scholars. This strong young man beside her, with his clear, natural look, seemed to get a hold of things which she did not quite understand, but approved of. It was fine to be so, as a man, she thought.

The conversation changed off to a book that was having its vogue at the time—"The Opening of a Chestnut Burr," by E. P. Roe. Mrs. Vance had read it. Vance had seen it discussed in some of the papers.

"A man can make quite a strike writing a book," said Vance. "I notice this fellow Roe is very much talked about." He was looking at Carrie as he spoke.

"I hadn't heard of him," said Carrie, honestly.

"Oh, I have," said Mrs. Vance. "He's written lots of things. This 'Opening of a Chestnut Burr' is pretty good."

"He doesn't amount to much," said Ames.

Carrie turned her eyes toward him as to an oracle.

"His stuff is nearly as bad as 'Dora Thorne,' " concluded Ames.

Carrie felt this as a personal reproof. She had read "Dora Thorne" in the past. It seemed only fair to her, but she thought that people thought it was very fine. Now this clear-eyed, fine-headed youth, who looked something like a student to her, made fun of it. It was poor to him—not worth reading. She looked down and for the first time felt the pain of not understanding.

Yet there was nothing sarcastic or supercilious in the way Ames spoke. He had very little of that in him. Carrie felt that it was just kindly thought of a high order—the right thing to think, and wondered what else was right according to him. He seemed to notice that she listened and rather sympathized with him, and from now on he talked mostly to her.

As the waiter bowed and scraped about, felt the dishes to see if they were hot enough, brought spoons and forks and did all those little attentive things calculated to impress the luxury of the situation upon the diner, Ames also leaned slightly to one side and told her of Indianapolis in an intelligent way. He really had a very bright mind, which was finding its chief development in electrical knowledge. His sympathies for other forms of information, however, and for types of people, were quick and warm. The red glow on his hair gave it a sandy tinge and put a pink tint in his eye. Carrie noticed all these things, as he leaned towards her, and felt exceedingly young. This man was far ahead of her. He seemed wiser than Hurstwood, saner and wiser than Drouet. He seemed innocent and clean, and she thought that he was exceedingly pleasant. Also she noticed that his interest in her was a far-off one. She was not in his life or any of the things that touched his life, and yet, now as he spoke of these things, they appealed to her.

"I shouldn't care to be rich," he told her as the dinner proceeded, and the supply of food warmed up his sympathies— "not rich enough to spend my money this way."

"Oh, wouldn't you?" said Carrie, the, to her, new attitude forcing itself distinctly upon her for the first time.

"No," he said. "What good would it do? A man doesn't need this sort of thing to be happy."

Carrie thought of this doubtfully, but coming from him it had weight with her.

"He probably could be happy," she thought to herself, "all alone. He's so strong."

Mr. and Mrs. Vance kept up a running fire of interruptions, and these impressive things by Ames came at odd moments. They were sufficient, however, for the atmosphere that went with this youth impressed itself upon Carrie without words. There was something in him, or the world he moved in, which appealed to her. He reminded her of scenes she had seen on the stage—the sorrows and sacrifices that always went with she knew not what. He had taken away some of the bitterness of the contrast between this life and her life, and all by a certain defiant indifference which concerned only him.

As they went out, he took her arm again and helped her into the coach, and then they were off again and so to the show.

During the acts Carrie found herself listening to him very attentively. He mentioned things in the play which she most approved of—things which swayed her deeply.

"Don't you think it's rather fine to be an actor?" she asked once.

"Yes—I do," he said. "To be a good one. I think the theatre's a great thing."

Just this little approval set Carrie's heart bounding. Ah, if she could only be an actress—a good one. This man was wise— he knew—and he approved of it. If she were a fine actress, such men as he would approve of her. She felt that he was good to speak as he had, although it did not concern her at all. She did not know why she felt this way.

At the close of the show, it suddenly developed that he was not going back with them.

"Oh, aren't you?" said Carrie, with an unwarrantable feeling.

"Oh, no," he said. "I'm stopping right around here in 33rd Street."

Carrie could not say anything else, but somehow this development shocked her. She had been regretting the wane of a pleasant evening, but she had thought there was a half-hour more. Oh, the half-hours—the minutes of the world. Ye gods, what miseries and griefs are crowded into them.

She said goodby with feigned indifference. What matter could it make? Still the coach seemed lorn.

When she went into her own flat, she had this to think about. She did not know whether she would ever see this man any more. What difference could it make— What difference could it make.

Hurstwood had returned and was already in bed. His clothes were scattered loosely about. Carrie came to the door and saw it, then retreated. She did not want to go in yet awhile. She wanted to think. It was disagreeable to her.

Back in the dining room she sat in her chair and rocked. Her little hands were folded tightly as she thought. Through a fog of longing and conflicting desires, she was beginning to see. Oh, ye legions of hope and pity—of sorrow and pain. She was rocking and beginning to see.

CHAPTER XXXVI.

The immediate result of this was—nothing. Results from such things are usually long in growing. Morning brings a change of feeling. The existent condition invariably pleads for itself. It is only at odd moments that we get glimpses of the misery of things. The heart understands when it is confronted with contrasts. Take them away and the ache subsides.

Carrie went on, leading much this same life for six months thereafter or more. She did not see Ames any more. He called once upon the Vances, but she only heard about it through the young wife. Then he went west, and there was a gradual subsidence of whatever personal attraction had existed. The mental effect of the thing had not gone, however, and never could any more entirely. She had an ideal to contrast men by—particularly men close to her.

During all this time, a period rapidly approaching three years, Hurstwood had been moving along in a path which might have been called even. There was no apparent slope downward and distinctly none upward, so far as the casual observer might have seen. But psychologically there was a change which was marked enough to suggest the future very distinctly indeed. This was in the mere matter of the halt his career had received when he departed from Chicago. A man's fortune, or material progress, is very much the same as his bodily growth. Either he is growing stronger, healthier, wiser, as the youth approaching manhood; or he is growing weaker, older, less incisive mentally, as the man approaching old age. There are no other states. Frequently there is a period between the cessation of youthful accretion and the setting in, in the case of the middle-aged man, of the tendency toward decay, when the two processes are almost perfectly balanced, and there is little doing in either direction. Given time enough, however, the balance becomes a sagging to the grave side. Slowly at first, then with a modest momentum, and at last the graveward process is in full swing. So is it, frequently, with man's fortune. If its process of accretion is never halted, if the balancing stage is never reached, there will be no toppling. Rich men are, frequently, in these days, saved from this dissolution of their fortunes by their ability to hire younger brains. These younger brains look upon the interests of the fortune as their own, and so steady and direct its progress. If each individual were left absolutely to the care of his own interests and were given time enough in which to grow exceedingly old, his fortune would pass as his strength and will. He and his would be utterly dissolved and scattered into the four winds of the heavens.

But now see wherein the parallel changes. A fortune, like a man, is an organism, which draws to itself other minds and other strength than that inherent in the founder. Besides the young minds drawn to it by salaries, it becomes allied with young forces which make for its existence, even when the strength and wisdom of the founder are fading. It may be conserved by the growth of a community, or of a state. It may be involved in providing something for which there is a growing demand. This removes it at once beyond the special care of the founder. It needs not so much foresight now, as direction. The man wanes, the need continues or grows, and the fortune, fallen into whose hands it may, continues. Hence some men never recognize the turning in the tide of their abilities. It is only in chance cases, where a fortune, or a state of success, is wrested from them that the lack of ability to do as they did formerly becomes apparent. Hurstwood, set down under new conditions, was in a position to see that he was no longer young. If he did not, it was due wholly to the fact that his state was so well-balanced that an absolute change for the worse did not show.

Not trained to reason or introspect himself, he could not analyze the change that was taking place in his mind and hence his body, but he felt the depression of it. Constant comparison between his old state and his new showed a balance for the worse, which produced a constant state of gloom, or at least depression. Now it has been shown experimentally that a constantly subdued frame of mind produces certain poisons in the blood, called katastates, just as virtuous feelings of pleasure and delight produce helpful chemicals, called anastates. The poisons, generated by remorse, inveigh against the system and eventually produce marked physical deterioration. To this Hurstwood was subject.

In the course of time, it told upon his temper. His eye no longer possessed that buoyant, searching shrewdness which had characterized it in Adams Street. His step was not as sharp and firm. He was given to thinking, thinking, thinking. The new friends he made were not celebrities. They were of a cheaper, a slightly more sensual and cruder grade. He could not possibly take the pleasure in their company that he had in that of those fine frequenters of the Chicago resort. He was left to brood.

Slowly, exceedingly slowly, his desire to greet, conciliate and make at home these people who visited the Warren Street place passed from him. More and more slowly the significance of the realm he had left began to be clear. It did not seem to be so wonderful to be in it when he was in it. It seemed very easy for anyone to get up there and have ample raiment and money to spend, but now that he was out of it, how far off it became. He began to see it as one sees a city with a wall about it. Men were posted at the gates. You could not get in. Those inside did not care to come out to see who you were. They were so merry inside there that all those outside were forgotten, and he was on the outside.

Each day he could read in the evening papers of the doings in this walled city. In the notices of passengers for Europe, he read the names of eminent frequenters of his old resort. In the theatrical column appeared, from time to time, announcements of the latest success of men whom he had known. He knew that they were at their old gayeties, Pullmans were hauling them to and fro about the land, papers were greeting them with interesting mentions, the elegant lobbies of hotels and the glow of polished dining rooms were keeping them close within the walled city. Men whom he had known, men whom he had tipped glasses with—rich men, and he was forgotten. Who was Mr. Wheeler? What was the Warren Street resort? Bah!

If one thinks that such thoughts do not come to so common a type of mind—that such feelings require a higher mental development, I would urge for their consideration the fact that it is the higher mental development which is the thing that does away with such thoughts. It is the higher mental development which induces philosophy and that fortitude which refuses to dwell upon such things—refuses to be made to suffer by their consideration. The common type of mind is exceedingly keen on all matters which relate to its physical welfare—exceedingly keen. It is the unintellectual miser who sweats blood at the loss of a hundred dollars. It is the Epictetus who smiles when the last vestige of physical welfare is removed.

The time came—in the third year,—when this thinking began to produce results in the Warren Street place. The tide of patronage dropped a little below what it had been at its best since he had been there. This irritated him, exceedingly, but it worried him also. He had never gotten along comfortably with his partner. That individual was too gross, too interested in other things. His relations with Hurstwood were strictly business, reaching down to the last cent and nothing more. He did not agree with any ideas of improvement or branching out, and Hurstwood could not save enough to branch out for himself. This went on until he hated his associate for the dullard that he was. He disliked to see him come around, wished a thousand times that he could buy him out.

There came a night when he confessed to Carrie that the business was not doing as well this month as it had the month before. This was in lieu of certain suggestions she had made concerning little things she wanted to buy. She had not failed to notice that he did not seem to consult her about buying clothing for himself. For the first time it struck her as a ruse, or that he said it so that she would not think of asking for things. Her reply was mild enough, but her thoughts were rebellious. He was not looking after her at all. She was depending for her enjoyments upon the Vances.

And now the latter announced that they were going away. It was approaching spring and they were going north.

"Oh yes," said Mrs. Vance to Carrie, "we think we might as well give up the flat and store our things. We'll be gone for the summer and it would be a useless expense. I think we'll settle a little farther downtown when we come back."

Carrie heard this with genuine sorrow. She had enjoyed Mrs. Vance's companionship so much. There was no one else in the house whom she knew. Again she would be all alone.

Hurstwood's gloom over the slight decrease in profits and the departure of the Vances came together. So Carrie had loneliness and this mood of her husband to enjoy at one and the same time. It was a grievous thing. She became restless and dissatisfied, not exactly, as she thought, with Hurstwood, but with life. What was it? A very dull round indeed. What did she have? Nothing but this narrow little flat. The Vances could travel, they could do the things worth doing, and here she was. For what was she made, anyhow? More thought followed and then tears—tears which seemed justified and the only relief in the world.

For another period this state continued, the twain leading a rather monotonous life, and then there was a slight change for the worse. One evening, Hurstwood, after thinking about a way to modify Carrie's desires for clothes and the general strain of their way of life upon his ability to provide, said:—

"I don't think I'll ever be able to do much with Shaughnessy."

"What's the matter?" said Carrie.

"Oh, he's a slow, greedy Mick. He won't agree to anything to improve the place and it won't ever pay without it."

"Can't you make him?" said Carrie.

"No, I've tried. The only thing I can see, if I want to improve, is to get hold of a place of my own."

"Why don't you?" said Carrie.

"Well, all I have is tied up in there just now. If I had a chance to save awhile, I think I could open a place that would give us plenty of money."

"Can't we save?" said Carrie.

"We might try it," he suggested. "I've been thinking that if we'd take a smaller flat down town and live economically for a year, I would have enough, with what I have invested, to open a good place. Then we could arrange to live as you want to."

"It would suit me all right," said Carrie, who nevertheless felt badly to think it had come to this. Talk of a smaller flat sounded like poverty.

"There are lots of nice little flats down around Sixth Avenue there, below 14th. We might get one in there."

"I'll look at them if you say so," said Carrie.

"I think I could break away from this fellow inside of a year," said Hurstwood. "Nothing will ever come of this arrangement as it's going on now."

"I'll look around," said Carrie, observing that the proposed change seemed to be a serious thing with him.

The upshot of this was that this change was eventually effected. Not without great gloom on the part of Carrie. It really affected her more seriously than anything that had yet happened. She began to look upon Hurstwood wholly as a man and not as a lover or husband. She felt thoroughly bound to him as a wife and that her lot was cast with his, whatever it might be, but she began to see that he was gloomy and taciturn, not a young, strong and buoyant man. He looked a little bit old to her about the eyes and mouth now, and there were other things which placed him in his true rank, so far as her estimation was concerned. She began to feel that she had made a mistake. Incidentally, she also began to recall the fact that he had practically forced her to fly with him.

The new flat was located in 13th Street, a half-block west of Sixth Avenue, and contained only four rooms. The furniture they had in the six rooms in 78th Street more than amply furnished it, and left a few pieces which they put in storage. The new neighborhood did not appeal to Carrie as much. There were no trees here, no west view of the river. The street was solidly built up, and these flats, only three years old, had been so flimsily built that they looked as bad as a sounder building would have appeared after fifteen years. There were twelve families here, respectable enough but nothing like the Vances. Richer people required more space.

Being left alone in this little place, Carrie did without a girl. She made it charming enough, but could not make it delight her. Hurstwood was not inwardly pleased to think that they should have to modify their state, but he argued that he could do nothing. He must put the best face on it, and let it go at that.

He tried to show Carrie that there was no cause for financial alarm, but only congratulation over the chance he would have at the end of the year, by taking her rather more frequently to the theatre and by providing a liberal table. This was for a time only. He was getting in the frame of mind where he wanted principally to be alone and to be allowed to think. The disease of brooding was beginning to claim him as a victim. Only the newspapers and his own thoughts were worth while. The delight of love had again slipped away. It was a case of live, now, making the best you can out of a very commonplace station in life.

The road downward has but few landings and level places. The very state of his mind, superinduced by his condition, caused the breach to widen between him and his partner. At last that individual began to wish that Hurstwood was out of it. It so happened, however, that a real estate deal on the part of the owner of the land arranged things even more effectually than ill will could have schemed.

"Did you see that?" said Shaughnessy one morning to Hurstwood, pointing to the real estate column in a copy of the "Herald," which he held.

"No, what is it?" said Hurstwood, looking down the items of news.

"The man who owns this ground has sold it."

"You don't say so," said Hurstwood.

He looked and there was the notice. Mr. August Viele had yesterday registered the transfer of the lot, 25 × 75 ft., at the corner of Warren and Hudson Streets, to J. F. Slawson, for the sum of $57,000.

"Our lease expires—when?" asked Hurstwood thinking— "next February isn't it?"

"That's right," said Shaughnessy.

"It doesn't say what the new man's going to do with it," remarked Hurstwood, looking back to the paper.

"We'll hear, I guess, soon enough," said Shaughnessy.

Surely enough it did develop. Mr. Slawson owned the property adjoining and was going to put up a modern office building. The present one was to be torn down. It would take probably a year and a half to complete the other one.

All these things developed by degrees, and Hurstwood began to ponder over what would become of the saloon. One day he spoke about it to his partner.

"Do you think it would be worth while to open up somewhere else in the neighborhood?"

"What would be the use?" said Shaughnessy. "We couldn't get another corner around here."

"It wouldn't pay anywhere else, do you think?"

"I wouldn't try it," said the other.

The approaching change now took on a most serious aspect to Hurstwood. Dissolution meant the loss of his thousand dollars, and he could not save another thousand in the time. He understood as well as anything that Shaughnessy was merely tired of the arrangement and would probably lease the new corner, when completed, alone. He began to worry about the necessity of a new connection and to see impending serious financial straits unless something turned up. This left him in no mood to enjoy his flat or Carrie, and consequently the depression invaded that quarter.

Meanwhile he took such time as he could to look about, but opportunities were not numerous. More, he had not the same impressive personality which he had when he first came to New York. Bad thoughts had put a shade into his eyes which did not impress others favorably. Neither had he thirteen hundred dollars in hand to talk with. About a month later, he found that he had not made any progress, and Shaughnessy reported definitely that Slawson would not extend the present lease.

"I guess this thing's got to come to an end," he said, affecting an air of concern.

"Well, if it has, it has," answered Hurstwood grimly. He

would not give the other a key to his opinions, whatever they were. He should not have the satisfaction.

A day or two later he saw that he must say something to Carrie.

"You know," he said, "I think I'm going to get the worst of my deal down there."

"How is that?" asked Carrie in astonishment.

"Well, the man who owns the ground has sold it and the new owner won't re-lease it to us. The business may come to an end."

"Can't you start somewhere else?"

"There doesn't seem to be any place. Shaughnessy doesn't want to."

"Do you lose what you put in?"

"Yes," said Hurstwood, whose face was a study.

"Oh, isn't that too bad," said Carrie.

"It's a trick," said Hurstwood, "that's all. They'll start another place there all right."

Carrie looked at him and gathered from his whole demeanor what it meant. It was serious, very serious.

"Do you think you can get something else?" she ventured timidly.

Hurstwood thought a while. It was all up with the bluff about money and investment. She could see now that he was broke.

"I don't know," he said solemnly. "I can try."

CHAPTER XXXVII.

Carrie pondered over this situation as consistently as Hurstwood, once she got the facts adjusted in her mind. It took several days for her to fully realize that the approach of the dissolution of her husband's business meant commonplace struggle and privation. Her mind went back to her early venture in Chicago, the Hansons and their flat, and her heart revolted. That was terrible. Everything about poverty was terrible. She wished she knew a way out. Her recent experiences with the

Vances had wholly unfitted her to view her own state with complacence. The glamour of the high life of the city had, in the few experiences afforded her by the former, seized her completely. She had been taught how to dress and where to go without having ample means to do either. Now these things, ever-present realities as they were, filled her eyes and mind. The more circumscribed became her state, the more entrancing seemed this other. And now poverty threatened to seize her entirely and to remove this other world far upward like a heaven to which any Lazarus might extend, appealingly, his hands.

So, too, the ideal brought into her life by Ames remained. He had gone, but here was his word that riches were not everything, that there was a great deal more in the world than she knew, that the stage was good and the literature she read poor. He was a strong man and clean—how much stronger and better than Hurstwood and Drouet she only half-formulated to herself, but the difference was painful. It was something to which she voluntarily closed her eyes.

During the last three months of the Warren Street connection Hurstwood took parts of days off and hunted, tracking the business advertisements. It was more or less depressing business, wholly because of the thought that he must soon get something or he would begin to live on the few hundred dollars he was saving, and then he would have nothing to invest—he would have to hire out as a clerk.

Everything he discovered in his line advertised as an opportunity was either too expensive or too wretched for him to join in on. Some squalid bars which he found for sale or bidding for an investment were such wretched places that they gave him the blues. Besides, winter was coming on, the papers were announcing hardships, and there was a general feeling of hard times in the air, or at least he thought so. In his worry, other people's worries became apparent. No item about a firm's failing, a family's starving, or a man's dying upon the streets, supposedly of starvation, but arrested his eye as he scanned the morning papers. Once the "World" came out with a flaring announcement about "80,000 people out of employment in New York this winter," which struck as a knife at his heart.

"Eighty thousand," he thought. "What an awful thing that is."

This was new reasoning for Hurstwood. He did not notice

it, but it was nevertheless true that this was the first time in his
life he had ever paid much attention to such things. In the old
days the world had seemed to be getting along well enough. He
had been wont to see similar things in the "Daily News" in
Chicago, but they did not hold his attention except for a few
seconds, and then were immediately forgotten. He had been so
much interested in other things. Now, however, these things
were like gray clouds hovering along the horizon of a clear day.
They threatened to cover and obscure his life with chill gray-
ness. He tried to shake them off, to forget and brace up. Sometimes he said to himself, mentally:—

"What's the use worrying. I'm not out yet. I've got six
weeks more. Even if worst comes to worst, I've got enough to
live on for six months," and then he would figure about how
much he would have when the end came, and how long it would
last him if nothing else turned up.

Came more doubts and misgivings on top of this—more
threats of a winter without any business connection, and then
his heart would sink. Already he was at the end, so far as
thought was concerned. What would he do?

Curiously, as he troubled over his future, his thoughts occasionally reverted to his wife and family. He had avoided such
thoughts for the first three years, as much as possible. He hated
his wife and he could get along without her. Let her go. He
would do well enough. Now, however, when he was not doing
well enough, he began to wonder what she was doing, how his
children were getting along. He could see them living as nicely
as ever, occupying the comfortable house and using his property.

"By George, it's a shame they should have it all," he
vaguely thought to himself on several occasions. "I didn't do
anything."

As he looked back now and analyzed the situation which
led up to his taking the money, be began mildly to justify himself. What had he done—what in the world that should bar him
out this way and heap such difficulties upon him? It seemed only
yesterday to him since he was comfortable and well-to-do, but
now, it was all wrested from him.

She didn't deserve what she got out of him, that was sure.
He hadn't done so much, if everybody could just know.

There was no thought that the facts ought to be advertised.

It was only a mental justification he was seeking from himself—something that would enable him to bear his state as a righteous man.

One afternoon five weeks before the Warren Street place closed up, he left the saloon to visit three or four places he saw advertised in the "Herald." One was down in Gold Street, and he visited that, but did not enter. It was such a cheap-looking place, he felt that he could not abide it. Another was up in the Bowery, which he knew contained many showy resorts. It was near Grand Street, and turned out to be very handsomely fitted. He talked around about investments for fully three-quarters of an hour with the proprietor, who maintained that his health was poor, and that was the reason he wished a partner.

"Well, now just how much money would it take to buy a half-interest here?" said Hurstwood, who saw seven hundred dollars as his limit.

"Three thousand," said the man.

Hurstwood's jaw fell.

"Cash?" he said.

"Cash."

He tried to put on an air of deliberation, as one who might really buy, but his eyes showed gloom. He wound up by saying he would think it over and came away. The man he had been talking to sensed his condition, in a vague way.

"I don't think he wants to buy," he said to himself. "He doesn't talk right."

The afternoon was as gray as lead, and cold. It was blowing up a disagreeable winter wind. He visited a place far up on the East Side near 69th Street, and it was five o' clock and growing dim when he reached there. A portly German kept this place.

"How about this ad of yours?" asked Hurstwood, who rather objected to the looks of the place.

"Oh, dat iss all over," said the German. "I vill not sell now."

"Oh, is that so?" said Hurstwood.

"Yes, der is nothing to dat. It iss all over."

"Very well," said Hurstwood, turning around.

The German paid no more attention to him, and it made him mad.

"The crazy ass," he said to himself. "What does he want to advertise for?"

Wholly depressed he started for 13th Street. The flat had only a light in the kitchen, where Carrie was working. He struck a match and, lighting the gas, sat down in the dining room, without even greeting her. She came to the door and looked in.

"It's you, is it?" she said, and went back.

"Yes," he said, without even looking up from the evening paper he had bought.

Carrie saw things were wrong with him. He was not so handsome when he was gloomy. The lines at the sides of the eyes were wrinkled. Naturally dark of skin, gloom made him look slightly sinister. He was quite a disagreeable figure.

Carrie set the table and brought in the meal.

"Dinner's ready," she said, passing him for something.

He did not answer, reading on.

She came in and sat down at her place, feeling exceedingly wretched.

"Won't you eat now?" she asked.

He folded his paper and drew near, silence holding for a time, except for the "pass me's."

"It's been gloomy today, hasn't it," ventured Carrie, after a time.

"Yes," he said.

He only picked at his food.

"Are you still sure to close up?" said Carrie, venturing to take up the subject, which they had discussed often enough.

"Of course we are," he said, with the slightest modification of sharpness.

This retort angered Carrie. She had had a dreary day of it herself.

"You needn't talk like that," she said.

"Oh!"—he exclaimed, pushing back from the table, as if to say more, but letting it go at that. Then he picked up his paper. Carrie left her seat, containing herself with difficulty. He saw she was hurt.

"Don't go 'way," he said, as she started back into the kitchen. "Eat your dinner."

She passed, not answering.

He looked at the paper a few moments and then rose up, and put on his coat.

"I'm going down town, Carrie," he said, coming out. "I'm out of sorts tonight."

She did not answer.

"Don't be angry," he said. "It will be all right tomorrow."

He looked at her, but she paid no attention to him, working at her dishes.

"Goodbye," he said finally, and went out.

This was the first strong result of the situation between them, but with the nearing of the last day of the business, the gloom became almost a permanent thing. Hurstwood could not conceal his feelings about the matter. Carrie could not help wondering where she was drifting. It got so that they talked even less than usual, and yet, it was not Hurstwood who felt any objection to Carrie. It was Carrie who shied away from him. This he noticed. It aroused the objection to her becoming indifferent to him. What he did object to was the fact that she could get mad at him and not say goodbye, as she had—that she could keep silence, could afford not to try to cheer him up. He made the possibility of friendly intercourse almost a giant task, and then noticed with discontent that Carrie added to it by her manner and made it more impossible.

At last the final day came. When it actually arrived, Hurstwood, who had got his mind into a state where a thunder clap and raging storm would have seemed highly appropriate, was rather relieved to find that it was a plain ordinary day. The sun shone, the temperature was pleasant. He felt, as he came to the breakfast table, that it wasn't so terrible after all.

"Well," he said to Carrie, "today's my last day on earth."

Carrie smiled in answer to his humor.

"What are you going to do with the fixtures and stock?" she asked.

"Oh, we've got a man to buy them," said Hurstwood.

"Are they going to tear down the building right away?"

"No. I guess they won't begin for a few weeks. We have five days to get our things out."

Hurstwood glanced over his paper rather gaily. He seemed to have lost a load.

"I'll go down for a little while," he said, after breakfast, "and then I'll look around. Tomorrow I'll spend the whole day looking about. I think I can get something, now this thing's off my hands."

He went out smiling and visited the place. Shaughnessy

was there. They had made all arrangements to share according to their interests. When, however, he had been there several hours, gone out three more and returned, his elation had departed. As much as he had objected to the place, now that it was no longer to exist, he felt sorry. He wished that things were different.

Shaughnessy was coolly business-like.

"Well," he said at five o' clock. "We might as well count the change and divide."

They did so. The fixtures had already been sold and the sum divided.

"The other people will look to getting their stuff out—I guess," said Hurstwood, referring to the people who had bought the goods.

"Ye may trusht them fer that," said Shaughnessy.

"Good night," said Hurstwood, at the final moment, in a last effort to be genial.

"So long," said Shaughnessy, scarcely deigning to notice.

Thus the Warren Street arrangement was permanently concluded.

Carrie had prepared a good dinner at the flat, but after his ride up, Hurstwood was in a solemn and reflective mood.

"Well?" said Carrie, inquisitively.

"I'm out of that," he answered, taking off his coat.

As she looked at him she wondered what his financial state was now. They ate and talked a little.

"Will you have enough to buy in anywhere else?" asked Carrie.

"No," he said. "I'll have to get something else and save up."

"It would be nice if you could get some place," said Carrie, prompted by anxiety and hope.

"I guess I will," he said reflectively.

For some days thereafter he put on his overcoat regularly in the morning and sallied forth. On these ventures he first consoled himself with the thought that with the seven hundred dollars he had, he could still make some advantageous arrangement. He thought about going to some brewery, which, as he knew, frequently controlled saloons which they leased, and getting them to help him. Then he remembered that he would have to make a number of hundreds of dollars of expenditures, with the result that he would have nothing left for his monthly expenses. It was costing him nearly eighty dollars a month to live, and if, after putting his money into a saloon, it did not pay, he would be worse off than ever.

"No," he said, in his sanest moments, "I can't do it. I'll get something else and save up."

This getting-something proposition complicated itself the moment he began to think of what it was he wanted to do. Manage a place? Where should he get such a position? The papers contained no requests for managers. Such positions, he knew well enough, were either secured by long years of service or were bought, with a half or third interest. Into a place important enough to need such a manager he had not money enough to buy.

Nevertheless he started out. His clothes were very good, and his appearance still excellent, but it involved the trouble of being deluding. People looking at him imagined instantly that a man of his age, stout and well-dressed, must be well-off. He was not seeking anything. He was a comfortable owner of something, a man from whom the common run of mortals could well expect gratuities. Being now forty-three years of age and comfortably built, walking was not easy. He had not been used to exercise of that kind for, lo, these many years. His legs tired, his shoulders ached and his feet pained him at the close of the day, even when he took street cars in almost every direction. The mere getting up and down, if long continued, produced this result.

The fact that people took him to be much better off than he was, he well understood. It was so painfully clear to him that it retarded his search. Not that he wished to be less well-appearing, but that he was ashamed to belie this fine appearance by incongruous appeals. So he hesitated, wondering what to do.

On the first day, he decided to visit a brewery and see what they had to offer.

"How much money have you to invest in a place in New York?" asked the secretary of the brewery in question.

"Well, I have a few hundred dollars," said Hurstwood.

"The only thing we have now would require five hundred dollars at the lowest. I couldn't offer you that yet."

Hurstwood came away. It had been a long journey uptown for nothing.

He tried to think of something else, but only impossibilities suggested themselves. He thought of being a hotel-clerk, but instantly he remembered that he had no experience, and, what was more important, no acquaintances or friends in that line to whom he could go. He did know some hotel owners in several cities, including New York, but they knew of his dealings with Hannah and Hogg—he could not apply to them. He thought of other lines, suggested by large buildings or businesses which he knew of—wholesale groceries, hardware, insurance concerns and the like, but he had no experience.

How to go about getting anything was a bitter thought. Would he have to go personally and ask; wait outside an office door, and then, distinguished and affluent-looking, announce that he was looking for something to do? He strained painfully at the thought. No, he could not do that.

He really strolled about, thinking, and then, the weather being cold, stopped into a hotel. He knew hotels well enough to know that any decent-looking individual was welcome to a chair in the lobby. This was in the Broadway Central, which was then one of the most important hotels in the city. Taking a chair here was a painful thing to him. To think he should come to this. He had heard loungers about hotels called chair-warmers. He had called them that himself in his day. It had always seemed a cheap, miserable thing to do. But here he was, despite the possibility of meeting someone who knew him, shielding himself from the cold, and the weariness of the streets, in a hotel lobby.

"I can't do this way," he said to himself. "There's no use my starting out mornings without first thinking up some place to go to. I'll think up some places and then look them up."

This thought offered some slight consolation, but only slight. As he sat there in the shaded lobby, he could not think of one single place to go to. All the time his mind would come back to saloons as a last resort, and for these he had no money. It occurred to him that the positions of bartenders were sometimes open, but he put this out of his mind. Bartender—he! the ex-manager.

It grew awfully dull sitting in the hotel lobby, and so at

four he went home. He tried to put on a business air as he went in, but it was a feeble imitation. The rocking chair in the dining room was comfortable. He sank into it gladly, with several papers he had bought, and began to read.

As she was going through the room to begin preparing dinner, Carrie said:—

"The man was here for the rent today."

"Oh, was he?" said Hurstwood.

The least wrinkle crept into his brow as he remembered that this was February 2nd, the time when the man always called. He fished down in his pocket for his purse, getting the first taste of paying out when nothing is coming in. He looked at the fat green roll as a sick man looks at the one possible saving cure. Then he counted off twenty-eight dollars.

"Here you are," he said to Carrie when she came through again.

He buried himself in his papers and read. Oh, the rest of it—the relief from walking and thinking. What Lethean waters were these floods of telegraphed intelligence. He forgot his troubles in part, reading the smart items about doings of all kinds. Here was a young, handsome woman, if you might believe the newspaper drawing, suing a rich, fat, candy-making husband in Brooklyn for divorce. Here was another item, detailing the wrecking of a vessel in ice and snow, off Princess Bay, on Staten Island. A long, bright column told of the doings in the theatrical world—the plays produced, the actors appearing, the managers making announcements. Fanny Davenport was just opening at the Fifth Avenue. Daly was producing "King Lear." He read of the early departure for the season of a party, composed of the Vanderbilts and their friends, for Florida. An interesting shooting affray was on in the mountains of Kentucky. So he read, read, read, rocking in the warm room, near the radiator and waiting for dinner to be served.

CHAPTER XXXVIII.

The next morning he looked over the papers but found nothing that would suit him. He began after breakfast at nine o'clock and studied the business chances:—

For sale. The chance of a life time. The old established corset business of Mergens, Azalea Corsets, established for 30 years; the right, good will, name, lease, stock and fixtures offered at a ridiculous price. For terms and particulars apply to Yaku, Harbin and Co., 16 West 14th.

Further on in the same column he read:—

A FEW DOLLARS invested in your own neighborhood according to our instruction will bring an income of $8 daily for three hours' work; we do not invest your money; we give you this information for 25¢. by mail; if not as represented will return it. F. T. ROE & CO., 127 East 83d St.

And then:—

$2,500 WILL BUY fully furnished saloon and hotel business, 3-story, 172 Newark Ave., Jersey City; includes six months' rent and license to July 1. Call between 8 and 10 p.m., or address OWNER, 81 Herald.

He waded through a long list of these, making a few notes. Then he turned to the male help-wanted column, but with disagreeable feelings. The day was before him—a long day in which to discover something, and this was how he must begin to discover. He scanned the long column, which mostly concerned bakers, bushelmen, cooks, compositors, drivers and the like, finding two things only which arrested his eye. One was a cashier wanted in a wholesale furniture house and the other a salesman for a whiskey house. He had never thought of the latter. At once he decided to look that up.

The firm in question was Alsbery and Company, whiskey brokers, whose offices were in Broome Street, near Centre. It was half-past ten when he started out. By eleven-fifteen he was there. The house looked successful enough, but Hurstwood suffered at the thought of applying. Still he went in. A salesmanship in such a house was not such a small thing to ask for. It was a good, respectable position.

He was admitted almost at once to the manager on his appearance.

"Good morning, sir," said the latter, thinking at first that he was encountering one of his out-of-town customers.

"Good morning," said Hurstwood. "You advertised, I believe, for a salesman."

"Oh," said the man, showing plainly the enlightenment which had come to him. "Yes. Yes, I did."

"I thought I'd drop in," said Hurstwood with dignity. "I've had some experience in that line myself."

"Oh, have you?" said the man. "What experience have you had?"

"Well, I've managed several liquor houses in my time. Recently I owned a third-interest in a saloon at Warren and Hudson."

"I see," said the man.

Hurstwood ceased, waiting for some suggestion.

"We did want a salesman," said the man, "and we are considering several applications that have been made. I don't know as it's anything you'd care to take hold of, though. We are only paying one hundred a month. We expected to get some young man."

"I see," said Hurstwood. "Well, I'm in no position to choose just at present. If it were open, I should be glad to get it."

The man did not take kindly at all to his "no position to choose." He wanted someone who wasn't thinking of a choice, or something better. Especially not an old man. He wanted some one young, active and glad to work actively for a moderate sum. Hurstwood did not please him at all. He had more of an air than his employers.

"Well," he said in answer, "we'd be glad to consider your application. We shan't decide for a few days yet. Supposing you send us your references."

"I will," said Hurstwood.

He nodded good morning and came away. At the corner he looked at the furniture company's address and saw that it was in West 23rd Street. Accordingly he went up there. The place was not large enough, however. It looked moderate, the men in it idle and small-salaried. He walked by, glancing in, and then decided not to go there.

"They want a girl, probably, at ten a week," he said.

At about one o'clock he thought of eating and went to Dorlon's. There he pondered over places which he might look up. He was tired. It was blowing up gray again. Across the way, through Madison Square Park, stood the Fifth Avenue Hotel, looking down upon a busy scene. He decided to go over there in the lobby and sit awhile. It was warm in there and bright. He had seen no one he knew at the Broadway Central. In all likelihood he would encounter no one here. Finding a seat on one of the red plush divans close to the great windows which look out on Broadway's busy rout, he sat there musing. His state did not seem so bad in here. Sitting still and looking out, he could take some slight consolation in the few hundred dollars he had in his purse. He could forget, in a measure, the weariness of the street and his tiresome search. Still, it was only escape from a severe to a less severe state. He was still gloomy and disheartened. These minutes seemed to go very slowly. An hour was a long, long time in passing. It was filled for him with observations and mental comments concerning the actual guests of the hotel who passed in and out, and those more prosperous pedestrians whose good fortune showed in their clothes and spirits as they passed along Broadway outside. It was nearly the first time since he had arrived in the city that his leisure afforded him ample opportunity to contemplate this spectacle. Now, being perforce idle himself, he wondered at the activity of others. How gay were the youths he saw, how pretty the women. Such fine clothes they all wore. They were so intent upon getting somewhere. He saw coquetish glances cast by magnificent girls. Ah, the money it required to train with such—how well he knew. How long it had been since he had had the opportunity to do so.

Coaches rolled to and fro across the fine opening triangle of space. The Fifth Avenue rout of carriages bearing the ladies, weary of shopping, and the gentlemen, hastening early from business, was beginning to blockade the way, all going north. Everyone seemed to be merry, everyone content. Now he began to envy these people a little. It was so hard to see so much comfort and yet lack it all. His very future glowered at him coldly. The approaching night offered nothing. All this company was hastening to pleasures. The evening!—where would he go.

Two gentlemen sat down beside him on the same seat. They were rich and prosperous, two big mining millionaires from the West.

"When did you get in?" said one.

"Oh, last Wednesday."

"Wife with you?"

"Yes."

"Going to Florida this year?"

"No, my wife doesn't care to. She's picked on France. We're going there for a few months."

"Well, I leave tonight."

"Do you?"

"Yes."

"Same old place?"

"Yes, Florida suits me. I feel very good down there."

Hurstwood listened and then arose. He was weary, rather disheartened. The clock outside registered four. It was a little early but he thought he would go back to the flat.

This going back to the flat was coupled with the thought that Carrie would think he was sitting around too much if he came home early. He hoped he wouldn't have to, but the day hung heavy on his hands. Over there he was on his own ground. He could sit in his rocking chair and read. It was more comfortable. This busy, distracting, suggestive scene was shut out. He could read his papers.

Accordingly he went home. Carrie was reading, quite alone. It was rather dark in the flat, shut in as it was.

"You'll hurt your eyes," he said when he saw her.

After taking off his coat, he felt it incumbent upon him to make some little report of his day.

"I've been talking with a wholesale liquor company," he said. "I may go out on the road."

"Wouldn't that be nice," said Carrie.

"It wouldn't be such a bad thing," he answered.

Always from the man at the corner now he bought two papers—the "Evening World" and "Sun." Already the Italian who kept the stand had suggested, because for one time when he could not make change, that Hurstwood pay weekly. So now he merely picked his papers up as he came by without stopping.

Carrie thought it time to be about dinner. Hurstwood drew up his chair near the radiator and lighted the gas. Then it was as the evening before. His difficulties vanished in the items he so well loved to read.

The next day was even worse than the one before, because now he could not think of where to go. Nothing he saw in the papers, which he studied till ten A.M., appealed to him. He felt that he ought to go out and yet he sickened at the thought. "Where to? where to?"

"You mustn't forget to leave me my money for this week," said Carrie quietly.

They had an arrangement by which he placed twelve dollars a week in her hands out of which to pay current expenses. He heaved a little sigh as she said this and drew out his purse. Again he felt the dread of the thing. Here he was taking off, taking off, and nothing coming in.

"Lord," he said in his own thoughts, "this can't go on."

To Carrie he said nothing whatsoever. She could feel that her request disturbed him. To pay her would soon become a distressing thing.

"Yet, what have I got to do with it?" she thought. "Oh, why should I be made to worry?"

Hurstwood went out and made for Broadway. He wanted to think up some place. Before long, though, he reached the Grand Hotel at 31st Street. He knew of its comfortable lobby. He was cold after his twenty blocks' walk.

"I'll go in their barber shop and get a shave," he thought.

Thus he justified himself in sitting down in here, after his tonsorial treatment.

Again, time hanging heavy, he went home early, and this continued for several days, each day the need to hunt paining him, and each day disgust, depression, shamefacedness driving him into lobby idleness.

At last three days came in which a storm prevailed and he did not go out at all. The snow began to fall late one afternoon. It was a regular flurry of large, soft, white flakes. In the morning it was still coming down with a high wind, and the papers announced a blizzard. From out the front windows one could see a deep, soft bedding.

"I guess I'll not try to go out today," he said to Carrie at breakfast.

"It's going to be awful bad, so the papers say."

"The man hasn't brought my coal, either," said Carrie, who ordered by the bushel.

"I'll go over and see about it," said Hurstwood. This was the first time he had ever suggested doing an errand, but somehow, the wish to sit about the house prompted it, as sort of compensation for privilege. He did not openly think of it in that light, but the subconscious suggestion was there.

All day and all night it snowed, and the city began to suffer from a general blockade of traffic. Great attention was given to the details of the storm by the newspapers, which played up the distress of the poor in large type. Italians, doing all the small-bushel business in coal throughout the city, raised the price. A vast excitement about cold, hunger, starvation and the like was really worked up by the papers until nearly everyone felt some of the terrors of winter, although they were not suffering at all.

Hurstwood sat and read by his radiator in the corner. He did not try to think about his need of work. This storm's being so terrific and tying up all things robbed him of the need. He made himself wholly comfortable and toasted his feet.

Carrie observed his ease with some misgiving. For all of the greatness of the storm, she doubted this comfort. He took his situation too philosophically. He was too well satisfied.

Hurstwood however read on and on. He did not pay much attention to Carrie. She fulfilled her household duties and said little to disturb him.

The next day it was still snowing and the next bitter cold. Hurstwood took the alarm of the paper and sat still. Now he volunteered to do a few other little things. One was to go to the butcher, another to the grocery. He really thought nothing of these little services in connection with their true significance. It seemed as if, being at home, it was the proper thing to do. He felt as if he were not wholly useless—indeed, in such a stress of weather, quite worth while about the house.

On the fourth day, however, it cleared and he read that the storm was over. Now, however, he idled, thinking how sloppy the streets would be. It was still cold. He hated to think of going out.

It was noon before he finally abandoned his papers and got under way. Owing to the slightly warmer temperature, the streets were sloppy and bad. He went across 14th on the car and got a transfer south on Broadway. One little advertisement he had relating to a saloon down in Pearl Street. When he reached the Broadway Central, however, he changed his mind.

"What's the use?" he thought, looking out upon the slop and snow. "I couldn't buy into it. It's a thousand to one nothing comes of it. I guess I'll get off," and off he got. In the lobby he took a seat and waited again, wondering what he could do.

While he was idly pondering, satisfied to be inside, a well-dressed individual passed up the lobby, stopped, looked sharply as if not sure of his memory and then approached. Hurstwood recognized Cargill, the owner of the large stables in Chicago of the same name, whom he had last seen at Avery Hall, the night Carrie appeared there. The remembrance of how this individual brought up his wife to shake hands on that occasion was also on the instant clear.

Hurstwood was greatly abashed. His eyes expressed the difficulty he felt.

"Why it's Hurstwood," said Cargill, remembering now, and sorry that he had not recognized him quick enough in the beginning to have avoided this meeting.

"Yes," said Hurstwood. "How are you."

"Very well," said Cargill, troubled for something to talk about. "Stopping here?"

"No," said Hurstwood, "just keeping an appointment."

"I knew you had left Chicago. I was wondering what had become of you."

"Oh, I'm here now," answered Hurstwood, anxious to get away.

"Doing well, I suppose?"

"Excellent."

"Glad to hear it."

They looked at one another, rather embarrassed.

"Well, I have an engagement with a friend upstairs. I'll leave you. So long."

Hurstwood nodded his head.

"Damn it all," he murmured, turning toward the door. "I knew that would happen."

He walked several blocks in the street. His watch only registered one-thirty. He tried to think of some place to go or something to do. The day was so bad he wanted only to be inside. Finally his feet began to feel wet and cold, and he boarded a car. This took him to 59th Street, which was as good as anywhere else. Landed here, he turned to walk back along Seventh Avenue, but the slush was too much. The misery of lounging about with nowhere to go became intolerable. He felt as if he were catching cold.

Stopping at a corner he waited for a car southbound. This was no day to be out; he would go home.

Carrie was surprised to see him at a quarter of three.

"It's a miserable day out," was all he said. Then he took off his coat and changed his shoes.

That night he felt a cold coming on and took quinine. He was feverish until morning and sat about the next day while Carrie waited on him. He was a helpless creature in sickness, not very handsome in a dull-colored bath gown and his hair uncombed. He looked haggard about the eyes and quite old. Carrie noticed this and it did not appeal to her. She wanted to be good-natured and sympathetic, but something about the man held her aloof.

Toward evening he looked so bad in the weak light that she suggested he go to bed.

"You better sleep alone," she said. "You'll feel better. I'll open your bed for you now."

"All right," he said.

As she did all these things she was in a most despondent state.

"What a life! What a life!" was her one thought.

Once during the day when he sat near the radiator, hunched up and reading, she passed through and, seeing him, wrinkled her brows. In the front room, where it was not so warm, she sat by the window and cried. This was the life cut out for her, was it? To live cooped up in a small flat with some one who was out of work, idle and indifferent to her? She was merely a servant to him now, nothing more. All love was dead. There was no praise, only medium good nature. He expected everything of her and in return offered nothing. For two weeks now he had done nothing. If he became seriously ill, what would they do? She buried her face in her hands and wept anew.

This crying made her eyes red and when, in preparing his bed, she lighted the gas, and having prepared it, called him in, he noticed the fact.

"What's the matter with you?" he asked, looking into her face. His voice was hoarse, and his unkempt head only added to its grewsome quality.

"Nothing," said Carrie weakly.

"You've been crying," he said.

"I haven't either," she answered.

It was not for love of him exactly, that he knew.

"You needn't cry," he said, getting into bed. "Things will come out all right."

In a day or two he was up again, but rough weather holding, he stayed in. The Italian now delivered the papers, and these he read assiduously. A few times after that he ventured out, but meeting another of his old-time friends, he began to feel uneasy sitting about hotel corridors.

Each day he came home early and at last made no pretence of going anywhere. Winter was no time to look for anything.

The increase of his home attendance was marked by a trait which grew with his home-staying habit. That was of observation and suggestion. Naturally, being about the house, he noticed the way Carrie did things. She was far from perfect in household method and economy, and her little deviations on this score first caught his eye. Not, however, before her regular demand for her allowance became a grievous thing. Sitting around as he did, the weeks seemed to pass very quickly. Every Tuesday Carrie asked for her money.

"Do you think we live as cheaply as we might?" he asked one Tuesday morning.

"I do the best I can," said Carrie.

Nothing was added to this at the moment but the very next day he said:—

"Do you ever go to this market over here?"

He referred to the Gansevoort Market at 11th on the West Side.

"I didn't know there was a market there," said Carrie.

"There is a big one there. They say you can get things lots cheaper there."

Carrie was very indifferent to the suggestion. These were things which she did not like at all.

"How much do you pay for a pound of meat?" he asked one day.

"Oh, there are different prices," said Carrie. "Sirloin steak is twenty-two cents."

"That's steep, isn't it?" he answered.

So he asked about other things, until finally, with the passing days, it seemed to become a mania with him. He learned the prices and remembered them.

His errand-running capacity also improved. It began in a small way of course. Carrie, going to get her hat one morning, was stopped by him.

"Where you going, Carrie?" he asked.

"Over to the baker's," she answered.

"I'd just as leave go for you," he said.

She acquiesced and he went. Each afternoon he would go to the corner for the papers.

"Is there anything you want?" he would say.

By degrees she began to use him. Doing this, however, she lost the weekly payment of twelve dollars.

"You want to pay me today," she said one Tuesday, around this time.

"How much?" he asked.

She understood well enough what it meant.

"Well, about five dollars," she answered. "I owe the coal man."

The same day he said:—

"I think this Italian up here on the corner sells coal at twenty-five cents a bushel. I'll trade with him."

Carrie heard this with indifference.

"All right," she said.

Then it came to be:—

"George, I must have some coal today," or "You must get some meat of some kind for dinner."

He would find out what she needed and order.

Accompanying this plan came skimpiness.

"I only got a half-pound of steak," he said, coming in one afternoon with his papers. "We never seem to eat very much."

These miserable details ate the heart out of Carrie. They blackened her days and grieved her soul. Oh, how this man had changed. All day and all day, here he sat, reading his papers. The world seemed to have no attraction. Once in a while he would go out. In fine weather it might be four or five hours between eleven and four. She could do nothing but view him with growing contempt.

It was true apathy with Hurstwood, resulting from his inability to see his way out. Each month drew from his small store. Now he only had five hundred dollars left and this he hugged, half-feeling as if he could stave off absolute necessity for an indefinite period. Sitting around the house he decided to wear some old clothes he had. This came first with the bad days. Only once he apologized, in the very beginning.

"It's so bad today. I'll just wear these around."

Eventually these became the permanent thing.

Also he had been wont to pay fifteen cents for a shave and a tip of ten cents. In his first distress he cut down the tip to five, then to nothing. Later he tried a ten-cent barber shop and, finding that the shave was satisfactory, patronized regularly. Later still he put off shaving each day to every other day, then to every third and so on, until once a week became the rule. On Saturday he was a sight to see.

Of course, as his own self-respect vanished, it perished for him in Carrie. She could not understand what had gotten into the man. He had some money, he had a decent suit remaining, he was not bad-looking when dressed up. She did not forget her own difficult struggle in Chicago, but she did not forget either that she had never ceased from trying. He never tried. He did not even consult the ads in the papers any more.

Finally a distinct impression escaped from her.

"What makes you put so much butter on the steak?" he asked her one evening, standing around in the kitchen.

"To make it good, of course," she answered.

"Butter is awful dear these days," he suggested.

"You wouldn't mind it if you were working," she answered.

He shut up after this and went in to his paper, but the retort rankled in his mind. It was the first cutting remark that had come from her.

That same evening, Carrie, after reading, went off to the front room to bed. This was unusual. When Hurstwood decided to go, he retired as usual without a light. It was then that he discovered Carrie's absence.

"That's funny," he said. "Maybe she's sitting up."

He gave the matter no more thought, but slept. In the morning she was not beside him. Strange to say, this passed without comment.

Night approaching and a slightly more conversational feeling prevailing, Carrie said, "I think I'll sleep alone tonight. I have a headache."

"All right," said Hurstwood.

The third night she went to her front bed without apologies.

This was a grim blow to Hurstwood but he never mentioned it.

"All right," he said to himself with an irrepressible frown, "let her sleep alone."

CHAPTER XXXIX.

The Vances, who had been back in the city ever since Christmas, had not forgotten Carrie; but they, or rather Mrs. Vance, had never called on her for the very simple reason that Carrie had never sent her address. True to her nature, she corresponded with Mrs. Vance so long as she still lived in 78th Street, but when she was compelled to move into 13th, her fear that the latter would take it as an indication of reduced circumstances caused her to study some way of avoiding the necessity of giving her address. Not finding any convenient method she sorrowfully resigned the privilege of writing to her friend entirely. The latter wondered at this strange silence, thought Carrie must have left the city and in the end gave her up as lost. So she was thoroughly surprised to encounter her in 14th Street, where she had gone shopping. Carrie was there for the same purpose.

"Why, Mrs. Wheeler," said Mrs. Vance, looking Carrie over in a glance, "where have you been? Why haven't you been to see me? I've been wondering all this time what had become of you. Really, I—"

"I'm so glad to see you," said Carrie, pleased and yet nonplussed. Of all times this was the worst to encounter Mrs. Vance. "Why, I'm living down-town here. I've been intending to come and see you. Where are you living now?"

"In 58th Street," said Mrs. Vance, "just up Seventh Avenue—218. Why don't you come and see me?"

"I will," said Carrie. "Really I've been wanting to come. I know I ought to. It's a shame. But you know—"

"What's your number?" said Mrs. Vance.

"13th Street," said Carrie, reluctantly. "112 West."

"Oh," said Mrs. Vance, "that's right near here, isn't it?"

"Yes," said Carrie. "You must come down and see me some time."

"Well, you're a fine one," said Mrs. Vance laughing, the while noting that Carrie's appearance had modified somewhat. "The address too," she added to herself. "They must be hard up."

Still she liked Carrie so well as to take her in tow.

"Come with me in here a minute," she exclaimed, turning into a store.

When Carrie returned home, all her feelings about the luxury and fastidiousness of the city revived, and the quality of her deprivations was emphasized. Worst of all, Mrs. Vance had declared, almost unasked, that she was going to call.

There was Hurstwood, reading as usual. He seemed to take his condition with the utmost nonchalance. His beard was at least four days old.

"Oh," thought Carrie, "if she were to come here and see him."

She shook her head in absolute misery. It looked as if her situation was becoming unbearable.

Driven to desperation she asked at dinner, "Did you ever hear any more from that wholesale house?"

"No," he said. "They don't want an experienced man."

Carrie dropped the subject, feeling unable to say more.

"I met Mrs. Vance this afternoon," she said after a time.

"Did, eh?" he answered.

"They're back in New York now," Carrie went on. "She did look so nice."

"Well, she can afford it, as long as he puts up for it," returned Hurstwood. "He's got a soft job."

Hurstwood was looking into the paper. He could not see the look of infinite weariness and discontent Carrie gave him.

"She said she thought she'd call down here some day."

"She's been long getting 'round to it, hasn't she?" said Hurstwood, with a kind of sarcasm.

The woman didn't appeal to him from her spending side.

"Oh, I don't know," said Carrie, angered by the man's attitude. "Perhaps I didn't want her to come."

"She's too gay," said Hurstwood significantly. "No one can keep up to her pace unless they've got a lot of money."

"Mr. Vance doesn't seem to find it very hard."

"He may not now," answered Hurstwood doggedly, well understanding the inference, "but his life isn't done yet. You can't tell what'll happen. He may get down like anybody else."

There was something quite knavish in the man's attitude. His eye seemed to be cocked with a twinkle upon the fortunate, expecting their defeat. His own state seemed a thing apart—not considered.

This thing was the remains of his old-time cocksureness and independence. Sitting in his flat and reading of the doings of other people, sometimes this independent, undefeated mood came upon him. Forgetting the weariness of the streets and the degradation of search he would sometimes prick up his ears. It was as if he said:—

"I can do something. I'm not down yet. There's lots of things coming to me if I want to go after them."

It was in this mood that he would occasionally dress up, go for a shave, and, putting on his gloves, sally forth quite actively. Not with any definite aim. It was more a barometric condition. He felt just right for being outside and doing something.

On such occasions his money went also. He knew of several poker rooms down town. A few acquaintances he had in down-town resorts and about the city hall. It was a change to see them and exchange a few friendly commonplaces.

"Hello, Wheeler, how are you?"

"Oh, very fair."

"You're looking good. What news?"

"Oh, nothing much."

Such little things as these made the world still tolerable, though they profited him nothing.

He had once been accustomed to hold a pretty fair hand at poker. Many a friendly game had netted him a hundred dollars or more at the time when that sum was merely sauce to the dish of the game—not the all in all. Now, on such a fair day as this, he would think somewhat of playing.

"I might win a couple of hundred. I'm not out of practise."

It is but fair to say that this thought had occurred to him several times before he acted upon it.

The poker room which he first invaded was over a saloon which he knew, in West Street, near one of the ferries. He had been there before. Several games were going on at the time. These he watched for a time and noticed that the pots were quite large for the ante involved.

"Deal me a hand," he said, at the beginning of a new shuffle. He pulled up a chair and studied his cards. Those playing made that quiet study of him which is so unapparent and yet invariably so searching.

Poor fortune was with him at first. He received a mixed collection without progression or pairs.

"I pass," he said.

On the strength of this he was content to lose his ante. The deals did fairly by him in the long run, causing him to come away with a few dollars to the good.

A little success, like a little wisdom, is certainly a dangerous thing. The very next afternoon he was back again, seeking amusement and profit. This time he followed up three of a kind to his doom. There was a better hand across the table, held by a pugnacious Irish youth, who was a political hanger-on of the Tammany district in which they were located. Hurstwood was surprised at the persistence of this individual, whose bets came with a sang-froid which, if a bluff, was excellent art. Hurstwood began to doubt, but kept, or thought to keep at least, the cool demeanor with which, in olden times, he deceived those psychic students of the gaming table who seem to read thoughts and moods, rather than exterior evidences, however subtle. He could not down the cowardly thought that this man had something better and would stay to the end, drawing his last dollar into the pot, should he choose to go so far. Still he hoped to win much—his hand was excellent. Why not raise it five more?

"I raise you three," said the youth.

"Make it five," said Hurstwood, fishing out his chips.

"Come again," said the youth, pushing out a small pile of reds.

"Let me have some more chips," said Hurstwood to the keeper in charge, taking out a bill.

A cynical grin lit up the face of his youthful opponent. When the chips were laid out, Hurstwood met the raise.

"Five again," said the youth.

Hurstwood's brow was wet. He was deep in now—very deep for him. Sixty dollars of his good money was up. He was ordinarily no coward, but the thought of losing so much weakened him. Finally he gave way. He would not trust to this fine hand any longer.

"I call," he said.

"Hearts straight," said the youth, showing a flush progression of high cards.

Hurstwood's hand dropped.

"I thought I had you," he said weakly.

The youth raked in his chips and Hurstwood came away, not without first stopping to count his remaining cash on the stair.

"Three hundred and forty dollars," he said.

With this loss and ordinary expenses, so much had already gone.

Back in the flat he decided he would play no more, and that he would look for something to do. The fact was, however, that pride stopped him—a keen remembrance of former days. He did go out, but a little aimless walking took the nerve out of him and made him as apathetic as before. He returned home and occupied his chair in the corner.

Remembering Mrs. Vance's promise to call, Carrie made one other mild protest. It was concerning Hurstwood's appearance. This very day, coming home, he changed his clothes to the old togs he sat around in.

"What makes you always put on those old clothes?" asked Carrie.

"What's the use wearing my goods around here?" he asked.

"Well, I should think you'd feel better." Then she added, "Some one might call."

"Who?" he said.

"Well, Mrs. Vance," said Carrie.

"She needn't see me," he answered sullenly.

This lack of pride and interest made Carrie almost hate him.

"Oh," she thought, "there he sits. 'She needn't see me.' I should think he would be ashamed of himself."

The real bitterness of this thing was added when Mrs. Vance did call. It was on one of her shopping rounds. Making her way up the commonplace hall, she knocked at Carrie's door. To her subsequent and agonizing distress, Carrie was out. Hurstwood opened, half-thinking that the knock was Carrie's. For once he was taken honestly aback. The last voice of youth and pride spoke in him.

"Why," he said, actually stammering, "how do you do?"

"How do you do?" said Mrs. Vance, who could scarcely believe her eyes. His great confusion she instantly perceived. He did not know whether to invite her in or not.

"Is your wife at home?" she inquired.

"No," he said, "Carrie's out. But, won't you step in? She'll be back shortly."

"No—o," said Mrs. Vance, realizing the change of it all. "I'm really very much in a hurry. I thought I'd just run up and look in, but I couldn't stay. Just tell your wife she must come and see me."

"I will," said Hurstwood, standing back and feeling intense relief at her going. He was so ashamed that he folded his hands weakly, as he sat in the chair afterwards and thought.

Carrie, coming in from another direction, thought she saw Mrs. Vance going away. She strained her eyes but could not make sure.

"Was anybody here just now?" she asked of Hurstwood.

"Yes," he said, guiltily, "Mrs. Vance."

"Did she see you?" she asked, expressing her full despair.

This cut Hurstwood like a whip and made him sullen.

"If she had eyes she did. I opened the door."

"Oh," said Carrie, closing one hand tightly out of sheer nervousness. "What did she have to say?"

"Nothing," he answered. "She couldn't stay."

"And you looking like that," said Carrie, throwing aside a long reserve.

"What of it?" he said, angering. "I didn't know she was coming, did I?"

"You knew she might," said Carrie. "I told you she said she was coming. I've asked you a dozen times to wear your other clothes. Oh, I think this is just terrible."

"Oh, let up," he answered. "What difference does it make? You couldn't associate with her anyway. They've got too much money."

"Who said I wanted to?" said Carrie fiercely.

"Well, you act like it, rowing around over my looks. You'd think I'd committed—"

Carrie interrupted:

"It's true," she said. "I couldn't if I wanted to—but whose fault is it? You're very free to sit and talk about who I could associate with. Why don't you get out and look for work?"

This was a thunderbolt in camp.

"What's it to you," he said rising, almost fiercely. "I pay the rent don't I? I furnish the—"

"Yes, you pay the rent," said Carrie. "You talk as if there was nothing else in the world but a flat to sit around in. You haven't done a thing for three months except sit around and interfere here. I'd like to know what you married me for."

"I didn't marry you," he said in a snarling tone.

"I'd like to know what you did do, then, in Montreal," she answered.

"Well, I didn't marry you," he answered. "You can get that out of your head. You talk as though you didn't know."

Carrie looked at him a moment, her eyes distending. She had believed it was all legal and binding enough.

"What did you lie to me for, then?" she asked fiercely. "What did you force me to run away with you for?"

Her voice became almost a sob.

"Force!" he said with curled lip. "A lot of forcing I did."

"Oh!" said Carrie, breaking under the strain and turning. "Oh, oh!" and she hurried into the front room.

Hurstwood was now hot and worked up. It was a great shaking-up for him, both mental and moral. He wiped his brow as he looked around and then went for his clothes and dressed. Not a sound came from Carrie, who ceased sobbing when she heard him dressing. She thought, at first, with the faintest alarm, of being left without money—not at losing him, though he might be going away permanently. She heard him open the top of the wardrobe and take out his hat. Then the dining-room door closed and she knew he had gone.

After a few moments of silence she stood up dry-eyed and looked out the window. Hurstwood was just strolling up the street, from the flat toward Sixth Avenue.

The latter made progress along 13th and across 14th to Union Square.

"Look for work," he said to himself. "Look for work. She tells me to get out and look for work."

He tried to shield himself from his own mental accusation, which told that she was right.

"What a cursed thing that Mrs. Vance's call was anyhow," he thought. "Stood right there and looked me over. I know what she was thinking."

He remembered the few times he had seen her in 78th Street. She was always a swell-looker, and he had tried to put on the air of being worthy of such as she, in front of her. Now to think she had caught him looking this way. He wrinkled his forehead in his distress.

"The devil!" he said, a dozen times in an hour.

It was a quarter after four when he left the house. Carrie was in tears. There would be no dinner that night.

"What the deuce," he said, swaggering mentally to hide his own shame from himself. "I'm not so bad—I'm not down yet."

He looked around the square and seeing the Morton House, decided to go there for dinner. He would get his papers and make himself comfortable there.

Accordingly he ascended into the fine parlor of the Morton House, then one of the best New York hotels, and finding a cushioned seat, read. It did not trouble him much that his decreasing sum of money did not allow of such extravagance. Like the morphine fiend, he was becoming addicted to his ease. Anything to relieve his mental distress, to satisfy his craving for comfort. He must do it. No thoughts for the morrow—he could not stand to think of it, any more than he could of any other calamity. Like the certainty of death, he tried to shut the certainty of soon being without a dollar completely out of his mind, and he came very near doing it.

Well-dressed guests moving to and fro over the thick carpets carried him back to old days. A young lady, a guest of the house, playing a piano in one alcove, pleased his eye. He sat there reading and posing, everyone imagining him to be some well-to-do, comfortable merchant, and he lulling himself by it all.

His dinner cost him $1.50. By eight o'clock he was through, and then, seeing guests leaving, and the crowd of pleasure-seekers thickening outside, wondered where he should go. Not home. Carrie would be up. No, he would not go back there this evening. He would stay out and knock around as a man who was independent—not broke—well might. He bought a cigar and went outside on the corner where other individuals were lounging—brokers, racing people, thespians—his own flesh and blood. As he stood there, he thought of the old evenings in Chicago and how he used to dispose of them. Many's the game he had had. This took him to poker.

"I didn't do that thing right the other day," he thought, referring back to his loss of sixty dollars. "I shouldn't have weakened. I could have bluffed that fellow down. I wasn't in form, that's what ailed me."

Then he studied the possibilities of the game as it had been played and began to figure how he might have won in several instances by bluffing a little harder.

"I'm old enough to play poker and do something with it. I'll try my hand tonight."

Visions of a big stake floated before him. Supposing he did win a couple of hundred—wouldn't he be in it. Lots of sports he knew made their living at this game, and a good living too.

"They always had as much as I had," he thought.

So off he went to a poker room in the neighborhood, feeling much as he had in the old days. In this period of self-forgetfulness, aroused first by the shock of argument and perfected by a dinner in the hotel, with cocktails and cigars, he was as nearly like the old Hurstwood as he would ever be again. It was not the old Hurstwood—only a man arguing with a divided conscience and lured by a phantom.

This poker room was much like the other one, only it was a back room in a better drinking resort. Hurstwood watched awhile, and then, seeing an interesting game, joined in. As before, it went easy for awhile, he winning a few times and cheering up, losing a few pots and growing more interested and determined on that account. At last the fascinating game took a strong hold on him. He enjoyed its risks and ventured on a trifling hand to bluff the company and secure a fair stake. To his self-satisfaction—intense and strong, he did it.

In the height of this feeling he began to think his luck was with him. No one else had done as well. Now came another moderate hand and again he tried to open the jack-pot on it.

There were others there who were almost reading his heart, so close was their observation.

"I have three of a kind," said one of the players to himself. "I'll just stay with that fellow to the finish."

The result was that bidding began.

"I raise you ten."

"Good."

"Ten more."

"Good."

"Ten again."

"Right you are."

It got to where Hurstwood had seventy-five dollars up. The other man really became serious. Perhaps this individual (Hurstwood) really did have a stiff hand.

"I call," he said.

Hurstwood showed his hand. He was done. The bitter fact that he had lost seventy-five dollars made him desperate.

"Let's have another game," he said grimly.

"All right," said the man.

Some of the other players quit, but observant loungers took their places. Time passed and it came to twelve o'clock. Hurstwood held on, neither winning nor losing much. Then he grew weary and on a last game lost twenty more. He was sick at heart.

At a quarter after one in the morning, he came out of the place. The chill, bare streets seemed a mockery of his state. He walked slowly west, little thinking of his row with Carrie. He ascended the stairs and went into his room as if there had been no trouble. It was his loss that occupied his mind. Sitting down on the bedside he counted his money. What with the regular household expenses that were going on constantly, there was but a hundred and ninety dollars and some change. He put it up and began to undress.

"I wonder what's getting into me anyhow," he said.

In the morning Carrie scarcely spoke, and he felt as if he must go out again. He had treated her badly, but he could not afford to make up. Now desperation seized him and for a day or two, going out thus, he lived like a gentleman, or what he conceived to be a gentleman, which took money. For his escapades he was soon poorer in mind and body, to say nothing of his purse, which lost thirty by the process. Then he came down to cold, bitter sense again.

"The rent man comes today," said Carrie, greeting him thus indifferently three mornings later.

"He does?"

"Yes, this is the 2nd," answered Carrie.

Hurstwood frowned. Then, in despair he got out his purse.

"It seems an awful lot to pay for rent," he said.

He was nearing his last hundred dollars.

CHAPTER XL.

It would be useless to explain how in due time the last fifty dollars was in sight. The seven hundred, by his process of handling, had only carried them into June. Before the final hundred mark was reached, he began to indicate that a calamity was approaching.

"I don't know," he said one day, taking a trivial expenditure for meat as a text. "It seems to take an awful lot for us to live."

"It doesn't seem to me," said Carrie, "that we spend very much."

"My money is nearly gone," he said, "and I hardly know where it's gone to."

"All that seven hundred dollars?" asked Carrie.

"All but a hundred."

He looked so disconsolate that it scared her. She began to see that she herself had been drifting. She had felt it all the time.

"Well, George," she exclaimed, "why don't you get out and look for something? You could find something."

"I have looked," he said. "You can't make people give you a place."

She gazed weakly at him and said:—"Well, what do you think you'll do? A hundred dollars won't last long."

"I don't know," he said. "I can't do any more than look."

Carrie became frightened over this announcement. She thought desperately upon the subject. Frequently she had considered concerning the stage as a door through which she might enter that gilded state which she had so much craved. Now, as in Chicago, it came as a last resource in distress. Something must be done if he did not get work soon. Perhaps she would have to go out and battle again alone.

She began to think concerning how one would go about it to get a place. Her experience in Chicago proved that she had not tried the right way. There must be people who would listen to and try you—men who would give you an opportunity.

Once she thought to ask Hurstwood but, inexplicably, she at the same time felt that he would object. She had become so much of a housewife; everything depended upon her. He would not like to let her drop all this for something else. Still she thought she could ask him in a round-about way.

They were talking at the breakfast table a morning or two later when she brought up the dramatic subject by saying that she saw that Sarah Bernhardt was coming to this country. Hurstwood had seen it too.

"How do people get on the stage, George?" she finally asked innocently.

"I don't know," he said. "There must be dramatic agents."

Carrie was sipping coffee and did not look up.

"Regular people who get you a place?"

"Yes, I think so," he answered.

Suddenly the air in which she asked attracted his attention.

"You're not still thinking about being an actress, are you?" he asked.

"No," she answered, "I was just wondering."

Without being clear there was something in the thought which he objected to. He did not believe any more, after three years of observation, that Carrie would ever do anything great in that line. She seemed too simple, too yielding. His idea of the art was that it involved something more pompous. If she tried to get on the stage she would fall into the hands of some cheap manager and become like the rest of them. He had a good idea of what he meant by *them.* Carrie was pretty. She would get along all right, but where would he be?

"I'd get that idea out of my head, if I were you. It's a lot more difficult than you think."

Carrie felt this to contain, in some way, an aspersion upon her ability.

"You said I did real well in Chicago," she rejoined.

"You did," he answered, seeing that he was arousing opposition, "but Chicago isn't New York by a big jump."

Carrie did not answer this at all. It hurt her.

"The stage," he went on, "is all right if you can be one of the big guns, but there's nothing to the rest of it. It takes a long while to get up."

"Oh, I don't know," said Carrie, slightly aroused.

In a flash he thought he foresaw the result of this thing. Now when the worst of his situation was approaching she would get on the stage in some cheap way and forsake him. Strangely, he had not conceived well of her mental ability. That was because he did not understand the nature of emotional greatness. He had never learned that a person might be emotionally instead of intellectually great. Avery Hall was too far away for him to look back and sharply remember. He had lived with this woman too long.

"Well, I do," he answered. "If I were you I wouldn't think of it. It's not much of a profession for a woman."

"It's better than going hungry," said Carrie. "If you don't want me to do that, why don't you get work yourself?"

There was no answer ready for this. He had got used to the suggestion.

"Oh, let up," he answered.

The result of this was that she secretly resolved to try. It didn't matter about him. She was not going to be dragged into poverty and something worse to suit him. She could act. She could get something and then work up. What would he say then? She pictured herself already engaged in appearing in some fine performance on Broadway, going every evening to her dressing room and making up. Then she would come out at eleven o'clock and see the carriages ranged about, waiting for the people. It did not matter whether she was the star or not. If she were only once in, getting a decent salary, wearing the kind of clothes she liked, having the money to do with and going here and there as she pleased—how delightful it would all be. Her mind ran over this picture all the day long. Hurstwood's dreary state made its beauty become more and more vivid.

Curiously, this idea soon took hold of Hurstwood. His vanishing sum suggested that he would need sustenance. Why could not Carrie assist him a little, until he could get something?

He came in one day with something of this idea in his mind.

"I met John B. Drake today," he said. "He's going to open a hotel here in the fall. He says that he can make a place for me then."

"Who is he?" asked Carrie.

"He's the man that runs the Grand Pacific in Chicago."

"Oh," said Carrie.

"I'd get about fourteen hundred a year out of that."

"That would be good, wouldn't it?" she said sympathetically.

"If I can only get over this summer," he added, "I think I'll be all right. I'm hearing from some of my friends again."

Carrie swallowed this story in all its pristine beauty. She sincerely wished he could get through the summer. He looked so hopeless.

"How much money have you left?" she asked.

"Only fifty dollars."

"Oh, mercy!" she exclaimed, "what will we do? It's only twenty days until the rent will be due again."

Hurstwood rested his head on his hands and looked blankly at the floor.

"Maybe you could get something in the stage line," he blandly suggested.

"Maybe I could," said Carrie, now that some one approved of the idea.

"I'll lay my hand to whatever I can get," he said very bravely, now that he saw her brighten up. "I can get something."

She cleared up the things one morning after he had gone, dressed as neatly as her wardrobe permitted and set out for Broadway. She did not know that thoroughfare very well. To her it was a wonderful conglomeration of everything great and mighty. The theatres were there—these agencies must be somewhere about.

She decided to stop in at the Madison Square Theatre and ask the man how to find the theatrical agents. This seemed the sensible way. Accordingly, when she reached that theatre, she applied to the clerk of the box office.

"Eh," he said looking out. "Dramatic agents. I don't know. You'll find them in 'The Clipper' though. They all advertise in that."

"Is that a paper?" said Carrie.

"Yes," said the clerk, marveling at such ignorance of a common fact. "You can get it at the newsstands," he added politely, seeing how pretty the inquirer was.

Carrie proceeded to get "The Clipper" and tried to find the agents by looking over it as she stood beside the stand. This could not be done easily. Then she decided to go back home with it and see, if by assiduous study, she could not detect the addresses of these individuals. Thirteenth Street was quite a number of blocks off, but she went back, carrying the precious paper and regretting the waste of time.

Hurstwood was already back again, sitting in his place.

"Where were you?" he asked.

"I've been trying to find some dramatic agents."

He felt a little diffident about asking concerning her success. The paper she began to scan attracted his attention.

"What you got there?" he asked.

" 'The Clipper.' The man said to find their addresses in here."

"Have you been way over to Broadway to find that out? I could have told you."

"Why didn't you?" she asked, without looking up.

"You never asked me," he returned.

She went hunting aimlessly through the crowded columns. Her mind was distracted by this man's indifference. The difficulty of the situation she was facing was only added to by all he did. Self-commiseration brewed in her heart. Tears trembled along her eyelids but did not fall. Hurstwood noticed something.

"Let me look."

To recover herself she went into the front room while he searched. Presently she returned. He had a pencil and was writing upon an envelope.

"Here's three," he said.

Carrie took it and found that one was Mrs. Bermudez,

another Marcus Jenks, a third Percy Weil. She paused only a moment and then moved toward the door.

"I might as well go right away," she said without looking back.

Hurstwood saw her depart with some faint stirrings of shame, which were the expression of a manhood rapidly becoming atrophied. He sat awhile and then it became too much. He got up and put on his hat.

"I guess I'll go out," he said to himself, and went, strolling nowhere in particular, but feeling somehow that he must go.

Carrie's first call was upon Mrs. Bermudez whose address was quite the nearest. It was an old fashioned residence turned into offices, without the slightest attempt at reconstruction or decoration. The wall paper was not even changed. Mrs. Bermudez' offices consisted of what formerly had been a back chamber and hall bedroom on the third floor. The hall bedroom was now an exclusive office marked "Private." In the larger room was railing and wire screen, reaching to the ceiling, which partitioned off the quarter of the room nearest the back windows for clerical purposes.

As Carrie entered she noticed several individuals lounging about—men who said nothing and did nothing. The girl clerk behind the counter paid some attention to her after a few moments, seeing that Carrie did not address her.

"What is it you want?" she asked.

"I want to see about getting a place on the stage," said Carrie.

"Oh," said the girl. "Perhaps you want to see Mrs. Bermudez."

"I do," answered Carrie.

"Well, she isn't in now. She's out to lunch."

"When will she be back?"

"About two, I should say."

Carrie turned and walked out, followed by the eyes of the men.

After this lunch announcement, she knew that the others would be out also but nevertheless called at the office of Mr. Jenks. The latter was far more insignificant than the one she had been in. It was located in one very small room in 27th

Street, at the head of a very winding stairs, which was not only dark, but dirty. Carrie climbed earnestly up here, and found another clerk, behind a screen, apparently writing. This individual was a Jew. Another individual was sitting beside a stove, which was located in one small corner.

"What is it?" said the individual.

"Is Mr. Jenks in?"

"No, he's out to lunch."

"Do you know when he'll be back?"

"About two o'clock."

It was the same with the third cheap, dingy office, and so Carrie decided to walk and wait.

By a quarter of two she returned to Mrs. Bermudez' office.

The same dull situation seemed to be prevailing here when she entered, but even while she was waiting to be noticed, the door of the hall bedroom opened and from it issued two very mannish looking women, very tightly dressed and wearing white collars and cuffs. After them came a portly lady of about forty-five, light-haired, sharp-eyed, and evidently good-natured. At least she was smiling.

"Now don't forget about that," said one of the mannish women.

"I won't," said the portly woman. "Let's see," she added, "where are you in the first week in February?"

"Pittsburgh," said the woman.

"I'll write you there."

"All right," said the other, and the two passed out.

Instantly the portly lady's face became exceedingly sober and shrewd. She turned about and fixed on Carrie a very searching eye.

"Well," she said, "young woman, what can I do for you?"

"Are you Mrs. Bermudez?"

"Yes."

"Well," said Carrie, hesitating how to begin, "do you get places for persons upon the stage?"

"Yes."

"Could you get me one?"

"Have you ever had any experience?"

"A very little," said Carrie.

"Who did you play with?"

"Oh, with no one," said Carrie. "It was just a show gotten—"

"Oh, I see," said the woman, interrupting her. "No, I don't know of anything now."

Carrie's countenance fell.

"You want to get some New York experience," concluded the affable Mrs. Bermudez. "We'll take your name, though."

Carrie stood looking while the lady retired to her office.

"What is your address?" inquired the young lady behind the counter, taking up the curtailed conversation.

"Mrs. George Wheeler," said Carrie, moving over to where she was writing. The woman wrote her address in full and then allowed her to depart at her leisure.

She encountered a very similar experience in the office of Mr. Jenks, only that individual varied it by saying at the close, "If you could play at some local house, or had a program with your name on it, I might do something."

In the third place the individual asked:—

"What sort of work do you want to do?"

"What do you mean?" said Carrie.

"Well, do you want to get in a comedy or on the vaudeville stage or in the chorus?"

"Oh, I'd like to get a part in a play," said Carrie.

"Well," said the man, "it'll cost you something to do that."

"How much?" said Carrie, who, ridiculous as it may seem, had not thought of this before.

"Well, that's for you to say," he answered shrewdly.

Carrie looked at him curiously. She hardly knew how to continue the inquiry.

"Could you get me a part if I paid?"

"If we didn't, you'd get your money back."

"Oh!" she said.

The agent saw that he was dealing with an inexperienced soul and continued accordingly.

"You'd want to deposit fifty dollars anyway. No agent would trouble about you for less than that."

Carrie saw a light.

"Thank you," she said. "I'll think about it."

She started to go and then bethought herself.

"How soon would I get a place?" she asked.

"Well, that's hard to say," said the man. "You might get one in a week or it might be a month. You'd get the first thing that we thought you could do."

"I see," said Carrie, and then half smiling to be agreeable, she walked out.

The agent studied a moment and then said to himself, "It's funny how anxious these women are to get on the stage."

Carrie found ample food for reflection in the fifty-dollar proposition. She had no fifty dollars and the more she thought of it the more she realized that she would have difficulty in getting it. Again, she did not like the looks of the man who made the offer.

"Maybe they'd take my money and not give me anything," she thought. This caused her hopes to grow small.

"It's funny how hard it is," she thought. "Maybe that's why that Mrs. Bermudez wouldn't talk. If I had fifty dollars with me, she might have."

She returned to the flat, recalling that she had some jewelry—a diamond ring and pin and several other pieces. She could get fifty dollars for those if she went to a pawn broker.

Hurstwood was there before her. He had not thought she would be so long seeking.

"Well," he said, not venturing to ask what news.

"I didn't find out anything today," said Carrie, taking off her gloves. "They all want money to get you a place."

"How much?" asked Hurstwood.

"Fifty dollars."

"They don't want anything, do they?"

"Oh, they're like everybody else. You can't tell whether they'd ever get you anything after you did pay them."

"Well, I wouldn't put up fifty on that basis," said Hurstwood, as if he were deciding, money in hand.

"I don't know," said Carrie. "I think I'll try some of the managers."

Hurstwood heard this, dead to the horror of it. He rocked a little to and fro and chewed at his finger. It seemed all very natural in such extreme states. He would do better later on.

CHAPTER XLI.

When Carrie renewed her search, as she did the next day, going to the Casino, she found that in the opera chorus, as in other fields, employment is difficult to secure. Girls who can stand in a line and look pretty are as numerous as laborers who can swing a pick. She found there was no discrimination between one and the other of applicants, save as regards a conventional standard of prettiness and form. Their own opinion or knowledge of their ability went for nothing.

"Where shall I find Mr. Gray?" she asked of a sulky doorman at the stage entrance of the Casino.

"You can't see him now. He's busy."

"Do you know when I can see him?"

"Got an appointment with him?"

"No."

"Well, you'll have to call at his office."

"Oh, dear!" exclaimed Carrie. "Where is his office?"

"1278 Broadway."

She knew there was no need of calling at that number now. He would not be in. Nothing remained but to employ the intermediate hours in search.

The office of Mr. Daniel Frohman was in the Lyceum Theatre at 24th and Fourth Avenue. The office of Mr. Charles Frohman was in the Empire Theatre at 41st Street and Broadway. Mr. Daly was at Daly's Theatre. The dismal story of ventures in these places is quickly told. Mr. Daly saw no one save by appointment. Carrie waited an hour in a dingy office, quite in spite of obstacles, to learn this fact of the placid, indifferent Mr. Dorney.

"You will have to write and ask him to see you."

So she went away.

At the Empire Theatre she found a hive of peculiarly listless and indifferent individuals. Everything ornately upholstered, everything carefully furnished, everything remarkably reserved.

"Mr. Frohman's office?—on the third floor." This from a fair typewriter who studied her with a distinct purpose—namely that of causing her to feel her insignificant and utterly incon-sequential position.

In Mr. Frohman's antechamber another young lady posed at a typewriter.

"Mr. Frohman? Oh, he isn't here. What is it you wish?"

"I wish to see about getting into a company," said Carrie.

"Oh, well, you have to apply downstairs. Mr. Barnaby tends to that."

Thus Carrie retired abashed to the floor below. Here Mr. Barnaby was out.

"When can I see him?"

"After three maybe. He's usually in at that time."

Mr. Daniel Frohman's office was even more retired—one of those secluded, under-stairway closets, be-rugged and be-paneled, which cause one to feel the greatness of all positions of authority. Here was reserve itself done into a box-office clerk, a doorman and an assistant, glorying in their fine positions.

"Ah, be very humble now, very humble indeed. Tell us what it is you require. Tell it quickly, nervously and without a vestige of self-respect. If no trouble to us in any way, we may see what we can do."

This was the atmosphere of the Lyceum—the attitude, for that matter, of every managerial office in the city. These little proprietors of businesses are lords indeed on their own ground.

Carrie came away wearily, somewhat more abashed for her pains. Mr. Frohman was not putting on a company just then.

"No, no—none for several months."

Hurstwood heard the details of weary and unavailing search that evening.

"I didn't get to see anyone," said Carrie. "I just walked and walked and waited around."

Hurstwood only looked at her.

"I suppose you have to have some friends before you can get in," she added disconsolately.

Hurstwood saw the difficulty of this thing and yet it did not seem so terrible. Carrie was tired and dispirited, but now she could rest. Viewing the world from his rocking chair, its bitter-ness did not seem to approach so rapidly. Tomorrow was another day.

Tomorrow came and the next and the next.

Carrie saw the manager once.

"Come around," he said, "the first of next week. I may make some changes then."

He was a large and corpulent individual, surfeited with good clothes and good eating, who judged women as another would horseflesh. Carrie was pretty and graceful. She might be put in, even if she did not have any experience. One of the proprietors had suggested that the chorus was a little weak on looks.

The first of next week was some days off yet. The first of the month was drawing near. Carrie began to worry as she had never worried before.

"Do you really look for anything when you go out?" she asked Hurstwood one morning as a climax to some painful thoughts of her own.

"Of course I do," he said pettishly, troubling only a little over the disgrace of the insinuation.

"I'd take anything," she said, "for the present. It will soon be the first of the month again."

She looked the picture of despair.

Hurstwood quit reading his paper and changed his clothes.

He would look for something, he thought. He would go and see if some brewery couldn't get him in somewhere. Yes, he would take a position as bartender if he could get it.

It was the same sort of pilgrimage he had made before. He couldn't get anything. One or two slight rebuffs and the bravado disappeared.

"No use," he thought. "I might as well go on back home."

Now that his money was so low he began to observe his clothes and feel that they were beginning to look commonplace. This was a bitter thought.

Carrie came in after he did.

"I went to see some of the variety managers," she said aimlessly. "You've got to have an act. They don't want anybody that hasn't."

"I saw some of the brewery people today," said Hurstwood. "One man told me he'd try and make a place for me in two or three weeks."

In the face of so much distress on Carrie's part, some showing he had to make, and it was thus he did so. It was lassitude's apology to energy.

Monday Carrie went again to the Casino.

"Did I tell you to come around today?" said the manager, looking her over as she stood before him.

"You said the first of the week," said Carrie, greatly abashed.

"Ever had any experience?" he asked again, almost severely.

Carrie owned to ignorance.

"Well, I don't know," he said, looking again and then stirring around among some papers. He was secretly pleased with this pretty, disturbed-looking young woman. "Come around to the theatre tomorrow morning."

Carrie's heart bounded to her throat.

"I will," she said with difficulty. She could see he wanted her, and turned to go.

Would he really put her to work? Oh, blessed fortune, could it be?

Already the hard rumble of the city through the open windows became pleasant.

A sharp voice answered her mental interrogation, doing away with all immediate fears on that score.

"Be sure you're there promptly," it said roughly. "You'll be dropped if you're not."

Carrie hastened away. She did not now quarrel with Hurstwood's idleness. She had a place—she had a place. This sung in her ears.

In her delight she was almost anxious to tell Hurstwood. But as she walked homeward and her survey of the facts of the case became larger, she began to think of the anomaly of her finding work in several weeks and his lounging in idleness for a number of months.

"Why don't he get something," she openly said to herself. "If I can, he surely ought to. It wasn't very hard for me."

She forgot her youth and beauty. The handicap of age she did not, in her enthusiasm, perceive.

Thus, ever, the voice of success.

Still she could not keep her secret. She tried to be calm and indifferent about it, but it was a palpable sham.

"Well?" he said, seeing her relieved face.

"I got a place."

"You have?" he said, breathing a better breath.

"Yes."

"What sort of a place is it?" he asked, feeling, in his veins, as if now he might get something good also.

"In the chorus," she answered.

"Is it the Casino show you told me about?"

"Yes," she answered. "I begin rehearsing tomorrow."

There was more explanation, volunteered by Carrie, because she was happy. At last Hurstwood said:—

"Do you know how much you'll get?"

"No, I didn't want to ask," said Carrie. "I guess they pay twelve or fourteen dollars a week."

"About that, I guess," said Hurstwood.

There was a good dinner in the flat that evening, owing to the mere lifting of the terrible strain. Hurstwood went out for a shave and returned with a fair-sized sirloin steak.

"Now tomorrow," he thought, "I'll look around myself," and with renewed hope he lifted his eyes from the ground.

On the morrow Carrie reported promptly and was given a place in the line. She saw a great, empty, shadowy play-house, still redolent of the perfumes and blazonry of the night, and notable for its rich, oriental appearance. The wonder of it awed and delighted her. Blessed be its wondrous reality. How hard she would try to be worthy of it. It was above the common mass, above idleness, above want, above insignificance. People came to it in finery and carriages to see. It was ever a centre of light and mirth. And here she was of it. Oh, if she could only remain, how happy would be her days.

"What is your name?" said the manager who was conducting the drill.

"Madenda," she replied, instantly mindful of the name Drouet had selected in Chicago. "Carrie Madenda."

"Well now, Miss Madenda," he said very affably, as Carrie thought. "You go over there."

Then he called to a young woman who was already of the company.

"Miss Clark, you pair with Miss Madenda."

This young lady stepped forward so that Carrie saw where to go, and the rehearsal began.

Carrie soon found that while this drilling had some slight

resemblance to the rehearsals as conducted at Avery Hall, the attitude of the manager was much more pronounced. She had marveled at the insistence and superior airs of Mr. Millice, but the individual conducting the present air had the same insistence coupled with almost brutal roughness. As the drilling proceeded, he seemed to wax exceedingly wroth over trifles and to increase his lung power in proportion. It was very evident that he had a great contempt for any assumption of dignity or innocence on the part of these young women.

"Clark," he would call, meaning, of course, Miss Clark, "why don't you catch step there?"

"By fours, right! Right, I said, right! For God's sake get onto yourself, *Right!*" and in saying this he would lift the last sounds into a vehement roar.

"Maitland! Maitland!" he called once.

A nervous, comely-dressed little girl stepped out. Carrie trembled for her out of the fullness of her own sympathies and fears.

"Yes, sir," said Maitland.

"Is there anything the matter with your ears?"

"No, sir."

"Do you know what column left means?"

"Yes, sir."

"Well, what are you stumbling around the right for? Want to break up the line?"

"I was just—"

"Never mind what you were just. Keep your ears open."

Carrie pitied, and trembled for her turn.

Yet another suffered the pain of personal rebuke.

"Hold on a minute," cried the manager, throwing up his hands, as if in despair. His demeanor was fierce.

"Elvers!" he shouted, "what have you got in your mouth?"

"Nothing," said Elvers, while some smiled and some stood nervously by.

"Well, are you talking?"

"No, sir."

"Well, keep your mouth still, then. Now all together again."

At last Carrie's turn came. It was because of her extreme anxiety to do all that was required, that brought on the trouble.

She heard someone called.

"Mason," said the voice. "Miss Mason."

She looked around to see who it could be. A girl behind shoved her a little, but she did not understand.

"You, you!" said the manager. "Can't you hear?"

"Oh," said Carrie, collapsing and blushing fiercely.

"Isn't your name Mason?" asked the manager.

"No sir," said Carrie, "it's Madenda."

"Well, what's the matter with your feet? Can't you dance?"

"Yes, sir," said Carrie, who had long since learned this art.

"Why don't you do it then? Don't go shuffling along as if you were dead. I've got to have people with life in 'em."

Carrie's cheeks burned with a crimson heat. Her lips trembled a little.

"Yes sir," she said.

It was this constant urging, coupled with irrascibility and energy, for three long hours. Carrie came away worn enough in body, but too excited in mind to notice it. She meant to go home and practise her evolutions as prescribed. She would not err in any way, if she could help it.

When she reached the flat Hurstwood was not there. For a wonder he was out, looking for work as she supposed. She took only a mouthful to eat and then practised on, sustained by visions of freedom from financial distress.

"The sound of glory ringing in her ears."

When Hurstwood returned he was not so elated as when he went away, and now she was called by her mind to drop practise and get dinner. Here was an early irritation. She would have her work and this. Was she going to act and keep house?

"I'll not do it," she said, "after I get started. He can take his meals out."

Each day thereafter brought its cares. She found it was not such a wonderful thing to be in the chorus, and she also learned that her salary would be twelve dollars a week. After a few days she had her first sight of those high and mighties—the leading ladies and gentlemen. Lillian Russell appeared upon the boards and Jefferson di Angeles. There were others not quite so important, but far, far above Carrie. She saw that they were privileged and deferred to. She was nothing—absolutely nothing at all.

At home was Hurstwood, daily giving her cause for thought. He seemed to get nothing to do, and yet he made bold to inquire how she was getting along. The regularity with which he did this smacked of some one who was waiting to live upon her labor. Now that she had a visible means of support this irritated her. He seemed to be depending upon her little twelve dollars.

"How are you getting along?" he would blandly inquire.

"Oh, all right," she would reply.

"Find it easy?"

"It will be all right when I get used to it."

His paper would then engross his thoughts.

"I got some lard," he would add as an afterthought. "I thought maybe you might want to make some biscuit."

The calm suggestions of the man astonished her a little bit, especially in the light of recent developments. Her dawning independence gave her more courage to observe, and she felt as if she wanted to say things. Still, she could not talk to him as she had Drouet. There was something in the man's manner of which she had always stood in awe. He seemed to have some sinister strength in reserve.

One day, after her first week's rehearsal, what she expected came openly to the surface.

"We'll have to be rather saving," he said, laying down some meat he had purchased. "You won't get any money for a week or so yet."

"No," said Carrie, who was stirring a pan at the stove.

"I've only got the rent and about thirteen dollars more," he added.

"That's it," she said to herself. "I'm to use my money here."

Instantly she remembered that she had hoped to buy a few things for herself. She needed clothes. Her hat was not nice.

"What will twelve dollars do towards keeping up this flat?" she thought. "I can't do it. Why don't he get something to do?"

Still things ran on, and now the to her important night came. Curiously, she did not suggest to Hurstwood that he come and see. He did not think of going. It would only be money wasted. She had such a small part.

The advertisements were already in the papers, the posters upon the bill-boards. Miss Lillian Russell and many members were cited. Carrie was nothing.

As in Chicago she was seized with stage fright as the very first entrance of the ballet approached, but later she recovered. The apparent and painful insignificance of the part took fear away from her. She felt that she was so obscure it did not matter. Fortunately she did not have to wear tights. A group of twelve were assigned pretty golden-hued skirts which came only to a line about an inch above the knee. Carrie happened to be one of the twelve.

In standing about the stage, marching and occasionally lifting up her voice in the general chorus, she had a chance to observe the audience and to see the inauguration of a great hit. There was plenty of applause, but she could not help noting how poorly some of the women of alleged ability did.

"I could do better than that," Carrie ventured to think to herself, in several instances. To do her justice, she was right.

After it was over she dressed quickly, and, as the manager had scolded some others and passed her, she imagined she must have proved satisfactory. She wanted to get out quickly because she knew but few, and the stars were gossiping. Outside were carriages and some *de rigueur* youths in attractive clothing, waiting. Carrie saw that she was scanned closely. But the flutter of an eyelash would have brought her a companion. That she did not give.

One experienced youth volunteered anyhow.

"Not going home alone, are you?" he said.

Carrie merely hastened her steps and took the Sixth Avenue car. Her head was so full of the wonder of it that she had time for nothing else.

At the end of the week her twelve dollars was paid to her. Small as it may seem, it was large to her. The one irritation included in the possession of it was how it must be disposed of. Hurstwood secretly expected that she would come to the fore with it, that somehow it would, without the need of open discussion, be used for their mutual sustenance. Carrie, however, said nothing, debating what to do. She had the whole situation clear now, with need of immediate decision.

"Did you hear any more from the brewery?" she asked, hoping by the question to stir him on to action.

"No," he answered, "they're not quite ready yet. I think something will come of that though."

She said nothing more then, objecting to giving up her

sure money, and yet feeling that such would have to be the case. Hurstwood felt the crisis and artfully decided to appeal to Carrie. He had long since realized how good-natured she was, how much she would stand. There was some little shame in him at the thought of doing so, but he justified himself with the thought that he really would get something. Rent day gave him his opportunity.

"Well," he said, as he counted it out, "that's about the last of my money. I'll have to get something pretty soon."

Carrie looked at him askance, half-suspicious of an appeal.

"If I could only hold out a little longer, I think I could get something. Drake is sure to open a hotel here in September."

"Is he?" said Carrie, thinking of the short month that still remained until that time.

"Would you mind helping me out until then?" he said appealingly. "I think I'll be all right after that time."

"No," said Carrie, feeling sadly handicapped by fate.

"We can get along if we economize. I'll pay you back all right."

"Oh, I'll help you," said Carrie, feeling quite hard-hearted at thus forcing him to humbly appeal, and yet her desire for the benefit of her earnings wrung a faint protest from her.

"Why don't you take anything, George, temporarily," she said. "What difference does it make? Maybe, after while, you'll get something better."

"I will take anything," he said, relieved and wincing under reproof. "I'd just as leave dig on the streets. Nobody knows me here."

"Oh, you needn't do that," said Carrie, hurt by the pity of it. "But there must be other things."

"I'll get something," he said, assuming determination.

Then he went back to his paper.

CHAPTER XLII.

What Hurstwood got as a result of this determination was more self-assurances that each particular day was not the day. His clothes took on a shabbier tinge and by September first he was rather poorly dressed at his best. At the same time Carrie passed with him through thirty gray days of mental distress.

Her need of clothes, to say nothing of her desire for ornaments, grew rapidly as the fact developed that for all her work, she was not to have them. The sympathy she felt for Hurstwood at the time he asked her to tide him over vanished with these newer urgings of decency. He was not always renewing his request, but this love of good appearance was. It insisted, and Carrie, wishing to satisfy it, wished more and more that Hurstwood was not in the way. When a man, however passively, becomes an obstacle to the fulfillment of a woman's desires, he becomes an odious thing in her eyes,—or will, given time enough.

Hurstwood reasoned, when he neared the last ten dollars, that he had best keep a little pocket change and not become wholly dependent for car fare, shaves, and the like, so when this sum was still in his hand he announced himself as penniless.

"I'm clean out," he said to Carrie one afternoon. "I paid for some coal this morning and that took all but ten or fifteen cents."

"I've got some money there in my purse."

Hurstwood went to get it, starting as he was for a can of tomatoes. Carrie scarcely noticed that this was the beginning of the new order. He took out fifteen cents and bought the can with it. Thereafter it was dribs and drabs of this sort until one morning Carrie suddenly remembered that she would not be back until close on to dinner time.

"We're all out of flour," she said. "You'd better get some this afternoon. We haven't any meat either. How would it do if we had liver and bacon?"

"Suits me," said Hurstwood.

"Better get a half or three-quarters of a pound of that."

"Half'll be enough," volunteered Hurstwood.

She remembered that he had no money, and, opening her purse, took out a half-dollar and laid it down. He pretended not to notice it. This inaugurated a special phase of the new order— that of her remembering, in special cases of this sort, to leave money.

Hurstwood bought the flour, which all grocers sold in three-

and-a-half-pound packages, for thirteen cents, and paid fifteen cents for a half-pound of liver and bacon mixed. This he paid for and brought home, leaving the packages together with the balance of twenty-two cents upon the kitchen table, where Carrie found it. It did not escape her that the change was accurate. There was something sad in realizing that, after all, all that he wanted of her was something to eat. She felt as if hard thoughts were unjust. Maybe he would get something yet. He had no vices.

That very evening, however, on going into the theatre, one of the chorus girls passed her all newly arrayed in a pretty mottled tweed suit which took Carrie's eye. The young woman wore a fine bunch of violets and seemed in high spirits. She smiled at Carrie good-naturedly as she passed, showing pretty even teeth, and Carrie smiled back.

"She can afford to dress well," thought Carrie, "and so could I, if I could only keep my money. What a shame to have to give up everything. I haven't a decent tie of any kind to wear."

She put out her toe and looked at her shoe reflectively.

"I'll get me a pair of shoes Saturday, anyhow. I don't care what happens."

One of the sweetest and most sympathetic little chorus girls of the company made friends with her because in Carrie she found nothing to frighten her away. She was a gay little Manon, unwitting of society's fierce conception of morality, but nevertheless good to her neighbor and charitable. Little license was allowed the chorus in the matter of conversation, but nevertheless some was indulged in.

"It's warm tonight, isn't it?" said this girl, arrayed in pink fleshings and an imitation golden helmet. She also carried a shining shield.

"Yes it is," said Carrie, pleased that someone should talk to her.

"I'm almost roasting," said the girl.

Carrie looked into her pretty face with its large blue eyes, and saw little beads of moisture.

"There's more marching in this opera than ever I did before," added the girl.

"Have you been in others?" asked Carrie, surprised at her experience.

"Lots of them," said the girl. "Haven't you?"

"This is my first experience."

"Oh, is it? I thought I saw you the time they ran 'The Queen's Mate' here."

"No," said Carrie, shaking her head, "not me."

Their little conversation was interrupted by the blare of the orchestra and the sputtering of the calcium lights in the wings as the line was called to form for a new entrance. No other opportunity for conversation occurred but the next evening when they were getting ready for the stage this girl appeared anew at her side.

"They say this show is going on the road next month."

"Is it?" said Carrie.

"Yes, do you think you'll go?"

"I don't know. I guess so, if they'll take me."

"Oh, they'll take you. I wouldn't go. They won't give you any more and it will cost you everything you make to live. I never leave New York. There's too many shows going on here."

"Can you always get in another show?"

"I always have. There's one going on up at the Broadway this month. I'm going to try and get in that if this one really goes."

Carrie heard this with aroused intelligence. Evidently it wasn't so very difficult to get on. Maybe she also could get a place if this show went away.

"Do they all pay about the same?" she asked.

"Yes. Sometimes you get a little more. This show don't pay very much."

"I get twelve," said Carrie.

"Do you?" said the girl. "They pay me fifteen and you do more work than I do. I wouldn't stand it if I were you. They're just giving you less because they think you don't know. You ought to be making fifteen."

"Well, I'm not," said Carrie.

"Well, you'll get more at the next place if you want it," went on the girl, who admired Carrie very much. "You do fine and the manager knows it."

To say truth, Carrie did unconsciously move about with an air pleasing and somewhat distinctive. It was due wholly to her natural manner and total lack of self-consciousness.

"Do you suppose I could get more up at the Broadway?"

"Of course you can," answered the girl. "You come with me when I go. I'll do the talking."

Carrie heard this, flushing with thankfulness. She liked this little gaslight soldier. She seemed so experienced and self-reliant in her tinsel helmet and military accoutrements.

"My future must be assured if I can always get work this way," thought Carrie.

Still in the morning when her household duties would impinge upon her, and Hurstwood sat there, a perfect load to contemplate, her fate seemed dismal and unrelieved. It did not take so very much to feed them under Hurstwood's close-measured buying, and there would possibly be enough for rent, but it left nothing else. Carrie bought the shoes, and some other things which complicated the rent problem very seriously. Suddenly, a week from the fatal day, Carrie realized that they were going to run short.

"I don't believe," she exclaimed, looking into her purse at breakfast, "that I'll have enough to pay the rent."

"How much have you?" inquired Hurstwood.

"Well, I've got twenty-two dollars, but there's everything to be paid for this week yet and if I use all I get Saturday to pay this, there won't be any left for next week. Do you think your hotel man will open his hotel this month?"

"I think so," returned Hurstwood. "He said he would."

They thought awhile and then Hurstwood said:—

"Don't worry about it. Maybe the grocer will wait. He can do that. We've traded there long enough to make him trust us for a week or two."

"Do you think he will?" she asked.

"I think so."

On this account, Hurstwood, this very day, looked Grocer Oeslagge clearly into the eye, as he ordered a pound of coffee, and said:—

"Do you mind carrying my account until the end of every week?"

"No, no, Mr. Wheeler," said Mr. Oeslagge. "Dat iss all right."

Hurstwood, still tactful in distress, added nothing to this. It seemed an easy thing. He looked out of the door and then gathered up his coffee, when ready, and came away. The game of a desperate man had begun.

Rent was paid and now came the grocer. Hurstwood managed by paying out of his own ten and collecting from Carrie at the end of the week. Then he delayed a day next time settling with the grocer, and so, soon he had his ten, or such of it as remained, with Oeslagge getting his pay on this Thursday or Friday for last Saturday's bill.

This entanglement made Carrie anxious for a change of some sort. Hurstwood did not seem to realize that she had a right to anything. He schemed to make what she earned cover all expenses, but seemed not to trouble over adding anything himself.

"He talks about worrying," thought Carrie. "If he worried enough he couldn't sit there and wait for me. He'd get something to do. No man could go seven months without finding something if he tried."

The sight of him always around, in his untidy clothes and gloomy appearance, drove Carrie to seek relief in other places. Twice a week there were matinées and then Hurstwood ate a cold snack which he prepared himself. Two other days there were rehearsals beginning at ten in the morning and lasting usually until one. Now to this, Carrie added a few visits to one or two chorus girls, including the blue-eyed soldier of the golden helmet. She did it because it was pleasant and a relief from the dullness of the home over which her husband brooded.

The blue-eyed soldier's name was Osborne—Lola Osborne. Her room was in 19th Street, near Fourth Avenue, a block now given up wholly to office buildings. Here she had a comfortable back room, looking over a collection of back yards in which grew a number of shade trees. Carrie used to enjoy coming here and looking out upon these trees from one of the girl's rocking chairs.

"Isn't your home in New York?" she asked of Lola one day.

"Yes, but I can't get along with my people. They always want me to do what they want. Do you live here?"

"Yes," said Carrie.

"With your family?"

Carrie was ashamed to own up that she was married. She had talked so much about getting more salary and confessed to so much anxiety about her future that now, when the direct question of fact was waiting, she could not tell this girl.

"With some relatives," she answered.

Miss Osborne took it for granted that, like herself, Carrie's time was her own. She invariably asked her to stay, proposed little outings and other things of that sort, until Carrie began neglecting her dinner hours. Hurstwood noticed it, but felt in no position to quarrel with her. Several times she came so late as scarcely to have an hour in which to patch up a meal and start to the theatre.

"Do you rehearse in the afternoons?" Hurstwood once asked, concealing almost completely the cynical protest and regret which prompted it.

"No, I was looking around for another place," said Carrie.

As a matter of fact she was, but only in such a way as furnished the least straw of an excuse. Miss Osborne and she had gone to the office of the manager who was to produce the new opera at the Broadway and returned straight to the former's room where they had been since three o'clock.

Carrie felt this question to be an infringement of her liberty. She did not take into account how much liberty she was securing. Only the latest step, the newest freedom, must not be questioned.

Hurstwood saw it all clearly enough. He was shrewd after his kind and yet there was enough decency in the man to stop him from making any effectual protest. In his almost inexplicable apathy he was content to droop supinely while Carrie drifted out of his life, just as he was willing supinely to see opportunity pass beyond his control. He could not help clinging and protesting in a mild, irritating and ineffectual way, however—a way that simply widened the breach by slow degrees.

A further enlargement of this chasm between them came when the manager, looking between the wings upon the brightly lighted stage, where the chorus was going through some of its glittering evolutions, said to the master of the ballet:—

"Who is that fourth girl there on the right—the one coming round at the end now."

"Oh!" said the ballet-master, "that's Miss Madenda."

"She's good-looking. Why don't you let her lead that line?"

"I will," said the man.

"Just do that. She'll look better there than the woman you've got."

"All right. I will do that," said the master.

The next evening Carrie was called out, much as if for an error.

"You lead your company tonight," said the master.

"Yes, sir," said Carrie.

"Put snap into it," he added. "We must have snap."

"Yes, sir," replied Carrie.

Astonished at this change, she thought that the heretofore leader must be ill, but when she saw her in the line, with a distinct expression of something unfavorable in her eye, she began to think that perhaps it was merit.

She had a chic way of tossing her head on one side, and holding her arms as if for action—not listlessly. In front of the line this showed up even more effectually.

"That girl knows how to carry herself," said the manager another evening. He began to think that he should like to talk with her. If he hadn't made it a rule to have nothing to do with the members of the chorus he would have approached her most unbendingly.

"Put that girl at the head of the white column," he suggested to the man in charge of the ballet.

This white column consisted of some twenty girls, all in snow-white flannel trimmed with silver and blue. Its leader was most stunningly arrayed, in the same colors, elaborated, however, with epaulets and a belt of silver, with a short sword dangling at one side. Carrie was fitted for this costume and a few days later appeared, proud of her new laurels. She was especially gratified to find that her salary was now eighteen instead of twelve.

Hurstwood heard nothing about this, as indeed he heard nothing at all about the eyes made at her from the front rows nor the individuals who were around to tempt after the show was over.

"I'll not give him the rest of my money," said Carrie. "I do enough. I am going to get me something to wear."

As a matter of fact, during this second month she had been buying for herself as recklessly as she dared, regardless of the consequences. There were impending more complications rent day, and more extension of the credit system in the neighborhood. Now, however, she proposed to do better by herself.

Her first move was to buy a shirt-waist, and in studying these she found how little her money would buy—how much if she could only use all. She forgot that if she were alone she would have to pay room and board and imagined that every cent of her eighteen could be spent for clothes and things that she liked.

At last she picked upon something which not only used up all her surplus above twelve, but invaded that sum. She knew she was going too far but her feminine love of finery prevailed. The next day Hurstwood said:—

"We owe the grocer five dollars and forty cents this week."

"Do we?" said Carrie, frowning a little.

She looked in her purse to leave it.

"I've only got eight dollars and twenty cents altogether."

"We owe the milk-man sixty cents," added Hurstwood.

"Yes, and there's the coal-man," said Carrie.

Hurstwood said nothing. He had seen the new things she was buying, the way she was neglecting household duties, the readiness with which she was stepping out afternoons and staying. He felt that something was going to happen. All at once she spoke.

"I don't know," she said. "I can't do it all. I don't earn enough."

This was a direct challenge. Hurstwood had to take it up. He tried to be calm.

"I don't want you to do it all," he said. "I only want a little help until I can get something to do."

"Oh yes," answered Carrie, "that's always the way. It takes more than I can earn to pay things. I don't see what I'm going to do."

"Well, I've tried to get something!" he exclaimed. "What do you want me to do?"

"You couldn't have tried so very hard," said Carrie. "I got something."

"Well, I did," he said, angered almost to harsh words. "You needn't throw up your success to me. All I asked was a little help until I could get something. I'm not down yet. I'll come up all right."

He tried to speak steadily but his voice trembled a little.

Carrie's anger melted on the instant. She felt ashamed.

"Well," she said, "here's the money," and emptied it out on the table. "I haven't got quite enough to pay it all. If they can wait until Saturday, though, I'll have some more."

"You keep it," said Hurstwood sadly. "I only want enough to pay the grocer."

She put it back and proceeded to get dinner early and in good time. Her little bravado made her feel as if she ought to make amends.

In a little while their old thoughts returned to both.

"She's making more than she says," thought Hurstwood. "She says she's making twelve, but that wouldn't buy all those things. I don't care. Let her keep her money. I'll get something again one of these days. Then she can go to the deuce."

He only said this in his anger, but it prefigured a possible course of action and attitude well enough.

"I don't care," thought Carrie. "He ought to be told to get out and do something. It isn't right that I should support him. I won't do it, that's all."

In these days Carrie was introduced to several individuals—friends of Miss Osborne, who were of the kind most aptly described as gay and festive. They called once to get Miss Osborne for an afternoon drive. Carrie was with her at the time.

"Come and go 'long," said Lola.

"No, I can't," said Carrie.

"Oh, yes, come go. What have you got to do?"

"I have to be home by five," said Carrie.

"What for?"

"Oh, dinner."

"They'll take us to dinner," said Lola.

"Oh, no," said Carrie, "I won't go. I can't."

"Oh, do come. They're awful nice boys. We'll get you back in time. We're only going for a drive in Central Park."

Carrie thought awhile and at last yielded.

"Now, I must be back by half-past four," she said.

The information went in one ear of Lola's and out the other.

After Drouet and Hurstwood, there was the least touch of cynicism in her attitude toward young men—especially of the gay and frivolous sort. She felt a little older than they. Some of their pretty compliments seemed silly. Still she was young in heart and body, and youth appealed to her.

"Oh, we'll be right back, Miss Madenda," said one of the chaps, bowing. "You wouldn't think we'd keep you overtime, now would you?"

"Well, I don't know," said Carrie, smiling.

They were off for a drive, she looking about and noticing fine clothing, the young men voicing those silly pleasantries and weak quips which pass for humor in coy circles. Carrie saw the great park parade of carriages, beginning at the 59th Street entrance and winding past the Museum of Art to the exit at 110th Street and Seventh Avenue. Her eye was once more taken by the show of wealth, the elaborate costumes, elegant harnesses, spirited horses and above all the beauty. Once more the plague of poverty galled her, but now she forgot in a measure her own troubles so far as to forget Hurstwood. That individual waited until four, five and even six. It was getting dark when he got up out of his chair.

"I guess she isn't coming home," he said grimly.

"That's the way," he thought. "She's getting a start now. I'm out of it."

Carrie had really discovered her neglect, but only at a quarter after five, and the open carriage was now far up Seventh Avenue, near the Harlem River.

"What time is it?" she inquired. "I must be getting back."

"A quarter after five," said her companion, consulting an elegant, open-faced watch.

"Oh, dear me!" exclaimed Carrie. Then she settled back with a sigh. "There's no use crying over spilt milk," she said. "It's too late."

"Of course it is," said the youth, who saw visions of a fine dinner now, and such ingratiating talk as would result in a reunion after the show. He was greatly taken with Carrie. "We'll drive down to Delmonico's now and have something there, won't we, Orrin?"

"To be sure," replied Orrin, gaily.

Carrie thought of Hurstwood. Never before had she neglected dinner without an excuse.

They drove back and at six-fifteen sat down to dine. It was the Sherry's incident over again, the remembrance of which came painfully back to Carrie. She remembered Mrs. Vance, who had never called again after Hurstwood's reception of her— Ames—Robert Ames.

At his figure her mind halted. It was a strong, clean vision. She could see his fine brow now, his dark hair and strong nose. He liked better books than she read, better people than she associated with. His ideal burned in her heart.

"It's fine to be a good actress," came distinctly back.

What sort of an actress was she?

"What are you thinking about, Miss Madenda?" inquired her merry companion. "Come now, let's see if I can guess."

"Oh, no," said Carrie. "Don't try."

She shook it off and ate. She forgot it in part and was merry. When it came to the after-theatre proposition, however, she shook her head.

"No," she said, "I can't. I have a previous engagement."

"Oh, now, Miss Madenda!" pleaded the youth.

"No," said Carrie, "I can't. You've been so kind, but you'll have to excuse me."

The youth looked exceedingly crestfallen.

"Cheer up, old man," whispered his companion. "We'll go around anyhow. She may change her mind."

CHAPTER XLIII.

There was no after-theatre lark, however, so far as Carrie was concerned. She made her way homeward, thinking about her absence. Hurstwood was asleep, but roused up to look as she passed through to her own bed.

"Is that you?" he said.

"Yes," she answered.

The next morning at breakfast she felt like apologising.

"I couldn't get home last evening," she said.

"Ah, Carrie," he answered, "what's the use saying that? I don't care. You needn't tell me that, though."

"I couldn't," said Carrie, her color rising. Then seeing that he looked as if he said, "I know," she exclaimed, "Oh, all right. I don't care!"

From now on her indifference to the flat was even greater. There seemed no common ground on which they could talk to one another. She let herself be asked for expenses. It became so with him that he hated to do it. He preferred standing off the butcher and baker. He ran up a grocery bill of sixteen dollars with Oeslagge, laying in a supply of staple articles so that they would not have to buy any of those things for some time to come. Then he changed his grocery. It was the same with the butcher-man and several others. Carrie never heard anything of this directly from him. He asked only for such as he could expect, drifting farther and farther into a situation which could have but one ending.

In this fashion September went by.

"Isn't your Mr. Drake going to open his hotel?" Carrie asked several times.

"Yes. He won't do it before October, though, now."

Carrie became disgusted. "Such a man," she said to herself frequently. More and more she visited. She put most of her spare money in clothes, which after all was not an astonishing amount. At last she got a place in another company. This happened because the opera she was with announced its departure within four weeks. "Last two weeks of the Great Comic Opera Success—The—" etc., was upon all bill-boards, and in the newspapers, before she acted.

"I'm not going out on the road," said Miss Osborne.

Carrie went with her to apply to another manager.

"Ever had any experience?" was one of his questions.

"I'm with the company at the Casino now."

"Oh, you are?" he said.

The end of this was another engagement at twenty per week.

Carrie was delighted. She began to feel that she had a place in the world. People recognized ability.

So changed was her state that the atmosphere of the flat was something she could not abide. It was all poverty and trouble there, or seemed to be, because it was a load to bear. It became a place to keep away from. Still she slept there and did a fair amount of work keeping it in order. At last it was a sitting place for Hurstwood. He sat and rocked, rocked and read, enveloped in the gloom of his own fate. October went by and November. It was the dead of winter almost before he knew, and here he sat.

Carrie was doing better, that he knew. Her clothes were improved now, even fine. He saw her coming and going, sometimes picturing to himself her rise. Little eating had thinned him somewhat. He had no appetite. His clothes, too, were poor man's clothes. Talk about getting something had become even too threadbare and ridiculous for him. So he folded his hands and waited—for what he could not anticipate.

Mental apathy of this sort is a marvelous thing. He was a fit case for scientific investigation. A splendid paper might be prepared on the operation of certain preconceived notions which he had concerning dignity in the matter of his downfall. We know that certain forms of life, used to certain conditions, die quickly when exposed. The common canary, hardy enough when captured, loses, after a few years of confinement in a gilded cage, its power to shift for itself. The house-dog, held until middle age in comfort, will die of starvation if turned out into the woods to hunt alone. The house-dog, turned out a puppy, becomes a wolf, or so much like one that the difference is one of appearance only. So man, held until middle age in peace and plenty, forgets the art of shifting and doing. The skill and wit of the mind is atrophied. He appears to be something and lo, the poor brain argues that it must live up to that something, else it is disgraced. Courage to belie its feelings is not there. It must sit and wonder, waiting for the thing which it can do. It can scarcely change itself sufficiently to do as the thing requires.

This was Hurstwood. The butcher knocked at his door, and he made excuses. The grocer called also. More excuses. He would return to his chair after one of these disagreeable and sharp encounters thinking that he must get some money from Carrie. When she gave him only what he constantly asked for, he would think of putting off the butcher. The absent trouble was always the easiest to deal with.

At last, however, these troubles became too thick. The hounding of creditors, the indifference of Carrie, the silence of the flat and presence of winter all joined to produce a climax.

It was effected by the arrival of Oeslagge, personally, when Carrie was there.

"I call about my bill," said Mr. Oeslagge.

Carrie was only faintly surprised.

"How much is it?" she asked.

"Sixteen dollars," he replied.

"Oh, that much," said Carrie. "Is this right?" she asked, turning to Hurstwood.

"Yes," he said.

"Well, I never heard anything about it."

She looked as if she thought he'd been contracting some needless expense.

"Well, he had it all right," he answered. Then he went to the door. "I can't pay you anything on that today," he said mildly.

"Well, when can you?" said the grocer.

"Not before Saturday anyhow," said Hurstwood.

"Huh!" returned the grocer. "This is fine. I must have that. I need the money."

Carrie was standing back farther in the room, hearing it all. She was greatly distressed. It was so bad and commonplace. Hurstwood was annoyed also.

"Well," he said, "there's no use talking about it now. If you'll come in Saturday I'll pay you something on it."

The grocery-man went away.

"How are we going to pay it?" asked Carrie, astonished by the bill. "I can't do it."

"Well, you don't have to," he said. "He can't get what he can't get. He'll have to wait."

"I don't see how we ran up such a bill as that," said Carrie.

"Well, we ate it," said Hurstwood.

"It's funny," she replied, still doubting.

"What's the use of your standing there and talking like that now?" he asked. "Do you think I've had it alone? You talk as if I'd taken something."

"Well, it's too much anyhow," said Carrie. "I oughtn't to be made to pay for it. I've got more than I can pay for now."

"All right," replied Hurstwood, sitting down in silence. He was sick of the grind of this thing.

Carrie went out and there he sat, determining to do something.

There had been appearing in the papers about this time rumors and notices of an approaching strike on the trolley lines in Brooklyn. There was general dissatisfaction as to the hours of labor required and the wages paid. As usual, and for some inexplicable reason, the men chose the winter for the forcing of the hand of their employers and the settlement of their difficulties.

Hurstwood had been reading of this thing and wondering concerning the huge tie-up which would follow. A day or two before this trouble with Carrie, it came. Of a cold afternoon, when every thing was gray and it threatened to snow, the papers announced that the men had been called out on all the lines.

Being so utterly idle and his mind filled with the numerous predictions which had been made concerning the scarcity of labor this winter, and the panicky state of the financial market, Hurstwood read this with interest. He noted the claims of the striking motormen and conductors, who said that they had been wont to receive two dollars a day in times past, but that for a year or more, "trippers" had been introduced which cut down their chance of livelihood one-half and increased their hours of servitude from ten to twelve and even fourteen. These "trippers" were men who were put on during the busy and *rush* hours to take a car out for one trip. The compensation paid for such a trip was only twenty-five cents. When the rush or busy hours were over, they were laid off. Worst of all no man might know when he was going to get a car. He must come to the barns in the morning and wait around in fair and foul weather, until such time as he was needed. Two trips were an average reward for so much waiting—a little over three hours' work for fifty cents. The work of waiting was not counted.

The men complained that this system was extending and that the time was not far off when but a few out of seven thousand employés would have regular two-dollar-a-day work at all. They demanded that the system be abolished and that ten hours be considered a day's work, barring unavoidable delays, with two dollars and twenty-five cents pay. They demanded immediate acceptance of these terms, which the various trolley companies refused.

Hurstwood at first sympathized with the demands of these men—indeed it is a question whether he did not always sympathize with them to the end, belie him as his actions might.

Reading nearly all the news, he was attracted first by the scare-heads with which the trouble was noted in the "World." He read it fully, the names of the seven companies involved, the number of men.

"They're foolish to strike in this sort of weather," he thought to himself. "Let 'em win if they can, though."

The next day there was even a larger notice of it. "Brooklynites Walk," said the "World." "Knights of Labor Tie Up the Trolley Lines Across the Bridge." "About Seven Thousand Men Out."

Hurstwood read this, formulating to himself his own idea of what would be the outcome. He was a great believer in the strength of corporations.

"They can't win," he said concerning the men. "They haven't got any money. The police will protect the companies. They've got to. The public has got to have its cars."

He didn't sympathize with the corporations, but strength was with them. So was property and public utility.

"Those fellows can't win," he thought.

Among other things, he noticed a circular issued by one of the companies which read:

Atlantic Avenue Railroad.
Special Notice.

The motormen and conductors and other employés of this company having abruptly left its service, an opportunity is now given to all loyal men who have struck against their will to be reinstated, provided they will make their applications by twelve o'clock noon on Wednesday, Jan. 16. Such men will be given employment (with guaranteed protection) in the order in which such applications are received, and runs and positions assigned them accordingly. Otherwise they will be considered discharged, and every vacancy will be filled by a new man as soon as his services can be secured.

(Signed) Benjamin Norton, President.

He also noted among the want ads one which read:—

Wanted—50 skilled motormen, accustomed to Westinghouse system, to run U.S. mail cars only, in the city of Brooklyn. Protection guaranteed.

He noted particularly in each the "Protection guaranteed." It signified to him the unassailable power of the companies.

"They've got the militia on their side," he thought. "There isn't anything those men can do."

While this was still in his mind, the incident with Oeslagge and Carrie occurred. There had been a good deal to irritate him before, but this seemed much the worst. Never before had she accused him of stealing—or very near that. She doubted the naturalness of so large a bill. And he had worked so hard to make expenses seem light. He had been doing butcher and baker in order not to call on her. He had eaten very little—almost nothing.

"Damn it all," he said. "I can get something. I'm not down yet."

He thought that he really must do something now. It was too cheap to sit around after such an insinuation as this. Why, after a little, he would be standing anything.

He got up and looked out the window into the chilly street. It came gradually in his mind, as he stood there, to go to Brooklyn.

"Why not?" his mind said. "Anyone can get work over there. You'll get two a day."

"How about accidents?" said a voice. "You might get hurt."

"Oh, there won't be much of that," he answered. "They've called out the police. Anyone who wants to run a car will be protected all right."

"You don't know how to run a car," rejoined the voice.

"I won't apply as a motorman," he answered. "I can ring up fares all right."

"They'll want motormen mostly," came the reply.

"They'll take anybody, that I know," he replied.

For several hours he argued pro and con with this mental counselor, feeling no need to act at once, in a matter so sure of profit.

"I'll go tomorrow," he said.

When Carrie came back that afternoon, he felt as if he ought to make the announcement, but put off, and put off, until finally she went out to the theatre. They never really made up after these little arguments. The trouble passed by a sort of silent agreement to ignore.

In the morning he put on his best clothes, which were poor enough, and began stirring about, putting some bread and meat into a page of a newspaper. Carrie watched him, interested in this new move.

"Where are you going?" she asked.

"Over to Brooklyn," he answered. Then seeing her still inquisitive, he added, "I think I can get on over there."

"On the trolley lines?" said Carrie, astonished.

"Yes," he rejoined.

"Aren't you afraid?" she asked.

"What of?" he answered. "The police are protecting them."

"The paper said four men were hurt yesterday."

"Yes," he returned, "but you can't go by what the papers say. They'll run the cars all right."

He looked rather determined now, in a desolate sort of way, and Carrie felt very sorry. Something of the old Hurstwood was here—the least shadow of what was once a shrewd and pleasant strength. Outside it was cloudy and blowing a few flakes of snow.

"What a day to go over there," thought Carrie.

Now he left before she did, which was a remarkable thing. She sat down and wondered what he would do if he really got work. He might, you know.

While she sat thinking, Hurstwood tramped eastward to 14th and Sixth Avenue, where he took the car. He had read that scores of applicants were applying at the office of the Brooklyn City Railroad Building at Montague and Clinton Streets and being received. He decided to go there. He made his way by horse-car and ferry, a dark, silent man, to the offices in question. It was a long way, for no cars were running, and the day was cold, but he trudged on. Once in Brooklyn he could clearly see and feel that a strike was on. People showed it in their manner. Along the routes of certain tracks, not a car was moving. About certain corners and nearby saloons, small groups of men were lounging. Especially was this true of the vicinities of car-barns and street-car offices. Several spring wagons passed him, equipped with plain wooden chairs and labeled "Flatbush" or "Prospect Park, Fare Ten Cents." He noticed cold and even gloomy faces. Labor was having its little war.

When he came near the office in question, he saw a few men standing about and some policemen. On the far corners were other men whom he took to be strikers, watching. All the houses were small and wooden, the streets poorly paved. After New York, Brooklyn looked naturally poor and hard-up.

He made his way into the heart of the small group, eyed by policemen and the men already there. One of the officers addressed him.

"What are you looking for?"

"I want to see if I can get a place."

"The offices are up those steps," said the blue-coat. His face was a very neutral thing to contemplate. In his heart of hearts he sympathized with the strikers and hated this scab. In his heart of hearts also, he felt the dignity and use of the police force, which commanded order. Its true social significance he never once dreamed of. His was not the mind for that. The two feelings, blended in him, neutralized one another and him. He would have fought for this man as determinedly as for himself, and yet only so far as commanded. Strip him of his uniform and he would have soon picked his side.

Hurstwood ascended a dusty flight of steps and entered a small, dust-colored office, in which were a railing, a long desk and several clerks.

"Well, sir," said the middle-aged man, looking up at him from the long desk.

"Do you want to hire any men?" inquired Hurstwood.

"What are you—a motorman?"

"No, I'm not anything," said Hurstwood.

He was not at all abashed by his position. He knew these people needed men. If one didn't take him, another would. This individual could take him or leave him, just as he chose.

"Well, we prefer experienced men, of course," said the man. He paused while Hurstwood smiled indifferently. Then he added, "Still, I guess you can learn. What is your name?"

"Wheeler," said Hurstwood.

The man wrote an order on a small card. "Take that to our barns," he said, "and give it to the foreman. He'll show you what to do."

Hurstwood went down and out. He walked straight away in the direction indicated, while the policemen looked after.

"There's another wants to try it," said Officer Kiely to Officer Macey.

"I have my mind he'll get his fill," returned the latter, quietly.

They had been in strikes before.

CHAPTER XLIV.

The barn at which Hurstwood applied was exceedingly short-handed, and was being operated practically by three men as directors. There were a lot of green hands around, queer hungry-looking individuals, who looked as if want had driven them to desperate means. They tried to be lively and willing, but there was an air of hang-dog diffidence about the place. Most all were awkward. All were silent, all poorly clothed.

Hurstwood presented the card given him.

"No experience, eh?" asked the man pleasantly enough.

"Not any," he replied.

"Well, I guess we'll have to teach you. Go out there in the yard and ask for Saunders. He'll show you."

Hurstwood went back through the barns and out into a large enclosed lot, where were a series of tracks and loops. A half-dozen cars were there, manned by instructors, each with a pupil at the lever. More pupils were waiting at one of the rear doors of the barn.

He took in the situation at once. Mr. Saunders need not be called for. All he had to do was stand here and wait his turn.

Presently one of the cars stopped near the barn end and a pupil got off.

"Next!" cried the teacher.

A shabby, thin-faced individual in a worn spring overcoat stepped away from Hurstwood's side and got on the platform. Then the teacher conferred with him quietly.

In silence Hurstwood viewed this scene and waited. His companions took his eye for awhile, though they did not interest him much more than the cars. They were an uncomfortable-looking group, however. One or two were very thin and lean. Several were quite stout. Several others were rawboned and sallow, as if they had been beaten upon by all sorts of rough weather.

"Did you see by the paper they are going to call out the militia?" Hurstwood heard one of them remark.

"Oh, they'll do that," returned the other. "They always do."

"Think we're liable to have much trouble?" said another, whom Hurstwood did not see.

"Not very."

"That Scotchman that went out on the last car," put in a voice, "told me that they hit him in the ear with a cinder."

A small nervous laugh accompanied this.

"One of those fellows on the Fifth Avenue line must have had a hell of a time, according to the papers," drawled another. "They broke his car windows and pulled him off into the street 'fore the police could stop 'em."

"Yes, but there are more police around today," was added by another.

Hurstwood hearkened without much mental comment. These talkers seemed scared to him. Their gabbling was feverish—things said to quiet their own minds. He only looked out into the yard and waited.

Two of the men got around quite near him, but behind his back. They were rather social and he listened to what they said.

"Are you a railroad man?" said one.

"Me, no. I've always worked in a paper factory."

"I had a job in Newark, until last October," returned the other, with reciprocal feeling.

There were some words which passed, too low to hear. Then the conversation became strong again.

"I don't blame these fellers for strikin'," said one. "They got the right of it all right, but by God, I had to get something to do."

"Same here," said the other. "If I had my job in Newark, I wouldn't be over here takin' chances like these."

"It's hell these days, ain't it," said the man. "A poor man ain't nowhere. You could starve, by Jesus, right in the streets and there ain't most no one would help you."

"Right you are," said the other. "The job I had I lost 'cause they shut down. They run all summer and lay up a big stock, and then shut down."

Hurstwood paid some little attention to this. Somehow he felt a little superior to these two, a little better-off. To him they were ignorant and commonplace, poor sheep in a driver's hand.

"Poor devils," he thought, speaking out of the thoughts and feelings of a bygone period of success.

He was still listening to more of the same sort, which was private opinion, when he was called.

"Next," said one of the instructors.

"You're next," said a neighbor, touching him.

He went out and climbed on the platform. The instructor took it for granted that no preliminaries were needed.

"You see this handle," he said, reaching up to an electric cut-off, which was fastened to the roof. "This throws the current off or on. If you want to reverse the car, you turn it over here. If you want to send it forward, you put it over here. If you want to cut off the power, you keep it in the middle."

Hurstwood smiled at the simple information.

"Now this handle here regulates your speed. To here," he said, pointing with his finger, "gives you about four miles an hour. This is eight. When it's full on, you make about fourteen miles an hour."

Hurstwood watched him calmly. He had seen motormen work before. He knew just about how they did it and was sure he could do as well, with a very little practise.

The instructor explained a few more details and then said:—

"Now we'll back her up."

Hurstwood stood placidly by, while the car rolled back into the yard.

"One thing you want to be careful about, and that is to start easy. Give one degree time to act before you add another. The one fault of most men is that they always want to throw her wide open. That's bad. It's dangerous too. Wears out the motor. You don't want to do that."

"I see," said Hurstwood.

He waited and waited, while the man talked on.

"Now you take it," he said finally.

The ex-manager laid hand to the lever and pushed gently, as he thought. It worked much easier than he imagined, however, with the result that the car jerked quickly forward, throwing him back almost against the door. He straightened up sheepishly, while the instructor stopped the car with the brake.

"You want to be careful about that," was all he said.

Hurstwood found, however, that handling a brake and regulating speed were not so instantly mastered as he had imagined. Once or twice he would have ploughed through the rear fence, if it had not been for the hand and word of his companion. The latter was rather patient with him, but he never smiled.

"You've got to get the knack of working both arms at once," he said. "It takes a little practise."

It came one o'clock while he was still on the car practising, and he began to feel hungry. The day set in snowing, and he was cold. He grew quite weary of running to and fro on the short track. He could see there was a knack to the thing which he had not quite mastered yet.

"Have you had your dinner yet?" asked the man, at last.

"No," he answered.

"Perhaps you'd better get it, then."

They ran the car to the end and both got off. Hurstwood went into the barn and sought a car step, pulling out his paper-wrapped lunch from his pocket. There was no water and the bread was dry, but he enjoyed it. There was no ceremony about dining. He swallowed and looked about, contemplating the dull, homely labor of the thing. It was disagreeable, miserably disagreeable, in all its phases. Not because he was better, but because it was hard. It would be hard to anyone, he thought.

After eating he stood about as before, waiting until his turn came. Among the men were those who impressed him as being against the strikers—grim, dull-looking individuals who maintained an unbroken silence. There was no index to the working of their minds. Hurstwood did not fancy these people. He was neutral himself, fairly well determined to work if he could, but willing to allow that the strikers had grievances. He would have preferred to see the others taking the situation in the same spirit.

When his turn came he perceived that he would not run a car this day. The intention was to give him an afternoon of practise, or such part of practise as he could get, along with others. A greater part of the time was spent in waiting about.

At last, evening came and with it hunger and a debate with himself as to how he should spend the night. It was half-past five. He must soon eat. If he tried to go home it would take him two hours and a half of cold walking and riding. Besides he had orders to report at seven the next morning, and going home would necessitate his rising at an unholy and disagreeable hour. More, he had only something like a dollar and fifteen cents of

Carrie's money, with which he had intended to pay the week's coal bill, before the present idea struck him.

"They must have some place around here," he thought. "Where does that fellow from Newark stay?"

Finally he decided to ask. There was a young fellow standing near one of the doors in the cold, waiting a last turn. He was a mere boy in years—twenty-one about, but with a body which was lankly long, only because of privation. A little good living would have made this youth plump and swaggering.

"How do they arrange this, if a man hasn't got any money?" inquired Hurstwood discreetly.

The fellow turned a keen, watchful face on the inquirer.

"You mean eat?" he replied.

"Yes, and sleep. I can't go back to New York tonight."

"The foreman'll fix that if you ask him, I guess. He did me."

"That so?"

"Yes. I just told him I didn't have anything. Gee, I couldn't go home. I live way over in Hoboken."

Hurstwood only cleared his throat by way of acknowledgement.

"They've got a place upstairs here, I understand. I don't know what sort of a thing it is. Purty tough I guess. He gave me a meal ticket this noon. I know that wasn't much."

Hurstwood smiled grimly and the boy laughed.

"It ain't no fun, is it?" he inquired, wishing vainly for a cheery reply.

"Not much," answered Hurstwood.

"I'd tackle him now," volunteered the youth. "He may go 'way."

Hurstwood did so.

"Isn't there some place I can stay around here tonight?" he inquired. "If I have to go back to New York, I'm afraid I won't—"

"There's some cots upstairs," interrupted the man, "if you want one of them."

"That'll do," he assented.

He meant to ask for a meal ticket, but the seemingly proper moment never came and he decided to pay himself that night.

"I'll ask him in the morning."

He ate in a cheap restaurant in the vicinity and, being cold and lonely, went straight off to seek the loft in question. The company was not attempting to run cars after nightfall. It was so advised by the police.

The room seemed to have been a lounging place for night workers. There were some nine cots in the place, two or three wooden chairs, a soap box and a small round-bellied stove in which a fire was blazing. Early as he was, another man was there before him. The latter was sitting beside the stove, warming his hands.

Hurstwood approached and held out his own toward the fire. He was sick of the bareness and privation of all things connected with this venture already, but was steeling himself to hold out. He fancied he could for awhile.

"Cold isn't it?" said the early guest.

"Rather."

A long silence.

"Not much of a place to sleep in is it?" said the man.

"Better than nothing," replied Hurstwood.

Another silence.

"I believe I'll turn in," said the man.

Rising, he went to one of the cots and stretched himself, removing only his shoes and pulling the one blanket and dirty old comforter over him in a sort of bundle. The sight disgusted Hurstwood, but he did not dwell on it, choosing to gaze into the stove and think of something else. Presently he decided to retire and picked a cot, also removing his shoes.

While he was doing so, the youth who had advised him to come here entered and, seeing Hurstwood, tried to be genial.

"Better'n nothin'," he observed, looking around.

Hurstwood did not take this to himself. He thought it to be an expression of individual satisfaction and so did not answer. The youth imagined he was out of sorts and set to whistling softly. Seeing another man asleep, he quit that and lapsed into silence.

Hurstwood made the best of a bad lot by keeping on his clothes, and pushing away the covering, which was dirty, from his head; but at last he dozed in sheer weariness. The covering became more and more comfortable; its character was forgotten and he slept.

In the morning he was aroused out of a pleasant dream by

several men stirring about in a cold, cheerless room. He had been back in Chicago in fancy, in his own comfortable home. Jessica had been arranging to go somewhere and he had been talking with her about it. She was so clear in his mind, that he was startled now by the contrast of this room. He raised his head, and the cold bitter reality jarred him into wakefulness.

"Guess I'd better get up," he said.

There was no water on this floor. He fastened on his shoes in the cold and stood up, shaking himself in his stiffness. His clothes felt disagreeable, his hair bad.

"Hell," he muttered, as he put on his hat.

Downstairs things were stirring again.

He found a hydrant with a trough which had once been used for horses, but there was no towel here and his handkerchief was soiled from yesterday. He contented himself with wetting his eyes with the ice-cold water. Then he sought the foreman, who was already on the ground.

"Had your breakfast yet?" inquired that worthy.

"No," said Hurstwood.

"Better get it then. Your car won't be ready for a little while."

Hurstwood hesitated.

"Could you let me have a meal-ticket?" he asked with an effort.

"Here you are," said the man, handing him one.

He breakfasted as poorly as the night before on some fried steak and bad coffee. Then he went back.

"Here," said the foreman, motioning to him when he came in. "You take this car out in a few minutes."

Hurstwood climbed up on the platform in the gloomy barn and waited for a signal. He was nervous, and yet the thing was a relief. Anything was better than the barn.

On this, the fourth day of the strike, the situation had taken a turn for the worse. The strikers, following the counsel of their leaders and the newspapers, had struggled peaceably enough. There had been no great violence done. Cars had been stopped, it is true, and the men argued with. Some crews had been won over and led away; some windows broken, some jeering and yelling done; but in no more than five or six instances had men been seriously injured. These by crowds whose acts the leaders disclaimed.

Idleness, however, and the sight of the company, backed by the police, triumphing, angered the men. They saw that each day more cars were going on, each day more declarations were being made by the company officials that the effective opposition of the strikers was broken. This angered the men and put desperate thoughts in their minds. Peaceful methods meant, they saw, that the companies would soon run all their cars, and those who had complained would be forgotten. There was nothing so helpful to the companies as peaceful methods.

All at once they blazed forth, and for a week there was storm and stress. Cars were assailed, men attacked, policemen struggled with, tracks torn up and shots fired, until at last street fights and mob movements became frequent, and the city was invested with militia.

Hurstwood knew nothing of the change of temper.

"Run your car out," called the foreman, waving a vigorous hand at him. A green conductor jumped up behind and rang the bell twice as a signal to start. Hurstwood turned the lever, and ran the car out through the door into the street in front of the barn. Here two brawny policemen got up beside him on the platform—one on either hand.

At the sound of a gong near the barn door, two bells were given by the conductor and Hurstwood opened his lever.

The two policemen looked about them calmly.

" 'Tis cold, all right, this morning," said the one on the left, who possessed a rich brogue.

"I had enough of it yesterday," said the other. "I wouldn't want a steady job of this."

"Nor I."

Neither paid the slightest attention to Hurstwood, who stood facing the cold wind, which was chilling him completely, and thinking of his orders.

"Keep a steady gait," the foreman had said. "Don't stop for anyone who doesn't look like a real passenger. Whatever you do, don't stop for a crowd."

The two officers kept silent for a few moments.

"The last man must have gone through all right," said the officer on the left. "I don't see his car anywhere."

"Who's on there?" asked the second officer, referring of course to its complement of policemen.

"Schaeffer and Ryan."

There was another silence in which the car ran smoothly along. There were not so many houses along this part of the way. Hurstwood did not see many people either. The situation was not wholly disagreeable to him. If he wasn't so cold, he thought, he would do real well.

He was brought out of this feeling by the sudden appearance of a curve ahead, which he had not expected. He shut off the current and did an energetic turn at the brakes, but not in time sufficient to avoid an unnaturally quick turn. It shook him up quite a bit and made him feel like making some apologetic remarks, but he refrained.

"You want to look out for them things," said the officer on the left, condescendingly.

"That's right," agreed Hurstwood, shame-facedly.

"There's lots of them on this line," said the officer on the right.

Around the corner, a more populated way appeared. One or two pedestrians were in view ahead. A boy coming out of a gate, with a tin milk bucket, gave Hurstwood his first objectionable greeting.

"Scab!" he yelled. "Scab!"

Hurstwood heard it but tried to make no comment, even to himself. He knew he would get that and much more of the same sort probably.

At a corner farther up a man stood by the track and signaled the car to stop.

"Never mind him," said one of the officers. "He's up to some game."

Hurstwood obeyed. At the corner he saw the wisdom of it. No sooner did the man perceive the intention to ignore him, than he shook his fist.

"Ah! you bloody coward!" he yelled.

Some half-dozen men, standing on the corner, flung taunts and jeers after the speeding car.

Hurstwood winced the least bit. The real thing was slightly worse than the thoughts of it had been.

Now came in sight, three or four blocks farther on, a heap of something on the track.

"They've been at work here, all right," said one of the policemen.

"We'll have an argument maybe," said the other.

Hurstwood ran the car close and stopped. He had not done so wholly, however, before a crowd was gathered about. It was composed of ex-motormen and conductors in part, with a sprinkling of friends and sympathizers.

"Come off the car, pardner," said one of the men in a voice meant to be conciliatory. "You don't want to take the bread out of another man's mouth, do you?"

Hurstwood held to his brake and lever, pale and very uncertain what to do.

"Stand back!" yelled one of the officers, leaning over the platform railing. "Clear out of this now. Give the man a chance to do his work."

"Listen, pardner," said the leader, ignoring the policeman and addressing Hurstwood. "We're all working men, like yourself. If you were a regular motorman and had been treated as we've been, you wouldn't want anyone to come in and take your place, would you? You wouldn't want anyone to do you out of your chance to get your rights, would you?"

"Shut her off! Shut her off!" urged the other of the policemen roughly. "Get out of this now," and he jumped the railing and landed before the crowd, and began shoving. Instantly the other officer was down beside him.

"Stand back now!" they yelled. "Get out of this. What the hell do you mean—out now!"

It was like a small swarm of bees.

"Don't shove me," said one of the strikers determinedly. "I'm not doing anything."

"Get out of this!" cried the officer, swinging his club. "I'll give ye a bat on the sconce! Back now!"

"What the hell!" cried another of the strikers, pushing the other way, adding at the same time some lusty oaths.

Crack came an officer's club on his forehead. He blinked his eyes blindly a few times, wobbled on his legs, threw up his hands and staggered back. In return a swift fist landed on the officer's neck.

Infuriated by this, the latter plunged left and right, laying about madly with his club. He was ably assisted by his brother of the blue, who poured ponderous oaths upon the troubled waters. No severe damage was done, owing to the agility of the strikers in keeping out of reach. They stood about the side walk now and jeered.

"Where is the conductor?" yelled one of the officers, getting his eye on that individual, who had come nervously forward to stand by Hurstwood. The latter had stood gazing upon the scene with more astonishment than fear.

"Why the hell don't you come down here and get these stones off the track?" inquired the officer. "What you standing there for? Do you want to stay here all day? Get down."

Hurstwood breathed heavily in excitement and jumped down with the nervous conductor, as if he had been called.

"Hurry up now," said the other policeman.

Cold as it was, these officers were hot and mad. Hurstwood worked with the conductor, lifting stone after stone and warming himself by the work.

"Ah, you scab you!" yelled the crowd. "You coward! Steal a man's job, will you? Rob the poor, will you—you thief! We'll get you yet, now. Wait!"

Not all of this was delivered by one man. It came from here and there, incorporated with much more of the same sort and curses.

"Work, you blackguards!" yelled a voice. "Do the dirty work! You're the suckers that keep the poor people down—you bastards!"

"May God starve ye yet!" yelled an old Irishwoman, who now threw open a nearby window and stuck out her head.

"Yes and you!" she added, catching the eye of one of the policemen. "You bloody, murtherin thafe! Crack my son over the head, will you, you hard-hearted murtherin divil! Ah, ye—"

But the officer turned a deaf ear.

"Go to the devil, you old hag," he half-muttered as he stared round upon the scattered company.

Now the stones were off and Hurstwood took his place again amid a continued chorus of epithets. Both officers got up beside him, and the conductor rang the bell, when, bang! bang! through window and door came rocks and stones. One narrowly grazed Hurstwood's head. Another shattered the window behind.

"Throw open your lever," yelled one of the officers, grabbing at the handle himself.

Hurstwood complied and the car shot away, followed by a rattle of stones and a rain of curses.

"That _____ _____ hit me in the neck," said one of the officers. "I gave him a good crack for it though."

"I think I must have left spots on some of them," said the other.

"I know that big guy that called me a _____ _____ ," said the first. "I'll get him yet for that."

"I thought we were in for it sure, once there," said the second.

Thus they talked. Hurstwood, warm and excited, gazed steadily ahead. It was an astonishing experience for him. He had read of these things but the reality seemed something altogether new. He was no coward in spirit. The fact that he had suffered this much now rather operated to arouse a stolid determination to stick it out. He did not recur in thought to New York or the flat. This one trip seemed a consuming thing.

They now ran into the business heart of Brooklyn uninterrupted, though not without reminders of the fact that they might expect more. People gazed at the broken windows of the car and at Hurstwood in his plain clothes. Voices called "scab" now and then, as well as other epithets, but no crowd attacked the car. At the down-town end of the line, one of the officers went to call up his station and report the trouble.

"There's a gang out there," he said, "laying for us yet. Better send some one over there and clean them out."

The car ran back more quietly, hooted, watched, flung at, but not attacked. Hurstwood breathed freely when he saw the barns.

"Well," he observed to himself, "I came out of that all right."

The car was turned in and he was allowed to loaf awhile, but at last he was again called. This time a new team of officers were aboard. Slightly more confident, he sped the car along the commonplace streets and felt somewhat less fearful. On one side, however, he suffered intensely. The day was raw, with a sprinkling of snow, and a gusty wind, which was made all the more intolerable by the speed of the car. His clothing was not intended for this sort of work. He shivered, stamped his feet and beat his arms as he had seen other conductors do in the past, but said nothing. The novelty and danger of the situation modified, in a way, his disgust and distress at being compelled to be here, but not enough to prevent him from feeling grim and sour. This was a dog's life, he thought. It was a tough thing to have to come to.

The one thought that strengthened him was the insult offered by Carrie. He was not down so low as to take all that, he thought. He could do something—this even—for awhile. It would get better. He would save a little.

A boy threw a clod of mud while he was thus reflecting and hit him upon the arm. It hurt sharply and angered him more than he had been any time since morning.

"The little cur," he muttered.

"Hurt you?" asked one of the policemen.

"No," he answered.

At one of the corners where the car slowed up because of a turn, an ex-motorman, standing on the sidewalk, called to him.

"Won't you come out, pardner, and be a man? Remember we're fighting for a decent day's wages, that's all. We've got families to support." The man seemed most peaceably inclined.

Hurstwood pretended not to see him. He kept his eyes straight on before and opened the lever wide. The voice had something appealing in it.

All morning this went on and long into the afternoon. He made three trips which were not any more difficult than the last described. The dinner he had was no stay for such work, and the cold was telling on him. Numb as he seemed to become to it, nevertheless it seemed to get worse. At each end of the line he stopped to thaw out, but he could have groaned at the anguish of it. One of the barn-men, out of pity, loaned him a heavy cap and a pair of sheepskin gloves, and for once he was extremely thankful. These were things he needed much.

On the second trip of the afternoon he ran into a crowd about half-way along the line, which blocked the car's progress with an old telegraph pole.

"Get that thing off the track!" shouted the two policemen.

"Yah, yah, yah!" yelled the crowd. "Get it off yourself!"

The two policemen got down and Hurstwood started to follow.

"You stay there," one called. "Some one will run away with your car."

Amid the babel of voices, Hurstwood heard one close beside him.

"Come down, partner, and be a man. Don't fight the poor. Leave that to the corporations."

He saw the same individual who had called to him from the corner. Now as before he pretended not to hear.

"Come down," the man repeated gently. "You don't want to fight poor men. Don't fight at all." It was a most philosophic and jesuitical motorman.

A third policeman joined the other two from somewhere, and someone ran to telephone for more officers. Hurstwood gazed about, determined but fearful.

A man grabbed him by the coat.

"Come off of that!" he exclaimed, jerking at him and trying to pull him over the railing.

"Let go!" said Hurstwood savagely.

"I'll show you—you scab!" cried a young Irishman, jumping up on the coupler and aiming a blow at Hurstwood. The latter ducked and caught it on the shoulder instead of the jaw.

"Away from here!" shouted an officer, hastening to the rescue and adding, of course, the usual oaths.

Hurstwood recovered himself, pale and trembling in the hands. It was becoming serious with him now. People were looking up and jeering at him. One girl was making faces.

"Ah, ya! ya!" she cried. It was the hissing, jeering mob of Christ's time.

He had begun to waver in his resolution when a patrol wagon rolled up and more officers dismounted. Now the track was quickly cleared and the release effected.

"Let her go now, quick," said the officer, and again he was off.

Another trial of the afternoon came when, delayed by a crowd, the officer commanded him to open up and plough his way through them.

"Run over 'em," he said, hoarsely.

Hurstwood complied and scattered a small throng, amid jeers.

The end came with a real mob which met the car on its

return trip a mile or two from the barns. It was an exceedingly poor-looking neighborhood. He wanted to run fast through it, but again the track was blocked. He saw men carrying something out to it when he was yet a half-dozen blocks away.

"There they are again!" exclaimed one policeman.

"I'll give them something this time," said the second officer, whose patience was becoming worn. Hurstwood suffered a qualm of body as the car rolled up to this.

As before the crowd began hooting, but now, rather than come near, they threw things. One or two windows were smashed and Hurstwood dodged a stone.

Both policemen ran out towards the crowd, but the latter replied by running toward the car. A woman, a mere girl in appearance, was among these, bearing a rough stick. She was exceedingly wrathful and struck at Hurstwood, who dodged. Thereupon her companions, duly encouraged, jumped on the car and pulled Hurstwood over. He had hardly time to speak or shout before he fell.

"Let go of me," he said, falling on his side.

"Ah, you sucker," he heard some one say. There were kicks and blows rained on him. He seemed to be suffocating. Then two men seemed to be dragging him off and he wrestled for freedom.

"Let up," said a voice. "You're all right. Stand up."

He was let loose, and sort of recovered himself. Now he recognized the two officers. He felt as if he would faint from exhaustion. Something was wet on his chin. He put up his hand and felt—then looked. It was red.

"They cut me," he said, foolishly, fishing for his handkerchief.

"Now, now," said one of the officers. "It's only a scratch."

His senses became clearer now and he looked around. He was standing in a little store where they left him for the moment. Outside, he could see, as he stood wiping his chin, the car and the excited crowd. A patrol wagon was there and another.

He walked over, and looked out. It was an ambulance, backing in.

He saw some energetic charging by the police and arrests being made.

"Come on now, if you want to take your car in," said an officer, opening the door and looking in.

He walked out, feeling rather uncertain of himself. He was very cold and frightened.

"Where's the conductor?" he asked.

"Oh, he's not here now," said the policeman.

Hurstwood went towards the car and stepped nervously on. As he did so, there was a pistol shot. Something stung his shoulder.

"Who fired that!" he heard an officer exclaim. "By God, who did that!" Both left him, running towards a certain building. He paused a moment and then got down.

"By God," he said vaguely—"this is too much for me."

He walked nervously to the corner and hurried down a side street.

"Wheh!" he said, drawing in his breath.

A half-block away, a small girl gazed at him.

"You better sneak," she called after him.

He walked homeward in a blinding snow storm, reaching the ferry by dusk. The cabins were filled with a few comfortable souls who studied him curiously. His head was still in such a whirl that he felt confused. All the wonder of the twinkling lights of the river in a white storm passed for nothing. He trudged doggedly on until he reached the flat. There he entered and found the room warm. Carrie was gone. A couple of evening papers were lying on the table where she left them. He lit the gas and sat down. Then he got up and stripped to examine his shoulder. It was a mere scratch. He washed his hands and face, still in a brown study, apparently, and combed his hair. Then he looked for something to eat, and finally, his hunger gone, sat down in his comfortable rocking chair. It was a wonderful relief.

He put his hand to his chin, forgetting for the moment the papers.

"Well," he said after a time, his nature recovering itself. "That's a pretty tough game over there."

Then he turned and saw the papers. With a half a sigh, he picked up the "World."

"Strike Spreading in Brooklyn," he read. "Rioting Breaks Out in All Parts of the City."

He adjusted his paper very comfortably and continued. It was the one thing he read with absorbing interest.

CHAPTER XLV.

Those who look upon Hurstwood's Brooklyn venture as an error of judgment will none the less realize the negative influence on him of the fact that he had tried and failed. Carrie got a wrong idea of it. He said so little that she imagined he had encountered nothing worse than the ordinary roughness. Quitting so soon, in the face of this, seemed trifling. He did not want to work.

During his absence, brief as it was—only from ten o'clock of one morning to seven o'clock of the next evening, she had felt intensely relieved. With him there passed out of the flat a great shadow. In its place came hopes for the future—hopes of freedom from annoyance and money-drain. She had got a taste of what it is to grow weary of the idler. Now, after a gleam of pleasant energy, he returned. Her heart sank at the sight.

It was not because hard-heartedness was a characteristic of her nature. It was weariness and an ache for change. When she saw him in bed that night, she knew that it imported failure. Coming on top of a further improvement in her own situation which must now be detailed, and as a destroyer of her hope that he had really roused himself, it was a shock. She could only shake her head in despair.

"Oh, me!" she sighed.

The improvement referred to concerned some attention her work had attracted. She was one of a group of oriental beauties who, in the second act of the comic opera, were paraded by the Vizier before the new potentate as the treasures of his harem. There was no word assigned to any of them, but on the evening when Hurstwood was housing himself in the loft of the street-car barn, the leading comedian and star, feeling exceedingly facetious, said in a profound voice, which created a ripple of laughter:—

"Well, who are you?"

It merely happened to be Carrie who was curtsying before

him. It might as well have been any of the others, so far as he was concerned. He expected no answer, and a dull one would have been reproved. But Carrie, whose experience and belief in herself gave her daring, curtsied sweetly again and answered:—

"I am yours truly."

It was a trivial thing to say, and yet something in the way she did it caught the audience, which laughed heartily at the mock-fierce potentate towering before the young woman. The comedian also liked it, hearing the laughter.

"I thought your name was Smith," he returned, endeavoring to get the last laugh.

Carrie almost trembled for her daring after she had said this. All members of the company had been warned that to interpolate lines or "business" meant a fine or worse. She did not know what to think.

As she was standing in her proper position in the wings, awaiting another entry, the great comedian made his exit past her and paused in recognition.

"You can just leave that in hereafter," he remarked, seeing how intelligent she appeared. "Don't add any more, though."

"Thank you," said Carrie humbly. When he went on, she found herself trembling violently.

"Well, you're in luck," remarked another member of the chorus. "There isn't another one of us has got a line."

There was no gainsaying the value of this. Everybody in the company realized that she had got a start. Carrie hugged herself when next evening the lines got the same applause. She went home rejoicing, knowing that soon something must come of it. It was Hurstwood, who by his presence, caused her merry thoughts to flee and replaced them with sharp longings for an end of distress.

The next day she asked him about his venture.

"They're not trying to run any cars except with police. They don't want anybody just now—not before next week."

Next week came, but Carrie saw no change. Hurstwood seemed more apathetic than ever. He saw her off mornings to rehearsals and the like with the utmost calm. He read and read. Several times he found himself staring at an item but thinking of something else. The first of these lapses that he sharply noticed concerned a hilarious party he had once attended at a driving club, of which he had been a member. He sat, gazing downward, mentating, and gradually he thought he heard the old voices and the clink of glasses.

"You're a dandy, Hurstwood," his good friend Walker said. He was standing again, well-dressed, smiling, good-natured, the recipient of encores for a good story.

All at once he looked up. The room was so still it seemed ghostlike. He heard the clock ticking audibly and half-suspected that he had been dozing. The paper was so straight in his hands, however, and the item he had been reading so directly before him that he rid himself of the doze idea. Still it seemed peculiar. When it occurred a second time, however, it did not seem quite so strange.

Butcher and groceryman, baker and coal man—not the group whom he was then dealing with, but those who had trusted him to the limit, called. He met them all blandly, becoming deft in excuse. At last he became bold, pretended to be out or waved them off.

"They can't get blood out of a turnip," he said. "If I had it, I'd pay them."

Carrie's little soldier friend, Miss Osborne, seeing her succeeding, had become a sort of satellite. Little Osborne could never of herself amount to anything. She seemed to realize it in a sort of pussy-like way, and instinctively concluded to cling with her soft little claws to Carrie.

"Oh, you'll get up," she kept telling Carrie with admiration. "You're so good."

Timid as Carrie was, she was strong in capability. The reliance of others made her feel as if she must, and when she must she dared. Experience of the world and of necessity were in her favor. No longer the lightest word of a man made her head dizzy. She had learned that men could change and fail. Flattery in its most palpable form had lost its force with her. It required superiority—kindly superiority, to move her—the superiority of a genius like Ames.

"I don't like the actors in our company," she told Lola one day. "They're all so stuck on themselves."

"Don't you think Mr. Barclay's pretty nice?" inquired Lola, who had received a condescending smile or two from that quarter.

"Oh—he's nice enough," answered Carrie, "but he isn't sincere. He assumes such an air."

Lola felt for her first hold upon Carrie in the following manner.

"Are you paying room-rent where you are?"

"Certainly," answered Carrie, "why?"

"I know where I could get the loveliest room and bath, cheap. It's too big for me but it would be just right for two and the rent only six dollars a week for both."

"Where?" said Carrie.

"In 17th Street."

"Well, I don't know as I'd care to change," said Carrie, who was already turning over the three-dollar rate in her mind. She was thinking, if she had only herself to support, this would leave her seventeen for herself.

Nothing came of this until after the Brooklyn adventure of Hurstwood, and her success with the speaking part. Then she began to feel as if she must be free. She thought of leaving Hurstwood and thus making him act for himself, but he had developed such peculiar traits, she feared he might resist any effort to throw him off. He might hunt her out at the show and hound her in that way. She did not wholly believe that he would, but he might. This she knew would be an embarrassing thing, if he made himself conspicuous in any way. It troubled her greatly.

Things were precipitated by the offer of a better part. One of the actresses, playing the part of a modest sweetheart, gave notice of leaving and Carrie was selected.

"How much are you going to get?" asked Miss Osborne, on hearing the good news.

"I didn't ask him," said Carrie.

"Well, find out. Goodness, you'll never get anything if you don't ask. Tell them you must have forty dollars anyhow."

"Oh, no," said Carrie.

"Certainly!" exclaimed Lola. "Ask 'em anyway."

Carrie succumbed to this prompting, waiting however until the manager gave her notice of what clothing she must have to fit the part.

"How much do I get?" she inquired.

"Thirty-five dollars," he replied.

Carrie was too much astonished and delighted to think of mentioning forty. She was nearly beside herself and almost hugged Lola, who clung to her at the news.

"It isn't as much as you ought to get," said the latter, "especially when you've got to buy clothes."

Carrie remembered this with a start. Where to get the money. She had none laid up for such an emergency. Rent day was drawing near.

"I'll not do it," she said, remembering her necessity. "I don't use the flat. I'm not going to give up my money this time. I'll move."

Fitting into this came another appeal from Miss Osborne, more urgent than ever.

"Come live with me, won't you?" she pleaded. "We can have the loveliest room. It won't cost you hardly anything that way."

"I'd like to," said Carrie frankly.

"Oh, do," said Lola. "We'll have such a good time."

Carrie thought awhile.

"I believe I will," she said, and then added, "I'll have to see first, though."

With the idea thus grounded, rent day approaching and clothes calling for instant purchase, she soon found excuse in Hurstwood's lassitude. He said less and drooped more than ever.

As rent day approached, an idea grew in him. It was fostered by the demands of creditors and the impossibility of holding up many more. Twenty-eight dollars was too much for rent. "It's hard on her," he thought. "We could get a cheaper place."

Stirred with this idea, he spoke at the breakfast table.

"Don't you think we pay too much rent here?" he asked.

"Indeed I do," said Carrie, not catching his drift.

"I should think we could get a smaller place," he suggested. "We don't need four rooms."

Her countenance, had he been scrutinizing her, would have exhibited the disturbance she felt at this evidence of his determination to stay by her. He saw nothing remarkable in asking her to come down lower.

"Oh, I don't know," she answered, growing wary.

"There must be places around here where we could get a couple of rooms, which would do us just as well."

Her heart revolted. "Never," she thought. Who would furnish the money to move? To think of being in two rooms with him. She resolved to spend her money for clothes quickly before something terrible happened. That very day she did it. Having done so, there was but one other thing to do.

"Lola," she said, visiting her friend, "I think I'll come."

"Oh, jolly!" cried the latter.

"Can we get it right away?" she asked, meaning the room.

"Certainly!" cried Lola.

They went to look at it. Carrie had saved ten dollars from her expenditures—enough for this and her board beside. Her enlarged salary would not begin for ten days yet—would not reach her for seventeen. She paid half of the six dollars with her friend.

"Now I've just enough to get on to the end of the week," she confided.

"Oh, I've got some," said Lola. "I've got twenty-five dollars if you need it."

"No," said Carrie. "I guess I'll get along."

They decided to move Friday, which was two days away. Now that the thing was settled, Carrie's heart misgave her. She felt very much like a criminal in the matter. Each day, looking at Hurstwood, she had realized that along with the disagreeableness of his attitude there was something pathetic. The winter was cold, his clothes were poor, he had no money. Moreover he looked less robust than formerly, as if confinement had bleached him.

Carrie had experienced too much of the bitterness of search and poverty, not to sympathize keenly with one about to be cast out upon his own resources. She remembered the time when she walked the streets of Chicago—and only recently when she searched here. Where would he go? Without money he must starve.

She looked at him the same evening she had made up her mind to go, and now he seemed not so much shiftless and worthless, but run-down and beaten upon by chance. His eyes were not keen, his face marked, his hands flabby. She thought his hair had a touch of gray. All unconscious of his doom, he rocked and read his paper while she glanced at him.

Thinking upon what she would take away with her, she

came to a just conclusion. The furniture he had bought and paid for—she would leave it. Her clothes, she had not so many, could go in the trunk which he had bought for her in Montreal.

"I'll only take the trinkets that belong to me," she thought.

These were upon mantel and chiffonier, dressing-table and stand. Little silver perfume bottles and silver-backed articles of toilet use, the fancy pieces of a manicure set, some belt buckles, jewelry and several lace table covers which she had made herself. All these she would take.

Knowing that the end was so near she became rather solicitous.

"Will you go over and get some canned peaches?" she asked Hurstwood, laying down a two-dollar bill.

"Certainly," he said, looking in wonder at the money.

"See if you can't get some nice asparagus," she added. "I'll cook it for dinner."

Hurstwood rose and took the money, slipping on his overcoat and getting his hat. Carrie noticed that both of these articles of apparel were old and poor-looking in appearance. It was plain enough before, but now it came home with peculiar force. Perhaps he couldn't help it after all. He had done well in Chicago. She remembered his fine appearance the days he met her in the park. Then he was so sprightly, so clean. Had it been all his fault? Far be it from her, at this decisive hour, to say.

He came back and laid the change down with the food.

"You'd better keep it," she observed. "We'll need other things."

"No," he said, with a sort of pride, "you keep it."

"Oh, go on and keep it," she replied, rather unnerved. "There'll be other things."

He wondered at this, not knowing the pathetic figure he had become in her eyes. She restrained herself with difficulty from showing a quaver in the voice.

To say truly, this would have been Carrie's attitude in any case. She had looked back at times upon her parting from Drouet and had regretted that she had served him so badly. She hoped she would never meet him again, but she was ashamed of her conduct. Not that she had had any choice in the final separation. She had gone willingly to seek him, with sympathy in her heart, when Hurstwood had reported him ill. There was something cruel somewhere, and not being able to track it mentally to its logical lair, she concluded with feeling that he would never understand what Hurstwood had done and would see hard-hearted decision in her deed—hence her shame. Not that she cared for him. She did not want to make anyone who had been good to her feel badly.

She did not realize what she was doing by allowing these feelings to possess her. Hurstwood, noticing the kindness, conceived better of her. "Carrie's good-natured, anyhow," he thought.

Going to Miss Osborne's that afternoon, she found that little lady packing and singing.

"Why don't you come over with me today?" she asked.

"Oh—I can't," said Carrie. "I'll be there Friday."

They talked awhile, Carrie constantly endeavoring to find a proper moment for introducing a thought she had. Finally she observed:—

"Would you mind loaning me the twenty-five dollars you spoke of?"

"Why no," said Lola, going for her purse.

"I want to get some other things," said Carrie.

"Oh, that's all right," answered the little girl good-naturedly, glad to be of service.

Towards dinner time, Carrie came away. She went back to her flat, thinking how on Friday she would get her things away. She did not propose to tell Hurstwood. She had no courage for that. Unless he went out of his own accord, she would have to invent some errand to get him out. That was something she had never done before. She had no time to think during the play that night, and the next day's thinking offered no suggestion. She began to think she would have to postpone her flight until a good opportunity presented itself. The weather came to her rescue.

It had been days since Hurstwood had done more than go to the grocery or to the newsstand. Now the weariness of indoors was upon him—had been for two days, but chill, gray weather had held him back. Friday broke fair and warm. It was one of those lovely harbingers of spring, given as a sign in dreary winter that earth is not forsaken of warmth and beauty. The blue heavens, holding their one golden orb, poured down a crystal wash of warm light. It was plain, from the voice of the sparrows, that all was halcyon outside. Carrie raised the front windows and felt the south wind blowing.

"It's lovely out today," she remarked.

"Is it?" said Hurstwood.

After breakfast he immediately got his other clothes.

"Will you be back for lunch?" asked Carrie, nervously.

"No," he said.

He went out into the streets and tramped north along Seventh Avenue, idly fixing upon the Harlem River as an objective point. He had seen some ships up there, the time he had called upon the brewers. He wondered how the territory thereabouts was growing.

Passing 59th he took the west side of Central Park, which he followed to 78th Street. There he remembered the neighborhood and turned over to look at the mass of buildings erected. It was very much improved. The great open spaces were filling up. Coming back, he kept to the park until 110th Street and then turned into Seventh Avenue again, reaching the pretty river by one o'clock.

There it ran winding before his gaze, shining brightly in the clear light between the undulating banks on the right and the tall, tree-covered heights on the left. The spring-like atmosphere waked him to a sense of its loveliness and for a few moments he stood looking at it, folding his hands behind his back. Then he turned and followed it toward the East Side, idly seeking the ships he had seen. It was four o'clock before the waning day, with its suggestion of a cooler evening, caused him to return. He was hungry and would enjoy eating in the warm room.

When he reached the flat by half-past five, it was still dark. He knew that Carrie was not there, not only because there was no light showing through the transom, but because the evening papers were stuck between the outside knob and the door frame. He opened with his key and went in. Everything was still dark. Lighting the gas he sat down, proposing to wait a little while. Even if Carrie did come now, dinner would be late. He read until six, then got up to fix something for himself.

As he did so, he noticed that the room seemed a little queer. What was it? He looked around, as if he missed something, and then saw an envelope right near where he had been sitting. It spoke for itself, almost without further action on his part.

Reaching over he took it, a sort of chill settling upon him even while he reached. The crackle of the envelope in his hands was loud. Green paper money lay soft within the note.

"Dear George," he read, crunching the money in one hand. "I am going away. I'm not coming back any more. It's no use trying to keep up the flat. I can't do it. I wouldn't mind helping you if I could, but I can't support us both and pay the rent. I need what little I make to pay for my clothes. I'm leaving twenty dollars. It's all I have just now. You can do whatever you like with the furniture. I won't want it. Carrie."

He dropped the note and looked quietly round. Now he knew what he missed. It was the little ornamental clock, which was hers. It had gone from the mantel-piece. He went into the front room—his bed-room, the parlor, lighting the gas as he went. From the chiffonier had gone the knick-knacks of silver and plate. From the table top, the lace coverings. He opened the wardrobe—no clothes of hers. He opened the drawers—nothing of hers. Her trunk was gone from its accustomed place. Back in his own room hung his old clothes, just as he had left them. Nothing else was gone.

He stopped in the parlor and waited for he knew not what. The silence grew oppressive. The little flat seemed wonderfully deserted. He wholly forgot that he was hungry, that it was only dinner-time. It seemed later in the night.

Suddenly he found that the money was still in his hands. There was twenty dollars in all, as she had said. Now he walked back, leaving the lights ablaze and feeling as if the flat were empty.

"I'll get out of this," he said to himself.

Then the sheer loneliness of his situation rushed upon him in full.

"Left me," he muttered and repeated, "left me."

The place that had been so comfortable, where he had spent so many days of warmth, was now a memory. Something colder and chillier confronted him. He sank down in his chair, resting his chin in his hand, mere sensation, without thought, holding him.

Then something like bereaved affection and self-pity swept over him.

"She needn't have gone away," he said. "I'd have got something." He sat a long while without rocking, and then added, quite clearly to himself—"I tried, didn't I?"

At midnight he was still rocking, staring at the floor.

CHAPTER XLVI.

When Hurstwood finally awoke from his reverie, it was with a dull feeling that he ought to go to bed. It was to nervous dreams that he returned. In the morning, sitting up in his bed, he looked gloomily about. The loneliness of the place was distasteful to him. If he had breakfast at all, he must cook it himself. He got up, dressed, and sat down, but there seemed nothing to stay for. The loneliness insisted that he should leave it.

The fact that he must accept the twenty dollars which Carrie had left was not agreeable, and yet he felt there was nothing else to do. He remembered that in the ad columns of the "World" he had seen the advertisements of men who buy out the furnishings of flats as they stand. That he would not be able to keep up this place he knew, and so he decided to sell it all out for what he could get. The first man who came to look at the place offered him forty dollars for all that was in it. The paltry offer made him mad. He had at least expected a hundred—

"Aw, come off," he said glumly. "I paid twenty dollars for that chiffonier."

"Vell," said the man, "I can't help id. I'm not puying of a department store. I haf got to make my profit."

"Well, you can't have it for forty dollars," said Hurstwood, and forthwith turned him out.

Then he made another pilgrimage to one of these merchant buyers. He was worse than the first.

"Tirty dollars," he said.

"I'd rather break it up for kindling," said Hurstwood.

"Vell, how much do you vant?" said the man.

"I'll take sixty or nothing."

His fancies about good prices were being rapidly modified.

Becoming cautious, he notified three such merchants to call.

The second one offered him the best terms he had yet received.

"Fifty dollars," he said.

Thoroughly discouraged by the indifference of these men, whom he considered vampires, he agreed.

It seemed a pitiful sum after all he had paid.

"All right," he said. "That stuff cost me two hundred dollars when it was new."

"Yes, but it is not new now," said the man.

"Well, it isn't damaged any," returned Hurstwood.

This bargain being struck, he waited gloomily for the furniture to be removed and the money paid.

It was the second morning after Carrie's flight before the man sent for the things and paid him the money. In the interim he sat in the flat waiting, gradually accommodating himself to the change. Out of things in the cupboard he prepared himself a little to eat—coffee, fried bacon, and the like, going once for a loaf of bread. Finally the man came and paid him as agreed.

Looking around on the two men who were preparing to pack things, Hurstwood decided not to stay and see the gloomy finish. He was afraid some of his creditors, seeing a moving van in front of the door, would come up and trouble him.

"Well, I guess you can get the things out without me," he observed to the buyer.

"Oh, yes, we won't be long about it," said the man.

Hurstwood put on his hat and went out. It was a trying moment. He felt as if he were being driven. The cold world held no place where he might go. He must now walk, he knew not where, ungreeted by a single friendly face.

At the corner he passed his Italian newsman.

The latter nodded genially, although Hurstwood owed him a dollar and a half which he would never get. He did not know this, however. Then the ex-manager turned his face toward the lower portion of the city. He knew where the cheap hotels were.

Installed in her comfortable room, Carrie wondered how Hurstwood had taken her departure. She arranged a few things hastily and then left for the theatre, half-expecting to encounter him at the door. Not finding him, her dread lifted and she felt more kindly toward him. She quite forgot him until she was about to come out after the show, when the chance of his being there frightened her. As day after day passed and she heard nothing at all, the thought of being bothered by him passed. In a little while she was, except for occasional thoughts, wholly free of the gloom with which her life had been weighted in the flat.

It is curious to note how quickly a profession absorbs one. Carrie became wise in theatrical lore, hearing the gossip of little Lola. She learned what the theatrical papers were, which ones published items about actresses and the like. She began to read the newspaper notices, not only of the opera in which she had so small a part, but of others. Gradually the desire for notice took hold of her. She longed to be renowned like others and read with avidity all the complimentary or critical comments made concerning others high in her profession. The showy world in which her interests lay completely absorbed her.

It was about this time that the newspapers and magazines were beginning to pay that illustrative attention to the beauties of the stage which has since become fervid. The newspapers and particularly the Sunday-newspapers indulged in large, decorative theatrical pages in which the faces and forms of well-known theatrical celebrities appeared, done about with artistic scrolls. The magazines also, or at least one or two of the newer ones, published occasional portraits of pretty stars, and now and again, photos of scenes from various plays. Carrie watched these with growing interest. When would a scene from her opera appear? When would some paper think her photo worth while?

The Sunday before taking her new part, she scanned the theatrical pages for some little notice. It would have accorded with her expectations if nothing had been said, but there in the squibs, tailing off several more substantial items, was a wee no-tice. Carrie read it with a tingling body.

> The part of Katisha, the country maid in "The Wives of Abdul" at the Broadway, heretofore played by Inez Carew, will be hereafter filled by Carrie Madenda, one of the cleverest members of the chorus.

Carrie hugged herself with delight. Oh, wasn't it just fine. At last! The first, the long-hoped-for, the delightful notice. And they called her clever. She could hardly restrain herself from laughing loudly. Had Lola seen it?

"They've got a notice here of the part I'm going to play tomorrow night," said Carrie, to her friend.

"Oh, jolly, have they?" cried Lola, running to her. "That's all right," she said, looking. "You'll get more now, if you do well. I had my picture in the 'World' once."

"Did you?" asked Carrie.

"Did I?—well, I should say," returned the little girl. "They had a frame around it."

Carrie laughed.

"They never published my picture."

"But they will," said Lola. "You'll see. You do better than most that get theirs in now."

Carrie felt deeply grateful for this. She almost loved Lola for the sympathy and praise she extended. It was so helpful to her—so almost necessary.

Fulfilling her part capably brought another notice in the papers that she was doing her work acceptably. This pleased her immensely. She began to think the world was taking note of her.

The first week she got her thirty-five dollars it seemed an enormous sum. Paying only three dollars for room-rent seemed ridiculous. After paying Lola her twenty-five she still had seven dollars left. With four left over from previous earnings, she had eleven. Five of this went to pay the regular installment on the clothes she had to buy. The next week she was even in greater feather. Now only three dollars need be paid for room rent, and five on her clothes. The rest she had for food and her own whims.

"You'd better save a little for this summer," cautioned Lola. "We'll probably close in May."

"I intend to," said Carrie.

The regular entrance of thirty-five dollars a week to one who has endured scant allowances for several years past is a demoralizing thing. Carrie found her purse bursting with good, green bills of comfortable denominations. Having no one dependant upon her, she began to buy pretty clothes and pleasing trinkets, to eat well and to ornament her room. Friends were not long in gathering about. She met a few young men who belonged to Lola's staff. The actors of the opera company made her acquaintance without the formality of introduction. One of these discovered a fancy for her. He was pleasant and she liked him for his genial good-nature, but there was nothing compelling about him.

On several occasions he strolled home with her.

"Let's stop in and have a rarebit," he suggested one midnight.

"Very well," said Carrie.

In the rosy restaurant filled with the merry lovers of late hours, she found herself criticizing this man. He was too stilted, too self-opinionated. He did not talk of anything which lifted her above the common run of clothes and material success. When it was all over, he smiled most graciously.

"Got to go straight home, have you?" he said.

"Yes," she answered with an air of quiet understanding.

"She's not so inexperienced as she looks," thought the lover, and thereafter his respect and ardor were increased.

She could not help sharing in Lola's love for a good time. There were days when they went carriage-riding, nights when after the show they dined, afternoons when they strolled along Broadway, tastefully dressed. She was getting in the metropolitan whirl of pleasure.

At last her picture appeared in one of the weeklies. She had not known of it, and it took her breath. "Miss Carrie Madenda," it was labeled. "One of the favorites of 'The Wives of Abdul' company." At Lola's advice she had had some pictures taken by Sarony. They had got one there. She thought of going down and buying a few copies of the paper, but remembered that there was no one she knew well enough to send them to. Only Lola, apparently, in all the world, was interested.

The metropolis is a cold place socially and Carrie soon found that a little money brought her nothing. The world of wealth and distinction was quite as far away as ever. She could feel that there was no warm, sympathetic friendship back of the easy merriment with which many approached her. All seemed to be seeking their own amusement, regardless of the possible sad consequence to others. So much for the lessons of Hurstwood and Drouet.

In April she learned that the opera would probably last until the middle or the end of May, according to the size of the audiences. Next season it would go on the road. She wondered if she would be with it. As usual Miss Osborne, owing to her moderate salary, was for securing a home engagement.

"They're putting on a summer play at the Casino," she announced, after figuratively putting her ear to the ground. "Let's try and get in that."

"I'm willing," said Carrie.

They tried in time and were apprised of the proper date to apply again. That was May 16th. Meanwhile, their own show closed May 5th.

"Those that want to go with the show next season," said the manager, "will have to sign this week."

"Don't you sign," advised Lola. "I wouldn't go."

"I know," said Carrie, "but maybe I can't get anything else."

"Well, I won't," said the little girl, who had a resource in her admirers. "I went once and I didn't have anything at the end of the season."

Carrie thought this over. She had never been on the road.

"We can get along," added Lola. "I always have."

Carrie did not sign.

The manager who was putting on the summer skit at the Casino had never heard of Carrie, but the several notices she had received, her published picture and the programme bearing her name had some little weight with him. He gave her a silent part at thirty dollars a week.

"Didn't I tell you?" said Lola. "It don't do you any good to go away from New York. They forget all about you if you do."

Now, because Carrie was pretty, the gentlemen who make up the advance illustrations of shows about to appear for the Sunday papers selected Carrie's photo along with others to illustrate the announcement. Because she was very pretty they gave it excellent space and drew scrolls about it. Carrie was delighted. Still the management did not seem to have seen anything of it. At least no more attention was paid to her than before. At the same time there seemed very little in her part.

It consisted of standing around in all sorts of scenes, a silent little Quakeress— The author of the skit had fancied that a great deal could be made of such a part, given to the right actress, but now, since it had been doled out to Carrie, he would as leave have had it cut out.

"Don't kick, old man," remarked the manager. "If it don't go the first week, we will cut it out."

Carrie had no warning of this halcyon intention. She practised her part ruefully, feeling that she was effectually shelved. At the dress rehearsal she was disconsolate.

"That isn't so bad," said the author, the manager noting the curious effect which Carrie's blues had upon the part. "Tell her to frown a little more when Sparks dances."

Carrie did not know it, but there was the least show of wrinkles between her eyes, and her mouth was almost puckered in sullenness.

"Frown a little more, Miss Madenda," said the stage-manager.

Carrie instantly brightened up, thinking he had meant it as a rebuke.

"No, frown," he said. "Frown as you did before."

Carrie looked at him in astonishment.

"I mean it," he said. "Frown hard, when Mr. Sparks dances. I want to see how it looks."

It was easy enough to do it. Carrie scowled. The effect was something so quaint and droll, it caught even the manager.

"That *is* good," he said. "If she'll do that all through, I think it will take."

Going over to Carrie, he said, "Suppose you try frowning all through. Do it hard. Look mad. It'll make the part really funny."

On the opening night it looked to Carrie as if there were nothing to her part, after all. The happy, sweltering audience did not seem to see her in the first act. She frowned and frowned, but to no effect. Eyes were riveted upon the more elaborate efforts of the stars.

In the second act, the crowd, wearied by a dull conversation, roved with its eyes about the stage and sighted her. There she was, gray-suited, sweet-faced, demure but scowling. At first the general idea was that she was temporarily irritated, that the look was genuine and not fun at all. As she went on frowning, looking now at one principal and now at the other, the audience began to smile. The portly gentlemen in the front rows began to feel that she was a delicious little morsel. It was the kind of frown they would have loved to force away with kisses. All the gentlemen yearned towards her. She was capital.

At last, the chief comedian, singing in the centre of the stage, noticed a giggle where it was not expected. Then another, and another. When the place came for loud applause, it was only moderate. What could be the trouble? He realized that something was up.

All at once, after an exit, he caught sight of Carrie. She was frowning alone on the stage and the audience was giggling and laughing.

"By George, I won't stand that," thought this thespian, thoroughly angered. "I'm not going to have my work cut up by some one else. Either she quits that when I do my turn or I quit."

"Why, that's all right," said the manager, when the kick came. "That's what she's supposed to do. You needn't pay attention to that."

"But she ruins my work."

"No she don't," returned the former soothingly. "It's only a little fun on the side."

"It is, eh?" exclaimed the big comedian. "She killed my hand all right. I'm not going to stand that."

"We'll wait until after the show. Wait until tomorrow. We'll see what we can do."

The next act, however, settled what was to be done. Carrie was the chief feature of the play. The audience, the more it studied her, the more it indicated its delight. Every other feature paled beside the quaint, teasing, delightful atmosphere which Carrie contributed while on the stage. Manager and company realized she had made a hit.

The critics of the daily papers completed her triumph. There were long notices in praise of the quality of the burlesque, touched with recurrent references to Carrie. The contagious mirth of the thing was repeatedly emphasized.

"Miss Madenda presents one of the most delightful bits of character work ever seen on the Casino stage," observed the sage critic of the "Sun." "It is a bit of quiet, unassuming drollery, which warms like good wine. Evidently the part was not intended to take precedence, as Miss Madenda is not often on the stage, but the audience, with the characteristic perversity of such bodies, selected for itself. The little Quakeress was marked for a favorite the moment she appeared, and thereafter easily held attention and applause. The vagaries of fortune are indeed curious."

The critic of the "Evening World," seeking as usual to establish a catch phrase, which should "go" with the town, wound up by advising, "If you wish to be merry, see Carrie's frown."

The result was miraculous so far as Carrie's fortune was concerned. Even during the morning she received a congratulatory message from the manager.

"You seem to have taken the town by storm," he wrote. "This is delightful. I am as glad for your sake as for my own."

The author also sent word.

That evening when she entered the theatre, the manager had a most pleasant greeting for her.

"Mr. Stevens," he said, referring to the author, "is preparing a little song which he would like you to sing next week."

"Oh, I can't sing," returned Carrie.

"It isn't anything difficult. It's something that is very simple—" he said, "and would suit you exactly."

"Of course, I wouldn't mind trying," said Carrie archly.

"Would you mind coming to the box office a few moments before you dress?" observed the manager in addition. "There's a little matter I want to speak to you about."

"Certainly," replied Carrie.

In that latter place the manager produced a paper.

"Now of course," he said, "we want to be fair with you in the matter of salary. Your contract here only calls for thirty dollars a week for the next three months. How would it do to make it, say, one hundred and fifty a week and extend it for twelve months?"

"Oh, very well," said Carrie, scarcely believing her ears.

"Supposing then you just sign this."

Carrie looked and beheld a new contract, made out as the other one, with the exception of the new figures of salary and time. With a hand trembling from excitement, she fixed her name.

"One hundred and fifty a week," she murmured when she was again alone. She found, after all, as what millionaire has not, that there was no realizing, in consciousness, the meaning of large sums. It was only a shimmering, glittering phrase, in which lay a world of possibilities.

Down in a third-rate Bleecker Street hotel, the brooding Hurstwood read the dramatic item covering Carrie's success, without at once realizing who was meant. Then suddenly it came to him, and he read the whole thing over again.

"That's her all right, I guess," he said.

Then he looked about upon a dingy, moth-eaten hotel lobby.

"I guess she's struck it," he thought, a picture of the old shiny, plush-covered world coming back, with its lights, its ornaments, its carriages and flowers. Ah, she was in the walled city now. Its splendid gates had opened, admitting her from a cold, dreary outside. She seemed a creature afar off—like every other celebrity he had known.

"Well, let her have it," he said. "I won't bother her."

It was the grim resolution of a bent, bedraggled but unbroken pride.

CHAPTER XLVII.

When Carrie got back on the stage she found that overnight her dressing room had been changed.

"You are to use this room, Miss Madenda," said one of the stage lackeys.

No longer any need of climbing several flights of steps to a small coop shared with another. Instead a comparatively large and commodious chamber, with conveniences not enjoyed by the small fry overhead. She breathed deeply and with delight. Her sensations were more physical than mental. In fact she was scarcely thinking at all. Heart and body were having their say.

Gradually the deference and congratulations gave her a mental appreciation of her state. She was no longer ordered but requested, and that politely. The other members of the cast looked at her enviously as she came out, arrayed in her simple habit which she wore all through the play. All those who had supposedly been her equals and superiors now smiled the smile of sociability, as much as to say, how friendly we have always been. Only the star comedian whose part had been so deeply injured stalked by himself. Figuratively he could not kiss the hand that smote him.

Doing her simple part, Carrie gradually realized the meaning of the applause which was for her, and it was sweet. She felt mildly guilty of something—perhaps unworthiness. When her associates addressed her in the wings, she only smiled weakly. The pride and daring of place was not for her. It never once crossed her mind to be reserved or haughty—to be other than she had been. After the performance she rode to her rooms with Lola, in a carriage provided.

Then came a week in which the first fruits of success were offered to her lips, bowl after bowl. It did not matter that her splendid salary had not begun. The world seemed satisfied with the promise. She began to get letters and cards. A Mr. Withers, whom she did not know from Adam, having learned by some hook or crook where she resided, bowed himself politely in.

"You will excuse me for intruding," he said, "but have you been thinking of changing your apartments?"

"I hadn't thought of it," returned Carrie.

"Well, I am connected with the Wellington—the new hotel on Seventh Avenue. You have probably seen notices of it in the papers."

Carrie recognized the name as standing for one of the newest and most imposing hostelries. She had heard it spoken of as having a splendid restaurant.

"Just so," went on Mr. Withers, accepting her acknowledgment of familiarity. "We have some very elegant suites of rooms at present which we would like to have you look at, if you have not made up your mind where you intend to reside for the summer. Our apartments are perfect in every detail—hot and cold water, private baths, special hall service for every floor, elevators and all that. You know what our restaurant is."

Carrie looked at him quietly. She was wondering whether he took her to be a millionaire.

"What are your rates?" she inquired.

"Well, now that is what I came to talk with you privately about. Our regular rates are anywhere from three to fifty dollars a day."

"Mercy," interrupted Carrie, "I couldn't pay any such rate as that."

"I know how you feel about it!" exclaimed Mr. Withers, halting. "But just let me explain. I said those are our regular rates. Like every other hotel we make special ones, however. Possibly you have not thought about it, but your name is worth something to us."

"Oh," ejaculated Carrie, seeing at a glance.

"Of course. Every hotel depends upon the repute of its patrons. A well-known actress, like yourself," and he bowed politely, while Carrie flushed, "draws attention to the hotel, and, although you may not believe it, patrons. Now we must have repute. It is what we live on. The common run of individuals will go where the celebrities are. Consequently we must have the celebrities. You can see that yourself."

"Oh, yes," returned Carrie vacantly, trying to arrange this curious proposition in her mind.

"Now," continued Mr. Withers, swaying his derby hat softly, and beating one of his polished shoes upon the floor, "I want to arrange, if possible, to have you come and stop at the Wellington. You need not trouble about terms. In fact we need hardly discuss them. Anything will do, for the summer—a mere figure—anything that you think you could afford to pay."

Carrie was about to interrupt but he gave her no chance.

"You can come today or tomorrow, the earlier the better, and we will give you your choice of nice, light, outside rooms, the very best we have. You need not occupy them this week if you do not wish to. That is a matter of your own choice. When you do come, we will see that you have every attention, and I am sure you will find everything to your taste. You know what the reputation of the house is already."

"You're very kind," said Carrie, touched by the agent's extreme affability. "I should like to come very much. I would want to pay what is right, however. I shouldn't want to—"

"You need not trouble about that at all," interrupted Mr. Withers. "We can arrange that to your entire satisfaction at any time. If three dollars a day is satisfactory to you, it will be so to us. All you have to do is to pay that sum to the clerk at the end of the week or month, just as you wish, and he will give you a receipt for what the rooms would cost if charged for at our regular rates."

The speaker paused.

"Suppose you come and look at the rooms," he added.

"I'd be glad to," said Carrie, "but I have a rehearsal this morning yet."

"I did not mean at once," he returned. "Any time will do. Would this afternoon be inconvenient?"

"Not at all," said Carrie.

Suddenly she remembered Lola, who was out at the time.

"I have a room-mate," she added, "who will have to go wherever I do. I forgot about that."

"Oh, very well," said Mr. Withers blandly. "It is for you to say whom you want with you. As I say, all that can be arranged to suit yourself."

He bowed and backed toward the door.

"At four, then, we may expect you."

"Yes," said Carrie.

"I will be there to show you," and so Mr. Withers withdrew.

After rehearsal Carrie informed Lola.

"Did they really!" exclaimed the latter, thinking of the Wellington as a group of managers. "Isn't that fine. Oh, jolly! It's so swell. That's where we dined, that night we went with those two Cushing boys. Don't you know?"

"I remember," said Carrie.

"Oh, it's as fine as it can be."

"We'd better be going up there," observed Carrie later in the afternoon.

The rooms which Mr. Withers displayed to Carrie and Lola were three and bath, a suite on the parlor floor. They were done in chocolate and dark red, with rugs and hangings to match. Three windows looked down into busy Broadway on the east, three into a side street, which crossed there. There were two lovely bedrooms, set with brass and white enamel beds, white ribbon-trimmed chairs, and chiffoniers to match. In the third room, or parlor, was a piano, a heavy piano lamp, with a shade of gorgeous pattern, a library table, several huge easy rockers, some dado book shelves, and a gilt curio case, filled with oddities. Pictures were upon the walls, soft turkish pillows upon the divan, foot stools of brown plush upon the floor.

"Oh, lovely!" exclaimed Lola, walking about.

"It is comfortable," said Carrie, who was lifting a lace curtain and looking down into crowded Broadway.

The bath was a handsome affair, done in white enamel, with a large, blue-bordered stone tub and nickel trimmings. It was bright and commodious, with a beveled mirror set in the wall at one end, and incandescent lights arranged in three places.

"Do you find these satisfactory?" observed Mr. Withers.

"Oh, very," answered Carrie.

"Well then, any time you find it convenient to move in, they are ready. The boy will bring you the keys at the door."

Carrie noted the elegantly carpeted and decorated hall, the marbled lobby, and showy waiting room. It was such a place as she had often dreamed of occupying.

"I guess we'd better move right away, don't you think?" she observed to Lola, thinking of the commonplace chamber in 17th Street.

"Oh, by all means," said the latter.

The next day her trunk left for the new abode.

Dressing, after the matinée on Wednesday, a knock came at her dressing-room door.

Carrie looked at the card handed by the boy and suffered a shock of surprise.

"Tell her I'll be right out," she said softly. Then looking at the card, added, "Mrs. Vance."

That merry soul had seen Carrie's picture in the paper only the Sunday before. Being slightly disguised by the Quaker costume and labeled "Madenda," she had not been at all sure, until today, when she visited the matinée to see.

"Why you little sinner!" she exclaimed as she saw Carrie coming toward her across the now vacant stage. "How in the world did this happen?"

Carrie laughed merrily. There was no trace of embarrassment in her friend's manner. You would have thought that the long separation had come about accidentally.

"I don't know," returned Carrie, warming in spite of her first troubled feelings toward this handsome, good-natured young matron.

"Well, you know I saw your picture in the Sunday paper, but your name threw me off. I thought it must be you or somebody that looked just like you, and I said, well now, I'll go right down there and see. I was never more surprised in my life. How are you, anyway?"

"Oh, very well," returned Carrie. "How have you been?"

"Fine. But aren't you a success. Dear, oh! All the papers talking about you. I should think you would be just too proud to breathe. I was almost afraid to come back here this afternoon."

"Oh, nonsense," said Carrie, blushing. "You know I'd be glad to see you."

"Well, anyhow, here you are. Can't you come up and take dinner with me now? Where are you stopping?"

"At the Wellington," said Carrie, who permitted herself a touch of pride in the acknowledgement.

"Oh, are you!" exclaimed the other, upon whom the name was not without its proper effect.

Tactfully Mrs. Vance avoided the subject of Hurstwood— of whom she could not help thinking. No doubt Carrie had left him. That much she surmised.

"Oh, I don't think I can," said Carrie, "tonight. I have so little time. I must be back here by seven-thirty. Won't you come dine with me?"

"I'd be delighted, but I can't tonight," said Mrs. Vance, studying Carrie's fine appearance. The latter's good fortune made her seem worthy and delightful in the other's eyes. "I promised faithfully to be home at six." Studying the small gold watch pinned to her bosom, she added, "I must be going too. Tell me when you're coming up, if at all."

"Why, any time you like," said Carrie.

"Well, tomorrow then. I'm living at the Chelsea now."

"Moved again?" exclaimed Carrie, laughing.

"Yes. You know I can't stay six months in one place. I just have to move."

It went on this way for fully ten minutes more, as fast as

tongues could talk, and at last Mrs. Vance departed, more taken with Carrie than ever.

"Remember now—half-past five."

"I won't forget," said Carrie, casting a glance at her as she went away. Then it came to her that she was as good as this woman now—perhaps better. Something in the other's solicitude and interest made her feel as if she were the one to condescend.

Now, as on each preceding day, letters were handed her by the doorman at the Casino. This was a feature which had rapidly developed since Monday. What they contained, she well knew. *Mash-notes* were old affairs in their mildest form. She remembered having received her first one far back in Columbia City. Since then, as a chorus girl, she had received others—gentlemen who prayed for an engagement. They were common sport between her and Lola, who received some also. They both frequently made light of them.

Now, however, they came thick and fast. Gentlemen with fortunes did not hesitate to note, as an addition to their own amiable collection of virtues, that they had their horses and carriage. Thus one:—

> I have a million in my own right. I could give you every luxury. There isn't anything you could ask for that you couldn't have. I say this not because I want to speak of my money, but because I love you and wish to gratify your every desire. It is love that prompts me to write. Will you not give me one half-hour in which to plead my cause?

Such of these letters as came while Carrie was still in the 17th Street place were read with more interest, though never delight, than those others which arrived after she was installed in her luxurious quarters in the Wellington. Even there, her vanity—or that self-appreciation, which in its more rabid form is called vanity, was not sufficiently cloyed to make these things wearisome. Adulation, being new in any form, pleased her. Only she was sufficiently wise to distinguish between her old condition and her new one. She had not had fame or money before. Now they had come. She had not had adulation and affectionate propositions before. Now they had come. Wherefore? She smiled to think that men should suddenly find her so much more attractive. In the least way it incited her to coolness and indifference.

"Do look here," she remarked to Lola. "See what this man says." Then she read parts of one of those effusive appeals of a sensual and desirous money-bags who was deeply smitten with her charms.

" 'If you will only deign to grant me one little half-hour,' " she repeated with an imitation of languor. "The idea. Aren't men silly."

"He must have lots of money, the way he talks," observed Lola.

"That's what they all say," said Carrie innocently.

"Why don't you see him," suggested Lola, "and hear what he's got to say?"

"Indeed I won't," said Carrie. "I know what he'd say. I don't want to meet anybody that way."

Lola looked at her with big, merry eyes.

"He couldn't hurt you," she returned. "You might have some fun with him."

Carrie shook her head.

"You're awfully queer," returned the little blue-eyed soldier.

Thus crowded fortune. For this whole week, though her large salary had not yet arrived, it was as if the world understood and trusted her. Without money—or the requisite sum at least, she enjoyed all the luxuries which money could buy. For her the doors of fine places seemed to open quite without the asking. These palatial chambers—how marvellously they came to her. The elegant apartments of Mrs. Vance in the Chelsea—these were hers. Men sent flowers, love notes, offers of fortune. And still her dreams ran riot. The one hundred and fifty! The one hundred and fifty! What a door to an Aladdin's cave it seemed to be. Each day, her head almost turned by developments, her fancies of what her future must be, with ample money, grew and multiplied. She conceived of delights which were not—saw lights of joy that never were on land or sea. Then, at last, after a world of anticipation, came her first installment of one hundred and fifty dollars.

It was paid to her in greenbacks—three twenties, six tens,

and six fives. Thus collected it made a very convenient roll. It was accompanied by a smile and a salutation from the cashier who paid it.

"Ah, yes," said the latter when she applied, "Miss Madenda—one hundred and fifty dollars. Quite a success the show seems to have made."

"Yes, indeed," returned Carrie.

Right after came one of the insignificant members of the company, and she heard the changed tone of address.

"How much?" said the same cashier sharply. One such as she had only recently been was waiting for her modest salary. It took her back to the few weeks in which she had collected, or rather had received, almost with the air of a donation, four-fifty per week from a lordly foreman in the shoe-factory: a man who in distributing the envelopes had the manner of a prince doling out favors to a servile group of petitioners. She knew that out in Chicago this very day, the same factory chamber was full of poor homely-clad girls working in long lines at clattering machines, that at noon they would eat a miserable lunch in a half-hour, that Saturday they would gather as they had when she was one of them and accept the small pay for work a hundred times harder than she was now doing. Oh, it was so easy now. The world was so rosy and bright. She felt so thrilled, that she must needs walk back to the hotel to think, wondering what she should do.

It does not take money long to make plain its impotence, providing the desires are in the realm of affection. With her one hundred and fifty in hand Carrie could think of nothing particularly to do. In itself, as a tangible, apparent thing which she could touch and look upon, it was a diverting thing for a few days, but this soon passed. Her hotel bill did not require its use. Her clothes had for some time been wholly satisfactory. Mash notes offered her more money. Another day or two and she would receive another hundred and fifty. It began to appear as if this were not so startlingly necessary, to maintain her present state. If she wanted to do anything better or move higher, she must have more—a great deal more.

Now a critic called to get up one of those tinsel interviews, which shine with clever observation, show up the wit of critics, display the folly of celebrities and divert the public. He liked

Carrie, and said so, publicly, adding however that she was merely pretty, good-natured and lucky. This cut like a knife. The "Herald," getting up an entertainment for the benefit of its free ice fund, did her the honor to beg her to appear, along with other celebrities, for nothing. She was visited by a young author who had a play which he thought she could produce. Alas, she could not judge. It hurt her to think it. Then she found she must put her money in her bank for safety, and, so moving, finally reached the place where it struck her that the door to life's perfect enjoyment was not open.

Gradually she began to think it was because it was summer. Nothing was going on much save such entertainments as the one in which she was a star. Fifth Avenue was boarded up where the rich had deserted their mansions. Madison Avenue was little better. Broadway was full of loafing thespians in search of next-season engagements. The whole city was quiet, and her nights were taken up with her work. Hence the feeling that there was little to do.

"I don't know," she said to Lola, one day, sitting at one of the windows which looked down into Broadway. "I get kinda lonely. Don't you?"

"No," said Lola, "not very often. You won't go anywhere. That's what's the matter with you."

"Where can I go?" asked Carrie.

"Why there's lots of places," returned Lola, who was thinking of her own lightsome tourneys with the gay youths. "You won't go with anybody."

"I don't want to go with these people who write to me. I know what kind they are."

"You oughtn't to be lonely," said Lola, thinking of Carrie's success. "There's lots would give their ears to be in your shoes."

Carrie looked out again at the passing crowd.

"I don't know," she said.

Unconsciously her idle hands were beginning to weary her.

CHAPTER XLVIII.

The gloomy Hurstwood, sitting in his cheap hotel where he had taken refuge, with seventy dollars between him and nothing, saw a hot summer out and a cool fall in, reading. He was not wholly indifferent to the fact that his money was slipping away. As fifty cents after fifty cents was paid out for a day's lodging, he became uneasy and finally took a cheaper room—thirty-five cents a day—to make his money last longer. Frequently he saw notices of Carrie. Her picture was in the "World" once or twice, and an old "Herald" he found in a chair informed him that she had recently appeared with some others at a benefit for something or other. He read these things with mingled feelings. Each one seemed to put her farther and farther away into a realm which became more imposing as it receded from him. On the bill-boards too, he saw a pretty poster, showing her as the Quaker maid, demure and dainty. More than once he stopped and looked at these, gazing at the pretty face in a sullen sort of way. His clothes were shabby, and he presented a marked contrast to all that she now seemed to be.

Somehow, so long as he knew she was at the Casino, though he had never an intention of going near her, there was sub-conscious comfort for him. He was not quite alone. The show seemed such a fixture that after a month or two he began to take it for granted that it was still running. In September it went on the road and he did not notice it. When all but twenty dollars of his money was gone, he moved to a fifteen-cent lodging house in the Bowery, where there was a bare lounging room filled with tables and benches, as well as some chairs.

Here his preference was to close his eyes and dream of other days, a habit which grew upon him. It was not sleep at first, but a mental harking back to scenes and incidents in his Chicago life. As the present became darker, the past grew brighter, and all that concerned it stood in relief.

He was unconscious of just how much this habit had gotten hold of him until one day he found his lips repeating an old answer he had made to one of his friends. They were in Hannah and Hogg's. It was as if he stood in the door of his elegant little office, comfortably dressed, talking to Sagar Morrison about the value of some South Chicago real estate in which the latter was about to invest.

"How would you like to come in on that with me?" he heard Morrison say.

"Not me," he answered, just as he had years before. "I've got my hands full now."

The movement of his lips aroused him. He wondered

whether he had really spoken. The next time he noticed any-thing of the sort, he really did talk.

"Why don't you jump, you bloody fool," he was saying—"jump."

It was a funny English story he was telling to a company of actors. Even as his voice recalled him, he was smiling. A crusty old codger, sitting nearby, seemed disturbed. At least he stared in a most pointed way. Hurstwood straightened up. The humor of the memory fled in an instant and he felt ashamed. For relief he left his chair and strolled out into the streets.

One day, looking down the ad columns of the "Evening World," he saw where a new play was at the Casino. Instantly he came to a mental halt. Carrie had gone. He remembered seeing a poster of her only yesterday, but no doubt it was one left uncovered by the new signs. Curiously, this fact shook him up. He had almost to admit that somehow he was depending upon her being in the city. Now she was gone. He wondered how this important fact had skipped him. Goodness knows when she would be back now. Impelled by a nervous fear, he rose and went into the dingy lavatory, where he counted his remaining money unseen. There was but ten dollars in all.

Sitting in the lodging-house room, it came down to his last fifty cents. He had saved and counted until his health was af-fected. His stoutness had gone. With it, even the semblance of a fit in his clothes. Now he decided he must do something, and walking about, saw another day go by, bringing him down to his last twenty cents—not enough to eat on for the morrow.

Summoning all his courage he crossed to Broadway and up to the Broadway Central. Within a block he halted, undecided. A big, heavy-faced porter was standing at one of the side-entrances looking out. Hurstwood proposed to appeal to him. Walking straight up, he was upon that individual before he could turn away.

"My friend," he said, recognizing even in his plight the man's inferiority, "is there anything about this hotel that I could get to do?"

The porter stared at him, the while he continued to talk.

"I'm out of work and out of money and I've got to get something—it doesn't matter what. I don't care to talk about what I've been, but if you'd tell me how to get something to do

I'd be much obliged to you. It wouldn't matter if it only lasted a few days just now. I've got to have something."

The porter still gazed, trying to look indifferent. Then seeing that Hurstwood was about to go on, he said:—

"I've got nothing to do with it. You'll have to ask inside."

Curiously this stirred Hurstwood to further effort.

"I thought you might tell me."

The fellow shook his head irritably.

Inside went the ex-manager, and straight to an office, off the clerk's desk. One of the managers of the hotel happened to be there. Hurstwood looked him straight in the eye.

"Could you give me something to do for a few days?" he said. "I'm in a position where I've got to get something at once."

The comfortable manager looked at him as much as to say, "Well, I should judge so."

"I came here," explained Hurstwood nervously, "because I've been a manager myself in my day. I've had bad luck in a way, but I'm not here to tell you that. I want something to do, if only for a week."

The man imagined he saw a feverish gleam in the applicant's eye.

"What hotel did you manage?" he inquired.

"It wasn't a hotel," said Hurstwood. "I was manager of Hannah and Hogg's place in Chicago for fifteen years."

"Is that so?" said the hotel man. "How did you come to get out of that?"

The figure of Hurstwood was rather surprising in contrast to the fact.

"Well, by foolishness of my own. It isn't anything to talk about now. You could find out if you wanted to. I'm broke now and if you will believe me, I haven't eaten anything today."

The hotel man was slightly interested in this story. He could hardly tell what to do with such a figure, and yet Hurstwood's earnestness made him wish to do something.

"Call Olsen," he said, turning to the clerk.

In reply to a bell, and a disappearing hall-boy, Olsen, the head porter, appeared.

"Olsen," said the hotel man, "is there anything down stairs you could find for this man to do? I'd like to give him something."

"I don't know, sir," said Olsen. "We have about all the help we need. I think I could find something, sir, though, if you like."

"Do. Take him to the kitchen and tell Wilson to give him something to eat."

"All right, sir," said Olsen.

Hurstwood followed. Out of the manager's sight, the head-porter's manner changed.

"I don't know what the devil there is to do," he observed.

Hurstwood said nothing. To him the big trunk-hustler was a subject for private contempt.

"You're to give this man something to eat," he observed to the cook.

The latter looked Hurstwood over, and seeing something keen and intellectual in his eyes, said:—

"Well, sit down over there."

Thus was Hurstwood installed in the Broadway Central. But not for long. He was in no shape or mood to do the scrub work that exists about the foundation of every hotel. Nothing better offering, he was set to aid the fireman, to work about the lavatory, and do anything and everything that might offer. Porters, cooks, clerks, all were over him. Moreover his appearance did not please these individuals—his temper was too lonely and they made it disagreeable for him.

With the stolidity and indifference of despair, however, he endured it all, sleeping in an attic at the roof of the house, eating what the cook gave him, accepting a few dollars a week, which he tried to save. His constitution was in no shape to endure. One day the following February he was sent on an errand to a large coal company's office. It had been snowing and thawing, and the streets were sloppy. He soaked his shoes in his progress and came back feeling dull and weary. All the next day he felt unusually depressed and sat about as much as possible, to the irritation of those who admired energy in others.

In the afternoon some boxes were to be moved to make room for new culinary supplies. He was ordered to handle a truck. Encountering a big box, he could not lift it.

"What's the matter there?" said the head-porter. "Can't you handle it?"

He was straining hard to lift it, but now he quit.

"No," he said weakly.

The man looked at him and saw that he was deathly pale.

"Not sick are you?" he asked.

"I think I am," returned Hurstwood.

"Well, you better go sit down then."

This he did, but soon grew rapidly worse. It seemed all he could do to crawl to his room, where he remained for a day.

"That man Wheeler's sick," reported one of the lackeys, to the night-clerk.

"What's the matter with him?"

"I don't know. He's got a high fever."

The hotel physician looked at him.

"Better send him to Bellevue," he recommended. "He's got pneumonia."

Accordingly he was carted away.

In three weeks the worst was over, but it was nearly the first of May before his strength permitted him to be turned out. Then he was discharged.

No more weak-looking object ever strolled out into the spring sunshine than the once hale, lusty manager. All his old corpulency had fled. His face was thin and pale, his hands white, his body flabby. Clothes and all, he weighed but one hundred and thirty-five pounds. Some old garments had been given him—a cheap brown coat, and a misfit pair of trousers. Also some change and advice. He was told to apply to the charities.

Again he resorted to a Bowery lodging house, brooding over where to look. From this it was but a short step to beggary.

"What can a man do?" he said. "I can't starve."

His first application was in sunny Second Avenue. A well-dressed man came leisurely strolling toward him out of Stuyvesant Park. Hurstwood nerved himself and sidled near.

"Would you mind giving me ten cents?" he said directly. "I'm in a position where I must ask someone."

The man scarcely looked at him, but fished in his vest pocket and took out a dime.

"There you are," he said.

"Much obliged," said Hurstwood, softly, but the other paid no more attention to him.

Satisfied with his success, and yet ashamed of his situation, he decided that he would only ask for twenty-five cents more since that would be sufficient. He strolled about, sizing up people, but it was long before just the right face and situation arrived. Then, when he asked, he was refused. Shocked by this result he took an hour to recover, and then asked again. This time a nickel was given him. By the most watchful effort he did get twenty cents more, but under circumstances which were painful.

The next day he resorted to the same effort, experiencing a variety of rebuffs and one or two generous receptions. At last it crossed his mind that there was a science of faces, and that a man could pick the liberal countenance if he tried.

It was no pleasure to him, however, this stopping of passers-by. He saw one man taken up for it and now troubled lest he should be arrested. Nevertheless he went on, vaguely anticipating that indefinite something which is always better.

It was with a sense of satisfaction, then, that he saw announced one morning the return of the Casino company, "with Miss Carrie Madenda." He had thought of her often enough in days past. How successful she was—how much money she must have. Even now, however, it took a severe run of ill-luck to decide him to appeal to her. He was truly hungry before he said:—"I'll ask her. She won't refuse me a few dollars."

Accordingly he headed for the Casino one afternoon, passing it several times in an effort to locate the stage entrance. Then he sat in Bryant Park, a block away, waiting.

"She can't refuse to help me a little," he kept saying to himself.

Beginning with half-past six he hovered like a shadow about the 39th Street entrance, pretending always to be a hurrying pedestrian, and yet fearful lest he should miss his object. He was slightly nervous, too, now that the eventful hour had arrived; but being weak and hungry, his ability to suffer keenly was modified. At last he saw that the actors were beginning to arrive, and his nervous tension increased until it seemed as if he could not stand it.

Once he thought he saw Carrie coming and moved forward, only to see that he was mistaken.

"She can't be long now," he said to himself, half-fearing to encounter her and equally depressed at the thought that she might have gone in by another way. His stomach was so empty that it ached.

Individual after individual passed him, nearly all well-dressed—almost all indifferent. He saw coaches rolling by, gentlemen passing with ladies—the evening's merriment was beginning in this region of theatres and hotels.

Suddenly a coach rolled up and the driver jumped down to open the door. Before Hurstwood could act, two ladies flounced across the broad walk and disappeared in the stage door. He thought he saw Carrie, but it was so unexpected, so elegant and far away, he could hardly tell. He waited awhile longer, growing feverish with want, and then seeing that the stage door no longer opened, and that a merry audience was arriving, he concluded it must have been Carrie and turned away.

"Lord," he said, hastening out the street into which the more fortunate were pouring, "I've got to get something."

At that hour when Broadway is wont to assume its most interesting aspect, a peculiar individual did in those days invariably take his stand at the corner of 26th Street and Broadway,—a spot which is also intersected by Fifth Avenue. This was the hour when the theatres were just beginning to receive their patrons. Fire signs announcing the night's amusements blazed on every hand. Cabs and carriages, their lamps gleaming like yellow eyes, pattered by. Couples and parties of three and four freely mingled in the common crowd which poured by in a thick stream, laughing and jesting. On Fifth Avenue were loungers—a few wealthy strollers; a gentleman in evening dress with his lady on his arm; some clubmen, passing from one smoking room to another. Across the way the great hotels (the Hoffmann House and the Fifth Avenue) showed a hundred gleaming windows, their cafés and billiard rooms filled with a comfortable, well-dressed, and pleasure-loving throng. All about was the night, pulsating with the thoughts of pleasure and exhilaration, the curious enthusiasm of a great city bent upon finding joy in a thousand different ways.

This individual was no less than an ex-soldier turned religionist, who, having suffered the whips and privations of our peculiar social system, had concluded that his duty to the God which he conceived lay in aiding his fellow-man. The form of aid which he chose to administer was entirely original with him-self. It consisted of securing a bed for all such homeless way-farers as should apply to him at this particular spot, though he had scarcely the wherewithal to provide a comfortable habita-tion for himself.

Taking his place amid this lightsome atmosphere, he would stand, his stocky figure cloaked in a great cape overcoat, his head protected by a broad slouch hat, awaiting the applicants who had in various ways learned the nature of his charity. For awhile he would stand alone, gazing like any idler upon an ever-fascinating scene. On the evening in question, a policeman, passing, saluted him as "Captain" in a friendly way. An urchin, who had frequently seen him there before, stopped to gaze. All others took him for nothing out of the ordinary save in the matter of dress, and conceived of him as a stranger whistling and idling for his own amusement.

As the first half-hour waned, certain characters appeared. Here and there in the passing crowd one might see, now and then, a loiterer, edging interestedly near. A slouchy figure crossed the opposite corner and glanced furtively in his direc-tion. Another came down Fifth Avenue to the corner of 26th, took a general survey and hobbled off again. Two or three no-ticeable Bowery types edged along the Fifth Avenue side of Madison Square but did not venture over. The soldier in his cape overcoat walked a short line of ten feet at his corner, to and fro, indifferently whistling.

As nine o'clock approached, some of the hubbub of the earlier hour passed. On Broadway the crowd was neither so thick nor so gay. Fewer cabs were passing. The atmosphere of the hotels was not so youthful. The air, too, colder. On every hand curious figures were moving, watchers and peepers, without an imaginary circle which they seemed afraid to enter—a dozen in all. Presently, with the arrival of a keener sense of cold, one figure came forward. It crossed Broadway from out the shadow of 26th Street and in a halting, circuitous way arrived close to the waiting figure. There was something shamefaced or diffident about the movement, as if the intention were to conceal any idea of stopping until the very last moment. Then suddenly, close to the soldier, came the halt.

The Captain looked in recognition, but there was no especial greeting. The newcomer nodded slightly and murmured something, like one who waits for gifts. The other simply motioned toward the edge of the walk.

"Stand over there," he said.

By this the spell was broken. Even while the soldier resumed his short, solemn walk, other figures shuffled forward. They did not so much as greet the leader but joined the one, sniffling and hitching and scraping their feet.

"Cold, ain't it?"

"I'm glad winter's over."

"Looks as though it might rain."

The motley company had increased to ten. One or two knew each other and conversed. Others stood off a few feet, not wishing to be in the crowd and yet not counted out. They were peevish, crusty, silent, eyeing nothing in particular and moving their feet.

There would have been talking soon but the soldier gave them no chance. Counting sufficient to begin, he came forward.

"Beds, eh, all of you?"

There was a general shuffle and murmur of approval.

"Well, line up, here. I'll see what I can do. I haven't a cent myself."

They fell into a sort of broken, ragged line. One might see now some of the chief characteristics by contrast. There was a wooden leg in the line. Hats were all drooping, a collection that would ill become a second-hand Hester Street basement collection. Trousers were all warped and frayed at the bottom and coats worn and faded. In the glare of the store lights, some of the faces looked dry and chalky. Others were red with blotches, and puffed in the cheeks and under the eyes. One or two were raw-boned and reminded one of railroad hands. A few spectators came near, drawn by the seemingly conferring group, then more and more and quickly there was a pushing, gaping crowd. Some one in the line began to talk.

"Silence!" exclaimed the Captain. "Now then, gentlemen, these men are without beds. They have got to have some place to sleep tonight. They can't lie out in the streets. I need twelve cents to put one to bed. Who will give it to me?"

No reply.

"Well, we'll have to wait here, boys, until some one does. Twelve cents isn't so very much for one man."

"Here's fifteen!" exclaimed a young man, peering forward with strained eyes. "It's all I can afford."

"All right, now I have fifteen. Step out of the line," and seizing one by the shoulder, the Captain marched him off a little way and stood him up alone.

Coming back, he resumed his place and began again.

"I have three cents left. These men must be put to bed somehow. There are," counting, "one, two, three, four, five, six, seven, eight, nine, ten, eleven, twelve men. Nine cents more will put the next man to bed,—give him a good, comfortable bed for the night. I go right along and look after that myself. Who will give me nine cents?"

One of the watchers, this time a middle-aged man, handed in a five-cent piece.

"Now I have eight cents. Four more will give this man a bed. Come, gentlemen. We are going very slow this evening. You all have good beds. How about these?"

"Here you are," remarked a bystander, putting coins into his hand.

"That," said the Captain, looking at the coins, "pays for two beds for two men and gives me five on the next one. Who will give me seven cents more?"

"I will," said a voice.

Coming down Sixth Avenue this evening, Hurstwood chanced to cross east through 26th Street toward Third Avenue. He was wholly disconsolate in spirit, hungry to what he deemed an almost mortal extent, weary and defeated. How should he get at Carrie now? It would be eleven before the show was over. If she came in a coach, she would go away in one. He would need to interrupt under most trying circumstances. Worst of all, he was hungry and weary, and at best a whole day must intervene for he had not heart to try again tonight. He had no food and no bed.

When he neared Broadway, he noticed the Captain's gathering of wanderers, but thinking it to be the result of a street preacher, or some patent-medicine faker, he was about to pass on. However, in crossing toward Madison Square Park, he noticed the line of men whose beds were already secured, stretching out from the main body of the crowd. In the glare of the neighboring electric light, he recognized a type—his own kind, the figures whom he saw about the streets and in the lodging houses, drifting in mind and body like himself. He wondered what it could be and turned back.

There was the Captain, curtly pleading as before. He heard with astonishment, and a sense of relief, the oft-repeated words, "These men must have a bed." Before him was the line of unfortunates whose beds were yet to be had, and, seeing a newcomer quietly edge up and take a position at the end of the line, he decided to do likewise. What use to contend? He was weary tonight. It was a simple way out of one difficulty at least. Tomorrow, maybe—he would do better.

Back of him, where some of those were whose beds were safe, a relaxed air was apparent. The strain of uncertainty being removed, he heard them talking with moderate freedom and some leaning towards sociability. Politics, religion, the state of the government, some newspaper sensations and the more notorious facts the world over found mouth-pieces and auditors there. Cracked and husky voices pronounced forcibly upon odd matters. Vague and rambling observations were made in reply. There were squints and leers and some dull, ox-like stares, from those who were too dull or too weary to converse.

Standing tells. Hurstwood became more weary waiting. He thought he should drop soon, and shifted restlessly from one foot to the other. At last his turn came. The man ahead had been paid for and gone to the blessed line of success. He was now first, and already the Captain was talking for him.

"Twelve cents, gentlemen—twelve cents puts this man to bed. He wouldn't stand here in the cold if he had any place to go."

Hurstwood swallowed something that rose to his throat. Hunger and weakness had made a coward of him.

"Here you are," said a stranger, handing money to the Captain.

Now the latter put a kindly hand on the ex-manager's shoulder.

"Line up over here," he said.

Once there, Hurstwood breathed easier. He felt as if the

world were not quite so bad with such a good man in it. Others seemed to feel like himself about this.

"Captain's a great feller, ain't he?" said the man ahead, a little, woe-begone, helpless-looking sort of individual, who looked as though he had ever been the sport and care of fortune.

"Yes," said Hurstwood indifferently.

"Huh! there's a lot back there yet," said a man farther up, leaning out and looking back at the applicants for whom the Captain was pleading.

"Yes. Must be over a hundred tonight," said another.

"Look at the guy in the cab," observed a third.

A cab had stopped. Some gentleman in evening dress reached out a bill to the Captain who took it with a simple thanks and turned away to his line. There was a general craning of necks as the jewel in the broad white shirt front sparkled and the cab moved off. Even the crowd gaped in awe.

"That fixes up nine men for the night," said the Captain, counting out as many of the line near him. "Line up over there. Now then, there are only seven. I need twelve cents."

Money came slowly. In the course of time the crowd thinned out to a meagre handful. Fifth Avenue, save for an occasional cab, passenger or pedestrian, was bare. Broadway was thinly peopled with pedestrians. Only now and then a stranger, passing, noticed the small group, handed out a coin and went away, unheeding.

The Captain remained stolid and determined. He talked on, very slowly uttering the fewest words, and with a certain assurance as though he could not fail.

"Come. I can't stay out here all night. These men are getting tired and cold. Some one give me four cents."

There came a time when he said nothing at all. Money was handed him and for each twelve cents he singled out a man and put him in the other line. Then he walked up and down as before, looking at the ground.

The theatres let out. Fire signs disappeared. A clock struck eleven. Another half-hour and he was down to the last two men.

"Come now!" he exclaimed to several curious observers. "Eighteen cents will fix us all up for the night. Eighteen cents.

I have six. Somebody give me the money. Remember, I have to go way over to Brooklyn yet tonight. Before that I have got to take these men down and put them to bed. Eighteen cents!"

No one responded. He walked to and fro, looking down for several minutes, occasionally saying, softly, "Eighteen cents." It seemed as if this paltry sum would delay the desired culmination longer than all the rest had. Hurstwood, buoyed up slightly by the long line, of which he was a part, refrained with an effort from groaning, he was so weak.

At last a lady in opera cape and rustling skirts came down Fifth Avenue, supported by her escort. Hurstwood gazed wearily, reminded by her both of Carrie, in her new world, and of the time when he had escorted his own wife in like manner.

While he was gazing she turned and, looking at the remarkable company, sent her escort over. He came, holding a bill in his fingers, all elegant and graceful.

"Here you are," he said.

"Thanks," said the Captain, turning to the two remaining applicants. "Now we have some for tomorrow night," he added.

Therewith, he lined the last two and proceeded to the head, counting as he went.

"One hundred and thirty-seven," he announced. "Now, boys, line up. Right dress there. We won't be much longer about this. Steady now."

He placed himself at the head and called out "Forward." With the line Hurstwood moved. Across Fifth Avenue, through Madison Square, by the winding paths, east on 23rd Street and down Third Avenue wound the long serpentine company. Midnight pedestrians and loiterers stopped and stared as the company passed. Chatting policemen, at various corners, stared indifferently or nodded to the leader, whom they had seen before. In Third Avenue they marched a seemingly weary way to 8th Street, where was a lodging house, closed apparently for the night. They were expected, however.

Outside in the gloom they stood, while the leader parleyed within. Then doors swung open and they were invited in with a "Steady now."

Some one was at the head, showing rooms, so that there was no delay for keys. Toiling up the creaky stairs, Hurstwood looked back and saw the Captain watching, the last one of the line being included in his broad solicitude. Then he gathered his cloak about him and strolled out into the night.

"I can't stand much of this," said Hurstwood, whose legs ached him painfully as he sat down upon the miserable bunk in the small, lightless chamber allotted him. "I got to eat or I'll die."

CHAPTER XLIX.

Playing in New York, one evening, on this her return, Carrie was putting the finishing touches to her toilet, before leaving for the night, when a commotion near the stage door caught her ear. It included a familiar voice.

"Never mind now. I want to see Miss Madenda."

"You'll have to send in your card."

"Oh come off. Here—"

A half-dollar was passed over, and now a knock came at her dressing-room door.

Carrie opened it.

"Well, well," said Drouet. "I do swear. Why how are you? I knew that was you, the moment I saw you."

Carrie fell back a pace, expecting a most embarrassing conversation.

"Aren't you going to shake hands with me? Well, you're a dandy. That's all right, shake hands."

Carrie put out her hand, smiling if for nothing more than the man's exuberant good nature. Though older, he was but slightly changed. The same fine clothes; the same stocky body; the same rosy countenance.

"That fellow at the door there didn't want to let me in, until I paid him. I knew it was you all right. Say, you've got a great show. You do your part fine. I knew you would. I just happened to be passing tonight and thought I'd drop in a few minutes. I saw your name on the programme, but I didn't remember it until you came on the stage. Then it struck me all at once. Say, you could have knocked me down with a feather. That's the same name you used out there in Chicago, isn't it."

"Yes," answered Carrie mildly, overwhelmed by the man's assurance.

"I knew it was, the moment I saw you. Well, how have you been, anyhow?"

"Oh, very well," said Carrie, lingering in her dressing-room. She was rather dazed by the assault. "How have you been?"

"Me? Oh, fine. I'm here now."

"Is that so?" said Carrie.

"Yes, I've been here for six months. I've got charge of a branch here."

"How nice!"

"Well, when did you go on the stage, anyhow?" inquired Drouet.

"About three years ago," said Carrie.

"You don't say so! Well, sir, this is the first I've heard of it. I knew you would, though. I always said you could act—didn't I?"

Carrie smiled.

"Yes, you did," she said.

It was very evident by now that the past did not make any difference to him. He was for ignoring it, if so be, or, at least, attaching no importance to it. The old affection, such as it was, did not seem to generate complaint. His attitude was such as would indicate his desire to retain her good favor—regardless.

"Well, you do look great," he said. "I never saw anybody improve so. You're taller, aren't you?"

"Me? Oh, a little, maybe."

He gazed at her dress, then at her hair, where a becoming hat was set jauntily, then into her eyes, which she took all occasion to avert. Evidently he expected to restore their old friendship at once and without modification.

It was her feeling, however, that it could not be. She understood him better now—understood the type. He was not anyone whom she could admire, or even associate with pleasantly. The world had taught her so much. She wondered that he did not appreciate the change.

"Well," he said, seeing her gather up her purse, handkerchief, and the like, preparatory to departing, "I want you to come out to dinner with me, won't you? I've got a friend out here—"

"Oh, I can't," said Carrie. "Not tonight. I have an early engagement tomorrow."

"Ah, let the engagement go. Come on. I can get rid of him. I want to have a good talk with you."

"No, no," said Carrie. "I can't. You mustn't ask me any more. I don't care for a late dinner."

"Well, come on and have a talk then, anyhow."

"Not tonight," she said, shaking her head. "We'll have a talk some other time."

As a result of this she noticed a shade of thought pass over his face, as if he were beginning to realize that things were changed. Good nature dictated something better than this for one who had always liked her.

"You come around to the hotel tomorrow," she said as a sort of penance for error. "You can take dinner with me."

"All right," said Drouet, brightening. "Where are you stopping?"

"At the Waldorf," she answered, mentioning the fashionable hostelry, then but newly erected.

"What time?"

"Well, come at three," said Carrie pleasantly.

The next day Drouet called, but it was with no especial delight that Carrie remembered her appointment. However, seeing him, handsome as ever, after his kind, and most genially disposed, her doubts as to whether the dinner would be disagreeable or not were swept away. He talked as volubly as ever.

"They put on a lot of lugs here, don't they?" was the first thing he said, as she came into the parlor where he was waiting.

"Yes, they do," said Carrie.

Genial egotist that he was, he went right off into a detailed account of his own career.

"I'm going to have a business of my own pretty soon," he observed in one place. "I can get backing now for two hundred thousand dollars."

Carrie listened most good-naturedly.

"Say," he said, when they had got far along into events and interests, "where is Hurstwood now?"

Carrie flushed a little.

"He's here in New York, I guess," she said. "I haven't seen him for some time."

Drouet mused a moment. He had not been sure until now that the ex-manager was not an influential figure in the background. He imagined not, but this assurance relieved him. It must be that Carrie had got rid of him, as well she ought, he thought.

"A man always makes a mistake, I think, when he does anything like that," he observed.

"Like what?" said Carrie, unwitting of what was coming.

"Oh, you know," and Drouet waved her intelligence, as it were, with his hand.

"No, I don't," she answered. "What do you mean?"

"Why that affair in Chicago, the time he left."

"I don't know what you are talking about," said Carrie, whose suspicions were now, however, fully aroused.

"Oho!" said Drouet, incredulous. "You knew he took ten thousand dollars with him when he left, didn't you?"

"What?" said Carrie. "You don't mean to say he stole money, do you?"

"Why," said Drouet, puzzled at her tone, "you knew that, didn't you?"

"Why, no," said Carrie, "of course I didn't."

"Well, that's funny," said Drouet. "He did, you know. It was in all the papers."

"How much did you say he took?" said Carrie.

"Ten thousand dollars. I heard he sent most of it back afterward, though."

Carrie looked vacantly at the richly carpeted floor. A new light was shining upon all the years since her enforced flight. She remembered now a hundred things that indicated as much. She also imagined that he took it on her account. Instead of hatred springing up, there was a kind of sorrow generated. Poor fellow—what a thing to have had hanging over his head all the time.

At dinner Drouet warmed up by eating and drinking, and, softened in mood, fancied he was winning Carrie to her old-time, good-natured regard for him. He began to imagine it would not be so difficult to enter into her life again, high as she was. Ah, what a prize, he thought. How beautiful, how elegant, how famous. In her theatrical and Waldorf setting, Carrie was, to him, the all-desirable.

"Do you remember how nervous you were that night at the Avery?" he asked.

Carrie smiled to think of it.

"I never saw anybody do better than you did then. Ah," he added ruefully, as he leaned an elbow on the table, "I thought you and I were going to get along fine those days."

Carrie saw the drift, and tried to change the subject. This sort of thing from Drouet today sounded mawkish and silly. Anyhow, Hurstwood was uppermost in her mind just at present, flashed upon, as he was, by information so newly imported.

"I don't suppose you care for anybody any more much, do you?" he said crudely, not to be dragged away from his idea.

"You mustn't talk that way," said Carrie, bringing in the least trace of coldness.

"Won't you let me tell you—"

"No," she answered, rising. "Besides, it's time I was getting ready for the theatre. I'll have to leave you. Come now."

"Oh, stay a minute," pleaded Drouet. "You've got plenty of time."

"No," said Carrie, gently.

Reluctantly Drouet gave up the bright table and followed. He saw her to the elevator and standing there said:—

"When do I see you again?"

"Oh, sometime, possibly," said Carrie. "I'll be here all summer. Good night."

The elevator door was open.

"Good night," said Drouet, as she rustled in.

Then he strolled sadly down the hall, all his old longing revived, because she was now so far off. The merry frou-frou of the place spoke all of her. He began to think that he was hardly dealt with. Carrie, however, had other thoughts.

That night it was that she passed Hurstwood, waiting at the Casino, without observing him.

"Did you see that miserable-looking man out there as we came in?" asked Lola, on the stage.

"No," said Carrie.

"He was awful hungry-looking. He stared at us the funniest."

"It's too bad, isn't it," said Carrie.

The next night, walking to the theatre, she encountered

Hurstwood face to face. He was waiting, more gaunt than ever, determined to see her if he had to send in word. At first she did not recognize the shabby, baggy figure. He frightened her, edging so close, a seemingly hungry stranger.

"Carrie," he half-whispered, "can I have a few words with you."

She turned and recognized him on the instant. If there ever had lurked any feeling in her heart against him, it deserted her now. Still she remembered what Drouet had said about his having stolen the money.

"Why George," she said, "what's the matter with you?"

"I've been sick," he answered. "I just got out of the hospital. For God's sake let me have a little money, will you?"

"Of course," said Carrie, her lip trembling in a strong effort to maintain her composure. "But what's the matter with you, anyhow?"

She was opening her purse and now pulled out all and the only bills in it—a five and two twos.

"I've been sick, I told you," he said, peevishly, almost resenting her excessive pity. It came hard to him to receive it from such a source.

"Here," she said. "It's all I've got with me."

"All right," he answered softly. "I'll give it back to you some day."

Carrie looked at him, while pedestrians stared at her. She felt the strain of publicity. So did Hurstwood.

"Why don't you tell me what's the matter with you?" she asked, hardly knowing what to do. "Where are you living?"

"Oh, I've got a room down in the Bowery," he answered. "There's no use trying to tell you here. I'm all right now."

He seemed in a way to resent her kindly inquiries—so much better had fate dealt with her.

"Better go on in," he said. "I'm much obliged, but I won't bother you any more."

She tried to answer but he turned away and shuffled off toward the east.

For days this apparition was a drag on her soul before it began to wear partially away. Drouet called again but now he was not even seen by her. His attentions seemed out of place.

"I'm out," was her reply to the boy.

So peculiar indeed was her lonely, self-withdrawing temper, that she was becoming an interesting figure in the public eye. She was so quiet and reserved.

Mrs. Vance was not to be kept away, however. Our lovely matron was more or less of a permanent factor in Carrie's life, coming always and sharing in her feelings.

"Do you know," she said one day, "Cousin Bob is making quite a strike out west. You remember Cousin Bob, don't you?"

"Of course," said Carrie, turning eyes that showed that they could lighten clearly. "What has he done?"

"Oh, he has invented something or other—I forget what. It's a new kind of light, though."

"You don't say so," said Carrie, evincing clear interest. "I always thought he would do something."

"So did we," said Mrs. Vance. "He's just as bright as he can be. He wants to open up a laboratory here in New York soon."

"Is that so?" said Carrie. She paused awhile, thinking. "Do you think he will?"

"Yes, indeed," answered Mrs. Vance, who had already got off onto something else in thought. "Bill and he are corresponding about it. He knows some electrical people here."

This was much to Carrie, in spite of herself. Reason had little to do with it.

Not long after, the management decided to transfer the show to London. A second summer season did not seem to promise well here.

"How would you like to try subduing London?" asked her manager one afternoon.

"It might just be the other way," said Carrie.

"I think we'll go in June," he answered.

Carrie almost forgot Hurstwood in arranging and executing this important departure. Both he and Drouet were left to discover that she was gone. The latter tried to console himself, after it was all over, by saying, "She isn't so much," but in his heart of hearts he did not believe this. Hurstwood shifted by curious means through a long summer and fall, by the aid of a small job he secured as a sort of a janitor of a dance hall, by begging and by resorting to those peculiar charities, several of which, in the press of hungry search, he accidentally stumbled upon. Toward the dead of winter Carrie came back in a new play, but he was not aware of it. Mrs. Vance was.

"You must come to dinner with us tomorrow night now," she said, after a long welcoming conversation, in which everything else was canvassed. "We'll have it early."

"That's the trouble," said Carrie. "You're awfully kind. I wish I didn't have to be at the theatre so early."

"Oh, that's all right," said Mrs. Vance. "Now you come."

She was quite out of the door, ready to finally depart, when she said suddenly:—

"Oh, I forgot to tell you. Bob's here, you know."

"Is that so?" said Carrie.

"Yes. He has a laboratory down in Wooster Street. He'll be there, too."

"I saw an article in one of the papers on his lamp," she said, remembering the keen interest an illustrated special in one of the New York papers, which reached her in London, had had for her.

"Oh yes, he's getting quite famous now," said Mrs. Vance. "He's doing fine."

"Isn't that nice," said Carrie.

For this dinner she arrayed herself with particular care, adding by almost unconscious touches to her demure type of beauty. Those little effects which the critics had noted concerning her as the Quaker maid she now duplicated. Work in the dressing room had taught her the value of a touch of cosmetics, the point for a jewel, the loveliness of a rose rightly placed. When her coach came, she was all that her type of beauty would allow.

"You look so sweet," said Lola, who was now more maid than actress, so essential and superior had Carrie become to her.

For answer Carrie showed her white teeth in a radiant smile. It did her good to be told so tonight.

Mrs. Vance welcomed her. "Of course you remember Bob, don't you?" she said, leading Carrie in from the foyer of their suite of rooms.

Ames was standing, well-formed and clean. He had donned a dress suit for the occasion, and now the white shirt front made the line of his face seem brown and strong.

"Why, how do you do?" said Carrie, giving him a merry smile.

"Very well," he said. "I needn't ask how you've been. I've been reading about you."

"Oh, have you?" said Carrie. "Well, I know what you've been doing. I read it all while I was in London."

"Yes, I know," said Ames. "I didn't want that published. It wasn't—"

"There you go again, Bob," put in Mrs. Vance. "Oh, dear, these celebrities."

Ames laughed. He was looking at Carrie in a pleased, straightforward way. As before she seemed to wait interestedly for what he would say.

"I haven't had an opportunity to see you yet," he said, after a few moments, in which he sat down near her. "I haven't been in New York very long."

"Well, I've only been back a little while," answered Carrie, not unmindful, however, that his interests ran far from hers. They were not even good friends enough for him to want to come to see her. Yet she had dressed thus carefully for him.

"I'm coming tonight, however, if that makes any difference to you." He smiled at what he considered his humor.

"Well," said Carrie, innocently ignoring it, "I don't know. Perhaps you won't like the play. It's only a kind of comedy."

"Oh, it isn't the play that I care about," he answered frankly. "It's you I'm coming to see."

"Oh!" said Carrie, pleased in spite of herself. "Perhaps you won't like what I'm doing now."

He looked at her as one does at a boquet of flowers.

"Very well then," he answered. "I'll not come any more."

Ames, however, was a poor figure as a wit. He had sufficient of the latter quality to realize it, however, and to express himself with that modesty which becomes the thinking man. Moreover, there was an accentuated seriousness about him, compared with what he had been when they first met.

"You two must come into dinner now," interrupted Mrs. Vance. "I want to tell you another thing," she added, shaking her finger at him. "No monopolizing the star, do you hear?"

"Do you hear?" repeated Ames, turning to Carrie. "Don't monopolize me."

Then all three laughed.

At table the tendency was to talk lightly of things in general, there being other guests, besides Carrie and Ames, but the latter was too much of an original thinker to have much regard for convention. The fact is, he was prone to forget the little niceties of attention unless constantly reminded. Now Carrie seemed the most pleasing character present. She extended to him that sympathy and attention which he needed to show his mind at its best. At its best it was speculative and idealistic—far above anything which she had as yet conceived, and yet, curiously, he could talk to her. She made him feel as if she understood, and he unconsciously strove to make himself plain. Thus the bond between them was drawn closer than they knew.

"I've been reading the books you suggested," she said in one place, when the conversation was between them alone.

He turned his serious eyes upon her, and a happy sense of having fulfilled a duty answered in her own, until he said:—

"What were they?"

His having forgotten stole away some of the charm for her.

" 'Saracinesca,' " she answered. " 'The Great Man from the Provinces.' 'The Mayor of Casterbridge.' "

"Oh, yes," he interrupted. "How do you like Balzac?"

"Oh, he's delightful to me. I liked 'The Mayor of Casterbridge,' though, as well as any," she answered.

"I should imagine you would," he said, submitting one of those keen observations which was the result of his comprehension of her nature.

"Why?" she asked.

"Well," he said, "you are rather gloomy in your disposition, and all of Hardy's novels have that in them."

"I?" asked Carrie.

"Not exactly gloomy," he added. "There's another word—melancholia, sad. I should judge you were rather lonely in your disposition."

For answer Carrie only looked.

"Let's see," put in Mrs. Vance, "didn't Hardy write 'Tess of the D'Urbervilles,' or something like that?"

"Yes," said Ames.

"Well, I couldn't see so much in that. It's too sad."

Carrie turned her eyes on Ames for a reply.

"No one who didn't feel the pathetic side of life would," he retorted.

"There!" thought Carrie triumphantly.

"Oh, I don't know," replied Mrs. Vance, rather shocked at the blunt reply. "I think I feel something of it."

"Not so very much," laughed Ames.

This served to ward off interference for awhile.

"I think you would enjoy 'Père Goriot,' " he said, turning to Carrie, "if you haven't read it. That's one of Balzac's."

"I haven't," said Carrie.

"Well, you get it." He was thinking to start her off on a course of reading which would improve her. Anyone so suscep-tible to improvement should be aided. Her mind seemed free and quick enough to grasp most anything. "Read all of Balzac's. They will do you good."

Carrie expressed something about the sadness of the failure of Lucien de Rubemfré in "The Great Man from the Provinces."

"Yes," he answered, "if a man doesn't make knowledge his object, he's very likely to fail. He didn't fail in anything but love and fortune, and that isn't everything. Balzac makes too much of those things. He wasn't any poorer in mind when he left Paris than when he came to it. In fact he was richer, if he had only thought so. Failure in love isn't so much."

"Oh, don't you think so?" asked Carrie, wistfully.

"No. It's the man who fails in his mind who fails com-pletely. Some people get the idea that their happiness lies in wealth and position. Balzac thought so, I believe. Many people do. They look about and wring their hands over every passing vision of joy. They forget that if they had that, they couldn't have something else. The world is full of desirable situations, but unfortunately we can only occupy one at a time. Most people occupy one and neglect it too long for the others."

Carrie looked at him, closely, but he did not see her. He seemed to be stating her case. Had not she done that very thing, and often?

"Your happiness is within yourself wholly if you will only believe it," he went on. "When I was quite young I felt as if I were ill-used because other boys were dressed better than I was, were more sprightly with the girls than I, and I grieved and grieved, but now I'm over that. I have found out that everyone is more or less dissatisfied. No one has exactly what his heart wishes."

"Not anybody?" she asked.

"No," he said.

Carrie looked wistfully away.

"It comes down to this," he went on. "If you have powers, cultivate them. The work of doing it will bring you as much satisfaction as you will ever get. The huzzas of the public don't mean anything. That's the aftermath—you've been paid and satisfied if you are not selfish and greedy long before that reaches you."

"Oh, I don't know," said Carrie, thinking of her own short struggle, and feeling as if her whole life had been one of turmoil, for which her present state was no reward.

Suddenly he seemed to have reached the state of her mind without talking.

"You ought not to be gloomy, however," he said, looking at her—"as young as you are."

"I'm not," she replied, "exactly. I don't know what it is. I don't seem to be doing what I want to do. I thought once I was, but now I—"

Their eyes had met, and for the first time Ames felt the shock of sympathy, keen and strong.

"You didn't go into comedy-drama after all, did you?" he observed after a time, remembering her interest in that form of dramatic art. It had been a source of wonder to him that she had not.

"No," she answered, wincing in conscience. "I haven't so far. I want to, though."

"You ought to," he returned in a speculative way, as if the position she had attained was nothing. "You have the sort of disposition that would do well in a strong comedy-drama."

He was looking directly at her now—studying her face, as it were. Her large, sympathetic eyes and pathetic mouth appealed to him as proofs of his judgement.

"Do you really think so?"

"Yes," he said, "I do. I don't suppose you're aware of it, but there is something about your mouth and eyes which would fit you for that sort of work."

Carrie thrilled to be taken so seriously. Here was praise, keen, strong, analytical. It was what her heart had craved for years. He was dwelling upon her as having qualities worthy of discussion.

"It's in your eyes and mouth," he went on. "I remember thinking, the first time I saw you, that your mouth looked as if you were about to cry."

"How odd," said Carrie, warm with delight. Her eyes were shining with suppressed fire.

"Then I noticed that that was really its mould, and I noticed it again tonight. There's a shadow about your eyes, too, which is pathetic. It's in the depth of them, I think. You probably are not aware of it."

She looked away, longing to be equal to this feeling written upon her countenance.

"I wasn't," she answered.

"That's why I think you would do well in some sympathetic part," he went on. "Your natural appearance would suggest more to the audience than the careful make-up of most people."

He paused and smiled—then looked away. Carrie saw how careful were his words. He was not talking to hear himself talk. This was *thought,* straight from that clean, white brow. She could have kissed his hands in thankfulness.

Others interrupted now and the meal went on to its conclusion, not, however, with much diminution of the feeling which Ames had aroused. In the parlor, the playing of one of the guests broke up the company into couples, who addressed each other, in undertones. Carrie fell to Ames, because he found her most congenial of all.

"Well," he said in a light way, to begin with, "what are you going to do about it?"

"I don't know," she replied. "Sometimes I don't seem able to do much of anything."

He was surprised to find her taking him so seriously. It threw him into the speculative contemplation of the ideal—the something better. To this, the undertone in the song then singing added.

"Well," he said, finding her both sweet to look upon and attentive, "perhaps you're too comfortable. That often kills a person's ambition. Many people fail because they succeed too quickly.

"I know why, if you tried, you would be a success, because I know the quality of that thing which your face represents. The world is always struggling to express itself—to make clear its hopes and sorrows and give them voice. It is always seeking the means, and it will delight in the individual who can express these things for it. That is why we have great musicians, great painters, great writers and actors. They have the ability to express the world's sorrows and longings, and the world gets up and shouts their names. All effort is just that. It is the thing which the world wants portrayed, written about, graven, sung or discovered, not the portrayer or writer or singer, which makes the latter great. You and I are but mediums, through which something is expressing itself. Now, our duty is to make ourselves ready mediums."

He stopped and looked at Carrie, but only in an intellectual way. Her eyes were turned steadily toward his face and her lips were apart. She was colorful and dainty—the perfect Carrie in mind and body, because now her mind was aroused.

"You and I," said Ames—"what are we? We don't know where we came from nor where we are going to. Tomorrow you might die and dissolve and I could search high and low in all the winds and waters and not find you. Here you are a mere expression of something—you know not what. It so happens that you have the power to act. That is no credit to you. You might not have had it. It isn't an excuse for either pride or self-glorification. You paid nothing to get it. But now that you have it, you must do something with it."

He paused again.

"What must I do?" said Carrie.

"Every person according to his light," said Ames. "You must help the world express itself. Use will make your powers endure. I should say turn to the dramatic field. You have so much sympathy and such a melodious voice—make them valuable to others. You will have them so long as they express something in you. You can preserve and increase them longer by using them for others. The moment you forget their value to the world, and they cease to represent your own aspirations, they will begin to fade. Mark that. The sympathetic look will leave your eyes, your mouth will change, your power to act will disappear. You may think they won't, but they will. Nature takes care of that. You can't become self-interested, selfish and luxurious, without having these sympathies and longings disappear, and then you will sit there and wonder what has become of them. You can't remain tender and sympathetic, and desire to serve the world, without having it show in your face and your art. If you want to do most, do good. Serve the many. Be kind and humanitarian. Then you can't help but be great."

He stopped again. Carrie gazed on into his eyes. Her little hands were folded in her lap, her lips sweetly parted.

"Well," he said, seeing her so interested, "I didn't mean to read you a lecture."

"Oh," she said, "you don't know how interesting it all was. It makes me feel as if I had never done anything at all."

"Oh, yes you have," he said. "No one gets up without doing something. It may seem at times as if people get up without effort, but if so, they were born with something in them which the world needed in a high place, or they wouldn't be there."

Carrie did not answer. She was thinking of the solution being offered her. Not money—he did not need that. Not clothes—how far was he from their pretension. Not applause—not even that—but goodness—labor for others.

Curiously, all he said appealed to her as absolutely true. Never had she seen such a man as this. He was not handsome, as dandies figure it. Most stage people would have thought him queer. But oh, she was weary of stage people. Had not even Drouet gone from her door? The memory of them was wearying.

"Well," said Mrs. Vance, "are you two nearly done arguing?"

"We weren't arguing," said Ames, "were we?"

"Not in the least," said Carrie solemnly.

"Well, do let Carrie talk with me now," she returned.

So Ames was left alone for a time, and it was not until Carrie was putting on her wraps that she came to give him goodbye.

"Well," he said. "I'll see more of you possibly." He seemed cooled off now, and once more reserved and far away.

"Yes, I hope so," she returned with an effort at a reserve which she could not feel.

He looked at her calmly, while she stood before him. Suddenly she added:—

"I know I shall be nervous tonight."

"Why?" he asked, getting a keen impression of her mental state.

"Oh, I don't know," she answered, and drooped her eyelashes. "Good night."

He looked after her sympathetically. What Mrs. Vance had told him about her husband's having disappeared, together with all he felt concerning the moral status of certain types of actresses, fled. There was something exceedingly human and unaffected about this woman—a something which craved neither money nor praise. He followed to the door—wide awake to her beauty.

"Good night," he said, looking mildly after her.

Carrie looked back, irrepressible feeling showing in her eyes, which she quickly shielded, with her lashes. She felt very much alone, very much as if she were struggling hopelessly and unaided, as if such a man as he would never care to draw nearer. All her nature was stirred to unrest now. She was already the old, mournful Carrie—the desireful Carrie,—unsatisfied.

Oh, blind strivings of the human heart. Onward, onward it saith, and where beauty leads, there it follows. Whether it be the tinkle of a lone sheep bell o'er some quiet landscape, or the glimmer of beauty in sylvan places, or the show of soul in some passing eyes, the heart knows and makes answer, following. It is when the feet weary in pursuit and hope is vain that the heartaches and the longings rise.

Carrie! Oh Carrie! ever whole in that thou art ever hopeful, know that the light is but now in these his eyes. Tomorrow it shall be melted and dissolved. Tomorrow it shall be on and further on, still leading, still alluring, until thought is not with you and heartaches are no more.

CHAPTER L.

In the city at that time there were a number of charities, similar in nature to the Captain's, which Hurstwood patronized in a similarly unfortunate way. One was a convent missionhouse of the Sisters of Mercy in 15th Street—a row of red brick family dwellings before the door of which hung a plain wooden contribution box, on which was painted the statement that every noon a meal was given free to all those who might apply and ask for aid. This simple announcement was modest in the extreme, covering as it did a charity so broad. Institutions and charities are so large and so numerous in New York that such things as this are not often noticed by the more comfortably situated. But to one whose mind is upon the matter, they grow exceedingly under inspection. Unless one were looking up this matter in particular, he could have stood at Sixth Avenue and 15th Street for days around the noon hour and never have noticed that out of the vast crowd that surged along that busy thoroughfare there turned out, every few seconds, some weatherbeaten, heavy-footed specimen of humanity, gaunt in countenance and dilapidated in the matter of clothes. The fact is none the less true, however, and the colder the day the more apparent it became. Space and a lack of culinary room in the mission house compelled an arrangement which permitted of only twenty-five or thirty eating at one time, so that a line had to be formed outside and an orderly entrance effected. This caused a daily spectacle which, however, had become so common by repetition during a number of years that now nothing was thought of it. The men waited patiently like cattle in the coldest weather, often for several hours, before they could be admitted. No questions were asked and no service rendered. They ate and went away again, some of them returning regularly day after day the winter through.

A big, motherly woman invariably stood guard at the door during the entire operation and counted in the admissible number. The men moved up in solemn order. There was no haste and no eagerness displayed. It was almost a dumb procession.

In the bitterest weather this line was to be found here. Under an icy wind there was a prodigious slapping of hands and a dancing of feet. Fingers and the features of the face looked as if severely nipped by the cold. A study of these men in broad light proved them to be nearly all of a type. They belonged to the class that sits on the park benches during the endurable days and sleeps upon them during the summer nights. They frequent the Bowery and those down-at-the-heels East Side streets where poor clothes and shrunken features are not singled out as curious. They are the men who are in the lodging house sitting rooms during bleak and bitter weather and who swarm about the cheaper shelters which only open at six in a number of the lower East Side streets. Miserable food, ill-timed and greedily eaten, had played havoc with bone and muscle. They were all pale, flabby, sunken-eyed, hollow-chested, with eyes that glinted and shone, and lips that were a sickly red by contrast. Their hair was but half attended to, their ears anæmic in hue, and their shoes broken in leather and run down at heel and toe. They were of the class which simply floats and drifts, every wave of people washing up one as breakers do driftwood upon a stormy shore.

For nearly a quarter of a century in another section of the city, Fleischmann, the caterer, had given a loaf of bread to anyone who would come for it to the rear door of his restaurant at the corner of Broadway and 9th Street, at midnight. Every night, during twenty years, about three hundred men had formed in line and at the appointed time marched past the doorway, picked their loaf from a great box, placed just outside, and vanished again into the night. From the beginning to the present time there had been little change in the character or number of these men. There were two or three figures that had grown familiar to those who had seen this little procession pass year after year. Two of them had missed scarcely a night in fifteen years. There were about forty more-or-less regular callers. The remainder of the line was formed of strangers. In times of panic and unusual hardships, there were seldom more than three hundred. In times of prosperity, when little is heard of the unemployed, there were seldom less. The same number winter and summer, in storm or calm, in good times and bad, held this melancholy midnight rendezvous at Fleischmann's bread box.

At both of these two charities, during the severe winter which was now on, Hurstwood was a frequent visitor. On one occasion it was peculiarly cold, and, finding no comfort in begging about the streets, he waited until noon before seeking this free offering to the poor. Already at eleven o'clock of this morning, several such as he had shambled forward out of Sixth Avenue, their thin clothes flapping and fluttering in the wind. They leaned against the iron railing which protects the walls of the 9th Regiment Armory, which fronts upon that section of 15th Street, having come early in order to be first in. Having an hour to wait, they at first lingered at a respectful distance, but others coming up, they moved closer in order to forfend against being forestalled in the matter of precedence. To this collection Hurstwood came up from the west out of Seventh Avenue and stopped close to the door, nearer than all the others. Those who had been waiting before him, but farther away, now drew near and by a certain stolidity of demeanor, no words being spoken, indicated that they were first. Seeing the opposition to his action he looked sullenly along the line and then moved out, taking his place at the foot. When order had been restored, the animal feeling of opposition relaxed.

"Must be pretty near noon," ventured one.

"It is," said another. "I've been waitin' nearly an hour."

"Gee but it's cold."

They peered eagerly at the door where all must enter. A groceryman drove up and carried in several baskets of edibles. This started some words upon grocerymen and the cost of food in general.

"I see meat's gone up," said one.

"If there wuz war it would help this country a lot."

The line was growing rapidly. Already there were fifty or more, and those at the head by their demeanor evidently congratulated themselves upon not having so long to wait as those at the foot. There was much jerking of heads and looking down the line.

"It don't matter much how near you get to the front so long as you're in the first twenty-five," commented one of the first twenty-five. "You all go in together."

"Hmph!" ejaculated Hurstwood, who had been so sturdily displaced.

"This here Single Tax is the thing," said another. "There ain't gone to be no order till it comes."

For the most part there was silence, gaunt men shuffling, glancing and beating their arms.

At last the door opened and the motherly sister looked out. She only looked an order. Slowly the line moved up and one by one passed in until thirty were counted. Then she interposed a stout arm and the line halted with six men on the steps. Of these the ex-manager was one. Waiting thus, some talked, some ejaculated concerning the misery of it, some brooded, as did Hurstwood. At last he was admitted and, having eaten, came away, almost angered because of his pains in getting it.

At eleven o'clock of another evening perhaps two weeks later, he was at the midnight offering of a loaf, waiting patiently. It had been an unfortunate day with him, but now he took his fate with a touch of philosophy. If he could secure no supper, or was hungry late in the evening, here was a place where he could come. A few minutes before twelve a great box of bread was pushed out and exactly on the hour a portly, round-faced German took position by it, calling "Ready." The whole line at once moved forward, each taking his loaf in turn and going his separate way. On this occasion the ex-manager ate his as he went, plodding the dark streets in silence to his bed.

By January he had about concluded that the game was up with him. Life had always seemed a precious thing, but now constant want and a weakened vitality had made the charms of earth rather dull and inconspicuous. Several times, when fortune pressed most harshly, he thought he would end his troubles, but with a change of weather, or the arrival of a quarter or a dime, his mood would change and he would wait. Each day he would find some old paper lying about and look into it to see if there was any trace of Carrie, but all summer and fall he had looked in vain. Then he noticed that his eyes were beginning to hurt him, and rapidly this ailment increased until in the dark chambers of the lodgings he frequented he did not attempt to read. Bad and irregular eating was sapping every function of his body. The one recourse left him was to doze, when a place offered and he could get the money to occupy it.

He was beginning to find, in his wretched clothing and meagre state of body, that people took him for a chronic type of bum and beggar. Police hustled him along, restaurant and lodging-house keepers turned him out promptly the moment he had his due, pedestrians waved him off. He found it more and more difficult to get anything from anybody.

At last he admitted to himself that the game was up. It was after a long series of appeals to pedestrians in which he had been refused and refused, everyone hastening from contact.

"Give me a little something, will you mister?" he said to the last one. "For God's sake do. I'm starving."

"Ah, get out," said the man, who happened to be a common type himself, holding a small official position under Tammany. "You no good. I'll give you nawthin."

Hurstwood put his hands, red from cold, down in his pockets. Tears came into his eyes.

"That's right," he said, "I'm no good now. I was all right. I had money. I'm going to quit this," and with death in his heart he started down toward the Bowery. People had turned on the gas before and died. Why shouldn't he? He remembered a lodging house where there were little closed rooms with gas jets in them, almost pre-arranged, he thought, for this which he wanted to do, which rented for fifteen cents. Then he remembered that he had no fifteen cents.

On the way he met a comfortable-looking gentleman coming clean-shaven out of a fine barber shop.

"Would you mind giving me a little something?" he asked this man boldly.

The gentleman looked him over and fished for a dime. Nothing but quarters were in his pocket.

"Here," he said, handing him one to be rid of him. "Be off now."

Hurstwood moved on, wondering. The sight of the large, bright coin pleased him a little. He remembered that he was hungry and that he could get a bed for ten cents. With this, the idea of death passed for the time being out of his mind. It was only when he could get nothing but insults that death seemed worth while.

One day in the middle of the winter, the sharpest spell of the season set in. It broke gray and cold on the first day and on the second snowed. Poor luck pursuing him, he had secured but ten cents by nightfall, and this he had spent for food. At evening he found himself at the Boulevard and 67th Street, where he finally turned his face Bowery-ward. Especially fatigued because of the wandering propensity which had seized him in the morning, he now half dragged his wet feet, slopping the soles upon the sidewalk. An old, thin coat was turned up about his red ears—his cracked derby hat was pulled down until it turned the same hearing organs outward. His hands were in his pockets.

"I'll just go down Broadway," he said to himself.

When he reached 42nd Street, the fire signs were already blazing bright. Crowds were hastening to dine. Through bright windows at every corner might be seen gay companies in luxuriant restaurants. There were coaches, and crowded cable cars.

In his weary and hungry state he should never have come here. The contrast was too sharp. Even he was recalled keenly to better things.

"What's the use," he thought. "It's all up with me. I'll quit this."

People turned to look after him, so uncouth was his shambling figure. Several officers followed him with their eyes to see that he did not beg of anybody.

Once he paused in an aimless, incoherent sort of way and looked through the windows of an imposing restaurant, before which blazed a fire sign and through the large plate windows of which could be seen the red and gold decorations, the palms, the white napery and shiny glassware, and above all, the comfortable crowd. Weak as his mind had become, his hunger was sharp enough to show the importance of this. He stopped stock still, his frayed pants soaking in the slush, and peered foolishly in.

"Eat," he mumbled. "That's right, eat. Nobody else wants any."

Then his voice dropped even lower and his mind half lost the fancy it had.

"It's mighty cold," he said. "Awful cold."

At Broadway and 39th Street was blazing, in incandescent fire, Carrie's name. "Carrie Madenda," it read, "and the Casino Company." All the wet, snowy sidewalk was bright with this radiated fire. It was so bright that it attracted Hurstwood's gaze. He looked up, and then at a large gilt-framed poster-board on which was a fine lithograph of Carrie, life-size.

Hurstwood gazed at it a moment, snuffling and hunching one shoulder as if something were scratching him. He was so run-down, however, that his mind was not exactly clear.

"That's you," he said at last, addressing her. "Wasn't good enough for you, was I? Huh."

He lingered, trying to think logically. This was no longer possible with him.

"She's got it," he said, incoherently, thinking of money. "Let her give me some."

He started around to the side door. Then he forgot what he was going for and paused, pushing his hands deeper to warm the wrists. Suddenly it returned. The stage door! That was it.

He approached that entrance and went in.

"Well," said the attendant, staring at him. Seeing him pause he went over and shoved him. "Get out of here," he said.

"I want to see Miss Madenda," he said.

"You do, eh!" the other said, almost tickled at the spectacle. "Get out of here," and he shoved him again.

Hurstwood had no strength to resist.

"I want to see Miss Madenda," he tried to explain, even as he was being hustled away. "I'm all right. I—"

The man gave him a last push and closed the door. As he did so Hurstwood slipped and fell in the snow. It hurt him and some old vague sense of shame returned. He began to cry and swear foolishly.

"God damned dog!" he said. "Damned old cur," wiping the slush from his worthless coat. "I—I hired such people as you once."

Now a fierce feeling against Carrie welled up—just one fierce, angry thought before the whole thing slipped out of his mind.

"She owes me something to eat," he said. "She owes it to me."

Hopelessly he turned back into Broadway again and slopped onward, and away, begging, crying, losing track of his thoughts, one after another, as a mind decayed and disjointed is wont to do.

It was a truly wintry evening a few days later when his one distinguished mental decision was reached. Already at four o'clock the sombre hue of night was thickening the air. A heavy snow was falling—a fine, picking, whipping snow, borne forward by a swift wind in long, thin lines. The streets were bedded with it, six inches of cold, soft carpet, churned to a dirty brown by the crush of teams and the feet of men. Along Broadway, men picked their way in ulsters and umbrellas. Along the Bowery, men slouched through it with collars up and hats pulled over their ears. In the former thoroughfare, business men and travellers were making for comfortable hotels. In the latter, crowds on cold errands shifted past dingy stores, in the deep recesses of which lights were already gleaming. There were early lights in the cable cars, whose usual clatter was reduced by the mantle about the wheels. The whole city was muffled by its fast-thickening mantle.

In her comfortable chambers at the Waldorf, Carrie was reading, at this time, "Père Goriot," which Ames had recommended to her. It was so strong, and Ames's mere commendation had so aroused her interest, that she caught nearly the full sympathetic significance of it. For the first time it was being borne in upon her how silly and worthless had been her earlier reading, as a whole. Becoming wearied, however, she yawned and came to the window, looking out upon the old unending procession of carriages rolling up Fifth Avenue.

"Isn't it bad," she observed to Lola.

"Terrible," said that little lady, joining her. "I hope it snows enough to go sleigh riding."

"Oh, dear," said Carrie, with whom the sufferings of father Goriot were still keen. "That's all you think of. Aren't you sorry for the people who haven't got anything tonight?"

"Of course I am," said Lola, "but what can I do? I haven't got anything."

Carrie smiled.

"You wouldn't care if you had," she returned.

"I would too," said Lola. "But people never gave me anything when I was hard up."

"Isn't it just awful," said Carrie, studying the winter's storm.

"Look at that man over there," laughed Lola, who had caught sight of someone falling down. "How sheepish men look when they fall, don't they?"

"We'll have to take a coach tonight," answered Carrie absently.

In the lobby of the Imperial, Mr. Charles Drouet was just

arriving, shaking the snow from a very handsome ulster. Bad weather had driven him home early and stirred his desires for those pleasures which shut out the snow and gloom of life. A good dinner, the company of a young woman, and an evening at the theatre were the chief things for him.

"Why hello, Harry," he said, addressing a lounger in one of the comfortable lobby chairs—"how are you?"

"Oh, about six and six," said the other.

"Rotten weather, isn't it."

"Well, I should say," said the other. "I've been just sitting here, thinking where I'd go tonight."

"Come along with me," said Drouet. "I can introduce you to something dead swell."

"Who is it?" said the other.

"Oh, a couple of girls over here in 40th Street. We could have a dandy time. I was just looking for you."

"Supposing we get 'em and take 'em out to dinner."

"Sure," said Drouet. "Wait'll I go upstairs and change my clothes."

"Well, I'll be in the barber shop," said the other. "I want to get a shave."

"All right," said Drouet, creaking off in his good shoes toward the elevator. The old butterfly was as light on the wing as ever.

On an incoming vestibuled Pullman, speeding at forty miles an hour through the snow of the evening, were three others, all related.

"First call for dinner in the dining car," a Pullman servitor was announcing, as he hastened through the aisle in snow-white apron and jacket.

"I don't believe I want to play any more," said the youngest, a black-haired beauty (turned supercilious by fortune) as she pushed a euchre hand away from her.

"Shall we go in to dinner?" inquired her husband, who was all that fine raiment can make.

"Oh, not yet," she answered. "I don't want to play any more, though."

"Jessica," said her mother, who was also a study in what good clothing can do for age, "push that pin down in your tie—it's coming up."

Jessica obeyed, incidentally touching at her lovely hair, and looking at a little jewel-faced watch. Her husband studied her, for beauty, even cold, is fascinating from one point of view.

"Well, we won't have much more of this weather," he said. "It only takes two weeks to get to Rome."

Mrs. Hurstwood nestled comfortably in her corner and smiled. It was so nice to be mother-in-law of a rich young man— one whose financial state had borne her personal inspection.

"Do you suppose the boat will sail promptly," asked Jessica, "if it keeps up like this?"

"Oh yes," answered her husband. "This won't make any difference."

Passing down the aisle came a very fair-haired banker's son, also of Chicago, who had long eyed this supercilious beauty. Even now he did not hesitate to glance at her, and she was conscious of it. With a specially conjured show of indifference she turned her pretty face wholly away. It was not wifely modesty at all. By so much was her pride satisfied.

The last of this small and once partially united company, however, was elsewhere, having reached a distinguished decision. Before a dirty four-story building in a side street quite near the Bowery, whose one-time coat of buff had been changed by soot and rain, he mingled with a significant crowd of men—a crowd which had been and was still gathering by degrees. It began with the approach of two or three who hung about the closed wooden doors and beat their feet to keep them warm. They had on faded derby hats with dents in them. Their misfit coats were heavy with melted snow and turned up at the collars. Their trousers were mere bags, frayed at the bottoms and wobbling over big, soppy shoes, torn at the sides and worn almost to shreds. They made no effort to go in but shifted ruefully about, digging their hands deep in their pockets and leering at the crowd and the increasing lamps. With the minutes increased the numbers. There were old men with grizzled beards and sunken eyes, men who were comparatively young but shrunken by diseases, men who were middle-aged. None was fat. There was a face in the thick of the collection which was as white as drained veal. There was another red as brick. Some came with thin, rounded shoulders; others with wooden legs; still others with frames so lean that clothes only flapped about them. There were great ears, swollen noses, thick lips, and above all, red, bloodshot eyes. Not a normal, healthy face in the whole mass; not a straight figure; not a straightforward, steady glance.

In the drive of the wind and sleet they pushed in on one another. There were wrists, unprotected by coat or pocket, which were red with cold. There were ears, half-covered by every conceivable semblance of a hat, which still looked stiff and bitten. In the snow they shifted, now one foot, now another, almost rocking in unison.

With the growth of the crowd about the door came a murmur. It was not conversation but a running comment directed at anyone in general. It contained oaths and slang phrases.

"By damn, I wisht they'd hurry up."

"Jesus."

"Look at the copper watchin'."

"Maybe it ain't winter, nuther."

"I wisht I was in Sing Sing."

Now a sharper lash of wind cut down and they huddled closer. It was an edging, shifting, pushing throng. There was no anger, no pleading, no threatening words. It was all sullen endurance, unlightened by either wit or good fellowship.

A carriage went jingling by with some reclining figure in it. One of the members nearest the door saw it.

"Look at the bloke, ridin'."

"He ain't so cold!"

"Eh! Eh! Eh!" yelled another, the carriage having long since passed out of hearing.

Little by little the night crept on. Along the walk a crowd turned out on its way home. Men and shop girls went by with quick steps. The cross-town cars began to be crowded. The gas lamps were blazing and every window bloomed ruddy with steady flames. Still the crowd hung about the door, unwavering.

"Ain't they ever goin' to open up?" queried a hoarse voice suggestively.

This seemed to renew general interest in the closed door, and many gazed in that direction. They looked at it as dumb brutes look, as dogs paw and whine and study the knob. They shifted and blinked and muttered, now a curse, now a comment. Still they waited and still the snow whirled and cut them with biting flakes. On the old hats and peaked shoulders it was piling.

It gathered in little heaps and curves and no one brushed it off. In the centre of the crowd the warmth and steam melted it, and water trickled off hat-rims and down noses, which the owners could not reach to scratch. On the outer rim the piles remained unmelted. Those who could not get in the centre lowered their heads to the weather and bent their forms.

A light appeared through the transom overhead. It sent a thrill of possibility through the watchers. There was a murmur of recognition. At last the bars grated inside and the crowd pricked up its ears. Footsteps shuffled within and it murmured again. Some one called: "Slow up there now," and then the door opened. It was push and jam for a minute, with grim, beast silence to prove its quality, and then it melted inward, like logs floating, and disappeared. There were wet hats and wet shoulders, a cold, shrunken, disgruntled mass pouring in between bleak walls. It was just six o'clock and there was supper in every hurrying pedestrian's face. And yet no supper was provided here—nothing but beds. Of these, Hurstwood was claiming one.

He laid down his fifteen cents and crept off with weary steps to his allotted room. It was a dingy affair, wooden, dusty, hard. A small gas jet furnished sufficient light for so rueful a corner.

"Hm," he said, clearing his throat and locking the door.

Now he began leisurely to take off his clothes, but stopped first with his coat and tucked it along the crack under the door. His vest he arranged in the same place. His old wet, cracked hat he laid softly upon the table. Then he pulled off his shoes and lay down.

It seemed as if he thought awhile for now he arose and turned the gas out, standing calmly in the blackness, hidden from view. After a few moments in which he reviewed nothing, but merely hesitated, he turned the gas on again, but applying no match. Even then he stood there, hidden wholly in that kindness which is night, while the uprising fumes filled the room. When the odor reached his nostrils he quit his attitude and fumbled for the bed.

"What's the use," he said wearily, as he stretched himself to rest.

HISTORICAL
COMMENTARY

SISTER CARRIE: *MANUSCRIPT TO PRINT*

The composition, publication, and subsequent "suppression" of Theodore Dreiser's first novel, *Sister Carrie,* is one of the most famous stories in American literary history. Like all controversial stories, it has been told many times and in many forms. Dreiser himself told the story frequently throughout his career—to interviewers, critics, correspondents, and biographers—and, as one might expect, his versions differed.[1] Indeed, the *Sister Carrie* story eventually took on a separate reality of its own and became a rallying point for intellectuals, a paradigm for the suppression of artistic freedom by Puritanism and Comstockery.

Most early Dreiser biographers and critics based their reconstructions of the *Sister Carrie* legend on Dreiser's own accounts. Later scholars have studied the extant documentary evidence and have corrected many of Dreiser's misstatements and lapses of memory.[2] The full story of the making of the novel, however, has not been told. In particular, the roles played by Dreiser's first wife, Sara, and his friend Arthur Henry have not been clearly understood. In this essay we shall attempt to tell that full story, to give a detailed account of the journey of *Sister Carrie* from manuscript to print. This essay is addressed in part to the seasoned Dreiser scholar, but it is intended even more for the teacher or advanced student who is investigating the background of *Sister Carrie* for the first time. Some information that is available elsewhere is included here, but much of the material in this essay is new. This account corrects many mistakes in previously published research and adds much fresh information and detail to existing versions. It is our aim in the pages that follow to examine and interpret the surviving evidence and to reconstruct, in as much detail as possible, the historical and textual background of Dreiser's first novel.

Preliminaries

Dreiser started writing *Sister Carrie* in the early fall of 1899, but the compositional history of the novel actually begins five years earlier. In March 1894 Dreiser had come to Toledo, Ohio, in search of employment on a newspaper. Since 1892 he had been working his way from Chicago east toward New York, serving as a reporter on various newspapers as he moved from city to city. Dreiser's immediate aim was to make contacts and gain experience as a journalist; his eventual goal was to write for one of the large New York metropolitan dailies. In Toledo, Dreiser applied for work at the *Toledo Blade*, and there he met Arthur Henry, the city editor. Henry was talkative, imaginative, and imbued with much boyish enthusiasm and natural charm. Like Dreiser, he wanted to be a successful writer. The two young men were attracted to one another, and they developed a close friendship almost immediately. "I became enamored of him," Dreiser later remembered, "the victim of a delightful illusion."[3] But Henry could offer Dreiser only a four-day job covering a streetcar strike, and when that employment was over Dreiser moved on to Cleveland, then to Buffalo, and finally to Pittsburgh, where he wrote for the *Pittsburgh Dispatch* until November 1894.

Dreiser arrived in New York late in November but found it impossible to secure a steady newspaper position. He went through a trying period of anxiety and disappointment but was eventually rescued by his brother, Paul Dresser, a successful songwriter and stage performer. (Paul had changed his name to the less Germanic "Dresser" when he had gone on stage years before.) Dreiser persuaded his brother's partners in a music-publishing firm to launch a monthly magazine as a vehicle for their sheet music. The magazine, called *Ev'ry Month*, first appeared in October 1895 with Dreiser as editor and chief contributor. The venture was a success, and Dreiser's literary career in New York was off to a favorable start.[4]

Dreiser had kept in touch with Arthur Henry and now solicited material from him for *Ev'ry Month*. Henry even came east during the summer of 1897 to visit Dreiser and to investigate the possibility of making a start as a professional writer in New York. Shortly thereafter Dreiser left *Ev'ry Month* to become a free-lance magazine author himself. His success with original articles and essays was promising, and by December 1898 he felt financially secure enough to marry Sara Osborne White, a schoolteacher from Missouri. Dreiser had proposed to her more than five years earlier; and although in the meantime his ardor had cooled, he went ahead with the marriage, in part from a sense of obligation. Sara—whose nickname was "Jug"—was a shy, reserved, and highly moral young woman. Dreiser was quite proud of her, though, for she had been brought up in a good family and was well educated for her time.

Dreiser was becoming a successful author for the magazines, but most of his writings so far had been articles and essays. He had published a few poems, and he had long wanted to try his hand at drama, but he seems to have had little inclination toward fiction. During the summer of 1899, however, Dreiser and Jug visited Arthur Henry and his wife in Maumee, Ohio, and during that visit Henry persuaded Dreiser to write some short stories for commercial sale. Dreiser was at first reluctant, but before the summer was out he had produced four stories, all of which he eventually sold to magazines.[5]

By the time Dreiser, Jug, and Henry returned to New York in September 1899, Henry had persuaded Dreiser to write a novel. He himself had begun a narrative called *A Princess of Arcady,* and he wanted Dreiser to write a novel too so that they could share the experience.[6] Accordingly Dreiser took a half-sheet of coarse yellow paper—the kind used in newspaper rooms of the day—and at the top he wrote the title "Sister Carrie." Then he began to compose the opening sentences of Caroline Meeber's story.[7]

Composition of the Manuscript

Dreiser progressed steadily, using materials from many sources. He drew most heavily on his journalist's knowledge of contemporary city life, on his personal experiences in Chicago and New York, and on his reading of such authors as Balzac, Hardy, and Spencer. Dreiser also seems to have decided from the outset that his novel would be as realistic as possible, and he therefore emulated Balzac by using real names for theaters, bars, streets, stores, plays, books, actors, singers, and other public figures and places. When a character went to the theater, Dreiser mentioned the name of the actual play he would see— Charles Hoyt's farce *A Hole in the Ground*. Or when Dreiser wished to describe a glittering theatrical crowd, he mentioned names of real actors—Joseph Jefferson III and Henry E. Dixey. Dreiser was determined to make his narrative a true reflection of American urban life of that period.

Dreiser also drew much material from his childhood experiences and from the checkered and impoverished lives of members of his own family. Particularly important was his sister Emma's involvement with L. A. Hopkins in a scandalous affair on which Dreiser based the story of Carrie and Hurstwood. Hopkins, married and the father of an eighteen-year-old daughter, was cashier in Chapin and Gore's tavern in Chicago. He became involved with Emma Dreiser, and when his wife learned of his infidelity he panicked, absconded with some thirty-five hundred dollars from his employers' safe, and fled to Montreal with Emma. The newspapers gave full and lurid coverage to the event. Hopkins later repented, returned most of the money, and took Emma to New York City, where they lived together for several years.[8] Although there are obvious superficial resemblances between the Hopkins-Emma affair and the Hurstwood-Carrie story, it is important to realize that here (as elsewhere in the novel) Dreiser made significant alterations, both in detail and in intensity, to transform real-life experience into fiction.[9]

When Dreiser had finished three chapters of his novel, he gave them to Jug for correction and criticism. She was apparently intrigued by the opening scenes of the story and took time to write down a list of queries about the historical accuracy of certain terms and facts in these chapters. Dreiser next showed the chapters to Henry, who penciled in a few changes of his own. Throughout the composition of the manuscript, in fact, Dreiser offered his drafts to Jug and Henry for revision and editing. This practice was by now habitual: during his apprentice years as a newspaper reporter, Dreiser had become accustomed to working with copy-editors and rewrite men, and he had never developed much sensitivity about his prose. He had always been a poor speller and an indifferent grammarian; Jug, who knew the mechanics of the language from her teaching days, could correct demonstrable errors in his drafts. Henry's function was different; he was a published author with some feeling for the style and rhythm of English prose, and Dreiser allowed him to identify and revise awkward spots in the drafts. The manuscript of *Sister Carrie* therefore exhibits, in nearly every chapter, markings by both Jug and Henry.[10]

Jug was the more attentive reader of the two. She added prepositions, articles, and pronouns where Dreiser, in the heat of composition, had forgotten to include them. She corrected a few misspellings, wrong verb tenses, and errors in grammar. She also caught characteristic Dreiserisms such as "your" for "you're" and "alright" for "all right." Jug did not do a full job of copy-editing, though. She left most of Dreiser's sketchy punctuation alone, and she did not correct many of his misspellings. Jug's alterations in manuscript were almost all minor; only in a few instances did she change meaning.

Henry's markings in the manuscript were of another character entirely. Unlike Jug, he seems to have read quickly, at some points only dipping and skipping. He descended now and then on an awkward phrase or sentence and "repaired" it, but he left most of the prose untouched. Many of his alterations, however, did affect meaning and characterization. His changes were bolder and more significant than Jug's, but his reading of the manuscript appears not to have been so thorough as hers.

Dreiser completed nine chapters before running into trouble.[11] He had managed to tell the story of Carrie Meeber and Charles Drouet successfully, and he had introduced George Hurstwood into the narrative, but he was unable to develop the relationship between Carrie and Hurstwood. Dreiser therefore put down the novel in mid-October 1899 and neglected it for almost two months. Henry kept after him, though, claiming among other things that he could not continue with *A Princess of Arcady* unless Dreiser got back to *Sister Carrie*. In mid-

December Dreiser therefore returned to his manuscript and wrote the chapters in which Hurstwood insinuates himself into Carrie's affections and persuades her to leave Drouet. Dreiser was again moving ahead with his novel.

In chapter XIX, Dreiser decided to put Carrie on stage for the first time. For her debut, he chose an Elks Club production of Augustin Daly's five-act melodrama *Under the Gaslight*. Dreiser, probably familiar with this popular play from his days as drama critic for the *St. Louis Republic,* remained faithful to reality by incorporating actual dialogue and stage directions from the play into his novel. He took a copy of the 1895 Samuel French "Author's Edition" of *Under the Gaslight* and copied whole sections into his narrative almost verbatim.[12]

At about this point Dreiser began using Jug in a new way by asking her to make fair copies of his heavily reworked drafts. Some of these fair copies survive in the manuscript of the novel. Dreiser even seems to have asked Jug's advice about using profanity in *Sister Carrie.* In chapter XXIV of the manuscript, Hurstwood is ruminating bitterly about his wife's persistent attempts to extract money from him. Dreiser wrote in manuscript, "The confounded   . Was she going to try to bull-doze him into submission" (p. 235).[13] Dreiser left the spot after "confounded" blank, apparently unsure whether he should use the word "bitch." Jug's counsel was conservative: in her own hand she wrote "wretch" at that spot in the manuscript.

All went well until some time in late January 1900 when Dreiser reached the end of manuscript chapter XXVII, the point at which Hurstwood must steal the money from his employers' safe and flee Chicago with Carrie. At this point, unable to work out Hurstwood's psychological motivations, Dreiser stalled again. Arthur Henry was not there to help this time. Although married and the father of a child, he was off with Anna Mallon, a woman several years his senior who would eventually become his second wife. A discouraged Dreiser gave up the project, shelved the novel, and made a trip south to gather information for magazine articles.

When he returned in February, he showed the completed chapters to Henry, who had been living with the Mallon family. Henry encouraged Dreiser to continue and even made some revisions in the manuscript in order to "improve" what had been written. Dreiser seems to have wanted this kind of attention and encouragement; this was his first attempt at a novel and he was conscious of his inexperience.

Jug also entered the compositional process at this point by doing some censoring. In chapter XVI, Carrie is blossoming into an attractive young beauty, and Dreiser took special pains to describe her:

> Her dresses draped her becomingly, for she wore excellent corsets and laced herself with care. Her hair had grown out even more luxuriantly than before, and she knew considerable concerning dressing it. She had always been of cleanly instincts and now that opportunity afforded, she kept her body sweet. Her teeth were white, her nails rosy, her hair always done up clear of her forehead. (p. 146)

This passage, with its sexual connotations and its mention of Carrie's "corsets" and "body," must have been too intimate for Jug. She toned down the description by revising it to read:

> Her dresses draped her becomingly. Her hair, always luxuriant, she now dressed prettily, rolling it back from her wide, clear brow. She had always been of cleanly instincts. Her teeth were white, her nails rosy.

Three pages later in the manuscript, Jug came upon this quintessentially Dreiserian sentence: "On her feet were yellow shoes and in her hands her gloves" (p. 147). Jug's revised version is smoother, but it is not characteristic of Dreiser's prose: "Her brown shoes peeped occasionally from beneath her skirt. She carried her gloves in her hand."

Dreiser pushed ahead and composed chapters XXVIII and XXIX, in which Hurstwood takes almost eleven thousand dollars from the safe at Hannah and Hogg's, lures Carrie onto the train with him, and flees to Montreal. Breaking through this jam seems to have had a positive effect; Dreiser was now relatively confident that he could finish his book. It was time to think about getting the novel in shape to show to a publisher.

Dreiser had not been having his drafts of *Sister Carrie* typed, because typing was expensive and, if he eventually aborted the novel, he would waste the typing fees. Henry's friendship with Anna Mallon, however, had produced an attractive side benefit. Mallon operated a large typing agency and was willing to have Henry's and Dreiser's writings typed for "next to nothing."[14] Dreiser took advantage of this arrangement. He had twenty-nine chapters ready for Mallon's typists: they were to work on these while he pressed ahead with his story and sent fresh manuscript chapters along as he finished them. Eventually the typists would catch up with him and would type the final few chapters immediately after they were composed. In this way Dreiser could show a complete typescript to a publisher a short time after finishing the manuscript of his novel. When Mallon's employees began typing and Dreiser resumed writing, he seems to have become confused about his chapter numbering and, thinking that he had given thirty chapters to Mallon instead of twenty-nine, he assigned the numeral XXXI to his next chapter.[15]

The typing job, unfortunately, was not very good. Dreiser's drafts were reasonably clean, but his hand was difficult to read, and consequently many words were misread or mistyped. A single typist might have become accustomed to Dreiser's cramped, backhanded script, but Mallon seems to have been fitting this job in where she could, and so the chapters were assigned to various typists as they had extra time.[16] The typists corrected most of Dreiser's misspellings and added whatever punctuation they thought appropriate. They did a good job on Dreiser's spelling but, as one might expect, had trouble punctuating his curiously Germanic prose. In an effort to apply conventional rules of punctuation to Dreiser's unconventional sentences, the typists punctuated the novel quite heavily, often backspacing to add more commas between words that had already been typed. There were also numerous instances of "eyeskip"—points at which the typist became distracted for a moment, took her eyes from the manuscript leaf, and resumed typing at the wrong spot further down the page.

These errors would have been of little consequence had Dreiser checked the finished typescripts carefully against the original manuscript. Indeed, he did just that with the first few chapters, but he seems to have tired of such meticulous work. He therefore adopted a more efficient method: when he came upon an odd word or an apparent error, he nearly always eliminated the word or interlined a fresh revision without going back to the manuscript for the original wording. This was unfortunate, because these makeshift revisions are almost invariably inferior to the original manuscript readings.[17]

Unlike her husband, Jug took considerable care with the typescripts when they first came back from the typing agency. As with the manuscript, she corrected grammar and verb tenses, caught misspellings, and added an occasional omitted word. She also removed some wordiness and repetition. Giving special attention to punctuation, she erased a few typed commas but added many new commas of her own and inserted numerous question marks—a punctuation mark which Dreiser almost never used in his holograph drafts. Jug's insistence on correctness was in many cases overly meticulous. She made numerous grammatical changes in dialogue—remedying split infinitives, removing prepositions from the ends of sentences, revising out the word "got," and taking out the colloquialism "he don't." As a result, Dreiser's characters were made to speak more formally than they had in the manuscript. Carrie's lines especially were altered: in manuscript her dialogue is that of a lower-middle-class Midwestern girl, but in typescript (after Jug's revisions) she often speaks much more stiffly and properly.[18]

Dreiser continued to work on his novel through February and on into March of 1900, bringing the narrative to its conclusion. In these closing chapters he tried especially hard to use realistic detail. He clipped advertisements from the classified sections of the New York newspapers and pasted them into his manuscript at the point where Hurstwood is searching for employment. And for details of the streetcar strike in which Hurstwood works as a scab, Dreiser borrowed information from back issues of the *New York Times* and even copied an announcement from that newspaper into his manuscript.[19]

In the final two chapters Dreiser also borrowed from his own previous writings. In the spring or summer of 1899 he had written a lengthy article called "Curious Shifts of the Poor" in which he had described various sources of food and lodging for the derelicts of New York City.[20] The article had been published in *Demorest's* in November 1899, but Dreiser had retained his original manuscript of the piece. He now took that manuscript—which was written in pencil on yellowish half-sheets identical to those he was using for *Sister Carrie*—and spliced parts of it into the manuscript of the novel. In the process of incorporation Dreiser revised a few of the pages from "Curious Shifts" so heavily that fresh copies had to be made, and Arthur Henry was pressed into service to inscribe them. Other leaves, however, needed only a bit of tinkering with verb tenses; this done, they were put into the manuscript and their original page numbers were simply altered to fit into the new pagination sequence.[21]

On 29 March 1900, Dreiser ended his novel—for the first time—with Hurstwood's suicide. Dreiser seems to have been satisfied with this ending after he composed it; he gave the final chapter to Anna Mallon to be typed. The initial act of composition was over—Dreiser now had a complete typescript of his novel before him. He, Arthur Henry, and Jug could turn their attention to revising the novel for submission to a publisher.

Revision of the Typescript

This typescript—which eventually served as printer's setting-copy for the first edition of *Sister Carrie*—is a fascinating document.[22] It exibits numerous levels of revision in three different hands—Dreiser's, Jug's, and Henry's.[23] From the evidence of the typescript, however, one cannot always deduce the precise sequence in which they made their corrections and revisions. Clearly, Jug did not first go over the typescript, then turn it over to Henry, and he, in turn, to Dreiser. Rather, all three seem to have gone through the typescript several times apiece. Many of Jug's corrections were made before Dreiser and Henry began revising and cutting, but beyond that, one cannot be certain.

Dreiser has been characterized by some of his biographers and critics as too undisciplined to edit his own prose carefully, but for *Sister Carrie* this is not true. In working through the Mallon typescript, Dreiser was clearly aware of the clumsiness of some of his writing and concentrated on revising many awkward spots. He changed individual readings, cut unnecessary wordiness, broke up long and unwieldy sentences, and polished rough phrasing. He also did some preliminary cutting. His numerous changes show careful attention to style and tone. In chapter III, for instance, he had written in manuscript: "No one, outside of making her uncomfortable by sidelong glances paid her the least attention." In the typescript he revised to a more graceful version: "Aside from making her uncomfortable by sidelong glances, no one paid her the least attention" (pp. 25–26). Dreiser's concentration did not falter; he made the same kinds of careful revisions in the later chapters of the novel that he had made in the earlier chapters. In chapter XXXIX, for example, he had begun a sentence in manuscript with unnecessary verbiage: "The upshot of this was that Carrie returned home, all her feelings about the luxury and fastidiousness of the city revived, and the quality of her deprivations emphasized." In the typescript Dreiser revised to: "When Carrie returned home, all her feelings about the luxury and fastidiousness of the city revived, and the quality of her deprivations was emphasized" (p. 367). These two revisions are typical of scores of similar changes made by Dreiser in the typescript.

Henry's revising, though not so careful as Dreiser's, was also meant to improve style and eliminate wordiness. Most of Henry's revisions were "internal"; that is, he excised clauses and phrases from groups of sentences and then tied them back together with new syntactical strategies. Henry attempted to rid the text of many awkward readings, and he altered typical Dreiser phrasings such as "this individual" and "the latter." Henry did a relatively thorough job, but his changes in the first two hundred or so pages of the typescript are much more careful than his alterations in the last three hundred and fifty pages. Evidently he tired of revising and hurried through the later chapters of the novel.

Some of Henry's alterations do indeed clarify Dreiser's prose. In chapter VII, for instance, Carrie is talking with her sister, Minnie, about how difficult it is to find work in Chicago. Carrie has lied to Minnie the day before by telling her that there is a chance she might be employed in a downtown department store. Minnie now sees that Carrie has not been offered the job. The original typescript reads: "Carrie looked at her out of the corner of her eye, after she had answered in the negative." Henry introduced a more direct approach: "Carrie looked at her out of the corner of her eye. 'No,' she answered" (p. 71).

Others of Henry's revisions, however, were perhaps not so successful. In chapter IV, for instance, Dreiser placed Carrie in a row of workers at a dreary shoe factory. In setting the scene he tried to emphasize the dull regularity of such toil: "[The foreman] seemed rather annoyed at having to bother with such help, but put down her name and then led her across to where a line of girls were sitting on a line of stools in front of a line of clacking machines" (p. 36). Henry seems not to have caught the significance of the repeated phrase "a line of." He revised the last part of the sentence to read ". . . across to where a line of girls occupied stools in front of clacking machines." Some of Henry's rewordings, then, were helpful, but others were not.

Revision of the Ending

The most significant revision occurred when Dreiser changed the original ending of *Sister Carrie*. The first ending—Hurstwood's suicide—had offered a bleak conclusion to the picture of human desire and tragedy that Dreiser painted. In manuscript Dreiser had ended chapter XLIX, the penultimate chapter, by having Carrie, now a successful actress, meet Robert Ames again at a party. An intelligent young inventor from the Midwest, Ames had known Carrie briefly before and had been her escort to dinner and the theater on one occasion. Clean-looking and independent, Ames disdains the materialism and meretriciousness of New York society. To Carrie he represents intellectuality, assurance, and self-awareness. When they again see each other, in the original ending, there is an immediate and electric attraction between them—partly mental and partly sexual. Ames seeks her out, and Carrie reveals that she has remembered their earlier meeting and has faithfully read the books he recommended. Their tête-à-tête has an exciting quality as it intensifies and they ignore the other guests. Carrie is radiant; she has prepared for this encounter with great attention to makeup and dress. When she leaves for the theater, Ames follows her to the door, "wide awake to her beauty." She looks at him, "irrepressible feeling showing in her eyes" (p. 487). Carrie and Ames are both aroused, and Dreiser strongly suggests that they will see each other again. A relationship may even develop between them. But Dreiser makes it plain in his first ending that any hopes Carrie might have for happiness and satisfaction with Ames are doomed. The original version of manuscript chapter XLIX finishes with this coda:

> Oh, blind strivings of the human heart. Onward, onward it saith, and where beauty leads, there it follows. Whether it be the tinkle of a lone sheep-bell o'er some quiet landscape, or the glimmer of beauty in sylvan places, or the show of soul in some passing eyes, the heart knows and makes answer, following. It is when the feet weary in pursuit and hope is vain that the heartaches and the longings rise.
> Carrie! Oh Carrie! ever whole in that thou art ever hopeful, know that the light is but now in these his eyes. Tomorrow it shall [be] melted and dissolved. Tomorrow it shall be on and further on, still leading, still alluring, until thought is not with you and heartaches are no more. (p. 487)

Dreiser is saying that a relationship between Ames and Carrie would only be a repetition of the cycle. Throughout the novel Carrie has longed for material objects and intangible qualities— "things" which she believes will make her happy. She has already allied herself with two men in her search for this elusive happiness. But Carrie, like most human beings, learns little from past disappointments. Instead she sets her sights on a new quality or a new man in the belief that if she can only possess that quality or that man, she will be permanently happy. Dreiser is saying that Carrie will follow this futile pattern over and over, always pursuing some vague emotion she cannot understand and can never retain.

In chapter L, the last chapter in the unrevised manuscript, Dreiser describes Hurstwood's final decline. Then—after a brief look at Drouet, at Hurstwood's former wife and daughter, and at Carrie—Dreiser shows us Hurstwood taking his own life in a Bowery flophouse:

> It seemed as if he thought awhile for now he arose and turned the gas out, standing calmly in the blackness, hidden from view.

After a few moments in which he reviewed nothing, but merely hesitated, he turned the gas on again, but applying no match. Even then he stood there, hidden wholly in that kindness which is night, while the uprising fumes filled the room. When the odor reached his nostrils he quit his attitude and fumbled for the bed.

"What['s] the use," he said wearily, as he stretched himself to rest. (p. 499)

Dreiser's original instinct was to end his novel here. At the bottom of the manuscript page he wrote "The End. | Thursday, March 29—1900—2.53 P.M." He sent this ending on to Anna Mallon, who had it typed. At some point during the revision of the typescript, however, Dreiser rewrote the endings of chapters XLIX and L. It is impossible now to discover precisely why he did so; the extant evidence is suggestive but inconclusive. The crucial question has to do with Dreiser's motivation: Did he become dissatisfied with the first ending on his own, or did Henry, or perhaps Jug, dislike the ending and persuade Dreiser to write another?

The documentary evidence which bears on this problem is intriguing. Preserved with the manuscript of *Sister Carrie* are thirteen sheets of extensive notes about the ending of the book. Except for the first sheet and the first sentence on the second sheet, which are in Dreiser's hand, these notes are all in Jug's handwriting. The wording of the notes and the hasty, sketchy quality of her writing suggest that they may have been dictated to her by someone—perhaps by Dreiser or Henry, but one cannot be sure. These notes emphasize two points: that Ames should not be cast as a "matrimonial possibility" for Carrie, and that the final scene of the novel should deal with Carrie, not with Hurstwood. Dreiser used the ideas and even some of the phrasings in these notes in his rewritten ending for *Sister Carrie*.

After Jug wrote out these notes, Dreiser began reworking parts of the last two chapters of his novel. First he went back to the middle of manuscript chapter XLIX and rewrote the entire scene between Carrie and Ames. In the new version, he destroyed the attraction between the two; now there is only a spark of interest which quickly dies, leaving Carrie puzzled and dissatisfied. Now she is not so strongly attracted to Ames: "She could hardly tell why the one-time keen interest in him was no longer with her" (p. 648). Ames's attitude is superior: "As a matter of fact her little newspaper fame was nothing at all to him. He thought she could have done better, by far" (p. 648). He is critical of Carrie's lack of ambition; when she asks him whether she liked her play, he tells her "Very good indeed . . . for a comedy" (p. 648). Carrie does not seem to understand what Ames is saying to her. He tells her that her talent "puts a burden of duty on you" (p. 651), but she does not grasp the significance of his comment. His last words to her are, "If I were you . . . I'd change" (p. 651). At the end of the chapter Carrie is in her rocking chair, troubling over her future. The final paragraph reveals a sad, uncertain Carrie: "Still, she did nothing, grieving. It was a long way to this better thing, or seemed to be, and comfort was about her. Hence the inactivity and longing" (p. 651). The chapter ends at this point; the "blind strivings" coda from the original version is left out.

In chapter L, Dreiser continued to revise by adding a lengthy passage after Hurstwood's suicide, apparently to throw the spotlight on Carrie at the end of the book. In this final passage—a meandering philosophical statement—Dreiser attempted to analyze what had happened to Carrie and to explain why she would never find her much-desired happiness. Dreiser seems to have been at a loss to end this final passage, however, and so for the last paragraph in his novel he simply took the "blind strivings" coda from the original version of chapter XLIX and moved it to the end of chapter L. In the process, though, he changed the coda to this more equivocal version:

Oh Carrie! Carrie! Oh, blind striving of the human heart, rather. Onward, onward it saith, and where beauty leads, there it follows. Whether it be the tinkle of a lone sheep-bell o'er some quiet landscape, or the glimmer of beauty in sylvan places, or the show of soul in some passing eyes, the heart knows and makes answer, following. It [is] when the feet weary and hope is vain, that the heartaches and the longings rise. Know then, that for you is neither surfeit nor content. In your rocking chair, by your window, dreaming, shall you long for beauty. In your rocking chair, by your window shall you still know such happiness as you may ever feel. (p. 655)

But this new ending for chapter L was not yet in shape for the typist, because Dreiser's draft was filled with strikeovers and interlineations. He therefore had Jug make a fair copy. She did so—the sheets, inscribed in her hand, also survive with the manuscript—but she did more than recopy. She made numerous changes in the text, some of them quite significant. Jug's version of the "blind strivings" coda, for instance, differs in several important readings from Dreiser's. Her changes in the last two sentences of the novel are highlighted here in italics: "In your rocking chair by your window dreaming, shall you long *alone*. In your rocking chair by your window shall you *dream* such happiness as you may *never* feel" (p. 659). Whether Dreiser was aware of Jug's revisions is not known, but it was Jug's ending, not Dreiser's, which was eventually typed, typeset, and printed in 1900. In fact, Jug's ending has appeared in every edition of *Sister Carrie* ever published.

Someone at Anna Mallon's agency typed the new passages, using Dreiser's draft of the new portion for chapter XLIX and Jug's draft of the new ending for chapter L. Then Dreiser spliced these passages into his typescript. This much is clear from the evidence of the manuscript and typescript, but the original question still remains: Why did Dreiser change the ending of his novel so drastically? Why did he become dissatisfied with what he had already written? Was it he who made the decision to revise, or was he persuaded by someone else to revise? Unless new evidence comes to light, these questions will never be answered definitively, but the available documents suggest that the impulse to change the ending did not spring from Dreiser alone.

Dreiser seems to have been confident about his first ending after he wrote it, but, as we have seen, once his novel was in typescript he began to accept practically all of Henry's suggestions for revision and cutting. Dreiser made almost no large revisions or cuts in the typescript on his own; nearly all major changes were initially suggested by Henry. There are the sheets of notes in Jug's hand: they may have been dictated to her by Dreiser, but there is no way to test that assumption. All they show is that someone—Dreiser, Henry, or Jug herself—was dissatisfied with the ending. We will probably never know precisely why Dreiser altered the last two chapters of *Sister Carrie*, but the extant evidence suggests that either Henry or Jug or perhaps both of them were closely involved in the decision to revise.

The Search for a Publisher

It was now time to find a publisher, and Dreiser decided to try a prestigious house first. He started by asking his friend Henry Mills Alden, editor of *Harper's Monthly*, to read the typescript of *Sister Carrie*. Alden, who frequently read manuscripts for Harper and Brothers, praised the novel but predicted that his employers would not publish it. Dreiser was not to be dissuaded, however, and so he had Alden submit the typescript to Harper early in April 1900.[24] About three weeks later, the novel was rejected with this comment:

> This is a superior piece of reportorial realism—of highclass newspaper work, such as might have been done by George Ade. It contains many elements of strength—it is graphic, the local color is excellent, the portrayal of a certain below-the-surface life in the Chicago of twenty years ago faithful to fact. There are chapters that reveal a very keen insight into this phase of life and incidents that disclose a sympathetic appreciation of the motives of the characters of the story. But when this has been said there remains the feeling that the author has not risen to the standard necessary for the efficient handling of the theme. His touch is neither firm enough nor sufficiently delicate to depict without offense to the reader the continued illicit relations of the heroine. The long succession of chapters dealing with this important feature of the story begin to weary very quickly. Their very realism weakens and hinders the development of the plot. The final scenes in New York are stronger and better—But I cannot conceive of the book arousing the interest or inviting the attention, after the opening chapters, of the feminine readers who control the destinies of so many novels.
> The style is uneven. At times singularly good (and generally so,) it is disfigured by such colloquialisms as "suspicioned," "pulled off on schedule time," "staved off," "it's up to you," etc.[25]

Dreiser must have been stung by these criticisms. He had poured much energy and emotion into *Sister Carrie* and had created what he believed to be a powerful novel in the tradition of Balzac and Hardy. The Harper reader, however, had called the story only "a superior piece of reportorial realism—of highclass newspaper work, such as might have been done by George Ade." The story had offended the Harper reader and, according to him, was potentially offensive to a female audience. Dreiser's touch was "neither firm enough nor sufficiently delicate to depict without offense to the reader the continued illicit relations of the heroine." The chapters dealing with Carrie he found wearying: "Their very realism weakens and hinders the development of the plot." The message was clear; Dreiser should cut and expurgate his typescript before showing it to another publisher. The narrative must be made to move more quickly, and the sexual aspects of the story must be toned down.

Dreiser seems to have accepted the Harper reader's criticisms as valid. He must have disliked the thought of having to shorten and expurgate his novel, but he must also have felt that the task was necessary if *Sister Carrie* was to see print. The actual cutting, though, would be a distasteful task, and so Dreiser enlisted Henry to do a preliminary job of it. Henry accordingly went through the typescript and marked more than thirty thousand words for excision. He followed directions well: almost without exception his cuts quicken narrative pace and tone down sexual passages. For example, Dreiser had included several lengthy paragraphs in the early chapters in which he paused to analyze Carrie's thoughts—in particular her ambivalent feelings about losing her virginity to Drouet in return for security and entertainment. Henry had Dreiser cut these passages. He also had Dreiser delete numerous paragraphs of factual data about Chicago, New York, the theater world, and lower-class working conditions. Henry evidently felt that these passages slowed the pace of the novel, and that their detail, while of interest to a reader in 1900, might be sacrificed. Henry's suggested cuts also had a strong effect on the philosophical message of *Sister Carrie*. Dreiser had written several long sections in which he outlined in some detail his harsh naturalistic beliefs. These passages slowed the story, though, and they might well put off many readers. Henry had Dreiser cut these passages, thereby speeding up the story but unfortunately removing much of the philosophical scaffolding of the book. At Henry's suggestion Dreiser also eliminated most of the dialogue and stage directions from *Under the Gaslight* in order further to speed up the story. This cutting, however, did away with one of Dreiser's special effects: it was now no longer apparent that Carrie's life paralleled the life of Laura, the rags-to-riches character she portrayed in the play. The lengthy quotations had also let the reader know that *Under the Gaslight* was popular, lightweight melodrama in the best nineteenth-century tradition. After the cuts, the reader is not sure what kind of play Carrie is appearing in.

The most significant cuts suggested by Henry had to do with sex. Henry himself was a reasonably sophisticated man and probably had no moral objections to a frank depiction of sex in fiction, but he knew that no publisher of the day would print Dreiser's novel as he had first written it. The treatment of sex was not explicit, but it was harsh and blunt. The Harper reader had been offended, and he had predicted that women readers would be shocked. Henry therefore marked for cutting a great many passages which dealt with sexual desire, seduction, or adultery. For instance, in the uncut typescript Drouet continues to pursue other women after he begins living with Carrie. Henry had Dreiser prune these passages heavily, and in the published book Drouet seems only to flirt innocently with other women while remaining faithful to Carrie. Hurstwood's character too was affected: in the original typescript, he is motivated much more strongly by erotic desire. Part of what attracts him to Carrie is her freshness and youth, but he is equally drawn by desire for her physical self. When Hurstwood begs Carrie to leave Drouet in chapter XVI, for example, his appeal is clearly sexual. He lets Carrie know that he needs her physically, and Carrie responds strongly to his desire. Henry marked these passages for heavy cutting, and so in the final version Hurstwood's love for Carrie appears idealistic and his behavior toward her courtly.

Carrie is subjected to numerous other sexual advances in the original text of the typescript. For example, when she goes looking for work in Chicago, after Drouet has left her, she is relentlessly propositioned almost everywhere she applies. She searches long and hard, but all she gets are blatant offers to carry her on the payroll if she will grant sexual favors. This disgusts her, but toward the end, weary and discouraged, she contemplates accepting such a position as a way out of her present difficulties. All of this material was cut at Henry's suggestion and does not appear in the published novel.[26]

The block cuts marked by Henry altered *Sister Carrie* significantly, but it is important to emphasize that these cuts had Dreiser's approval. Henry marked most of them only tentatively: for short passages he would draw light pencil lines through the words or sentences he wanted taken out; for longer passages he would mark a light "X" or a zig-zag line through the undesirable passage. And for long, block cuts, he would pencil a bracket in the left-hand margin around the section he wished Dreiser to remove. Dreiser would then follow behind and make the cuts himself by striking through the typed words with a heavy back-and-forth motion of a soft, blunt pencil. So far as we can tell, Dreiser agreed to all block cuts in *Sister Carrie*, but it must be mentioned that he almost never disagreed with Henry. In only two or three instances in the entire typescript did Dreiser not make a block cut that had been recommended by Henry, and Dreiser erased only a scattered few of Henry's revisions and re-wordings. The report from the Harper reader had a strong effect on both men.[27]

A New Publisher

Harper and Brothers was obviously too well established and conservative for *Sister Carrie*; Dreiser would have to find a younger and more experimental house. Alden suggested Doubleday, Page and Company, which had been formed less than a year before from the old firm of Doubleday and McClure, and which had recently published a successful realistic novel called *McTeague* by a young author named Frank Norris. Dreiser took his typescript to Doubleday, Page sometime in May. The novel was read by Norris himself, whose reaction was immediate and affirmative: he thought *Sister Carrie* an excellent piece of fiction, and he wholeheartedly favored publication. On 28 May 1900, he wrote as follows to Dreiser:

My Dear Mr. Dreiser:

My report of *Sister Carrie* has gone astray and I cannot now put my hand on it.

But I remember that I said, and it gives me pleasure to repeat it, that it was the best novel I had read in M.S. since I had been reading for the firm, and that it pleased me as well as any novel I have read in *any* form, published or otherwise. . . .

You may rest assured I shall do all in my power to see that the decision is for publication. I shall rush it through as fast as may be and possibly you will hear from me by the end of this week.[28]

Naturally Dreiser was delighted. He had just read *McTeague* and had been much taken by it; praise from a successful author like Norris was welcome.[29] Henry Lanier, senior editor at Doubleday, Page, read the typescript of *Sister Carrie* next, and he seems also to have liked it well enough, though he objected to Dreiser's use of real names and did not care for the title. From Lanier the typescript went to Walter Hines Page, junior partner in the firm. (Frank Doubleday, the senior partner, was in Europe and would not return until early July.) Whether Page actually read the typescript is not known; it is likely that he simply acted on Norris's enthusiasm for the book. He wrote Dreiser this note on 9 June 1900:

Dear Sir:

As, we hope, Mr. Norris has informed you, we are very much pleased with your novel. If you will be kind enough to call here on Monday—preferably later than two o'clock, we shall be glad to talk it over with you.[30]

The conference at the offices of Doubleday, Page went pleasantly. Page assured Dreiser that his book was as good as accepted and that it would be out in the fall. Dreiser later remembered that Page even talked of holding a dinner in his honor as a boost for sales of the book. No formal contract for publication was signed, however—an important point to remember in the dispute which would follow.[31]

Dreiser must have been pleased—his future as a novelist looked bright. He decided to take a vacation with his wife in Missouri, and they left New York and stayed in Montgomery City nearly the entire summer. Unfortunately, this was a bad time for Dreiser to be absent, for had he been in New York he might have forestalled much of the trouble that followed.[32]

Sometime early in July 1900, Frank Doubleday and his wife returned from abroad. Precisely what happened next has never been established. Doubleday may have read the typescript and disliked it, or he may have asked his wife to read it and, after she expressed her distaste for the story, he may then have read it himself.[33] For whatever reason, he developed a strong antipathy toward *Sister Carrie* and decided that his firm should not publish it. As the senior partner, Doubleday seems to have forced his decision on Page and Norris. Page apparently went along readily; Norris was unhappy, but there was little he could do. On 19 July, Page sent a letter to Dreiser asking that he release Doubleday, Page from its unwritten obligation to publish *Sister Carrie.*

Arthur Henry, still in New York, acted as Dreiser's representative in the dispute, and he wrote Dreiser urging him not to take back the typescript. Henry may have taken this stance because of previous experience. Ten years before, he had run into similar difficulties with his own first book, a rabidly anti-Negro novel called *Nicholas Blood, Candidate*. A publisher had accepted the book, had it set in type, and had the type cast into plates. But at that point the publisher had backed down on his commitment, and Henry had not pressed him for fulfillment of his obligations. Henry eventually found another publisher, Oliver Dodd, who agreed to handle the book; copies were manufactured and marketed, but the novel flopped abysmally. Now, ten years later, Henry must have felt that his friend was facing an almost identical situation. Henry could not allow his own earlier mistake to be repeated; he must not permit the same fate to befall *Sister Carrie* that had befallen *Nicholas Blood.*[34] Henry's letters to Dreiser were therefore insistent: "Hold Doubleday and Page to their agreement," he counselled. "They admit that they are bound to publish it, if you say so and Norris agrees with me that if they do so Doubleday will soon get over his kick and that it will be a great seller."[35] Dreiser followed Henry's advice and in his subsequent lengthy correspondence with Page stood firm on his demand that the book be brought out in the fall. Dreiser's argument was that he had spread word of the forthcoming publication of *Sister Carrie* to friends and family and also to his associates in the journalistic and literary fields. To admit now that his book had been turned down would be embarrassing and would injure his career and reputation. Page offered to place *Sister Carrie* with another publishing house, but Dreiser did not want the typescript to leave Doubleday, Page, and he rejected Page's offer.[36] Frank Doubleday therefore consulted with the firm's lawyer, Thomas H. McKee, about his legal obligation to Dreiser. Doubleday learned that if Dreiser insisted, *Sister Carrie* must indeed be published—that is, copies must be manufactured and orders must be filled. But the firm was under no obligation to advertise or otherwise to promote the book. Doubleday therefore capitulated and on 20 August 1900 a contract, or "Memorandum of Agreement," was finally drawn up between Doubleday, Page and Company and Theodore Dreiser for publication of a novel called "The Flesh & the Spirit." Apparently Lanier had won out temporarily in the matter of the title. Dreiser signed the contract but added the words "or Sister Carrie" on the title line.

On 4 September 1900, Doubleday sent the typescript of *Sister Carrie* to Dreiser for final revisions. Doubleday allowed Dreiser to keep the title *Sister Carrie*, but he insisted that all real names be altered and that much profanity be removed.[37] Someone—perhaps Doubleday himself, or perhaps Lanier—had already gone through the typescript and had queried, in blue pencil, the spots which needed attention. Dreiser went along with most of Doubleday's requests and changed many real names to fictitious ones and revised much suggestive wording. Dreiser balked at some of the blue pencillings, however, leaving pugilist John L. Sullivan's name unchanged and refusing to alter such mild profanity as "by the Lord."[38] It also seems to have been at this point that Dreiser and Henry added chapter titles to *Sister Carrie*. Their reasons for doing so are unknown, but the typescript does show that the chapter titles were a collaborative enterprise. Some of them were written in Dreiser's hand, some in Henry's, and some in a combination of both hands.[39]

Typesetting, Proofing, and Publication

In order to get *Sister Carrie* out in time for the fall publishing season, the printers had to typeset the novel quickly. They worked from the Mallon typescript: their markings, spike-holes, and inky fingerprints are still visible on its leaves. By 22 September they had already set ninety-four galleys, which brought them to a point about midway through chapter XXXI.[40] If the printers held to that approximate pace, they finished setting the book late in September. They did an adequate job: there were some obvious errors—Carrie wears a "string of pears" instead of a "string of pearls," for instance—but relatively few fresh corruptions were introduced.[41] Some spellings were altered and much punctuation was again added or changed, but only a few words were misread or left out.

The extant correspondence indicates that Dreiser saw both galleys and page proofs. Neither stage of the text survives today, but by collating the setting-copy typescript with the first printing one can uncover the changes that were made between the two forms. Assigning responsibility for the variants is more difficult, however, and requires some reconstruction of the proofing process. Normal procedure would have been for the printer to send two sets of proofs to Doubleday, Page—an author's set for Dreiser and a master set for the publisher. The correspondence, in fact, shows that Dreiser did receive his proofs from Doubleday, Page and not from the printer. Dreiser would have marked his corrections and revisions on his sets of proofs and then have returned them to the publisher. Dreiser's markings would have been transferred to the master proofs, on which the publisher would also have marked changes. Doubleday, Page would thus have final control over the revisions that were marked for the printer on the master proofs.

In an amicable relationship, the publisher will transfer all of the author's changes to the master proofs, or if he does not he will explain to the author why every revision cannot be made. A friendly publisher will also seek approval for significant alterations beyond those requested by the author. Feelings between Dreiser and Doubleday, Page, however, were hardly friendly, and so it is probable that Dreiser did not see the master proofs. It is therefore especially important to scrutinize all variants between the setting copy and the first printing in search of changes, introduced by the publisher, which Dreiser would not have approved.

Many of the variants do appear to be Dreiser's. Several

single-word revisions were made where the original word was inappropriate, and, more important, there was some revising done to smooth over ragged edges where the typescript had been cut. Dreiser was probably responsible for these changes. Jug may also have worked on the proofs, because the grammar in several passages of dialogue was "improved." The single most important proof revision came almost at the end of the novel. The passage in question comes just before Hurstwood's suicide and has symbolic overtones about "men who fall." In manuscript and typescript, the passage reads:

> Isn't it just awful, said Carrie, changing the drift of the conversation slightly. "Look at that man over there," and she began to laugh at a young man who had executed a comic fall.
> "How sheepish men look when they fall, don't they," said Lola.
> "We'll have to take a coach tonight," answered Carrie absently.

This passage was altered in proof, however, so that Carrie would no longer laugh at the young man. That bit of action went to Lola:

> "Isn't it just awful," said Carrie, studying the winter's storm.
> "Look at that man over there," laughed Lola, who had caught sight of someone falling down. "How sheepish men look when they fall, don't they?"
> "We'll have to take a coach tonight," answered Carrie absently. (p. 495)

This late revision makes Carrie less callous and slightly more abstracted and aloof. One assumes that Dreiser made the change, since the publisher would have had no motive for making it.

But it is highly likely that someone at Doubleday, Page did make other changes in the proofs, probably without consulting Dreiser. Some of the real names that he had refused to alter in typescript, for example, were changed in proof. There are also several new instances of censoring. In chapter I, Dreiser had written that Drouet had a "mind free of any consideration of the problems or forces of the world and actuated not by greed but an insatiable love of variable pleasure—woman—pleasure" (p. 6).

The wielder of the blue pencil at Doubleday, Page had queried "variable pleasure—woman—pleasure" in typescript, but Dreiser had made no change. The Doubleday, Page reader seems eventually to have come back to the reading in proof, however, and to have altered it to read "variable pleasure."[42] The reading "you bastards!"—shouted during the streetcar strike—was cut in proof,[43] and a reference to a "dingy lavatory" in which Hurstwood counts his money was changed to "dingy hall."[44] The most startling bit of censorship, though, occurs in chapter XXXII. In manuscript and typescript, Hurstwood and Carrie spend the night together in the Montreal hotel room before they go through the marriage ceremony the next day. This was rewritten in proof, however, so that in the published book the two are married on the afternoon of the day they reach Montreal and then sleep together that night in the hotel room.[45] This censoring was almost surely done by the publisher.

The master proofs were returned to the printer, who presumably made the requested changes in the text. Stereotype plates were cast from the standing type. The total cost of typesetting and plating came to $715.00. Printing and binding were executed at a cost of $.10 per copy for the printing and paper, and $.07 per copy for the binding. Bound copies were probably ready by late October. *Sister Carrie* was formally published by Doubleday, Page on 8 November 1900. The press run for the first printing was modest—only 1,008 sets of sheets.[46] The book retailed for $1.50 per copy, a standard price in 1900 for a novel the size of *Sister Carrie*. Doubleday, Page apparently did not expect a large sale, however, because 450 sets of sheets were left unbound.[47]

As Dreiser had feared, the publisher did little to promote the book. There were no space ads, no sales pitches to booksellers, and no honorary dinners. Frank Norris tried to help *Sister Carrie* by sending out 127 review copies to newspapers, magazines, and influential literary persons.[48] The resulting notices were generally favorable: some reviewers objected to the unpleasantness of Dreiser's story, which they found pessimistic and depressing, but most liked the skillful realism of the book and acknowledged its power. The picture of Hurstwood's gradual decline was singled out for special praise.[49] Despite its generally favorable critical reception, however, *Sister Carrie* was not a commercial success. Of the first printing, only some 456 copies were sold between November 1900 and February 1902. Dreiser collected a meager $68.40 in total royalties.[50] In later years he would blame this poor showing on the publisher; indeed, this experience with Doubleday, Page embittered Dreiser and contributed significantly to his later distrust of publishers in general.

The British Edition

The story of *Sister Carrie* in England is more pleasant. George A. Brett of Macmillan praised the novel to a partner in the London publishing firm of William Heinemann, and in early May 1901 Heinemann himself offered to bring out a British edition.[51] He wanted *Sister Carrie* for his "Dollar Library of American Fiction," a series which published an American novel every month for the British market. Heinemann's Dollar Library was meant to "give to English readers a representative selection of the best American fiction of the day."[52] Hamlin Garland's *Her Mountain Lover* had already been published, and Heinemann wanted to bring out volumes by Harold Frederic and Stephen Crane in the months to come. Clearly he wished to introduce the works of American realists and naturalists to British readers. *Sister Carrie*, however, presented a problem; it was too long. The Dollar Library offered inexpensive fiction; one could subscribe to a series of twelve of the volumes for two guineas, or one could purchase any single title for four shillings—about the equivalent of one American dollar.[53] The price was already set, no matter how expensive the book might be for Heinemann to manufacture. At 557 pages in its American edition, *Sister Carrie* was simply too long to be included in the Dollar Library. Typesetting and printing costs for a book that long could not be recovered if individual copies had to be sold at only four shillings. Heinemann therefore stipulated that *Sister Carrie* be shortened, and even specified how the cutting be done: the first 200 pages must be condensed into approximately 80 pages.[54]

Dreiser was probably not especially happy over the prospect of abridging *Sister Carrie,* but Heinemann was enthusiastic about the book and Dreiser was in no position to quibble. He therefore accepted Heinemann's offer and again persuaded Arthur Henry to make the necessary cuts, this time using a copy of the Doubleday, Page first printing.[55] Heinemann set type from this copy and published *Sister Carrie* in late July 1901.[56] Heinemann sent out 219 review copies[57] and advertised the book extensively. The British notices were mostly favorable,[58] and *Sister Carrie* did relatively well at the bookshops. By October over 1,000 of the 1,500 copies of the first printing had been sold. Encouraged by this showing, Heinemann ordered a second printing of 1,000 additional copies, of which 280 were bound up. Heinemann had misread the market, however, because sales of *Sister Carrie* dried up soon thereafter, and he was left with unsold stock. (He continued to carry *Sister Carrie* until 1912, when the remaining bound copies of the novel were sold to the publisher Grant Richards for remaindering. The unbound gatherings had already been disposed of in January 1911 when they were covered in pictorial wrappers and sold to W. H. Smith and Sons to be marketed as paperbacks.)[59]

The Heinemann *Sister Carrie* is an important textual artifact. Collation of the Doubleday, Page edition against the Dollar Library setting reveals that Arthur Henry did just what Heinemann asked—and no more. The first 195 pages were condensed into about 90 pages, and the rest of the book was left alone. Henry did a workmanlike job: he made heavy cuts and then smoothed over the resulting gaps with smaller revisions. He also shifted the location of a few blocks of text. He made no changes in style, nor did he polish wording or alter the events of the story. *Sister Carrie* was changed considerably, however, just by the cutting. Jack Salzman, who edited a facsimile of the Heinemann *Sister Carrie* in 1969, comments that "the section which was concerned primarily with Carrie" was shortened, thereby bringing the reader "more quickly to the story of Hurstwood. . . . The overall effect of the condensation was to not only make the novel less prolix but to also give it a sharper focus. . . . In the Heinemann edition, more so than in the American edition, it is the tragedy of George Hurstwood that dominates the novel."[60]

The story of *Sister Carrie* from this point on is uncompli-
cated. Dreiser was convinced that with a proper send-off from
a friendly publisher, the novel would draw attention and sell in
the United States. In the fall of 1901, Doubleday, Page sold the
plates and remaining stock of *Sister Carrie* (both bound copies
and unbound sheets) to the publisher J. F. Taylor and Company
for $500.[61] Dreiser was at that time working on his second novel,
Jennie Gerhardt, which was under contract to Taylor. Dreiser
wanted Taylor to reissue *Sister Carrie* immediately, but Taylor
declined to do so. He preferred to wait until *Jennie Gerhardt* had
been published and had "made a success"; *Sister Carrie* could
then be reissued as a follow-up to *Jennie*.[62] Dreiser was at that
time, however, unable to complete *Jennie Gerhardt*, and Taylor
therefore never republished *Sister Carrie*.

Soon after, Dreiser fell into a period of nervous collapse
which lasted until late in 1903. He eventually re-entered the
New York literary scene, however, and renewed his efforts to
have *Sister Carrie* brought out by another publisher. In January
1905 Dreiser's friend Charles A. MacLean bought the plates and
stock of the novel from Taylor for $500,[63] but MacLean also
failed to reissue the novel. Dreiser himself purchased the plates
and stock from MacLean in June 1906 for $550 and persuaded
B. W. Dodge and Company, a new publishing house with which
he was associated, to issue *Sister Carrie*.[64] The Dodge impression
(the second from the original plates) appeared in May 1907.
The novel sold well enough for Dodge to order another impression,[65] and in 1908 Grosset and Dunlap, which specialized in
reprints, agreed to market a fourth impression.[66] In 1911 Harper
and Brothers published *Jennie Gerhardt*, which Dreiser had finally
completed. To capitalize on the success of *Jennie*, Harper re-
printed *Sister Carrie* and thus became the fourth publisher to
market the novel.[67] For this reprinting Dreiser wanted to remove
the chapter titles, but apparently he forgot to convey these instructions to the publisher and so the titles remained.[68] Dreiser
kept control of the original plates for the rest of his life and
leased them out to various publishers, such as Boni and Liveright, Horace Liveright, and Random House for the Modern Library.[69]

There was only one other American typesetting of *Sister Carrie* during Dreiser's lifetime. In 1939, the Limited Editions Club produced a handsome edition with illustrations by Reginald Marsh and an introduction by Burton Rascoe. Dreiser might have taken this opportunity to revise *Sister Carrie*, but in 1939, nearly four decades after its original publication, Dreiser probably felt very far removed from his first novel. He was sixty-eight years old; his interests had shifted to politics and social reform, and he seems to have felt no inclination to rework *Sister Carrie*. The Limited Editions Club therefore produced an exact resetting of the 1900 text, with no authorial changes and, interestingly, with almost no printer's errors or corruptions.[70]

Dreiser died in 1945. All posthumous editions of *Sister Carrie* have been based on the 1900 Doubleday, Page setting. Some textual work has been done on the novel, but until now no attempt has been made to re-edit it. The manuscript of the novel preserves Dreiser's text in an uncorrupted state—before Arthur Henry, Jug, the typists, the publishers, and the printers began adding layers of censoring, cutting, editing, and error. The Pennsylvania edition, based on this manuscript, presents a text of *Sister Carrie* which is very close to what Dreiser first conceived and wrote. The Pennsylvania edition also restores Dreiser's original ending for the novel, the ending that his initial instinct told him was right.

The Pennsylvania Edition

The Pennsylvania edition of *Sister Carrie* is much more than a new version of the novel. It is in fact a new work of art, heretofore unknown, which must be approached freshly and interpreted anew. The Pennsylvania *Sister Carrie* differs from the Doubleday, Page *Sister Carrie* most markedly in characterization, philosophy, and theme. In its expanded form, *Sister Carrie* is infinitely richer, more complex, and more tragic than it was before.

Of the characters in the novel, Carrie herself is altered most significantly in this new edition. In the 1900 text she seems almost mindless, with little personality, practically no moral conscience, and no awareness of her course in life. She is almost ignorant of sex and is unaware of her ability to awaken desire in men. She seems especially to lack the emotional depth necessary for success as an actress. Carrie has been much criticized in the past for being shallow, fickle, and unthinking, but examination of the textual history of the novel reveals that this impression of her was created in large part by Henry's and Dreiser's cutting of the typescript. With the full text restored, a new Carrie emerges, much more complex and sexually aware than before.

This new Carrie has more of a conscience than the old Carrie. Passages now restored to the text show that she is unhappy about her liaison with Drouet and very much aware of her position in the eyes of society. The new Carrie is tougher: after Drouet leaves her she tries much harder to find work, and after Hurstwood tricks her onto the train she resists him more strongly and for a longer time. She is also a better actress. With the passages from *Under the Gaslight* restored, the reader can now watch Carrie transform that piece of lightweight melodrama into something emotional and moving and can see her capture an audience with her winsome beauty and innate stage presence. The new Carrie is determined to gain fame and money, but she also wants happiness and love in the bargain. It is this conflict which gives emotional depth to Carrie and gives her face the melancholy, dissatisfied look that so intrigues Ames.

Hurstwood is also changed in the new *Sister Carrie*. In the 1900 edition, his decline is puzzling. There is virtually no hint of his weakness, his essential vulnerability to decay, prior to his meeting with Carrie. It is as though he becomes a different man, merely by being infatuated with this small-town girl. Even though the progress of his decline is fully described, there remains this question: How could a man who seemed so stable, so willing to sacrifice all for the sake of respectability and affluence, have allowed himself to be placed in a position from which he could not escape, which could lead only to the loss of everything he valued? The Pennsylvania edition reveals that Dreiser did, in fact, presage Hurstwood's decline, for he portrays quite a different Hurstwood, a man who brings in women after hours ("Is she a blonde?" asks Drouet) and who pays visits with some regularity to "those more unmentionable resorts of vice—the gilded chambers of shame with which Chicago was then so liberally cursed" (pp. 48, 44). Hurstwood certainly was gambling with his fate, for respectability was the key to holding his job. He thus becomes more believable as the man who finally risks everything for a chance at immediate gratification.

Drouet is also changed in this new edition, though not so significantly. He remains the genial egotist, but because we are given a clearer and harsher portrayal of his sexuality, he comes off a bit less favorably. To him women exist only to be pursued, charmed, and seduced. The new Drouet pursues several other women while he is living with Carrie, and we come to realize that she is little more than a pretty diversion he can count on when he is home in Chicago. In the new *Sister Carrie*, Drouet's sexual morality is nonexistent.

Even Ames is changed in this new edition. In the 1900 *Sister Carrie* he seems impossibly aloof. Haughty and scornful, he is immune to Carrie's charms. In the new edition, by contrast, he responds strongly to her and sees in her the emotional depth that Drouet and Hurstwood miss. He is more believable. He is, in fact, not so very different from Hurstwood in that his dormant sexual and emotional urges are awakened by Carrie— an additional testament to her effect on men. It may be that Carrie and Ames will form a relationship or even fall in love, but Dreiser makes it clear that no lasting happiness will result because, in this life, lasting happiness is impossible.

All of the major characters in this new *Sister Carrie* are more complex, which is to say, they are more human. Carrie displays more emotional depth, Hurstwood shows more passion; Drouet is less likable, Ames is more vulnerable. Presented as Dreiser originally meant them to be, these characters are a fascinating group, motivated by conflicting urges they cannot understand and at the mercy of fates they cannot control.

Dreiser had taken special pains in the original manuscript of *Sister Carrie* to set forth, in several lengthy and discursive passages, his pessimistic Spencerian philosophy, his belief in man's fundamental insignificance and inability to control his own destiny. At Henry's suggestion, however, he cut nearly all of these sections from the typescript. With the philosophical underpinning restored in the Pennsylvania edition, the reader now has a stronger sense that the characters in this novel are in the grip of an indifferent fate they can neither control nor comprehend. And in what will likely be its most controversial decision, the Pennsylvania edition reinstates Dreiser's original ending for *Sister Carrie*. This ending is bleaker and philosophically more deterministic than the equivocal ending of the 1900 text. It follows naturally and appropriately, however, from the rest of the restored text, throughout which Dreiser's deterministic view of the human condition is reflected. It is a tribute to Dreiser's original concept that even cut, censored, and corrupted *Sister Carrie* retained enough strength to engage three generations of literary critics and readers; but in its purified form, presented here for the first time, *Sister Carrie* emerges as a more balanced and compelling novel, a new and more tragic work of art by one of the major American novelists of this century.

J.L.W.W. III
J.C.B.
A.M.W.

Notes

1. The significant accounts either written by Dreiser or based on interviews with him are: "Author of 'Sister Carrie' Formerly Was a St. Louisan," *St. Louis Post-Dispatch*, 26 January 1902, p. 4; " 'Sister Carrie' Theodore Dreiser," *New York Herald*, 7 July 1907, Literary and Art Sect., p. 2; Dreiser to H. L. Mencken, 13 May 1916, in *Letters of Theodore Dreiser: A Selection*, edited by Robert H. Elias, 3 vols. (Philadelphia: University of Pennsylvania Press, 1959), 1: 210–14; Dreiser to Fremont Older, 27 November 1923, *Letters*, 2: 417–21; Vrest Orton, *Dreiserana: A Book about His Books* (New York: Chocorua Bibliographies, 1929), pp. 12–25; Dreiser, "The Early Adventures of *Sister Carrie*," *Colophon*, pt. 5 (March 1931), republished on pp. v–vii of the 1932 Modern Library reprinting of *Sister Carrie*; Dorothy Dudley, *Forgotten Frontiers: Dreiser and the Land of the Free* (New York: Smith and Haas, 1932), pp. 160–94.

2. The major scholarly accounts of the composition and publication of *Sister Carrie* are found in: Robert H. Elias, *Theodore Dreiser: Apostle of Nature* (New York: Knopf, 1949; emended ed. Ithaca and London: Cornell University Press, 1970); W. A. Swanberg, *Dreiser* (New York: Scribner, 1965); Richard Lehan, *Theodore Dreiser: His World and His Novels* (Carbondale and Edwardsville: Southern Illinois University Press, 1969); Ellen Moers, *Two Dreisers* (New York: Viking Press, 1969); Donald Pizer, *The Novels of Theodore Dreiser: A Critical Study* (Minneapolis: University of Minnesota Press, 1976); and Stephen C. Brennan, "The Making of *Sister Carrie*" (Ph.D. diss., Tulane Uni-

versity, 1979). Useful source materials, correspondence, and commentary are available in vol. 1 of Elias's edition of Dreiser's *Letters*, and Pizer's edition of *Sister Carrie* (New York: W. W. Norton, 1970), hereafter referred to as the Norton Critical edition. The footnotes to the discussion that follows record our specific debts to these various scholars, but it seems proper at this point to express our general gratitude to these Dreiserians who have prepared the way for much of our own work.

3. *A Book about Myself* (New York: Boni and Liveright, 1922), p. 374.

4. See Joseph Katz, "Theodore Dreiser's *Ev'ry Month,*" *Library Chronicle* 38 (1972): 46–66.

5. The four were "When the Old Century Was New," "The Shining Slave Makers," "Nigger Jeff," and "Butcher Rogaum's Door." For citations to the periodical appearances of these stories, see Donald Pizer, Richard W. Dowell, and Frederic E. Rusch, *Theodore Dreiser: A Primary and Secondary Bibliography* (Boston: G. K. Hall, 1975), entries C01–2, 7, 9, and 11. Pizer discusses the four stories in the introduction to *Novels.*

6. *A Princess of Arcady* was published by Doubleday, Page and Company in 1900. Dreiser later claimed to have written the last chapter of *A Princess* (see Dreiser to Mencken, 13 May 1916; also see Orton, *Dreiserana,* pp. 12–13).

7. The manuscript of *Sister Carrie* is housed at the Manuscripts Division of the New York Public Library. Dreiser gave the manuscript to Mencken in 1914, and Mencken later donated it to the NYPL.

8. See George Steinbrecher, Jr., "Inaccurate Accounts of *Sister Carrie,*" *American Literature* 23 (1952): 490–93.

9. For information about Dreiser's sources for *Sister Carrie,* see the discussion in pts. 1 and 2 of Moers, *Two Dreisers;* see also Joseph Katz, "Theodore Dreiser and Stephen Crane: Studies in a Literary Relationship," in *Stephen Crane in Transition: Centenary Essays,* edited by Katz (DeKalb: Northern Illinois University Press, 1972), pp. 174–204; D. B. Graham, "Dreiser's Maggie," *American Literary Realism* 7 (Spring 1974): 169–70; Pizer, *Novels,* pp. 3–95; and Thomas P. Riggio, "Notes on the Origins of 'Sister Carrie,'" *Library Chronicle* 44 (1979): 7–26.

10. Some of Dreiser's manuscript chapters are free of nonauthorial markings, but these appear to be fair copies of earlier drafts which had presumably already been read and marked by Jug and Henry. Curiously, Jug's handwriting is similar enough to Henry's to deceive even a careful observer. Donald Pizer, for instance, mistakenly attributes Jug's alterations and notes in the manuscript to Henry. See *Novels,* pp. 45–47. Neda M. Westlake first identified the presence of Jug's hand in the manuscript; see Appendix B of Jack Salzman's edition of *Sister Carrie* (New York: Bobbs-Merrill, 1970), p. 481. Stephen C. Brennan has successfully differentiated Jug's hand from Henry's and has analyzed some of her contributions to the novel in "The Composition of *Sister Carrie:* A Reconsideration," *Dreiser Newsletter* 9 (Fall 1978): 17–23.

11. Dreiser stalled at either two or three different points during the composition of *Sister Carrie,* but his memory varied in later years about the precise places at which he stopped writing. The discussion which follows is largely based on two accounts: Dreiser to Mencken, 13 May 1916, and his comments as reported by Dudley in *Forgotten Frontiers,* chap. 31. Both accounts are sketchy and probably unreliable for specific details. Brennan ("Making,"

p. 27) argues that Dreiser stopped for the first time after chapter X rather than chapter IX, but there is no hard evidence to support this assertion.

12. For discussion of theatrical elements in *Sister Carrie* and extensive examination of *Under the Gaslight*, see Hugh Witemeyer, "Gaslight and Magic Lamp in *Sister Carrie*," *PMLA* 86 (March 1971): 236–40.

13. Quotations from the manuscript of *Sister Carrie* are reproduced verbatim, *with errors and irregularities intact*. When a chapter number is cited for a manuscript quotation, it is the chapter number in the manuscript, which is not necessarily the same in the Doubleday, Page first edition or the Pennsylvania edition. The manuscript quotations are followed, however, by parenthetical references to the page in the Pennsylvania edition on which the passage is printed.

14. The quotation is from Dreiser's "Rona Murtha," one of the quasi-autobiographical sketches in *A Gallery of Women*, 2 vols. (New York: Horace Liveright, 1929), 2: 582. The character of Rona is based on Anna Mallon and the character of Winnie on Arthur Henry. Dreiser undoubtedly imagined many of the details of the sketch, but one assumes that his recollections about typing fees are reliable.

15. This reconstruction is partly speculative. It is now impossible to know at what precise point Dreiser began giving chapters to Anna Mallon, but his misnumbering of chapter XXX—and the fact that he remembered having difficulty composing manuscript chapters XXVIII and XXIX—makes the theory plausible. We also know that Mallon's typists caught up with Dreiser and were working on the final chapters very shortly after he wrote them. On 22 March 1900, only a week before Dreiser finished composing *Sister Carrie*, Mallon's typists sent him this playful note:

> Dear Mr. Author:
> We have finished the last iniquitous chapter of Sister Carrie, and are now ready for something hot and sizzling. So please send her down.
> Impatiently,
> THE INFANT CLASS.

Mallon herself wrote to Dreiser a few days later, praising the first version of chapter XLIX and adding that she would "impatiently await the closing chapter." These two letters are in the Dreiser Collection, University of Pennsylvania Library.

16. Several items of evidence suggest that more than one typist worked on *Sister Carrie*. (Mallon employed approximately fifteen women.) The typed chapters were done on several different typewriters. Too, as Mallon's typists finished chapters of *Sister Carrie* they would mark a total page count across the top of the first manuscript leaf of the chapter. One of the typists always wrote "done" on her completed chapters. The page counts and notations on the manuscript chapters are in several hands, and each chapter is paginated separately, the typed page numbers always beginning with "1."

17. For example, in chapter XI of the manuscript, Dreiser had written this sentence: "Once these things were in her hand, on her person, she might dream of giving them up; the method by which they came might intrude itself so forcefully that she would ache to be rid of the canker of it, but she would not give them up" (p. 98). The typist, however, could not decipher "canker" and so left a blank space in the typescript at that point. Dreiser apparently did not check his holograph draft for the missing word; rather, he simply wrote the less evocative word "thought" in the blank space.

18. One of the best examples occurs in chapter XXIV, where Carrie and Drouet argue about Hurstwood's visits. In the manuscript, Carrie tells Drouet, "You've lied to me—thats what you've done. You've brought your old friends out here under false pretences" (p. 226). But Jug, like all proper young women of her day, knew that "to lie," in the sense of "to tell an untruth," was a verb which one simply did not use. She therefore altered "lied" to "deceived" in the typescript and diluted the force of Carrie's accusations, making her seem controlled and prim.

19. Donald Pizer first called attention to Dreiser's use of the *New York Times* reports in the Norton Critical edition of *Sister Carrie*, p. 297n.

20. Moers, in her lengthy examination of "Curious Shifts," presents a convincing argument about the composition date of the article. She concludes that it "could not have been completed before January or February 1899" and that "Dreiser may have worked it up into final form as late as the summer of 1899." See Moers, *Two Dreisers*, pp. 66–67n.

21. Moers speculates that Dreiser "first wrote down a slightly revised version of the *Demorest's* piece ['Curious Shifts'] and *then* corrected it to conform more closely to the magazine version" (p. 67n). Analysis of the pagination and inscription of the drafts, and collation of the manuscript text against the *Demorest's* text, show that Dreiser was instead revising the original draft to the readings which finally appeared in *Demorest's*. An interesting sidelight: either Dreiser or a *Demorest's* editor cut the text heavily before publishing it. By using his original manuscript leaves in *Sister Carrie*, however, Dreiser restored the excised passages.

22. The typescript is in the Dreiser Collection at the University of Pennsylvania Library. Dreiser kept it throughout his career.

23. Elias, in *Letters*, 1: 52n, maintains that Mary Annabel Fanton helped edit the manuscript of *Sister Carrie*. Swanberg, apparently using Elias's note as his source, repeats this statement (*Dreiser*, p. 85). But Miss Fanton's hand appears neither in the manuscript nor in the typescript of *Sister Carrie*. It is possible, of course, that she read the novel in some prepublication form and made oral or written suggestions to Dreiser. Miss Fanton did edit some of Dreiser's later writings; see *Letters*, 1: 66–67.

24. Orton, *Dreiserana*, pp. 13–14.

25. *Letters*, 1: 210n. Dreiser saved a copy of this report; it is in Box 317 of the Dreiser Collection. The report is dated 2 May 1900 in his hand.

26. Richard Lehan, in *Theodore Dreiser: His World and His Novels*, pp. 60–66, sees the cuts as a conscious effort by Dreiser to make Carrie more moral and Hurstwood more idealistic. Pizer disagrees with Lehan—correctly, we believe—and argues that the motive for much of the cutting in typescript was "salability." According to Pizer, Lehan "ignores . . . the strong possibility that much of the cutting of the typescript was by Henry" (*Novels*, p. 47 and p. 352, n. 31).

27. In his 13 May 1916 letter to Mencken, Dreiser wrote, "After [*Sister Carrie*] was done considerable cutting was suggested by Henry and this was done. I think all of 40,000 words came out." (Dreiser's estimate was fairly accurate. A check reveals that he and Henry cut approximately thirty-six thousand words from the typescript.) Over twenty years later Dreiser gave this slightly different account to Louis Filler: "As for *Sister Carrie* being cut, it happened this way. When I finished the book, I realized it was too long, and I went over it and marked what I thought should be cut out. Then I consulted with a friend, Arthur Henry, who suggested other cuts, and whenever I agreed

with him I cut the book. It was thus shortened to its present length" (Pizer, *Novels*, p. 48).

28. This letter was first published in *The Letters of Frank Norris*, edited by Franklin D. Walker (San Francisco: Book Club of California, 1956), pp. 60–61. It is more readily available in the Norton Critical *Sister Carrie*, p. 434.

29. Dreiser to Mencken, 13 May 1916.

30. Norton Critical *Sister Carrie*, p. 435.

31. In "The Early Adventures of *Sister Carrie*," Dreiser stated that a contract had been signed and copies of the book printed before Doubleday tried to halt publication. Other versions of the *Sister Carrie* legend have Doubleday and his wife reading the book in galleys. The dates of the extant correspondence and of the contract, however, prove that no contract had been signed and no type set when Doubleday read the novel. He must therefore have read it in typescript.

32. Jack Salzman has straightened out much of the controversy between Dreiser and Doubleday, Page in "The Publication of *Sister Carrie*: Fact and Fiction," *Library Chronicle* 33 (1967): 119–33. Salzman's article contains much useful information, but he misidentifies a typewritten account of the dispute in the Dreiser Collection as "an unpublished article on the suppression of *Sister Carrie*" written by Arthur Henry "some time before 8 February 1901" (pp. 121 and 129 n). Neda M. Westlake, in "The *Sister Carrie* Scrapbook," *Library Chronicle* 44 (1979): 71–84, has demonstrated that the typewritten account was actually prepared in 1907 by Dreiser himself to publicize the reprinting of *Sister Carrie* by B. W. Dodge & Co.

33. Several tellers of the *Sister Carrie* story (especially Dorothy Dudley in *Forgotten Frontiers*) point an accusing finger at Mrs. Doubleday, but all known evidence against her is hearsay.

34. See James L. W. West III, "*Nicholas Blood* and *Sister Carrie*," *Library Chronicle* 44 (1979): 32–42.

35. Henry to Dreiser, ca. 25 July 1900, Norton Critical *Sister Carrie*, p. 446.

36. Dreiser would later regret this decision; see Dreiser to Fremont Older, 27 November 1923, in *Letters*, 2: 417–21.

37. Doubleday's covering letter has been published in *Letters*, 1: 63–64, and in the Norton Critical *Sister Carrie*, p. 452.

38. Dreiser's incomplete copy of his letter to Doubleday, explaining which changes he has made and which he has not made, has been published in *Letters*, 1: 64–65, and in the Norton Critical *Sister Carrie*, p. 453.

39. See Philip Williams, "The Chapter Titles of *Sister Carrie*," *American Literature* 36 (1964): 359–65.

40. This information is taken from a card (saved by Dreiser) which was attached by Doubleday, Page to one batch of the author's galleys. Because the galley "takes" were marked by the printer on the setting-copy typescript, one can tell how far the compositors had progressed.

41. Doubleday, Page edition, p. 205. The reading should actually have been "string of imitation pearls" (p. 190). Dreiser tried to stress the artificiality of Carrie's looks in this manuscript passage, but Henry persuaded Dreiser to excise "imitation" in the typescript. Henry also had Dreiser cut the phrase "made so by a touch of blue under the eyes" which was to modify Carrie's "pale face."

42. The unusually wide spacing between words in lines 4.33–35 and

5.1–3 of the Doubleday, Page first edition indicates that the compositor had to reset these six lines in order to rejustify the passage after the expurgation had been made.

43. Doubleday, Page text, p. 466; Pennsylvania text, p. 424.

44. Doubleday, Page text, p. 510; Pennsylvania text, p. 460.

45. Doubleday, Page text, p. 317; Pennsylvania text, p. 301.

46. This production and publication information was extracted from the Doubleday, Page records on 27 February 1901, shortly after Dreiser asked how much it would cost for him to acquire the plates and unsold stock of *Sister Carrie*. A three-panel folding card bearing this information (written and dated in an unknown hand) survives in the Dreiser Collection. A notation at the bottom of the card indicates that Doubleday, Page would sell plates and stock to Dreiser for "cost less 15%."

47. Royalty report from Doubleday, Page to Dreiser dated 1 February 1901, Dreiser Collection.

48. Royalty report, 1 February 1901.

49. For texts of the reviews, see *Theodore Dreiser: The Critical Reception*, edited by Jack Salzman (New York: David Lewis, 1972), pp. 1–18.

50. Royalty reports from Doubleday, Page to Dreiser dated 1 February 1901, 1 August 1901, and 1 February 1902, Dreiser Collection.

51. Brett to Dreiser, 21 September 1901, Dreiser Collection. The offer was relayed to Dreiser by Doubleday, Page in a letter dated 6 May 1901, Dreiser Collection.

52. Quoted from the prospectus for the Dollar Library printed in the Heinemann *Sister Carrie*, p. ii.

53. Prospectus, p. i. Four shillings were worth about 96 cents at the 1901 exchange rate.

54. Doubleday, Page to Dreiser, 6 May 1901, Dreiser Collection.

55. John C. Berkey and Alice M. Winters have demonstrated that Henry alone did the cutting; see "The Heinemann Edition of *Sister Carrie*," *Library Chronicle* 44 (1979): 43–70.

56. Orton (*Dreiserana*, p. 22) gives the publication date as 31 July 1901 but reveals no source for the date. C. S. Evans of Heinemann to Dreiser, 16 April 1924, gives the publication date simply as July 1901.

57. Royalty report, Doubleday, Page to Dreiser, 8 April 1902, Dreiser Collection.

58. The British reviews are republished in *Critical Reception*, edited by Salzman, pp. 18–24. See also Jack Salzman, "The Critical Recognition of *Sister Carrie*, 1900–1907," *Journal of American Studies* 3 (1969): 123–33.

59. This information is taken from three letters, written by various members of the firm of Heinemann to Dreiser, dated 11 December 1911, 11 October 1923, and 16 April 1924. Dreiser had written to Heinemann in 1911 to ask how much it would cost for him to purchase their plates of *Sister Carrie*. In the 11 December 1911 letter, Heinemann offered Dreiser the papier-mâché molds and the clothbound stock for £15, but Dreiser did not buy them. The 1923 and 1924 letters were prompted by Dreiser's having chanced to see a copy of the 1911 wrapper-covered remainder. He immediately feared that a paperback reprint of *Sister Carrie* was being marketed in England without his consent. The two letters from Heinemann were explanations.

60. *Sister Carrie*, edited by Jack Salzman (New York and London: Johnson Reprint Corp., 1969), p. viii.

61. Contract between Doubleday, Page and J. F. Taylor and Company, ca. 30 Sept. 1901, Dreiser Collection.

62. The question of reissuing *Sister Carrie* is discussed at length in several 1901 letters between Dreiser and R. B. Jewett of J. F. Taylor; Taylor himself finally refuses to reissue *Sister Carrie* in a letter to Dreiser dated 4 December 1901. See West, "*Nicholas Blood* and *Sister Carrie*," pp. 38–40.

63. Contract between J. F. Taylor and Company and Charles A. MacLean, 19 January 1905, Dreiser Collection.

64. Contract between Charles A. MacLean and Dreiser, 19 June 1906, Dreiser Collection. Dreiser worked for Dodge as a director of the firm and was paid in stock rather than money. See the agreement between Dreiser and Dodge dated 6 June 1907, Dreiser Collection.

65. See Orton, *Dreiserana*, pp. 23–25.

66. Ibid., pp. 24–25.

67. Dreiser's contract with Harper and Brothers for *Jennie Gerhardt* specifies that Dreiser will deliver the plates of *Sister Carrie* to Harper without charge, and that Harper will publish a new "edition" (i.e., a new impression) on the same terms as those agreed upon for *Jennie Gerhardt*.

68. Dreiser to Frederick A. Duneka (secretary of Harper and Brothers), 20 February 1912, *Letters*, 1: 135.

69. Dreiser ordered only one change in the original plates of *Sister Carrie* through its many reprintings, as Historical Editors Berkey and Winters have confirmed by machine-collating exemplars of all known pre-1945 printings of *Sister Carrie* against the original 1900 Doubleday, Page text. See the entry and textual note at 6.17–7.2 of Selected Emendations in the Copy-Text. See also Jack Salzman, "Dreiser and Ade: A Note on the Text of *Sister Carrie*," *American Literature* 40 (1969): 544–48. At some point Dreiser apparently contemplated making extensive alterations in the plates, and he even marked changes on the first 69 pages of a copy of the Doubleday, Page first printing. For an unknown reason, however, he dropped the idea. The marked copy survives: see James L. W. West III, "John Paul Dreiser's Copy of *Sister Carrie*," *Library Chronicle* 44 (1979): 85–93.

70. There was only one other complete typesetting of *Sister Carrie* during Dreiser's lifetime; in 1927 the London publisher Constable brought out an edition based on the complete 1900 Doubleday, Page text rather than on the abridged 1901 Heinemann text. Extensive spot collations indicate that Dreiser made no revisions for the Constable edition and took no part in its preparation, other than giving his consent for publication.

MAPS

In order to help the reader follow the action of the novel through the cities of Chicago and New York, the Pennsylvania edition includes an artist's rendering of maps of these cities. These are specialized maps that label only the streets and the hotels, theaters, restaurants, and other public places that Dreiser specifically mentions in the novel. Rand McNally maps and others of the 1880s and 1890s were used to outline the cities. If a street is mentioned in the novel, it is labeled on the map. If the street immediately intersecting it or adjacent to it is not mentioned, it is not labeled. Some fictional places are noted—for example, Carrie's and Hurstwood's apartment in New York. If Dreiser fails to mention a particular street, it is not labeled on the map.

Dreiser's remarkable feat is evident: in an unobtrusive way he has placed in the novel enough material to create what is virtually a complete map of Chicago in the 1880s; it encompasses the various economic areas from poor working-class through middle-class and elite neighborhoods and covers the entertainment and commercial areas in the center of the city.

The reader follows Carrie around the whole city, from the Hansons' flat situated among working-class homes at 354 West Van Buren Street, through her job-seeking among the factories and industrial buildings, on to her life with Drouet among the restaurants and shops and theaters, and then finally, in the carriage with Hurstwood, to the outskirts of the Chicago yet-to-be.

When Carrie moves to New York, Dreiser's scope encompasses virtually all of Manhattan in the 1890s. Once again the novel covers the economic spectrum, as Carrie and Hurstwood move from middle-class respectability and addresses to, for Hurstwood, the very dregs of the Bowery and, for Carrie, the theater and restaurant environment of the privileged classes.

J.C.B.
A.M.W.

SISTER CARRIE'S CHICAGO
MAP LEGEND

CARRIE'S RESIDENCES

1. 354 West Van Buren (the Hansons' flat). [Fictional]
2. No. 29 Ogden Place (Carrie and Drouet's flat). [Fictional]

COMMERCIAL ENTERPRISES

3. Bartlett, Caryoe and Co. (Drouet's employer). Corner of State and Lake. [Fictional]
4. Rhodes, Morgenthau and Scott (shoe company where Carrie is employed). Adams and Fifth Avenue. [Fictional]
5. The Boston Store. 118–20 State.
6. Schlesinger and Mayer. State at southeast corner of Madison.
7. Carson, Pirie, Scott and Co. 234 W. Madison.
8. The Fair. State, Adams, and Dearborn.
9. Sea and Co. 122–24 State.
10. Siegel, Cooper and Co. 185–89 Madison.

THEATERS

11. Grand Opera House. Clark, near Washington.
12. Criterion Theater. 87 Sedgwick.
13. McVicker's Theater. Madison, between State and Dearborn.
14. Hooley's Theater. Randolph, near La Salle.
15. Chicago Opera House. Washington, between Clark and LaSalle.
16. Columbia Theater. Monroe, between Clark and Dearborn.
17. Avery Hall. Madison and Throop
    (Carrie makes her acting debut here in *Under the Gaslight*). [Fictional]
18. H. R. Jacob's. Halstead and Madison.
19. Standard Theater. 169 S. Halstead.

HOTELS AND RESTAURANTS

20. Tremont Hotel. Dearborn and Lake.
21. Grand Pacific Hotel. Jackson and Clark.
22. Palmer House. State, southeast corner Monroe.
23. Windsor Hotel (Drouet and Carrie dine here before the seduction). Dearborn, between Madison and Monroe.
24. Rector's (Hurstwood and Drouet favor this restaurant). Clark and Monroe.
25. Hannah and Hogg's (Hurstwood is manager of this resort). Adams, opposite Federal Building.
26. Kinsley's Restaurant. 106–7 Adams.

PUBLIC BUILDINGS

27. The Exposition. Michigan Avenue at Adams.
28. Michigan Central Railroad Depot (Carrie is tricked by Hurstwood into boarding the train from this depot). Michigan and Lake.

Sources: *Map of the Business and Central Portions of Chicago* (Chicago: Rufus Blanchard, 1890).
Chicago Tribune's Map of Chicago and the World's Fair (1893).

SISTER CARRIE'S
CHICAGO

SISTER CARRIE'S NEW YORK
MAP LEGEND

HOTELS

1. Imperial Hotel. Broadway and 32d.
2. Waldorf Astoria (where Carrie lives with her friend Lola at the end of the novel). Fifth Avenue and 33d.
3. Broadway Central (Hurstwood takes a menial position here). 671 Broadway.
4. Grand. Broadway and 31st.
5. Gilsey. 1202 Broadway.
6. Fifth Avenue Hotel. Fifth Avenue at 26th.
7. Wellington Hotel (Carrie accepts a complimentary suite here after her initial success in the theater). Seventh Avenue and 55th.
8. Plaza. Fifth Avenue and 59th.
9. Hoffman House. Broadway and 25th.
10. Continental Hotel. Broadway and 20th.
11. Morton House Hotel. Broadway and 14th.

THEATERS AND RESTAURANTS

12. Casino Theater (Carrie joins the chorus at this theater for her first professional stage engagement). Broadway and 39th.
13. Broadway Theater. Broadway and 41st.
14. Empire Theater. Broadway and 40th.
15. Madison Square Theater. Madison Avenue and 26th.
16. Lyceum Theater. Fourth Avenue, between 23d and 24th.
17. Tony Pastor's Theater. 14th, near Third Avenue.
18. Fifth Avenue Theater. 28th off Fifth Avenue.
19. Daly's Theater. Broadway, at 28th.
20. Wallack's Theater. Broadway and 30th.
21. Delmonico's. Fifth Avenue and 26th.
22. Sherry's. Fifth Avenue and 37th.
23. Shaughnessy's saloon. Warren and Hudson Streets (the saloon in which Hurstwood bought a third interest for $1,000 and ultimately lost his investment). [Fictional]

RESIDENCES AND PUBLIC BUILDINGS

24. 78th, near Amsterdam Avenue (Carrie and Hurstwood's first apartment in New York). [Fictional]
25. Sisters of Mercy (Hurstwood received handouts here). 15th and Sixth Avenue.
26. Stuyvesant Park. 15th and Second Avenue.
27. Bellevue Hospital. 26th and First Avenue.
28. City Hall. City Hall Park.
29. Metropolitan Museum. Fifth Avenue and 83d.
30. Grand Central Station. 42d and Vanderbilt Avenue.
31. 112 W. 13th (Carrie and Hurstwood's last apartment in New York). [Fictional]

Source: *Guide Map of New York City* (New York: Rand, McNally and Co., 1894).

SISTER
CARRIE'S
NEW
YORK

"Taken about the time I wrote Sister Carrie—1900." Dreiser Collection, University of Pennsylvania Library

First page of the holograph manuscript of Sister Carrie. New York Public Library

First page of the typescript of Sister Carrie. Dreiser Collection, University of Pennsylvania Library

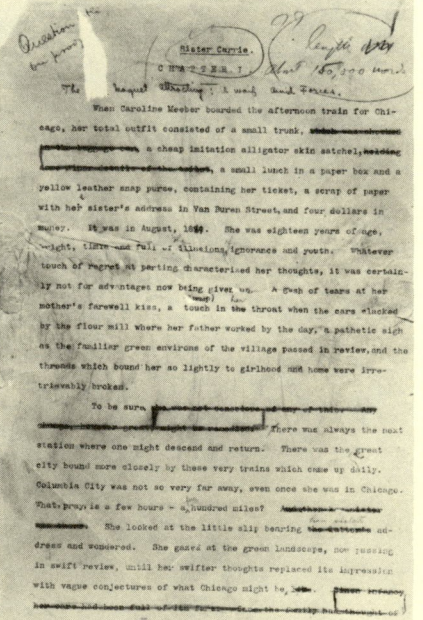

Chapin and Gore. Emma Dreiser's lover, Hopkins, was the cashier here. Chicago Historical Society

Hurstwood managed this establishment, Hannah and Hogg's. Chicago Historical Society

McVicker's Theatre, 25 W. Madison, Chicago. Chicago Historical Society

The Palmer House Hotel, State and Madison Streets, Chicago, rebuilt in 1873 after the Chicago fire of 1871. Chicago Historical Society

"On the Bow'ry you can make a front,
In a suit of hand me down
But don't think you're the real thing till
You mingle in up town"
Library of Congress

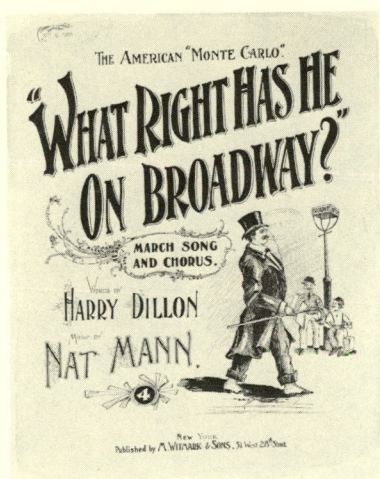

Casino Theatre, at Broadway and Thirty-ninth Street, New York, where Carrie made her theatrical debut in the chorus line. Museum of the City of New York

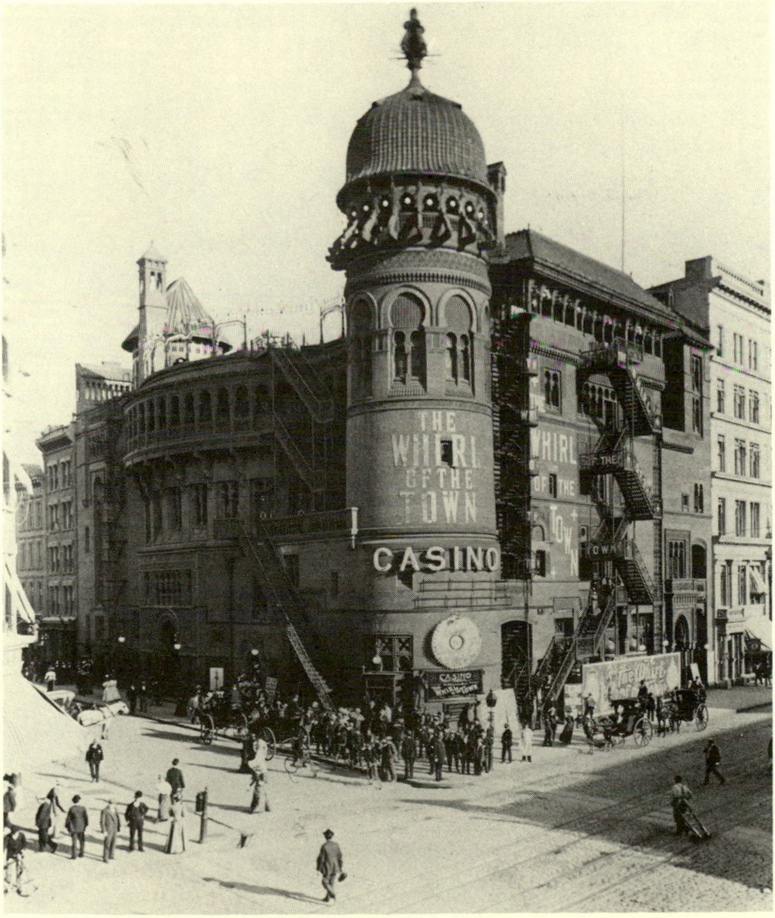

Trolley strike in Brooklyn, 1899, with police guards. Byron Collection, Museum of the City of New York

A dinner at Sherry's. Museum of the City of New York

HISTORICAL NOTES

Proper names and phrases that require factual, historical, or literary documentation have been annotated. These annotations provide the reader not only with clarification of unfamiliar place names, terminology, and historical fact, but also with an appreciation for the significance of the myriad details in *Sister Carrie*, for Dreiser did not use detail whimsically.

The factual material is so rich, and Dreiser's almost photographic mind retained so much of what he saw, that even passing references can be of considerable interest in understanding the historic qualities of the novel. For example, in a description of central Chicago, Dreiser mentions that "large plates of window glass . . . were then rapidly coming into use." These windows were in fact unique to Chicago at one time. Called "Chicago windows" they featured a large fixed center-pane with movable sashes on either side, and were a direct outgrowth of the use by Chicago architects of the skeleton frame. This reference illustrates Dreiser's close attention to factual detail. The research for the annotations has proven that it is nearly always safe to trust Dreiser. If he refers to Hurstwood's $1.50 dinner, it is safe to assume that the price of a good meal at the restaurant described will have been just that. Another example of Dreiser's use of authentic background is his description of the narrow and joyless household of the Hansons. Just such lower-middle-class families lived in the Union Park area of Chicago on the West Side, an area Dreiser knew well. Their lives were bound to work and home, their pleasures were few, and their outside contacts were minimal. (See Richard Sennett, *Families Against the City: Middle Class Homes of Industrial Chicago, 1872–1890* [Cambridge: Harvard University Press, 1970], pp. 48–59.)

Another example of significant small detail is the mention of the popular song "What Right Has He On Broadway." The verse is a rueful but humorous plaint of a man who knows that his clothes must be proper when he appears on that illustrious street. He is in reality a derelict who stays in the lobbies of hotels until he is asked to leave, then sleeps in the park. The parallel with Hurstwood's condition is unmistakable. (For verse and chorus of this song, see the historical note at 323.16.)

Dreiser describes the world of the theater in great detail. The plays of the period are recorded along with the opulent throngs, the brilliant lights, and the surge of movement on the streets. Together these details provide an artist's vision of the authentic atmosphere of the time. Unless Dreiser's references are examined carefully, however, it is not immediately apparent that there is virtually no mention of serious theater, that the great actors of the day such as Edwin Booth and John Drew are never mentioned, that no one goes to the opera or sees a Shakespearean play. Dreiser recorded one form of drama only, the light frothy fare of the popular theater. He was surely aware of other forms of theater, but in the context of *Sister Carrie* he deemed these forms inappropriate. He selected his material to suit his novel.

Another instance of Dreiser's discrimination lies in the fact that he eliminated a segment of society he knew well, the wealthy, successful men such as Marshall Field and Philip D. Armour about whom he wrote regularly for periodicals. Robert Ames is the only character in the novel who could be considered famous. Dreiser wrote an article on Thomas Alva Edison just a few months before he started writing *Sister Carrie*, and it is possible that Ames was modelled after Edison. The resemblances are striking. Ames is an inventor; he has just invented a new lamp; he is a celebrity of sufficient note to achieve newspaper acclaim. He is not handsome in the theatrical sense, but he has strong features and a direct gaze and is a man of superior intellect. All of these qualities can be ascribed to Edison. Furthermore, Edison came from the West, as did Ames; he set up a laboratory in the East, as did Ames.

Dreiser frequently drew on real-life experiences but altered the details to suit his story. For example, his sister Emma ran away from Chicago to New York with her lover after he had stolen thirty-five hundred dollars from Chapin and Gore, a low-class tavern with overhead oscillating fans above the bar, and a distinctly working-class clientele. Dreiser upgraded this escapade for *Sister Carrie*. Carrie ran away from Chicago to New York with her lover-to-be after he had stolen ten thousand dollars from Hannah and Hogg's, an elaborate nineteenth-century establishment with a curved marble bar, a beautiful ceramic tile floor, and a well-to-do clientele. While both of these drinking establishments were real places (as photographs from the Chicago Historical Society substantiate) it suited Dreiser's purpose to choose a more glamorous life for Carrie than his sister Emma had ever experienced.

Dreiser seems to have had a general rule that when he issued a pejorative or derogatory judgment of a person or place he used a fictitious name for this person or place. On the other hand, if his statement was neutral or complimentary he used actual names. He used a fictitious name for Carrie's place of employment, Rhodes, Morgenthau and Scott, which is branded by Drouet as a "cheap outfit," for example, but real names for theaters and department stores.

For the convenience of the reader, annotations are listed in the notes with reference to the chapter, page, and line where they occur. Specifically, the following have been annotated: (1) proper names, (2) geographical locations, (3) literary references, (4) slang words or phrases, and (5) quotations. There are no annotations for streets, theaters, restaurants, public buildings, or Carrie's residences in the novel unless they are of special significance. These locations are marked on the maps of Carrie's Chicago and New York included in this edition. Whenever a specific reference does not appear either in the annotations or on the maps, historical documentation has been inconclusive or nonexistent for the note or reference, or the matter referred to has been found to be fictitious in nature.

These annotations, like "*Sister Carrie*: From Manuscript to Print," are directed not to the scholar already familiar with Dreiser's novel but to the advanced reader who may well need some aid in understanding the era of *Sister Carrie*. The time span encompasses the years between 1884, when Dreiser first visited

Chicago as a boy of thirteen, and 1900, when he finished writing *Sister Carrie*. Bold-face type signals the annotated term or name as quoted from the text.

J.C.B.
A.M.W.

Notes

CHAPTER I

3.7   **August, 1889**   This is the only specific date mentioned in the novel. In the holograph, Dreiser originally gave the date of Carrie's arrival in Chicago as "1894," then erased that date and wrote "1884" over the erasure. The typist read the smeared manuscript incorrectly and typed "1894." This date was in turn crossed out in the typescript and written over in pencil in Dreiser's hand with the date "1889." Most scholars have agreed that Dreiser was trying to settle on a date which would most nearly represent his actual experiences in Chicago and New York.

3.21   **Columbia City**   In *Sister Carrie*, Dreiser places the town in Wisconsin, but it is in fact in Indiana, approximately thirty miles from Warsaw, where the Dreiser family lived.

4.38   **Waukesha**   A resort town in Wisconsin, on the Little Fox River, sixteen miles west of Milwaukee and approximately fifty miles north of Chicago. It is noted for its mineral springs. White Rock Water and other bottled waters were shipped from there.

5.24   **"drummers"**   Traveling salesmen.

5.29   **"masher"**   A male flirt.

5.40   **the secret insignia of the Order of Elks**   The insignia features a clock pointing to the hour of eleven, the ceremonial hour for toasting deceased members.

6.17–7.2   **Let . . . regard.**   This passage was adapted by Dreiser from George Ade's sketch "The Fable of the Two Mandolin Players and the Willing Performer" in Ade's *Fables in Slang* (Chicago and New York: Herbert S. Stone & Co., 1899), pp. 181–94. The borrowing did not go unnoticed; a reviewer for the *Syracuse Post-Standard* remarked that Dreiser had clipped "a page entire from Mr. Ade's 'Fables in Slang' " (see *Theodore Dreiser: The Critical Reception*, edited by Jack Salzman [New York: David Lewis, 1972], p. 12). Dreiser had the passage altered in the plates of *Sister Carrie* for the 1907 B. W. Dodge reprinting. This revised passage appeared in all subsequent impressions from those plates. In 1926, when Dreiser became embroiled in another plagiarism controversy over a passage that he took from Sherwood Anderson, Ade was asked in an interview to comment. He gave Dreiser this handsome tribute: "We

Hoosiers are proud of him, for he erects literary skyscrapers while we're busy pounding out chicken coops or bungalows" (*New York Herald Tribune*, 9 September 1926). The textual history of the Ade passage is traced in the emendation note at 6.17–7.2 of this edition. For commentary on this much-discussed matter, see W. A. Swanberg, *Dreiser* (New York: Scribner, 1965), p. 314, and Ellen Moers, *Two Dreisers* (New York: Viking Press, 1969), pp. 130–32.

CHAPTER II

12.26 **a cleaner of refrigerator cars**   Dreiser attempted this occupation in 1887 when fellow lodgers urged him to apply for a job in the stockyards. He was dismissed after a half day of drudgery. See *Dawn* (New York: Horace Liveright, 1931), pp. 301–2.

15.5–6 **a city of over 500,000**   The population of Chicago in 1880 was approximately 500,000. In 1889, however, with the annexation of Hyde Park, Lake Cicero, Jefferson, and part of Lake View, the population (according to the school census) was 1,066,213.

CHAPTER III

18.20 **screwing up her courage to the sticking point**   The passage is a reference to *Macbeth* I.vii.60: "But screw your courage to the sticking place."

18.30 **"Storm and King"**   Probably a fictitious name. There was a J. A. King dry goods store at 669 W. Lake Street.

21.40 **The first three [department stores] in the United States, established about 1884, were in Chicago.**   Actually Marshall Field was established in 1868 on State Street in Chicago in a six-story building named Palmer's Marble Palace. It was a retail store that sold not only dry goods, but also a wide variety of other merchandise. In New York City, Claflin's and Stewart's Department Stores predated Marshall Field. (Bessie Louise Pierce, *A History of Chicago* [New York: Knopf, 1940], 2:109.)

22.3 **the "Daily News"**   Victor F. Lawson and Company, proprietor, was located at 123–25 Fifth Avenue, Chicago. George Ade and Eugene Field, both admired by Dreiser, wrote for this newspaper.

CHAPTER IV

38.10 **"Mark"**   Slang for an object of ridicule or abuse.

38.25 **"Duffer"**   A dull, mischievous, or unrealistic person.

38.27 **"Rubber"**   Short for "rubberneck." A person who stares or gawks at something or someone.

40.12–13 **"you'll jar your back hair"**   Ruffle your composure.

CHAPTER V

41.32 **Hannah and Hogg's**   The "resort" Dreiser refers to was actually located at 146 Madison Street, opposite the Federal Building.

Other locations of this chain of "resorts" were 88 LaSalle, 190 W. Madison, and 220 Clark Streets, according to the Chicago Directory of that period.

42.14   **Joseph Jefferson** III (1829–1905)   A third generation member of a theatrical family, he achieved international acclaim for his portrayal of the title role in *Rip Van Winkle*, a play adapted for him by Dion Boucicault in London in 1865. He performed this role throughout his lifetime.

42.15   **Henry E. Dixey**   An actor (1859–1943) who appeared in musical comedies and became famous for his performance in the title role of *Adonis*, first performed and introduced in Hooley's Theater. The Elks Lodge No. 4 met regularly in Hooley's to conduct meetings. Carrie makes her acting debut later in the novel in a theater production sponsored by the Elks.

42.19   **"rounders"**   Persons who frequent or make the rounds of saloons and other resorts; debauchers.

45.13   **Old Hennessy**   The 1900 edition printed this name as Old Pepper, probably at the insistence of Doubleday, Page, since Hennessy is the name of an actual imported cognac. The query "real?" is scribbled next to "Old Hennessy" in the margin of the Mallon typescript.

46.24   **"A Hole in the Ground"**   Subtitled "A Wail for the Woes of a Wayfarer," it was one of seventeen farces written by Charles Hoyt (1860–99), a skillful writer and producer of farce. The first production was in 1887 in Philadelphia. The first Chicago production was in 1889.

48.9   **Jules Wallace**   A spiritualist who professed to heal the sick. Dreiser wrote a series of articles about him for the *St. Louis Republic* in 1898: "Jules Wallace, Fake, Fraud, Medium, Healer," 9 September 1898, pp. 1–2; "Wallace on Wallace," 10 September 1898, p. 6; and "A Spiritualist Fraud," 11 September 1898, p. 3.

CHAPTER VI

53.20   **"You're a daisy."**   A shortened slang term for "Daisy Miller-ism," which suggests bold or unconventional behavior on the part of women. Henry James's novel *Daisy Miller* was published in 1878. The term "daisy" was in common use by the late 1880s, but the man on the street would have been unaware of the literary allusion.

54.32   **"Eight Bells"**   A pantomime comedy that opened in Union Square Theater, New York, on 7 September 1891. It was an acrobatic reworking of an old farce entitled *To Paris and Back for Five Francs*.

55.5   **Plasterers or Woodworkers Unions**   Craft unions that formed the nucleus for the American Federation of Labor founded in Columbus, Ohio, in December 1880. The A.F.L. was a loose confederation of autonomous unions.

59.21   **Rhodes, Morgenthau and Scott**   Probably a fictitious name. There was a Morgenthau Company listed in the 1895 Chicago Directory at 163 State and 47–51 Monroe.

CHAPTER VII

64.12   **"He keepeth His creatures whole."**   An unidentified reference. Though biblical in phrasing, it does not derive from any specific passage in the Bible, nor does it seem to have its derivation in religious books of devotion such as *The Book of Common Prayer*.

CHAPTER VIII

76.7   **"The Mikado"**   A Gilbert and Sullivan light opera, also called *The Town of Titipu*, it was first produced at the Savoy in London on 14 March 1885. According to Sheila Hope Jurnak in "Popular Art Forms in *Sister Carrie*," *Texas Studies in Literature and Language* 12 (Summer 1971): 314, the version to which Dreiser refers was "probably the Sydney Rosenfeld production which appeared in Chicago. A contemporary review called the performance 'wholly discreditable.' "

78.24   **"There are more things . . ."**   *Hamlet*, I. v. 166–67.

80.25   **euchre**   A card game played by two, three, or four people. It can also be a verb meaning to outwit, or get the better of, as by scheming. Dreiser may have had both definitions in mind when he created this scene.

80.26   **Sec**   A dry wine.

CHAPTER IX

83.15   **Fox Lake**   A summer resort about thirty-five miles north of Chicago.

83.23   **Vega-cura**   Probably a patent medicine with some vegetable base. Patent medicines were extremely popular and were daily advertised in newspapers.

84.1   **lyceum**   A generic term for a lecture hall.

86.19   **perfection vests**   See p. 94 for a description of the one Hurstwood is wearing.

CHAPTER X

87.34   **Spencer**   Herbert Spencer (1820–1903) was an English philosopher who attempted to work out a philosophy, based on the scientific discoveries of his day, which could be applied to all subjects. Dreiser read his *First Principles* (1862) in 1894 in Pittsburgh. For an analysis of Spencer's effect on Dreiser's own philosophy see W. A. Swanberg, *Dreiser*, pp. 60–61; Robert H. Elias, *Theodore Dreiser: Apostle of Nature* (New York: Knopf, 1949), pp. 80–83; and for the fullest discussion see Ellen Moers, *Two Dreisers*, pp. 134–45.

88.33   **A good Brussels carpet**   The carpet is woven on a Brussels power loom and is made with three-ply or four-ply worsted yarn drawn up in uncut loops to form a pattern over the entire surface (body Brussels). A cheaper version is made of worsted or woolen yarns on which a pattern is printed (tapestry Brussels). The loom was developed in the United States by Erastus B. Bigelow in 1848.

CHAPTER XI

98.31   **Pardridge's**   C. W. & E. Pardridge's was a store with branches
at 114–16 State Street and 284 W. Madison.

100.26   **Armour**   Philip D. Armour (1832–1901) was the first of the
modern meat packers. He came to Chicago in 1875 to supervise
his brother's firm, which dealt in meats and grain. By the time
Dreiser wrote *Sister Carrie*, Armour's products were known throughout the world. See Dreiser's magazine article "Philip D. Armour,"
Success, October 1898, pp. 3–4.

100.26   **Pullman**   George M. Pullman (1831–97) began remodeling
sleeping cars in 1859. By 1880 the Pullman Palace Car Company
was building freight cars and street cars as well as sleeping cars, and
in Dreiser's time was the largest car-building company in the country. Dreiser discussed the company town Pullman created, in "The
Town of Pullman," *Ainslee's*, 18 March 1899, pp. 189–200.

100.26–27 **Potter Palmer** (1826–1902)   He was a Chicago merchandiser
who developed State Street and made it the present street of department stores. The first Palmer House (a hotel) was built in
1869–70 but was destroyed by the Chicago Fire, which began on
the night of 9 October 1871. The second Palmer House was built
on the same location in 1873. See map.

100.27   **Marshall Field** (1834–1906)   He came to Chicago in 1856 and
worked as a clerk for Cooley, Wadsworth and Company. He eventually bought Potter Palmer's merchandising business, which he
developed into the largest department store in the world. See note
on department stores, 21.40. See also Dreiser's article "Marshall
Field," *Success*, December 1898, pp. 7–8.

103.11–12 **Bertha M. Clay**   Pseudonym of Charlotte M. Braeme
(1836–84), a popular English Roman Catholic writer. She wrote
sixty-eight novels during her lifetime. *Dora Thorne* was her most
popular novel. Her pseudonym was carried on after her death by
other writers for her publisher, Street and Smith. Dreiser expressed
his low opinion of American literary taste in "Why Not Tell Europe
about Bertha Clay," *New York Call*, 24 October 1921, p. 6.

CHAPTER XII

109.5–6   **The Exposition**   This was a permanent exposition housed in
the Inter-State Industrial Exposition Building. A collection of modern paintings and sculpture was permanently on display, and dry
goods, millinery, and manufactured items were exhibited each autumn. In one wing was an indoor beer garden where symphonic
concerts and grand opera were occasionally performed. James Garfield was nominated for the Presidency in this building.

CHAPTER XIII

113.27   **"Rip Van Winkle"**   See note on Joseph Jefferson, 42.14.

114.23   **Kinsley's**   Kinsley's Restaurant and Catering Establishment was
constructed in 1885 in Moresque architectural style and patterned
after the Alhambra at Grenada. It was located at 105–7 Adams

562 · HISTORICAL COMMENTARY

Street and was the first building in Chicago to be lighted with
electricity.

116.14–15 **philosophy of the grapeless fox**   A reference to the Aesop fable
"The Fox and the Grapes," wherein the fox consoles himself by
saying the unattainable object is worthless.

119.8–13 **That it is not true of beauty alone that**
     ". . . it speaketh through the landscape
     And it speaketh through the sky."
but that
     "All its realms are earth and heaven
     Good and evil, thou and I."
The poetry in this passage has not been identified. Dreiser may
be quoting a popular poem of the period.

CHAPTER XIV

121.32 **Bowery Hell**   Probably the sort of low-class tavern that catered
to the needs of the most depraved segment of society; also called
a hell-hole. The Bowery is a district that runs north-south on the
lower tip of Manhattan; it became associated with derelicts in the
1890s.

121.33 **Sisters of Mercy**   A religious order of the Roman Catholic
Church founded in 1827 by Catharine McAuley and dedicated to
the spiritual and temporal welfare of the poor, the sick, and the
ignorant.

125.13 **horse car**   Chicago had eighty-six miles of cable tracks by
March 1894, but on the West Side, where Carrie lived, no cable
service was available until 1890, and then it was limited. The
South Side was the first area to receive cable car service with the
State Street and Cottage Grove lines, which reached 63d and 67th
Streets by 1887. A year later the North Side got its first cable
service on Clark and Wills Streets.

126.20–21 **macadamized road**   John Loudon McAdam (1756–1836), a
Scottish inventor, lent his name to the system of road building
called "macadamizing." He developed the modern paved road, and
from this development came this country's system of national roads.

CHAPTER XVI

140.36 **the Derby**   American Derby Day took place annually in late
spring, from 1884 to 1904, at the Washington Park Race Track,
61st Street and Cottage Grove Avenue. The coaching set, in all
its finery, attended this event.

142.35 **Wheaton**   A town twenty miles west of Chicago.

CHAPTER XVII

152.13 **a way-up Mason**   Under the Scottish Rite of Freemasonry, the
highest-ranking mason is the 33d degree, which is conferred by the
Consistory of Master Masons in good standing.

153.6–7 **"Over the Hills"**   A reference to Will Carleton's poem "Over
the Hill to the Poor-house." Dreiser was fond of the poem and

mentioned in *Dawn*, p. 105, that it was "a poem that always reminded me of my brother Paul's attitude toward his mother." The poem begins as follows:

Over the hill to the poor-house I'm trudgin' my weary way—
I, a woman of seventy, and only a trifle gray—
I, who am smart an' chipper, for all the years I've told
As many another woman that's only half as old.

Over the hill to the poor-house—I can't quite make it clear!
Over the hill to the poor-house—it seems so horrid queer!
Many a step I've taken a-toilin' to and fro,
But this is a sort of journey I never thought to go.

What is the use of heapin' on me a pauper's shame?
Am I lazy or crazy? am I blind or lame?
True, I am not so supple nor yet so awful stout;
But charity ain't no favor, if one can live without.

I am willin' and anxious an' ready any day
To work for a decent livin', an' pay my honest way;
For I can earn my victuals, an' more too, I'll be bound,
If any body only is willin' to have me round.

Will Carleton, *Farm Ballads* (New York: Harper & Brothers, 1875), pp. 51–62.

This long poem continues for many stanzas, in which the old woman describes how she was rejected by her children, one by one. Dreiser's brother Paul probably resembles the loving jailbird son who finally rescues his mother from poverty in a sequel called "Over the Hill from the Poorhouse."

153.13   **"Under the Gaslight"**   This melodramatic play by Augustin Daly was first performed in 1867 at the Worrell Sisters Theater in New York. It was the first of many productions to use the device of a hero or heroine tied to a railroad track by the villain just as the express train is due, although Dreiser eliminates this scene. See Donald Pizer's analysis of the play in *The Novels of Theodore Dreiser: A Critical Study* (Minneapolis: University of Minnesota Press, 1976), pp. 41–42. See also Hugh Witemeyer, "Gaslight and Magic Lamp in *Sister Carrie*," PMLA 86 (1971): 236–40, and Moers, *Two Dreisers*, pp. 109–11.

153.14   **Augustin Daly** (1838–99)   One of America's most successful playwright-producers and a staunch supporter of the "star system," he operated one or more theaters in New York for thirty years and a theater in London for several years as well.

154.31–32 **Custer Lodge of the Order of Elks**   This seems to be a contrived name. The only Elks Lodge listed in the 1889 City Directory appears in the entry: "BPOE Chicago Lodge No. 4, meets every Thursday at 8 P.M. at lodge room, Hooley's Theater Building, 149 Randolph." Several other fraternal orders in Chicago had "Custer" lodges, but these were on the South Side and other outlying areas far from the action of the novel. These lodges were named in honor of George Armstrong Custer (1839–76), who led the attack on the Sioux Indians in 1876 in the Battle of Little Bighorn, which came to be known in folklore as "Custer's Last Stand." He and his entire center column of 264 men were killed in the battle.

159.5	**Scanlan**	William J. Scanlan (1856–98) was a popular Irish co-median and vocalist born in Springfield, Massachusetts. At the age of thirteen, he became known as "the Temperance Boy Songster" and traveled throughout the country.

CHAPTER XVIII

165.22	**John L. Sullivan, the pugilist** (1858–1918)	He was the last bare knuckle World's Heavyweight Champion. He won the heavy-weight title in 1882 and lost it in 1892 to James J. Corbett.

CHAPTER XIX

172.1	**Avery Hall**	The description of this theater matches that of the Waverly Theater situated opposite the Dreiser apartment on West Madison Street at Throop, where Dreiser lived as a boy in 1884. Dreiser described the Waverly as follows: "Across the street in front and covering the entire block was the old—but now disappeared—Waverly Theater and, in summer, open-air beer garden, where nightly was to be heard music and the applause of a pleasurably entertained public. For here, too, was dancing—in the mornings roller-skating for the young—and along its roof's edge, on all three sides, bright-colored flags—of all nations, I presume" (*Dawn*, pp. 157–58).

CHAPTER XXIII

211.19	**Chesterfieldian arts**	The practice of elegant deportment and vanity in speech and dress originally espoused by Philip Dormer Stanhope Chesterfield (1694–1773), 4th Earl of Stanhope. He is noted as the author of *Letters to His Son*, posthumously published in 1774, in which he emphasizes the importance of honesty, learn-ing, and elegant manners.

218.15	**Chicago and Detroit** [baseball] **teams**	In 1871 the Chicago White Stockings participated in the formation of the National Professional Base-ball Association and five years later in the orga-nization of the National Base-ball League. During 1887, the year Dreiser went to Chicago to look for work, the closeness of the final standings between Chicago and Detroit created intense interest in the rivalry. Detroit was the final victor, winning seventy-nine games to Chicago's seventy-one.

218.30	**Bunko-steerer**	A member of a confidence team who conducts his victim to a remote spot or prearranged location for the purpose of fleecing or robbing him.

219.7–8	**suit to compel the Illinois Central**	The lawsuit to eject the Illinois Central Railroad from the lakefront was settled in 1887 by the United States Supreme Court. The decision was overwhelming for the city's claims in support of the railroad's right-of-way. An act of ejectment was first sought in 1852.

CHAPTER XXVII

250.22   **Mr. Francis Wilson** (1854–1935)   An actor who made his debut in Philadelphia in 1878 and achieved stardom in musical comedy.

252.10   **Charles Frohman** (1854–1915)   The first of America's theatrical tycoons, he operated five theaters in New York City, one in London, and several hundred others throughout the United States.

252.32–33 **Nat Goodwin** (1857–1919)   A popular comic actor and one of Charles Frohman's stars. He was noted for his roles in the field of burlesque and light comedy, although he did perform in some serious drama.

CHAPTER XXVIII

255.5–6   **Mr. Wilson's company at the Chicago Opera House**   The repertory company of Francis Wilson.

255.13   **"The Old Homestead"**   A play written by Denman Thompson, the actor, and first produced as a sketch in 1875. It was a comedy of country folk, popular in the eighties and nineties.

257.16   **the "Great American Art Company"**   This name is contrived. The 1895 Chicago Directory lists the "Great Western Art Company" at 170 Madison Street, but no further information on this enterprise is available.

CHAPTER XXIX

264.23   **William Gillette** (1855–1937)   He made his debut in 1875 and became not only an outstanding actor but a playwright as well. The zenith of his career came in 1899 with his portrayal of the lead role in the play *Sherlock Holmes.*

271.35   **At the first drug store he stopped, seeing a long-distance telephone booth.**   Dreiser may have been referring to the Sargeant Drug Store on Wabash, a few blocks from Hannah and Hogg's. There were very few public phone booths available in the late 1880s.

272.1   **1643**   Telephone number of the Michigan Central Railroad Depot. The Chicago directory of 1882 lists the number as 510. In 1887, when Dreiser lived in Chicago, the number was 5569.

CHAPTER XXX

280.8   **Michigan City**   A town in Indiana, near Lake Michigan, about forty miles from Chicago.

CHAPTER XXXII

296.23   **Pinkerton**   Allan Pinkerton (1819–84) established in Chicago the first private detective agency in the United States. He guarded Abraham Lincoln on his journey from Springfield, Illinois, to Washington, D.C., to be inaugurated as President. Shortly after the outbreak of the Civil War, Pinkerton assisted in organizing the

Federal Secret Service, of which he became chief, while still operating his private agencies in various cities.

296.23 **Mooney and Boland**   The Mooney and Boland Detective Agency was a national detective firm with offices in major cities in the United States.

303.12 **Spuyten Duyvil**   The part of the Harlem River nearest the Hudson was called Spuyten Duyvil Creek. It was expanded into a ship canal, which was opened for traffic 17 June 1895. Before the construction of the canal, the tides raced through the creek, and when the two tides from the Harlem and Hudson met, the tide rips thus formed caused so great a turbulence in the creek that the water "spouted" or was thrown into the air. In ancient maps and records many variants are found, such as: "Spitting devil," "Spiking devil," "Spitten devil," "Spouting devil," and "Spiken devil." See Stephen Jenkins, *The Greatest Street in the World* (New York: G. P. Putnam's Sons, 1911), p. 336.

304.1 **a million or more**   According to the official census of 1890, the population of New York City was a million and a half.

304.13 **the Continental hotel**   Situated at Broadway and 20th. The name was changed in the 1900 edition to the Belford.

CHAPTER XXXIII

304.25 **Vanderbilt, Gould, and Russell Sage**   Cornelius Vanderbilt (1794–1877), Jay Gould (1836–92), and Russell Sage (1816–1906) attained their huge fortunes primarily in transportation. Steamboats and ferries were parts of their lucrative businesses, but these men built railroads primarily and manipulated their wealth in ways advantageous to themselves.

304.30 **Howells**   William Dean Howells (1837–1920), literary critic and novelist, was known by Dreiser and his contemporaries as the dean of American letters. As editor of *Harper's Magazine*, he championed realistic fiction and encouraged writers such as Hamlin Garland, Stephen Crane, and Frank Norris. Dreiser wrote two articles about Howells, one for *Success*, April 1898, entitled "How William Dean Howells Climbed Fame's Ladder," and the other for *Ainslee's*, March 1900, entitled "The Real Howells." Howells's career as a novelist spanned over forty years, during which time he wrote novels of manners, and later serious works of realistic fiction that deal with the problems of contemporary industrial society. See Moers, *Two Dreisers*, pp. 43–56.

304.30 **Z. G. A. Ward**   Dreiser may have been referring to J. Q. A. Ward. John Quincy Adams Ward (1830–1910) was a friend of Howells and a well-known sculptor who became president of the National Academy of Design. He is famous for his sculpture "The Indian Hunter," which was placed in Central Park in New York City.

304.30 **John LaFarge (1835–1910)**   A talented painter who worked in oils and water colors, on wood and with stained glass. He traveled widely, studied at the Louvre, and visited Japan and the South Seas.

304.31 **Edison** Thomas Alva Edison (1847–1931) invented the phonograph and the electric lamp before 1900. In the 1880s he personally installed the electric lighting system for the Madison Square Theater, managed by Steele McKaye.

304.31 **Dana** Charles Anderson Dana (1819–1897) was a journalist who became a national figure as editor of the *New York Sun*. His paper specialized in the human interest story. Earlier in his career he wrote for the *Harbinger*, the newspaper associated with the Brook Farm Experiment.

304.31 **Conklin** Probably Edwin Grant Conklin (1863–1952), noted American biologist and author of many books, including *Heredity and Environment, Biology and Democracy*, and *Freedom and Responsibility*.

304.31 **John Kelly** Successor to "Boss" Tweed in the leadership of Tammany Hall, he induced many leading reformers to serve as his advisers.

304.32 **Tammany Hall** Founded as a fraternity of patriots by William Mooney in 1789, it became a political machine wielding vast power in New York. William M. Tweed initiated complete boss domination of the Hall in 1868. Under Tweed, New York City was plundered of over two hundred million dollars, and the name Tammany Hall became synonymous with political dominance and corruption.

CHAPTER XXXIV

316.24 **tenderloin** A district in New York City noted for corruption and vice; so called because police there could eat well from their bribes.

323.16 **"What Right Has He On Broadway"** This was a popular song with words by Harry Dillon and music by Nat Mann. It was copyrighted 4 September 1895. The three stanzas and chorus are as follows:

1. On the Bow'ry you can make a front,
In a suit of hand me down,
But don't think you're the real thing till
You mingle in up town.
On Broadway that's the place to note,
The shabby from the fad,
And if you're in a misfit,
Why it makes you look quite sad.

2. On a bicycle [*sic*] I look a dream,
I ride one in my sleep!
Yes that's about the only way,
But still it's very cheap,
And when I spin along up town,
How good it makes me feel,
To hear the ladies whisper,
There's a gent that's got a Wheel.

3. I always stop at good hotels,
For I'm a son of rest,

I stay until the porter says,
These seats are for the guests,
Like swallows then I homeward fly,
I'm not out after dark.
My room is always open,
For I'm sleeping in the park.

CHORUS:
When you're on Broadway,
There you must look the part,
Of a man that owns a mine,
And can open lots of wine,
If you're not dressed complete,
They'll say what right has he on Broadway.

CHAPTER XXXV

326.40	**"A Gold Mine"** A play written in 1889 by Brander Matthews and George H. Jessop.
327.35 and 328.4	**Altman's, Stewart's** These department stores were two of the most exclusive and expensive stores in New York. In the 1900 edition "Stewart's" was changed to "Lord and Taylor's."
329.40	**Florence** W. J. Florence (1831–91) was a popular comedy actor. His most famous role was the vulgar Yankee politician, the Hon. Bardwell Slate, in Benjamin E. Woolf's *The Mighty Dollar.*
330.34	**the Plaza Square** A city square named for the Plaza Hotel, which opened in 1890.
334.34	**"The Opening of a Chestnut Burr"** A popular novel of the day, by Edward Payson Roe (1838–88), published in 1874. In the 1900 edition the title was changed to *Moulding a Maiden* by Albert Ross, pseudonym of Linn Boyd Porter (1851–1916). Porter's novel was published in 1891.

CHAPTER XXXVI

339.13–14	**katastates . . . anastates** According to Donald Pizer, these "were terms in common usage among physiologists in the 1890s. Anastates were stored energy substances in the metabolic process; katastates were the waste products of energy use. Dreiser derived his specialized (and generally unaccepted) concept of these substances from Elmer Gates, an eccentric scientist about whom he was attempting to write an article in early 1900." See Pizer's edition of *Sister Carrie* (New York: Norton, 1970), p. 240. For a detailed study of Dreiser's commitment to this theory see Moers, *Two Dreisers,* pp. 160–69.
340.20	**Epictetus** An ethical philosopher (ca. A.D. 60–110), who taught the love of good and hatred of evil, obedience to the dictates of conscience, and perfect trust in a wise and merciful Providence.

CHAPTER XXXVII

346.37	**"80,000 people out of employment . . ."** There was wide-

spread unemployment in New York in the 1890s during a period of severe depression.

354.18   **Lethean waters**   In Greek mythology the Lethe was one of the rivers of Hades. It was the river of oblivion, the waters of which caused anyone who drank thereof to forget his former existence.

354.24   **Princess Bay**   In the holograph and the original Mallon typescript this place name was spelled correctly. In the 1900 edition, however, it was changed to "Prince's Bay."

354.27   **Fanny Davenport (1850–98)**   One of Augustin Daly's prominent stock actresses. Born in London, she was discovered by Daly in 1869 and trained by him. She left Daly in the 1880s to form her own company.

CHAPTER XXXVIII

335.27   **Alsbery and Company, whiskey brokers**   This may be Asbury and Company, an importing house where Henry George, a noted socialist, worked for a time. For more on George, see note on "single tax," 491.1.

356.40   **Dorlon's**   Dorlon's Oyster House was located at 6 E. 23d Street.

CHAPTER XL

377.17   **Sarah Bernhardt (1844–1923)**   "The Divine Sarah" was born in Paris and made her acting debut at la Comédie-Française in 1862. Her roles covered a wide range in both French and English drama, and she became one of the most acclaimed actresses in the world. Between 1880 and 1917 she toured America nine times.

379.5   **John B. Drake**   Dreiser depicts him as being about to open his well-known hotel in New York. He also managed the Grand Pacific Hotel in Chicago.

380.10   **"The Clipper"**   A theatrical newspaper published in New York between 1853 and 1924. It evolved into the current theatrical publication *Billboard Magazine*.

CHAPTER XLI

385.2   **the opera chorus**   These "operas" were not grand opera, but light, frothy forerunners of the musical comedy.

385.21   **Daniel Frohman (1851–1940)**   Brother of American theater tycoon Charles Frohman, he became the manager of the Lyceum Theater, Fourth Avenue and 23d Street, in 1886.

385.23   **the Empire Theatre**   Opened in 1893 at Broadway and 41st Street under the aegis of Charles Frohman. Dreiser incorrectly located the theater on 40th Street and Broadway in the manuscript and typescript.

385.28   **Dorney**   Richard Dorney was Augustin Daly's business manager.

391.36   **Lillian Russell (1861–1922)**   She was famous for her beauty as well as her talent as an actress and a singer. She sang ballads in New York City theaters, and later appeared as leading lady in the comic opera productions of the McCaull Opera Company. She left

McCaull to organize her own company with which she toured the United States and England. Her real name was Nellie Leonard.

391.37 **Jefferson di Angeles**   A member of a theatrical family from California and star of the Broadway Theater production of *Caliph* in 1896. He appeared with Lillian Russell in *The Wedding Day* that same year.

CHAPTER XLII

396.25 **Manon**   The heroine of the novel *Manon Lescaut*, written in 1731 by Antoine François Prévost (1697–1763), known as Abbé Prévost. Dreiser is implying that Carrie's friend has the same characteristics of innocence and a frivolous attitude toward morality as did the young heroine in the novel. The novel became the basis for operas by Auber (1856), Massenet (1884), and Puccini (1893).

397.4 **"The Queen's Mate"**   A light opera by Henry Paulton, first performed in 1888. It was a revision of Lecocq's *La Princesse de Canaries*.

CHAPTER XLIII

409.2 **strike on the trolley lines in Brooklyn**   The event Dreiser draws on for his story began on 14 January 1895 and was marked by violence. It was thoroughly covered by the New York papers. The "Special Notice" paragraph on p. 410 is a direct quotation from the *New York Times* of 15 January 1895, although in the *Times* there was no headline that read "Special Notice."

The men were striking not only to have their wages raised from $2.00 a day to $2.25, but also to protest against the company policy that they each make fifteen or more trips a day, a requirement that caused them to have to travel at hazardous speeds. They were also protesting the policy of hiring "trippers" to work during rush hours and run perhaps three trips a day. The strikers were fearful that eventually the union men would be phased out and "trippers," who worked for lower wages, would take their jobs.

Dreiser had covered the story of a local trolley strike in March 1894 for the *Toledo Blade*, but that strike was uneventful.

412.22 **the Brooklyn City Railroad Building at Montague and Clinton**   Mentioned in a *New York Times* article on the strike (16 January 1895).

CHAPTER XLVI

444.31 **Sarony**   Napoleon Sarony was a leading theatrical photographer in the 1890s.

CHAPTER XLVII

450.26 **Wellington**   This hotel was located at 7th Avenue and 55th Street. The present Wellington, at the same site, was built in 1930.

453.2 **dado book shelves**   Shelves adorned with decorative molding.

454.35   the Chelsea   This hotel is located at 222 W. 23d Street. It has historically been favored by people of the theater.

CHAPTER XLVIII

465.22   **Fire signs**   Outdoor electrical lighting.
465.35   **a thousand different ways**   Dreiser recalled this scene on Broadway in an article entitled "The Color of Today," *Harper's Weekly*, 14 December 1901, pp. 1272–73.

CHAPTER XLIX

481.20   **"Saracinesca"**   A novel written by Francis Marion Crawford (1854–1909), who was born in Italy of American parents. The novel was first published in *Blackwood's Magazine* in England in 1887. Macmillan published the American edition in May of the same year. Crawford was a prolific and popular author, essentially a storyteller, whose works were found consistently in the best literary journals in England and America. He wrote four novels about the Saracinesca family: *Saracinesca* (1887), *Sant' Ilario* (1889), *Don Orsino* (1892), and *Corleone* (1898). Dreiser spelled this title "Sor a cenesca" in the holograph.

481.20–21   **"The Great Man from the Provinces"**   A novel by Honoré de Balzac (1799–1850). Dreiser admired Balzac's writing and his philosophy. Balzac argued that just as differences of environment and heredity produce various species of animals, so do the varying pressures of society produce differentiations among human beings.

481.21   **"The Mayor of Casterbridge"**   This novel and *Tess of the D'Urbervilles* were written by the renowned English novelist Thomas Hardy (1840–1928). Hardy's characters are motivated primarily by sex or "nature," and he portrays women in a frank and open manner, much as Dreiser portrays Carrie. *The Mayor of Casterbridge* was serialized in the *London Graphic* from 2 January to 15 May 1886, and in America in *Harper's Weekly*. It appeared in book form in New York in 1886, published by Henry Holt and Company. It is the tragic story of a man of character caught in the inexorable workings of fate. *Tess of the D'Urbervilles*, Hardy's most famous novel, was published in 1891.

482.9   **"Père Goriot"**   A novel by Honoré de Balzac which elucidates the constant theme of Balzac's novels, that of the young provincial struggling for advancement in the competitive world of Paris, where the demoralizing effects of contemporary life were at their most extreme.

482.18   **Lucien de Rubemfré**   A promising young man from the provinces, a poet and journalist, who appears and reappears in most of the novels of Balzac's "La Comédie humaine." He goes to Paris to realize his fortune but, finding the path to success full of difficulties, grows despondent. He appears in *Les Illusions perdues*, *Les Splendeurs et misères des courtisanes*, and *La Dernière Incarnation de Vautrin*.

488.4   **Sisters of Mercy**   These nuns were probably associated with Saint Francis Xavier Roman Catholic Church at 15th Street near 6th Avenue. For more on this religious order, see note for 121.33.

489.23   **Fleischmann the caterer . . . Broadway and 9th Street**   In the 1900 edition this address is listed as Broadway and 10th Street. Fleischmann's Vienna Model Bakery did, in fact, give bread to whoever needed it.

491.1   **single tax**   A concept popularized by Henry George (1839–97), economist and land reformer, in his book *Progress and Poverty* (1879). He espoused the position that the government should tax only land and income from real estate and should abolish all other taxes. From this "single tax" the government's annual income would be so large that there would be a surplus for expansion of public works, from roads to universities.

496.33   **euchre**   This card game is being played by three people in this scene, just as it was in the beginning of the novel (see note for 80.25). Dreiser originally wrote that Mrs. Hurstwood, her daughter, and her son-in-law were playing whist, then he crossed out "whist" and replaced it with "euchre."

498.17   **Sing Sing**   The state prison at Ossining, New York.

J.C.B.
A.M.W.

TEXTUAL
COMMENTARY

EDITORIAL PRINCIPLES

The Pennsylvania edition of *Sister Carrie* has been established according to modern copy-text principles of scholarly editing. The basic procedures are simple: the editor first collects all surviving forms of the text, both prepublication and post-publication, and then identifies the form closest to the author's hand. This text usually becomes the "copy-text" on which the edition is based. The copy-text is the general authority for "accidentals"—such features as punctuation, spelling, word-division, and paragraphing. The actual words are called "substantives." The editor collates the copy-text against all important subsequent versions of the work in search of later substantive changes introduced by the author. Such changes can then be emended back into the copy-text. Variants which appear to be nonauthorial are usually excluded from the text. The edition is therefore eclectic: whenever possible it follows the author's own accidentals, or those closest to his hand, but imposes on the text later changes proved or conjectured to be the author's. An extensive apparatus presents the textual evidence and records the editorial emendations. The interested scholar is thereby enabled to check the editorial work and question all decisions.[1]

Copy-Text

The selection of copy-text for *Sister Carrie* is simple. Dreiser's manuscript of the novel automatically becomes the base text for this edition. No other choice is possible: the typescript was corrupted by Anna Mallon's typists and was revised and cut by Sara Dreiser and Arthur Henry. The first printing was further flawed by editorial interference and censoring by Doubleday, Page and Company. Only the manuscript preserves the original text of *Sister Carrie*, the text that was most nearly under Dreiser's complete control. A further distinction must be made, however: copy-text for the Pennsylvania *Sister Carrie* is the original form of the manuscript *before* Jug and Henry made revisions in it. Some of their changes have been accepted into the text of this edition, but for theoretical reasons the copy-text must be defined as Dreiser's original manuscript, before nonauthorial alterations were introduced.

Substantive Emendations

The creation of *Sister Carrie* was a complicated and, in part, a collaborative enterprise. Dreiser allowed Jug and Henry to make revisions in the manuscript and typescript of his novel, and he accepted nearly all of their changes. His motives for doing so, however, must be examined carefully. *Sister Carrie* was Dreiser's first novel. He had high hopes that it would bring him literary success—favorable reviews and substantial royalties— and he was willing to accept advice and editing to achieve these goals. He must have believed that Jug's and Henry's changes would increase the marketability of his novel. Dreiser was young and unknown; his experience as a writer had been in newspaper reporting, where he had always worked with a rewrite man, and in freelance journalism, where his manuscripts had frequently been revised and cut by magazine editors. He had been conditioned to accept extensive nonauthorial alterations before he began composing *Sister Carrie*.

Dreiser's working relationship with Henry also demands close examination. In one important sense Henry was invaluable to Dreiser: he persuaded him to begin *Sister Carrie* and urged him to continue with the manuscript when he became discouraged. But one must realize that Henry was little more than a dilettante, an intellectual lightweight whose long suit was his boyish charm. Careful study of Henry's revisions in the manuscript and typescript of *Sister Carrie* leads to the inescapable conclusion that he did not really understand what Dreiser was trying to do in the novel. Dreiser was composing a serious work of art; Henry was trying to revise it into saleable fiction. Dreiser did not recognize, however, with what lack of depth Henry was reading the novel: to him Henry was an educated writer with a knowledge of the market and a practiced instinct about what kind of fiction would sell. Dreiser was much under Henry's spell during the composition of *Sister Carrie;* the typescript shows that Dreiser was inclined to accept whatever changes Henry proposed, no matter what effect these revisions had on the novel. Shortly after the publication of *Sister Carrie,* however, Dreiser began to see Henry more clearly and their friendship began to crumble. Years later Dreiser gave this retrospective portrait of Henry:

> As I saw him then and see him now, he was a dreamer of dreams, a spinner of fine fancies, a lover of impossible romances which fascinated me by their very impossibility. Also he was jolly, generous, a lover of life and of play, mostly play as I later came to think. His weakest and most irritating trait was a vaulting egotism which caused him to imagine, first, that he was as great a thinker and writer as had ever appeared; second, that he was at the same time practical, a man of the world, a man of affairs. Let him but give his solemn attention to any muddle and it must come straight. Let him but think seriously, and every philosophic as well as practical riddle was solved. In short, he loved to direct and control as well as argue. Because I liked him much, as did nearly every one else with whom he came in contact, I was inclined to let him have his way in everything. He was too delightful and interesting not to humor.[2]

Dreiser wrote this quasi-fictional characterization long after he and Henry had fallen out, but it still has a strong ring of truth about it.

Dreiser's relationship with Jug was quite different. His was the dominant personality in their marriage, but in one important area he was distinctly her inferior: Jug's formal education was much better than his. As early as the seventh grade, Dreiser had become painfully aware of his deficiencies in grammar, spelling, and other mechanical aspects of the language.[3] He never remedied these shortcomings and remained, throughout life, unable to spell and punctuate properly. Later in his career he would leave these features of his writing to secretaries and editors, but during the composition of *Sister Carrie* he used Jug as copy-editor and grammarian. For the most part she performed her duties well, but sometimes she overstepped her role. Particularly damaging was her insistence that Dreiser's characters observe grammatical niceties in dialogue. Dreiser, however, seems to have bowed readily to her knowledge of the formal rules of syntax. He adopted nearly all of her changes without question.

In accepting advice, cuts, and revisions from Jug and Henry, Dreiser was acting more as editor than as author. In the strictest sense, his authorial function ceased after he inscribed the holograph draft of *Sister Carrie*. Thereafter he acted as an editor and revised his own prose and decided what nonauthorial alterations, by Jug and Henry, to adopt. It is Dreiser's editorial judgment, with regard to Jug and Henry, that we question in this edition. Dreiser, Jug, and Henry were all working under various pressures, some self-imposed and some imposed by the times in which they lived. Their motives for revising and cutting *Sister Carrie* were sometimes artistic, but just as often they were not.

It has therefore been the policy of the Pennsylvania edition to examine each nonauthorial change made in Dreiser's text subsequent to the original inscription of the manuscript. It does not matter who made the change: Jug, Henry, or by extension the typists or compositors. For each alteration, the Pennsylvania editors have sought to determine the reason for the change. Was the revision made to remove a grammatical or mechanical problem? Was it made to "improve" the style? Was it made to streamline the narrative? Was it made to remove a factual reference? Was it made to tone down or remove a sexual reference? It is impossible to pinpoint a specific reason for every change, of course, but in a surprising number of instances the intention behind the revision is readily apparent. Moreover, the revisions and cuts (especially those by Henry) fall into predictable patterns.

Dreiser's own revisions, those he made without outside prompting, are simple to deal with. He was the creator of the novel, the artist from whose mind came the characters, plot, and theme of *Sister Carrie*. His revisions are nearly always accepted. When evidence in the typescript shows that Henry or Jug influenced Dreiser to make a revision, however, that revision is treated more circumspectly and is not always incorporated into the Pennsylvania text. It is important to realize that Dreiser almost never cut, and never censored, the text of *Sister Carrie* on his own. In virtually every instance he was prompted to cut and censor by Henry (or, later, by the Doubleday, Page editor).

Jug's revisions likewise present few problems. In most instances, she simply added necessary articles and prepositions, altered incorrect verb forms, and caught obvious typos. Most of her minor substantive alterations are necessary for simple correctness or clarity, and they have therefore been admitted to the Pennsylvania text. If Jug's alterations of these readings were not adopted, a scholarly editor would have to make the identical emendations. Where Jug made more significant changes, where she tinkered with Dreiser's prose style, corrected his grammar unnecessarily, or censored his references to sex, her alterations are rejected.

Henry's changes were bolder and more significant than Jug's. He frequently introduced fancied improvements in style, but unfortunately his own style was undistinguished. The sentences which he revised usually flow more smoothly, but they lack the force and weight of Dreiser's prose. As a result the Doubleday, Page text, which incorporates Henry's revisions, is a pastiche. Dreiser's Germanic rhythms and cumulative sentence structures dominate most of the narrative, but Henry's "improvements" crop up throughout, altering and often emasculating the original writing. The Pennsylvania edition has as one of its goals the preservation, wherever possible, of Dreiser's original prose, with its awkward power and forcefulness intact. Henry's stylistic revisions are therefore as a rule rejected. If Henry's changes are necessary for simple correctness or clarity, they are accepted, just as Jug's are, but if his changes are merely rewordings of Dreiser's awkward style, they are rejected.

The cuts suggested by Henry and made by Dreiser are nearly all rejected. Most of them were made simply to speed up the narrative or to remove sexually offensive material. The impetus for these cuts seems to have come from the Harper reader's report—a decidedly exterior influence. Dreiser undoubtedly agreed to these excisions because he felt that they would make his novel more saleable to potential readers and therefore more attractive to a publisher. He must have known that he was weakening his novel by cutting it in this fashion, but he apparently felt that he had no choice, given the circumstances of American publishing in 1900. The Pennsylvania text, with these cut passages restored, is approximately thirty-six thousand words longer than the Doubleday, Page text—an addition of some seventy pages. The narrative pace of the Pennsylvania edition is thereby slowed a bit, but its character development, realistic detail, and philosophical message are significantly broadened and deepened.

Anna Mallon's typists made changes in Dreiser's text as they worked. Most of these alterations were simple mistakes—typos and misreadings—but on a few occasions a typist spotted a demonstrable error in Dreiser's grammar, spelling, or punctuation and corrected it properly. In such instances the typist's revision has been carried over into the Pennsylvania text.

Some of the substantive alterations made in the manuscript and typescript are necessary for correctness, but it is difficult to identify the hand by which they are made. In such instances (most of them small cuts) the change is adopted and attributed in the apparatus to an *"unidentified hand."* The reader should not, however, jump to the conclusion that there was yet another person working on Dreiser's text. The alteration is by Dreiser, Jug, or Henry; it is simply impossible to tell which person made the revision. Other cuts in the typescript present a similar problem. These cuts were clearly Dreiser's work: they were made with the heavy back-and-forth motion of a blunt pencil characteristic of his revising. But it is often possible to discern Henry's lighter preliminary cutting strokes beneath Dreiser's heavy markings, and in such instances the cut is usually rejected.

Substantive variants in proof present a different problem because the marked proofs do not survive. The printer's setting copy (the Mallon typescript) does survive, though, and by collating it with the first printing one can identify compositorial and proof alterations. The problem is to decide which proof alterations are Dreiser's and which are not. Some of the decisions are easy: most of the stylistic revision, for instance, was probably introduced by Dreiser, and the additional censoring was almost certainly done by Doubleday, Page. But there are several variants between typescript and first print for which it is difficult to assign responsibility. It has been the policy of the Pennsylvania edition to treat such variants very conservatively. Doubleday, Page would have had no qualms about meddling with the proofs of *Sister Carrie*, and many of these doubtful changes were surely introduced by them. Only those proof revisions which can be attributed with confidence to Dreiser are accepted in the Pennsylvania text.

In the final reckoning, some 404 substantive revisions by Dreiser have been emended into the copy-text. There are fewer acceptable changes by Jug: 87 substantive alterations in her hand have been incorporated. Only 49 of Henry's many substantive alterations have been judged necessary. Each one of these necessary revisions has been recorded in the apparatus of this volume.[4]

Special Substantive Problems

Two substantive cruxes must be addressed separately: the chapter titles and the revised ending. The chapter titles were the work of Dreiser and Henry. No surviving document reveals why the titles were added, but they appear to represent an attempt to restore some part of the philosophical message of the book after the typescript had been cut. Because the Pennsylvania edition retains most of the excised passages, however, the chapter titles become superfluous. Since the Pennsylvania text also follows the original chapter divisions from the manuscript, there are three untitled chapters. It would be presumptuous to manufacture titles for these chapters and awkward to leave them untitled. In 1912 Dreiser expressed a desire to have the chapter titles removed from the plates of *Sister Carrie*, but he never carried through on this idea. For these various reasons, the Pennsylvania edition prints the chapters as they were written in manuscript—without titles. The titles, however, are part of the textual history of the novel, and they are included in a separate apparatus table.

The most difficult decision has been whether to accept or reject Dreiser's revised endings for chapters XLIX and L. No hard evidence exists to guide the editor here. The leaves of notes in Jug's hand do survive, but they reveal nothing conclusive. Of potential interest is the following account, which Dreiser gave to an interviewer for the *New York Herald* in 1907.

"There is one odd circumstance about the book. When I finished it I felt that it was not done. It was a continuous strip of life to me that seemed to be driven onward by those logical forces that had impelled the book to motion. The narrative, I felt, was finished, but not completed. The problem in my mind was not to round it out with literary grace, but to lead the story to a point, an elevation where it could be left and yet continue into the future. The story had to stop, and yet I wanted in the final picture to suggest the continuation of Carrie's fate along the lines of established truths.

"The note, the exact impression that I sought, evaded me. The drain of sustained imagination was beginning to tell. Finally, with note book and pencil I made a trip to the Palisades, hoping that the change of scene would bring out just what I was trying to express.

"Finding a broad, overhanging shelf, I stretched out flat on my back and allowed my thoughts to wander—gave them a sort of open air holiday.

"Two hours passed in a delicious mental drifting. Then suddenly came the inspiration of its own accord. I reached for my note book and pencil and wrote. And when I left the Palisades 'Sister Carrie' was completed."[5]

The value of this interview must be assessed carefully. Dreiser gave this account seven years after he had revised the ending of his novel. The wording does not come to us directly from Dreiser but reaches us indirectly through the *Herald* interviewer. The first paragraph appears to refer to the revised ending; but the remainder of the account, with its emphasis on mystical inspiration, seems quite contrived—of a piece with Dreiser's frequent insistence that he began *Sister Carrie* with no notion of what the novel would contain. The *Herald* account makes no mention of influence from Henry or Jug, but one must remember that Dreiser waited sixteen years before divulging Henry's role in the composition of the book and that he never acknowledged the important role Jug had played. The *Herald* interview, though intriguing, ultimately provides no firm evidence on which to base a decision about the ending of *Sister Carrie.*

The Pennsylvania edition therefore takes the conservative course and retains the original endings for chapters XLIX and L. These are clearly Dreiser's own endings, written without outside prompting. They are consistent with the rest of *Sister Carrie;* they grow naturally out of what has come before. The revised endings, by contrast, are suspect on a number of counts. They are contrived and unnatural—more like clumsy graftings than natural parts of the novel—and they were almost surely added on the advice of Henry or Jug.

Accidental Emendations

The manuscript is copy-text and its accidentals are in general authoritative, but they are in rough form. Dreiser expected to exercise no real control over accidentals and paid little attention to them. It might therefore be argued that the punctuation supplied by Jug, by Anna Mallon's typists, and by the typesetters at the print shop should be accepted *en bloc* because Dreiser gave it his tacit approval. The Pennsylvania editors, however, reject this line of reasoning. Our belief is that experienced scholarly editors who have studied Dreiser's manuscripts and become familiar with his prose style will be able to punctuate more carefully and intelligently than the hired typists and compositors who worked on *Sister Carrie* in 1900.

Dreiser punctuated very lightly in his manuscript drafts, but fortunately his pointing (or lack of it) is predictable. For instance, he usually omitted the apostrophe in a contraction and left out the period after an abbreviation. He was casual about dialogue and often used no quotation marks or terminal punctuation. Such cases are simple: the proper punctuation is supplied. One minor matter is that Dreiser sometimes put the comma or period inside his quotation marks (American practice), and at other times he put it outside (British practice). Because he seems to have had no particular preference, the Pennsylvania edition follows American practice and places all commas and periods inside quotation marks.

Dreiser's written prose falls into certain syntactical patterns, and his punctuation for some of these patterns is predictably odd or incorrect. Four examples are discussed below.

1. Dreiser often used a modifying element in the middle of a sentence. His punctuation was consistent: "He was capable of strong feelings—often poetic ones, and under a stress of desire, such as the present, he waxed eloquent" (p. 128). The modifying element "often poetic ones" is set off by a dash at the beginning but by only a comma at the end. This feature has been retained in the Pennsylvania edition. Standard practice would probably be to change the comma to a dash, but wherever the meaning of the sentence is clear, Dreiser's punctuation has been preserved.

2. In similar fashion, Dreiser sometimes omitted the closing comma in a modifying construction: "On this Friday afternoon, scarcely two days after his previous visit he made up his mind that he would go out and talk with Carrie" (p. 124). A second comma is necessary for clarity and is therefore always added in this edition.

3. Dreiser rarely put a comma before the conjunction in a compound sentence. This habit occasionally caused trouble, particularly when the word immediately before the conjunction was the main verb of the first clause. When a comma is needed to avoid confusion it has been added, but whenever possible the sentence has been left unpunctuated, as Dreiser wrote it.

4. Dreiser sometimes separated his subject and verb with a comma. This idiosyncrasy is retained when possible, but it usually disturbs the meaning of the sentence so significantly that the comma has been removed.

In the Pennsylvania text, Dreiser's manuscript punctuation is preserved if at all possible. When punctuation must be added, it is added conservatively and with a light hand. Dreiser's prose reads more smoothly when it is not heavily punctuated, and he appears to have preferred free or open pointing.

Word division is a special problem with Dreiser. He was inconsistent, usually writing "someone," for instance, but occasionally writing "some one." When such inconsistencies occur on the same page of printed text in this edition, they have been regularized to Dreiser's most common spelling. Otherwise they have been allowed to stand. Dreiser generally did not hyphenate compound words, even when the hyphen was clearly necessary. Here the editors, bearing in mind that compound words were more commonly hyphenated in 1900 than they are today, have added hyphens according to their own sense of the rhythm and meaning of the passage in question.

A hands-off policy has been followed with spelling. Dreiser's misspellings are predictable: he nearly always wrote "ei" for "ie" (and vice versa) and he regularly wrote "opourtunity" and "alright." His misspellings are corrected. The authority consulted in questionable cases has been the *Oxford English Dictionary*. Interestingly, many of Dreiser's spellings, such as "coquetish" and "nostalgy," are archaic forms. These have been allowed to stand. Occasional British spellings such as "centre" and "practise" have also been preserved. No attempt has been made to regularize orthography; variant spellings such as "grey" and "gray" are left unemended when both are correct.[6] The names of numbered avenues in New York City are spelled out; numbered streets are given in numerals. Hence "Seventh Avenue," but "42nd Street."

Apparatus

The Pennsylvania *Sister Carrie* has two textual apparatuses, an abbreviated or "selected" apparatus printed at the end of this volume and a comprehensive apparatus at the Rare Books Room of the University of Pennsylvania Library.[7] Because both the manuscript and typescript of *Sister Carrie* survive, this comprehensive apparatus is very long indeed, much too lengthy to be printed in this volume. The comprehensive apparatus contains many minor emendations and variants which are of interest only as matters of record. In fact, it contains so many variants that it is difficult for a user to extract significant information from it. The Pennsylvania edition therefore prints only a selected apparatus which records all significant emendations in the copy-text, together with other useful data about the textual history of *Sister Carrie*.

The major table in the apparatus of this volume is "Selected

Emendations in the Copy-Text," a list of all significant substantive and accidental emendations made in the copy-text to produce the text of this edition. For each emendation, this table gives the change in wording, tells who made it, and records the stage of composition (manuscript, typescript, proof) in which it was made. Other tables in the abbreviated apparatus are "Block Cuts Marked by Arthur Henry and Accepted by Dreiser," "Chapter Titles," "Word Division," and "Pedigree of Editions."

It must not be inferred, however, that the comprehensive apparatus is a massive compilation of inconsequential textual data. It is, rather, the backbone of this edition—the record on which its text ultimately stands. The major table in this larger apparatus is "Emendations in the Copy-Text," a comprehensive list of all emendations, both accidental and substantive, made in the copy-text. Other tables in the full apparatus are "Rejected Proof Alterations," and "Selected Historical Collation." The full apparatus does not include a table of "Alterations in the Manuscript," traditionally part of a scholarly edition for which manuscript survives. Theoretically such a table would record all revisions in the manuscript (and the typescript) of *Sister Carrie*, thereby enabling the scholar to study the author's revising and rewriting habits. But for *Sister Carrie*, the revising was so complicated, multi-handed, and multi-leveled that it cannot be recorded usably in a textual table. Any scholar who wishes fully to trace the revision of *Sister Carrie* must work with the actual documents—the manuscript at the New York Public Library and the typescript at the University of Pennsylvania.

Future Editions

There are many types of scholarly editions: photo-facsimile, type facsimile, variorum, parallel text, clear text, and so on. The Pennsylvania *Sister Carrie* might best be described as a copy-text edition based on the manuscript. The reader should realize, however, that there are other possible editions of *Sister Carrie*.[8] Annotated photo-facsimile editions of both the manuscript and the typescript would be valuable to Dreiser scholarship. A variorum edition of *Sister Carrie*, with textual information at the bottom of each page, would give critics ready access to the changing textual history of the novel. A parallel-text edition, with manuscript and typescript passages on facing pages, would illustrate graphically the changes made by Dreiser, Jug, and Henry.

It would even be possible to produce other copy-text editions by following other editorial principles. A different editor, for instance, might well accept many more of Jug's and Henry's revisions and cuts. This policy might be valid, so long as the editor defended his reasoning intelligently, recorded his emendations, and included the cut passages in his apparatus. Another editor might keep the chapter titles. And there are several possible approaches to the endings of chapters XLIX and L. One might accept the revised endings for both chapters, or one might restore the original ending (minus the coda) for chapter XLIX but print the revised ending for chapter L. One might even devise an argument for using Jug's ending for chapter L rather than Dreiser's. The same requirements, however, would hold: the editor would have to defend his rationale and record his emendations.

Since the Pennsylvania edition of *Sister Carrie* is the first full-dress scholarly edition of the novel, it has been deemed appropriate to follow a relatively conservative editorial policy. The resulting text, though, should not be thought of as "definitive." There will never be a "definitive" text of *Sister Carrie*. Its textual history is so complicated and, in places, so conjectural, that the ideal of a "definitive" text will never be achieved. Differently edited texts of this novel may appear in future years; if they do, they will be based in part on the information presented here. One hopes that such editions do appear. Dreiser studies will benefit from lively debate about his texts, provided such debate is backed by careful research and tempered by rational thought.

J.L.W.W. III

Notes

1. This description of copy-text editing is very much simplified. The *locus classicus* for copy-text editing is W. W. Greg's "The Rationale of Copy-Text," *Studies in Bibliography* 3 (1950–51). Greg's thinking has subsequently been extended by Fredson Bowers in "Current Theories of Copy-Text, with an Illustration from Dryden," *Modern Philology* 68 (1950–51); "A Preface to the Text," in *The Scarlet Letter*, Centenary Edition (Columbus: Ohio State University Press, 1962); "Established Texts and Definitive Editions," *Philological Quarterly* 41 (1962); "Some Principles for Scholarly Editions of Nineteenth-Century American Authors," *Studies in Bibliography* 17 (1964); "Old Wine in New Bottles: Problems of Machine Printing," in *Editing Nineteenth Century Texts*, edited by John M. Robson (Toronto: University of Toronto Press, 1967); "Practical Texts and Definitive Editions," in *Two Lectures on Editing* (Columbus: Ohio State University Press, 1969); and "Greg's 'Rationale of Copy-Text' Revisited," *Studies in Bibliography* 31 (1978). G. Thomas Tanselle has defended Greg-Bowers theory in "Greg's Theory of Copy-Text and the Editing of American Literature," *Studies in Bibliography* 28 (1975); and "The Editorial Problem of Final Authorial Intention," *Studies in Bibliography* 29 (1976).

2. "Rona Murtha," *A Gallery of Women* (New York: Horace Liveright, 1929), 2: 567–68.

3. See Dreiser, *Dawn* (New York: Horace Liveright, 1931), pp. 192–95.

4. Approximately fifty accidental changes in Jug's hand are so minor that they are not recorded in the apparatus of this volume, but they are present in the comprehensive apparatus.

5. " 'Sister Carrie' Theodore Dreiser," *New York Herald*, 7 July 1907, Literary and Art Sect., p. 2.

6. For comments about spelling and punctuation in scholarly editions, see Hershel Parker, "Regularizing Accidentals: The Latest Form of Infidelity," *Proof* 3 (1973): 1–20.

7. Copies of this apparatus are also on deposit at the Library of Congress, the Lilly Library, and the Huntington Library.

8. Donald Pizer speculates about two possible types of editions in "Dreiser's Novels: The Editorial Problem," *Library Chronicle* 38 (1972): 7–24.

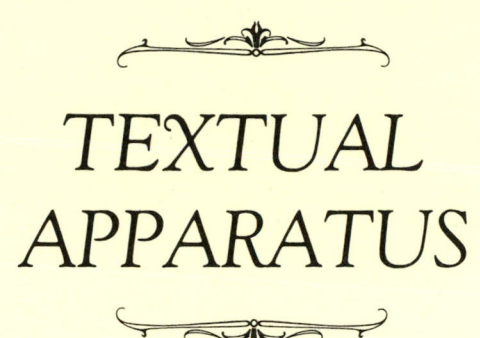

TEXTUAL
APPARATUS

SELECTED EMENDATIONS
IN THE COPY-TEXT

Copy-text for the Pennsylvania edition of *Sister Carrie* is Dreiser's manuscript of the novel. Listed below are all significant substantive and accidental emendations made in that copy-text for this edition.

Each entry begins with a page-line reference to the location of the reading in the Pennsylvania edition. This first reading in the entry is the emended reading, that which is printed in the text of this edition. There follows a bracket, which can be read "emended from." The second reading is the rejected reading from the copy-text. The final siglum, within parentheses, indicates who first introduced the change into the novel and in what stage that person made the change. The following sigla are used:

(MS—SWD)	A revision in the manuscript by Sara White Dreiser.
(MS—AH)	A revision in the manuscript by Arthur Henry.
(TS—TD)	A revision in the typescript by Dreiser.
(TS—SWD)	A revision in the typescript by Sara White Dreiser.
(TS—AH)	A revision in the typescript by Arthur Henry.
(TS—-AM)	A change made by one of Anna Mallon's typists in the process of typing the text of the novel.
(TS—*unidentified hand*)	A revision in the typescript (usually a cut) made in a hand that cannot be identified.

(DP)   A reading that appears initially in
                              the Doubleday, Page first printing of
                              Sister Carrie. Emendations followed
                              by this siglum are believed to be
                              Dreiser's proof revisions.

(P)   An emendation introduced first in
                              the Pennsylvania edition.

Below are sample entries:

7.17   felt] felt, though she did not then see, (TS—TD)

This entry indicates that in the TS, Dreiser deleted the clause
"though she did not then see", together with the two commas
that set it off. The word "felt", which was not affected by the
revision, is printed at 7.17 of the Pennsylvania edition.

90.23   color] hue (MS—SWD)

This entry records a change by Sara White Dreiser in the MS;
she deleted "hue" and substituted "color". This particular
change has been adopted for the text of this edition because it
removes an awkward repetition. The word "color" appears at ·
90.23 of the Pennsylvania text.

·98.39   canker] *stet*

This entry indicates a refusal to emend a reading that might
possibly be emended. The word "canker" in the manuscript is
retained without change at 98.39 of the Pennsylvania edition.
The asterisk indicates that a note has been written to explain
the decision. All such notes are grouped together at the end of
the table, keyed to the emendations list by page-line numbers.
Several other non-*stet* emendations are also explained by asterisk
notes.

3.13   her father] *unreadable* (MS—SWD)

This entry indicates that Sara White Dreiser erased or struck
through a reading in Dreiser's hand in the manuscript and substituted "her father". SWD's erasures or excision marks were so
thorough that it is now impossible to recover the original read-

ing. The revision "her father" in SWD's hand must therefore be accepted; it is printed at 3.13 of the Pennsylvania text.

All ellipsis points (. . .) in this table are editorial and stand for omitted words in quotations from the Pennsylvania text. None of the ellipsis points is punctuation by Dreiser.

A wavy dash (~) in the rejected reading indicates repetition of the same word or words from the reading in the Pennsylvania text. The subscript caret (ʌ) indicates the absence of punctuation. For example:

118.22   it,] ~ʌ   (TS—AM)

This entry indicates that one of Anna Mallon's typists added a necessary comma after "it" in the typescript. The wavy dash stands for "it", and the caret denotes the absence of punctuation immediately after "it" in the copy-text.

The paragraph-mark (¶) indicates a paragraph indentation at that point in either the copy-text or the Pennsylvania text.

Selected Emendations in the Copy-Text

*v.—   no dedication] stet

*3.7   1889] 1884 (TS—TD)

3.13   her father] unreadable (MS—SWD)

3.21   Columbia City] unreadable (MS—SWD)

3.27   might be.] might be like. (TS—TD)

4.16   or "Sister Carrie"] or Carrie (MS—SWD, and P)

4.17   termed by the family] termed (MS—SWD)

4.38   Waukesha] unreadable (MS—SWD)

5.23   which] who (TS—SWD)

5.23	was] were (TS—SWD)
5.34	high white] *unreadable* (MS—SWD)
•6.17–7.2	Let . . . regard.] *stet*
6.37	the porter bring her a footstool.] a porter bring a footstool for her. (TS—TD)
6.38	would] would bestir himself to (TS—TD)
7.7	young she is] young (P)
7.17	felt] felt, though she did not then see, (TS—TD)
8.32	purse . . . slip.] purse, in which the address slip was, nervously. (TS—SWD, and TD)
9.11	on, pointing . . . it—"corner] on,—"corner (TS—TD)
9.18	354 West Van] 354 Van (TS—SWD)
9.25	Here . . . two,] Now here were these two individuals (TS—TD)
•9.28	was] *stet*
9.34	relaxed.] relaxed. She was more interested in what he said. (TS—TD)
9.38	fields] open feilds (TS—TD)
10.26	crossings] street corners (TS—SWD)
11.25	looking] looking on (TS—TD)
12.16	and] or (TS—TD)
13.12	were covered with] were (MS—SWD)
14.14	twenty] *unreadable* (MS—SWD)
14.35	it ran] she wrote (TS—TD)
15.18	considerably since . . . now a] considerably, a (TS—SWD, and AH)
16.19	regions] regions which were (TS—SWD)
16.37	"nobby"] $_\wedge$ ~ $_\wedge$ (TS—*unidentified hand*)
17.22	nothing] nothing about (P)
17.25	river, and] river, with (TS—TD)

17.26	edge. Through] edge and through (TS—TD)
17.27	windows] windows of which (TS—TD)
18.11	an air] the air (TS—TD)
18.24	because] because that (TS—*unidentified hand*)
22.10	by that] by (TS—TD)
22.19	along] on (TS—TD)
22.25	stationery, jewelry. Each] stationary, jewelry and so on, each (TS—TD)
22.25	was] made into (TS—TD)
22.27	each] each individual (TS—TD)
23.18	their . . . their . . . their] its . . . its . . . its (TS—TD)
23.28	compared poorly.] compared but poorly in the matter of appearence. (TS—*unidentified hand*)
24.4	lends—girls] lends girls, (P)
25.24	Co., makers . . . caps, occupied] Co, was makers . . . caps and occupied (TS—TD)
25.25	in depth] deep (MS—SWD)
25.39	Aside from making . . . glances, no one paid] No one, outside of making . . . glances paid (TS—TD)
26.1	waited] waited quite a few minutes, (TS—TD)
26.6	already] somehow already (TS—TD)
26.21	half] half a week (DP)
26.29	added] said (TS—TD)
27.10	cloak manufacturing] manufacturing cloak (P)
27.15	sensual-faced] sensuous-faced (TS—AH)
27.22	went] went both (TS—*unidentified hand*)
28.29	informed, "Well, I] informed, "Do you live in the city?" "Not long, though, Ah!" he went on as Carrie informed him concerning herself. "Well," he concluded I (TS—TD)
29.9	say!] ~. (TS—AM)

29.9	say!] say. What would not the family think at home. (TS—TD)
30.15	delight] delights (TS—*unidentified hand*)
30.26	enthusiasm. Disposed . . . diminution, she was happy.] enthusiasm, being disposed . . . diminution. In short she really indulged in those unsophisticated fore-runnings which would in any less fanciful situation, have required an income of a thousand instead of 4.50 per week. (TS—TD)
30.38	Carrie.] Carrie who was naturally of a more or less vivacious turn. (TS—TD)
31.7	questions] questions as to the location of the shoe company etc, (TS—TD)
31.20	nothing.] nothing. She was not a close fisted woman by nature, but her husband's small income and saving disposition confined her money expenditures within a very narrow limit. Hanson would seldom join in on even the smallest pleasures if they cost money. So the attractions she now noted were confined to public buildings, the fine boulevards and the Parks. (TS—TD)
32.16	topic.] topic. That she did or did not care to go was an inconsiderable factor in the light of her knowledge of her husband. He could not have been forced, let alone persuaded, to spend so much money on anything of that sort. (TS—TD)
32.19	Carrie] Carrie's woman's instinct (TS—TD)
32.23	softly, rattling] softly and rattling (P)
32.38	was her coming . . . profit them?] was coming . . . profit her. (TS—TD)
34.8	work. She dressed] work. An express package made up of a change of clothing not quite as good as that which she had on had followed her on Saturday. She now dressed (TS—TD)
*34.10	faded] worn (TS—AH)
34.13	impart] imparts (DP)
34.32	She] Somehow she (TS—TD)
34.34	men] men should (TS—TD)
34.38	cents a week for car] cents car (TS—SWD)
35.14	like a walled cañon] like walled a cañons (TS—AM)

36.24	shoulder] shoulders (DP)
36.34	(which . . . shoe)] $_\wedge$ ~ . . . ~ $_\wedge$ (P)
36.37	clicks, cutting circular] clicks, circular (TS—TD)
37.1	Seeing] Eventually, seeing (TS—TD)
37.3	The pieces . . . left.] The peices of leather thus to be operated upon came from the girl at the machine at her left, and were passed on, after being operated upon as shown to the girl at her right. (TS—TD)
37.9	feelings, and, in a way, tried] feelings, in a way, and tried (TS—TD)
37.14	light. It] light and it (TS—TD)
38.25	Aw] Ah (TS—TD)
38.31	seemed] would seem (TS—TD)
38.37	less mental] less of mental (TS—TD)
39.8	into] in (P)
39.23	then taken hold upon manufacturing companies.] then gotten its hold upon the manufacturing companies it has since acquired. Built with broad, high ceiled rooms, amply lighted by windows and swept by plenty of fresh air such a task would not be so difficult to follow. It has since been proved that work can be made both pleasant and profitable by the many successful companies which have made their manufactories the central architectural crown of a lovely park settlement. But here was nothing except crude space, poorly lighted and set back from the street in such a manner that fresh air was impossible. The windows were small and looked out upon walls of other buildings not a score of feet away. By putting your head out and looking upward you could see the sky—not otherwise. (TS—TD)
40.17	felt] could not help but feel (TS—TD)
40.18	feared] became afraid (TS—TD)
40.25	over and . . . whirr again] over again and . . . whirr (P)
42.5	not] not even (TS—TD)
42.32	*they*] they (TS—*unidentified hand*)
42.39	wood, which . . . light,] wood, (which . . . light) (TS—*unidentified hand*)

*43.9   under forty] over thirty (TS—*unidentified hand*)

43.14   bar] store (TS—TD)

43.15   cigar.] cigar or several of them. (TS—TD)

43.23   altitude.] altitude, where his sole duties now consisted in ·
               looking after the general welfare of this magnificent resort.
               (TS—TD)

44.18   two children who were] two small sons (TS—TD)

46.15   him.] him, evidently friends. (TS—TD)

47.20   splendid] splendiferous (TS—TD)

49.3   trying] and trying (P)

49.10   its] the flats (TS—TD)

49.15   satisfied.] satisfied. He came home as usual reserved in man-
               ner, having little to say and nothing about him to indicate
               his frame of mind. (TS—TD)

49.24   Carrie ¶ It] Carrie. ¶ "Um", said Hanson. ¶ It (TS—TD)

49.27   for Carrie to be pleased.] that Carrie should have been
               pleased. He wanted her to work. It would be so much better
               all around. He was thinking how nice it would be if she
               could only pay her board easily and be happy. (TS—TD)

50.5   people. Minnie] people. ¶ At the supper table and thereafter
               until bed time nothing pleasing or soothing came, although
               it is equally true that there was nothing said which was
               directly unpleasent. The three lacked sympathy for one an-
               other and there was not that in their natures which made
               communication with and social enjoyment of each other
               possible. Minnie (TS—TD)

50.19   Now . . . were, she hoped he would not.] She was not
               sure—she hoped not—now . . . were. (TS—TD, and SWD)

52.5   itself.] itself in a peculiar manner. (TS—TD)

52.11   to him] to Hanson (TS—TD)

52.29   for] but (TS—SWD)

52.31   arrangement.] arrangement, in so far as she felt this its first
               direct effect, but it was not for long. (TS—TD)

52.31   But the] The (TS—AH)

53.17	her] Carrie (TS—TD)
53.21	yourself!] ~, (DP)
54.10	quickly and had seen] quick and seen (TS—SWD)
54.31	had visited] visited (P)
57.7	very ill] *unreadable* (MS—SWD)
58.6	different.] different. Somehow he liked the girl. She was of his own mould of flesh—his feminine counterpart. (TS—*unidentified hand*)
60.39	closer.] closer, to be nearer. (TS—TD)
61.16	What are] What (TS—AM)
61.28	hand] palm (TS—TD)
63.2	to take] to have taken (TS—TD)
63.6	got] gotten (TS—TD)
˙63.41	A Madame Sappho would have called him a pig;] *stet*
64.15	not, then] not (P)
65.12	necessary] absolutely necessary (TS—TD)
65.14	brought] brought into the flat (TS—TD)
65.35	home] home a little (TS—TD)
66.6	work, the taking of it now seemed dreadful.] work made the taking of the money now seem dreadful. (TS—AH, and AM)
66.21	have.] have it. (TS—*unidentified hand*)
67.24	proper one] one (MS—SWD)
68.28	was pleasing] pleasing (P)
68.32	words in Carrie's mind a . . . left.] words a . . . left in Carrie's mind. (MS—SWD)
71.8	along] out (TS—AH)
71.26	eye. "No," she answered.] eye after she had answered in the negative. (TS—AH)
73.1	Carrie," he said,] Carrie", (TS—TD)

73.5	stage—] ~, (P)
73.32	do they] does it (TS—AH)
73.34	are they] is it (P)
75.16	Aw] Ah (TS—TD)
77.11	throng] crush (TS—AH)
77.19	Great] Um (TS—TD)
79.17	no!"] ~", (P)
81.20	They] He (P)
81.23	they] he (TS—AH)
81.38	telling each] telling (TS—SWD)
82.11	seventeenth] *unreadable* (MS—SWD)
82.24	twentieth] *unreadable* (MS—SWD)
84.14	among] between (P)
85.9	well] nice (TS—TD)
86.21	bought] got (TS—TD)
86.29	but when] and when (TS—TD)
•88.23	Avenue, where stood] Avenue, were (TS—AM, and TD)
88.40	is] was (TS—TD)
90.11	fearful] fearsome (TS—SWD)
90.23	color] hue (MS—SWD)
90.30	load, feel the . . . winter.] load and feeling the . . . winter understand. (TS—AH)
91.4	without it.] without. (TS—TD)
92.34	get back] get (TS—SWD)
92.40	more clever] really cleverer (TS—TD)
93.10	more clever] cleverer (TS—TD)
94.25	after . . . conversation.] after he had indulged in a little round of conversation about life in Chicago. (TS—TD)

94.26	everything] anything (TS—TD)
94.34	don't] do not (TS—TD)
95.1	than ever before.] than he had ever felt. (TS—TD)
95.2	Her] That little soldier's (TS—TD)
95.29	considered] considered that (TS—*unidentified hand*)
95.34	quicker] quickest (TS—SWD)
96.7	perceptible] *unreadable* (MS—SWD)
*96.22	Carrie and then Drouet] Carrie and Drouet (MS—AH)
98.18	by men] men (MS—SWD)
*98.39	canker] *stet*
100.4	not with] not (P)
100.6	older, wiser woman] *unreadable* (MS—SWD)
101.8	of a] of (P)
*102.7–29	In . . . company.] There was a young girl and her mother there—two citizens of Evansville Indiana who were in the city—the daughter to study music—the mother to look after and keep her company. The father was treasurer of some railroad terminating in that city, and was kept at home, save for an occasional visit, by his important duties. (TS—TD)
102.9	wife, a] wife—the latter a (TS—*unidentified hand*)
102.16	Carrie] she (P)
102.36	was] was of such a nature as to be (TS—TD)
103.1	ruminations] rumination (TS—AH)
103.1	chords. They awoke] chords. For instance the Suwanee River would wake old memories or create longings in her which she could not understand. She would listen to some popular tune played in a simple manner and soon there would steal into her bosom the yearning which all mortals feel at one time or another for—they scarce know what. Vague unrest is one term for it. The German *Saensucht* is another. ¶ Now this feeling is as unaccountable as the drifts of the ocean, or the wanderings of the stars. Nearly all men have it. In some it is rudimentary, in others exaggerated. The greatest musicians, poets and artists are probably exaggeratively responsive. We see however that it is a thing which

works out in more material objects than men. Strains of music will cause dogs to howl. Certain notes of the fifth octave of the piano will make a zinc coal scuttle, unevenly balanced vibrate. It has long been known that a moderate rate of vibration long continued will crack a bell. Other notes or strains will affect other objects similarly, so that not long ago the biblical statement concerning the blast which shattered the walls of Jericho was discussed from the point of the scientists as a natural possibility, whether it ever happened or not. This was the result of the investigations into the vibratory powers of the notes of a cornet. They were found to be of wonderful and far reaching nature, effecting molecular displacement in several kinds of material. ¶In Carrie, such music staged in such a place by such a superior person, while it pained, still sweetened her state for her. It awoke (TS—TD)

103.3   They] It (TS—TD)

103.5   parlor] floor (TS—TD)

104.4   mistake.] mistake. ¶ The result of her sentimental imaginings was not unfavorable to the preservation of that mental process which gradually made her content to accept her new condition. They affected her ambition in such a way that she felt it impossible to go back, felt it necessary to go forward, even though she could not see in what direction. She wanted to be such a girl as that, to be able to play beautifully, as she assumed that playing to be. (TS—TD)

104.17   taste] grace and taste (TS—TD)

105.8   to. The] to. There was in her that longing which is always beautiful in woman. The (TS—TD)

105.9   passed] passed away (TS—TD)

105.9   graceful] half graceful (TS—TD)

105.12   to] for (P)

106.27   however] on the other hand (TS—TD)

106.37   himself. He . . . individuality. He was] himself. Her large innocent eyes dwelt in his memory. Her rounded, half-pensive face touched a chord in his nature which aroused him completely. That he must see her again was a constant thought. He must attempt to impress her. It was a strange thrill of delight that raced through his well nourished body as he construed some of her surprised looks into a composite, coquetish current which contained some slight appreciation of him and his capabilities. He . . . individuality. There was no need of anything like that. He had done nothing concerning which anything could be said. He was (TS—TD)

107.3   A few days later,] It so chanced that (TS—TD)

107.4   Chicago] the very city of Chicago (TS—TD)

107.29   troubled] troubled in thought (TS—TD)

108.17   there. I'll get a box for Joe Jefferson.] there. (DP)

108.27   he would just . . . it would settle] he just . . . he would
             have settled (TS—TD)

•108.37–40   quarter. ¶ That . . . glass. ¶ "Cad," said he, catching her,
             ] quarter. ¶ The fact is that the effect of her changed rela-
             tionships and surroundings was to make Carrie more wom-
             anly in carriage and appearance. She dropped many of her
             girlish ways, because of her mere power of observation; and
             by considering her state and consulting her ambition took
             on a seriousness which was not with her before. It was not
             a wise seriousness by any means, but it was better than airy
             ignorance. It made her much more attractive, and by a
             roundabout process brought her that fruit of attractiveness
             which is self knowledge and a faint breath of self love. ¶ In
             the same house with her, lived an official of one of the
             theatres, Mr. Frank A. Hale, manager of the Standard, and
             his wife—the latter a pleasing looking brunette of thirty-five.
             They were people of a sort very common in America today
             who live respectably from hand to mouth. Hale recieved a
             salary of forty-five dollars a week. His wife, quite attractive,
             affected the feeling of youth and objected to that form of
             home life which means the care of a house and the raising
             of a family. Like Drouet and Carrie they also occupied three
             rooms on the floor above. The same were comfortably fur-
             nished. Mrs. Hale was the possessor of many knick-knacks.
             She had a few jewels. For her age she got herself up rather
             smartly and went about with an air of being somebody. For
             all that they had no friends worthy consideration, as who,
             in so modern a city could have. They lived, rather more
             forced than preferably, to themselves, both being long since
             disillusioned by their own lack of intellectual breadth or
             ingrained sympathies as to the enduring qualities of love.
             Hale went about his affairs of a morning with relief. There
             was more diversion there than at home. Mrs. Hale, left con-
             siderably to herself, read the cheap love stories of the calibre
             of Dora Thorne, cultivated a lap-dog for a time, went to
             theatres with her husband, and not infrequently, in season,
             to the races, which to her seemed a gathering place for elite
             people. She ventured a dollar now and then for the excite-
             ment of the thing and so in the end stimulated her interest
             in the affair that it became one of her chief pleasures through

the long, monotonous summer season. Hale had his friends, of an order of mind suitable to the world in which his wife moved. ¶ It was not long after Carrie arrived until Mrs. Hale was aware of a good many of her characteristics. She was not irritated by Carries appearence, whereas the airs which the treasurers daughter gave herself made her long for an opourtunity to wreak some sort of social vengeance upon her. She met Carrie a few times in the halls, apologized profusely for little nothings, and soon became familiar enough to strike up a conversation. The next thing was a visit to Carries room, and thereafter they were on social terms of a slightly elastic order. ¶ Carrie had never enjoyed the companionship or the confidences of women—and especially of a woman of this sort, who was apparently far removed above the station she had occupied. She was no keen judge of nature. While she had *feelings* concerning people which were accurate enough if she had accepted them unwaveringly, she was too little assured of her own judgment not to readily fall a victim. ¶ Mrs. Hale's manner of entering upon this friendly relationship was simple enough. Knocking at Carries door one afternoon, she began with:—¶ "You'll excuse me, wont you, but I was wondering whether you wouldn't want to go to the theatre with me this evening. I'm alone and I believe you're alone—that is, I haven't seen Mr—¶ "Yes," put in Carrie, pleased by this attention, "wont you come in." ¶ "I can only stay a few moments," said the other walking in. "I thought you might like to go. It's so lonely when one is alone and Mr. Hale is out of town now." ¶ "Yes, it is very lonely," returned Carrie, sympathetically. ¶ The two sat and talked for nearly half an hour. The visitor took this occasion to find out as much as she could. ¶ "So your husband travels does he", she went on in one place. "I shouldn't think that would be so awfully pleasent for you. Have you been long in Chicago." ¶ "Not so very long," answered Carrie, slightly nervous at any approach to specific interrogation Her visitor had some tact of her own. She veered to the more general subjects of dress and amusements. ¶ "Now we must start by seven-thirty," she said at parting, "and you must come up and see me sometime." ¶ "I will," said Carrie. ¶ The saving element for Carrie in all such encounters lay in the fact that she could not talk. She had no way of expressing herself and yet the general impression she made was pleasing. Consequently she involved herself in but few of the difficulties of the gossip. ¶ After this meeting there was more of the same sort, and Mrs Hale made herself agreeable to Carrie in many ways. ¶ "My dear", she said "you must go about more. You won't remain strong if you don't. You look a little pale". ¶ Carrie heard this plea with solicitation. She was alone a good deal. Not long after Mrs. Hale invited her to go with her to the downtown stores of an afternoon. Carrie accepted and the two visited a number of places together. Mrs Hale was rather familiar with Chicago life and imparted a host of interesting facts concerning events and people. She was rich in that half knowledge of life which concerns the material and concerned herself much over scandals and public displays. She had a habit of pointing out the first striking looking person that came along and declaring him or her to be such and such a person of repute. Upon this assumed fact she would hang a host of gossip which soon filled Carries head with large ideas of the fine thing it was to be some such person and recieve individual notice of this sort. ¶ All this helped to fix the younger woman's sphere of thought. It created illusions concerning what constitutes position in this world. Naturally the intellectual and spiritual side were ignored. The things which constitute noble effort were never once approached. This managers wife had no conception of them whatever. She was simply a silly, deteriorating influence upon her pupil. ¶ One day they were in Marshall Field's one of the better dry goods stores of the town, when a very dressy individual passed along the aisle accompanied by one of those elaborately harnessed young women who form the bulk of the middle class actresses of our stage. ¶ "Look", said Mrs. Hale, "there's Scalan." ¶ "The actor", queried Carrie, who was familiar with the name of the Irish melodramatic singer. ¶ "That must be one of the members of his company" continued Mrs. Hale. "Isn't she vain". ¶ Unquestionably the young lady was carrying herself with an air. Her form was garnished conspicuously with those little ornaments of gold and silver which the vanity of fashion concieves. She was slightly haughty and keenly alive to her own physical merits. ¶ "Oh, he is such a delightful singer", went on Carries companion. "He is just charming". ¶ Carrie gazed after them with mingled feelings of awe and admiration. That seemed to be a high plane to be upon. When people point and stare, and you may walk on aware of but indifferent that the silent admiration is for yourself—ah, that must be bliss. The continued elucidation of Mrs. Hale, made the superiority of the state all the more certain. ¶ The standard of merit in such minds is very low. In most cases it does not involve merit of mind at all. Men were pointed out as gentlemen and elegant individuals who were of Hurstwood's manner and dress. Fine clothing wherever seen, was admired and commended. The person who wore it must be something. Those who did not were nothing. ¶ Carrie, in the presence of Mrs Hale, saw the shop girls in a different light. ¶ "The insignificant little two dollar a week nobody", she exclaimed to Carrie, when one of the girls waited upon her somewhat indifferently. "They put their last cent on their backs and then pass as ladies. I'll go to the manager and have her discharged". ¶ They had not seemed such miserable creatures to Carrie before, but this woman seemed to consider them nothing, and to Carrie she represented a better stratum of society. ¶ There was another point which was forever coming up. It was the value of having money. ¶ "If you have money, my dear", said Mrs. Hale, "you're alright. You can do what you please". ¶ This idea is one which seems to take ready root in most minds ¶ "It is said," Mrs Hale remarked one afternoon when Carrie was spending an hour in her room at her invitation, "that she never was married to him at all." ¶ She was speaking of some local celebrity. ¶ "You dont say so," said Carrie. ¶ "Yes indeed, but that doesn't make any difference. She has her carriage and plenty of fine clothes and she can go where she wants to. No one remembers such things when you have money." ¶ Carrie treasured up this last as a sort of self-justification. She had no money, but some how it seemed that there was still salvation somewhere. Perhaps her state was not so bad. If money would do this thing, perhaps the world was right in judging the error trivial. She busied herself thinking and then went before her mirror. There was considerable consolation in certain developing prettiness which she saw there. ¶ "Cad", said Drouet, catching her at it, (TS—TD)

113.33	have created] create (P)
114.1	had asked] asked (P)
114.21	wanting.] wanting. That she could not control. (TS—TD)
114.33	time] *unreadable* (MS—AH)
115.6	not grow in] not (MS—AH)
115.7	awakened] did awaken (MS—AH)
115.9	wealth.] wealth. One of the most interesting lessons of this kind was learned in the following manner. (TS—TD)
115.10	loved] dearly loved (TS—TD)
115.22	that . . . were] this . . . are (P)
115.25	mellow] soft (TS—TD)
115.32	seemed to be] seemed (TS—SWD)
116.6	quickly would] quick [*unreadable word*] (MS—AH)
117.10	below.] below. It was just 8:30 P. M. (TS—TD)
117.35–36	it. ¶ There] it. ¶ It would be almost impossible to explain the climax of this visit without introducing the atmosphere of half a dozen other encounters which are scarcely worth the space. It was not the first time he had called, but it is no more than the third. ¶ There (TS—TD)
118.16	behind. When the] behind. Thus we speak of the "unspeakable." When words are dumb then invisible currents are

substituted. Through these every feeling cries aloud and all the senses make answer. We understand best when least is said—when the (TS—TD)

118.17	removed,] removed and (TS—TD)
118.18	In this conversation she heard] It might be said of this conversation between Carrie and Hurstwood that the distraction of words was removed. She heard (TS—TD)
118.22	it,] ~∧ (TS—AM)
121.10	is probable that Carrie represented] is questionable whether Carrie did not represent (TS—SWD)
121.22	him] her (MS—SWD)
121.31	her] their (MS—SWD)
123.11	conclusion to another] conclusion (MS—SWD)
124.8	be.] be. If ever there was a time when he was anxious to leave the office it was now. (TS—*unidentified hand*)
124.11	his position] his own position his (TS—SWD)
124.11	out was] out were (TS—SWD)
124.16	successfully . . . take.] most successfully . . . take off. (TS—TD)
124.17	which was most essential] which it was most essential that it should have (TS—*unidentified hand*)
125.14	carried] got (TS—TD)
126.8	both] do (TS—TD)
126.30	when] before (MS—SWD)
128.21	worry] *unreadable* (MS—SWD)
131.18	the cook was] was the cook (TS—SWD)
133.12	gift] gift which he could enjoy (TS—*unidentified hand*)
133.13	had—] ~∧ (P)
135.5	drummer] drummer after all (TS—TD)
135.7	but . . . with] and . . . without (TS—TD)
135.41	head] head Caddie (TS—TD)

137.1	Drouet. "I] Drouet. He had been under the impression that the visit Hurstwood referred to had taken place sometime before. His thoughts on the subject stirred himself sufficiently to say "I (TS—*unidentified hand*)
138.24	a] a little (TS—TD)
138.26	walk] walk away (TS—TD)
140.15	young.] young. Oh, the awe of inexperience. Oh, the anticipation of desire which has never yet suffered fulfillment. If but we could go back to this. How, forever, would the world remain young. (TS—TD)
141.30	and later] and (TS—TD)
141.35	because of] for (TS—TD)
142.11	said Jessica another day] she said the next morning after the quarrel about the racing ticket (TS—TD)
142.13	No. Where] No, where (TS—AM)
143.34	evenings, and thought how charming] evenings with her and Drouet. He rejoiced in thoughts of how much more charming (TS—TD)
*144.12–13	penmanship. ¶ Hurstwood] penmanship. ¶ The desire to write letters which marks all victims of a passion of this sort is sometimes thought to be a singular thing but we must not forget that under the influence of a contagion as subtle, expansive, and pervasive as love, the mind is above the normal in its power of imagination. This yearning toward another being gives a feeling to the body which reacts upon the mental state or vice versa, the mind upon the physical state, as you will. The spirit of the body we must remember is a subtle thing. It is a breath of wind, a wave of electricity. It is affected by love as air is affected by heat. There follows an expansion which is power—which finds relief in overflow and expression. These too quick succeeding thoughts of the mind need freedom,—they need to be poured off in order that the mind may be relieved and left free to generate new richness. Thus we find the lover breathing those ardent phrases which are nothing save the pointless mumurings of a blissful spirit—the spreading perfume of a sun-warmed flower. Thus we find him grasping the significance of a strain of music, percieving readily, almost brilliantly, things which were before abstruse, receiving full impressions of all subtle beauties, giving them forth again in rounded form—by tongue or pen. Things said or written under such circumstances should have no more significance attached to them than is attached to a ripple of laughter or a burst of song. They are above the ordinary purposes of life. They are the

expression of a superior state which is not comprehensible in the ordinary stress of affairs. And in a true comprehension of life man may not be bound by these, for he has not expressed them in the spirit in which ordinary life is taken. What he contracts in a soberer, less elveated frame of mind, he should in justice be held to. But to condemn on the higher plane the entire world should be in love. For these things after all are the art of the soul—the perfect expression of enjoyment and should so be considered. ¶ Hurstwood (TS—*unidentified hand*)

144.27	the human] human (P)
145.31	strength—] ~∧ (P)
145.39	up—] ~, (P)
146.15	fresh] freshen (TS—*unidentified hand*)
147.2	children were] were (MS—SWD)
148.34	replied] said (TS—TD)
148.41	decision] decision anyhow (TS—TD)
149.3	little] little upon it (TS—TD)
149.20	be] was (TS—TD)
149.20	entangling.] entangling. The more difficult things became, the more delightful it was. (TS—TD)
150.9	weight,] weight—oh how that (TS—TD, and P)
153.28	Drouet got . . . Mr. Quincel had] he got . . . the latter had (P)
154.27	"drop in"] *drop in* (P)
155.7	"On the sixteenth."] "A week from next Friday". (DP)
155.35	added] said (TS—TD)
158.36	had exercised . . . thousand dollars.] exercised . . . thousand. (MS—SWD)
158.38	suffering] bedampened (TS—TD)
159.4	sorrow] woe (TS—TD)
159.8	ebb. She] ebb. She looked upon this suggestion of Drouets as an opourtunity. Why, she did not know. If seemed to her that it would be a delightful thing. Indeed she (TS—TD)

159.17	pulled] promptly pulled (TS—TD)
*161.10–163.9	She read . . . expression.] *stet*
161.33	expression] repression (P)
161.39	She has been cared for until nineteen years old, and now the villain] Now having been cared for until 19 years old the villian (P)
*163.3	Heaven's blow!] heavens blow, (P)
164.30	possessor.] possessor. Men lean toward the individual who is burning *to do*. There is contagion in the fire of hope, which enflames all hearers. The upspringing of an enthusiasm is like the breath of returning youth or spring. It restores the fibres of the weary to freshness. It reaches the aged, warming as we say, the cockles of the heart. It is a part of the suns own radiance, a handful of the fiery ball itself, done over into nerves, bright eyes, a beating heart. It is *youth* in the truest sense of the word and he who is truly ambitious is forever young. (TS—TD)
165.6	him] Charlie (TS—TD)
165.9	he] Charlie (TS—TD)
166.16	he said] said Drouet (TS—TD)
166.19	short] short one (TS—TD)
170.3	lines] part (TS—TD)
170.32	ended] was gotten through with (TS—TD)
170.38–39	up. The] up. ¶ "Well," he said "how did you come out, Cad." ¶ "Alright. I guess." ¶ "Have any trouble to recite your part". ¶ "Not at all," she said easily. ¶ The (TS—TD)
171.4	worry] worry on that score (TS—TD)
171.5–8	irritating. She . . . worthy were . . . done.] irritating. At the very time when he should have given her the benefit of his enthusiasm his mind was caught up with something else—a thing very common in individuals so unstable. She . . . worthy was . . . done. The feeling which properly approved, could have cemented their kindly relationship more closely was now at low ebb. He could not quite restore it. Only the superior influence of Hurstwood could awaken her delight in herself again, and it did. (TS—TD, and SWD)
171.26	while] while alright (TS—TD)

*171.29   fondly. "Now] fondly, "and I'll see what I can do. Wont
           you need any special dresses". ¶ "I think not," said Carrie
           ¶ "Remember I want you to look your best. You'd better take
           this," he said to Carrie pulling a thin clean roll of new $100⁰⁰
           bills out of his vest and handing her one." ¶ "Oh, I dont
           need it," said Carrie. ¶ "You might," said Hurstwood. "Bet-
           ter take it and if you dont use it you can give it to the poor
           for me". ¶ Carrie could hardly refuse the offer he was so
           tactful about. He put it in her little green leather purse and
           closed it up. (MS—AH)

171.32   She] She almost (TS—TD)

172.3   to disuse] to use or disuse (P)

172.21   of the] of Friday the (TS—TD)

175.4   performance] occasion (DP)

176.15   with] *unreadable* (MS—SWD)

*180.20–30 nature . . . was.] nature. Seats clicked, gentlemen were
           ushered to their places, hands were shaken. Through it all
           one could see the standing of the man Hurstwood. He was
           evidently a light among his kind. He reflected in his person-
           ality the ambition of the men who greeted him or they would
           not have been so cordial. He was acknowledged, fawned
           upon, in a way lionized, for was he not of much influence.
           Look at him anytime within the half hour before the curtain
           was up;—he was a member of an eminent group—a rounded
           company of five or more, whose stout figures, large white
           bosoms and shining pins bespoke the character of their suc-
           cess. The gentleman who brought their wives called him out
           to shake hand. ¶ "I say George, here is my wife—she wants
           to meet you" ¶ "Delighted, I am sure," he would answer,
           coming forward most graciously. "How do you do Mrs Car-
           gill. Well this is pleasure. I've known your husband here for
           years." ¶ "No." "Certainly not." "No, my wife couldn't come
           tonight." "Sorry. Such a chance to meet with old friends"—
           these and more were sample fragments of the running con-
           versation with which he recieved and entertained the merry
           company. (TS—TD)

183.27   rehearsal, but] rehearsel however, but (TS—AM, and *uni-
           dentified hand*)

185.8   here at work] at work here (TS—TD)

*185.11   Ray!] *stet*

*185.23   suffer long] *stet*

185.38   his feelings] they (P)

186.1	said Drouet] he said (TS—AH)
186.36	Hurstwood] he (P)
187.40	under the] *unreadable* (MS—SWD)
194.6	was] was almost (TS—TD)
194.17	We'll see tomorrow.] Tomorrow, if I can. (TS—TD)
*195.9–27	It was . . . said] *stet*
*197.34	She did not love him.] *stet*
201.28	had] have (TS—AM)
206.22	to weigh] *unreadable* (MS—SWD)
206.31	you] *unreadable* (MS—AH)
212.37	secretiveness] secretion (P)
214.1	prey] a prey (P)
215.17	time as] time for special puppy-love conversation as (TS—TD)
216.38	walked] walking (TS—TD)
216.40	her] the (TS—TD)
218.2	to all] all (P)
219.3	tell her] tell (TS—SWD)
219.15	something] something not exactly clear (TS—TD)
219.27	evening.] evening, seemingly as it was to him. (TS—TD)
220.1	feel so] feel (TS—TD)
220.4	else?" she exclaimed,] else", (TS—TD, and AM)
220.20	of his head to one side] to one side of his head (MS—SWD)
221.5	airs have] air has (TS—*unidentified hand*)
221.14	have] got (MS—SWD)
223.25	at five] which was about five (TS—AH)
223.37	diplomat.] diplomat, no Rochefoucauld. (TS—TD)

225.21	confusedly.] confusedly. Anyone who could have looked upon them there would have gained a clear perception of wherein they resembled each other. (TS—TD)
225.39	added.] added, noting something in her appearence which looked like explanations. (TS—TD)
227.1	mildly conscious . . . but certain] slightly sensible . . . somewhere, and yet certain (TS—TD)
*227.25	toy] *unreadable* (MS—SWD)
228.25	insulting . . . "or] insulting coward or (TS—TD)
228.27	secured] gotten (TS—TD)
228.27	the latter] it (TS—AH)
229.3	Aw] Ah (TS—TD)
229.10	he] she (TS—*unidentified hand*)
*233.21	the floor] his office floor (MS—SWD)
234.2	usual.] usual and he could arrange accordingly as he felt when the hour came. (TS—TD)
234.4	could] could not (TS—TD)
234.9	outside] outside of (TS—*unidentified hand*)
234.10	way,] way, and soon, (TS—TD)
*235.31	bitch!] wretch! (P)
235.32	have it out with her] *unreadable* (MS—SWD)
236.2	once.] once. He would be visited by attorneys of the law. Then what. She would not only keep all his property which was technically hers, but make him pay alimony besides. Perhaps he would ruin his position in the bargain. (TS—TD)
236.23	once.] once. He'd see about this thing. (TS—TD)
237.7	but] but it was (TS—TD)
237.14	waited. Finally] waited, and finally (TS—TD)
237.16	the cabby] that individual (P)
238.31	endurance.] endurance. He thought he should get a headache if something did not come to soothe him. (TS—TD)

238.37   it the] *unreadable* (MS—SWD)

239.3   then, tipped . . . smoking, decided that] then decided, tipped . . . smoking that (MS—SWD)

239.16   turned] *unreadable* (MS—SWD)

240.19   two.] two. This was a great deal. (TS—TD)

241.8   He . . . was, but] Carrie was, he well knew where, but (MS—SWD)

241.29   adjust] adjudicate (TS—AH)

242.2   affected most miserably] most miserably affected (MS—SWD)

242.2   all] all this (TS—AM)

242.12   him.] him. Oh the lovely vision of her bending to forgiveness. It compensated for all complications, all distress. He wouldn't mind what his wife did if he could arrange this affair with her. (TS—TD)

242.17   nothing.] nothing. He could think of no remedy. Go out. He might encounter Drouet. He might encounter facts of a more disturbing nature. Supposing—to this word he added all the endings imaginable, with the result that he shoved his hands deeper in his pockets and thought the harder. It would seem as if the endless circle of worry would wear him out, without result. ¶ More, the letter of McGreggor, James and Hay affected his ability to plan regarding Carrie. Not infrequently he took it out and scanned it anew. When had she gone to these people. What was it she wanted to do with the property. He knew what the *susetnance* referred to. They were going to demand alimony and attach his salary. ¶ "To the deuce with them". he thought. "I'll not call there. I'll see a lawyer—thats what I'll do". ¶ Then he thought of the legal fight he would have to go into. It would affect his standing with the firm and perhaps lose him his place. She had the property anyhow—what could he get. Anyhow, he didn't want her. He would rather not live with her. It would be a long round of war and come to nothing. He could not live with her after this and he knew well enough she did not want to live with him. Thus he went trotting about the ring of sequence, worrying all the time because he could come to know conclusion. ¶ Monday also passed and with it almost his power to act. No word came from Carrie—he gained no courage to go out there. He did not know what to do. (TS—TD)

244.16   alone] alone. It was some relief to have a comfortable chamber and rocking chair in which to think it over, but nevertheless it grew and grew. (TS—TD)

244.16   Suppose. . . . Suppose] Supposing. . . . Supposing (TS—TD)

244.18   them] this (TS—TD)

244.19   Hurstwood.] Hurstwood in these earlier thoughts. (TS—TD)

244.21   regret.] regret. Oh, that he should have decieved her so grossly—he whom she liked so well. (TS—TD)

244.25   manners.] manners. Every moment something would turn up in her mind, relative to him and it was not disagreeable. (TS—TD)

245.16   would] *unreadable* (MS—SWD)

247.38   she put] put (P)

248.3   day.] day. She filled out her idle time with ruminations which were as sombre colored as one of so volatile a nature could make them. She saw her fate trembling in the balance and moved from one phase of the situation to another regretting Drouet's attitude toward her in decieving her regarding Hurstwood as much as she did the managers duplicity. She made up her mind that men were cruel and indifferent and that there was no goodness in their attitude toward her. Then she decided that she must act for herself and concluded that on the morrow she would go forth seek work as before. (TS—TD)

248.4   Saturday,] Saturday, however, (TS—TD)

248.15   Hurstwood, but] Hurstwood—so she tried to make herself believe—, but (TS—TD)

248.26   part] part again (TS—TD)

248.37   appearance.] appearence. She looked well. (TS—*unidentified hand,* and AM)

248.39   before had] had (MS—SWD)

249.1   eyes.] eyes. There were engaging smiles from various quarters and that general interestedness and make-wayish spirit on all sides which shows a woman that she is pretty. (TS—TD)

249.3   nothing] nothing in that quarter (TS—TD)

249.6   honestly.] honestly and she was experienced enough to know that any effort of that sort was difficult unless a woman had some special qualifications, she knew not what. (TS—TD)

249.13   at which] which (P)

249.30   and] and really (TS—TD)

249.30   would see] saw (P)

249.34   good impression.] good. (MS—SWD)

*250.14   David] John (DP)

250.23   week] week in some production or other (TS—TD)

250.38   be.] be. Indeed she felt as though she had applied a thousand times and had been as regularly, and with great coldness, repulsed. (TS—TD)

251.19   she rebuked] she felt that not a moment must be lost. She rebuked (TS—TD)

251.21   before.] before in coming away from the Chicago Opera House without at least having made some inquiry as to how women secured places on the stage. She decided that she would certainly do better today, and that if nothing offered there she would do the best she could looking in other places. (TS—TD)

251.21   to revisit] and soon reached (TS—TD)

251.22   House] House vicinity (TS—TD)

251.25   was] was somewhat (TS—TD)

252.18   office. ¶ In the manager's office were] office. ¶ Carrie went upstairs and found a man who was the personification of the word authoritative. He was about thirty-six years of age, smooth-shaven, rather prominent in the matter of jaw-bone and dressed about as showily as Drouet. He had a large turquoise pin in his necktie, and a seal ring upon his right hand. ¶ Carrie saw the office indicated to her at the head of the first flight of steps. In it were (TS—TD, and AH)

252.36   Made quite a curtain address at Hooley's last night.] Had quarrel with the people at Hooleys. (DP)

254.40   game.] game he had played. (P)

*255.—   Chapter XXVIII.] stet

255.7   mind] time (TS—AM)

255.23   tense complaint] a tense note of complaint (TS—TD)

255.33   difficult.] difficult, for the tender relations they had so recently maintained, made her waver between gentle phraseology and harsh. At last she wrote: (TS—TD)

255.34   "You] "I know all. You (TS—TD)

255.35   you," she wrote in part. "How] you. How (TS—TD, and DP)

*256.2–3   circumstances. ¶ "Oh] circumstances." Oh (P)

*256.6–7   Goodbye." ¶ She signed the letter "Carrie."] Goodbye. [centered, one line below] Carrie." (P)

256.7–8   Carrie." ¶ She took the letter the next morning and] Carrie." ¶ She addressed an envelope and sealed this but did not mail it. Even in this she must give her self time to think and so Tuesday evening passed away. ¶ Wednesday she found herself in lower spirits than ever for now she felt that her histrionic ability was nothing and that she would need to look elsewhere. She could not brook the thought of the shops. She remembered what the managers of the wholesale houses had once told her about people who were not prepared to do especial lines of work. Her only hope was the stores—the possibility of obtaining a position waiting behind a counter. She decided to try for that and failing—but she prayed that she might not fail. ¶ Unfortunately Mrs. Hale came down and detained her a few minutes, asking whether she would not accompany her shopping that day. Carrie pleaded other engagements. ¶ "Its alright" Mrs. Hale remarked. "I thought if you were going we might go together. How is your husband." ¶ "He's quite well, thank you. He's gone away for a day or two." ¶ "I thought I saw him go out with his valise". ¶ Carrie hurried out after this little visit, anxious to be underway. She took her letter to Hurstwood and (TS—TD)

257.5   in a most covert manner as she went out] as she went out in a most covert manner (P)

257.10   or] and (MS—SWD)

257.25   twenty-six] twenty (MS—SWD)

257.29   weak] weakly (P)

259.17   compared with] by (MS—SWD)

*259.34–40   staying. What . . . made. She put] staying. He had probably come when he was sure she was not at home. These things which he left could signify nothing. He might not have wanted them sufficiently to carry them away. This observation threw her into the deepest gloom—she did not know why. Often before she had argued with herself that it could not matter if he came back, that she would want, would have to go inevitably and yet, now that the fact that he would not return seemed most wholly assured she could not view it with anything less than dread. What . . . made. She looked about her utterly distressed. She would have to move out quietly soon. Oh, the misery of it. She put (P, and TS—TD)

260.8   peace.] peace. At least, he wanted to see if she was there yet and to have a word with her. He could not exactly explain his motives for coming to himself, but equivical as they were, they were sufficient. He had reached the place where he could scarcely endure her silence any longer. (TS—TD)

261.10   me] me a little (TS—TD)

261.12   wording] word (TS—AM)

262.3   the attorneys] perhaps they (TS—TD)

*263.35–37   after supper. . . . out to lunch.] *stet*

264.1   Mr. Drouet] Drouet (MS—SWD)

264.10   girl, who had heard Carrie tell this to Mrs. Hale.] girl. (DP)

264.34   This] There is no question but that this (TS—TD)

265.4   office.] office. It was not long before the entanglement of all his affairs began to trouble him exceedingly and he spent a good hour, meditating, alone. (TS—TD)

265.40   abundance] abundance on to themselves (TS—TD)

266.9   "take something."] *"take something."* (TS—*unidentified hand*)

266.37   left] departed (DP)

267.16   tomorrow," he thought.] tomorrow. (TS—TD)

267.36   one hundred] hundreds (DP)

268.1   words] answer (MS—SWD)

268.10   down] up (TS—TD)

269.5   he partly] he (TS—AH)

269.30   back] back and closed the door (TS—TD)

270.10   from] from off (TS—*unidentified hand*)

270.27   they] it (P)

*270.29   had] had gotten (TS—TD)

*270.33   took] got (TS—TD)

271.9	While the money was in his hand] Suddenly (TS—TD)
271.20	action.] action. His situation frightened him a little. (DP)
271.30	doors] the door (TS—TD)
272.6	sleeper. Yes, there is too," he added. "There's] sleeper. Theres (TS—TD)
272.30	emphatic manner.] emphatic. (MS—SWD)
277.8	quickly.] quickly. The train was rushing on at a great rate. There was no hope of stopping it. (TS—TD)
277.30	you after] you (MS—SWD)
278.24	could not] could (P)
279.21	difficulty] difficulty of her situation for her (TS—TD)
279.32	to stay] to (MS—SWD)
280.3	go back] back (MS—SWD)
280.9	the long] its long (MS—AH)
282.34	might come? . . . might they] might not come. . . . might not they (P)
284.29	could foretell] could (MS—SWD)
284.37	have done as I did] *unreadable* (MS—SWD)
285.28	staring at his shoes] *unreadable* (MS—SWD)
285.33	so. She turned her head away.] so. (MS—SWD)
286.14	think about it] *unreadable* (MS—AH)
287.20	That sum, or any other, could never] That sum, nor any other could not (MS—SWD)
291.1	The following morning] In the morning (TS—TD)
291.2	be] be thus safely (TS—TD)
292.19	taking] laying of (TS—AM)
292.29	on."] on. I love you. I'll do right by you". (TS—TD)
294.37	toward the stairs] upstairs (DP)
295.17	cold] old (TS—AH)
*296.6	This city] The city (P)

296.10	clothes as soon as breakfast is over and . . . York soon.] clothes today and . . . York. (DP)
297.9	and, seated] and sat (TS—TD)
298.1	Look] Lookee (TS—TD)
299.39	he could] possible (TS—TD)
300.7	something—]~, (DP)
300.8	money, his] money, (P)
300.36	smiling] smiling weakly (TS—TD)
301.9	broke] to break (TS—TD)
301.22	it."] it," said Carrie. (TS—TD)
302.17	had] had and so on (TS—TD)
*304.22–305.17	The . . . great] stet
306.9	gathered] foregathered (TS—TD)
306.16	hundred or five hundred thousand] hundred thousend or five hundred (TS—TD)
309.23	Hogg's in Chicago] Hoggs (TS—TD)
309.29	had thought] thought (P)
311.2	remark—]~, (P)
*311.6	Carrie . . . large.] stet
313.33	and] and without much else it (TS—TD)
315.27	months] weeks (DP)
316.8	acting] act (P)
316.23	look again] look (TS—TD)
316.28	him] him in Chicago (TS—TD)
316.37	with] with and so on (TS—TD)
317.7	then came] came (P)
319.17	friendship] acquaintenceship (DP)
322.6–8	flat one morning, still . . . arising.] flat, still . . . arising one morning. (TS—SWD)

323.33	stared at and ogled.] stared and ogled at. (DP)
324.12	imagine that it] imagine that she was making a poor show-ing, that it (TS—TD)
324.25	Chicago] Chicago quite two years before (DP)
325.8	Amid] In (DP)
•326.40	A Gold Mine] The Sheen of Garnet (DP)
330.34	Square] there (TS—TD)
331.2	their wraps] hats, coats and canes (DP)
332.2	latter] head waiter (DP)
334.18	brooch] pin (DP)
335.7	She had read "Dora Thorne" in the past.] She read Dora Thorne, or had a great deal in the past. (P)
338.32	are] is (DP)
340.9	Bah!] Bah! And oh, oh, by what secret gate or passage way should he ever get back. (TS—TD)
341.7	north] South (DP)
343.22	his mind] his (TS—AM)
344.7	The present one was to be torn down.] He was going to tear down the buildings. (DP)
344.22	arrangement] connection (DP)
344.32	later, he found . . . progress, and] later, finding . . . prog-ress, (P)
345.8	and the new owner] and (DP)
346.32	so.] so. This was due to the mental state, which is aptly shadowed forth by the old saw which states that "misery loves company". (TS—unidentified hand)
346.38	his] its (DP)
•347.13	if worst comes to worst] stet
347.24	wife and] wife but (TS—SWD)
348.12	the proprietor] this individual (DP)
349.28	had had] had (TS—SWD)

352.3	It] As it (TS—AH)
353.13	anything] them (TS—TD)
353.17	that.] that. No, no, that would be too awful. (TS—TD)
353.26	always seemed] always (TS—AM)
354.5	begin] be beginning (TS—AM)
*354.36	chances:— ¶ For sale. The] chances. "For sale" he read. "The (P)
355.19	him—] ~; (DP)
*356.10	a third-interest] half interest (DP)
356.39	At] Being (TS—AH)
357.1	up. He] up, but he could think of none. Already he (TS—TD)
357.4	awhile.] awhile. Accordingly, when through he passed over. (TS—TD)
357.5	one he knew] one (TS—AH)
357.18	showed] shown (TS—AM)
359.8	twelve] eleven (TS—TD)
361.22	Chicago. I] Chicago," said Cargill, weakly. "I (TS—TD)
361.30	with] to (TS—AH)
361.38	inside.] inside. Still he walked on thinking. (TS—TD)
362.21	she was] he was (TS—unidentified hand)
364.14	twelve] ten (TS—TD)
364.26	came] became (TS—unidentified hand)
364.27	get some] some (TS—AM)
*365.10	ten cents] cents (TS—AM)
*365.34	go, he] go he lit he (TS—AM)
367.13	When Carrie] The upshot of this was that Carrie (TS—TD)
367.15	was emphasized] emphasized (P)
367.20	thought] said (TS—AH)

369.4	pots were] pot was (TS—AH)
369.22	bets] antes (TS—AH)
369.37	a bill] bill (TS—AM)
370.11	chips] checks (DP)
370.23	call,] ⌢ (TS—AM)
370.37	thought] said (TS—AH)
372.23	you for] you (TS—AM)
373.22	parlor of the Morton House, then] collection of parlors, in what was then (DP)
374.26	the old] the (TS—AH)
374.34	game took] took (TS—AH)
374.36	secure] secured (DP)
375.3	have] have got (TS—TD)
376.11	how] that (TS—AH)
376.19	"It] "I don't know," said Carrie. "It (TS—TD)
376.19	me," said Carrie, "that] me that (TS—AH)
377.8	right way.] right. (TS—AM)
378.4	It] It was something which (TS—TD)
378.30	going] of going (P)
378.31	out at] out (TS—SWD)
379.28	idea.] idea. If he had only encourged her in the least bit before. He did not know the jewel he had. (TS—*unidentified hand*)
379.34	that] what that (TS—AM)
380.4	You'll] You'd (DP)
381.9	and went] and thereupon suited action to word (TS—TD)
382.13	returned to Mrs. Bermudez' office.] returned (P)
382.36	"Yes."] "Yes" Mrs. Bermudez. (TS—TD)
383.16	play at] place (TS—AH)

384.19   other pieces] others (DP)

384.35   to the] to (TS—AM)

*384.37   on.] on. ¶ It is curious how thinking along a certain a line
almost invariably produces developments along that line—
developments which frequently having nothing about them
capable of being rationally connected with the process of
thought. Thus Carrie had discovered some time before that
on the floor below her dwelt an actress of some sort. This
came about in the same curiously trivial methods with en-
compassed her acquaintence with Mrs. Vance. ¶ It so happened that one day, owing to her having forgotten the drip
pan, which caught the waste water of her ice box it over-
flowed, and soaked through the cieling of the flat below,
dripping slightly. Of course, as is made and provided in all
such cases, the lady below appealed to the janitor to investigate. The latter, a stout German, came duly puffing up the
steps to inquire. ¶ "Ter lady sess as wot your ice box iss
leaken" ¶ "Who," said Carrie, scarcely understanding. ¶
"Ter actress underneat you—yes." ¶ "Oh, my ice-box," said
Carrie. "Goodness me, so I have. I'm so sorry. Tell her I'll
stop it right off." ¶ Now it so happened that the actress in
question was listening at her own door below to see what
would be the result of the janitors inquiry. When she heard
this kindly expression on the part she immediately concieved
well of her. She really did not want to create a fuss—only
to have the water stopped. Of course both knew each others
names. They got them from the bells. So at the earliest
opourtunity the actress, almost lying in wait for Carrie, managed to come out just in time to meet her and apologize. ¶
She was a very thin young woman, rather taller than Carrie,
and anything but good looking. She was a well-meaning
soul, after her sort forever playing small parts, and forever
rehearsing for new plays which did not stay out long. ¶ "I'm
so sorry about that ice-box the other day," she said. "I didn't
mean to complain." ¶ "Oh" said Carrie, you had good right.
It was all my fault." ¶ "I was afraid you would think I was
complaining. I meant for the janitor only to tell you of it."
¶ "Your very kind," said Carrie, feeling that the woman was
generous in the matter. "I'll try and not let it happen any
more." ¶ "Oh, thats alright," said the woman. "It really
wasn't anything to speak about". ¶ This womans name was
Wilson—Mattie Wilson, whose husband was of a nameless
disappearing sort. Carrie never met him nor indeed anything
concerning him, in all their short acquaintence. Of course
after this, whenever chance caused them to meet, they exchanged a few conventional greetings. ¶ Now Carrie bethought herself of this woman. Why not ask her. It would
be better than pawning her few jewels. Perhaps this woman
could tell her. ¶ Next morning, after screwing up her courage, Carrie ventured to timidly knock at the door below. ¶

"Why, do you do Mrs. Wheeler", said Mrs. Wilson, pleased by this call, "won't you come in". ¶ Carrie entered. ¶ "Wont you have a chair", said the hostess. "I'm glad you've called". ¶ "I didn't want to intrude upon you said Carrie, after a few conventionalities but I knew you were connected with the stage and I wanted to ask your advice". ¶ "Why certainly," said Mrs. Wilson, beaming kindly. "What is it". ¶ "I want to know how you go about it to get on the stage", said Carrie. ¶ "Oh" said Mrs. Wilson, "why it isn't so hard I guess. Do you want to get on". ¶ "I've often thought I'd like to try", returned Carrie. ¶ "Have you been around any," asked Mrs. Wilson. ¶ "I went to two or three dramatic agents," said Carrie. ¶ "I guess you didn't get anything out of them." ¶ "No, I didn't," said Carrie. ¶ "Well, I don't think you will either. I would bother with them. All they want is your money. They'll take your fifty dollars and then you can wait for your engagement". ¶ Mrs. Wilson spoke sharply and Carrie concluded that at some time or other she must have been taken in. ¶ "I kinda thought they might do that" said Carrie. ¶ "Oh, they do", said Mrs. Wilson, "dont I know. They've got money out of me, already." ¶ Carrie could scarcely refrain from smiling at the old maidish seriousness of the woman. ¶ "I have never had any experience" volunteered Carrie. ¶ "Do you want to get on the variety stage or in a company," asked Mrs. Wilson. ¶ "I thought I'd like to get in a company" said Carrie. ¶ "Well I don't know", said the woman, "a company is easier to begin with, I know, if you've never had any experience, but they're harder to get into. You've haven't seen any of the managers." ¶ "No," said Carrie. ¶ "Well, you ought to try some of the managers, I think. It oughtn't to be very hard for you to get a part Your so good looking". ¶ "Thank you," said Carrie, coloring a little. "Where do you find the managers." ¶ "I can give you their addresses" said Mrs. Wilson. ¶ The two looked at one another rather oddly and then Mrs. Wilson says. ¶ "It would be easy if you had a specialty" ¶ "Why" ¶ "Well, they give rehearsels every Monday morning at Pastors, Keiths and those places. You can go right on then and show what you can do and if they like your act, they'll take you." ¶ "I haven't any *act*," said Carrie simply ¶ "No, thats the trouble", said Mrs Wilson, reflectively. "You've got to have a pretty good act. Lots of people start right down in the gardens" added Mrs. Wilson, "but you wouldn't want to do that. They're not very nice—people drinking beer all around, but you dont need to know much. All you've got to do is to sing and dance a little. You wouldn't want to do that if you could get experience any other way." ¶ Carrie revolted a little at this picture. She said nothing however, not knowing what she might want to do. ¶ "You wouldn't go in the chorus, wouldn't you", said Mrs. Wilson. ¶ "I don't know", said Carrie, "I wouldnt mind if I could get a start that way." ¶ "It isn't so very hard to get in the chorus", said

Mrs. Wilson. "You know it depends mostly upon the figure. You have to wear tights, but then you get used to that. Lots of women get their start that way". ¶ "I know they do," said Carrie, who had heard of this method most of all. ¶ "Oh, you can get in," said Mrs. Wilson, "if you want to. It isn't very hard. I shouldn't think you'd want to." ¶ Carrie realized that this woman felt that this was just a desire on her part, backed up by no need. Her whole attitude showed it. Yet she did not have the heart disabuse her acquaintences mind. The chiefest distress of her life was the fear that she might be thought poor and in want. ¶ "I'd like to try it, so much" said Carrie. ¶ "There putting on a new Opera at the Casino" observed Mrs. Wilson. "You might get in there". ¶ "I think I'll try", said Carrie. ¶ Mrs. Wilson gave her the addresses of several managers offices and invited her down again. ¶ "I hope you'll have success," she said. (TS—TD)

385.2   to the] to seek the manager of the opera being staged at the (TS—*unidentified hand*)

385.2   the opera chorus] this (TS—AH, and TD)

385.3   secure. Girls] secure. Common labor is so plentiful. Girls (TS—*unidentified hand*)

385.8   nothing.] nothing. It remained for them to force their ability upon individuals whose sole object at times would seem to be that of preventing any opourtunity for a display of cleverness, by any except a favored few. (TS—*unidentified hand*)

385.23   Empire] Lyceum (TS—TD)

387.40   energy. ¶ Monday Carrie went again to the Casino. ¶ "Did] energy. ¶ That evening Mrs. Wilson called and suggested to Carrie a new idea. Her engagement with the new company, which had only reached the rehearsal stage, had fallen through. She was rather hard up herself and in her distress had cast about and thought of joining with Carrie. Here was a girl who was pretty. She could teach her to dance. Maybe they could get up an *act* which they could do on the vaudeville stage. ¶ "Would you like to", she asked, after explaining very fully her idea. ¶ "Why, yes," said Carrie, who saw a a a cessation of her lone and helpless wanderings. Surely, with this experienced woman for aid she could do a great deal. Mrs. Wilson seemed wonderfully generous and kind. ¶ The latter, poor soul, had been brooding out a comic sketch, a synopsis of which she now invited Carrie down to hear, and so this evening was passed. ¶ In her fancies that night the miserable difficulty was solved. All worries were over. The terrible necessity for Mrs. Wilson's skit to be funny and clever made it seem so. In her fear of want Carrie forced herself to see many delightful and pleasant things therein. ¶ Rehearsels of this thing replaced in part other efforts for a little while, but Carrie did not forget that the manager of the opera chorus had told her to come back the first of the week. Clearer observation of Mrs. Wilson and her skit, made her feel less hopeful. To Carrie, the poor woman seemed at times to pump up a semblance of humor which any audience would see was unreal and silly. It was pitiful. ¶ At the time then she felt as if she ought to go and see the manager. ¶ "Did (TS—TD)

388.2   said the manager] he said (TS—AH)

388.24   away. She did . . . ears.] away. No more rehearsels with Mrs. Wilson. She thought of that poor soul, but now the skit loomed up in its true light. It was not clever; it would have failed. Oh, the delight of being free of the need of depending on it. She did not think how Mrs. Wilson would feel. She did . . . ears. The stage too. Oh, now they would not starve. No, no. Now she would be independent and free. (TS—TD)

388.33–36   me." ¶ She forgot her youth and beauty. The handicap of age she did not, in her enthusiasm, perceive. ¶ Thus] me." ¶ Thus (DP)

389.2   "Yes."] "Um, huh!" (TS—TD)

389.9–10   said:— ¶ "Do . . . get?"] said:— ¶ "What about the act you and Mrs. Wilson were going to do." ¶ "Oh, I don't know," said Carrie. "I'll have to give that up, I guess. ¶ "Do . . . get," asked Hurstwood. (TS—TD)

389.12   week."] week. Mrs. Wilson says they do." (TS—TD)

389.21   perfumes and] perfumes of the (TS—TD)

389.31   "Madenda," she replied,] "Madenda," (TS—TD)

389.32   Drouet] she (TS—TD)

389.32   selected in Chicago] selected (MS—SWD)

390.4   the same] the (MS—AH)

392.6   her. He] her. To be sure she had earned nothing as yet but she soon would. He (TS—TD)

392.11   "It] "Well, kinda. It (TS—TD)

392.24   laying down] laying (MS—AH)

394.34   first] one (MS—SWD)

•395.2   distress.] distress. Outside, in her new sphere of action she gained hope and the glimpse of a future. These two things

militated one against the other, and so against the contin-
uance of the worst. (TS—TD)

395.4	fact developed that . . . them.] fact that . . . them, devel-oped. (TS—AH)
396.4	twenty-two] thirty-two (P)
396.12	The] In addition the (TS—TD)
397.3	it? I] it," said the girl. "I (TS—TD, and AM)
397.15	know. I] know", said Carrie. "I (TS—TD)
397.19	show?"] show? asked Carrie. (TS—TD, and AM)
397.29	I] I only (TS—TD)
397.39	air] air which was (TS—TD)
398.29	she asked] asked Carrie (TS—TD)
398.30	so."] so," said Hurstwood. (TS—TD)
398.39	looked] looked away (TS—TD)
399.1	came] came paying (TS—TD)
400.22	clearly] clear (TS—SWD)
401.6	he added] said the man (DP)
401.11	merit.] merit. With this feeling in her heart she tried to do as good as ever and succeeded admirably. (TS—TD)
401.12	tossing . . . and holding . . . listlessly] holding . . . holding . . . listless (DP)
401.18	chorus] company (MS—AH)
402.3	all. She] all. She hated to think that she was handicapped in this way, and that she could not use all her money. She (TS—TD)
403.11	Hurstwood.] Hurstwood, who had heard her tell of her pro-motion to be captain of a line. (DP)
405.2	the Sherry's . . . again, the remembrance of which came] the large Sherry . . . again, only that that affair came (DP, and P)
405.6	It was a strong] Oh, the strong (TS—TD)
•405.6–8	vision. She . . . nose. He] stet

405.9	in] into (TS—TD)
405.29–32	said. ¶ "Yes," she answered. ¶ The next morning at breakfast she felt like apologising. ¶ "I . . . evening," she said.] said. ¶ The next morning was rehearsel. ¶ I . . . night", said Carrie. (DP)
405.33	answered] said (DP)
•406.17	your Mr. Drake] you Drake (MS—SWD, and P)
406.29	apply to another manager.] apply. (TS—TD)
407.10	clothes.] clothes now. (TS—TD)
407.11	him] him to talk about (TS—*unidentified hand*)
408.3	call] called (TS—TD)
408.17	"Not] "Well not (TS—*unidentified hand*)
409.33	have] have no (TS—*unidentified hand*)
•410.27	provided] providing (P)
•410.27	o'clock noon] ~, ~, (P)
•410.31	discharged,] ~∧ (P)
412.21	where he] and (TS—TD)
420.26	breakfasted] dined (DP)
420.28	Here] Here you are (TS—*unidentified hand*)
420.28	to him ∧] him, (P)
420.31	nervous] slightly nervous (DP)
421.22	gong] gong which struck (TS—TD)
423.9	pale] a little pale (DP)
•425.3	That _____ _____] *stet*
•425.7	a _____ _____] *stet*
•425.30–32	all right." ¶ The] alright". ¶ "How did you come out", asked the foreman, as the car stopped. ¶ "Oh, alright," he said. "Had a Little trouble at one place. ¶ The (TS—TD)
425.39	intended] calculated (DP)
426.14	one of the policemen] the policeman (DP)

427.29	had begun.] began (P)
428.5	one policeman] the policemen (DP)
428.21	on him] as if by a hundred (TS—AH, and DP)
428.26	the two] two (P)
432.15	he was then dealing] he dealt (TS—TD)
437.4	deed—] ~, (P)
437.40	their] its (P)
438.34	door frame] door (P)
439.6	lay soft] late safe (TS—AM)
•440.7–441.15	When . . . paid.] stet
440.34	Vell] Well (P)
441.40	left] departed (TS—TD)
442.1	him] Hurstwood (TS—TD)
442.2	until she was] until (P)
444.2	were not] were also (MS—SWD)
444.30	At] She remembered now that at (TS—TD)
•444.31	Sarony] Falk (TS—TD)
445.27	Carrie, but the] Carrie. The (DP)
446.29	Suppose] supposing (DP)
447.16	thoroughly angered.] thoroughly. (P)
448.6	easily held] easily (MS—SWD)
448.34	dollars a week] dollars (DP)
•449.12–23	"That's . . . pride.] stet
450.12	associates] confreres (DP)
454.35	the Chelsea] Chelsea (TS—AH)
454.36	"Moved again?"] "Again," (DP)
454.37	Yes.] Yes, I had to move. (DP)
454.37	can't] couldnt (DP)

•455.15	prayed] payed (TS—TD)
459.29	in relief] out (DP)
459.31	hold of] hold (TS—AM)
459.39	I've] I (P)
460.19	rose] got up (TS—TD)
460.27	eat on] eat (P)
463.19	weak-looking] weakly looking (P)
465.8	Hurstwood] he (DP)
465.15	Lord] I dont know (TS—TD)
466.6	¶ Taking] ¶ His method was as follows:— ¶ Taking (TS—TD)
466.9	charity] bounty (TS—TD)
466.29	Fewer] Less (P)
467.3	something,] ~∧ (P)
467.10	ain't] isn't (DP)
468.4	Here's] Here is (DP)
•468.21	coins] a coin (P)
•468.23	coins] coin (P)
470.22	cab . . . pedestrian] cab or foot passenger (P)
472.25	older] a decade older (DP)
•473.10–23	"Yes . . . was,] *stet*
474.1	tonight] this evening (DP)
474.14	a sort] sort (P)
476.20	gently] gently, but firmly (TS—TD)
477.9	had said] said (P)
477.12	hospital] hospital not long ago (DP)
477.32–33	her. ¶ "Better] her. ¶ On her part she was not only distressed for him, but because of the figure she made. He looked so dreadful. People were staring. ¶ "Better (DP)

478.2	eye] eye on this account (TS—TD)
*478.21	Bill] ———— (P)
478.30	Carrie] Carrie mildly (DP)
482.10	read it] it (P)
484.29	her] in her a (P)
488.2	to the] to that of the (P)
488.3	similarly] similar (P)
*489.29–39	night . . . in] *stet*
489.32	had] have (TS—TD)
490.25	where] whence (TS—AH)
492.5	the game] it (DP)
492.19	closed] close (P)
493.10	hastening] turning into it (DP)
493.11	seen] *unreadable* (MS—SWD)
493.11	companies] companies dining (DP)
493.25	above all] above (TS—AM)
494.13	went in] went (TS—AH)
495.1	long] lone (TS—TD)
495.32	But people] People (DP)
495.34–39	"Isn't . . . they?" ¶ "We'll] Isn't it just awful," said Carrie, changing the drift of the conversation slightly. "Look at that man over there," and she began to laugh at a young man who had executed a comic fall. ¶ "How sheepish men look when they fall, don't they," said Lola. ¶ "We'll (DP)
496.30	jacket] jumper (DP)
496.33	euchre] whist (TS—TD)
496.38	mother] elderly lady companion (DP)
497.7	smiled] smiled out across the field (TS—TD)
497.19	this] the (P)

498.40–499.14 flakes. On . . . disappeared.] flakes. ¶ A light appeared through the transom overhead where some one was lighting the gas. It sent a thrill of possibility through the watcher. There was a little louder murmur of recognition when it appeared, a dark, smothered "ah." On the old hats and peaked shoulders snow was piling. It gathered in little heaps and curves and no one brushed it off. In the centre of the crowd the warmth and steam melted it and water trickled off hat-rims and down noses which the owners could not reach to scratch. On the outer rim the piles remained unmelted. Those who could not get in the centre lowered their heads to the weather and bent their forms. ¶ At last the bars grated inside and the crowd pricked up its ears. Footsteps shuffled within and the crowd murmured. There was some one who called, "Slow up there now," and then the door opened. It was push and jam for a minute, with grim, beast silence to prove its quality, and then the crowd lessened. It melted inward, like logs floating, and disappeared. (DP)

499.23 door.] door. "Whats the use." (DP)

648.19 in such a peculiar way that she] with the wild eyes of the thinker and she (TS—TD)

648.38 floor, when] floor, as if he had been neglected when (DP)

649.22 melancholy," he said.] melancholy however." (DP)

650.4 abstractedly] abstractly (TS—*unidentified hand*)

650.9 heart craved] heart had craved for years (TS—TD)

*651.29 roiling] riding (DP)

TEXTUAL NOTES

v.— There is no dedication in either the MS or the TS, but the Doubleday, Page and Company first printing of *Sister Carrie* is dedicated "TO MY FRIEND | ARTHUR HENRY | WHOSE STEADFAST IDEALS AND SERENE | DE-VOTION TO TRUTH AND BEAUTY | HAVE SERVED TO LIGHTEN THE METHOD | AND STRENGTHEN THE PURPOSE OF | THIS VOLUME." The 1901 Hei-nemann edition carries no dedication, though this may have been a space-saving feature introduced by the British pub-lisher for the Dollar Library. The 1907 B. W. Dodge impres-sion and all impressions subsequent to it carry no dedication, probably because TD had fallen out with Henry by that time. The only other fresh typesettings of *Sister Carrie* during TD's lifetime—the 1927 Constable and 1939 Heritage Press edi-tions—are likewise without dedications. It appears that TD did not wish his novel to be published with the dedication to Henry. The Pennsylvania edition honors his wishes.

3.7 See the historical note at 3.7

6.17–7.2 **Let . . . regard.**   In composing this passage in MS, TD borrowed heavily from George Ade's "The Fable of the Two Mandolin Players and the Willing Performer," which was first printed in the *Chicago Record* on 7 October 1899 and was republished shortly thereafter in Ade's *Fables in Slang* (Chicago and New York: Herbert S. Stone & Co., 1899), pp. 181–94. Ellen Moers has shown that TD actually went back to his opening chapter (probably as much as two or three months after composing it) and patched the Ade pas-sage into his MS with scissors and paste. See Moers, *Two Dreisers* (New York: Viking Press, 1969), pp. 130–31. The original passage from Ade reads:

> He was the Kind of Fellow who would see a Girl twice, and then, upon meeting her the Third Time, he would go up and straighten her Cravat for her, and call her by her First Name.
>
> If a Fair-Looker on the Street happened to glance at him Hard he would run up and seize her by the

Hand, and convince her that they had Met. And he always Got Away with it, too.

In a Department Store, while waiting for the Cash Boy to come back with the Change, he would find out the Girl's Name, her Favorite Flower, and where a Letter would reach her.

Upon entering a Parlor Car at St. Paul he would select a Chair next to the Most promising One in Sight, and ask her if she cared to have the Shade lowered.

Before the Train cleared the Yards he would have the Porter bringing a Foot-Stool for the Lady.

At Hastings he would be asking her if she wanted Something to Read.

The entire Ade passage was deleted by AH in the process of cutting *Sister Carrie* for the 1901 Heinemann British edition. When the novel was reissued in 1907 by B. W. Dodge, TD wrote a substitute passage and had the plates altered to incorporate it into the text. The Ade passage, however, represents TD's intention in MS, and so it has been retained in the text of the Pennsylvania edition. The substitute passage in the 1907 reprinting reads:

Let him meet with a young woman once and he would approach her with an air of kindly familiarity, not unmixed with pleading, which would result in most cases in a tolerant acceptance. If she showed any tendency to coquetry he would be apt to straighten her tie, or if she "took up" with him at all, to call her by her first name. If he visited a department store it was to lounge familiarly over the counter and ask some leading questions. In more exclusive circles, on the train or in waiting stations, he went slower. If some seemingly vulnerable object appeared he was all attention—to pass the compliments of the day, to lead the way to the parlor car, carrying her grip, or, failing that, to take a seat next her with the hope of being able to court her to her destination. Pillows, books, a footstool, the shade lowered; all these figured in the things which he could do. If, when she reached her destination he did not alight and attend her baggage for her, it was because, in his own estimation, he had signally failed.

The plate alteration in the 1907 reprinting was first noted by Michael Millgate; see "Note on the Text" (pp. xxv–xxvi) and "Variant Readings" (p. 461) in *Sister Carrie*, edited by Millgate (London: Oxford University Press, 1965). Jack Salzman has commented further on the textual history of the passage in "Dreiser and Ade: A Note on the Text of *Sister Carrie*," *American Literature* 40 (1969): 544–48. For additional information, including Ade's reaction to TD's borrowing, see the explanatory annotation at 6.17–7.2 of the historical notes.

9.28 **was** TD revised to "were" in TS, but that reading is grammatically incorrect and is rejected here.

34.10 **faded** AH's revision of "worn" to "faded" in TS is accepted to avoid the repetition of "worn . . . worn" in lines 9–10.

43.9 **under forty** Either SWD or AH made this alteration in TS. It is a necessary change, because if Hurstwood were "slightly over thirty" at this point he would probably still have enough youthful vitality in New York to avoid his final decline. The reading is interesting because it shows us that TD initially conceived of Hurstwood as a younger man. A few pages farther on in the MS, for instance, TD originally gave Hurstwood "two small sons"—a detail which was also altered in TS (see entry 44.18 in Selected Emendations).

63.41 **A Madame Sappho would have called him a pig;** TD seems to be mixing two classical references here. The first is to Sappho, the Greek poetess (born ca. 612 B.C.) who lived on the isle of Lesbos as the center of a group of young women. The second reference, suggested by the word "pig," is to Circe, a goddess who appears in Book 10 of the *Odyssey* and Book 7 of the *Aeneid*. Circe likewise lives on an island (Aeaea); she entices men to her abode and transforms them into beasts. In a famous scene in the *Odyssey*, she turns Odysseus' men into swine. It might be possible to emend "Sappho" to "Circe" here, but the confusion seems harmless and has been allowed to stand.

88.23 **Avenue, where stood** The typist noticed the odd reading "Avenue, were" in MS, and on her own typed "Avenue, where were". TD then altered "were" to "stood" for stylistic purposes. (TD later cut the entire sentence at AH's suggestion, but that cut has been rejected.)

96.22 **Carrie and then Drouet** TD originally wrote "Carrie and Drouet" in MS. AH struck through "and" and substituted "then"—a necessary change which clarifies the sentence. It was not necessary, however, to cut "and", and the word is therefore restored to the Pennsylvania text.

98.39 **canker** TD inscribed "canker" in the MS, but his lettering was nearly illegible. The typist therefore left a blank in the TS. TD apparently did not refer back to the MS for his original reading; instead, he simply filled the blank with the less evocative word "thought". The MS reading "canker" is restored.

102.7–29 **In . . . company.** TD took the actual typed text of the first paragraph of this passage from the next chapter (XII) and moved it back to this chapter. He then inscribed the next two paragraphs in holograph and pasted them into the Mallon TS. These two paragraphs are condensations of longer passages, originally inscribed in the MS but cut from the TS by TD, without AH's prompting.

108.37–40   TD apparently made this cut without AH's prompting. He saved the second paragraph of the cut passage and relocated it in the previous chapter (XI). See the textual note for 102.7–29, directly above.

144.12–13   **penmanship. ¶ Hurstwood**   This cut was made in TS with scissors and paste. No markings remain, and so it is impossible to know whether TD made the cut on his own or at AH's suggestion. The passage is not, however, sexually offensive; Dreiser probably removed it because it is highly digressive. The cut is honored in the Pennsylvania text.

161.10–163.9   **She read . . . expression.**   Throughout this passage, TD copied dialogue into his MS from the "Author's Edition" of Daly's *Under the Gaslight* (New York and London: Samuel French, 1895). In the process, however, TD miscopied some words and punctuation. Since most of these errors are quite minor, they have no effect on meaning and are probably unintentional. In these instances, the Pennsylvania text has been emended to conform to the Samuel French edition. In three other instances, however, TD's MS text seems deliberately altered from the printed edition in order to create a particular effect, and therefore the MS reading has been preserved. A note below defends the refusal to emend.

163.3   **Heaven's blow!**   The Samuel French edition reads "Heaven's own blow". The capitalization of "Heaven's" is transferred to the Pennsylvania text, but the word "own" is not, since TD may deliberately have omitted it to make the last line of this scene more forceful. There is no terminal punctuation in either the MS or the Samuel French edition; the exclamation point has therefore been added as a (P) emendation.

171.29   **fondly. "Now**   This passage was cut in MS by AH, but there was good reason for the cut. Hurstwood's gift of a one-hundred-dollar bill to Carrie was an excellent touch because it paralleled Drouet's earlier gift of two ten-dollar bills. But Carrie could hardly have used the money for clothes without Drouet's knowing it, and if she had hidden the money away, she could have fallen back on it when Drouet walked out on her. With one hundred dollars, Carrie would not have become desperate so quickly. The cut must therefore stand.

180.20–30   **nature . . . was.**   Chapter XIX is unusually long in MS— sixty-one pages of holograph draft. TD therefore decided, in TS, to divide the original chapter into two shorter chapters. He gave the first of the two new chapters this different ending.

185.11   **Ray!**   TD changed the comma in the Samuel French edition to an exclamation point in his MS, apparently for effect. In his rendering, Pearl is to "cry" the line. The MS punctuation is therefore preserved.

185.23   **suffer long**   The Samuel French edition reads "suffer the disgrace long!" but TD's version in the MS is more direct and forceful. He writes that Carrie spoke the line with "utter simplicity". The MS reading is therefore preserved.

195.9–27   **It was . . . said**   This passage was copied into the MS by SWD, apparently from an earlier draft of TD's. TD then went back over the passage and made three very minor revisions in wording.

197.34   **She did not love him.**   TD struck out this sentence in the Mallon TS, without AH's prompting, but his probable reasons for doing so must be examined. He very likely meant to suggest in the sentence that Carrie did not "make love" to Drouet—that is to say, that she did not have sexual intercourse with him. This interpretation is supported by the next sentence: "She kept him at such lengths as she could . . ." and by the one following: "She felt Hurstwood's passion as a delightful background. . . ." We already know that Hurstwood is tormented by the fear that Carrie and Drouet will sleep together after they leave him. It would seem wrong, however, to emend "love" to "make love" or to "submit". By the same token, it would be equally wrong to accept TD's excision of the sentence, since his action would seem to have been prompted by fear of censoring. The best course is preservation of the original MS reading, with its ambiguity intact.

227.25   **toy**   SWD erased TD's original word at this spot in the MS and substituted the word "toy", and then further added "—a plaything." The reading "toy" must be accepted because TD's original word is now unrecoverable, but "—a plaything." need not be incorporated into the text.

233.21   **the floor**   SWD made the change in MS, but with justifiable reason. At 233.5–6, Hurstwood moves from his office to his room at the Palmer House for the night, and it would be illogical to have him back in his office a few lines later.

235.31   **bitch!**   TD left this spot blank in MS. He apparently wanted to use the word "bitch!" but wondered if he dare do so. Evidently he consulted SWD, because the reading "wretch!" (which is, in sound, fairly close to "bitch") is written into the blank spot in her hand. The reading "bitch!" is published here as a conjectural emendation.

250.14   **David**   The MS and TS read "John", but the first printing reads "David". David A. Henderson was in fact manager of the Chicago Opera House, and TD (apparently wishing to use Henderson's real name) must have made the correction in proof. Doubleday, Page seems not to have noticed that TD was using Henderson's real name.

255.— Chapter XXVIII.   At AH's suggestion TD made substantial cuts in this chapter in TS, but his cuts were clearly attempts to clean up the chapter, since Carrie is propositioned in the excised passages. Killing those sections made the chapter too short to stand alone, and so TD attached the uncut material to the end of the previous chapter. The "offensive" material is restored here, however, and so the original chapter division is preserved.

256.2–7 TD was confused about how he wanted to have Carrie's letter rendered by the printer—as a block quotation, or as quoted matter in the text. The latter method has been chosen for this edition, and emendations have been made accordingly.

259.34–40 **staying. What . . . made. She put**   TD originally made even more extensive cuts in the TS, all apparently without AH's prompting. Some of these excisions have therefore been honored, as the emendation entry indicates. But the three-sentence passage "She would have . . . been made." has been retained because it refers to the unsavory proposition that has been offered to Carrie and suggests that if she becomes desperate enough, she might consider taking it. TD very likely cut these sentences to clean up his text.

263.35–37 **after supper. . . . out to lunch.**   TD seems to have followed nineteenth-century practice in calling the three meals of the day "breakfast," "dinner," and "supper." He used "lunch" to mean a small meal at any time of the day, often at night. Hence at several points in *Sister Carrie* the characters have after-theater "lunches," and Drouet purchases a portable gas stove for the Ogden Place flat so Carrie can prepare "small lunches" there (p. 89). There is potential confusion for the modern reader—who thinks of "lunch" as a midday meal—in having Hurstwood decide to go to "supper" in line 35 and then, two lines below, go "out to lunch" at 6:00 P.M. One could avoid the difficulty by emending "lunch" to "supper," but to do so would remove an entirely acceptable 1900 usage. The reading has therefore been allowed to stand.

270.29,33 **had** and **took**   At some point in the revising process, someone apparently told TD that the word "got" was grammatically improper, and so TD began revising "got" out of his text. This is justifiable for passages in which the omniscient author is narrating, but in passages of dialogue it gives a false primness to the speech of the characters. In the dia-

logue that follows in the novel, TD's removal of "got" is
therefore ignored.

296.6   **This city**   In the margin of the TS beside this sentence,
SWD wrote "which", meaning "which city?" The problem
is that the sentence can be interpreted two ways: either that
Carrie does not like Montreal (the meaning TD intended),
or that she does not like *any* city (which is certainly not
true). Instead of clearing up the difficulty, TD simply struck
out the sentence. But by emending "The" to "This", the
problem is solved, and the sentence can be preserved.

304.22–305.17   **The . . . great**   Six pages are missing at this point in the
MS. They were apparently missing when TD gave the MS
to Mencken, because Mencken's note "6 pp. missing HLM"
is inscribed at the top of p. 7. The entire passage was cut
from the TS at AH's suggestion. The TS of all but the last
paragraph of the cut passage was apparently thrown away,
and so it is lost forever. It survives neither in MS nor in TS.
The last paragraph, however, still survives on Mallon TS p.
352, where it is lined out in TD's hand. This paragraph—an
important one, because it mentions numerous real persons
and sets the financial scene in New York City—is therefore
restored. Above this paragraph a four-line fragment of the
previous paragraph also survives, but because it is a fragment,
it cannot be incorporated into the reading text of the Pennsylvania edition. This fragment reads as follows:

> the heaviest crush of population. Above that for a
> space of four miles already straggled the forerunners
> of the vast home district which was so soon to follow,
> the five story flat buildings, standing out like sentinels
> upon a windy common.

311.6   **Carrie . . . large.**   This sentence seems illogical, but neither SWD nor AH queried it, and TD did not revise it in
MS, TS, or proof. The sentence is therefore allowed to stand
unemended.

326.40   **A Gold Mine**   The MS and TS read " 'The Sheen of
Garnet'," an apparently fictitious title. The first printing,
however, reads " 'A Gold Mine'," which is the title of an
actual play (see the historical note at 326.40). The real title
was likely added in proof by TD and escaped notice by Doubleday, Page. The Pennsylvania edition prints the title of
the real play.

347.13   **if worst comes to worst**   The expression should properly
be "if worse comes to worst," but the popular corruption is
"if worst comes to worst." Emendation might be called for
if the words appeared in a passage of authorial narration, but
here they are part of Hurstwood's mental comment to himself. Hurstwood uses many other slang, popular, or ungram-

matical expressions in the novel; it would therefore seem proper to leave this one unemended.

354.36 **chances:— ¶ For sale. The** Rendering the entire advertisement as an extract is a P emendation. TD originally ran the advertisement into the text in paragraph form.

356.10 **a third-interest** Hurstwood owned a one-third interest in the Warren Street saloon. TD may possibly have wanted Hurstwood to lie to the manager, but if so, TD did not call attention to the falsehood by omniscient authorial comment. It seems more likely that TD forgot what percentage Hurstwood had owned and then later corrected his error in proof.

365.10 **ten cents** In MS, TD erroneously wrote "tip of cents". The typist improvised to "tip of ten cents". Someone drew a line beneath "ten" in the TS and put a question-mark in the margin, as if to question the amount. Someone else, perhaps TD, crossed out both the underlining and the question-mark, as if to indicate that the amount was correct. Hurstwood would have been a big tipper in better days, able to pay a quarter for a shave. The amount has been left at "ten cents".

365.34 **go, he** In inscribing the MS, TD started to have Hurstwood light the gas but changed his mind. TD forgot, however, to cross out "he lit"—hence the odd reading in the MS.

384.37 **on.** This and subsequent cuts remove from the novel a character named Mrs. Wilson, a second-rate actress with whom Carrie tries to work up a vaudeville act. This material added little to the novel, and TD apparently decided to cut it from the TS without prompting from AH. See also the cuts at 387.40, 388.24, and 389.9–10.

395.2 **distress.** TD made this cut in TS at AH's suggestion, but AH was probably right. The two sentences are quite vague and confusing, and so the cut as been adopted for the Pennsylvania text.

405.6–8 **vision. She . . . nose. He** The sentence "She could see his fine brow now, his dark hair and strong nose." was cut in TS by TD without AH's prompting. But the cut appears to have been made in order to de-emphasize Carrie's physical attraction to Ames. It is likely that TD cut the sentence after he rewrote the ending of chapter XLIX because in rewriting that ending he lessened the sexual magnetism between Carrie and Ames. The original ending of chapter XLIX is restored to the Pennsylvania text, and so it is proper to restore this sentence as well.

406.17   **your Mr. Drake**   TD originally wrote "you Drake" for "your Drake" in MS. SWD crossed through "you" and substituted "Mr." in the MS. SWD's addition of "Mr." is justifiable, but her deletion of "you[r]" is not; therefore, "your" has been retained.

410.27, 31   TD copied this notice into his MS from the 15 January 1895 issue of the *New York Times*, but he made four minor errors in copying. These emendations correct his copying errors.

425.3, 7   TD marked two equal-sized blanks in his MS at each of these points in order to suggest unprintable profanity. The Doubleday, Page edition, however, prints four blanks in both places ("— — — —") in order to suggest "son of a bitch." But Dreiser wanted two blanks, not four. One can attempt to imagine what words Dreiser had in mind, but it would be presumptuous to print these terms in the text. In fact, he probably wanted these blanks to remain in his text so that each reader could imagine his own profane words. The two blanks from the MS are therefore retained here.

425.30–32   **all right." ¶ The**   TD made this cut in TS at AH's suggestion, but the passage was repetitive of wording directly above and should therefore have been removed.

440.7–441.15   **When . . . paid.**   This entire passage was copied by SWD into the MS, apparently from an earlier draft of TD's. TD made no changes in the text after SWD had copied it.

444.31   **Sarony**   In the typescript, TD changed "Falk," an apparently fictitious name, to "Sarony." Napoleon Sarony was an actual theatrical photographer of the day, and his name has therefore been adopted into the Pennsylvania text.

449.12–23   **"That's . . . pride.**   The page that bears this text is missing from the MS, and so copy-text for this passage shifts to the TS. That TS text is followed exactly here, with a few minor emendations in accidentals. No one made revisions in this passage of the Mallon TS.

455.15   **prayed**   TD wrote "payed" for "prayed" in MS. The typist typed "paid", which is also a logical reading, but TD struck through "paid" and substituted "prayed" on the TS sheet.

468.21,23   **coins**   There must be more than one coin involved, unless there was a twenty-one-cent piece in circulation in 1900.

473.10–23   **"Yes . . . was,**   The page that bore this text is missing from the MS, and so copy-text for this passage shifts to the Mallon TS.

478.21   **Bill**   TD left a blank at this point in the MS because he could not remember the first name he had earlier given Vance. TD discarded the TS of this particular passage when he revised the ending of this chapter, and so the name he filled in is not known. Vance's name is William; the nickname "Bill" is therefore used in the Pennsylvania text.

489.29–39   **night . . . in**   This entire passage in the MS is in AH's hand. The passage "night . . . strangers." at 489.29–35 is taken from the published text of TD's essay "Curious Shifts of the Poor." The remainder of the passage is either AH's own addition or is an addition by TD in the text that AH was copying. The second possibility seems more likely, since TD picked up the draft at the middle of a sentence in the MS and finished it out. The entire passage is therefore accepted for the Pennsylvania text.

651.29   **roiling**   TD's "riding" in MS makes no sense. The typist first typed "riling" and then, unsure of that reading, interlined "roiling" above. Someone erased "roiling" in the TS, however, and the compositor must therefore have set "riling", which was then presumably changed to "roiling" in proof.

DREISER'S REVISED ENDING FOR
CHAPTER XLIX

NOTE: In typescript Dreiser substituted the following passage for "Carrie almost forgot Hurstwood . . . heartaches are no more." at 478.32–487.35 of the Pennsylvania edition. The text below has been emended with recourse to the Mallon typescript and the Doubleday, Page and Company first edition; substantive emendations have been recorded in the apparatus.

In the hurry of departure Hurstwood was forgotten. Both he and Drouet were left to discover that she was gone. The latter called once and exclaimed at the news. Then he stood in the lobby chewing the ends of his mustache. At last he reached a conclusion. The old days had gone for good.

"She isn't so much," he said, but in his heart of hearts he did not believe this.

Hurstwood shifted by curious means through a long summer and fall. A small job as janitor of a dance hall helped him for a month. Begging, sometimes going hungry, sometimes sleeping in the park, carried him over more days. Resorting to those peculiar charities, several of which in the press of hungry search he accidentally stumbled upon, did the rest. Toward the dead of winter Carrie came back, appearing on Broadway in a new play, but he was not aware of it. For weeks he wandered about the city begging, while the fire sign, announcing her engagement, blazed nightly upon the crowded street of amusements. Drouet saw it but did not venture in.

About this time Ames returned to New York. He had made a little success in the West and now opened a laboratory in Wooster Street. Of course he encountered Carrie through Mrs. Vance, but there was nothing responsive between them. He thought she was still united to Hurstwood, until otherwise informed. Not knowing the facts then, he did not profess to understand and refrained from comment.

With Mrs. Vance he saw the new play and expressed himself accordingly.

"She ought not to be in comedy," he said. "I think she could do better than that."

One afternoon they met at the Vances' accidentally and began a very friendly conversation. She could hardly tell why the one-time keen interest in him was no longer with her. Unquestionably it was because at that time he had represented something which she did not have, but this she did not understand. Success had given her the momentary feeling that she was now blessed with much that he would approve. As a matter of fact her little newspaper fame was nothing at all to him. He thought she could have done better, by far.

"You didn't go into comedy-drama after all, did you," he said, remembering her interest in that form of art.

"No," she answered, "I haven't so far."

He looked at her in such a peculiar way that she realized that she had failed. It moved her to add, "I want to though."

"I should think you would," he said. "You have the sort of disposition that would do well in comedy-drama."

It surprised her that he should speak of disposition. Was she then so clearly in his mind?

"Why?" she asked.

"Well," he said, "I should judge you were rather sympathetic in your nature."

Carrie smiled and colored slightly. He was so innocently frank with her that she drew nearer in friendship. The old call of the ideal was sounding.

"I don't know," she answered, pleased nevertheless beyond utter concealment.

"I saw your play," he remarked. "It's very good."

"I'm glad you liked it."

"Very good indeed," he said, "for a comedy."

This was all that was said at the time owing to an interruption, but later they met again. He was sitting in a corner, after dinner, staring at the floor, when Carrie came up with another of the guests. Hard work had given his face the look of

one who is weary. It was not for Carrie to know the thing in it
which appealed to her.

"All alone?" she said.

"I was listening to the music."

"I'll be back in a moment," said her companion, who saw
nothing in the inventor.

Now he looked up in her face, for she was standing a moment, while he sat.

"Isn't that a pathetic strain?" he inquired, listening.

"Oh, very," she returned, also catching it, now that her
attention was called.

"Sit down," he added, offering her the chair beside him.
They listened a few moments in silence, touched by the same
feeling, only hers reached her through the heart. Music still
charmed her as in the old days.

"I don't know what it is about music," she started to say,
moved to explain the inexplicable longings which surged within
her, "but it always makes me feel as if I wanted something—I—"

"Yes," he replied. "I know how you feel."

Suddenly he turned to considering the peculiarity of her
disposition, expressing her feelings so frankly.

"You ought not to be melancholy," he said.

He thought a while and then went off into a seemingly
alien observation which, however, accorded with their feelings.

"The world is full of desirable situations but, unfortunately,
we can occupy but one at a time. It don't do us any good to
wring our hands over the far-off things."

The music ceased and he arose, taking a standing position
before her, as if to rest himself.

"Why don't you get into some good, strong comedy-
drama," he said. He was looking directly at her now, studying
her face. Her large sympathetic eyes and pain-touched mouth
appealed to him as proofs of his judgement.

"Perhaps I shall," she returned.

"That's your field," he added.

"Do you think so?"

"Yes," he said, "I do. I don't suppose you're aware of it, but
there is something about your eyes and mouth which fits you for
that sort of work."

Carrie thrilled to be taken so seriously. For the moment, loneliness deserted her. Here was praise which was keen and analytical.

"It's in your eyes and mouth," he went on abstractedly. "I remember thinking the first time I saw you that there was something peculiar about your mouth. I thought you were about to cry."

"How odd," said Carrie, warm with delight. This was what her heart craved.

"Then I noticed that that was your natural look, and to-night I saw it again. There's a shadow about your eyes, too, which gives your face much the same character. It's in the depth of them, I think."

Carrie looked straight in his face, wholly aroused.

"You probably are not aware of it," he added.

She looked away, pleased that he should speak thus, longing to be equal to this feeling written upon her countenance. It unlocked the door to a new desire.

She had cause to ponder over this until they met again. Several weeks or more. It showed her she was drifting away from the old ideal which had filled her in the dressing rooms of the Avery stage, and thereafter for a long time. Why had she lost it?

"I know why you would be a success," he said another time, "if you had a more dramatic part. I've studied it out."

"What is it," said Carrie.

"Well," he said, as one pleased with a puzzle, "the expression in your face is one that comes out in different things. You get the same thing in a pathetic song, or any picture which moves you deeply. It's a thing the world likes to see because it's a natural representation of its longings."

Carrie gazed without exactly getting the import of what he meant.

"The world is always struggling to express itself," he went on. "Most people are not capable of voicing their feelings. They depend upon others. That is what genius is for. One man expresses their desires for them in music, another one in poetry, another one in a play. Sometimes nature does it in a face—it makes the face representative of all desire. That's what has happened in your case."

He looked at her with so much of the impact of the thing in his eyes that she caught it. At least she got the idea that her look was something which represented the world's longing. She took it to heart as a creditable thing until he added:—

"That puts a burden of duty on you. It so happens that you have this thing. It is no credit to you—that is, I mean, you might not have had it. You paid nothing to get it. But now that you have it, you must do something with it."

"What?" asked Carrie.

"I should say turn to the dramatic field. You have so much sympathy and such a melodious voice. Make them valuable to others. It will make your powers endure."

Carrie did not understand his last. All the rest showed her that her comedy success was little or nothing.

"What do you mean?" she asked.

"Why just that. You have this quality in your eyes and mouth, and in your nature. You can lose it, you know. If you turn away from it and live to satisfy yourself alone, it will go fast enough. The look will leave your eyes, your mouth will change, your power to act will disappear. You may think they won't, but they will. Nature takes care of that."

He was so interested in forwarding all good causes that he sometimes became enthusiastic, giving vent to these preachments. Something in Carrie appealed to him. He wanted to stir her up.

"I know," she said absently, feeling slightly guilty of neglect.

"If I were you," he said, "I'd change."

The effect of this was like roiling helpless waters. Carrie troubled over it in her rocking chair for days.

"I don't believe I'll stay in comedy so very much longer," she eventually remarked to Lola.

"Oh, why not?" said the latter.

"I think," she said, "I can do better in a serious play."

"What put that idea in your head?"

"Oh, nothing," she answered. "I've always thought so."

Still she did nothing, grieving. It was a long way to this better thing, or seemed to be, and comfort was about her. Hence the inactivity and longing.

DREISER'S REVISED ENDING FOR CHAPTER L

NOTE: Dreiser wrote this passage to be substituted in the typescript immediately after Hurstwood's death (p. 499 of the Pennsylvania edition).

And now Carrie had attained that which in the beginning seemed her object, or at least such fraction of it as human beings ever attain of their original desires. She could look about her on her furniture and dresses, her carriage and her bank account. Friends there were, or at least those who would bow and smile in acknowledgment of her merits, and these she had once craved for. Applause there was and publicity—those once wonderful, far-off, essential things. Beauty also,—her type of loveliness, and yet she was lonely. In her rocking chair she sat, when not otherwise engaged—singing, rocking and dreaming.

Strange as this may seem we must not forget that in life there is ever the intellectual and the emotional nature—the mind which reasons and the mind which feels. Of one comes the men of action—generals and statesmen—of the other the poets and dreamers, artists all, in that which they do. Hung as a harp in the wind, the latter respond to every breath of fancy, voicing in their mood all the ebb and flow of the ideal.

Man has not yet comprehended the dreamer any more than he has the ideal. For the latter the laws and morals of the world are unduly severe. Hearkening to the sound of beauty, ever waiting the flash of its distant wings, he watches to follow—wearying his feet in traveling. So watched Carrie—so followed, rocking and singing.

And it must be remembered that reason had little part in this. She saw that the city offered more of loveliness than she had known, and instinctively, by force of her moods, she clung to the city. She saw that in fine raiment and elegant surroundings men seemed to be comfortable. Hence she drew near to that. Chicago and New York, Drouet and Hurstwood—the world of society and the world of the stage, these were but mere incidents. It was not these which she wanted. Time proved that. It was the thing which they once seemed to represent.

Oh, the tangle of human life! How dimly, as yet, we see. Here was Carrie, poor, unsophisticated, desirous, responding as a harp to all that is lovely in this life, yet finding herself bound as by a wall. Laws to say, "Be allured if you will to yon lovely scene but draw not nigh unless by righteousness." Convention to say, "So and so is right." If the "so and so" of convention seemed hard to endure; if in struggling to follow where beauty leads and the heart is whole, her hands were torn, her feet wearied; if she abandoned that strict observance of the admired way for the despised path which should let her in, who shall cast the first stone of reproach? Not evil, but longing for that which is better, too often directs the steps of the erring. Not evil but goodness too often allures the mind which does not reason at all.

Amid the tinsel and shine of her state Carrie was unhappy. As when Drouet took her, she thought, "Now am I lifted into that which is best." As when Hurstwood seemingly offered her the better way—"Now am I happy." But since the world goes its way past all save those who have much to give, and scatter their trail lavishly, Carrie was left alone. Her honor she kept decently. Her purse was open to him whose need was most. Going down Broadway now, she did not think of the elegance of the creatures who passed, as far as clothes were concerned. Were they better than she?—oh, that was still sharp. Had they more of that peace and beauty which glinted afar off? Then were they to be envied.

Drouet went his way, and was seen no more. Of Hurstwood's death she never heard. A slow, black boat setting out from 27th Street upon its regular nightly journey bore his nameless body, with many others, up the East River to the Potters' Field. The item which mentioned him she saw, but did not read. It was not labeled so that she might know.

Thus passed all that was of interest concerning these twain in their relation to her. Their influence upon her life is explicable, alone, by the knowledge of her longings. Time was when both represented for her all that was most worth while in earthly success. They were the personal representatives of that thing— the titled ambassadors of comfort and peace—aglow with their own credentials. It is but natural that when the world which they represented no longer allured her, its ambassadors should be discredited. Even had Hurstwood returned now, in his original beauty and glory, he could not have allured her. She had learned that in his world at least was not happiness.

Sitting now alone she was an illustration of the devious ways by which one who feels, rather than reasons, may be led, in the pursuit of beauty. Still young, but several times disillusioned, she was still waiting for that mysterious day when she should be led forth among dreams merely. Ames had pointed out a farther step, but on and on, beyond that if accomplished, would lie others for her. It was forever to be the pursuit of that radiance which tints the distant hilltop—Radiance which moves onward as succeeding heights are attained.

Oh Carrie! Carrie! Oh, blind striving of the human heart, rather. Onward, onward it saith, and where beauty leads, there it follows. Whether it be the tinkle of a lone sheep-bell o'er some quiet landscape, or the glimmer of beauty in sylvan places, or the show of soul in some passing eyes, the heart knows and makes answer, following. It is when the feet weary and hope is vain, that the heartaches and the longings rise. Know then, that for you is neither surfeit nor content. In your rocking chair, by your window, dreaming, shall you long for beauty. In your rocking chair, by your window shall you still know such happiness as you may ever feel.

SARA WHITE DREISER'S REVISED ENDING
FOR CHAPTER L

NOTE: Dreiser's wife made a fair copy of his revised ending for chapter L. In the process of copying she made numerous changes in the text. Her version was typed by the typist, set by the compositor, and published in the first edition of *Sister Carrie*. Her ending, reproduced below without emendation, has appeared in all subsequent editions of the novel until the present one.

And now Carrie had attained that which in the beginning seemed life's object, or at least such fraction of it as human beings ever attain of their original desires. She could look about on her gowns & carriage, her furniture and bank account. Friends there were, as the world takes it—those who would bow and smile in the acknowledgement of her success. For these she had once craved. Applause there was, and publicity, once far off essential things, but now grown trivial and indifferent. Beauty also, her type of lovliness, and yet she was lonely. In her rocking chair she sat, when not otherwise engaged—singing and dreaming.

Thus in life there is ever the intellectual and the emotional nature. The mind that reasons, and the mind that feels. Of one come the men of action—generals and statesmen: of the other the poets and dreamers—artists all,

As harps in the wind the latter respond to every breath of fancy, voicing in their moods all the ebb & flow of the ideal.

Man has not yet comprehended the dreamer any more than he has the ideal. For him the laws and morals of the world are unduly severe. Ever hearkening to the sound of beauty, straining for the flash of its distant wings, he watches to follow, wearying his feet in travelling. So watched Carrie, so followed, rocking and singing.

And it must be remembered that reason had little part in

this. Chicago dawning, she saw the city offering more of loveliness than she had ever known, and instinctively, by force of
her moods alone, clung to it. In fine raiment and elegant surroundings, men seemed to be contented. Hence she drew near
these things.

Chicago, New York. Drouet, Hurstwood. The world of
fashion and the world of stage. These were but incidents. Not
them, but that which they represented, she longed for. Time
proved the representation false.

Oh, the tangle of human life! How dimly as yet we see.
Here was Carrie in the beginning poor, unsophisticated, emotional; responding with desire to everything most lovely in life,
yet finding herself turned as by a wall; laws to say, "Be allured,
if you will, by everything lovely, but draw not nigh unless by
righteousness;" convention to say, "You shall not better your
situation save by honest labor." If honest labor be unremunerative and difficult to endure, if it be the long, long road which
never reaches beauty but wearies the feet and the heart, if the
drag to follow beauty be such that one abandons the admired
way, taking rather the despised path leading to her dreams
quickly, who shall cast the first stone? Not evil, but longing for
that which is better, more often directs the steps of the erring.
Not evil but goodness more often allures the feeling mind unused
to reason.

Amid the tinsel and shine of her state walked Carrie, unhappy. As when Drouet took her she had thought, "Now am I
lifted into that which is best;" as when Hurstwood seemingly
offered her the better way—"Now am I happy." But since the
world goes its way past all who will not partake of its folly, she
now found herself alone. Her purse was open to him whose need
was greatest. In her walks on Broadway, she no longer thought
of the elegance of the creatures who passed her. Had they more
of that peace and beauty which glimmered afar off, then were
they to be envied.

Drouet abandoned his claim and was seen no more. Of
Hurstwood's death she was not even aware. A slow black boat
setting out from the pier at Twenty Seventh Street upon its
weekly errand bore, with many others, his nameless body to the
Potter's Field.

Thus passed all that was of interest concerning these twain

in their relation to her. Their influence upon her life is explicable alone by the nature of her longings. Time was when both
represented for her all that was most potent in earthly success.
They were the personal representatives of a state most blessed
to attain—the titled ambassadors of comfort and peace—aglow
with their credentials. It is but natural that when the world
which they represented no longer allured her its ambassadors
should be discredited. Even had Hurstwood returned in his original beauty and glory, he could not now have allured her. She
had learned that in his world, as in her own present state, was
not happiness.

Sitting alone, she was now an illustration of the devious
ways by which one who feels rather than reasons, may be led in
the pursuit of beauty. Tho' often disillusioned, she was still waiting for that halcyon day when she should be led forth among
dreams become real. Ames had pointed out a farther step, but
on and on beyond that, if accomplished, would lie others for
her. It was forever to be the pursuit of that radiance of delight
which tints the distant hilltops of the world.

Oh, Carrie, Carrie! Oh, blind strivings of the human heart.
Onward, onward it saith, and where beauty leads there it follows. Whether it be the tinkle of a lone sheep-bell o'er some
quiet landscape or the glimmer of beauty in sylvan places, or the
show of soul in some passing eye, the heart knows and makes
answer, following. It is when the feet weary and hope seems
vain that the heartaches and the longings rise. Know then that
for you is neither surfeit nor content. In your rocking chair by
your window dreaming, shall you long alone. In your rocking
chair by your window shall you dream such happiness as you
may never feel.

SARA WHITE DREISER'S REVISED END-

ING FOR CHAPTER L · 659

BLOCK CUTS MARKED BY ARTHUR HENRY
AND ACCEPTED BY DREISER

The table below records the block cutting suggested by Arthur Henry in the Mallon typescript. In each instance, Dreiser accepted Henry's suggestions. Dreiser struck through most of the passages himself, but the preliminary excision marks are by Henry. This cutting quickened the pace of *Sister Carrie* and toned down sexual references in the novel.

The entries below record only the cuts; they do not show the later repairs, usually by Henry, which smoothed over the spots where cutting had been done. And this table records none of the smaller excisions and changes in wording that Henry introduced in typescript.

The page-line numbers in each entry below indicate the location in the Pennsylvania text at which the cut passage has been restored. Then follow the first and last words of the cut passage, separated by ellipses.

3.27–32	Since . . . there.
6.19–24	If . . . further.
7.3–5	Those . . . clothes.
7.18–20	He . . . him.
10.20–28	Already . . . off.
13.16–19	Too . . . commonplace.
15.8–10	She . . . street.
17.21–23	It . . . understand.
18.26–29	After . . . about.
23.1–19	or . . . dress.

24.33–25.23	thinking . . . ascended.
27.15–21	In . . . refuge.
29.20–26	An . . . purse.
29.30–30.6	It . . . break.
46.1–31	"Hello . . . prevailing.
51.7–31	Meanwhile . . . false.
52.35–40	The . . . introduction.
54.25–55.10	Another . . . Fair.
56.18–24	She . . . her.
64.13–16	That . . . itself?
64.20–25	Evil . . . all.
72.14–16	Then . . . room.
74.28–39	We . . . comes.
77.22	He . . . desire.
78.11–28	the subject . . . calculated.
81.16–20	of . . . They
87.24–27	It . . . not.
88.23–26	Across . . . well-to-do.
88.28–31	No . . . Side.
90.13–17	We . . . atmosphere.
90.31–34	The . . . cheerless.
91.7–38	"Dawdler . . . truth?
93.34–40	Ah . . . necessity.
97.1–98.20	In . . . them.
99.28–33	It . . . eye.
100.18–102.4	One . . . Side."
104.27–105.6	She . . . display.
105.29–106.36	Drouet . . . Carrie.

111.1–112.2	If . . . it.
113.35–38	Beside . . . did.
114.4–6	"George . . . tonight."
118.31–119.13	Let . . . I."
122.15–20	"Ah . . . reach.
123.3–6	Ah . . . fountain.
123.22–26	No . . . feeling.
123.34–40	Carrie . . . do.
124.37–125.10	He had . . . hat.
126.9–18	"Very . . . going."
126.24–30	He . . . conspicuous.
126.33–39	"Supposing . . . idea.
129.1–4	It . . . perfect.
132.3–133.5	That . . . evil.
133.24–30	He . . . were.
133.34–134.3	It . . . it.
135.34–37	He . . . round.
138.3–17	Her . . . itself.
140.1–8	Oh . . . outside.
141.32–142.10	He . . . mother.
143.26–29	Out . . . Carrie.
144.20–28	An . . . them.
146.23–34	With . . . upon.
147.38–148.9	so . . . off."
148.14–17	They . . . ridiculous.
152.3–8	attending . . . forth.
153.27–154.15	It . . . people."
158.6–32	Dramatic . . . began.

159.23–36	Both . . . Drouet.
160.9–10	"There . . . pages.
161.10–163.9	She . . . expression.
172.1–20	Avery . . . out.
172.28–31	from . . . way.
173.9–28	"They're . . . Hurstwood.
173.32–174.17	His . . . say?"
174.19–29	He . . . acquaintances.
175.5–33	She . . . easy."
176.13–17	From . . . society.
176.27–32	The . . . stage.
176.37–177.4	They . . . her.
177.26–31	Ah . . . should.
177.33–178.2	The . . . appearance.
187.14–19	Her . . . ransom.
187.33–188.6	In . . . designs.
188.8–189.6	Drouet . . . results.
189.8–10	He . . . matter.
189.11–14	for . . . entered.
190.16–24	This . . . play.
192.4–7	now . . . about.
197.1–14	Why . . . interesting."
198.30–199.7	He . . . it."
203.6–28	To . . . back.
205.5–22	"Don't . . . expression.
207.12–209.20	"I . . . woman.
211.9–15	No . . . atmospheres.

211.18–23	He . . . detection.
212.36–213.2	He . . . too.
217.9–28	His . . . disorder.
223.7–17	The . . . distress.
234.33–40	Such . . . her.
237.24–238.5	What . . . demands.
238.38–239.8	He . . . finally
240.33–241.13	The . . . avail.
243.17–244.4	The . . . later.
245.27–247.29	The . . . do.
247.34–36	She . . . resources.
248.18–25	She . . . alone.
249.7–11	She . . . least.
250.5–11	Besides . . . thought.
252.6–10	Once . . . House.
256.19–33	In . . . now."
256.38–259.29	There . . . life.
259.36–40	She . . . made.
261.19–25	He . . . that
262.7–35	It . . . understand.
263.2–8	He . . . thought.
264.22–24	Carrie . . . running.
265.23–38	There . . . manager.
266.24–29	"Did . . . came.
270.10–11	He . . . it.
270.39–271.8	Could . . . brow.
273.7–9	The . . . know.

279.4–8	"You . . . more.
279.22–28	"You'll . . . answer.
280.7–13	"Won't . . . you."
281.4–8	The . . . be."
281.33–287.8	During . . . once.
287.14–17	Already . . . it.
287.31–288.23	Wild . . . have.
290.3–7	It . . . wound.
290.13–17	To . . . traveling.
290.30–36	Hurstwood . . . passed.
291.8–16	to . . . walls.
291.25–35	"Anything . . . place.
296.26–297.2	His . . . Carrie.
299.10–20	What . . . spirits.
299.27–29	"I . . . book.
300.37–38	He . . . both.
301.31–302.14	Hurstwood . . . him.
303.7–11	She . . . it.
304.22–34	The . . . strong.
305.3–4	the . . . were.
307.21–24	"Suppose . . . it?"
309.25–28	It . . . here.
309.31–35	He . . . it.
310.1–6	In . . . contain.
311.2–4	The . . . Hurstwood.
311.24–37	It . . . mentally.
312.18–20	It . . . about.

312.24–26	All . . . them.
313.1–4	Between . . . follow.
314.15–24	This . . . well.
314.39–315.4	The . . . eyes.
317.1–28	When . . . decisions.
317.39–318.9	It . . . there,
318.20–24	"Has . . . sweet."
318.29–30	"I've . . . Carrie.
319.35–320.13	"Perfectly . . . me."
320.17–35	This . . . her.
321.30–36	The . . . attractive."
333.24–29	Young . . . will."
340.26–34	He . . . out.
347.14–20	and . . . do?
350.28–33	"What . . . out."
351.12–15	"The . . . Shaughnessy.
352.34–353.4	On . . . themselves.
353.33–36	This . . . money.
354.34–355.16	but . . . Herald.
355.28–33	whose . . . position.
357.29–358.14	Coaches . . . disheartened.
358.33–35	Already . . . weekly.
360.9–13	Italians . . . all.
362.30–34	All . . . anew.
367.13–16	When . . . call.
368.27–32	"Hello . . . nothing.
370.17–22	and . . . corner.

377.10–14	Once . . . way.
381.22–382.15	The . . . even
384.9–12	She . . . offer.
384.14–18	This . . . that
385.21–24	The . . . Theatre.
385.34–386.13	"Mr. Frohman's . . . retired—
386.26–27	Mr. Frohman . . . months."
393.29–36	At . . . decision.
394.35–395.1	His . . . best.
395.10–13	When . . . enough.
407.13–37	Mental . . . with.
411.33–38	"I'll . . . ignore.
414.7–12	Most . . . you."
414.18–25	He . . . quietly.
416.1–2	He . . . called.
417.9–13	He . . . then."
417.23–31	Among . . . day.
427.34–39	Another . . . jeers.
430.10–26	During . . . attracted.
435.24–33	The . . . starve.
435.40–436.9	Thinking . . . take.
437.15–17	They . . . observed:—
437.24–33	Towards . . . rescue.
440.7–441.37	When . . . were.
451.16–19	Now . . . yourself."
451.31–35	You . . . already."
453.31–34	That . . . see.

454.39–455.2   It . . . ever.

456.6–8   Then . . . charms.

473.21–25   It . . . regardless.

473.33–37   It . . . change.

476.7–12   Carrie . . . idea.

476.34–39   "Did . . . Carrie.

478.4–24   Mrs. Vance . . . it.

CHAPTER TITLES

The table below records the chapter titles that were printed in the 1900 Doubleday, Page and Company edition of *Sister Carrie*. In each entry, the title in small capitals is the title that appeared in the Doubleday, Page text. When that printed title varies substantively from the title that Dreiser and Henry inscribed in the Mallon TS, the TS title also appears (in roman upper and lowercase), after the Doubleday, Page title. Roman numerals record the chapter numbers for each title. The numeral to the right of the virgule refers to the Doubleday, Page text. The numeral to the left of the virgule refers to the corresponding chapter (or chapters) in the Pennsylvania edition. In revising the Mallon TS, Dreiser and Henry cut and expurgated three chapters so heavily that they were too brief to stand alone. These three shortened chapters (XII, XXVIII, and XXXI in the Pennsylvania edition) were therefore merged by Dreiser, in the Mallon TS, with the chapters that immediately preceded them. The Pennsylvania edition ignores nearly all of this cutting, however, and the three chapters are allowed to stand alone, as Dreiser originally wrote them. The double numerals below in entries XI–XII / XI, XXVII–XXVIII / XXVI, and XXX–XXXI / XXVIII reflect this restoration of cut material.

Chapter Numbers
Penn / DP

I / I	THE MAGNET ATTRACTING: A WAIF AMID FORCES
II / II	WHAT POVERTY THREATENED: OF GRANITE AND BRASS] What Poverty Threatened: Granite and Brass
III / III	WE QUESTION OF FORTUNE: FOUR-FIFTY A WEEK
IV / IV	THE SPENDINGS OF FANCY: FACTS ANSWER WITH SNEERS] The Spendings of Fancy: Sordid Facts Reprove

WORD DIVISION

Dreiser rarely hyphenated compound words at the ends of lines in the MS of *Sister Carrie*. Those few instances in which he did so have been resolved by reference to his usage in other parts of the MS. Numerous hyphenated compounds (or possible hyphenated compounds) are divided at the ends of lines in the Pennsylvania edition, however, and the critic using this text must know how to render these words when quoting for publication. The words in the list below are all divided at the ends of lines in the Pennsylvania text. In quoting these words, Dreiser's hyphenation should be preserved. All other compounds divided at the ends of lines in this edition should be quoted as one word.

5.37	cat's-eyes
7.22	dry-goods
13.14	patched-together
23.2	rosy-cheeked
27.15	sensual-faced
33.3	half-hearted
37.12	hum-drum
42.38	dark-polished
42.39	stucco-work
52.29	four-fifty
54.25	stay-at-home-ishness
79.32	far-away-sounding

88.25	well-to-do
95.34	ten-cent
104.30	self-conscious
111.13	money-making
121.18	well-grounded
128.33	well-positioned
139.19	twenty-eight
145.18	white-faced
145.33	half-light
165.15	dress-suit
165.21	be-scarf-pinned
176.3	self-confident
176.13	dressing-room
182.16	one-armed
202.11	good-naturedly
228.30	grief-stricken
250.6	over-experienced
267.17	half-hour
283.16	well-situated
293.7	half-dissolved
293.26	barber-shop
295.4	ex-manager
306.12	self-centered
308.10	well-appearing
308.14	well-dressed
314.2	self-important
314.7	white-covered
318.11	night-gown

320.33	dumb-waiter
325.6	knick-knacks
330.30	pleasure-seeking
332.25	robin's-egg
335.9	fine-headed
352.31	well-appearing
353.24	chair-warmers
360.9	small-bushel
361.5	well-dressed
368.24	down-town
382.18	forty-five
386.14	be-paneled
395.40	three-and-a-half-pound
398.11	close-measured
410.1	scare-heads
414.1	short-handed
414.28	uncomfortable-looking
417.15	paper-wrapped
430.30	street-car
437.3	hard-hearted
437.22	good-naturedly
446.17	stage-manager
460.30	side-entrances
462.7	head-porter's
463.28	well-dressed
464.12	passers-by
465.3	well-dressed
466.2	way-farers

466.10	ever-fascinating
473.5	dressing-room
475.35	old-time
485.27	self-glorification
488.3	mission-house
649.30	comedy-drama

PEDIGREE OF EDITIONS

New York: Doubleday, Page & Co., 1900.
London: Heinemann, 1901. Abridged.
London: Constable, 1927.
New York: Heritage Press/Limited Editions Club, 1939.
New York: Pocket Books, 1949. Abridged.
New York: Holt, Rinehart and Winston, 1957.
New York: Sagamore, 1957.
New York: Bantam, 1958.
Boston: Houghton Mifflin, 1959.
New York: Dell, 1960.
New York: New American Library/Signet, 1961.
London: Oxford University Press, 1965.
New York: Harper and Row, 1965.
New York: Airmont, 1967.
New York: Norton, 1970.
Indianapolis and New York: Bobbs-Merrill, 1970.
Cambridge, Mass.: Robert Bentley, 1971.